OXFORD DATA PROTECTION AND PRIVACY LAW

Series Editors

CHRISTOPHER KUNER

Professor of Law, VUB Brussels

GRAHAM GREENLEAF

Professor of Law and Information Systems, University of New South Wales

Privacy and the Role of International Law in the Digital Age

OXFORD DATA PROTECTION AND PRIVACY LAW

Series Editors

Christopher Kuner, Professor of Law, VUB Brussel
Graham Greenleaf, Professor of Law and Information Systems,
University of New South Wales

The aim of this series is to publish important and original books on legal issues of data protection and privacy. This includes many different areas of law, including comparative law, EU law, human rights law, international law, privacy on the Internet, and others.

Prospective authors are welcome to submit proposals for the series, as outlined on the series website: global.oup.com/academic/content/series/o/oxford-data-protection-and-privacy-law-odppl/

Privacy and the Role of International Law in the Digital Age

KINFE YILMA

Addis Ababa University School of Law

OXFORD
UNIVERSITY PRESS

UNIVERSITY PRESS

Great Clarendon Street, Oxford, OX2 6DP,
United Kingdom

Oxford University Press is a department of the University of Oxford.
It furthers the University's objective of excellence in research, scholarship,
and education by publishing worldwide. Oxford is a registered trade mark of
Oxford University Press in the UK and in certain other countries

Published in the United States of America by Oxford University Press
198 Madison Avenue, New York, NY 10016, United States of America

British Library Cataloguing in Publication Data

Data available

Library of Congress Control Number: 2022946704

ISBN 978–0–19–288729–0

DOI: 10.1093/oso/9780192887290.001.0001

Printed and bound by CPI Group (UK) Ltd, Croydon, CR0 4YY

Series Editors' Preface

Data protection and privacy have increasingly become matters of global interest. This is reflected in the growth of data protection legislation around the world and the globalisation of data processing. These factors have led to concern about how privacy and data protection rights can be protected across national borders; interest in ways to avoid conflicts between the data protection laws of different jurisdictions; and examination of the tension between allowing data flows and protecting privacy on a global scale.

The present book by Kinfe Yilma addresses these issues in a scholarly yet original way. The author first examines the history and structure of international legal regimes for privacy protection under both international human rights law and data protection law. He then focuses on three initiatives designed to strengthen the rights to privacy and data protection in public international law, namely Internet bills of right, ongoing discussions at the United Nations (UN), and transnational data protection standards. The author finally argues that challenges to the global protection of privacy can best be dealt with through the use of "soft law".

Particularly noteworthy is the fact that the author does not limit himself to describing the problems and deficiencies of the current international legal framework, but also presents concrete and pragmatic solutions to them. He analyses instruments of traditional international law (such as treaties) and also considers how privacy can be protected through non-binding instruments such as resolutions of the UN General Assembly, human rights declarations, corporate governance principles, and others. He thus goes beyond analysis of traditional sources of international law to examine how the protection of privacy rights can be improved through non-binding mechanisms as well.

There has long been a need for a scholarly examination of the place of privacy and data protection rights in international law together with an imaginative treatment of how they can be protected in practice. This book fills that gap and represents an important contribution to data protection scholarship.

Christopher Kuner and Graham Greenleaf

Preface

This book grew out of a PhD research completed at the University of Melbourne Law School in mid-2019. A few years before I moved to Melbourne, several global media outlets broke, in early June 2013, the news of sweeping foreign and domestic surveillance practices of the United States and its 'Five Eyes' partner States. Provided with over a million classified documents by Edward Snowden, the revelations brought to light post 9/11 large-scale digital surveillance measures surreptitiously installed in those countries. On many fronts, the Snowden debacle has been a watershed moment, but its role in igniting a debate on how best to protect the right to privacy in the digital age is perhaps where its lasting mark lies. The revelations unearthed the ominous nature of transnational privacy threats enabled by technology companies as well as States with unprecedented levels of technological capabilities. This is what one may call the 'privacy problem' in the digital age. While the privacy problem is not all new, the scale of the surveillance and data collection practices revived longstanding calls for an 'international' privacy framework by various actors, including governments, civil society organizations, and even technology companies.

Such calls take various forms, and of course, predate the revelations. But proposals on and calls for an international law response to the privacy problem in the digital age have grown exponentially since the revelations. From calls for a bill of rights for the Internet age to initiatives to transform regional systems of privacy protection into universal standards and a multi-level privacy discourse at the United Nations, the Snowden debacle has put to the forefront the need for an international law response to the challenges of upholding the right to privacy in the digital age. But the nature and scope of such initiatives remain little studied. In particular, the ways in which such initiatives may evolve to assume the role of or contribute to the development of the long sought-after international law response to the privacy problem is yet to receive serious scholarly treatment. This relates to the broader void in the privacy literature as to the role of international law in the protection of privacy and data protection in the digital environment. This book is an attempt to address this lacuna in the broader scholarly and public policy debates.

In examining the question of how international law should respond to the challenges of securing the right to privacy in the digital age, the book takes the novel approach of exploring the role of international privacy initiatives in making international privacy law better-equipped in the digital age. Three global privacy initiatives are used as case studies in the book. The Internet bill of rights movement is one of the multi-level initiatives that postulate a progressive vision for privacy and data protection. The second initiative is the ongoing post-Snowden discourse on the 'right to privacy in the digital age' which tends to reimagine privacy in international law. A slightly different but equally notable initiative is the potential universalization of transnational standards, particularly the Council of Europe data protection framework.

As part of a broader examination of the role of international law in upholding digital privacy, the book situates such initiatives in international law. The aim, in so doing, is to explore the extent to which such initiatives may remedy shortcomings of international privacy law. But the book takes the investigation even further. Having shown limitations of the three initiatives in attending to international law's problem, it proposes a pragmatic approach to international law of privacy. A bundle of pragmatic reform measures is proposed that would reimagine international privacy to make it fit for purpose in the digital age. Building on the merits of post-Snowden reform measures, the book lays out virtues of an international soft law and a dialogical approach to digital privacy as practical remedies to the normative and institutional limitations of international law. The book, in that sense, hopes to inform long-running academic and policy debates with practical reform proposals.

Acknowledgements

Many people have been supportive in the course of researching for and writing this monograph. As a book that grew out of a PhD thesis, I am deeply grateful to my supervisors, Professors Andrew Kenyon, Megan Richardson, and John Tobin, who were very supportive and patient. In particular, I am grateful to my principal supervisor Andrew for his consistent and balanced supervision throughout my candidature—and for his ongoing support; to Megan for her generosity from the start to the end; and to John for the encouragement. Professor Tim Lindsay, who was the chair of my Advisory Committee for the entire period of my candidature, was extraordinarily supportive and provided highly valuable advice, for which I am thankful. I am also thankful to Professors Hilary Charlesworth and Mark Taylor, who have been academic assessors at my confirmation and completion seminars, for the highly useful feedback and insightful suggestions.

The University of Melbourne, Melbourne Law School, and Addis Ababa University Law School provided various forms of support at the different stages of writing this book, for which I remain indebted. I am grateful to my colleagues at AAU Law School, especially Dr Aschalew Ashagre for his encouragement and eagerness to see the completion of this work. My friend Bereket Abayneh has also been very supportive all along. I am also highly thankful to the exceptionally kind Professor Ben Chigara for his relentless support over the years.

Many thanks to Professors Christopher Kuner and Graham Greenleaf for supporting the publication of this monograph as part of the Oxford Data Protection and Privacy Law Series. Graham has been not only extremely kind and supportive but also an inspiration to me. OUP's Merel Alstein has been extraordinarily kind all along for which I am deeply grateful. Working with my editors at OUP Jo Dymond, Matt Williams, and Sam Bailey has been smooth and I thank them for all their excellent work.

Shorter and older versions of the two chapters in this book have appeared in other publications. Parts of chapter 3 are based on KM Yilma, 'The United Nations Data Privacy System and Its Limits' (2019) 33 International Review of Law, Computers and Technology 224 and a shorter version of chapter 5 appeared as KM Yilma, 'The Right to Privacy in the Digital Age': Boundaries of the "New" UN Privacy Discourse' (2018) 87 Nordic Journal of International Law 485. A special thanks to the editors of these journals for allowing the publication of these articles in the book.

Contents

Table of Cases   xv
Table of Legislation   xvii
List of Abbreviations   xxi
Note to Readers   xxiii

1. The 'Privacy Problem' in the Digital Age   1
   1. Imperatives of an 'International Law' Response   3
   2. International Law's Privacy Problem   5
      2.1. Normative Limits   5
      2.2. Institutional-Jurisprudential Limits   7
   3. Promises of Global Privacy Initiatives   7
   4. State of the Art and the Book's Argument   10
      4.1. The Status Quo Approach   10
      4.2. The Hard Legalization Approach   11
      4.3. The Institutionalist Approach   16
      4.4. The Soft Legalization Approach   18
      4.5. The Book's Argument   19
   5. Method and Analytical Framework   21
   6. A Note on Terminologies and Concepts   24

PART I—INTERNATIONAL LAW OF
PRIVACY IN THE DIGITAL AGE

2. The Reach of Human Rights Law   29
   1. Introduction   29
   2. The Human Right to Privacy and the Cold War   30
      2.1. The Cold War Effect   30
      2.2. The Privacy Inattention Effect   34
   3. Normative Sources   37
      3.1. Treaty Law   38
      3.2. Custom   43
      3.3. General Principles   47
      3.4. Soft Law   51
   4. 'Blind Spots'   52
      4.1. Normative Gaps   53
      4.2. Institutional-Structural Gaps   67
      4.3. Jurisprudential Gaps   69
   5. Conclusion   76

3. **Boundaries of International Data Privacy Law**   79
    1. Introduction   79
    2. Data Privacy and the Cold War   81
        2.1. The Cold War Effect   82
        2.2. The Data Privacy Inattention Effect   86
    3. Normative Sources   88
        3.1. Treaty Law   89
        3.2. Custom   97
        3.3. General Principles   99
        3.4. Soft Law   102
    4. Falling into Disuse   104
        4.1. Problems of Substance and Approach   105
        4.2. Problems of Institutionalization   118
    5. Conclusion   124

PART II—GLOBAL PRIVACY INITIATIVES AND INTERNATIONAL LAW

4. **Internet Bills of Rights**   129
    1. Introduction   129
    2. Making Sense of Internet Bills of Rights   131
        2.1. Origins of a Constitutional Project   131
        2.2. Locating Convergence in IBRs Initiatives   133
        2.3. Legal Sources and Forms in IBRs   143
        2.4. Privacy in IBRs   147
    3. Situating IBRs in International Law   151
        3.1. Freestanding Role   151
        3.2. Contributory Role   163
        3.3. Catalytic Role   167
    4. Conclusion   168

5. **Emergent Privacy Standards**   169
    1. Introduction   169
    2. Mapping the Discourse   170
        2.1. Background to the Discourse   171
        2.2. Novelties of the Discourse   176
    3. Situating the Discourse in International Law   190
        3.1. Elaborative and Interpretive Functions   190
        3.2. Universalizing Privacy Standards   195
        3.3. Charting Normative and Methodological Directions   203
    4. Conclusion   208

6. **Transnational Privacy Standards** 210
   1. Introduction 210
   2. Background to the Convention 108(+) System 212
   3. Norm Universalization 214
      3.1. Meaning 214
      3.2. Virtues 216
   4. Avenues of Norm Universalization 221
      4.1. Accession 221
      4.2. Accretion of General International Law 228
      4.3. Jurisprudential Cross-influence 233
   5. Prospect of other Regional Standards 242
   6. Conclusion 245

PART III—TOWARDS A PRAGMATIC APPROACH

7. **Virtues of Soft Legalization** 251
   1. Introduction 251
   2. Virtues of a Soft Law Supplement 253
      2.1. Reimagining the Right to Privacy in the Digital Age 253
      2.2. Globalizing Emergent Privacy Standards 257
      2.3. Facilitating Progressive Development of Privacy Law 259
   3. Normative Structures of the Soft Law 262
      3.1. Clarifying Scope of the Right to Privacy 263
      3.2. Core Privacy Principles 267
      3.3. Defining Obligations and Responsibilities 269
   4. Questions of Form 282
   5. Conclusion 286

8. **Virtues of a Dialogical Approach** 287
   1. Introduction 287
   2. Virtues of a Dialogical Approach 288
      2.1. Dialogue as a Pragmatic Future 288
      2.2. Dialogue as a Responsive Strategy 291
   3. Ways of Conversation 292
      3.1. Foundations of the Privacy Forum 293
      3.2. Roles of the Privacy Forum 297
      3.3. Procedural Considerations 300
      3.4. The Forum and Limits of Multistakeholderism 302
   4. Conclusion 305

Summary and Conclusion 306
   1. The 'Privacy Problem' and the Role of International Law 306
      1.1. In Search for a Role 306
      1.2. Looking Through the Lens of Global Emergent Law 307

2. Findings in the Book 308
   2.1. International Law of Privacy and Its Shortcomings
      in the Digital Age 309
   2.2. Global Privacy Initiatives and Their Limits 310
   2.3. Reimagining International Privacy Law in the Digital Age 312
3. Seizing the Moment for Practical Reform 313

Appendices 317
Select Bibliography 339
Index 365

Table of Cases

INTERNATIONAL COURT OF JUSTICE

Certain Expenses of the United Nations, Advisory Opinion,
ICJ Reports 1962 (20 July 1962) 224–25
South West Africa: Ethiopia and Liberia v South Africa, Second Phase,
ICJ Reports 1966 (18 July 1966) 47–48
*Legal Consequences for States of the Continued Presence of South Africa in
Namibia Notwithstanding Security Council Resolution 276 (1970)*
[Advisory Opinion] ICJ Reports 1971 (21 June 1971). 160–61
*Legal Consequences of the Construction of a Wall in the Occupied
Palestinian Territory*, ICJ Reports 2004 (9 July 2004). 63
*Interpretation of the Agreement of 25 March 1951 between
The WHO and Egypt*, ICJ Reports 1980 (20 December 1980). 224–25

HUMAN RIGHTS COMMITTEE

HR Committee, *A.B. v Canada*, Communication No 2387/2014 (16 March 2017) 61
HR Committee, *Al-Gertani v Bosnia and Herzegovina*,
Communication No. 1955/2010 (6 November 2013) 56–57, 70–71
HR Committee, *Antonius Cornelis Van Hulst v The Netherlands*,
Communication No 903/1999 (15 November 2004) 70–71
HR Committee, *D.T. v Canada*, Communication No 2081/2011
(29 September 2016) 56–57
HR Committee, *Dušan Vojnović v Croatia*,Communication
No 1510/2006 (30 March 2009) 56
HR Committee, *H.S. v Australia*, Communication No 2015/2010 (13 May 2015). 70–71
HR Committee, *Herbert Potter v New Zealand*,
Communication No 632/1995 (6 April 1995). 192
HR Committee, *I Elpida v Greece*, Communication No 2242/2013
(26 February 2014). 61
HR Committee, *I.P. v Finland*, Communication No 450/1991 (26 July 1993). 70–71
HR Committee, *Kalamiotis et al v Greece*, Communication No 2242/2013
(3 January 2017) 56
HR Committee, *Kenneth McAlpine v United Kingdom*,
Communication No 6/2011 (13 November 2012) 70
HR Committee, *Maharajah Madhewoo v Mauritius*,
Communication No 3163/2018 (21 July 2021). 236–38
HR Committee, *Marouf v Algeria*, Communication No 1889/2009
(29 April 2014) 70–71
HR Committee, *N.K. v The Netherlands*, Communication
No 2326/2013 (10 January 2018) 38–39, 120–21, 236–37
HR Committee, *Nabil Sayadi and Patricia Vinck v Belgium*,
Communication No 1472/2006 (29 December 2008) 236–37

HR Committee, *Petr Gatilov v Russia*, Communication No 2171/2012
(30 August 2017) 57–58
HR Committee, *Sergio Euben Lopez Burgos v Uruguay*,
Communication No R.12/52 (29 July 1981) 63

EUROPEAN COURT OF HUMAN RIGHTS

ECtHR, *Barbulescu v Romania*, Application No 61496/08 (5 September 2017) 120–21
ECtHR, *Big Brother Watch and Others v UK*, Application Nos 58170/13,
62322/14 and 24960/15 (13 September 2018)...........................202, 292
ECtHR, *Chapman v The United Kingdom*, Application No 27238/95
(18 January 2001)..56
ECtHR, *Ekimdzhiev v Bulgaria*, Application No 62540/00 (28 June 2007) 154
ECtHR, *Golder v The United Kingdom*, Application No 4451/70
(21 February 1975)..59
ECtHR, *Hamalainen v Finland*, Application No 37359/09 (16 July 2014)...........56–57
ECtHR, *Karako v Hungary*, Application No 39311/05 (28 April 2009) 55–56
ECtHR, *L.H. v Latvia*, Application No 52019/07 (29 April 2014)......... 122–23, 237–38
ECtHR, *Leander v Sweden*, Application No 9248/81 (26 March 1987) 181–82, 238–39
ECtHR, *Leyla Sahin v Turkey*, Application No 44774/98
(10 November 2005) 237–38
ECtHR, *Malone v UK*, Application No 8691/79 (26 April 1985)...................180–81
ECtHR, *Rachwalski and Ferenc v Poland*, Application No 47709/99
(28 July 2009) 56
ECtHR, *Roman Zakharov v Russia*, Application No 47143/06
(4 December 2015)...192, 241
ECtHR, *S. and Marper v United Kingdom*, Applications Nos 30562/04 and
30566/04 (4 December 2008) 235–36, 237
ECtHR, *Szabo and Vissy v Hungary*, Application No 37138/14 (12 January 2016).......165
ECtHR, *Uner v The Netherlands*, Application No 46410/99 (18 October 2006) 56–57
ECtHR, *Uzun v Germany*, Application No 35623/05 (2 September 2010)..........122–23
ECtHR, *W v Netherlands*, Application No 20689/08 (20 January 2009) 236–37
ECtHR, *Z v Finland*, Application No 22009/93 (25 February 1997)...............238–39

EUROPEAN UNION

Digital Rights Ireland and Stetlinger et al v Minister for
Communication and et al (C-293/12 and C-594/12) [2014] ECLI 238.............122
Google v Agencia Española de Protección de Datos (AEPD) v Mario
Costeja González (C-131/12) [2014] ECLI 317............................141–42

NATIONAL

Bundesverfassungsgericht (1983) *BVerfGE 65* 141–42
Bundesverfassungsgericht (2008) *BVerfG 822* 141
Justice K.S. Puttaswamy (Retd) v Union of India, Writ Petition
(Civil) No 494 OF 2012 (24 August 2017)...............................44–45
STC 292/2000, de 30 de noviembre de 2000 del Tribunal Constitucional 113

Table of Legislation

INTERNATIONAL

Charter of the United Nations
(1945)...................31, 193, 226
Constitution of the International Labour
Organization (1919)...........86–87
Constitution of the United Nations
Educational, Scientific and Cultural
Organization (16 November 1945)
[as amended]...................110
Convention Establishing the World
Intellectual Property Organization,
opened for signature 14 July 1967
(entered into force 1 June 1984)
[as amended in 1979].............17
Convention on Environmental Impact
Assessment in a Transboundary
Context, opened for signature 1 March
1991, 1989 UNTS 309 [entered into
force 10 September 1997] 115
Convention on the Rights of Persons
with Disabilities, opened for
signature 30 March 2007, 2515
UNTS 3 (entered into
force 3 May 2008)......... 29, 41–42,
58–59, 77–78, 89–90,
91, 92–93, 118–19
Convention on the Rights of the Child,
opened for signature 20 November
1989, 1577 UNTS 3 (entered into force
2 September 1990) 29, 39–40
Guidelines for the Regulation of
Computerized Personal Data Files,
GA Res 45/95, UNGAOR, 45th sess,
68th plen mtg (14 December
1990) 6, 79–80, 85,
102–3, 112–13, 114
Guiding Principles on Business and Human
Rights: Implementing the United
Nations 'Protect, Respect and Remedy'
Framework, 17th sess, Agenda
item 3 (6 June 2011) 6, 52, 64–65
International Convention for the Protection
of All Persons from Enforced
Disappearance, opened for signature
on 6 February 2007, 2716 UNTS
3 (entered into force 23 December
2010) 94
International Convention on the Protection
of the Rights of All Migrant Workers
and Members of Their Families, opened
for signature 18 December 1990, 2220
UNTS 3 (entered into force 1 July
2003) 29, 40–41, 77–78
International Covenant on Civil and
Political Rights, opened for signature
16 December 1966, 999 UNTS 171
(entered into force 23 March
1976) 1, 29, 38–39, 53,
61–62, 67–68, 72
International Health Regulations
(3rd ed, 2005) 95–96
Marrakesh Treaty to Facilitate Access to
Published Works for Persons Who Are
Blind, Visually Impaired, or Otherwise
Print Disabled, opened for signature
28 June 28 2013 (entered into
force 30 September 2016) 96–97
OECD Guidelines on the Protection of
Privacy and Transborder Flows of
Personal Data (23 September 1980)
[as updated in 2013]..........113–14
Optional Protocol to the Convention on
the Rights of the Child on the Sale of
Children, Child Prostitution and Child
Pornography, opened for signature
25 May 2000, 2171 UNTS 227
(entered into force 18 January
2002) 77–78
Optional Protocol to the International
Covenant on Civil and Political Rights,
GA Res 200A (XXI) , opened for
signature 19 December 1966, 999
UNTS 171 (entered into force
23 March 1976) 227
Statute of the International Court of
Justice (18 April 1946) 199, 232
Statute of the International Law
Commission (21 November
1947) 9, 226

The Right to Privacy in the Digital Age,
GA Res 68/167, 68th sess, Agenda item
69(b) (21 January
2014) 169, 172, 183, 187, 207
The Right to Privacy in the Digital Age,
GA Res 69/166, 69th sess, Agenda
item 68(b) (10 February
2015) .171, 185
The Right to Privacy in the Digital Age,
GA Res 71/199, 71[st]sess, Agenda
item 68(b) (25 January
2017) 164, 173–74, 187–88,
269, 290–91, 301
The Right to Privacy in the Digital Age,
GA Res 73/179, 73rd sess, Agenda
Item 74(b) (21 January
2019) 73, 173–74, 177–80, 181,
182, 184, 185–86, 187–88, 189,
201–2, 205, 207, 270–71
The Right to Privacy in the Digital Age,
GA Res 75/176, 75th sess, Agenda
item 72(b) (28 December
2020) 173–74, 175–76, 178–79,
180–81, 182, 183, 184,
185–87, 188–89, 205, 207–8
The Right to Privacy in the Digital Age,
HRC Res 28/16, 28[th]sess, Agenda
Item 3 (26 March
2015) 67, 68, 124, 174
The Right to Privacy in the Digital Age,
HRC Res 34/7, 34[th]sess, Agenda
Item 3 (22 March
2017) 174, 180–81, 184
The Right to Privacy in the Digital Age,
HRC Res 42/15, 42nd sess, Agenda
item 3 (7 October
2019) 175–76, 178–79, 186
The Right to Privacy in the Digital Age,
HRC Res 48/4, 48th sess, Agenda
item 3 (13 October
2021) 45–46, 173–76, 178–79,
180–82, 183, 184, 185–87,
188, 189, 205, 240
*Treaty on Principles Governing the Activities
of States in the Exploration and Use of
Outer Space, including the Moon and
Other Celestial Bodies,* opened for
signature 27 January 1967 (entered
into force 10 October) 204
Universal Declaration of Human Rights, GA
Res 217A(III), UN GAOR, 3[rd]sess,
183[rd]plen mtg (10 December
1948) .1, 29, 77

REGIONAL

*A Supplementary Act on Personal
Data Protection within ECOWAS,*
A1SA.1f01f10 (16 February
2010) 245
*Additional Protocol to the Convention for the
Protection of Individuals with regard to
Automatic Processing of Personal Data,
regarding Supervisory Authorities and
Transborder Data Flows,* opened for
signature 8 November 2001,
181 ETS (entered into force
1 July 2004) 121–22, 211–12
*Additional Protocol to the Convention
on Human Rights and Biomedicine
Concerning Biomedical Research,*
opened for signature 25 January
2005, 195 CETS (entered into
force 1 September 2007) 117
*Additional Protocol to the Convention
on Human Rights and Biomedicine
Concerning Genetic Testing for Health
Purposes,* opened for signature 27
November 2008, 203 CETS
(entered into force 1 July
2018) 117
*African Union Convention on Cybersecurity
and Personal Data Protection
Convention* (June 2014) 117
American Convention on Human Rights,
opened for signature 22 November
1969, OAS, Treaty Series No 36
(entered into force 18 July 1978). . . .45
*Asia Pacific Economic Cooperation
Privacy Framework*
(2014). 114–15, 244–45
*Charter of Fundamental Rights of the
European Union,* proclaimed on
7 December 2000 [2000]
OJ C 326/ 393 (entered into force
1 December 2009) 45
*Charter on the Rights and Welfare of the
Child,* opened for signature 11 July
1990, OAU Doc CAB/LEG/24.9/49
(entered into force 29 November
1999) .45, 159
*Convention for the Protection of Human
Rights and Fundamental Freedoms,*
opened for signature 11 April 1950,
European Treaty Series - No 5
(entered into force 9 March
1953) 45

Convention for the Protection of Individuals
    with Regard to Automatic Processing
    of Personal Data, opened for signature
    28 January 1981, ETS No 108
    (entered into force 1 October
    1981) 11–12, 211–12,
                  213–14, 216–17, 235
Convention on Cybercrime, opened for
    signature 23 November 2001, opened
    for signature 23 November 2001,
    European Treaty Series No 185
    (entered into force 1 July
    2004) 217–18
Convention on Human Rights and
    Biomedicine, opened for signature
    4 April 1997, 164 ETS (entered
    into force 1 December
    1999) 117, 118–19
Directive (EC) 2002/58 of the European
    Parliament and of the Council of 12 July
    2002 on the Protection of Privacy in
    the Electronic Communications Sector
    [2002] OJ L 201/37 ....111, 141
Directive (EU) 2016/680 of the European
    Parliament and of Council of 27 April
    2016 on the Protection of Natural
    Persons with regard to the Processing
    of Personal Data by Competent
    Authorities for the Purposes of the
    Prevention, Investigation, Detection or
    Prosecution of Criminal Offenses or the
    Execution of Criminal Penalties and on
    the Free Movement of such Data
    [2016] OJ L 119/89 111
European Convention on the International
    Classification of Patents for Inventions,
    opened for signature 19 December
    1954, European Treaty Series No. 017
    (entered into force 1 August
    1955) 217–18
Modernized Convention for the Protection
    of Individuals with Regard to the
    Processing of Personal Data,
    opened for signature 10 October 2018,
    CETS No. 223 (not yet in
    force) 11–12, 117, 123–24,
              211–12, 216–18, 221, 224–25

Regulation (EU) 2016/679 of the European
    Parliament and of the Council of 27
    April 2016 on the Protection of Natural
    Persons with regard to the Processing
    of Personal Data and on the Free
    Movement of Such Data [2016] OJ L
    119/1 ......113, 114–15, 117, 122–23,
              141–42, 155–56, 181–82, 183
Regulation (EU) 2018/1725 of the
    European Parliament and of
    Council of 23 October 2018 on the
    Protection of Natural Persons with
    regard to the Processing of Personal
    Data by the Union Institutions,
    Bodies, Offices and Agencies and on
    the Free Movement of such Data
    [2018] OJ L 295/39 111
Standards for Personal Data Protection for
    Ibero-American States (20 June
    2017) 243–44
Statute of the Council of Europe
    (5 May 1949) 216
Treaty of Lisbon, Amending the Treaty
    on EU and the Treaty Establishing
    the European Community, opened
    for signature 13 December 2007
    [2007] OJ C 306/1 (entered into force
    1 December 2009) 122–23

NATIONAL

Australian Privacy Act
    1988 (Cth) 113–14
Basic Law of the Federal Republic of
    Germany (1949) [as amended in
    2014] 141
Brazilian Civil Framework for the
    Internet (2014) 149
Constitution of Ecuador (2008)
    [as amended]...................159
Constitution of Mexico (1917)
    [as amended]...................159
FREEDOM Act of 2015, Pub L No 114-23,
    129 Stat 268 201
Presidential Policy Directive 28: Signals
    Intelligence Activities (17 January
    2018) 200–1

List of Abbreviations

ACHR	American Convention on Human Rights
ACLU	American Civil Liberties Union
ACRWC	African Charter on the Rights and Welfare of the Child
AI	Artificial Intelligence
APEC	Asia Pacific Economic Cooperation
AU	African Union
CAHDI	Committee of Legal Advisors on Public International Law
CIL	Customary International Law
CJEU	Court of Justice of the European Union
CoE	Council of Europe
CoM	Committee of Ministers
CRC	Convention on the Rights of the Child
CRD	Convention on the Rights of Persons with Disabilities
DRIP	Declaration on the Rights of Indigenous Peoples
ECHR	European Convention on Human Rights and Fundamental Freedoms
ECtHR	European Court of Human Rights
EFF	Electronic Frontier Foundation
EU	European Union
GC	General Comment
GDPR	General Data Protection Regulation
GNI	Global Network Initiative
GPsL	General Principles of Law
HR Committee	Human Rights Committee
HR Council	Human Rights Council
IAB	Internet Architecture Board
IBRs	Internet Bills of Rights
ICANN	Internet Corporation for Assigned Names and Numbers
ICCPR	International Covenant on Civil and Political Rights
ICESCR	International Covenant on Economic, Social and Cultural Rights
ICJ	International Court of Justice
ICJs	International Commission of Jurists
ICRMW	International Convention on the Rights of Migrant Workers and Members of their Families
ICTs	Information and Communication Technologies
IEEE	Institute of Electrical and Electronics Engineers
IETF	Internet Engineering Task Force
IGF	Internet Governance Forum
IHRs	International Health Regulations
ILC	International Law Commission

ILO	International Labour Organization
INTERPOL	International Criminal Police Organization
IOM	International Organization for Migration
IRP Charter	Charter of Internet Rights and Principles
OECD	Organization for Economic Cooperation and Development
OEI	Organization of Ibero-American States
OHCHR	Office of the High Commissioner for Human Rights
PACE	Parliamentary Assembly of the Council of Europe
PETs	Privacy Enhancing Technologies
PPD	Presidential Policy Directive
SDGs	Sustainable Development Goals
SRP	Special Rapporteur on the Right to Privacy
TLS	Transport Layer Security
UDHR	Universal Declaration of Human Rights
UN	United Nations
UNCITRAL	United Nations Commission on International Trade Law
UNDP	United Nations Development Program
UNESCO	United Nations Educational, Scientific and Cultural Organization
UNGA	United Nations General Assembly
UNHCR	United Nations High Commission for Refugees
UNICEF	United Nations Children's Fund
UPR	Universal Periodic Review
WFP	World Food Program
WHO	World Health Organization
WIPO	World Intellectual Property Organization
WSIS	World Summit on Information Society
WTO	World Trade Organization

Note to Readers

A characteristic feature of the privacy field is that it has to grapple with fast-moving developments, be it technological or legal. This makes it difficult for any scholarly undertaking to capture all developments. More so regarding themes explored in this book. Initiatives for Internet bill of rights routinely emerge at multiple levels, and in reaction to a certain privacy scandal, crisis, or emergent technologies. The ongoing privacy discourse at the United Nations is still in a state of flux. The prospect of universalizing transnational standards is also hard to accurately predict. Add to these inevitable jurisprudential developments in other processes such as human rights treaty bodies stimulated, in part, by the bill of rights and related initiatives. A lot has occurred since the PhD thesis, from which this book grew, was completed in mid-2019. But it has been substantially revised with new material added, including a newly written chapter 6 and all chapters revised substantially, to capture developments that have occurred in the interim couple of years. While the analysis in the book will (hopefully) remain relevant in the context of future developments, all care has been taken to capture developments both in law and practice until early May 2022. All URL links were last visited on 30 June 2022.

1

The 'Privacy Problem' in the Digital Age

The human right to privacy is one of the fundamental rights guaranteed in national, regional, and international law.[1] It is widely considered to be an 'enabling' right in that its protection facilitates the enjoyment of other fundamental rights such as freedom of expression, religion, and association.[2] Securing the right to privacy is not only an end in itself but also a means for the realization of these other civil and political rights. But upholding the right to privacy in the digital age faces novel challenges thereby impacting the enjoyment of a broad range of human rights. Unlike the pre-digital era, the threats that the right faces in the digital age are complex, dynamic, geographically unbounded, and involve multiple, and often obscure actors. What is here referred to as the 'privacy problem' in the digital age exhibits three mutually reinforcing dimensions that capture the new ways in which the right to privacy is undermined.[3] As shall be outlined below, not only does interference with the right to privacy occur increasingly in the transnational context but it also involves little regulated private actors that hold key roles in the rapidly shifting technological ecosystem.

One obvious manifestation of the digital environment is that it creates a range of new possibilities for cross-border violation of the right to privacy. The global nature of communication technologies enables State and non-State actors to violate the right to privacy of individuals located in different jurisdictions. While cross-border human rights violations are not entirely new, the breadth of transnational privacy violations has grown exponentially with the global Internet. As the Snowden revelations have shown, American and British intelligence agencies engage in far-reaching mass domestic and foreign surveillance, including against leaders of foreign countries.[4] The prevailing business model in cyberspace also entails routine corporate collection, processing, aggregation, and repurposing of

---

[1] See, eg, *Universal Declaration of Human Rights*, GA Res 217A(III), UN GAOR, 3rd sess, 183rd plen mtg, UN Doc A/810 (10 December 1948) art 12; *International Covenant on Civil and Political Rights*, opened for signature 16 December 1966, 999 UNTS 171 (entered into force 23 March 1976) art 17.

[2] See, eg, Eric Barendt, 'Privacy and Freedom of Speech' in Andrew Kenyon and Megan Richardson (eds), *New Dimensions in Privacy Law: International and Comparative Perspectives* (Cambridge University Press 2006) 11–12, 26–7, 30.

[3] cf Lilian Edwards, 'Reconstructing Consumer Privacy Protection Online: A Modest Proposal' (2004) 18 International Review of Law, Computers and Technology 313, 319 [applying the term 'privacy problem' (narrowly) to capture loss of consumer trust and erosion of privacy in cyberspace due to 'multinational corporatism and ubiquitous transnational data flows']; see also G B F Niblett, Digital Information and the Privacy Problem, OECD Information Studies No 2 (1971).

[4] See generally David Fidler (ed), *The Snowden Reader* (Indiana University Press 2015) part II.

Privacy and the Role of International Law in the Digital Age. Kinfe Yilma, Oxford University Press. © Kinfe Yilma 2023.
DOI:10.1093/oso/9780192887290.003.0001

personal data on a transnational scale.[5] In the digital context, personal privacy can be and often is, therefore, invaded by actors located in jurisdictions well beyond the remit of national legal systems. With the largely borderless nature of communication networks, these international actors can reach, unlike their 'brick-and-mortar' equivalents, billions of users worldwide without any physical presence in the jurisdiction in question. That is what is referred to in this monograph as transnationalization of privacy threats in the digital age.

Compounding the transnationalization phenomenon is the rise of little-regulated transnational private power in the digital space.[6] Much of the Internet's core physical and technical infrastructure as well as services are now owned and served by private corporations.[7] But while Internet users around the world rely on their infrastructures and services, most of these corporations are governed by the law of one or more States, which may themselves adopt diverging approaches.[8] Furthermore, many of the goods and services offered in the Internet space are governed through private contractual mechanisms between Internet corporations and individual users.[9] And often, these terms of use are not only unilaterally imposed and changed (and hence non-negotiable) but also incomprehensible to lay users.

This state of affairs is increasingly transforming technology companies, to use Eichensehr's words, into 'competing centers of power', seemingly on par with governments when it comes to their ability to impact the enjoyment of human rights.[10] With unprecedented access to and use of personal data of billions of users worldwide, technology companies wield considerable influence on the enjoyment of the right to privacy.[11] In a 1974 landmark report, the Danish Committee on Private Registers quipped that the 'privacy problem' is a problem of other persons and entities making decisions relating to individuals, including their work and private life.[12] But the problem has grown far more ominously since with the attendant sophistication of communication technologies. But as shall be demonstrated in this book, international (human rights) law has little to offer in constraining the

---

[5] See, eg, Christopher Millard, 'Data Privacy in the Clouds' in Mark Graham and William Dutton (eds), *Society and the Internet: How Networks of Information and Communication are Changing Our Lives* (Oxford University Press 2014) 333 et seq.

[6] See Angela Daly, *Mind the Gap: Private Power, Online Information Flows and EU Law* (Hart 2016) 18–21.

[7] See Laura DeNardis, *The Global War for Internet Governance* (Yale University Press 2014) chs 1 and 2.

[8] See Chris Reed, *Making Laws for Cyberspace* (Oxford University Press 2012) 14.

[9] See Lee Bygrave, *Internet Governance by Contract* (Oxford University Press 2015) 2–3 [noting that 'contracts provide the legal bricks and mortar of the present structure' of Internet governance].

[10] Kristen Eichensehr, 'Digital Switzerlands' (2019) 167 University of Pennsylvania Law Review 665, 670–85. In a claim (later attributed to a rogue employee), Zuckerberg stated that Facebook now is like a nation-state. Quoted in Jonathan Zittrain, A Bill of Rights for the Facebook Nation (The Chronicle of Higher Education, 20 April 2009) <https://bit.ly/2Jj8gpq>.

[11] See Orla Lynskey, 'Grappling with "Data Power": Normative Nudges from Data Protection and Privacy' (2019) 20 *Theoretical Inquiries in Law* 189, 201–2.

[12] Excerpted in Privacy Developments in Europe and Their Implications for United States Policy: A Staff Report of the Committee on Government Operations, United States Senate (March 1975) 71, 118.

influence of corporations generally.[13] What complicates this even more is that, as shown by the Snowden disclosures, corporations operate in tandem with governments in their transnational privacy invasive practices.[14] The problem, then, is not solely privatization of privacy threats but also abdication by States of their roles to regulate private actors and hence 'protect' the right to privacy.[15]

Sophistication of privacy threats is another aspect of the privacy problem in the digital age. Invasive practices of both States and corporations are increasingly being reinforced by new technologies such as big data analytics, Artificial Intelligence (AI), machine learning, spyware, and malware.[16] The ways in which the right to privacy could be undermined is becoming more seamless, surreptitious, and accessible. Not only are these technologies accessible by anyone with the economic means but they can be, and are indeed, deployed to invade privacy across borders. The proliferation of markets for surveillance technologies, which remains little regulated, best illustrates this phenomenon.[17] The 'privacy problem' caused by the rapid spread of computer technology is heightened by the incessant rise in data-driven technologies such as AI and machine learning. Sophistication of privacy threats, presented by transnational actors, not only facilitates privacy violations and complicates avenues for remedies but also tends to normalize otherwise privacy invasive practices. More crucially, such dynamism of the digital environment undercuts the effectiveness of orthodox protection mechanisms such as time-taking adjudicative processes.

1. Imperatives of an 'International Law' Response

Highlights of the 'privacy problem' in the digital age, outlined above, reveal that the right to privacy in the digital age cannot effectively be secured only through national and regional systems of protection. Part of the challenge relates to the *ability* of these systems of protection to address the privacy problem. At the national level, for example, most jurisdictions either face jurisdictional limits or lack of resources

---

[13] See, eg, Andrew Clapham, *Human Rights Obligations of Non-State Actors* (Oxford University Press 2006) 25–41.

[14] See Neil Richards, 'The Dangers of Surveillance' (2013) 126 Harvard Law Review 1934, 1958.

[15] For purposes of this book, the term 'Internet corporations'—alternatively referred to as 'technology companies' or 'Internet companies'—refer to those private corporations such as Google and Meta that provide web-based digital services and products which, in the process, involve the routine collection and processing of personal data.

[16] See, eg, Normann Witzleb and others, 'An Overview of Emerging Challenges in Privacy Law' in Norman Witzleb and others (eds), *Emerging Challenges in Privacy Law: Comparative Perspectives* (Cambridge University Press 2014) 2 [noting that 'rapid technological developments are a major driver of the current concern with privacy']; Omer Tene, 'Privacy: The New Generations' (2011) 1 International Data Privacy Law 15, 16–21 [discussing the impact of a 'new generation of technologies' on data privacy].

[17] See, eg, The Global Surveillance Industry (Privacy International, 16 February 2018) <https://bit.ly/2Isqqde>.

to counter the challenge. In jurisdictions where there may be fewer jurisdictional challenges—for instance the United States as the home to many big technology companies, political *will* is wanting. US courts have constantly rejected the extra-territorial reach of the right to privacy in international law and drew distinction between citizens/permanent residents and foreigners.[18] The same can often be seen in surveillance legislation of other 'Five Eyes' States.[19] Such discriminatory legal approaches leave citizens of foreign countries without meaningful remedies for arbitrary invasion of privacy.

Jurisdictional limits similarly undercut the ability of even relatively effective systems of regional protection. The success stories of both the Council of Europe (CoE) and the European Union (EU) are circumscribed by, inter alia, case backlog and compliance deficit.[20] And of course, no comparable regime exists, for example in the Asia-Pacific.[21] Where such a regime exists, for instance in Africa, it often lacks the necessary resources to meet the challenges.[22] Thus, the lack of jurisdiction over transnational actors, coupled with resource constraints and absence of political will, leaves billions of individuals without any meaningful recourse and remedies at the national or even regional level. Critically, the characteristically dynamic nature of the digital space where the nature and extent of privacy threats shift constantly as well as the identity and role of actors, challenges the effectiveness of adjudication as a redress mechanism in the digital age.[23] The international relations literature also rightly cautions that regional mechanisms could be impediments towards seeking a more global solution to critical global challenges like the privacy problem.[24]

Aspects of the 'privacy problem' outlined above largely underpin the often-made case for,[25] and initiatives on,[26] an international law response. But such recurring calls for an international privacy framework of some sort give rise to a series of questions, including the following: whether current international law is ill-equipped, in the first place, to address the privacy problem; and if that is really the case, what role(s), or rather place, do these initiatives have in addressing the problem? More broadly, how should international law respond to the 'privacy

---

[18] See chs 2 and 7.

[19] New Zealand, for instance, sets lower standards of protection for aliens, for example by allowing surveillance without judicial warrant. See, eg, New Zealand Must Respect Its International Human Rights Obligations (Privacy International, 2018) <https://bit.ly/3fyhNPr>.

[20] See ch 7.

[21] See, eg, Dinah Shelton and Paolo Carozza, *Regional Protection of Human Rights* (Oxford University Press Vol I, 2nd edn, 2013) 90 et seq.

[22] ibid, 73 et seq.

[23] See ch 8.

[24] See, eg, Ian Goldin, *Divided Nations: Why Global Governance is Failing, and What We Can Do About It* (Oxford University Press 2013) 91–2.

[25] See, eg, Ronald Krotoszynski Jr, *Privacy Revisited: A Global Perspective on the Right to Be Left Alone* (Oxford University Press 2016) 9–10; Konard Lachmayer, 'Rethinking Privacy Beyond Borders: Developing Transnational Rights on Data Privacy' (2015) 20 Tilburg Law Review 78.

[26] See more in section 3 below and further in chs 4–6.

problem' in the digital age? This book examines such questions surrounding the need for an international law response to the privacy problem from the perspective of three international privacy initiatives: proposals for Internet Bills of Rights (IBRs), the ongoing United Nations (UN) discourse on the 'right to privacy in the digital age', and the potential universalization of the CoE Data Protection Convention. It interrogates the respective role of these initiatives in reimagining international privacy law to make it better equipped in the digital age.

2. International Law's Privacy Problem

By and large, the absence of a robust international privacy framework has been the rallying cry of the persistent calls for an international law response to the privacy problem. And indeed, as this book will demonstrate, international law has so far proved ill-equipped to attend to the privacy problem in the digital age. Gaps in the current international law of privacy include a range of normative and institutional weaknesses that cumulatively created a jurisprudential dearth on the right to privacy. The proliferation of various international privacy initiatives in the past few decades, especially in the aftermath of the Snowden revelations is, in part, an attempt to address international law's privacy problem. This book examines the suitability of such initiatives in attending to the various gaps in international privacy law, foreshadowed below and explored further in chapters 2 and 3.

2.1. Normative Limits

International law of privacy has not moved beyond high-level abstract principles contained in human rights treaties, and practically less significant soft data privacy instruments. Since its recognition in 1948 by the Universal Declaration of Human Rights (UDHR), the right to privacy has been successively recognized in a number of binding human rights treaties. But the right has been formulated in an exceedingly vague manner in high-level abstract principles. As shall be shown in chapter 2, the formulation of the right to privacy is even weaker than the rather common tendency of framing human rights vaguely in human rights treaties.[27] The net result is that the uncertainty of scope severely limits the possibility of remedial measures in individual cases.[28] Ambiguity of scope also obscures the respective obligations of States and non-State actors vis-à-vis the right to privacy.

---

[27] On this tendency, see John Tobin, 'Seeking to Persuade: A Constructive Approach to Human Rights Treaty Interpretation' (2010) 23 Harvard Human Rights Journal 1, 1.

[28] See Daniel Cooper and Christopher Kuner, 'Data Protection Law and International Dispute Resolution' (2017) 382 Recueil des Cours 1, 48.

The UN data privacy framework, the second segment of international privacy law, is also riddled with several weaknesses. The Guidelines for Computerized Personal Data Files (Data Privacy Guidelines),[29] the principal UN data privacy instrument adopted in 1990, not only has become slightly obsolete but has also been practically ineffective.[30] A number of other soft law instruments adopted under the auspices of the UN also do not offer a sound basis for data privacy protection.[31] More recently, a number of UN specialized and related agencies have adopted internal data protection policies which apply when personal data are processed by these agencies.[32] While these policies are modern, and largely based on European data privacy standards, the intra-agency nature of these instruments limits their normative value in international law.

Another major normative gap concerns the regulation of the private sector. International human rights law does not impose direct human rights obligations on corporations.[33] It is only through the positive obligation of States that corporations are held to account for human rights violations. But, this vertical application of human rights by which States would 'protect' individuals against private sector infringements falters in the face of recent disturbing revelations. Technology companies routinely collaborate with State actors in various forms, including through granting unfettered access to user data or supplying surveillance technologies.[34] What is more, the existing international framework for the private sector, ie the Ruggie Principles, barely covers human rights in the digital context.[35] The ongoing UN treaty process to translate the Guiding Principles into a binding instrument, besides its little hope of materializing soon, also does not appear to address the human rights obligations of technology companies.[36]

The weak structure of international privacy law has historical roots. Most of the drafting work of the relevant instruments was undertaken during the ideologically divided Cold War era. The political controversies between the West and the East have had direct impact in the way these instruments were formulated. The

---

[29] *Guidelines for the Regulation of Computerized Personal Data Files*, GA Res 45/95, UNGAOR, 45th sess, 68th plen mtg, UN Doc A/Res/45/95 (14 December 1990). Note that the UN Data Privacy Guidelines are referred to in the singular throughout this book deliberately so as to capture the fact that it is *a* single instrument.

[30] See Lee Bygrave, 'International Agreements to Protect Personal Data' in James Rule and Graham Greenleaf (eds), *Global Privacy Protection: The First Generation* (Edward Elgar 2008) 30.

[31] See, eg, *Fundamental Principles of Official Statistics*, GA Res 68/261, 68th sess, Agenda item 9, UN Doc A/RES/68/261 (29 January 2014).

[32] See, eg, *Policy on the Protection of Personal Data of Persons of Concern to the UNHCR* (UNHCR, May 2015).

[33] See HR Committee, *General Comment 31: Nature of Legal Obligation Imposed on State Parties to the Covenant*, 80th sess, UN Doc CCPR/C/21/Rev.1/Add.13 (26 May 2004) para 8.

[34] See, eg, generally Alan Rozenshtein, 'Surveillance Intermediaries' (2018) 70 Stanford Law Review 99; see also Surveillance Technologies (EFF) <https://bit.ly/1fFUpH9>.

[35] *Guiding Principles on Business and Human Rights: Implementing the United Nations 'Protect, Respect and Remedy' Framework*, 17th sess, Agenda item 3, UN Doc A/HRC/RES/17/4 (6 June 2011).

[36] See ch 2.

now vaguely worded provisions of the human right to privacy in international human rights law were results of deliberate political compromises reached between political rivals of the time.[37] The setback caused by ideological differences was further exacerbated by the little attention paid to the right to privacy, in a stark contrast to other rights, by the drafters of the instruments. Similarly, the drafting of the UN Data Privacy Guidelines was also plagued by ideological controversy which derailed the process for over two decades, and ultimately resulted in merely Guidelines whose rather progressive content was significantly watered-down.[38]

2.2. Institutional-Jurisprudential Limits

Little has been forthcoming when it comes to the jurisprudence developed so far around these high-level abstract principles of the human right to privacy. Propelled by structural problems of the UN human rights system, treaty bodies—particularly the Human Rights Committee (HR Committee)—are yet to produce a robust jurisprudence on the right to privacy. Unlike the relatively effective systems of human rights protection at regional levels in Europe and the Americas, structural problems have hampered the development of a robust privacy jurisprudence. The case law of the Committee offers limited guidance on the right to privacy.[39] Other avenues for developing jurisprudence such as concluding observations of treaty bodies are not best-suited to unpack the content of the right to privacy in the digital context. The General Comment (GC) on the right to privacy, adopted in 1988, is largely obsolete and does not adequately cover important aspects of the right to privacy. And little has emerged so far from the work of the recently installed Special Rapporteur on the Right to Privacy (SRP). The lack of any institutional machinery in the international data privacy framework has also meant limited development of data privacy jurisprudence.

3. Promises of Global Privacy Initiatives

As hinted above, the cross-border nature of the Internet, and the lack of a robust privacy framework has long prompted calls for an 'international' framework,[40] and

---

³⁷ ibid.
³⁸ See ch 3.
³⁹ See ch 2.
⁴⁰ For an earlier call for an 'international' framework, see *Montreux Declaration: The Protection of Personal Data and Privacy in A Globalized World—A Universal Right Respecting Diversities* (International Conference of Privacy and Data Protection Commissioners, Montreux, Switzerland, 2005) cum *Madrid Privacy Declaration* (3 November 2009); see also Catherine Rampell, Google Calls for International Standards on Internet Privacy (The Washington Post, 15 September 2007) <http://wapo.st/2kXZAZz>. See also generally Christopher Kuner, 'An International Legal Framework for Data Protection: Issues and Prospects' (2009) 25 Computer Law and Security Review 307; Ariel Wade, 'A

indeed, concrete proposals have also been launched.[41] While academia has been at the forefront of such calls[42] other actors including civil society groups, UN bodies, and a coalition of domestic data protection authorities have taken concrete initiatives. The imperatives for an international privacy framework emerged with some force (and substance) in the wake of the Snowden revelations in 2013. For instance, shortly after his appointment—and in the aftermath of the Snowden debacle, the SRP has called for a 'Geneva style convention'.[43] In a direct response to this call, what came to be called the 'Snowden Treaty' has been reportedly drafted by 'experts in international law and legal experts on Internet freedoms and surveillance', through a process that involved Snowden himself.[44]

High-level proposals have also emerged. One, for instance, suggests negotiation of a 'social compact' among governments, private corporations, individuals, and the technical community to adequately protect privacy rights in the digital age.[45] A related development is the set of recommendations put forward by the (then) UN Secretary-General Ban Ki-moon's Expert Advisory Group assembled to provide recommendations on taking advantage of the 'data revolution' to achieve the Sustainable Development Goals (SDGs).[46] The Group's report provided recommendations, including one for 'global standards on data privacy', and highlighted some data privacy principles.[47]

New Age of Privacy Protection: A Proposal for An International Personal Data Privacy Treaty' (2010) 42 George Washington International Law Review 659. Perhaps, the earliest formal call for a seemingly international (privacy) law was made by the Nigerian delegation at the 1968 Tehran Conference on Human Rights. In a draft Resolution, which the Conference unfortunately was unable to consider due to 'lack of time', Nigeria had proposed for a study group to be created to study the impact of modern technologies on human rights, and then to draw up an 'appropriate convention'. As shall be considered in chapter 3, the Tehran Conference is where the process that led to the adoption of the UN Data Privacy Guidelines originated. See Nigeria: Draft Resolution in Annex to the Final Act of the Tehran Conference on Human Rights, UN Doc A/CONF.32/C.2/L.28 (May 1968) para 18. Another is a proposal by a Task Force established by the Canadian government. See Privacy and Computers, Report of a Task Force Established Jointly by the Department of Communications and the Department of Justice of the Federal Canadian Government (Information Canada, 1972) 173–74.

[41] See, eg, Joint Proposal for a Draft of International Standards on the Protection of Privacy and Personal Data: The Madrid Resolution (November 2009) <https://bit.ly/3SIhRtZ>.
[42] See section 4 below for a critique of scholarship in the field.
[43] Quoted in Adam Alexander, Digital Surveillance 'Worse than Orwell', Says New UN Privacy Chief (The Guardian, 25 August 2015) <http://bit.ly/2h2bEYF>.
[44] The Snowden Treaty: A New International Treaty on the Right to Privacy, Protection Against Improper Surveillance and Protection of Whistle-blowers (September 2015) <http://www.snowdentreaty.org/>; see also Murtaza Hussain, 'Snowden Treaty' Calls for End to Mass Surveillance, Protections for Whistle-blowers (The Intercept, 25 September 2015) <http://bit.ly/1OZZn3I>.
[45] See, eg, *Toward a Social Compact for Digital Privacy and Security: Statement by the Global Commission on Internet Governance* (Chatham House 2015) 13; cf Simon Chesterman, *One Nation Under Surveillance: A New Social Contract to Defend Freedom Without Sacrificing Liberty* (Oxford University Press 2011) ch 9.
[46] Data Revolution Advisory Group Named by UN Secretary General (UN Media Release, 29 August 2014) <http://bit.ly/2mycqzs>.
[47] A World That Counts: Mobilizing the Data Revolution for Sustainable Development, Report Prepared at the Request of the UN Secretary General by the Independent Expert Advisory Group on a Data Revolution for Sustainable Development (November 2014) 3, 21–3. The (then) Secretary-General's

More substantive and focused initiatives that seek to introduce a new or expanded set of privacy standards have also emerged. This book focuses on three of such initiatives that are normatively substantive, and with some potential to foster the progressive development of international law.[48] One post-Snowden initiative takes the form of IBRs. While the idea of IBRs predates the Snowden revelations,[49] IBRs initiatives of various forms and types have emerged in the wake of the revelations. While some are already adopted—or are tabled—in the form of national legislation, most are launched as advocacy and hortatory instruments.[50] Most IBRs documents embody a set of digital rights, principles, and governance forms, including on the right to privacy which is often broken down into several rights and principles.

The other major post-Snowden initiative is the ongoing discourse at the UN on the 'right to privacy in the digital age'.[51] As part of this discourse, the UN has so far adopted a series of Resolutions which incrementally flag some substantive privacy principles. In what appears to be a cross-fertilization of norms, these soft law instruments tend to further develop the corpus of the human right to privacy in international law based on various sources, including IBRs. The appointment of a SRP is also one outcome of this developing discourse. Further, and importantly, the series of Resolutions adopted both by the UN General Assembly (UNGA) and the Human Rights Council (HR Council) are gradually, albeit less coherently, elucidating the content of right to privacy. More importantly, the Resolutions tend to specify the role of Internet corporations.

A different version of the momentum towards an international law response to the 'privacy problem' is through the globalization of regional data protection instruments. This is particularly the case for the CoE Data Protection Convention 108 (as modernized in 2018). The possibility of accession to the Convention system by non-CoE member States—currently fifty-five State parties and counting—puts it in a unique position to gradually evolve into a truly international data protection Convention. To a lesser extent, regional and sub-regional data protection instruments are also emerging in other parts of the world that add up to the overall

---

final report, however, does not go beyond emphasizing the need to uphold the protection of privacy in making use of data for achieving the SDGs. See The Road to Dignity by 2030: Ending Poverty, Transforming All Lives and Protecting the Planet, Synthesis Report of the Secretary-General on the Post-2015 Agenda, UN Doc A/69/700 (December 2014) 39.

[48] For purposes of this book, the expression 'progressive development of international law' is not intended to represent its technical meaning in the Statute of the International Law Commission. The use here is in its ordinary meaning by which it captures the development of international law (of privacy), including but not limited to, through legislative, quasi-legislative, and judicial mechanisms. cf *Statute of the International Law Commission* (21 November 1947) art 15.

[49] For an earlier discussion on IBRs, see Stefano Rodotà, 'A Bill of Rights for the Internet Universe' (2008) 21 The Federalist Debate 15.

[50] See ch 4.

[51] See ch 5.

globalization of data protection standards. The African Union (AU) adopted a Cybersecurity and Personal Data Protection Convention (also referred as the Malabo Convention) in 2014, and sub-regional organizations in Western and Southern Africa have also adopted data protection instruments. With data privacy laws worldwide converging into a set of common rights, principles, and norms, the potential universalization of Convention 108 (and other regional instruments) is the third important global privacy initiative with a prospect of shaping the normative directions of international law.[52]

4. State of the Art and the Book's Argument

Scholarship that considers questions around an international privacy framework predates the Snowden revelations. One finds incidental scholarly commentary on whether, and in what form, an international (data) privacy framework is needed.[53] The debate on the need for, and pertinent form of such framework, has, however, taken on a new force in the wake of the revelations. And as yet, there is little consensus, despite a general agreement on the need for a global privacy framework, on the nature and form of such a framework. Moreover, a closer review of the literature reveals that the role of emerging privacy initiatives in fulfilling the goals of that long-sought 'global privacy framework' or more generally in reimagining the international law of privacy in the digital age is barely considered. Nor has it been part of a sustained discussion, as almost every scholarly viewpoint emerged in isolation of the others. Nevertheless, some common themes can be discerned. The scholarship in this area can be subsumed into four broad categories. What follows offers a brief critique of scholarship in the field and positions the book's argument in the broader debate on the role of international law in the protection of privacy in the digital age.

4.1. The Status Quo Approach

In the first category, one finds scholarship that appears to favour maintaining the status quo. It simply assesses the compatibility or otherwise of the surveillance practices disclosed by the Snowden revelations with present international human rights law.[54] In so doing, it assumes that existing standards are fit for purpose in the

---

[52] See ch 6.
[53] See, eg, Kuner (n 40).
[54] See, eg, Ilina Georgieva, 'The Right to Privacy Under Fire—Foreign Surveillance under the NSA and the GCHQ and Its Compatibility with Art. 17 ICCPR and Art. 8 ECHR' (2015) 31 Utrecht Journal of International and European Law 104, 104–30; Stephen Schulhofer, 'An International Right to Privacy? Be Careful What You Wish For' (2016) 14 International Journal of Constitutional Law 238, 239–61.

digital age, and hence leaves aside investigating the value of new normative stand-ards. Part of the reason for reliance on existing law appears to be challenges of real-izing any stronger international framework in the present political reality. But this also means that the potential of emerging initiatives is overlooked in this literature.

A version of the status quo perspective, prompted partly by the uncertainties of or gaps in treaty law, reaches to other sources of (international) law. One viewpoint holds that the right to privacy is now a rule of customary international law, and hence applies against all States.[55] The existence of a rule of customary international privacy law is argued for based on the wider recognition of the right to privacy in domestic and regional law as well as the recent adoption of Privacy Resolutions by the UN. Another viewpoint, advanced by Sourgens, holds that the right to privacy has attained the status of 'general principles of law' because of the widespread rec-ognition of the right to privacy in the private law of major legal systems of the world.[56]

Such attempts to look beyond treaty law, but still within the existing (inter-national) law, appear to settle for the status quo in terms of standards. That is, there is no suggestion that a new set of human rights standards is necessary, or even if necessary—due to perhaps the usual feasibility concerns associated with establishing new treaty law—that rules of general international law would provide adequate protection to digital privacy. As discussed further in chapters 2–6, such attempts to draw from rules of customary international law, or general principles of law, would do little to remedy the inadequacy of the international law of privacy. To what degree the existence of a customary norm or general principles would assist in reimagining international privacy law is thus not entirely clear. Because the purported customary norm(s) draws from existing privacy standards, the role of emergent privacy law in strengthening international privacy law's normative architecture is also not considered. Sourgens' argument even raises a question of whether general principles of law could be distilled from domestic private laws. This is precisely because the right to privacy, as an international human right, is a matter of (international) public law.

4.2. The Hard Legalization Approach

A second category of literature, which opts for some form of hard law option, comes in various forms. One argues for 'internationalizing' a regional law, a

---

[55] See, eg, Alexandra Rengel, *Privacy in the 21st Century* (Martinus Nijhoff, 2013) 108; Monika Zalnieriute, 'An International Constitutional Moment for Data Privacy' (2015) 23 International Journal of Law and Information Technology 99, 121 et seq.

[56] Frédéric Sourgens, 'The Privacy Principle' (2017) 42 Yale Journal of International Law 345, 367–92.

common candidate being the CoE Data Protection Convention 108.[57] This view-point sees the Convention as the most, if not the only, viable option towards an international (data) privacy law through accession by States that are not members of the CoE. The accession mechanism has so far brought a handful of countries within the Convention System.[58] But, the potential of the Convention as a future of international law of privacy may be overestimated. For one, it evidently focusses only on an aspect of the right to privacy—ie, processing of personal data—and does not address other important aspects of digital privacy such as government surveillance practices. Indeed, as in many data privacy instruments, the Convention does not apply in cases where processing of personal data is undertaken, inter alia, for national security purposes. State parties could make a declaration that exempts data processing for national security purposes.[59] Regulation of government surveillance measures, including by spy agencies, law enforcement, and immigration authorities as well as domain-specific regulatory agencies, falls in a separate area of law sometimes referred to as—in the domestic context—'law of national security surveillance'.[60] And, no comprehensive international treaty regulating government surveillance, including intelligence sharing between governments, currently exists.[61] The recently adopted modernized convention, Convention 108+, slightly rolls back the current national security exemption. But it still permits exceptions under certain conditions when personal data is processed for national security purposes.[62]

Secondly, the CoE Convention is not a self-executing, or self-contained, instrument. This means that no institutional regime tailored to enforce it is envisaged. The Convention, and its Additional Protocol, provides for a set of data privacy principles and mandates the creation of domestic data protection authorities by State parties. The modernization of the Convention has not also gone far enough in strengthening the role of the 'Consultative Committee', now renamed as the 'Convention Committee'. To a large extent, the Committee retains its advisory role.[63] Thus, the lack of a dedicated enforcement machinery reduces the Convention's potential to, by and large, a model law. In countries where rule of law

---

[57] See, eg, Graham Greenleaf, 'A World Data Privacy Treaty? "Globalisation" and "Modernisation" of Council of Europe Convention 108' in Norman Witzleb and others (eds), *Emerging Challenges in Privacy Law: Comparative Perspectives* (Cambridge University Press 2014) 92–138.

[58] See details at <https://bit.ly/2Mh8tvp>.

[59] See *Convention for the Protection of Individuals with Regard to Automatic Processing of Personal Data*, opened for signature 28 January 1981, ETS No 108 (entered into force 1 October 1981) art 3(2).

[60] See, eg, Francesca Bignami and Giorgio Resta, 'Human Rights Extraterritoriality: The Right to Privacy and National Security Surveillance' in Eyal Benvenisti and Georg Nolte (eds), *Community Interests Across International Law* (Oxford University Press 2018) 357–58.

[61] See Ashly Deeks, 'Regulating Foreign Surveillance Through International Law' in Fred Cate and James Dempsey (eds), *Bulk Collection: Systematic Government Access to Private-Sector Data* (Oxford University Press 2017) 351–53.

[62] *Modernized Convention for the Protection of Individuals with Regard to the Processing of Personal Data*, opened for signature 10 October 2018, CETS No 223 (not yet in force) art 11(1(a)).

[63] ibid, art 23.

is not sufficiently upheld, relevant institutions lack independence and resources, and where there are no robust civil society networks, the Convention—once acceded to—might not bring about significant difference in terms of (data) privacy protection. Many countries, particularly in Africa, where data privacy legislation has recently been introduced are also yet to install data protection authorities.

One possibility by which provisions of the Convention may find some enforcement is through the European Court of Human Rights (ECtHR) by which the Court draws from the Convention in interpreting Article 8 of the European Convention on Human Rights and Fundamental Freedoms (ECHR). But this also comes with its own limitations. One is that the jurisdiction of the ECtHR is limited to the forty-seven CoE member States, and secondly, whether the Court could rely on an extraneous instrument in applying the Article 8 is open to debate on legitimacy grounds.[64] Greenleaf, who has long advocated for the 'globalization' of Convention 108 through accession by non-CoE member States, recently suggested a way to address this institutional gap. He argues that once acceding States are required by the CoE to simultaneously ratify the First Optional Protocol to the International Covenant on Civil and Political Rights (ICCPR), which mandates a complaints procedure, the CoE 108's provisions could be enforced by the HR Committee.[65]

Given that the Committee's mandate is to apply only the ICCPR, the suggestion raises a question of competence. But importantly, the slow pace in which the accession by non-State parties have moved so far reduces the appeal of Greenleaf's idea of globalizing Convention 108. Since 2013, only a handful of non-CoE member States have acceded to the Convention.[66] And, the accession so far—like the recent surge in adoption of national data privacy legislation worldwide—is arguably prompted by pragmatic economic considerations, particularly with a view to facilitate trade with the EU.[67] Human rights considerations have thus taken the back seat. Making accession to the Convention conditional upon ratifying another, less favoured, treaty may also reduce the appeal of accession as a 'globalization' device. These contexts reduce the potential of globalizing the CoE data privacy Convention. Moreover, the prospect of a global privacy treaty mediated by the

---

[64] For legitimacy questions in the context of ECtHR, see Michael Hamilton and Antoine Buyse, 'Human Rights Courts as Norm-Brokers' (2018) 18 Human Rights Law Review 205, 207, 212, 216.

[65] Graham Greenleaf, The UN Special Rapporteur: Advancing A Global Privacy Treaty? (2015) 136 Privacy Laws and International Business Report 7–9; for a recent iteration, see Graham Greenleaf, The UN Should Adopt Data Protection Convention 108 as Global Treaty, University of New South Wales Law Research Series No 24 (2018) 2–5.

[66] See <https://bit.ly/2JPrMPr>.

[67] See, eg, Orla Lynskey, The Foundations of EU Data Protection Law (Oxford University Press 2015) 43; on the recent proliferation of data privacy legislation in Africa prompted by trade consideration, see Alex Makulilo, 'The Future of Data Protection in Africa' in Alex Makulilo (ed), African Data Privacy Laws (Springer 2016) 371–73. One of the driving factors for the enactment of the Australian Privacy (Private Sector) Amendment Act 2000 was a similar trade consideration. See, eg, Explanatory Memorandum, Privacy (Private Sector) Amendment Bill 2000 (Cth) 11.

CoE, as Bygrave aptly notes, will be affected by its regional status and bias.[68] We return to this point in chapter 6.

A regional approach to global governance of critical issues like digital privacy can also be problematic more generally. The international relations literature cautions that regional mechanisms could be, as alluded to above, impediments towards seeking a more global solution to critical global challenges like the 'privacy problem'.[69] States with strong bureaucratic structures and economic power may resist the pursuit of an international response. Add to this the fact that regional mechanisms generally have uneven capacities to respond even at the regional level. As noted above, regional bodies such the AU are not as institutionally capable as the CoE is in addressing the 'privacy problem' in the digital age.

A related proposal seeks to show the plausibility of introducing a global (data) privacy treaty negotiated under the auspices of the World Trade Organization (WTO).[70] Nomination of the WTO as a possible forum relies on three points: its organizational mandate of lowering global trade barriers, its robust institutional apparatus, and its 'all-in organizational structure' covering most trade-related matters.[71] Sinnreich suggests that the proposed treaty must be restricted to setting the 'minimum thresholds' for data privacy laws in member States such as a maximum period of data retention and the required text of privacy policies.[72] Besides the feasibility concern particularly given the ongoing trade wars, the proposal faces a number of other hurdles.

As Sinnreich himself admits, the primary objection to the proposal would come from the WTO which consistently distanced itself from being a forum for addressing digital privacy matters.[73] The institutional mandate of the WTO, ie, to facilitate free international trade, including transborder data flows, makes it also less pertinent for data privacy legislation whose underlying goal rather is to protect (data) privacy without unnecessarily limiting free trade. This point relates to what Bygrave ascribes to the 'commercial bias' of the WTO to sufficiently and impartially uphold data privacy interests.[74] The likelihood of a WTO-based data privacy treaty seems even less when considering the fact that its resources are already absorbed by administering numerous trade-related agreements.

---

[68] Lee Bygrave, *Data Privacy Law: An International Perspective* (Oxford University Press 2014) 206–07.

[69] See, eg, Goldin (n 24) 91–2.

[70] Aram Sinnreich, An International Approach to Data Privacy, Center for Media and Social Impact, American University Policy Briefing Note (August 2018) 8–9; for an earlier contemplation of the WTO as a possible forum for international (data) privacy treaty, see Colin Bennett and Charles Raab, *The Governance of Privacy: Policy Instruments in Global Perspective* (MIT Press 2006) 108.

[71] ibid.

[72] ibid.

[73] See The WTO and Internet Privacy, Fact and Fiction: Misunderstanding and Scare Stories <https://bit.ly/2P9arPD> (noting that 'the WTO has had nothing whatsoever to do with Internet privacy').

[74] Bygrave (n 30) 48.

Narrower treaty options are argued for in the other area of scholarship on government surveillance, be it under the auspices of the CoE,[75] a global instrument built around a set of procedural norms on surveillance drawn from domestic laws of western countries,[76] a treaty exclusively among western democratic countries,[77] a merely EU-US 'no-spy' agreement,[78] or just an additional protocol to Article 17 of the ICCPR that clarifies the issue of extraterritoriality.[79] Scholarship in this group not only is limited to 'digital surveillance' but also narrower in scope, both in terms of who gets to join the treaty and normative sources. But importantly, this category mostly overlooks emerging initiatives such as IBRs and the UN privacy discourse, and hence their normative significance in filling the void in global surveillance regulation.

A smaller section of the scholarship in this category advocates a broader treaty option. One, for instance, calls for 'global privacy standards' that primarily embrace a general right to privacy that, among other themes, recognizes the extraterritorial application of the right.[80] Specifics of this proposal, however, are left wanting: for instance, what content the general right would have, how such a right would be adopted, and in what form? Also unclear is how such a right would interact with existing international rules/rights such as Article 17 of the ICCPR—would it repeal these or be a supplemental/ amendment sub-right? Another related proposal has been for an IBRs to be adopted by a 'public supranational legislator' based on input from the private sector.[81] Similar problems of ambiguity as to the scope and authority of the instrument, and at which level it would be adopted, arise here as well.

Other broader concerns bedevil this category of scholarship. One is that no plausible reason is offered as to why, and whether, such a proposed treaty is feasible in the present reality of international politics. As Bygrave rightly notes, the prospects of a (data) privacy treaty will be frustrated by a host of factors, including ideological differences, other policy considerations such as national security and trade as well as the lack of a pertinent body to broker the instrument.[82] And whether a

---

[7]   Eliza Watt, 'The Right to Privacy and the Future of Mass Surveillance' (2017) 21 The International Journal of Human Rights 773, 773–99.

[7]   Ashley Deeks, 'An International Legal Framework for Surveillance' (2015) 55 Virginia Journal of International Law 291, 293 et seq.

[7]   See generally Ian Brown and others, Towards Multilateral Standards for Surveillance Reforms, Oxford Internet Institute Discussion Paper (2015).

[7]   David Cole and Federico Fabbrini, 'Bridging the Transatlantic Divide? The United States, the European Union, and the Protection of Privacy Across Borders' (2016) 14 International Journal of Constitutional Law 220, 220–37; see also Ian Brown, 'The Feasibility of Transatlantic Privacy-protective Standards for Surveillance' (2015) 23 International Journal of Law and Information Technology 23.

[7]   Jordan Paust, 'Can You Hear Me Now? Private Communication, National Security and the Human Rights Disconnect' (2015) 15 Chicago Journal of International Law 612, 612–51.

[8]   Valsamis Mitsilegas, 'Surveillance and Digital Privacy in the Transatlantic "War on Terror": The Case for A Global Privacy Regime' (2016) 47 Columbia Human Rights Law Review 1, 73–7.

[8]   Giovanna De Minico, 'Towards an Internet Bill of Rights' (2015) 37 Loyola of Los Angeles International and Comparative Law Review 1, 19–30.

[8]   Bygrave (n 68) 205–07; see also Lauren Saadat and Shannon Ballard, 'A Way Ahead for Global Privacy Standards?—Thoughts on a UN Convention on Data Protection, International Standards and International Agreements: Which is the Best Option?' (2007) 89 Privacy Laws and Business 15.

proposed treaty, once drafted and adopted, would be signed and ratified by a critical mass of States is highly uncertain.[83] The wider membership of the UN might also emerge as a challenge in building consensus around a global instrument.[84] Indeed, one of the reasons the UN itself had been hesitant in proposing an international (privacy) instrument is the perceived divergence of opinion on how such an instrument would fare with other existing rights and the different legal contexts in which such legislation would operate.[85] The extent of this challenge might have multiplied over the past few decades or so due to the phenomenon called in the international relations literature 'multipolarity'.[86] The number of States, added to the diversity of their interests and the complexity of modern global problems, has grown exponentially thereby making the prospect of global consensus on critical global issues less likely.

The common feasibility concern aside, the constant failure to reconcile the proposed treaty option with the existing treaty (and soft law) regime is a limitation of the literature. This is significant in that any reform idea, unless it explicates how it interacts with or complements, or even supplants, the existing framework, is unlikely to materialize, or be effective if/when introduced.

4.3. The Institutionalist Approach

Another area of scholarship favours an institutional rearrangement, either through the creation of a new monitoring body or revitalization of existing institutions. De Hert and Papakonstantinou argue that the missing link in global (data) privacy protection is the lack of an agency tasked to oversee protection of data privacy in the context of transnational data processing.[87] In their view, once the institutional gap is filled, existing law, particularly the UN Data Privacy Guidelines, already offers—at least tentatively—sufficient normative guidance. De Hert and Papakonstantinou suggest that the proposed agency could be fashioned like the

---

[83] ibid, 206.

[84] See Perry Keller, *European and International Media Law: Liberal Democracy, Trade and the New Media* (Oxford University Press 2011) 349.

[85] See Respect for the Privacy of Individuals and Integrity and Sovereignty of Nations in the Light of Advances in Recording and Other Techniques, Report of the Secretary-General, UN Doc E/CN.4/1116 (23 January 1973) para 177.

[86] See, eg, Thomas Hale and others, *Gridlock: Why Global Cooperation Is Failing When We Need It Most* (Polity 2013) 34–40.

[87] Paul De Hert and Vagelis Papakonstantinou, 'Moving Beyond the Special Rapporteur on Privacy with the Establishment of a New, Specialized United Nations Agency: Addressing the Deficit in Global Cooperation for the Protection of Data Privacy' in Dan Svantesson and Dariusz Kloza (eds), *Transatlantic Privacy Relations as a Challenge to Democracy* (Intersentia 2017) 521–32. For an earlier (and longer) rendition of the argument, see Paul De Hert and Vagelis Papakonstantinou, 'Three Scenarios for International Governance of Data Privacy: Towards an International Data Privacy Organization, Preferably a UN Agency?' (2013) 9 I/S: A Journal of Law and Policy for the Information Society 271 et seq.

World Intellectual Property Organization (WIPO), an intergovernmental specialized agency of the UN.

While the authors do not explicitly call for a data privacy treaty *per se*—at least as a matter of urgency, their support for a new agency presupposes the negotiation and adoption of a treaty. The WIPO is an inter-governmental agency created through a treaty: the WIPO Convention.[88] It is also not fully clear whether the idea of a new agency seeks to use relevant existing treaties such as the ICCPR as legal basis in lieu of negotiating one anew. But even this would be a peculiar proposition, not least because some form of legislative measure, most likely an amendment to the ICCPR, would be required to create the proposed agency.[89] This, in turn, raises the same issue of feasibility associated with a treaty solution.

To what extent the proposed data privacy agency would address institutional concerns associated with the right to privacy is also questionable. The possible functions of the proposed agency, for example whether it would also be an adjudicative body, are not clear. Based on the WIPO analogy, the most the agency could do is promotion of global data privacy protection and facilitating cooperation among States.[90] The rather desirable options for access to remedies, for example available through domestic data privacy authorities and courts, cannot be achieved through a WIPO-type data privacy agency. WIPO's alternative dispute resolution services also do not seem to be ideal for matters concerning data privacy.

Moreover, the argument—at least in its updated version—springs from the perception that the appointment of a SRP is an inadequate institutional response. In that sense, it appears to underestimate the potential of the already existing institutional arrangements such as the HR Committee. But more fundamentally, the institutionalist perspective overvalues the UN Data Privacy Guidelines which, as shall be shown in chapter 3, is mostly superseded by progressive data privacy standards elsewhere. As such, it does not consider whether and the ways in which emergent privacy standards may complement or revitalize extant UN data privacy standards to bring them up to speed with post-1990 developments in the data protection arena.

A slightly varied version of the institutionalist perspective expects existing institutional structures to step up and adapt existing privacy standards to the new realities of the digital age. Fischer-Lescano argues that the HR Committee should apply the right to privacy directly in the context of interference both by States and Internet corporations.[91] In light of the considerable influence of these corporations

---

[88] *Convention Establishing the World Intellectual Property Organization*, opened for signature 14 July 1967 (entered into force 1 June 1984) [as amended in 1979].

[89] Another concern associated with WIPO is bias. It is said to be 'beholden to intellectual property interests'. See, eg, Jack Goldsmith and Tim Wu, *Who Controls the Internet? Illusions of a Borderless World* (Oxford University Press 2006) 170.

[90] See WIPO Convention (n 88) art 4.

[91] Andreas Fischer-Lescano, 'Struggles for a Global Internet Constitution: Protecting Global Communication Structures Against Surveillance Measures' (2016) 5 Global Constitutionalism 145, 145–72.

in the digital space, the traditional 'statist' scope of human rights law is unsustainable, and they must be held directly accountable. He further suggests that the Committee must interpret the right to privacy broadly to encompass a 'right to cryptography' that imposes an obligation on both States and corporations to 'promote opportunities for use of cryptography'.[92] The Committee could—within its limited capacity and resources—pursue, the argument goes, doctrinal adaptations of the ICCPR to cyberspace.

While this view pragmatically builds on the present framework, it leaves open some fundamental issues. One is that it offers little as to how, and on what basis, such 'doctrinal adaptation' would be pursued by the Committee. Is it through progressive interpretation of the ICCPR, or drawing from comparative sources? Secondly, it tends to overvalue the capacity of the Committee, a part-time body of experts that operates through three sessions annually, each held just for four weeks. Thirdly, the legal basis to unilaterally impose direct human rights obligations on corporations is doubtful. In the absence of some form of legislative support that gives such a new mandate, and of course political support of States and the private sector, it appears to be an untenable proposition.

As will be discussed in chapter 2, both early and ongoing UN efforts of introducing a legally binding instrument on business and human rights have met stiff resistance from many States and transnational corporations. Fischer-Lescano's call for a 'right to cryptography' echoes the IBRs project's trademark 'right to (use) encryption' but nowhere is there a mention of IBRs or the UN Privacy Resolutions where the use of encryption is increasingly emerging as an important theme. The purported obligation of 'promoting opportunities' is also ambiguous as to, for instance, whether it would involve just a negative obligation or positive obligation as well. A related institutionalist viewpoint supports a multi-level 'transnationalization of rights', including the right to privacy. Alwicker recommends that progressive interpretation of international human rights by relevant stakeholders, including courts, transnational civil society actors, and legislatures. Details of the proposed interpretive approach are, however, left wanting.[93]

4.4. The Soft Legalization Approach

A final area of the literature favours a soft law approach towards reimagining privacy in the digital age. The fledgling scholarship on IBRs appears to envision a sort of cosmopolitan 'Internet constitution' that shapes policy and judicial practice at the local level. Rodotà, for instance, envisions a charter of rights for the Internet

---

[92] ibid, 170.
[93] See Tilmann Alwicker, 'Transnationalizing Rights: International Human Rights Law in Cross-Border Contexts' (2018) 29 European Journal of International Law 581, 604–6.

that a 'crowd of judges' in each jurisdiction would apply in addressing questions of human rights on the Internet.[94] But to which such instrument reference will be made is not clear. Whether it is envisioning a newer instrument to be adopted, or just referring to one or more of the existing IBRs such as the one launched under the auspices of the UN Internet Governance Forum (IGF), is not readily clear.[95] If it is the latter, a question of competence arises—on what legal basis would domestic courts refer to an external instrument like IBRs in their interpretive exercises? A variant of the 'soft legalization'[96] approach is the support for a 'model law' that would provide guidance to domestic lawmakers,[97] or a soft law in the form of a treaty body GC.[98] The model law proposal is based on several of the United Nations Commission on International Trade Law's (UNCITRAL) model laws. But as in the case of the 'internationalizing regional law' approach discussed above, this proposal substantially relegates the matter to States, to adopt and apply the law. That the model law would be non-binding further reduces the impact of the law in bringing about tangible results.

4.5. The Book's Argument

In addition to the specific points about each area of literature discussed above, there are three overarching limitations. First, the debate was not always part of a sustained discourse. Some scholarly viewpoints emerged in total isolation of, or without any visible engagement with, other viewpoints. One may attribute this disjoint in the academic debate to two factors. A primary factor could be the fledgling nature of the literature on the international aspect of the right to privacy. As the above survey of the literature illustrates, a robust body of scholarship on

---

[94] See Rodotà (n 49) 17; see also Rikke Jorgensen, 'An Internet Bill of Rights?' in Ian Brown (ed), *Research Handbook on Governance of the Internet* (Edward Elgar 2013) 369–70. For a related argument for a 'non-hierarchical' IBRs to be created in a multi-stakeholder fashion, see Wolfgang Benedek and others, The Humanization of Internet Governance: A Roadmap Towards a Comprehensive Global (Human) Rights Architecture for the Internet, Paper Presented at the 3rd Annual GigaNet Symposium, Hyderabad, India (2 December 2008).

[95] See *Charter of Human Rights and Principles for the Internet* (7th edn, 2019); see also ch 4. In an earlier work, Rodotà had flagged the idea of drafting an 'informational constitution' or 'information bill of rights' but did not go beyond casually mentioning that the said bill of rights would guarantee the 'right to search for, receive and distribute information, the right to informational self-determination and the right to informational privacy'. As such, common IBRs are not envisaged in the 'informational constitution'. See Stefano Rodotà, 'Protecting Informational Privacy: Trends and Problems' in Willem Ates and others (eds), *Information Law Towards The 21st Century* (Kluwer Law and Taxation 1992) 264.

[96] With apologies to Abbott and others for the term 'soft legalization', which captures the codification of international rules in soft law. See Kenneth Abbott and others, 'The Concept of Legalization' (2000) 54 International Organization 401, 401–02.

[97] See Christopher Kuner, 'The European Union and the Search for an International Data Protection Framework' (2014) 2 Groningen Journal of International Law 54, 66–7.

[98] See, eg, Rikke Jorgensen, 'Can Human Rights Law Bend Mass Surveillance?' (2018) 3 Internet Policy Review 1, 6.

international privacy law is yet to emerge. The other factor relates to the short life-span of the Internet and related technologies. This would mean that the legal dis-course around it is at the early stages in examining the implications of the Internet on international law and vice versa.[99] As Raustiala rightly notes, 'despite its global importance, the Internet remains little studied by international lawyers'.[100] This means that the role of international law in attending to the 'privacy problem' has not been a subject of comprehensive and sustained inquiry.

Secondly, the literature fails to provide a complete perspective on the inadequa-cies of international privacy law in protecting digital privacy. As the above dis-cussion suggests, each proposal addresses only an aspect of the right to privacy in international law. No major attempt has, therefore, been made to look at the questions regarding the right to privacy in a comprehensive manner. Thirdly, the existing scholarship does not address the role of emerging initiatives such as IBRs and the ongoing UN privacy discourse in reimagining the right to privacy in inter-national law. As shall be examined in chapters 4, 5, and 6 these initiatives tend to envision the right to privacy in a new light that would partly respond to gaps in present international privacy law. The book draws upon the progressive tenden-cies of these initiatives, exploring the ways in which international privacy may be reimagined in the digital age.

The book joins the debate on the appropriateness of global privacy standards but approaches it in a particular manner, ie, from the perspective of three global privacy initiatives. It examines the roles of these emerging initiatives in reimagining the international law of privacy in a manner that accommodates the new realities of the digital age. The book adopts a three-level framework of analysis, focusing on the 'freestanding', 'contributory', and 'catalytic' roles of the initiatives. The 'freestanding role' concerns the way in which the respective initiative would evolve as an autono-mous international law response to the privacy problem. The 'contributory role' relates to the possibility of shaping the development of law (international, regional, or national), judicial and industry practice. By 'catalytic role', the reference is to the potential of the relevant initiative in shaping the 'normative and methodological direction' of future reform efforts of international privacy law.[101]

The book argues that emergent privacy norms envisioned in progressive privacy initiatives have a potential in further developing the right to privacy based on the new realities of the digital environment. But it contends that a number of factors limit the extent to which these initiatives may contribute towards reimagining international privacy law in the digital age. To address this impasse, the book

---

[99] See Michael Schmitt, 'Introduction' in Nicholas Tsagourias and Russell Buchan (eds), *Research Handbook on International Law and Cyberspace* (Edward Elgar 2015) 2–3.

[100] Kal Raustiala, 'Governing the Internet' (2016) 110 The American Journal of International Law 491, 492.

[101] The term 'normative direction' is borrowed from Koh. See Harold Koh, 'Rosco Pound Lecture: Transnational Legal Process' (1996) 75 Nebraska Law Review 181, 207.

argues that what is needed now is an approach that builds on, but goes beyond, the merits of these initiatives. Mapped against the UN human rights framework, the book proposes a pragmatic, but principled, approach to international privacy law that is suitable to deal with the 'privacy problem' in the digital age.[102]

The book chooses to use IBRs, the ongoing UN Privacy discourse, and the Convention 108(+) system as case studies for the following reasons. First, these initiatives have the potential to spur the progressive development of international law of privacy. As shall be shown in chapters 4 and 5, the IBRs project and the UN privacy discourse cast the right to privacy in a more sophisticated and elaborate manner. This departs from the high-level nature of other privacy initiatives, or proposals. And, this makes them appropriate case studies to examine their role in reimagining international law of privacy in the digital age. Second, the initiatives are generally global in scope, and hence, offer a useful vantage point in examining the role of international law in securing the right to privacy in the digital age. The series of UN Privacy Resolutions, for instance, are international soft laws that tend to elaborate the existing international privacy standards. Third, unlike other initiatives highlighted above, the case studies are part of a relatively sustained and coherent global privacy discourse. As shall be shown, both initiatives have incrementally evolved over the years, particularly since the Snowden revelations. The UN Privacy discourse, for example, is still ongoing with new and substantive resolutions being adopted both by the UNGA and HR Council. Fourth—and in a slightly different way, the Convention 108(+) system is designed with a clear ambition of gradually evolving into a universal standard. If its universal potential were to accrue over time, it would be the only truly international data privacy treaty.

5. Method and Analytical Framework

The book primarily adopts a doctrinal research method, examining the role of *current* international law of privacy and *emergent* standards in upholding digital privacy. Thus, the focus is on existing and emergent norms, rights, and principles on the right to privacy in international law. These include relevant privacy rules of international human rights and data privacy laws as well as emergent privacy norms enshrined in IBRs initiatives and UN Privacy Resolutions. Reference is also made to a range of relevant literature from diverse areas of law, including public international law, human rights law, data privacy law, Internet law, and theories of rights. That the applicable digital privacy norms draw from multiple sources means

---

[102] cf Alexandra Huneeus, 'Human Rights and the Future of Being Human' (2018) 112 AJIL Unbound Symposium on UDHR at 70 and the Future of Being Human 324, 328 [noting that human rights law (and discourse) generally offers a framework for varying conversations and serves as a 'site of cross-fertilization'].

that the literature is also diverse. For example, the relevant literature on theories of rights is considered in examining the nature and legal significance of IBRs.

To some extent, the book also employs a comparative approach. It does so mainly in two respects. One is when it examines gaps in international privacy law. The law and practice of regional systems of human rights and data privacy protection are referred to where applicable. The second is in investigating the nature and scope of IBRs initiatives and UN Privacy Resolutions. Both the IBRs project and the Privacy Resolutions are products of cross-fertilization of norms, including norms and principles borrowed from domestic and regional laws. In examining these emergent privacy norms, incidental references are made to their counterparts in domestic or regional law and judicial decisions with a view to properly explicate the nature, scope, and significance of these norms.

This book proceeds from the premise that the right to privacy *is* a fundamental and universally accepted human right, subject to restriction only under legally prescribed conditions.[103] But as flagged above—and further explored in chapters 2 and 3, current international law of privacy is largely unfit for purpose in the digital age. In the process of exploring ways of reimagining the law in the digital age, the book adopts a pragmatic approach. This pragmatic orientation of the book has parallels with the little-known pragmatic approach to international law articulated by Schieder.[104] While his theoretical approach is premised on the traditional 'statist' nature of international law, its five key elements largely coincide with the book's analytical framework.[105] Thus, the pragmatic approach to international privacy law explored in the book has four key components: incremental and historically minded, practical, programmatic, and multi-faceted.[106] These features orient the examination throughout the book.

A primary component of the book's pragmatic approach is that it is *incremental and historically minded*. Its 'incremental' nature captures that fact that it is mapped onto, builds on, and is supplementary to present structures of privacy law in general and international privacy law in particular.[107] Reform ideas explored in chapters 7 and 8 are meant to fill gaps—both normative and institutional—in

---

[103] See, eg, generally Beate Roessler, 'Privacy as a Human Rights' (2017) 117 Proceedings of the Aristotelian Society 187.

[104] See Siegfried Schieder, 'Pragmatism and International Law' in Harry Bauer and Elisabetta Brighi (eds), *Pragmatism in International Relations* (Routledge 2009); see also Siegfried Schieder, 'Pragmatism as a Path Towards A Discursive and Open Theory of International Law' (2000) 11 European Journal of International Law 663. [Translated by Iain Fraser].

[105] These five key elements are: instrumentalism, historicism, contextualism, perspectivism, and eclecticism.

[106] Note also that these elements of pragmatism correspond to the four features of the 'constructive approach' to human rights treaty interpretation developed by Tobin: principled, clear and practical, coherent in reasoning, and context sensitivity. See Tobin (n 27) 15–48. These are noted further below.

[107] cf 'principled interpretation'. Tobin at 15, citing also Maarten Bos, 'Theory and Practice of Treaty Interpretation' (1980) 27 Netherlands International Law Review 135 (stating that for a treaty interpretation to be persuasive, it must be made in light of principles agreed upon by the interpretative community).

international law explored in chapters 2 and 3. This supports the overall 'historically minded' orientation of the book, capturing the idea that answers to existing and emerging challenges are usefully informed by history. In particular, the book emphasizes on relevant historical occurrences in international human rights law in looking to the future of the right to privacy. Chapters 2 and 3, for instance, look back at the drafting history of the respective regimes for the protection of the rights to privacy and data privacy in order to properly appreciate the present framework. Normative and institutional reform ideas proposed in chapters 7 and 8 are also historically minded. The proposed soft law is inspired by several precedents in the UN practice, as is the proposed privacy forum.

The second component is *practical* which conveys the relative suitability of measures for implementation.[108] As noted already, the primary objective of the book is to propose a set of measures that would effectively address international law's privacy problem. In that spirit, chapters 7 and 8 propose a suite of practical measures designed to lessen normative and institutional gaps in international privacy law. *Programmatic* is the third component which reflects the anti-formalist feature of pragmatism in that law and juridical decision making must be open to new experiences and reversibility to adjust to new developments.[109] This makes it a dynamic and progressive approach as opposed to an approach that sees law as a fixed set of rules and processes. The book's approach to the right to privacy seeks to clarify the ways in which international law can be moulded to remain fit for purpose in securing digital privacy. Informed by contemporary challenges that privacy faces, this book explores responsive mechanisms for protecting digital privacy. The proposed institutional reform of creating a multistakeholder forum, for instance, would help the UN privacy regime remain adaptive to changing circumstances.

The fourth aspect of the book's pragmatic approach is *multi-faceted*. A multifaceted approach is one that is informed by and builds on components drawn from multiple sources.[110] A primary virtue of heterogeneity is that it benefits from insights borrowed from different sources. The book broadly reflects eclecticism with elements drawn from a variety of sources, including insights from various areas of law, and scholarship. In examining UN privacy standards, the book examines, for example, a broad range of instruments, including relevant human rights treaties and the attendant case law as well as general and domain-specific data privacy

---

[108] cf 'clear and practical interpretation'. See at 25, citing also Bos (n 107) [noting the need for a treaty interpretation to yield a meaning capable of being applied in daily life].

[109] cf 'context sensitive interpretation'. See at 40–48, citing also Martti Koskenneimi, *From Apology to Utopia: The Structure of International Legal Argument* (Cambridge University Press 2006) [noting that treaty interpretation should be context-sensitive and hence it must be applicable to the relevant context].

[110] cf 'coherent interpretation'. See at 28–39, citing also Leanor Soriano, 'A modest Notion of Coherence in Legal Reasoning: A Model for the European Court of Justice' (2003) 16 Ratio Juris 296 (noting that the interpretation should draw from the views and expertise of relevant actors and ensure system coherence).

instruments. Chapters 4 and 5 examine the legal significance of IBRs and a series of UN Privacy Resolutions. Reform ideas explored in chapters 7 and 8 are also informed by and draw insights from heterogeneous sources.

6. A Note on Terminologies and Concepts

In this book, the phrase 'international privacy law'—alternatively referred to as 'international law of privacy'—is meant to capture all rules of international law concerning the right to privacy. This includes relevant UN treaties and soft law instruments that touch on aspects of the right to privacy, including data privacy; but deliberately excludes (a) a set of UN soft laws on consumer protection and competition regulation that are not only less known but also faintly address (consumer) privacy and (b) regional privacy laws such as EU law, which are referred to only for comparative purposes.[111] In that sense, it is a subcategory of international law dealing with privacy and data protection. It is primarily made up of two sources of law: international human rights law and international data privacy law. The international human right to privacy framework draws primarily from the major international human rights instruments such as the UDHR, the ICCPR, and subsequent human rights treaties.

Also forming part of this legal framework is the privacy jurisprudence, albeit thin, developed by relevant UN treaty bodies such as the HR Committee and Special Procedures of the HR Council, particularly the Special Rapporteurs on the Rights to Privacy and Freedom of Expression. International data privacy law, on the other hand, consists of a set of international soft laws governing the protection of personal data. Key among such instruments is the UN Data Privacy Guidelines. The Guidelines has been supplemented, over the years, with domain/subject specific data privacy guidelines, and more recently, with agency-level internal data protection policies. Whether privacy and data protection now form part of general international law is a question considered at length in the book: see chapters 2, 3, 5, and 6. In that sense, international custom and general principles are potential sources of international law of privacy.

In European (data) privacy discourse, a distinction is often drawn between the notions of 'privacy' and 'data protection' in the light of recognition of the distinct rights to privacy and to data protection in the EU Fundamental Rights Charter. The prevailing view is that while the two rights overlap to a greater degree, data protection protects more than privacy interests, and that privacy may not protect all types of personal data.[112] Moreover, privacy encompasses more than the protection

---

[111] See, eg, *UN Guidelines for Consumer Protection*, GA Res 70/186, 70th sess, Agenda item 18(a) UN Doc A/RES/70/186 (4 February 2016).

[112] See, eg, Orla Lynskey, 'Deconstructing Data Protection: The "Added-Value" of A Right to Data Protection in the EU Legal Order' (2014) 63 International and Comparative Law Quarterly 569.

of personal data. Against this backdrop, the book will treat the 'human right to privacy' and 'data privacy' as sources for the protection of privacy in the digital age. The reference to 'data protection' as a 'regulatory field of data privacy' is meant to capture the bureaucratic and mechanical nature of data protection legislation governing the collection, storage, processing, and disclosure of personal data.[113] The book follows Wack's description of the notion of privacy as the right not to be subject to incursions into one's private domains understood more broadly.[114] Whereas the rather nuanced phrase 'digital privacy' is used in the book to denote privacy in the context of digital communications.

---

[113] See, eg, Maria Tzanou, *The Fundamental Right to Data Protection: Normative Value in the Context of Counter-Terrorism Surveillance* (Hart 2017) ch 1.

[114] See Raymond Wacks, *Privacy: A Very Short Introduction* (Oxford University Press 2015) 2; see also Andrea Monti and Raymond Wacks, *Protecting Personal Information: The Right to Privacy Reconsidered* (Hart 2019) 125.

PART I

INTERNATIONAL LAW OF PRIVACY IN THE DIGITAL AGE

This part undertakes a 'regime analysis' by which the extent to which international privacy law offers effective protection to the right to privacy in the digital age is examined. In chapter 2, the reach of the human right to privacy framework is examined where it is argued that international human rights law is ill-equipped to uphold digital privacy. It traces the reasons behind its present weak structures to the drafting history of formative human rights instruments during the Cold War era. In chapter 3, the boundaries of the second but often overlooked source of international privacy law are examined: international data privacy law. The chapter argues that, plagued by deep normative fragmentation and the lack of a robust institutional framework, the international data privacy framework offers little protection to data privacy. It further locates the causes for the present weak structure of the data privacy framework in the political controversies of the Cold War period.

2

The Reach of Human Rights Law

1. Introduction

This chapter examines whether, and to what extent, international human rights law is well-equipped to uphold the right to privacy in the digital age. The right to privacy is guaranteed in a number of international human rights instruments. The primary sources of privacy rights are the Universal Declaration of Human Rights (UDHR) and the International Covenant on Civil and Political Rights (ICCPR) which guarantee the right to privacy in an almost identical manner.[1] The right to privacy is also guaranteed in other specialized United Nations (UN) instruments such as the Convention on the Rights of the Child (CRC), the Convention on the Rights of Persons with Disabilities (CRD), and the International Convention on the Rights of Migrant Workers and Members of their Families (ICRMW).[2] The chapter investigates the scope of the right to privacy in these instruments, and the accompanying jurisprudence, to show whether international human rights law is fit for purpose in the digital age. It finds that current international human rights law provides weak protection for digital privacy.

As shall be shown in this chapter, the human right to privacy in international law is formulated in vague and high-level abstract principles, thereby making its scope uncertain. The poor formulation of the right to privacy is exacerbated by the lack of a robust and dynamic institutional machinery. The monitoring of the right to privacy is left to a Committee of experts that operates on a part-time basis, and for a short duration. These factors have cumulatively led to a stagnation in the development of a privacy jurisprudence that responds to the threats present in the digital environment. The chapter further uncovers that the present weak structures of the right to privacy in international human rights have some historical antecedents. It locates the root causes of these gaps in the controversies of the Cold War period and the apparently little attention paid to the right to privacy during the drafting of earlier human rights accords. A vaguely crafted privacy provision in the

---

[1] *Universal Declaration of Human Rights*, GA Res 217A(III), UN GAOR, 3rd sess, 183rd plen mtg, UN Doc A/810 (10 December 1948) art 12; *International Covenant on Civil and Political Rights*, opened for signature 16 December 1966, 999 UNTS 171 (entered into force 23 March 1976) art 17.

[2] *Convention on the Rights of the Child*, opened for signature 20 November 1989, 1577 UNTS 3 (entered into force 2 September 1990) art 16; *Convention on the Rights of Persons with Disabilities*, opened for signature 30 March 2007, 2515 UNTS 3 (entered into force 3 May 2008) arts 22–23; *International Convention on the Protection of the Rights of All Migrant Workers and Members of Their Families*, opened for signature 18 December 1990, 2220 UNTS 3 (entered into force 1 July 2003) art 14.

Privacy and the Role of International Law in the Digital Age. Kinfe Yilma, Oxford University Press. © Kinfe Yilma 2023.
DOI: 10.1093/oso/9780192887290.003.0002

hastily adopted UDHR was simply replicated in the ICCPR, and other subsequent treaties, without any improvement of form or substance.

In undertaking a 'regime analysis', the chapter seeks to provide a background against which the roles of global privacy initiatives are considered in chapters 4, 5, and 6. The examination reveals where gaps lie in the existing law that may be addressed by these initiatives. The chapter concludes that despite the ambivalence at the UN whether existing privacy standards are adequate—exhibited mainly in the ongoing UN privacy discourse, international human rights law acutely needs some form of reform, and emerging initiatives offer, to a degree, an alternate way forward. A caveat is in order. References in this chapter of international human rights law does not concern regional human rights mechanisms. Incidental references are, however, made to the case law of the European Court of Human Rights (ECtHR) for comparative purposes.

2. The Human Right to Privacy and the Cold War

A look back at the history of the negotiation, drafting, and adoption of the UDHR and the ICCPR in general and their privacy provisions in particular offers useful insight regarding the current structure of the right to privacy in international law. This section discusses two major issues that left significant marks in the present structure of the human right to privacy: (a) the impact of political and ideological divisions that clouded the gestation of the right; and (b) the possible impact of drafting missteps, or inattention, of the privacy provisions in the present normative and institutional structures.

2.1. The Cold War Effect

The end of the Second World War undoubtedly was a watershed moment particularly in leading to the revival of an interest in international co-operation to prevent similar devastating wars.[3] But the post-war period during which the UDHR was drafted and particularly the Cold War period during which most of the work on the ICCPR was carried out were largely periods of deep political and ideological division.[4] Major multilateral efforts in the human rights field would not move far enough unless significant political compromises were struck to meet the demands of each side of the political spectrum. As this section illustrates, these compromises

---

[3] See William Edmundson, *An Introduction to Rights* (Cambridge University Press 2004) 105.
[4] See Christopher Roberts, *The Contentious History of the International Bill of Human Rights* (Cambridge University Press 2014) 66–71.

are reflected in at least two defining features of the current international human rights regime.

One is the resort to softer treaty monitoring mechanisms. With a view to enlist as many States as possible, it was imperative to introduce softer systems of human rights monitoring.[5] States were opposed to a regime that posits a strong international monitoring machinery.[6] The UN Charter's cardinal principle of non-intervention in matters of domestic jurisdiction particularly played out strongly in this regard.[7] The current human rights regime is, as a result, premised on the recognition of peaceful co-existence of divergent polities and respect for the national sovereignty of States.[8] Indeed, as Forsythe writes, even before the idea of the UDHR surfaced, the superpowers were not keen on international human rights at the start of the San Francisco Conference in 1945.[9]

An indication for the lack of interest in stronger monitoring under the ICCPR is that the individual communications procedure was strongly resisted by State parties.[10] The procedure was pushed to the eleventh hour during the negotiation, and finally tucked away in an Optional Protocol. The issue of international monitoring had, of course, been controversial from the outset of drafting universal instruments in general. The UN General Assembly (UNGA), for instance, had considered the idea of introducing a 'right to petition' into the then draft UDHR but later abandoned so that it could be addressed under the forthcoming Covenants.[11] The former Commission on Human Rights also had reportedly resisted the pressure from the UNGA to introduce an individual petitioning procedure.[12] Instead, in 1956 the Commission installed—in response to pressures from the UN Economic and Social Council—a softer reporting procedure based on the UDHR but was terminated later because it brought little results.[13] Similar complaint procedures

---

[5] Henry Steiner, 'Individual Claims in A World of Massive Violations: What Role for the Human Rights Committee?' in Philip Alston and James Crawford (eds), *The Future of the UN Human Rights Treaty Monitoring* (Cambridge University Press 2000) 17, 19–23.

[6] See Boutros Boutros-Ghali, 'Introduction' in *United Nations and Human Rights (1945–1995)* (United Nations Blue Book 1995) 46.

[7] See *Charter of the United Nations* (1945) art 2(7).

[8] See Yogesh Tyagi, *The Human Rights Committee: Practice and Procedure* (Cambridge University Press 2011) 38–41.

[9] David Forsythe, 'The United Nations and Human Rights: 1945–1985' (1985) 100 Political Science Quarterly 249, 251.

[10] See Boutros-Ghali (n 6) 46.

[11] *Right to Petition*, GA Res 217 B(III), UNGAOR, 3rd sess, 183rd plen mtg, UN Doc A/810 (10 December 1948); see also John Humphrey, 'The International Bill of Rights: Scope and Implementation' (1976) 17 William and Mary Law Review 527, 536, 540.

[12] See Vratislav Rechota, 'The Development of the Covenant on Civil and Political Rights' in Louis Henkin (ed), *The International Bill of Rights: The Covenant on Civil and Political Rights* (Columbia University Press 1981) 48–49.

[13] See Philip Alston, 'The Commission on Human Rights' in Philip Alston (ed), *The United Nations and Human Rights: A Critical Appraisal* (Oxford University Press 1992) 183–84; see also Tom Farer and Felice Gaer, 'The UN and Human Rights: At the End of the Beginning' in Adam Roberts and Benedict Kingsbury (eds), *United Nations, Divided World: The UN's Roles in International Relations* (Clarendon Press 2nd edn, 1993) 273.

introduced in 1967 and 1970, which respectively allowed individual and group petitions on 'patterns of gross violations', were rescinded for lack of success.[14]

The Commission's resistance was, however, merely a reflection of the wishes of States. This is because the Commission, which was an inter-governmental body, had solicited views of States on possible 'international supervision and complaints monitoring mechanisms' as well as the propriety of a global human rights court during the drafting of the ICCPR.[15] But States' lack of political will to be subjected to stronger international supervision had led to proposals based on compromises. The monitoring of the ICCPR ultimately fell in the hands of eighteen part-time experts with largely advisory roles. The present monitoring system essentially is a co-operative framework rather than adversarial, and relies on the good faith of State parties.[16] The individual communications procedure, which is relegated to an optional instrument, has unsurprisingly garnered relatively lower ratification by State parties.[17] This, in practice, meant that notorious violators of privacy rights such as the US have not ratified the Protocol. But this politically induced weak system of monitoring has had a more nuanced ramification to the present structures of international law of privacy. As the analysis below will show, the right to privacy provisions in international human rights law are framed in an exceedingly vague manner. But, because Cold War politics created a softer monitoring mechanism, this normative obfuscation could not be addressed by powerless treaty bodies. Hampered by structural problems, the Human Rights Committee (HR Committee), for instance, has not been able to develop a robust privacy jurisprudence.

Terminological vagueness is the second area where the influence of political compromises is strongly felt. Human rights are, of course, often framed in vague terms and deliberately so with a view to leave room for the technical details and exceptions to be determined by State parties.[18] Such deferrals would permit accommodating socio-economic, cultural, political and religious divergences among nation-states. This approach had particularly animated the drafting of the UDHR's privacy provision whose speedy adoption generally was made possible because it

---

[14] See Antonio Cassese, *International Law in a Divided World* (Clarendon Press 1986) 304–05.

[15] See Hersch Lauterpacht, *International Law and Human Rights* (Stevens and Sons Limited 1950) 278.

[16] See Jack Donnelly, 'International Human Rights: A Regime Analysis' (1986) 40 *International Organization* 599, 609–10; see also Makau Mutua, 'Looking Past the Human Rights Committee: An Argument for De-Marginalizing Enforcement' (1998) 4 Buffalo Human Rights Law Review 211, 216; Eric Posner, *The Twilight of Human Rights Law* (Oxford University Press 2014) 96.

[17] At the time of writing, the Optional Protocol has been ratified only by 116 States, compared to 173 ratifications of the ICCPR. This, of course, holds true also for the Optional Protocols to the other UN treaties that guarantee the right to privacy such as the CRD the Optional Protocol of which has merely 100 State parties and the CRC's Optional Protocol which has only forty-eight State parties. See <http://indicators.ohchr.org/>.

[18] See Oliver Diggelmann and Maria Cleis, 'How the Right to Privacy Become a Human Right' (2014) 14 Human Rights Law Review 441, 451.

couches rights in 'general principles'.[19] As will be shown further below, vagueness of the privacy provision is more acute than other rights in the ICCPR. The almost identical right to privacy provision of the Covenant was also quickly adopted because, as reportedly noted by the Philippine delegate, there was already agreement on the general principles involved.[20] Indeed, it was already acknowledged at the 9th session of the Covenant's drafting Committee in 1957 that translating the 'general principles' articulated under Article 12 of the UDHR into precise legal terms is difficult.[21]

This reveals two important points in understanding the present structure of the human right to privacy in international law. One is that it was known from the very start that the privacy provision was 'general' (and perhaps made so deliberately). Secondly, its replication under the ICCPR is partly because the drafters were not sure how best to put the right in a less generic manner. The ultimate reproduction into the ICCPR without any significant change might also speak more about the level of importance the drafters had attached to the right to privacy. This also runs counter to what drafters of the UDHR had hoped. In writing before the drafting of the ICCPR began, Malik—one of the drafters of the UDHR—had noted that the then impending Covenant would 'define with a greater degree of legal precision at least some of the rights proclaimed in the Declaration'.[22]

A closer look at the drafting history of the ICCPR sheds more light onto the present terminological make-up of the privacy provision. As the UN set out to translate the UDHR into binding treaties, there were two competing proposals on the form and content of these upcoming instruments. The first proposal favoured the drafting of a general human instrument and then the particulars would be addressed through subsequent specific instruments.[23] The second view, which vied for a rather detailed instrument, maintained that a general instrument would be a mere replication of the UDHR.[24] Doubtless, the first view is reflected in the current version of the ICCPR's privacy provision, which is a sheer replication of Article 12 of the UDHR. The truncated nature of the privacy provisions of both the UDHR and the ICCPR, framed in high-level abstract principles, is significant. Significant because it raises the central question of whether such principles must be seen as 'carved in stone'—and continuing to apply across changing times. Could a right crafted with the post-war twentieth century in mind be fit for purpose to the new realities of the digital age?

---

[19] ibid, 443–44.
[20] ibid, 451.
[21] See Marc Bossuyt, *Guide to the 'Travaux Preparatoires' of the International Covenant on Civil and Political Rights* (Martinus Nijhoff 1987) 339 [It remains unclear, however, whether the difficulty emanated from the lack of political will or inherent conceptual ambiguities].
[22] Charles Malik, 'Human Rights in the United Nations' (1951) 6 International Journal 275, 278.
[23] See Boutros-Ghali (n 6) 44.
[24] ibid.

The fact that post-ICCPR human instruments, as shall be noted later, appear to respond to technological developments suggests that the aim, while crafting the UDHR (and essentially the ICCPR), might have been more than articulating eternal general principles. One also traces interest among drafters of the Covenant in crafting the right to privacy based on the conditions of the day. An example is that an Israeli delegate had suggested including protection of 'telegraphic and telephonic communications' under Article 17 as these were common media of communication at the time.[25] This lends weight to the argument that the present human rights standards needed reforms based on the new realities of the digital age.[26] The now prevalent proposals for a new set of human rights for the digital age in the form of IBRs or international data privacy treaty proceed from the assumption that the digital age dictates new human rights norms or major translation and adaptation in the context of the digital environment. In today's world of digital connectivity, proponents of new privacy standards appear to suggest that there is a need for something which goes beyond mere evolution of a 'living document'.

In sum, the present weak structure of the UN framework on the human right to privacy is partly a result of Cold War politics. Deep ideological divisions that clouded the climate under which the Covenant was drafted forced the use of terms that would intrude as little as possible into the sovereign rights of Cold War foes.

2.2. The Privacy Inattention Effect

The UDHR and the ICCPR's general propensity to vague language is mainly attributable, as discussed above, to the deliberate decision of its drafters to reflect the political compromises of the time. But that is not the complete story. The right to privacy provision of the Covenant, and the other UN human rights treaties that reproduce the right, has been particularly affected by drafting inattention. This can best be illustrated by, first, looking at the account of the drafters and secondly, by simply comparing the text of privacy provisions with other rights in the ICCPR. The right to privacy has not received as much attention during the drafting as other rights that found relatively clear formulation in the Covenant.

One finds useful insights on this point from the account of figures who played key roles during the drafting of the UDHR. Malik's account, for instance, reveals that not only the drafting exercise was plagued by urgency but also that themes that received significant discussion during the drafting of the UDHR did not include the right to privacy. Instead, rights that had received attention were the right to life,

---

[25] See Diggelmann and Cleis (n 18) 450, footnote 56.
[26] Indeed, the former UN Secretary-General had conceded that the UDHR indeed entails 'some gaps' and that it touches only peripherally certain human rights problems particularly those caused by 'scientific and technical developments'. See Boutros-Ghali (n 6) 27.

rights of the accused, freedom of religion and the right to free speech, particularly the conditions under which they may be limited.[27] This suggests that the right to privacy, let alone possible restriction clauses, had received little attention during the drafting of the UDHR. Malik further wrote that '... the archetype of what we were trying to ensure was freedom from discrimination and from arbitrary arrest, and freedom of religion and speech. It never occurred to us that anything else was as important as these.'[28]

He further added that when the emphasis shifted, it shifted towards socio-economic and cultural rights.[29] Arguably, the neglect shown towards the right to privacy has affected the way how the provision was formulated in the UDHR. This point finds support in the admission of another important figure, Humphrey, who at the time was the Director of the UN Human Rights Division and more importantly, one who compiled the initial draft of the UDHR. Humphrey wrote that '...some of the rights would have been enunciated differently had the Declaration been prepared by learned legal draftspersons (sic); and it is possible that its style might have been improved ...'[30] This is an important insight when one considers the fact that UDHR's privacy provision was simply replicated later (almost) verbatim into the ICCPR.

Beyond these insights and admissions, sheer textual comparison of the right to privacy and other Covenant rights speaks volumes about the 'privacy inattention effect'. Covenant rights such as freedom of religion, expression and association are far better formulated than the right to privacy. These rights are stipulated in a more direct and elaborate manner particularly in terms of the grounds under which restrictions apply.[31] This is in contrast with the omission of a limitation clause from the privacy provision of the ICCPR. Imprecise terms such as 'arbitrary' are also not attached to these rights thereby avoiding potential interpretive difficulties. In the context of the right to freedom of expression for instance, there was also reportedly thorough discussion on the substance of the right, including on the linguistic details among members of the drafting committee.[32] This strengthens the claim that Article 17 of the ICCPR was haphazardly crafted, and the drafters seemingly attached little importance to the right to privacy.[33]

---

[27] Charles Malik, 'Human Rights in the United Nations with Text of Draft Covenants' (1952) 1 United Nations at Work 1, 12; see also Megan Richardson, *The Right to Privacy: Origins and Influence of a Nineteenth Century Idea* (Cambridge University Press 2017) 113 [noting the little discussion about the inclusion of the right to privacy during the drafting].

[28] ibid.

[29] ibid.

[30] John Humphrey, 'The Universal Declaration of Human Rights' (1949) 4 International Journal 351, 355–56.

[31] ICCPR (n 1) arts 18–21.

[32] See Molly Land, 'Toward International Internet Law' (2013) 54 Harvard International Law Journal 394, 418–21.

[33] Of a similar view, Diggelmann and Cleis (n 18) 457.

As noted above, the drafting Committee merely replicated Article 12 of the UDHR into the ICCPR because there was already agreement on the principles. No such replication, however, occurred when the other rights of the Covenant were drafted. Like the right to privacy, the rights to freedom of speech, religion and association were formulated in an understandably 'general principles' under the UDHR.[34] But these principles were later translated into fairly elaborate rights under the ICCPR. Consider Article 19 of the UDHR which reads as follows:

> Everyone has the right to freedom of opinion and expression; this right includes freedom to hold opinions without interference and to seek, receive and impart information and ideas through any media and regardless of frontiers.

This general proviso was later translated into a fairly elaborate provision Article 19 of the ICCPR, with a fully fledged limitation clause.

Not just the compromise-induced vagueness that this suggests but also, perhaps mainly, the inattention during the drafting of Article 17 of the ICCPR. What makes this more unfortunate is that the Covenant merely replicated Article 12 of the UDHR, the drafting of which also had exhibited some element of haste. Due to ideological impasse of the time, the former Commission on Human Rights had reportedly pushed for the Declaration to be adopted as quickly as possible.[35] The Commission had even rejected requests by some delegates to postpone the adoption of the Declaration to the following year so that it could be examined more closely.[36] This later led to eight abstentions from some of these delegates. In considering the fact that these abstentions were made mainly by countries from the 'Eastern' bloc led by the Soviet Union,[37] one might arguably state that problems of 'ideological divisions' and 'haphazard drafting' fed each other in producing the current normative structure of the right to privacy. Along similar lines, there was a concern during the drafting of the UDHR that the Declaration might not achieve meaningful consensus, and that modest goals be pursued instead.[38]

In summary, the present normative and institutional structures on the right to privacy are negatively affected by two factors. These are ideological divisions that dictated political compromises and an element of haphazard drafting of the relevant human rights treaties in general and the right to privacy provisions in particular. The two factors have resulted in a normatively vague right to privacy rules and an institutionally weak regime that cumulatively hampered the development

---

[34] UDHR (n 1) arts 18–20.

[35] See Farer and Gaer (n 13) 248–49.

[36] ibid.

[37] See Johannes Morsink, *The Universal Declaration of Human Rights: Origins, Drafting and Intent* (University of Pennsylvania Press 1999) 21–24.

[38] See Benedetto Croce, 'The Rights of Man and the Present Historical Situation' in *Human Rights: Comments and Interpretations* (Columbia University Press 1949) 93–95.

of a robust jurisprudence on the right to digital privacy. Nor has the Tehran Conference, which was held to commemorate the twentieth anniversary of the adoption of the UDHR—and held two years after the adoption of the ICCPR, led to steps in addressing the problem. Indeed, apart from its role in setting in motion a protracted UN process in the field of data privacy—considered in chapter 3, the meeting is generally considered to be a failure in furthering the UDHR and the ICCPR.[39] A meeting report of the International Commission of Jurists, for instance, stated that the Tehran Proclamation addressed 'less than half of the rights enumerated in the Universal Declaration', and failed further in 'defining and enlarging these rights', and even 'in some cases may even be said to limit the pronouncements of the Universal Declaration'.[40]

3. Normative Sources

Normative sources of the human right to privacy in international law can generally be grouped into four categories: treaties, international custom, general principles and soft law. In discussing these sources, this section—and the corresponding section in chapter 3 on sources of international data privacy law—draws mainly upon formal sources of international law envisaged in Article 38(1) of the Statute of the International Court of Justice (ICJ). Originally, this provision was meant to outline sources of law to be applied by the Permanent Court of International Justice—and later by its successor, the ICJ—but it has since been accepted widely to represent the main formal sources of international law.[41] Against this backdrop, the section discusses three of the sources indicated in the Statute. Treaty law is the first and the principal source of international human rights. The right to privacy is guaranteed in a number of international human rights treaties, be it omnibus or specialized treaties. Customary international law is the second potential source of the human right to privacy in international law. The third but least explored sources are general principles of law. Soft law constitutes the fourth but an increasingly important normative source of the human right to privacy in international law although it is not among the sources indicated in Article 38(1) of the ICJ Statute. A caveat is, however, in order. As shall become clear, these sources are not always mutually

---

[3] See generally Samuel Moyn, *The Last Utopia: Human Rights in History* (The Belknap Press 2010) ch 4.

[40] United Nations Conference on Human Rights: Report, Secretary-General of the International Commission of Jurists, S.2021, 22, excerpts reproduced in Moses Moskowitz, *International Concern for Human Rights* (Oceana Publications 1974) 179–80.

[41] See, eg, generally Samantha Besson and Jean d'Aspermont, 'The Sources of International Law: An Introduction' in Samantha Besson and Jean d'Aspermont (eds), *The Oxford Handbook on the Sources of International Law* (Oxford University Press 2017); Hugh Thirlway, *The Sources of International Law* (Oxford University Press 2nd edn, 2019) ch 1; James Crawford, *Brownlie's Principles of Public International Law* (Oxford University Press 9th edn, 2019) 18.

exclusive. For instance, treaties and soft law may contribute to the formation of customary international law.

3.1. Treaty Law

Human rights treaties are the primary normative sources of the right to privacy in international law. The ICCPR is the principal treaty of universal scope that guarantees the right to privacy: Article 17 provides as follows:

1. No one shall be subjected to arbitrary or unlawful interference with his privacy, family, home or correspondence, nor to unlawful attacks on his honour and reputation.
2. Everyone has the right to the protection of the law against such interference or attacks. [Emphasis added].

As shall be explored further in the next section and chapter 7, this provision protects a number of values as well as the right privacy. One such set of values is honour and reputation. In considering this expansive formulation of the provision, it might be said that Article 17 guarantees what is commonly known in continental legal systems as the 'rights of personality'. The way in which the provision is framed suggests that 'family', 'home', and 'correspondence' are distinct from 'privacy'. But it is widely established that family, home, and correspondence are 'zones' of protections of the right to privacy. This vague formulation of the right relates to the drafting history of the ICCPR in general and the privacy provision in particular highlighted in the preceding section.

Three additional points can be made about Article 17 of the ICCPR. First, apart from the generic qualifying terms of 'arbitrary' and 'unlawful', the provision does not provide a limitation clause. This is in contrast with other covenant rights such as freedom of expression. As alluded to above, this relates to the drafting history of the provision during which the right to privacy enjoyed little attention. Indeed, the HR Committee has interpreted these terms in General Comment (GC) 16,[42] its case law[43] and concluding observations[44] in a way that resembles the three-part test of legality, necessity, and legitimacy. Second, in bestowing the right to 'everyone' regardless of exclusionary grounds such as nationality and residence, the provision

---

[42] HR Committee, *General Comment 16: Article 17—The Right to Respect of Privacy, Family, Home and Correspondence, and Protection of Honour and Reputation*, 32nd sess, UN Doc HRI/GEN/1/Rev.9 (Vol I) (8 April 1988) paras 3–4.

[43] See, eg, HR Committee, *NK v The Netherlands*, Communication No 2326/2013 (10 January 2018) paras 9.4–9.11.

[44] See, eg, Concluding Observations of the HR Committee: Germany, UN Doc CCPR/C/DEU/CO/7 (30 November 2021) para 43.

appears to envision an extraterritorial right. But whether the Covenant applies extraterritorially has been a longstanding controversy. This stems from the text of the Covenant which provides that State human rights obligations pertain to individuals within their 'territory *and* subject to its jurisdiction'.[45] This would mean that a State party's obligation in respecting and protecting the right to privacy would not apply when the individual is outside its geographic territory but within its effective jurisdiction. Partly to prevent such contention, some post-ICCPR treaties—as shall be highlighted below—are designed deliberately to permit extraterritorial protection of rights.

Third, the right embodies both negative and negative dimensions in that it imposes a duty to 'respect' and 'protect' on State parties. The reference in the second sub-article, ie, 'right to the protection of the law', relates to the positive duty of State parties. This clause should be read together with Article 2(2) which defines the general duty of State parties under the Covenant, including to adopt legislation or other measures as may be necessary to give effect to the rights recognized in the Covenant. Among such laws key for the protection of the right to privacy in the digital age is data privacy legislation. Indeed, this is implied in GC 16 where it is stated that the 'gathering and holding of personal information on computers, data banks and other devices, whether by public authorities or private individuals or bodies, must be regulated by law'.[46] As shall be noted below, post-ICCPR human rights treaties tend to explicitly require the adoption of data privacy legislation which is instrumental in the protection of the right to privacy in the digital age.

Post-ICCPR specialized human rights treaties guarantee the right to privacy. While the privacy provisions of some of these treaties largely replicate the Covenant, others depart from it to a degree. One such treaty is the CRC which is one of the human rights treaties to achieve near universal ratification. Although adopted two decades after the ICCPR, the Convention simply replicates the privacy provision of the Covenant.[47] This meant replication with all the defects of Article 17 of the ICCPR. Indeed, there was a proposal to omit the word 'arbitrary' for being 'vague and subjective' during the drafting process.[48] But the proposal was declined with a view to ensure conformity with the Covenant. The verbatim replication occurred under a 'process already begun by the Working Group of incorporating provisions from the ICCPR (sic) into the draft convention'.[49] This was also the case regarding

---

[45] See ICCPR (n 1) art 2(1).

[46] GC 16 (n 42) para 10 cum para 9.

[47] See CRC (n 2) art 16. Note that the Convention provides further protection of children's privacy in the context of criminal proceedings. See art 40(2(vii)).

[48] Legislative History of the Convention on the Rights of the Child, Vol I (OHCHR, 2007) paras 56–57, excerpt from the Report of the Working Group to the Commission on Human Rights, UN Doc E/CN 4/1988/28 (1988) paras 35–38 and 55–59.

[49] ibid, 36; see also John Tobin and Sarah Field, 'Art. 16—The Right to Protection of Privacy, Family, Home, Correspondence, Honour, and Reputation' in John Tobin (ed), *The Convention on the Rights of the Child: A Commentary* (Oxford University Press 2019) 556.

the inclusion of protection against attacks on honour and reputation. As Tobin and Field rightly note, this 'appears to be the result of a decision to simply import the equivalent of Article 17 of the ICCPR into the Convention without any real evaluation as to merit of doing so'.[50] Not only that this reinforces the point made above about the overall privacy inattention effect during early standard setting processes but also its persistence two decades later when the CRC was drafted.

Despite the inherited ambiguities, the jurisprudence of the Committee on the Rights of the Child has been relatively progressive. This is especially so in elaborating the scope of the right to privacy in the digital context. A general comment on the right to privacy is yet to be adopted by the Committee. However, in a recent general comment, the Committee has elaborated rights of the Convention, including the right to privacy, in the digital context.[51] Without directly invoking Article 16, the Committee addresses digital privacy in different respects. First, it provides that States are required under the Convention to protect children's right to privacy against actions of digital corporations, including in the context of predatory marketing and targeting practices.[52] Second, it provides that States are required under the Convention to enact data protection legislation to effectively regulate processing of children's personal data.[53] In this regard, it outlines a series of data privacy principles that should be observed in the processing personal data of children. Finally, it addresses digital surveillance of children which should not be conducted routinely, indiscriminately or surreptitiously.[54] A product of cross-fertilization of norms and extensive consultation with various stakeholders,[55] this GC slightly unpacks the vaguely word treaty provision on the right to privacy.

Adopted a year after the CRC, the ICRMW is the other specialized human rights treaty that guarantees the right to privacy.[56] Like CRC, this Convention replicates Article 17 of the Covenant, the only change being the addition of 'other communications' as a 'zone' of protection alongside 'correspondence'. The addition of this phrase appears to have the objective of embracing modern means of communications, but the *travaux préparatoires* of the treaty offers little explanation. What emerges from the *travaux*, instead, is that the right to privacy—in contrast with the other rights—was not a subject of any discussion in the Open-ended Working Group that drafted the treaty. During second review of the draft treaty at the Working Group's 8th meeting in September 1986, for instance, the original text was adopted without any changes—and unlike other provisions, this provision

---

[50] See Tobin and Field (n 49) 592.
[51] See Committee on the Rights of the Child, *General Comment 25: Children's Rights in relation to the Digital Environment*, 86th sess, UN Doc CRC/C/GC/25 (March 2021).
[52] ibid, paras 35–42.
[53] ibid, paras 69–74
[54] ibid, paras 75–78.
[55] ibid, para 5.
[56] ICRMW (n 2) art 14.

drew no comments from representatives.[57] The draft article on freedom of expression had, in contrast, ignited fairly extensive discussion among members of the Working Group at the second reading.[58]

This is more evidence reinforcing the point about antipathy towards the right to privacy at the UN during the period of key human rights standard setting. Like in the case of nigh verbatim replication of Article 17 of the ICCPR in the CRC, drafters of the ICRMW were intent on ensuring normative alignment with the ICCPR. In the initial working paper drafted by the chairperson of the Working Group where an outline of the future convention was provided, one reads the following:[59]

> Provisions in the area of fundamental rights should constitute a reaffirmation of all inalienable rights recognized in the basic instruments and documents in this field, including the Universal Declaration, the Covenants on Civil and Political Rights ... (Emphasis Added).

In seeking to ground the proposed Convention in the Covenant, the drafters appear to have lost the opportunity to bring a level of clarity on the nature and scope of the right to privacy. What best explains such an oversight—as alluded to above— is the overall limited attention paid to the right to privacy and cognate norms during major milestones in international human rights standard setting processes.

Over a decade later, the right to privacy finds expression in another specialized human rights treaty: the CRD.[60] True to tradition, its privacy provision replicates almost verbatim Article 17 of the ICCPR. Just like ICRMW, it extends the 'zone' of privacy protection to include 'other types of communication' alongside 'correspondence'. As explicitly stated in its *travaux préparatoires*, the rationale for the inclusion of this phrase was to capture 'more recent communication technologies' such as the Internet and allied technologies.[61] In so doing, the drafters directly drew inspiration from ICRMW but with addition of the phrase 'other types' which is not part of Article 14 of the ICRMW.[62] But the privacy provision of CRD departs from the Covenant in that it explicitly guarantees the protection of privacy of

---

[57] Report of the Open-ended Working Group on the Drafting of an International Convention on the Protection of the Rights of All Migrant Workers and Members of Their Families, UN Doc A/C.3/41/3 (10 October 1986) para 176.

[58] ibid, paras 158–75; see also Measures to Improve the Situation and Ensure the Human Rights and Dignity of All Migrant Workers, Report of the Open-ended Working Group, UN Doc A/C.3/36/10 (23 November 1981) para 45.

[59] Outline for An International Convention on the Protection of the Rights of All Migrant Workers and Their Families, Working Paper Presented by the Chairman of the Working Group, UN Doc A/C.3/35/WH.1/CRP.5 (12 November 1980) Annex V, 3.

[60] CRD (n 2) art 22(1).

[61] Report of the Ad Hoc Committee on a Comprehensive and Integral International Convention on the Protection and Promotion of the Rights and Dignity of Persons with Disabilities on its Fifth Session, UN Doc A/RES/60/232 (31 January 2006) para 92(b).

[62] ibid.

'personal, health and rehabilitation information'.[63] This innovative but ambiguous clause essentially branches out data privacy as a subset of the right to privacy in international law.[64]

As shall be explored closely in chapter 3, this data protection clause is further reinforced by the procedural provision of the Convention dealing with the collection of statistical data about persons with disabilities.[65] But the question of whether such progressive standards in CRD are a reflection of an increase in attention to privacy in international human rights standard setting arises. That the Convention was adopted as recently as 2006 means a broader conception of the right to privacy, including protection of personal data, is to be expected. Global diffusion of legislation governing processing of personal data was already in motion at the turn of the century. Civil society groups had played an important role during the drafting of the Convention, which would generally involve bringing to bear international best practices.[66] That would mean drafters of the Convention would not be spared from influence of this global phenomenon, more so in light of the fact that collection and processing of personal data is key in the protection and promotion of rights of persons with disabilities.[67] In that sense, it may be said that the adoption of the CRD marked an important milestone post-Tehran in reviving interest in the value of the right to privacy in UN human rights standard setting processes.

As the above overview illustrated, the human right to privacy is firmly guaranteed in international law. Despite its vague formulation in human right treaties, the right now forms part of the corpus of binding international treaties. This would mean that the question of whether the human right to privacy has attained the status of customary international law makes it less exigent. The ICCPR and the CRC have attained almost universal ratification, but the other specialized treaties— especially the CRD which embodies a sub-right to data privacy—are yet to achieve wider accession. This is what makes an examination of the customary law status of the human right to privacy particularly important. In that spirit, what follows briefly considers the question of whether the right to privacy has become a rule of customary international law.

---

[63] See CRD (n 2) art 22(1).

[64] cf Frédéric Mégret, 'The Disabilities Convention: Towards a Holistic Concept of Rights' (2008) 12 The International Journal of Human Rights 261, 266 [mistakenly referring to this clause as an 'economic right' tucked in a civil right].

[65] CRD (n 2) art 31.

[66] Eilionoir Flynn, *From Rhetoric to Action: Implementing the UN Convention on the Rights of Persons with Disabilities* (Cambridge University Press 2011) 26–33.

[67] See, eg, Raymond Lan and others, 'Implementing the United Nations Convention on the Rights of Persons with Disabilities: Principles, Implications, Practice and Limitations' (2011) 5 ALTER: European Journal of Disability Research 206, 209.

3.2. Custom

International custom is the second primary source of international law listed in Article 38(1(b)) of the ICJ Statute. In the wake of the Snowden debacle, whether the right to privacy has become part of Customary International Law (CIL) has been a recurring question in the literature.[68] One also finds pertinent discussions in earlier international law scholarship—and its recent iterations—that engages the question. This relates mainly to popular arguments that the UDHR as whole, or at least some of its rights and principles, have become part of general international law. With the incorporation or invocation in national constitutions, subsidiary legislation and judicial decisions worldwide, the UDHR—the argument goes—has attained the status of CIL.[69] Applied to the question at hand, this simply would mean that because the right to privacy is guaranteed in the UDHR—a soft law, it is a rule of CIL. If taken even further, it would mean that Article 17 of the ICCPR—which replicates the UDHR's privacy provision almost verbatim—is also part of CIL.

Notwithstanding ideological controversies during its drafting, the UDHR has undoubtedly garnered universal acceptance since. Despite its soft law status, it has provided the basis for subsequent human rights standards at the international, regional and national levels. Indeed, the ICCPR which, codified into hard law civil and political rights, is also on course to enjoy the same level of global acceptance. If it were to be judged by the number of State ratifications, the ICCPR has been ratified by 173 countries at the time of writing in early 2022.[70] Although at an obviously slow rate—and differing motives of States, this attests to the global acceptance of the treaty. In light of the fact that subsequent specialized treaties largely replicate its privacy provision, the same observation applies—to a degree—to those treaties too. Or, so at least with respect to their respective provision on the right to privacy. In that sense, scholarly arguments about the customary law status of the right to privacy seem sensible. But it is also vital to 'stress test' whether such arguments still hold water in light of recent developments.

---

[68] See, eg, Alexandra Rengel, *Privacy in the 21st Century* (Martinus Nijhoff 2013) 108; Michael Schmitt (ed), *Tallinn Manual 2.0 on the International Law Applicable to Cyber Operations* (Cambridge University Press 2017) 180, 189.

[69] See, eg, John Humphrey, 'The Universal Declaration of Human Rights: Its History, Impact and Juridical Character' in Bertrand Ramcharan (ed), *Human Rights Thirty Years After the Universal Declaration* (Brill 1979) 21, 37; Louis Sohn, 'The Human Rights Law of the Charter' (1977) 12 Texas International Law Journal 129, 129, 133; M Cherif Bassiouni, 'Human Rights and International Criminal Justice in the Twenty-First Century The End of the Post-WWII Phase and the Beginning of an Uncertain New Era' in Margaret de Guzman and Diane Amann (eds), *Arcs of Global Justice: Essays in Fonour of William A. Schabas* (Oxford University Press 2018) 14, 18; see also John Humphrey, 'The Implementation of International Human Rights Law' (1978) 24 New York Law School Law Review 31 (1978) 32–33 [noting the 'juridical consensus' that has emerged since the adoption of the UDHR in 1948]. For a more recent rendition of the argument, see William Schabas, *The Customary International Law of Human Rights* (Oxford University Press 2021) 218–30.

[70] See details at <https://indicators.ohchr.org/>.

One such development is the adoption by the UN International Law Commission (ILC) of the Draft Conclusions on Identification of Customary Law.[71] The Draft Conclusions, which are yet to be formally adopted by the UNGA,[72] are instructive in the ways in which the existence and content of a rule of CIL can be ascertained. Can the customary law status of the right to privacy be established per the Draft Conclusions? Determining the existence and content of CIL requires ascertainment of the two constituent elements of custom: *general state practice* and *opinio juris*. What follows briefly considers whether the two constitutive elements can be ascertained when it comes to the right to privacy. But the focus here is only in determining the existence, not the content, of the customary international law of privacy. This is primarily because the exact normative contours of the right to privacy are difficult to establish due to the inherently nebulous nature of the notion of privacy as well as its divergent protection in domestic law. A more concrete example would be divergence over the extraterritorial scope of the right to privacy in international law. The US, for instance, has consistently rejected the holding, including by international courts and tribunals, that State obligations under the ICCPR apply exterritoriality. While such a clear and consistent objection makes the State a 'persistent objector'—and hence not bound by that particular rule,[73] it would not obviate the existence of a customary international law of privacy. Add to this the inevitable variations in the legal protection of the right to privacy in different legal traditions. The aim here, then, is attempting to establish the existence of a right to privacy in CIL.

The first requirement to be established is whether there is relevant general state practice.[74] State practice refers primarily to the practices of States, and sometimes international organizations, that may be expressed in different forms.[75] But essentially, relevant state practice relates to one that is exhibited in the course of discharging legislative, executive, and judicial state functions.[76] The Draft Conclusions envisage an illustrate list of forms of state practice, but particularly relevant to the question at hand are legislative and administrative acts as well as decisions of national courts.[77] Such state practices should, however, be 'general' in that they are sufficiently widespread, consistent and representative.[78] As alluded to above, the right to privacy is now recognized in the constitutions and subsidiary legislation of almost all States. In countries where it finds no explicit constitutional

---

[71] Draft Conclusions on Identification of Customary International Law, Adopted by the International Law Commission at its Seventieth Session (2018).

[72] The UNGA has simply 'noted', short of adopting the Draft Conclusions, and brought them to the attention of States. See *Identification of Customary International Law*, GA Res 73/203, 73rd sess, Agenda item 82, UN Doc A/RES/73/203 (11 January 2019) para 4.

[73] See Draft Conclusions (n 71) Conclusion 15.

[74] ibid, Conclusions 4, 8.

[75] ibid, Conclusion 4(2).

[76] ibid, Conclusion 5.

[77] ibid, Conclusion 6(2).

[78] ibid, Conclusion 8.

recognition such as in India, courts have read the right to privacy in other broader human rights.[79] Arguably, there is ample evidence to attest to the existence of state practice that is general when it comes to right to privacy.

Further reinforcing this point are three additional pieces of evidence as to the existence or reflections of the existence of the right to privacy in CIL. One is the stipulation of the right to privacy in a number of treaties.[80] From the European Convention on Human Rights and Fundamental Freedoms (ECHR),[81] several UN human rights treaties discussed above, the American Convention on Human Rights (ACHR)[82] and the EU Fundamental Rights Charter[83] to the African Charter on the Rights and Welfare of the Child (ACRWC),[84] the right to privacy is guaranteed extensively in treaty law. In line with the Draft Conclusions, this widespread recognition of the right to privacy in treaty law arguably *reflects* the existence of the right to privacy in CIL. The second piece of evidence concerns resolutions adopted by international organizations such as the UN. Such Resolutions may provide additional evidence for the existence of or contribute to the development of a rule of CIL.[85] Chapter 5 explores at length the normative values of the series of UN resolutions on the 'right to privacy in the digital age', including their potential in the formation of customary international law of privacy. But, a common thread in the Resolutions is that they consistently reaffirm the human right to privacy guaranteed in the ICCPR, and that it should be upheld online as well as offline.[86] Even if these Resolutions would not contribute for the creation of a rule of CIL, they certainly lend additional evidence in determining the existence of the right to privacy in CIL.

What is now left is determining whether the general state practice established above is undertaken with a sense of legal right or obligation, ie, *opinio juris*.[87] Ascertaining this element of custom is much harder than establishing general state practice owing mainly to the fact that it relates to a psychological matter. Among forms of evidence of *opinio juris* indicated in the Draft Conclusions include public

---

[79] See, eg, *Justice KS Puttaswamy (Retd) v Union of India*, Writ Petition (Civil) No 494 OF 2012 (24 August 2017) para 183 [holding that 'privacy has been held to be an intrinsic element of the right to life and personal liberty under Article 21 and as a constitutional value which is embodied in the fundamental freedoms embedded in Part III of the Constitution'].

[80] See Draft Conclusions (n 71) Conclusion 11(2).

[81] *Convention for the Protection of Human Rights and Fundamental Freedoms*, opened for signature 11 April 1950, European Treaty Series—No 5 (entered into force 9 March 1953) art 8.

[82] *American Convention on Human Rights*, opened for signature 22 November 1969, OAS, Treaty Series No 36 (entered into force 18 July 1978) art 11.

[83] *Charter of Fundamental Rights of the European Union*, proclaimed on 7 December 2000 [2000] OJ C 326/393 (entered into force 1 December 2009) art 7.

[84] *Charter on the Rights and Welfare of the Child*, opened for signature 11 July 1990, OAU Doc CAB/LEG/24.9/49 (entered into force 29 November 1999) art 10.

[85] See Draft Conclusions (n 71) Conclusion 12(2).

[86] See, eg, *The Right to Privacy in the Digital Age*, HRC Res 48/4, 48th sess, Agenda Item 3, UN Doc A/HRC/RES/48/4 (13 October 2021) para 4.

[87] See Draft Conclusions (n 71) Conclusion 9.

statements made on the behalf of States, official publications, government legal opinions, diplomatic correspondence, decisions of national courts, treaty provisions, and conduct in connection with resolutions adopted by an international organization.[88] But discerning the legal position of States in such instruments is a cumbersome exercise. As ILC's Commentary on the relevant Conclusion suggests, evidence of *opinio juris* as wells state practice may be found in the same material.[89] One such source is national legislation by the sheer adoption of which the legal position of a State about a particular rule is being expressed.[90] One may take this point even further and state that the recognition of the right to privacy in a constitution is the most expressive of a State's legal position. A State's conduct in relation to resolutions of an international organization is another possible evidence. In this regard, one may point to the adoption by consensus, as opposed to voting, of the series of UN resolutions on the right to privacy in the digital age.[91]

Taken all together, one may generally conclude that the right to privacy forms part of CIL. But what really is the value in the elevation of the human right to privacy into a rule of CIL? As highlighted above, the near universal ratification of the ICCPR lessens the importance of the right being part of CIL. Except for the CRC, post-ICCPR specialized treaties are yet to obtain as much acceptance by States. But that these treaties largely replicate near verbatim the Covenant's privacy provision further reduces the value of accretion into CIL. More importantly, claims often made about the undisputed customary law status of the right to privacy overestimate the value of a customary norm based on existing international privacy norms. As shall be shown later in this chapter, the right to privacy in international law is formulated in an exceedingly vague and abstract manner. Boundaries of the international right to privacy are, then, too vague to make its elevation to customary norm appealing. A major virtue of a norm becoming a rule of CIL is that it would bind all States that are not parties to the relevant human rights treaties. In asserting the customary law status of the right to privacy, one may also fall into the traps of minimal reform in international law of privacy. As alluded to in chapter 1, hard legalization is not probably a suitable avenue in the international law response to the 'privacy problem' in the digital age. Add to this the inherent uncertainty and fluidity of custom as a source of international law as well as its overall application in the context of inter-state relations.

---

[88]   ibid, Conclusion 10(2).
[89]   See Commentary to Conclusion 10(3) in Commentaries of the Draft Conclusions (2018) 141.
[90]   ibid, para 5.
[91]   See, eg, HRC Res 48/4 (n 86) 7 ('adopted without a vote').

3.3. General Principles

General Principles of Law (GPsL) are the third potential sources of the right to privacy in international law. GPsL are the least utilized sources of international law, including by international courts.[92] Part of the reason for its nigh disuse is that treaties and custom already provide rules for the regulation of international affairs.[93] Indeed, the drafters of the ICJ Statute envisaged GPsL to have mainly a 'gap filling' role in the event conventional and customary international law offer no rules.[94] This will most likely be in new areas of law where state practice is yet to extensively emerge or treaty law is adopted.[95] The heterogeneous nature of the international community would also mean that commonly shared principles are few and far between.[96]

While expressing surprise in the lack of attention to general principles as a source of human rights, Meron predicted in 1989 that this source will increasingly become one of the principal methods for the maturation of such standards into the mainstream of international law.[97] Three decades later, can it now be said that human rights in general and the right to privacy in particular form part of general principles? Scholarship and jurisprudence often tend to associate general principles generally with human rights as a concept. In one of the rarest instances where general principles are considered by the ICJ, Judge Tanaka argued in his dissenting opinion that the 'concept of human rights and of their protection is included in the general principles mentioned in that Article'—ie, Article 38(1(c)).[98] Writing in 1978, Schachter suggested that 'many' of the rights guaranteed in the UDHR now form part of general principles on account of their incorporation in national legal systems.[99] Humphrey likewise argued that the UDHR enunciates general principles.[100] But this raises the question of whether the right to privacy—by extension—has become part of general principles of law. If so, what is its normative

---

[92] See, eg, Catherine Redgwell, 'General Principles of International Law' in Stefan Vogenauer and Stephen Weatherill (eds), *General Principles of Law: European and Comparative Perspectives* (Hart 2017) 12–13; Giorgio Gaja, 'General Principles in the Jurisprudence of the ICJ' in Mads Andenas and others (eds), *General Principles and the Coherence of International Law* (Brill 2019) 36.

[93] Gennady Danileko, *Law-making in the International Community* (Martins Nijhoff 1993) 181.

[94] See Alain Pellet, 'Article 38' in Andreas Zimmermann and others (eds), *The Statute of the International Court of Justice: A Commentary* (Oxford University Press 2nd edn, 2012) 832.

[95] See Beatrice Bonafe and Paolo Palchetti, 'Relying on General Principles in International Law' in Catherine Brölmann and Yannick Radi (eds), *Research Handbook on the Theory and Practice of International Law Making* (Edward Elgar 2016) 172.

[96] See Danileko (n 93) 180–81.

[97] See Theodor Meron, *Human Rights Instruments and Customary Law* (Clarendon Press 1989) 88.

[98] Dissenting Opinion of Judge Tanaka in *South West Africa: Ethiopia and Liberia v South Africa*, Second Phase, ICJ Reports 1966 (18 July 1966) 298.

[99] Oscar Schachter, 'International Law Implications of U.S. Human Rights Policies' (1978) 24 New York Law School Law Review 63, 68.

[100] See Humphrey (n 30) 357.

value? This section briefly considers this in light of the most recent work of the ILC in the identification of GPsL.

A recurring debate in connection with general principles relates to source— should the principle be distilled from national law? If so, should reference be made to all aspects of domestic law such as constitutional, administrative, procedural, public and privacy law? Or, can general principles be drawn from international law itself? The question of source has been a bone of contention even during the drafting of the ICJ statute, but the overall agreement was that domestic law shall be the prime source of general principles.[101] Among such principles envisioned, then, included principles of procedure, good faith, estoppel, *res judicata*, *pacta sunt servanda* and other 'maxims' of law derived from national legal orders.[102] And the role of such principles is to offer interpretive guidance when substantive provisions of conventional or customary law are vague or ambiguous.[103] This is, of course, in keeping with the terms of Article 38(1(c)) which refers to 'general principles of law recognized by civilized nations'.[104] Recent scholarship deviates from this original conception of the terms. O'Boyle and Lafferty, for instance, suggest that 'respect for fundamental rights' constitutes a general principle of 'international' law.[105] In his dissenting opinion in *South West Africa Case*, Justice Tanaka of Japan argued that the universal nature of human rights *ipso facto* makes their protection general principles of law.[106] In certain instances, more emphasis is paid to the role of private law as opposed to public law in the development of general principles.[107]

To bring more clarity and certainty on the identification of general principles, the ILC has been working on the topic since 2018.[108] Thus far, its special rapporteur, Vázquez-Bermúdez, has presented two reports, in the second of which he proposed a set of draft conclusions on the identification of general principles.[109] In his first report, the special rapporteur argues that principles originating from the

---

[101] See, eg, Imogen Saunders, *General Principles as a Source of International Law: Article 38(1)(c) of the Statute of the International Court of Justice* (Hart 2020) 38–47; Redgwell (n 92) 7–11.

[102] See Danileko (n 93) 173–74; see also Gregory Kerwin, 'The Role of United Nations General Assembly Resolutions in Determining Principles of International Law in US Courts' (1983) Duke Law Journal 876, 878.

[103] See Samuel Bleicher, 'The Legal Significance of Re-Citation of General Assembly Resolutions' (1969) 63 The American Journal of International Law 444, 451.

[104] See also Bertrand Ramcharan, 'The Law-Making Process: From Declaration to Treaty and Custom' in Dinah Shelton (ed), *Oxford Handbook of International Human Rights Law* (Oxford University Press 2013) 514.

[105] See Michael O'Boyle and Michelle Lafferty, 'General Principles and Constitutions as Sources of Human Rights Law' in Dinah Shelton (ed), *The Oxford Handbook of International Human Rights Law* (Oxford University Press 2013) 196.

[106] Dissenting Opinion of Judge Tanaka in *South West Africa* (n 98) 298.

[107] See Frédéric Sourgens, 'The Privacy Principle' (2017) 42 Yale Journal of International Law 345, 367–92.

[108] See Other Decisions and Conclusions of the Commission, 70th session held in (July 2018) Chapter XIII, Para A <https://legal.un.org/ilc/reports/2018/english/chp13.pdf>.

[109] Second Report on General Principles of Law by Marcelo Vázquez-Bermúdez, Special Rapporteur, UN Doc A/CN.4/741 (9 April 2020) Annex.

international legal system should be taken as the second sources of general principles.[110] He bases this claim on the practices of States, international courts and the literature where general principles of international law increasingly are recognized to be important sources of general principles.[111] But such principles typically emerge out of international instruments such as treaty law, CIL, and international soft law but should be accepted as binding by the international community of States as a whole.[112] In this light, the proposed Draft Conclusions envisage separate processes in the identification of general principles drawn from domestic and international legal systems.[113]

With respect to domestic law sourced principles, two requirements need to be met.[114] First, the relevant principles should be common to principal legal systems of the world. In ascertaining whether a particular principle is common in the principal legal systems of the world, a fairly comprehensive comparative survey of national law and judicial decisions is required.[115] As several studies demonstrated, there is little doubt that the right to privacy is invariably recognized in all legal systems of the world.[116] Where it finds no explicit recognition in constitutional law, courts have read them within the rubric of other rights or subsidiary legislation provides some level of protection. Regardless of variations in the form and scope of protection, it may safely be said that the right to privacy is commonly recognized in principal, if not all, legal systems of the world.

The second requirement is that the relevant principles should be capable of transposition to the international legal system.[117] In assessing suitability of transposition, regard must be had to two factors. One relates to the compatibility of the relevant principles with the fundamental principles of international law. Among such fundamental principles alluded to by the special rapporteur in his report include the principles of sovereignty, territorial sovereignty, continental shelf entitlement, and the principles set out in the Friendly Relations Declaration.[118] The other concerns whether the attendant conditions for the effective application of the principles in the international plane exist. This pertains to the existence of procedural structures in the international legal system to give effect to the principles without distortion or abuses.[119] There is no reason to believe that human rights principles

---

[110] First Report on General Principles of Law by Marcelo Vázquez-Bermúdez, Special Rapporteur, UN Doc, A/CN.4/732 (5 April 2019) paras 231–53.
[111] ibid.
[112] ibid, paras 233–34; see also Bruno Simma and Philip Alston, 'The Sources of Human Rights Law: Custom, Jus Cogens, and General Principles' (1989) 12 Australian Year Book of International Law 82, 104–07.
[113] Consolidated Draft Conclusions, Conclusion 3, Annex to the Second Report of Vázquez-Bermúdez (n 109).
[114] ibid, Conclusion 4.
[115] ibid, Conclusion 5.
[116] See, eg, generally Rengel (n 68).
[117] Consolidated Draft Conclusions (n 113) Conclusion 6.
[118] See Second Report of Vázquez-Bermúdez (n 109) paras 75–83.
[119] ibid, para 85.

in general and the right to privacy in particular are not capable of transposition to the international legal system. One might even claim that the respect and protection of human rights already form a central part of the international legal order. One way this is vividly illustrated is through the host of human rights treaties and the attendant institutional framework currently in place in the international legal system. In that sense, it may safely be said that the right to privacy is a general principle of law.

Separate requirements apply when it comes to general principles originating from the international legal system.[120] The first requirement is that the relevant principles should be either (a) widely recognized in treaties or other international instruments, (b) underlie conventional or CIL, or (c) inherent in the basic features and fundamental requirements of the international legal system. Relevant to the discussion at hand is the first requirement in light of the widespread recognition of the right to privacy in treaties and international soft law. As highlighted above in the context of CIL, the right to privacy is recognized in key human rights treaties such as the ECHR, ACHR, and ACRWC as well as several UN human rights treaties. The right to privacy is further reaffirmed in the series of UN resolutions on the 'right to privacy in the digital age' adopted as part of an evolving discourse. In that sense, it may well be said that the right to privacy forms part of GPsL.

As the above brief sketch suggests, there is little doubt that the right to privacy is indeed part of general principles. What, then, follows, is the value that this adds in normative terms, namely in attending to the exigencies of the 'privacy problem' in the digital age. In becoming a rule of GPsL, a principle becomes part of general international law binding all States. Put differently, the prime value of elevation to the status of general principles is bindingness. But what lacks in international law is not hard law binding most or enough number of States. Indeed, as the discussion above on treaty law illustrated, the right to privacy is recognized in a number of binding international treaties of universal scope such as the ICCPR. Moreover, the right to privacy becoming a general principle should not arguably be considered beneficial. The human right to privacy in international law suffers from several ambiguities. If it indeed becomes a general principle, it does so with all its weaknesses. This is, of course, on top of the inherent uncertainty of general principles as a source of international law as well as its underlying conception as *a* principle governing inter-state relations. As shall be argued in chapter 7, soft law—as opposed to a new hard law—that elaborates the right to privacy in international hard law in light of the new realities of the digital age is the best way forward. For that reason, the elevation of the right to privacy to general principles is of little importance.

---

[120] Consolidated Draft Conclusions (n 113) Conclusion 7.

3.4. Soft Law

Soft law has been central in the development of the right to privacy in international law. As alluded to above, the right to privacy found its first recognition in the UDHR, a soft law adopted through a resolution of the UNGA. Not only has this latter been translated into a hard law with the adoption of the ICCPR but also that most of its rights arguably have become rules of general international law. But even after the right to privacy found recognition in international law, soft law continues to play a vital role in further elaborating the right. That is what makes it all the more an important normative source of the human right to privacy in international law. The elaborative role of soft legalization can be seen more vividly in two respects. One is in reimagining the right to privacy to make fit for purpose in the digital age. Treaty body jurisprudence in this regard has been instrumental, to a degree, in revitalizing the right to privacy in the digital age. An example is GC 16 of the HR Committee, albeit in an exceedingly abbreviated manner, interprets Article 17 to accommodate the advent of new technologies. GC 25 of the Committee on the Rights of the Child is, as highlighted above, a more recent example where the right to privacy finds a rather elaborate interpretation.[121] Although to a lesser degree—and informed by national and regional jurisprudence, other jurisprudential materials of treaty bodies such as case law are also increasingly introducing evolutive interpretations of the rather truncated provision of the right to privacy in international law. We return to these points throughout the book.

But it is through the post-Snowden privacy discourse at the UN that soft law is playing a significant role in elaborating the right to privacy in international law. Consisting mainly of a series of Resolutions adopted by both UNGA and the Human Rights Council (HR Council), the discourse—which is still ongoing—introduces progressive standards on the right to privacy. The Resolutions read into the right to privacy principles and governance norms which find no formulation or articulation in international law. Apart from modern data privacy norms, the Resolutions address important issues in digital privacy such as digital surveillance. Further addressed in the Resolutions are the specific human rights responsibilities of technology companies vis-à-vis the right to privacy.[122] We return to discuss at length the normative values of this evolving discourse in chapter 5.

---

[12]   It is also to be noted that the HR Committee's latest GC on freedom of assembly touches on the right to privacy, the protection of which, including in the digital context, is instrumental for the enjoyment of freedom of assembly. See HR Committee, *General Comment 37: Article 21—The Right of Peaceful Assembly*, 129th sess, UN Doc CCPR/C/GC/37 (17 September 2020) paras 98–99 cum paras 10, 54, 60–63, 94.

[12]   See Kinfe Yilma, The United Nations' Evolving Privacy Discourse and Corporate Human Rights Obligations (ASIL Insights 2019) <https://bit.ly/3tGg3bV>.

Related to this, and the second elaborative role of soft law, relates to the role of corporations in the protection of human rights. International human rights law does not directly regulate the conduct of non-State actors including companies. That means companies owe no human rights obligations to individual rights holders. In the light of enormous powers that corporations wield, this remains to be one of the challenges in securing human rights, more so in a transnational context. After several attempts at introducing a regime that directly binds corporations failed, the international community has settled—for now—on a soft law: the UN Guiding Principles.[123] The Guiding Principles is currently the only international instrument that directly addresses corporations in human rights language.[124] A soft law, the Ruggie Principles sets forth a series of corporate human rights responsibilities such as due diligence to mitigate or prevent human rights impact of business activities. In the past few years, there has been an ongoing process under the auspices of the UN to translate the Ruggie Principles into an international treaty. Part of the reason for this effort is that bindingness would curb the deepening and complex problem of corporate human rights infringements. We return to these issues throughout the book, including later in this chapter. But the central argument of this book is that soft legalization, as opposed to hard legalization, is the most pragmatic response to the 'privacy problem' in the digital age. As shall be shown in chapter 7, a soft law grounded on existing binding instruments such as the ICCPR, would go a long way in addressing international law's privacy problem in the digital age.

4. 'Blind Spots'

Building on the above discussion on the normative structures of the human right to privacy in international law, this section explores the reach of international human rights law in securing privacy in the digital age. It shows that the current international human rights law framework on the right to privacy exhibits three major gaps: normative, institutional, and jurisprudential dearth. What follows lays out how these gaps have made the international law of privacy ill-equipped in securing digital privacy. In so doing, it draws upon the history of its making and comparative law.

---

[123] *Guiding Principles on Business and Human Rights: Implementing the United Nations 'Protect, Respect and Remedy' Framework*, 17th sess, Agenda item 3, UN Doc A/HRC/RES/17/4 (6 June 2011).
[124] Note that the Guiding Principles or the Ruggie Principles are referred to in the singular throughout this book deliberately so as to capture the fact that it is *a* single instrument.

4.1. Normative Gaps

Normative limitations of the present regime relate mainly to two major issues. The primary limitation concerns the vague manner in which the right to privacy is formulated in UN human rights instruments. Terminological and conceptual vagueness inherent in existing privacy norms obscures the scope of the right, and as a result, hinders proper implementation of the right. The second limitation relates to the lack of clear and strong normative standards regarding the human rights responsibilities of Internet corporations vis-à-vis right to privacy. What follows considers these two normative limitations of international human rights law.

4.1.1. Problems of Scope

The right to privacy in existing international human rights instruments is framed in an exceedingly vague language. It finds the initial articulation in Article 12 of the UDHR:

> No one shall be subjected to arbitrary interference with his privacy, family, home or correspondence, nor to attacks upon his honour and reputation. Everyone has the right to the protection of the law against such interference or attacks.

This provision is replicated near verbatim in the ICCPR except that the term 'unlawful' is introduced to the privacy provision right next to 'arbitrary', and at the limb of the provision that protects 'honour' and 'reputation'.[125] It reads:

1. No one shall be subjected to arbitrary or unlawful interference with his privacy, family, home or correspondence, nor to unlawful attacks on his honour and reputation.
2. Everyone has the right to the protection of the law against such interference or attacks.

Such formulation of the right to privacy is followed in subsequent human rights too. But the manner in which the right to privacy is formulated both under the UDHR and the ICCPR—and other subsequent UN human rights instruments for that matter—raises three issues of scope. What follows considers these three issues of scope, along with the rather broader issue of the extraterritorial scope of the right to privacy.

---

[125] ICCPR (n 1) art 17.

4.1.1.1. (De)coupling Privacy and Reputation

The present terminological make-up of Article 17 of the ICCPR—and privacy provisions of the CRD, ICRMW, and CRC—indicates that the provision is more than a privacy provision.[126] In addition to privacy, it protects two broad set of interests: 'reputation' and 'honour'. This has, however, created confusion as to the possible link between the right to privacy on the one hand and reputation or honour on the other. A look back at the drafting history of the Covenant offers little but one learns from background documents of the UDHR that the nexus between privacy and reputation/honour was a topic of some discussion.[127] But the debate was primarily about whether the inclusion of reputation and honour into the privacy provision might affect the protection of free speech.[128] Michael reports that there was indeed a discussion at the UNGA's Third Committee regarding the inclusion of 'reputation and honour' in Article 17 of the ICCPR but offers no further details.[129]

The HR Committee, the treaty body that monitors the ICCPR, sends mixed signals in its GC 16 regarding the possible link between privacy and reputation/honour. The very heading of the GC, titled 'right to privacy', suggests that Article 17 is a solely privacy provision, and by extension, reputation and honour are not, as such, privacy interests or values. But the GC's paragraph on 'reputation and honour' appears to suggest otherwise, as it presents the latter as distinct interests.[130] The Committee's GC 31 further hints that Article 17 comprises 'privacy-related' guarantees but offers no clarification on how these interests, assuming these include honour and reputation, relate to privacy.[131] The Committee's GC on Freedom of Expression provision of the ICCPR, where 'reputation' is one ground of restriction, also does not clarify the meaning of reputation in the context of privacy.[132] In describing the right to privacy only in terms of 'privacy, family, home and correspondence', the series of post-Snowden UN Privacy Resolutions suggest that Article 17 of the ICCPR is solely a privacy provision. And as such, reputation and honour have little to do with privacy. A report of the Special Rapporteur on the Right to Privacy (SRP) adds to the confusion in vaguely stating that the 'right to protection

---

[126] Cf Myres McDougal and others, 'Aggregate Interest in Shared Respect and Human Rights: The Harmonization of Public Order and Civic Order' (1977) 23 New York Law School Law Review 183, 229 (stating that art 12 of the UDHR is 'broader than the technical concept of privacy and pregnant with potentiality for further expansion').

[127] See Lars Rehof, 'Article 12' in Asbjorn Eide and others (eds), *The Universal Declaration of Human Rights: A Commentary* (Scandinavian University Press 1992) 188–89.

[128] ibid.

[129] James Michael, *Privacy and Human Rights: An International and Comparative Study with Special Reference to Developments in Information Technology* (Dartmouth 1994) 21.

[130] GC 16 (n 42) para 11.

[131] HR Committee, *General Comment 31: Article 2—Nature of Legal Obligation Imposed on State Parties to the Covenant* 80th sess, UN Doc CCPR/C/21/Rev.1/Add.13 (26 May 2004) para 8.

[132] HR Committee, *General Comment 34: Article 19—Freedom of Opinion and Expression*, 102nd sess, UN Doc CCPR/C/GC/34 12 (September 2011) paras 21, 28.

of 'reputation' under Article 12 of the UDHR and Article 17 of the ICCPR is 'distinct from yet akin to privacy'.[133]

Thus, whether privacy has any conceptual link with reputation and honour is unclear. Doubtless, reputation and honour are, as Griffin rightly notes, matters of legitimate interest but relate rather to the law of defamation.[134] Even where reputation and honour are worthy of protection as fundamental rights, it is not clear why they are lumped together with privacy. Furthermore, given the fact that Article 19(3)(a) of the Covenant mentions 'respect of the rights or reputation of others' as one legitimate ground for the restriction of the right to free speech, the inclusion of reputation within the privacy provision might be seen as a redundancy.[135] But again, a strict reading of Article 19(3)(a)—especially the disjunctive 'or'—could also lend an argument that even the reference to reputation here is not as a *right* as such. Or, it is not at least conceived as a right recognized under the Covenant or in international human rights law in general.

This viewpoint finds support when one considers how the ECHR, the privacy provision of which was fashioned based on Article 12 of the UDHR, treats the matter. Background documents of the ECHR reveal that references to reputation and honour were deliberately excluded from the privacy provision and ultimately taken to Article 10 as an exception to the right to freedom of expression.[136] One account holds that the deliberate exclusion by the drafters was mainly due to the 'vagueness' of the terms.[137] In elaborating the drafting Committee's approach in transposing the UDHR into the Convention, a member of the Committee noted that the approach pursued was not to 'refer to all the provisions of the article in question but only to those specifying the content of the freedom'.[138] Moreover, while the ECtHR has considered 'reputation' claims under Article 8 of the ECHR in some cases, it has definitively ruled that 'reputation' and 'private life' are conceptually distinct.[139] Even for cases that implicate 'reputation' to be considered under the

[133] Report of the Special Rapporteur on the Right to Privacy, Joseph Cannataci, UN Doc A/HRC/34/60 (24 February 2017) para 46(i).

[134] See James Griffin, *On Human Rights* (Oxford University Press 2009) 703. Griffin further notes that provisions stipulating the right to reputation and honour are 'badly drawn' to the extent that 'they need interpretation tantamount to redrafting'. See at 209. Note also the Tallinn Manual where the International Group of Experts treated 'protection of defamation' separately from the right to privacy, see Tallinn Manual 2.0 (n 68) 187.

[135] Of a related view, see Michael (n 129) 20.

[136] See Tanya Alpin and Jason Bosland, 'The Uncertain Landscape of Article 8 of the ECHR: The Protection of Reputation as a Fundamental Right?' in Andrew Kenyon (ed), *Comparative Defamation and Privacy Law* (Cambridge University Press 2016) 265.

[137] See Gloria Fuster, *The Emergence of Personal Data Protection as a Fundamental Right of the EU* (Springer 2014) 38, citing Carlos Ruiz, *La Configuración Constitucional del Derecho a la Intimidad* (1992) 99.

[138] Quoted in Jacques Velu, 'The European Convention on Human Rights and the Right to Respect for Private Life, The Home and Communications' in Arthur Robertson (ed), *Privacy and Human Rights* (Manchester University Press 1973) 15–6.

[139] See, eg, ECtHR, *Karako v Hungary*, Application No 39311/05 (28 April 2009) paras 22–23.

right to private life, the Court has set a higher threshold of seriousness, ie the harm to reputation must be one capable of causing prejudice to private life.

4.1.1.2. Privacy and Its Zones of Protection

Privacy provisions of UN human rights treaties are couched in a manner that appears to detach the umbrella term 'privacy' from specific zones or grounds of protection—ie, 'family', 'home', and 'correspondence'—that it normally embraces. The way the provisions are formulated gives the impression that these terms are not covered under the umbrella term 'privacy'. This has been a source of confusion, and has been a subject of differing interpretations, including by the HR Committee. In an unprecedented interpretation, the Committee, for instance, has applied the term 'home' to cover tenancy rights.[140] Another decision of the Committee similarly held that eviction from one's home engages Article 17 because the measure presents a risk of homelessness.[141] GC 16 does not provide any clarification beyond stating that the term 'home' is to be understood to cover the place where 'a person resides or carries out his usual occupation'.

Such exceedingly broad interpretations of 'home' appear to be influenced by the case law of the ECtHR, which has long addressed similar cases under Article 8 of the Convention.[142] Perhaps in cognizance of this overstretched approach, the Court routinely reminds that there is nevertheless no right to be provided with a home/housing under Article 8. But even this caveat raises a question. If there is no right to be provided with a home—ie, a positive right to home, it is impliedly recognizing a 'negative' right to home. A right not to be evicted from one's home technically would mean a negative freedom of home. To be sure, the Court has on several occasions entertained cases relating to search and seizure under Article 8, which concern the classic right to the privacy of home.[143]

The term 'family' has also been interpreted by the Committee broadly to include family rights such as the right of foreigners not to be separated from their families by an expulsion order under immigration regulations.[144] But this interpretation is well beyond the usual understanding of privacy. The Committee's GC 16 has not adequately clarified the meaning of these terms either. It simply provides that the term 'family' must be given broad interpretation to include 'all those comprising the family as understood in the society of the State party concerned'.[145] Like

---

[140] See, eg, HR Committee, *Dušan Vojnović v Croatia*, Communication No 1510/2006 (30 March 2009).

[141] See HR Committee, *Kalamiotis and others v Greece*, Communication No 2242/2013 (3 January 2017) paras 12.4, 12.8.

[142] See, eg, ECtHR, *Chapman v The United Kingdom*, Application No 27238/95 (18 January 2001) para 99.

[143] See, eg, ECtHR, *Rachwalski and Ferenc v Poland*, Application No 47709/99 (28 July 2009).

[144] See, eg, HR Committee, *Al-Gertani v Bosnia and Herzegovina*, Communication No 1955/2010 (6 November 2013).

[145] See GC 16 (n 42) para 5.

in the case of 'home', the approach of the Committee might have been influenced by the case law of the ECtHR. The Court has on numerous occasions treated cases involving expulsion orders under the 'family life' proviso of Article 8, although a separate 'right to family' is guaranteed under Article 12 of the Convention.[146] The Court treats Article 12 as a *lex specialis* and proceeds to consider a case under Article 12 only when it finds no violation under Article 8.[147] The Committee has also increasingly adopted a similar approach of applying ICCPR's Article 23 on right to marry/family alongside Article 17 in matters that relate to 'family life'.[148] But it is worth noting that the Court's now established practice of considering the two provisions together has some precedent. During the drafting of the ECHR, both provisions were considered together, with almost absolute focus given to Article 8.[149] This might have influenced the current practice. But whether a similar path should be taken by Committee, without any such justification, is questionable.

Scholarly interpretations are also divergent, reflecting the general confusion about the present makeup of the provision. Volio, for instance, writes that Article 17 of the ICCPR protects both 'privacy and the family, home, correspondence, honour, and reputation'.[150] Another instance of the confusion is that mere reference to the term 'family' under Article 17, a provision mainly addressing privacy, led to the assumption that it relates to the right to form a family, a right separately guaranteed under Article 23 of the Covenant.[151] Kalin and Kunzli write that Article 17 protects 'the right to live together within a family'. This view sees Article 23 as a mere supplement to Article 17 of the Covenant. Sartor notes rightly that Article 17 of the ICCPR embodies a 'cluster of rights' but wrongly suggests that the right to privacy stands in this cluster distinctly than the others such as the right to correspondence.[152]

Nevertheless, it appears to be the case that references to 'privacy', 'home', 'family', and 'correspondence' aim to cover zones of privacy protection rather than to provide for individuated distinct rights to privacy, home, family, *and*

---

[146] See, eg, ECtHR, *Uner v The Netherlands*, Application No 46410/99 (18 October 2006).

[147] ECtHR, *Hamalainen v Finland*, Application No 37359/09 (16 July 2014) para 96.

[148] See, eg, HR Committee, *DT v Canada*, Communication No 2081/2011 (29 September 2016); see also Sarah Joseph and Melissa Castan, *The International Covenant on Civil and Political Rights: Cases, Materials and Commentary* (Oxford University Press 3rd edn, 2013) para 16.24.

[149] See William Schabas, *The European Convention on Human Rights: A Commentary* (Oxford University Press 2015) 582–4.

[150] See Fernando Volio, 'Legal Personality, Privacy and the Family' in Louis Henkin (ed), *The International Bill of Rights: The Covenant on Civil and Political Rights* (Columbia University Press 1981) 192.

[151] See Walter Kalin and Jorg Kunzli, *The Law of International Human Rights Protection* (Oxford University Press 2009) 14.

[152] See Giovanni Sartor, 'Human Rights and Information Technologies' in Roger Brownsword and others (eds), *The Oxford Handbook of Law, Regulation and Technology* (Oxford University Press 2017) 440.

correspondence.[153] Home, family, and correspondence must be seen as spheres of privacy protection—or 'institutional structures' as Nowak calls them.[154] When one refers to these terms within the context of privacy, they designate privacy of home, family and correspondence. As such, no distinct protection exists for these zones of privacy protection. The term home under Article 17, for instance, does not protect the right to home for two plain reasons. One is that the right to housing is far removed from privacy interests, and second, such right is protected under the International Covenant on Economic, Social and Cultural Rights (ICESCR) [Article 11] and the UDHR (Article 25). In one isolated occasion, a case concerning eviction, the HR Committee ironically held that the sanctioned eviction interfered with the author's 'right to the privacy of his home'.[155]

With increasing migration of people's personal lives to the digital space, privacy protection of the home must extend to these new spheres. Traditional privacy protection of individuals' personal effects in their homes must now cover aspects of personal effects situated in digital accounts. This is also in accord with emerging initiatives such as IBRs, considered in chapter 4, that embody a right to the 'inviolability of electronic systems, devices and domiciles'.[156] As Nowak notes, the right to privacy of home under Article 17 covers a broad range of interests including protection against 'forced or clandestine trespassing' as well as 'digital surveillance' through listening devices and hidden camera.[157] The increasing reliance on cloud computing services has made the cloud a 'digital home', worthy of protection under Article 17.[158]

The same is true with the term 'family' which, in several cases, has been applied to protect the right to family life. It is to be noted that none of UN human rights treaties that embody the right to privacy contain the term 'family life', except the CRD. And when the CRD refers to 'family life', which is explicitly mentioned in Article 8 of ECHR, it refers explicitly to the right to marry and form a family.[159] But, the right to family is recognized under Article 23 of the Covenant, and under Article 10(1) of the ICESCR. In that sense, the meaning of the term 'family' within the privacy provision should be different from the 'right to marry and form a family'. A more appropriate construction of the term—in the context

---

[153] Of a related view see, Privacy in the Digital Age: A Proposal for a New General Comment on the Right to Privacy under Article 17 of the International Covenant on Civil and Political Rights (American Civil Liberties Union, March 2014) 32.

[154] See Manfred Nowak, *UN Covenant on Civil and Political Rights: CCPR Commentary* (NP Engel 2005) 378. For a similar holding, in the context of 'correspondence', see Tallinn Manual 2.0 (n 68) 189, footnote 417.

[155] HR Committee, *Petr Gatilov v Russia*, Communication No 2171/2012 (30 August 2017) para 9.4.

[156] See *Italian Declaration of Internet Rights* (2015) art 7.

[157] Nowak (n 154) 400.

[158] Cf Mark Zuckerberg, A Privacy-Focused Vision for Social Networking (Facebook, 6 March 2019) <https://bit.ly/2TmiQWv> (noting the need for a digital equivalent to the 'living room' to protect privacy in social media).

[159] See CRD (n 2) art 23(3).

of digital privacy—should be right to privacy of family life. In the present realities of the Internet, family lives of individuals are represented in the digital sphere and equally merit protection under Article 17.

It is more straightforward with respect to 'correspondence' in the digital context. It essentially concerns secrecy of digital communications although it initially was meant for 'written letters'.[160] The term 'correspondence' must also be understood in the context of the right to privacy of correspondence. Similar understanding must be extended to these terms in the context of digital communications. The Committee is yet to examine cases that directly concern privacy of correspondence in the digital context. But it remains to be seen to what extent the case law of the ECtHR would inform its decisions. This is because the Court has made a number of decisions that read a far-reaching 'right to respect for correspondence' based on Article 8.[161]

But there are reasons to suggest that the ill-formulation, and the mis-drafting in between, of privacy vis-à-vis its zones of protection might have been partly a result of drafting and redrafting. A June 1947 draft of the UDHR—the third draft considered by the drafting Committee—was relatively accurate in its use of the umbrella term privacy. It reads that 'privacy of the home and of correspondence and respect for reputation shall be protected by law'.[162]

This formulation was accurate in applying the umbrella term privacy for the protection of specific zones of privacy protection—ie, home and correspondence. It removed the term 'family' for unknown reason, but it perhaps was because 'family' receives protection under another provision of the Declaration (Article 16). Similarly, an earlier draft version of Article 8 of ECHR reflected a more accurate version of the right to privacy: '... the right to privacy in respect of family, home and correspondence'.[163] One can argue that had these earlier fairly accurate formulations of the right to privacy were adopted, expansive interpretations of the right to privacy would not have ensued.

Overall, the expansive interpretive approach of the ECtHR seems to be influencing the Committee. In addition to reference by the Committee to the case law of the Court, its European members might also bring to the table the recipe of the jurisprudence. But the question is whether this is warranted and to what extent. The Court's expansive interpretation of Article 8 might have grown out of the

---

[160] See Nowak (n 154) 401; see also Tallinn Manual 2.0 (n 68) 189, footnote 417.

[161] See, eg, ECtHR, *Golder v The United Kingdom*, Application No 4451/70 (21 February 1975) [See particularly the Separate Opinions of Judges Zeika and Gerald]. The Court held that any measure that impedes someone from initiating correspondence interferes with the 'right to correspondence'. This far-reaching decision borderlines the right to free speech, which perhaps embraces the spirit of such a right to correspondence.

[162] Qouted in Mary Glendon, *A World Made New: Eleanor Roosevelt and the Universal Declaration of Human Rights* (Random House 2001) 283.

[163] See Preparatory Work on Article 8 of the European Convention on Human Rights [DH (56) 12] (1956) 6, footnote 2.

specific contexts in which the Court operates or the Council of Europe in general. For one, the way in which Article 8 is structured, particularly the terms 'private and family life' may have invited a broader interpretive approach. That the Court's jurisdiction does not embrace socio-economic rights like the right to housing perhaps encouraged an expansive approach. The Court has applied the notion of 'private life' in relation to areas that normally fall under other socio-economic rights such as the right to health, the right to work, and even the right to a clean and healthy environment.[164]

But when one considers that the Court has addressed issues relating to bodily and psychological integrity, eg rape and domestic violence, under the rubric of 'private life', one wonders to what extent that such an overly elastic approach should be relied upon by the Committee.[165] The Convention already guarantees a right to liberty and security of person, which even the Committee, based on relevant provisions of the ICCPR, interpreted to cover attacks against bodily and psychological integrity.[166] The concern with this approach is that the provision would lose one underlying notion that binds various interests together that is privacy.

4.1.1.3. Privacy and Limitation Clauses

Article 17 of the Covenant does not provide a fully fledged 'limitation clause' that stipulates conditions under which the right may be restricted. A limitation clause is key in ascertaining the scope of the human right to privacy. A vaguely formulated clause opens the door for wider construction of the conditions where restriction is permissible. The only phrases in Article 17 of the ICCPR that could be seen through the lens of a 'limitation clause' are the terms 'arbitrary' and 'unlawful'. If these terms were to be solely relied upon in assessing the legality of certain restrictions, measures that are neither arbitrary nor unlawful would not amount to interference with the right to privacy. But again, the meaning of these terms, particularly the term 'arbitrary', is not entirely clear. During the drafting of Article 12 of the UDHR, the term 'arbitrary' was controversial—and alternative terms such as 'unreasonable'—were suggested by delegates.[167] But such suggestions were not included in the final text.

---

[164] For a summary of case law on this, see Guide on Article 8 of the European Convention on Human Rights: Right to Respect for Private and Family (CoE, 31 August 2021) paras 129–41, 90–103, 158–66.

[165] Note, though, that the Court's expansive approach under Article 8 has already attracted widespread criticism. See, eg, Lord Sumption, The Limits of Law, 27th Sultan Azlan Shah Lecture, Kuala Lumpur (20 November 2013) 7–8 [noting how the Court 'went well beyond interpretation, and well beyond the language, object or purpose' of the ECHR to create 'new rights' relating to, inter alia, 'law of landlord and tenant' and questions best addressed in a 'social convention' out of a 'perfectly straightforward provision' (ie art 8) which was intended to protect 'private and family life, the privacy of the home and of personal correspondence'].

[166] See HR Committee, *General Comment 35: Article 9—Liberty and Security of Person*, 112th sess, UN Doc CCPR/C/GC/35 (16 December 2014) para 3.

[167] See Morsink (n 37) 137.

The High Commissioner's 2014 report on the right to privacy appears to play down the lack of an explicit limitation clause by pointing to the guidance offered by the Siracusa Principles on the meaning of the terms 'arbitrary' and 'unlawful' under the ICCPR.[168] The Siracusa Principles, however, provide no guidance on these two notions but provide a rather complex set of interpretive principles relating to limitations.[169] This is, of course, notwithstanding the question of whether these Principles are authoritative enough to warrant reference.[170] Instead, the HR Committee's jurisprudence has offered some clarification on the meaning of the term 'arbitrary' both under the right to privacy and the right to liberty and security of person provisions. But, when it comes to the right to privacy, the Committee has not been consistent in the way in which it interpreted the conditions for restriction. In some instances, it relied upon the organic limitation clauses of arbitrary and unlawful,[171] while in many others it applied the less organic three-part tests of legality, legitimate aim, and necessity.[172]

Problems of scope persisted due to this lack of coherence. A former UN Special Rapporteur on Human Rights and Counter-terrorism, Scheinin, suggested that despite the lack of a proper limitation clause under Article 17 of the ICCPR, the terms 'unlawful' and 'arbitrary' fulfil the requirements of legality and 'legitimate aim and/or necessary in a democratic society' respectively.[173] However, some States like the US have consistently rejected the reliance by the HR Committee of any limitation clauses other than the organic clauses of 'arbitrariness' and 'unlawfulness'.[174] This uncertainty and interpretive inconsistency underlines the need for an explicit and authoritative limitation clause that clearly demarcates the scope of the right to privacy.

Background documents indicate that there were initial proposals to incorporate a fully fledged limitation clause within Article 17 of the ICCPR benchmarked after Article 8(2) of the ECHR.[175] The political compromises that clouded the overall drafting of the Covenant led, however, to the rejection of the proposals without much discussion. The US delegation had even proposed a general limitation clause

---

[168] See The Right to Privacy in the Digital Age, Report of the High Commissioner for Human Rights, UN Doc A/HRC/27/37 (30 June 2014) para 22.

[169] See Siracusa Principles on the Limitation and Derogation Provisions in the International Covenant on Civil and Political Rights, American Association for the International Commission of Jurists (1988) Par I.

[170] The Siracusa Principles were not formally adopted by the UN, but the former Commission on Human Rights tacitly endorsed them when, inter alia, it assigned UN symbols and circulated them to member States. See UN Doc E/CN.4/1985/4.

[171] See, eg, HR Committee, I Elpida v Greece, Communication No 2242/2013 (26 February 2014).

[172] See, eg, HR Committee, AB v Canada, Communication No 2387/2014 (16 March 2017).

[173] See Report of the Special Rapporteur on the Promotion and Protection of Human Rights and Fundamental Freedoms while Countering Terrorism, Martin Scheinin, UN Doc A/HRC/13/37 (28 December 2009) para 16.

[174] See United States Response to OHCHR Questionnaire on the Right to Privacy in the Digital Age (20 4) <https://bit.ly/1FNq6r4>.

[175] See Nowak (n 154) 381–82.

similar to one provided for in Article 29(2) of the UDHR.[176] The majority of the delegates held however that State parties are best placed to prescribe grounds under which the right to privacy could be restricted based on their unique domestic circumstances.[177] This reason behind the rejection of a limitation clause does not, however, fully provide the complete story when one considers that other Covenant provisions were equipped with such a clause. Why would States agree for a limitation clause for the right to assembly,[178] but not for the right to privacy, unless the omission in the latter case was a result of an apparent lack of concern for privacy? This reinforces the point about the privacy inattention alluded to in the preceding section.

The ICCPR does not also contain a general limitation clause of a kind provided under UDHR which applies to all rights guaranteed under the Declaration. Article 29(2) of the UDHR reads:

> In the exercise of his rights and freedoms, everyone shall be subject only to such limitations as are determined by law solely for the purpose of securing due recognition and respect for the rights and freedoms of others and of meeting the just requirements of morality, public order and the general welfare in a democratic society.

While this has partly remedied the lack of a clearer limitation clause within Article 12 of the UDHR, it is not unfortunately repeated in the ICCPR. Although the resistance to including a proper 'limitation clause' within Article 17 of the ICCPR was due to political impasse of the time, the omission of a general limitation clause of a kind found in UDHR is probably a reflection of the haphazard drafting of the provision as well as the overall dearth of attention to privacy as a value.

4.1.1.4. The Extraterritorial Scope of the Right to Privacy

The fourth problem of scope relates to the extraterritorial scope of the right to privacy. The question of whether international human rights law in general and the ICCPR in particular apply extraterritorially has been contentious. The issue stems from the ambiguous way in which Article 2 of the ICCPR is framed. The provision partly reads as follows:

> Each State Party to the present Covenant undertakes to respect and to ensure to <u>all individuals within its territory and subject to its jurisdiction</u> the rights recognized in the present Covenant ... (Emphasis added).

---

[176] See Maya Randall, 'The History of the Covenants: Looking Back Half a Century and Beyond' in David Moeckli and others (eds), *Human Rights Covenants At 50: The Past, Present and Future* (Oxford University Press 2018) 13.

[177] ibid; see also Bossuyt (n 21) 347.

[178] See ICCPR (n 1) art 18(3).

Some States, particularly the United States, argue that this provision circumscribes the scope of States' human rights obligations to respect and protect the rights of individuals that are within their territory *and* jurisdiction.[179] According to this literal interpretation of the jurisdictional clause, States owe no human rights obligations vis-a-vis individuals outside their geographic borders. In the context of the right to privacy, this reading would mean that States would not be held accountable for unlawful foreign digital surveillance activities. This interpretation has been rejected by the HR Committee in its case law and concluding observations as well as GC 31.[180] In GC 31 adopted in 2004, the Committee held that Covenant rights apply extraterritorially and States owe an obligation to 'respect and ensure to all persons who may be within their territory and to all persons subject to their jurisdiction'.[181] In practice, this means that State obligations extend to anyone within the power or effective control of that State Party, even if not situated within the territory of the State party.[182]

In the years since the adoption of GC 31, the Committee has consistently affirmed this position in a number of concluding observations. But this primarily concerned the extraterritorial application of Covenant rights in the non-digital context. It was only in the wake of the Snowden revelations that the Committee considered the extraterritoriality of Article 17 in the context of digital communications. In a 2014 concluding observation on the periodic report of the United States, it held that the right to privacy applies extraterritorially, especially when a State party engages in foreign surveillance.[183] This position has later found some expression, as shall be noted in chapter 5, in the UN Privacy Resolutions.

Notwithstanding the above affirmations of the HR Committee (and UN Privacy Resolutions), the issue remains controversial. As noted above, the United States' position on this point relies very much on rigid textual reading of Article 2 of the ICCPR. And, in the absence of political will, the Committee's position is unlikely to resolve the contention. While the United States' position is now a minority view, it should not be a reason to underestimate the extent of the controversy. This is mainly because of the unique position the US holds in the global Internet governance more broadly, and particularly, in being home to major actors involved in the provision and ownership of Internet infrastructures, products and services.

[179] See Marko Milanovic, 'Human Right Treaties and Foreign Surveillance: The Right to Privacy in the Digital Age' (2014) 56 Harvard International Law Journal 81, 102–08.

[180] See, eg, GC 31 (n 131); HR Committee, *Sergio Euben Lopez Burgos v Uruguay*, Communication No R.12/52 (29 July 1981); note also that the ICJ has affirmed the extraterritorial scope of the ICCPR more generally. See, eg, *Legal Consequences of the Construction of a Wall in the Occupied Palestinian Territory*, ICJ Reports 2004 (9 July 2004) 136.

[181] ibid, para 10.

[182] ibid.

[183] See Concluding Observations of the HR Committee: The United States of America, UN Doc CCPR/C/USA/CO/4 (23 April 2014).

In part, the non-binding nature of GC 31 (and concluding observations) appears to lend weight to the argument that the meaning of a clear provision cannot be altered, and more so, through a soft law. This means that apart from political will, the problem of scope regarding Article 17 ICCPR should be addressed through a mechanism that carries higher normative force. As shall be argued in chapter 7, the best way to address this is by codifying the position of the HR Committee as well as other bodies and the growing state practice on the extraterritoriality of the ICCPR—especially the right to privacy—in a UNGA Declaration. Such a Declaration, while enjoying all the benefits of 'softness', would place the extraterritoriality scope of Article 17, in the context of digital communications, on a firm legal basis.

4.1.2. The Curious Case of Internet Corporations

The second major normative gap in international privacy law concerns the lack of clear normative guidance on the human rights obligations or responsibilities of technology companies. The primary obligation in human rights law lies on States, and as such, non-State actors owe no direct human rights obligations in human rights law.[184] It is through the general duty of States to 'protect' that private actors are held to account for human rights infringements. This obligation involves putting in place the requisite legal and institutional framework to regulate the conduct of private actors. But, the increasing influence that transnational corporations exercise over individuals has raised the question of whether the latter should be held to account directly under human rights law. This is more so in the case of Internet corporations such as Google and Facebook that wield tremendous power over the digital lives of their billions of users.

Recent revelations that mass digital surveillance has been carried out by governments in concert with these Internet businesses cast doubt on whether States could genuinely ensure respect for the right to privacy by private actors. Indeed, the lack of a direct human rights obligation of corporations, particularly in the area of privacy, is partially addressed through data privacy law. Progressive data privacy legislation in Europe regulates the behaviour of Internet corporations, and even guarantees enforceable data subject rights. While the scope of data privacy legislation is more nuanced, it essentially imposes direct obligation on corporations. But the absence of an enforceable international data privacy framework, considered further in chapter 3, means that the gap in international human rights law vis-à-vis Internet corporations remains unaddressed.

The question of how best to envisage the possible human rights obligations of transnational corporations has been controversial. A major UN attempt in this field was the adoption in 2003 of the 'Norms and Responsibilities of Transnational

---

[184] See GC 31 (n 131) para 8.

Corporations'.[185] These norms had envisaged 'periodic reporting' and 'verification' by the UN as monitoring mechanisms.[186] Because these 'norms' were framed in terms of strict 'obligations', they were not well received by stakeholders, particularly corporations.[187] This later forced the former Commission to abandon these norms and the matter received little attention for a while until the possibility of a 'soft law' measure was considered. The only applicable norms currently at the international level are envisaged in the Ruggie Principles adopted by the HR Council in 2011.[188]

The Guiding Principles does not strictly introduce new human rights obligations on businesses but rather 'elaborate' already existing State obligations in international human rights law. Paragraph 12 of the Guiding Principles states that the 'corporate responsibility of businesses to respect human rights' emanates from, inter alia, the international bill of human rights which includes the ICCPR and the UDHR. The human rights responsibilities of businesses are of four types: (1) to refrain from infringing human rights; (2) to prevent infringement of human rights; (3) to mitigate the impact of measures that impinge on human rights; and (4) to remedy violations of human rights. The practical utility of these Principles in addressing the role of Internet businesses vis-à-vis the right to privacy is limited. For one, the Guiding Principles being soft law and hence bereft of any legally binding force, makes it less effective.

The UN currently is in the process of translating these soft laws into a binding instrument. The HR Council created an open-ended Intergovernmental Working Group in 2014 to craft a 'binding international legal instrument' within the purview of international human rights law to regulate the activities of transnational corporations and other business enterprises.[189] While this might address the first concern by introducing an enforceable hard law, it appears not to adequately respond to the second concern. The Working Group has so far held several sessions but reports of the Group reveal that the discussions have not considered the case of internet corporations.[190] The focus rather was on the depletion of natural resources and its impact on the rights of workers and vulnerable groups such as indigenous peoples, children and disabled persons.[191]

---

[185] See *Norms and Responsibilities of Transnational Corporations and Other Business Enterprises with regard to Human Rights*, UN ESCOR, 55th sess, 22nd mtg, Agenda item 4, UN Doc E/CN.4/Sub.2/2003/12/Rev.2 (13 August 2003).

[186] ibid, para 16.

[187] ibid, para 4; see also Hurst Hannum, 'Reinvigorating Human Rights for the 21st Century' (2016) 16 Human Rights Law Review 409, 427–28.

[188] See Guiding Principles on Business and Human Rights (n 123).

[189] See *Elaboration of an International Legally Binding Instrument on Transnational Corporations and Other Business Enterprises with respect to Human Rights*, HRC Res 26/9, 26th sess, Agenda item 3, UN Doc A/HRC/RES/26/9 (14 July 2014) para 1.

[190] See, eg, Report on the Second Session of the Open-ended Intergovernmental Working Group on Transnational Corporations and other Business Enterprises with respect to Human Rights, UN Doc A/HRC/34/47 (4 January 2017).

[191] ibid, paras 32–33, 65.

In mid-2018, the 'zero draft' was released by the Working Group for substantive negotiation by States.[192] And several drafts have since been presented by the Working Group. But all drafts, including the latest version,[193] mostly read like a version of the Ruggie Principles, albeit in treaty form. Unlike a preceding document released by the Working Group that purported to impose direct obligations on corporations,[194] the latest draft treaty is mainly addressed to States. Considering that the retraction was due to opposition from some States and business organizations,[195] the prospect of an instrument being adopted seems doubtful. It is also worth noting, in this regard, that the Council's Resolution that creates the Working Group was curiously voted down by the United States and the United Kingdom, along with twelve other countries.

The negative votes of the United States and the United Kingdom should not come as surprise given their strongly held view that even the little disputed obligation of States to 'protect' against abuses by third parties is limited, and not grounded in customary international law of human rights.[196] But it is still striking that the Resolution was adopted by twenty to fourteen votes, with thirteen abstentions.[197] Almost all States who voted in favour of the Resolution were developing countries. Even some of the States like Russia that initially voted in favour of the Resolution have since opposed a treaty on business and human rights.[198] Reports of the Working Group also reveal that the level of participation, both from States and private actors, during the drafting of the instrument was limited. For instance, only a few States made submissions while no civil society working in the field of (digital) rights participated.[199]

---

[192] See Legally Binding Instrument to Regulate, in International Human Rights Law, the Activities of Transnational Corporations and Other Business Enterprises, Zero Draft (16 July 2018) <https://bit.ly/2Ly1nT0>.

[193] Legally Binding Instrument to Regulate, in International Human Rights Law, the Activities of Transnational Corporations and Other Business Enterprises, Third Revised Draft (17 August 2021) <https://bit.ly/3i2yTD1>.

[194] See Elements of the Draft Legally Binding Instrument on Transnational Corporations and Other Business Enterprises with respect to Human Rights (September 2017) Sec 3.2 <https://bit.ly/2fF5crq>.

[195] See Doug Cassel, 'The Third Session of the UN Intergovernmental Working Group on a Business and Human Rights Treaty' (2018) 3 Business and Human Rights Journal 277, 281.

[196] See, eg, Letter from David Bethlehem, Legal Advisor to UK's Foreign and Commonwealth Office, to John Ruggie, Special Representative of the Secretary General on Human Rights and Transnational Businesses and Other Business Enterprises (9 July 2009); Observation of the United States on General Comment 31 of the Human Rights Committee (December 2007) paras 10–18, 27.

[197] See HRC Res 26/9 (n 189) Annex.

[198] See Cassel (n 195) 283.

[199] See details at <https://bit.ly/2IemLOR>; see also Report on the Third Session of the Open-ended Intergovernmental Working Group on Transnational Corporations and other Business Enterprises with Respect to Human Rights, UN Doc A/HRC/37/67 (24 January 2018); see also Text of the Third Revised Draft Legally Binding instrument with the Concrete Textual Proposals Submitted by States during the Seventh Session, UN Doc A/HRC/49/65/Add.1 (January 2022); Report on the Sixth Session of the Open-ended Intergovernmental Working Group on Transnational Corporations and Other Business Enterprises with Respect to Human Rights, UN Doc A/HRC/46/73 14 (January 2021).

Moreover, the process appears to be moving without any heed to the ongoing discussion at the UN on the 'right to privacy in the digital age', which is gradually addressing the role of corporations vis-à-vis the right to privacy. The likelihood of such an instrument being adopted, in the face of such widespread lack of enthusiasm as well as possible resistance from businesses, appears to be low. At the Working Group's sixth session, a number of States expressed reservations and outright opposition to the draft text as well as the whole treaty process. The United Kingdom delegation, for instance, noted that while the draft has noble aims, they remain sceptical that this text can gather the political support.[200] The United States, on the other hand, not only maintained objection to the process but also called on the Working Group to abandon in favour of alternative approaches.[201] This makes more uncertain the possibility of clear and strong international normative standards that determine the nature of responsibilities that Internet businesses owe in respecting and protecting the right to privacy of their users.

4.2. Institutional-Structural Gaps

The second type of gap in international privacy law is institutional. The current regime for the monitoring of human rights treaties relies primarily on panels of independent experts organized in the form of committees, working groups and special procedures. When it comes to privacy, the monitoring of the right to privacy is undertaken mainly by the HR Committee and other treaties bodies such as the Committees that monitor CRD, ICRMW, and CRC as well as the Working Group that oversees the UN Guiding Principles.[202] The SRP also has some role in the promotion and protection of the right to privacy.[203]

But these human rights bodies operate in a framework that does not permit the development of a robust privacy jurisprudence. The Committees and Working Groups are composed of experts that work part-time. The HR Committee, for instance, is a Committee of 18 part-time experts who meet only three times per year, and only for four weeks each time.[204] And, these part-time experts are expected to review State periodic reports (and adopt concluding observations), examine individual communications, develop GCs, hear reports of Rapporteurs on follow-up of views and concluding observations. Add to that the frequent reshuffle of members

[200] Annex to the Report on the Seventh Session of the Open-ended Intergovernmental Working Group on Transnational Corporations and other Business Enterprises with respect to Human Rights, UN Doc A/HRC/49/65 (January 2021) para 22.

[201] ibid, para 23.

[202] See Human Rights and Transnational Corporations and Other Business Enterprises, HRC Res 17/4, 17th sess, Agenda item 3, UN Doc A/HRC/RES/17/4 (16 June 2011) para 6.

[203] See The Right to Privacy in the Digital Age, HRC Res 28/16, 28th sess, Agenda Item 3, UN Doc A/HRC/RES/28/16 (26 March 2015) para 4.

[204] See ICCPR (n 1) art 28.

of the Committee, due to term limits and other factors, which affects develop-ment of a coherent rights jurisprudence.[205] Interpretive inconsistencies, discussed above, regarding 'home' as well as the application of 'arbitrariness' are probably results of this institutional problem. What may follow from this state of affairs is that the Committee is not in a position to examine individual communications, periodic reports or GCs as rigorously as could be done with better resources. The broad range of Covenant rights that the Committee must address further works against full and proper examination of certain matters that implicate rights such as the right to privacy.

This adds to the broader challenge that these bodies do not have the power to pronounce legally binding decisions that impose sanctions against States found to be in breach of privacy rights. The HR Committee—like other Committees—is tasked under the ICCPR to adopt mere unbinding 'views' and 'concluding observa-tions' under the individual communications and reporting procedures respectively. The SRP's mandate is also only to promote the right to privacy through various mechanisms and to offer recommendations to the HR Council for the better pro-tection of the right to privacy.[206] The other relevant platform is the HR Council's Universal Periodic Review (UPR) mechanism, which also has similar institutional limitations. But, vesting the HR Committee, as shall be argued in chapter 7, with the power to make binding decisions would not necessarily improve the protection of human rights. But it is reflective of the larger institutional-structural problem in international privacy law.

These institutional weaknesses translate into two practical challenges that re-duce the effectiveness of the UN treaty monitoring framework. One is that the level of compliance by States found to be in violation of privacy rights is bound to be lower. States are likely to give deaf ears to non-binding views of the HR Committee, openly reject recommendations offered at the UPR or through concluding obser-vations.[207] This has, of course, occurred in practice. The level of State compliance with the views of the Committee has, for instance, been generally low. Its annual reports to the UNGA routinely complains not only that 'many' State parties have failed to implement views adopted under the Optional Protocol but also fail to co-operate with the Committee in providing observations on allegations submitted by authors.[208] Similar non-compliance tendencies have been detected at the UPR. Studies have shown that two years after the review process commenced States had

---

[205] Of a related view, see Steiner (n 5) 28–29.

[206] HRC Res 28/16 (n 203) para 4.

[207] Of a related view, see Martin Sheinin, 'The International Covenant on Civil and Political Rights' in Geir Ulfstein and others (eds), *Making Treaties Work: Human Rights, Environment and Arms Control* (Cambridge University Press 2007) 66.

[208] See, eg, Annual Report of the Human Rights Committee to the General Assembly, UNGAOR 75th sess, UN Doc A/75/40 (April 2020) paras 37, 30; Annual Report of the Human Rights Committee to the General Assembly, UNGAOR 70th sess, UN Doc A/70/40 (April 2015) para 40.

acted only on 40 per cent of the recommendations given.[209] Moreover, only 43 per cent of the recommendations were accepted by States under review at the 14th session of the second cycle.[210]

Secondly, the lack of discretion to pronounce binding and enforceable decisions against recalcitrant States also has the effect of limiting recourse by individuals whose privacy rights have been violated. Partly, this is because there are relatively effective regional courts that are empowered to issue enforceable decisions in Europe and the Americas. It is conceivable that Europeans would be more inclined to resort to, for example, the ECtHR than a rather powerless Committee to seek remedy against their States.[211] This explains why individuals and civil society groups mount several successful legal challenges in the wake of the Snowden revelations against mass digital surveillance before these European courts, not the HR Committee. It is also interesting to note that most digital privacy cases against European governments considered by the Committee, highlighted below, have initially been submitted to either the former European Commission on Human Rights or the ECtHR but declared inadmissible. This lends weight to the argument, then, that European authors filed complaints with the HR Committee (mainly) because their cases were declared inadmissible by the more effective regional bodies.

To summarize, the overall 'cooperative framework' that animates the UN human rights system renders human rights monitoring bodies' roles to be merely advisory rather than judicial. But the problem is not solely the lack of authority to issue legally binding decisions. Indeed, the way forward in strengthening the UN privacy system lies in rebuilding its central dialogical approach. We return to consider in chapter 8 the way in which the existing regime based on co-operative dialogue must be entrenched and enhanced in the digital age.

4.3. Jurisprudential Gaps

The third major limitation of the human right to privacy framework is jurisprudential, which flows from the normative and institutional limitations considered above. Not only are normative texts vague and ill-conceived but also the jurisprudence developed around these norms by a rather weak institutional framework has been thin and stagnant. A closer look at the practices of the UN Committees that monitor relevant human rights treaties such as the ICCPR, CRD, ICRMW and CRC as well as the HR Council and Working Group installed to monitor the UN Guiding Principles reveal that a coherent and progressive digital privacy

---

[209] See, eg, Roland Chauville, 'The Universal Periodic Review's First Cycle: Successes and Failures' in Hilary Charlesworth and Emma Larking (eds), *Human Rights and the Universal Periodic Review: Rituals and Ritualism* (Cambridge University Press 2015) 93.

[210] See 'Universal Periodic Review' (2013) 1 Human Rights Monitor Quarterly 1, 27.

[211] Of a related view, see Steiner (n 5) 34.

jurisprudence is yet to emerge. This section provides some highlights of the jurisprudence, or the lack thereof, on digital privacy to illustrate the jurisprudential dearth. The discussion explores, first, the privacy jurisprudence, or the lack thereof, of relevant UN treaty bodies, and second, the HR Council and associated bodies such as the UPR.

4.3.1. Treaty Body Jurisprudence

4.3.1.1. Case Law

Cases that implicate the right to privacy in the digital context have been few and far between in the international fora. Cases relating to the right to privacy under the ICCPR are considered mainly by the HR Committee. The other treaty bodies that monitor the CRC, ICRMW, and CRD are yet to consider digital privacy cases. At the time of writing, there was one privacy case considered by the Committee that monitors the CRD but it concerned physical privacy, and was ultimately declared inadmissible *ratio temporis*.[212] The required number of declarations recognizing the competence of Committee that monitors the ICRMW has not been achieved means that the individual communications procedure under Article 77 of the Convention has not yet entered into force.[213] The Committee that monitors CRC is also unlikely to consider digital privacy cases anytime soon as its Optional Protocol on Individual Communications has only forty-eight State parties.[214] Another possible avenue for consideration of privacy cases is the complaints procedure of the HR Council which allows lodging complaints concerning 'consistent patterns of gross and reliably attested violations of human rights'.[215] Mass digital surveillance by governments and corporations of the scale revealed by Snowden might arguably meet the threshold to be scrutinized by the Council. But there is no record of such complaints so far, unsurprisingly, because the threshold appears to invite mostly gross human rights violations such as torture, enslavement, and enforced disappearance.

The case law of the HR Committee, which is best placed to address digital privacy, is also yet to arrive. Most privacy cases adjudged by the HR Committee concern the right to 'family life' of foreigners facing expulsion orders, the right to not to be subjected to unreasonable search and seizure or interference with the secrecy of prisoners' correspondence.[216] A review of the Committee's case docket results in only four cases relating to privacy that centre around digital communications such as the Internet and telecommunications as well as disclosure of personal

---

[212] See HR Committee, *Kenneth McAlpine v United Kingdom*, Communication No 6/2011 (13 November 2012).

[213] See details at <https://www.ohchr.org/EN/HRBodies/TBPetitions/Pages/HRTBPetitions.aspx>.

[214] See details at <http://indicators.ohchr.org/>

[215] See *Institution Building of the United Nations Human Rights Council*, HRC Res 5/1, 5th sess, 9th mtg, UN Doc A/HRC/RES/5/1 (18 June 2007) para 85.

[216] See, eg, *Al-Gertani v Bosnia and Herzegovina* (n 144); HR Committee, *Marouf v Algeria*, Communication No 1889/2009 (29 April 2014).

information.[217] Even these cases touch on digital privacy only peripherally. More often, the Committee reviewed these cases in the context of reputation and honour than privacy per se. And where some of these cases concern digital privacy, the Committee has barely addressed them in full context, and as such the decisions are not preceded by thorough examination. With an emerging trend by which the HR Committee draws upon the case law of the ECtHR, rather progressive data privacy decisions are on the horizon. We return to this point in chapter 6 where this emerging trend of jurisprudential cross-influence is considered.

4.3.1.2. Concluding Observations

Concluding observations are another source of jurisprudence in the international human rights framework. The observations are basically concluding views of the treaty bodies after periodic reports of State parties are reviewed, and an interactive dialogue is held with the State under review. A typical feature of concluding observations is that, after a paragraph that briefly outlines concerns regarding a given piece of national law or practice that impinges on provisions of the relevant human rights treaty, the relevant treaty body urges the State party to ensure that the law or the practice is aligned with the treaty. Often, States are called upon to provide remedies, amend laws to make them in accord with the relevant human rights instrument and provide an independent oversight mechanism, for example, for surveillance measures.

Digital privacy has relatively received frequent attention through concluding observations at the HR Committee in contrast with case law.[218] Since its early days—and more so since the Snowden revelations, the Committee has adopted concluding observations that relate to wiretapping of telephones,[219] data privacy,[220] domestic laws that authorize warrantless and excessive surveillance,[221] and more

---

[217]   See HR Committee, *IP v Finland*, Communication No 450/1991 (26 July 1993); HR Committee, *Antonius Cornelis Van Hulst v The Netherlands*, Communication No 903/1999 (15 November 2004); HR Committee, *Nabil Sayadi and Patricia Vinck v Belgium*, Communication No 1472/2006 (29 December 2008); HR Committee, *HS v Australia*, Communication No 2015/2010 (13 May 2015). No individual communication alleging violation of the ICCPR through surveillance has been made to the Committee. See Yuval Shany, Online Surveillance in the Case Law of the Human Rights Committee, The Hebrew University of Jerusalem Center for Cybersecurity Research (13 July 2017) <https://bit.ly/2MECR7m>.

[218]   It is to be noted that no privacy related concluding observation has been adopted by the other treaty bodies, except one on the right to family life by the Committee that monitors the CRD. For a list of Concluding Observations by the Committee, see <http://bit.ly/2fUo4lZ>.

[219]   See, eg, Comments of the HR Committee: Russian Federation, UN Doc CCPR/C/79/Add.54 (26 July 1995) para 19; Concluding Observations of the HR Committee: Jamaica, UN CCPR/C/79/Add.83 (19 November 1997) para 20; Concluding Observations of the HR Committee: Poland, UN Doc CCPR/C/79/Add.110 (29 July 1999) para 22; Concluding Observations of the HR Committee: The Netherlands, UN Doc CCPR/C/NLD/CO/4 (25 August 2009) para 14; Concluding Observations of the HR Committee: Bulgaria, UN Doc CCPR/C/BGR/CO/3 (19 August 2011) para 22.

[220]   See, eg, Concluding Observations of the HR Committee: Sweden, UN Doc CCPR/C/SWE/CO/6 (7 May 2009) para 18; Concluding Observations of the HR Committee: Hungary, UN Doc CCPR/C/HUN/CO/5 (16 November 2010) para 6; Concluding Observations of the HR Committee: France, UN Doc CCPR/C/FRA/CO/4 (31 July 2008) para 22.

[221]   See, eg, Concluding Observations of the HR Committee: Poland, UN Do CCPR/C/POL/CO/7 (23 November 2016) para 39; Concluding Observations of the HR Committee: France, UN Doc CPR/C/

recently mass digital surveillance.[222] A survey by a former member of the HR Committee reveals that concluding observations relating to digital surveillance have increased by 25 per cent since the Snowden revelations.[223] Concluding observations are not, however, structurally best placed to expound and give content to the right to privacy provision of the relevant human rights treaties. The inherent limitation of the reporting procedure—and hence concluding observations—is that these observations, unlike case law, do not examine a particular scenario in the light of the specific human rights in question, and as such, they add little to the development of jurisprudence on digital privacy. The brief nature of concluding observations further robs them of jurisprudential significance.

4.3.1.3. General Comments

GCs adopted by the relevant treaty bodies are the other sources of jurisprudence in international human rights law. The comments are meant to elaborate the specific content of human rights, and as such, they are sometimes referred to as 'restatements' or 'authoritative interpretations' of treaty provisions.[224] GCs are drafted based on the jurisprudence developed by the relevant treaty body particularly from its concluding observations on periodic reports submitted by State parties.[225] The primary purpose of GCs is to offer guidance for States in the course of complying with their human rights treaty obligations.

GCs relating to digital privacy have so far been adopted by the HR Committee and the Committee on the Rights of the Child.[226] But it is GC 16 of the HR Committee that offers some guidance on the right to privacy although it was adopted as far back as 1988 and written in truncated forms. It addresses the right to privacy in two levels. First, it provides that the right to privacy of correspondence should be protected de jure and de facto, and surveillance is prohibited under Article 17.[227] Second, the GC addresses privacy of personal data to some degree. It provides that States' positive obligation under Article 17 includes the regulation by law of automated collection and processing of personal information both by the

---

SR.3193 (17 August 2015) para 12; Concluding Observations of the HR Committee: New Zealand, UN Doc CCPR/C/NZL/CO/6 (28 April 2016) paras 15–16.

[222] See, eg, Concluding Observations of the HR Committee: The United Kingdom of Great Britain and Northern Ireland, UN Doc CCPR/C/GBR/CO/7 (17 August 2015) para 24; Concluding Observations of the HR Committee: The United States of America (n 183) para 22.

[223] See Shany (n 217).

[224] See Tyagi (n 8) 285, 302.

[225] See, eg, ICCPR (n 1) art 40(4).

[226] See Section 3 above for a discussion on the recent GC dealing with children's rights in the digital context. Earlier GCs of the Committee also address privacy, albeit peripherally. The GC on the HIV/ AIDS and the Rights of the Child, for instance, emphasizes the need to respect and protect the privacy of medical data of the child. See Committee on the Rights of the Child, *General Comment 3: HIV/ AIDS and the Rights of the Child*, 32nd sess, UN Doc CRC/GC/2003/1 (17 March 2003) paras 6, 20, 24, 29, 40(c).

[227] See GC 16 (n 42) para 8.

public and private sectors.[228] This can be taken to mean that Article 17 requires States to pass data privacy legislation. Furthermore, the GC briefly reflects four principles of data privacy law.[229] The principle of 'data security' is implicit when the Comment states 'information concerning a person's private life does not reach the hands of persons who are not authorized by law to receive, process and use it'. The GC's stipulation that information concerning a person's private life must not be 'used for purposes incompatible with the Covenant' mirrors the 'use limitation principle'. The 'principle of data subject participation' is also partially envisaged under the GC where it empowers data subjects to ascertain the identity of the person who holds data on them and what information. The GC's proviso allowing data subjects to request rectification of incorrect information about them held by third parties highlights the 'principle of data quality'.

GC 16 has three inherent limitations, however. One is that it recognizes only some of the basic data privacy principles, and even those reflected in the GC are not adequately elaborated.[230] This is mainly due to the truncated nature of the comment. Second, GC 16—as for other GCs—is not a legally binding document, and as a result, it is difficult for individuals to invoke its provisions to challenge privacy violations. Third, the GC was adopted by the HR Committee in 1988, before modern technologies, including the Internet, were introduced or entered the mainstream. This reduces its pertinence to new threats to privacy posed by rapid technological advances. Recent calls and initiatives for a new GC are prompted by this outmoded state of the present GC.[231]

But the jurisprudence of the HR Committee to date, as noted above, appears to be too thin to lead to a new GC. It is not also straightforward whether the Committee could simply develop a new GC based on, say, draft proposals tabled by civil society groups or even on its own accord drawing on comparative (case) law. Also unclear is how/if a new GC would improve the protection of digital privacy or more generally induce better State behaviour. As shall be discussed in chapter 7, a GC is amongst the various types of soft law explored as the best way of addressing the 'normative gap' in international privacy law. But the adoption of a new GC without any reform in the institutional arrangements will not result in substantial progress in global privacy protection.

---

[228] ibid, para 10.

[229] ibid.

[230] Of a related view, see Lee Bygrave, 'Data Protection Pursuant to the Right to Privacy in Human Rights Treaties' (1998) 6 International Journal of Law and Information Technology 247, 253.

[231] See, eg, Report of Scheinin (n 173) paras 19, 74; Report of the High Commissioner (n 168) para 10; American Civil Liberties Union (n 153) 3–10 and annex of a Draft GC. The latest request for a new GC came from the UNGA which, for instance in the 2019 Resolution, noted the 'need to discuss the right to privacy in view of the challenges in the digital age' that emerged since its adoption in 1988. See *The Right to Privacy in the Digital Age*, GA Res 73/179, 73rd sess, Agenda Item 74(b), UN Doc A/RES/73/179 (21 January 2019) Preamble, para 10.

4.3.1.4. Jurisprudence of HR Council Bodies

The dearth in privacy jurisprudence is also present when it comes to HR Council bodies. One is the UPR mechanism. It is a recent human right monitoring mechanism within the HR Council that reviews human rights performance of all UN member States irrespective of ratification of any of the human rights treaties.[232] The review mechanism relies, like the bulk of the UN human rights monitoring system, on 'cooperative and interactive dialogue' and is devoid of any remedial procedure.[233] The ultimate consequence for 'persistent non-cooperation' is that the Council would pass a decision or resolution condemning the non-co-operative State.[234] When it comes to the review of States in relation to the right to digital privacy, there is little to be said. The review process, which will soon enter the fourth cycle, has so far reviewed quite a few countries regarding their digital surveillance practices post-Snowden.[235] Inherent structures of the UPR mechanism as well as the *modus operandi* of the Council, however, makes it an unlikely candidate to address concerns regarding digital privacy more directly. The fact that the reviews are often made by high-level government delegates means that little could be anticipated of the UPR in elaborating the right to privacy in the digital context.

A second potential source of privacy jurisprudence under the HR Council is the work of the Working Group that monitors the Ruggie Principles. However, a survey of the Working Group's reports suggests that there is little to be said. A 2016 report of the Working Group, for instance, focuses on the 'human rights impacts of agroindustry operations, particularly the production of palm oil and sugarcane, on indigenous peoples and local communities'.[236] An earlier report from 2014 even indicated that its areas of priority for the future will be promoting the incorporation of the Guiding Principles in the policy framework of 'international institutions'.[237] A recent 'stocktaking' report of the Working Group explicitly acknowledges the hitherto exclusive focus on brick-and-mortar corporations and signals a shift

---

[232] For details on the UPR mechanism, see <https://bit.ly/1dSvPEw>.

[233] See HRC Res 5/1 (n 215) paras 33–38; see also *Human Rights Council*, GA Res 60/251, 60th sess, Agenda items 46 and 120, UN Doc A/RES/60/251 (3 April 2006) para 5(e).

[234] ibid.

[235] See, eg, Australia: Report of the UPR Working Group, UN Doc A/HRC/31/14 (13 January 2016) para 136.226 cum Australia: Addendum to the Report of the UPR Working Group, UN Doc A/HRC/31/14/Add.1 (29 February 2016) para 28; United States of America: Report of the UPR Working Group, UN Doc A/HRC/30/12 (20 July 2015) para 176.296 cum Addendum to the Report of the UPR Working Group, UN Doc A/HRC/30/12/Add.1 (14 September 2015) paras 14–15; India: Report of the UPR Working Group, UN Doc A/HRC/36/10 (17 July 2017) para 161.145.

[236] See Report of the Working Group on the Issue of Human Rights and Transnational Corporations and Other Business Enterprises, UN Doc A/71/291 (4 August 2016).

[237] See Report of the Working Group on the Issue of Human Rights and Transnational Corporations and Other Business Enterprises, UN Doc A/HRC/26/25 (5 May 2014) paras 84, 87; see also The Guiding Principles on Business and Human Rights: Guidance on Ensuring Respect for Human Rights Defenders, Report of the Working Group on the Issue of Human Rights and Transnational Corporations and other Business Enterprises, UN Doc A/HRC/47/39/Add.2 (22 June 2021).

towards technology companies.[238] This might gradually go some way in bringing technology companies within the radar of the Working Group.

Indeed, the Guiding Principles has been adapted by Global Network Initiative (GNI), a civil society organization that promotes privacy and free speech on the Internet, to be applied by the technology sector. GNI's 'Principles on Freedom of Expression and Privacy', adaptations of the Ruggie Principles, outline general norms that could voluntarily be followed by technology companies.[239] Of major Internet companies, Google, Microsoft and Yahoo! have accepted the principles and undergo independent reviews of their systems, processes and policies for the protection of freedom of expression and privacy.[240] The review is made by 'accredited assessors' that conduct the assessment based on a predetermined assessment criteria and report to GNI Board, which is a composed of various stakeholder representatives, for review and determination.[241] That the review relies on good faith self-reporting by corporations means that it can only be a supplementary mechanism of holding corporations into account. GNI's early work had, indeed, drawn criticism, particularly due to lack of robust assessment mechanisms.[242] In sum, there currently exists no concrete jurisprudence on the human rights responsibilities of Internet businesses. But as shall be explored in chapter 5, the series of Privacy Resolutions adopted by the UNGA and the HR Council have, to an extent, elaborate responsibilities of corporations vis-à-vis the right to privacy.

The SRP is the other HR Council body with a potential to progressively develop international privacy jurisprudence. But, added with the largely 'promotional' role of UN special procedures—and partly because the SPR was appointed only in 2015, the mandate is yet to meaningfully contribute towards filling the jurisprudential gaps. Reports of the SRP have yet to offer intellectual guidance on the scope and meaning of the right to privacy in international law. The mandate's work thus far has focused primarily on creating a number of 'task forces' dealing with specific aspects of the right to privacy.[243] And, the outcome of these task forces, and the way in which they would address the jurisprudential gaps are yet to arrive. One tangible outcome so far has been a draft recommendation released by the task force working on the theme 'privacy and health data'.[244] While this draft may later evolve

---

[238] See Guiding Principles on Business and Human Rights at 10: Taking Stock of the First Decade, Report of the Working Group on the Issue of Human Rights and Transnational Corporations and other Business Enterprises, UN Doc A/HRC/47/39 (22 April 2021) paras 66, 74.

[239] See Principles on Freedom of Expression and Privacy (Global Network Initiative, 2008) <https://bit.ly/2FKiCwQ>.

[240] See, eg, Global Network Initiative: 2015 Annual Report (2015) 4.

[241] See details at <https://bit.ly/2HSY3EB>.

[242] See, eg, Sarah Joseph, 'Social Media, Political Change and Human Rights' (2012) 35 Boston College International and Comparative Review 145, 184.

[243] See, eg, Report of the Special Rapporteur on the Right to Privacy, Joseph Cannataci, UN Doc A/72 540 (19 October 2017).

[244] Draft Recommendation on the Protection and Use of Health-Related Data, Mandate of the United Nations Special Rapporteur on the Right to Privacy—Task Force on Privacy and the Protection of Health-Related Data (June 2019).

into an international soft law, it does little in filling the jurisprudential gaps addressed in the book. As it currently stands, the draft outlines a range of principles applicable to processing of health-related personal data. This observation applies to other stalled initiatives of the mandate such as the soft law that deals with protection of personal data in the context of artificial intelligence.[245]

5. Conclusion

This chapter argued that international human rights law is currently ill-equipped to respond to the 'privacy problem' in the digital age. Mainly due to political controversies that clouded the drafting of relevant standards—and exacerbated by poor drafting, the human right to privacy framework exhibits several weaknesses. The chapter examined the principal normative, institutional, and the resultant jurisprudential gaps. This attests to the need for a progressive development of existing privacy standards to adapt them to the digital age. Nevertheless, recent developments at the UN reveal an ambivalent approach as to whether existing standards require some form of progression or translation.

Post-Snowden revelation discussions at the UN proceed from the assumption that the right to privacy in international human rights law is fit for purpose in the digital age. In stating that international human rights law provides *the* universal privacy framework, former High Commissioner Pillay implied that there are no blind spots in the current legal framework.[246] The problem, or rather gap, is in the domestic law and practices of States.[247] Resolutions of the UNGA and the HR Council on the 'right to privacy in the digital age' routinely call upon States to ensure that their national laws and practices comply with international human rights law. This viewpoint maintains that mere abstract high-level general principles provided in the UDHR and the ICCPR are adequate to set international standards. Latent in this supposition is the idea that present international privacy norms set forth under the UDHR (and the ICCPR) are eternal principles that apply across changing times.[248] The belief, it seems, is that no change in technology or other developments would render these principles obsolete.

---

[245] See Data Privacy Guidelines for the Development and Operation of Artificial Intelligence Solutions (2020) <https://www.ohchr.org/EN/Issues/Privacy/SR/Pages/CFI_data_privacy_guidelines.aspx>.

[246] See Press Conference on the Right to Privacy in the Digital Age, UN High Commissioner for Human Rights Navi Pillay (16 July 2014) <https://www.ohchr.org/en/statements/2014/07/press-conference-right-privacy-digital-age-un-high-commissioner-human-rights>.

[247] See, eg, The Right to Privacy in the Digital Age, Report of the High Commissioner for Human Rights, UN Doc A/HRC/39/29 (3 August 2018) para 58 [noting that 'the international human rights framework provides a strong basis for shaping the responses to the manifold challenges arising in the digital age'].

[248] See, eg, Gordon Brown (ed), *The Universal Declaration of Human Rights in the 21st Century: A Living Document in A Changing World* (Open Book 2016) 14, 25, 29; Paul Lauren, *The Evolution of International Human Rights: Visions Seen* (University of Pennsylvania Press 3rd edn, 2011) 226 (stating

A more benign interpretation of this assumption is that these 'eternal principles' will just have to be applied to a new set of circumstances by, for example the HR Committee, through evolutive interpretation. Seibert-Fohr, a former member of the Committee, argues that there is no 'blind spot' in the international law of privacy and what is lacking is national-level regulation.[249] She suggests that the Committee's 'evolutive interpretation' has allowed it to 'confront new challenges and keep human rights protection alive and effective based on the existing legal framework'. As this chapter has demonstrated, that is not really the case. Not only is the (international) human right to privacy framework replete with normative 'blind spots'[250] but also that the HR Committee, strapped by structural shackles, has not been able to develop a robust digital privacy jurisprudence.

This suggests that gradual normative progression is both possible and desirable in the human rights movement. As Alston notes, 'gradualism' is an inherent characteristic of the international human right system.[251] The UDHR also hints the gradualist nature of rights protection when it states that 'States shall strive ... to promote respect for these rights and freedoms by progressive measures, national and *international*.'[252]

Such progressive measures arguably include gradual development of international human rights norms. This is, indeed, reflected partly in the privacy provisions of post-ICCPR human rights instruments.[253] The CRD and the ICRMW, for instance, appear to be progressive, to some degree, especially in suggesting inclusion of modern forms of 'communication' as new media of correspondence.[254] The Conventions, in so doing, follow other progressive regional instruments such as the EU Fundamental Rights Charter of 2000.[255] The CRD also addresses protection of data privacy at some length.[256] With the adoption of an Optional Protocol to the

---

the UDHR is targeted at the future); William Schabas (ed), *The Universal Declaration of Human Rights: The Travaux Préparatoires* (Cambridge University Press Vol I, 2013) xxiii [stating that the drafters of the UDHR were 'sensitive' to the evolving nature of human rights].

[249] Anja Seibert-Fohr, 'Digital Surveillance, Meta Data and Foreign Intelligence Cooperation: Unpacking the International Right to Privacy' in Joseph David and others (eds), *Strengthening Human Rights Protections in Geneva, Israel, the West Bank and Beyond* (Cambridge University Press 2021) 40, 56.

[250] Cf John Tobin, 'Seeking to Persuade: A Constructive Approach to Human Rights Treaty Interpretation' (2010) 23 Harvard Human Rights Journal 1, 44 (describing 'blind spots' in human rights treaties as 'issues that were overlooked or unanticipated in the drafting process but that are essential to the effective operation of the relevant provision and thus require the development of an appropriate interpretive response').

[251] Philip Alston, 'Beyond Them and Us: Putting Treaty Body Reform into Perspective' in Philip Alston and James Crawford (eds), *The Future of the UN Human Rights Treaty Monitoring* (Cambridge University Press 2000) 522.

[252] See UDHR (n 1) Preamble.

[253] Note, though, that these Conventions also backtracked in some respects, one instance being the CRD intriguingly omits 'home' from the zones of privacy protection.

[254] See CRD (n 2) art 22(1); see also ICRMW (n 2) art 14.

[255] See Charter of Fundamental Rights of the European Union (n 83) art 7.

[256] See CRD (n 2) art 22(2) cum art 31(1). For more, see ch 3.

CRC on the Sale of Children, Child Prostitution and Child Pornography, the CRC has also progressed to protect digital privacy of child victims of abuse, particularly in the context of criminal proceedings.[257] Considering limitations of the present regime explored in this chapter, there is a need to reimagine the human right to privacy framework to make it better equipped in the digital age. Chapter 7 will address the question of how best to meet this need.

---

[257] See *Optional Protocol to the CRC on the Sale of Children, Child Prostitution and Child Pornography,* opened for signature 25 May 2000, 2171 UNTS 227 (entered into force 18 January 2002) art 8(1(e)) cum para 6 of the preamble; see also a recent UN Resolution affirming this right, *Rights of the Child: Information and Communications Technologies and Child Sexual Exploitation,* HRC Res 31/7, 31st sess, Agenda item 3, UN Doc A/HRC/RES/31/7 (23 March 2016).

3
Boundaries of International Data Privacy Law

1. Introduction

This chapter turns to consider boundaries of international data privacy law in securing digital privacy. In undertaking this regime analysis, it seeks to show the extent to which present international data privacy standards supplement the human right to privacy framework. Unlike the much-developed European data privacy regime, the origins of the international data privacy framework are closely related to the human rights system. Early United Nations (UN) work in the field of data privacy emerged at the Tehran Conference in 1968 on the occasion of the twentieth anniversary of the Universal Declaration of Human Rights (UDHR). Held merely two years after the adoption of the International Covenant on Civil and Political Rights (ICCPR), the Conference was seized with issues surrounding 'scientific and technological developments', and their impact on human rights, particularly the right to privacy. In his opening address at the Conference, the then UN Secretary-General, U Thant, broached the subject with what now reads like a forward-looking speech:[1]

> The promise which science offers is understandably high but having invented and perfected the machine, is man going to become himself the slave of the machine or of those few in number who will be in the position to manipulate it? *Can man end his essential right to minimum of privacy be protected against the ever-present listening and seeing electronic or other devices?* […] [Emphasis Added]

U Thant's speech not only foresaw the now widely touted 'existential threats' posed by rapidly developing technologies like Artificial Intelligence (AI) but also present threats to democracy posed by digital platforms. Beyond being remarkably forward-looking, this speech ushered the first meaningful global discussions on the interplay between new technologies and human rights. This was followed by

[1] Address Delivered by the Secretary General of the United Nations, U Thant, in Commemoration of the Twentieth Anniversary of the Adoption of the Universal Declaration of Human Rights in Annex II(B) of the Final Act of the International Conference on Human Rights, Tehran 22 April to 13 May 1964 (May 1968) 37–38.

Privacy and the Role of International Law in the Digital Age. Kinfe Yilma, Oxford University Press. © Kinfe Yilma 2023. DOI: 10.1093/oso/9780192887290.003.0003

a Resolution that called upon the UN to conduct studies on the impact of modern technological developments on the right to privacy, a point later reiterated in the Proclamation of Tehran at the conclusion of the Conference.[2] After decades of protracted process—caused mainly by Cold war politics, visions of the Conference were translated into the Guidelines for Computerized Personal Data Files (Data Privacy Guidelines) adopted by the UN General Assembly (UNGA) in December 1990.[3] The Guidelines is the principal UN instrument in the field of data privacy to date. That makes the Tehran Conference the place where the 'first serious discussion of data protection law' took place.[4]

A year before the Tehran Conference, a largely regional, but by no means less momentous conference, took place in Stockholm, Sweden. Held under the auspices of the International Commission of Jurists (ICJs), the Nordic Conference on the Right to Privacy is probably where the seeds of the Tehran (data) privacy agenda were originally planted.[5] The discussions at the conference focused on the right to privacy more broadly. Nor was any express mention of data protection in the comparative Working Paper which served as the basis for the discussion at the Conference.[6] But protection of personal data was considered—albeit remotely—as one aspect of privacy rights. Part of the description of the right to privacy envisaged in the Conclusions of the Conference, for instance, was 'disclosure of information given to, or received from, professional advisers or to public authorities bound to observe secrecy'.[7] Albeit remote, such references to data privacy may have helped take the agenda further in the following year. To be sure, no national or subnational data protection legislation that would have been surveyed in the comparative study existed until 1970 when the Land Hesse adopted the first comprehensive data protection legislation.[8] In that sense, the Nordic Conference can be taken to be an important step in the development of international data privacy

---

[2] Human Rights and Scientific and Technological Developments, Resolution XI, adopted at the Tehran Conference, 25th plenary mtg (12 May 1968) para 2(a); see also *The Proclamation of Tehran*, UN Doc A/CONF.32/41 (13 May 1968) para 18.

[3] *Guidelines for the Regulation of Computerized Personal Data Files*, GA Res 45/95, UNGAOR, 45thsess, 68th plen mtg, UN Doc A/Res/45/95 (14 December 1990).

[4] Fred Cate, 'The EU Data Protection Directive, Information Privacy and the Public Interest' (1995) 80 Iowa Law Review 431.

[5] For more details, see <https://www.icj.org/the-right-to-privacy-conference-outcomes/>. The Conference was attended by 'jurists' from Nordic and non-Nordic countries as well as observers from international organizations such as the Council of Europe. See the list of participants in the Conclusions of the Nordic Conference on the Right to Privacy (23 May 1967) 10–11.

[6] Stig Strümholm, Right to Privacy and Rights of Personality: A Comparative Survey, Working Paper Prepared for the Nordic Conference on Privacy Organized by the International Commission of Jurists, Stockholm 22–23 May 1967 (Instituti Upsaliensis Iurisprudentiae Gomparativae, 1967).

[7] Conclusions of the Nordic Conference on the Right to Privacy (23 May 1967) Part I(3(xi)).

[8] A 1972 report of the ICJs commissioned by the UNESCO that surveyed privacy legislation in ten countries did address not only emergent data privacy laws around the world, including Germany, but also the role of the Tehran Conference in being the 'turning point' in the development of law in the area. See 'The Legal Protection of Privacy: A Comparative Survey of Ten Countries by the International Commission of Jurists' (1972) 24 International Journal of Science 417, 421.

law. It is also to be noted that the ICJs was an active participant during the Tehran Conference, including through written submissions.[9]

Against this backdrop, this chapter explores the current state of the international data privacy framework. It argues that the framework is normatively outdated, highly fragmented, and devoid of clear institutional arrangements to be considered an important source of international privacy law. A characteristic feature of the framework is that it is made up of highly dispersed rules embodied in a number of instruments. In addition to the 1990 Data Privacy Guidelines, present international data privacy rules are to be found in other instruments, including major human rights treaties and a range of soft law instruments adopted by various specialized and related agencies of the UN. Drawing a parallel to the human right to privacy framework, the chapter further locates factors for the present weak structures of international data privacy law in Cold War political controversies and the overall apathy towards privacy at the UN. The chapter concludes that the gradual prominence of data privacy themes in the ongoing UN privacy discourse, explored in chapter 5, bears—to an extent—a potential of reviving and modernizing international data privacy law.

References in this chapter to international data privacy law or framework should not be conflated with transnational data privacy standards. For purposes of this book, international data privacy law refers to a branch of international law with a clear universal scope of application. As such, it precludes transnational or regional frameworks such as the Council of Europe (CoE) Data Protection Convention system which lack inherent universal character.[10] With a view to properly appreciate limits of the international data protection framework, comparative references are made in this chapter to the relatively developed data protection regimes of the European Union (EU) and the CoE.

2. Data Privacy and the Cold War

UN initiatives in the field of data privacy began relatively early, shortly after the human right to privacy was enshrined in a binding treaty. These initiatives were, however, caught up in protracted processes of negotiation and a major UN data privacy instrument was adopted long after regional organizations enacted influential instruments that set the tone of data privacy law worldwide. Ideological differences that resulted in a weak regime for the protection of the human rights to digital privacy, considered in chapter 2, have had a similar negative impact on the

---

[9] See Lucian Weeramantry, *The International Commission of Jurists: The Pioneering Years* (Kluwer Law International 2000) 251–54.

[10] Chapter 6 considers, however, the question of whether—and how—the CoE's Data Protection Convention may evolve into a 'universal' data protection treaty.

international data privacy framework. In part, this has to do with the human rights origins of the data privacy framework. As noted above, UN efforts in the field of data privacy were set in motion in the context of human rights as the UN moved to renew the commitment pledged by States with the adoption of the UDHR. But the overall reluctant approach to privacy in the UN system has compounded the effects of the ideological factor. An overview of these historical episodes offers context to fully bring out the limits of international data privacy law. This section explores, first, the impact of the Cold War in shaping the current structures of international data privacy law and, second, a series of factors that led to a limited attention to issues of data privacy during that period.

2.1. The Cold War Effect

As the UN began to consider the impact of 'scientific and technological developments' on human rights in the wake of the Tehran Conference, the debate was divided along the North-South and the East-West ideological lines.[11] Countries in the South/East camp which mostly included developing countries insisted on the need to emphasize the socio-economic benefits of scientific and technological discoveries whereas those in the North/West bloc, mainly industrial nations, argued for priority to be given to the negative impact of these technologies on human rights, including the right to privacy.[12] These divisions could be seen partly as reverberations of the broader debate on the 'generation of human rights' that divided States between those that argued for the priority of civil and political rights—ie, first generation rights—and those that put thrust on socio-economic and cultural rights—ie, 'second generation rights'.[13] As Burke notes, it was difficult to arrive at a consensus about the balance of political and social rights between the ideological blocs.[14]

Despite initial references to (data) privacy as one area deserving of further study post-Tehran,[15] ideological divisions later pushed the matter to the edges. The South/Easter bloc led by the Soviet Union pushed, instead, for an international instrument that emphasized the use of modern technologies for positive ends. This later led to the adoption by the UNGA of the 'Declaration on the Use of Scientific and Technological Progress in the Interests of Peace and for the Benefit of

---

[11] See Sadako Ogata, 'Introduction: United Nations Approaches to Human Rights and Scientific Developments' in Christopher Weeramantry (ed), *Human Rights and Scientific and Technological Development* (United Nations University Press 1990) 3–4.

[12] See Moses Moskowitz, *International Concern for Human Rights* (Oceana Publications 1974) 14–15.

[13] See William Edmundson, *An Introduction to Rights* (Cambridge University Press 2004) 173–74.

[14] Ronald Burke, *Decolonization and the Evolution of Human Rights* (Pennsylvania University Press 2010) 94.

[15] See, eg, *Human Rights and Scientific and Technological Developments*, GA Res 2450 (XXIII), 1748th plenary mtg, UN Doc A/RES/2450(XXIII) (19 December 1968) para 1(a).

Mankind' in 1975.[16] The Declaration slightly diverted the question of human rights particularly privacy, and directed its focus on the need to gear technological innovations to positive economic ends.[17] The Declaration was initially recommended by a group of experts assembled by the Secretary-General, but the expert's recommendation appeared to have had more emphasis on human rights.[18]

The Declaration's reference to human rights in general and privacy in particular is slightly remote. It, for instance, requires States to take all measures, including legislative measures to prevent the use of modern technologies by State organs in a manner or for purposes that limit the rights recognized in the UDHR and the ICCPR.[19] The right to privacy, one of the main areas initially identified for further study, and possible international legal response, also similarly received less attention. The Declaration states partly:

> All states shall take measures ... to protect [all strata of the population] from harmful effects of the misuse of science and technological developments including their misuse to infringe upon the rights of the individual ... particularly with regard to respect for privacy ....[20]

Unlike States' widely accepted human rights obligations in international law both to 'respect' and 'protect', this provision appears to recognize only an obligation to 'protect', ie a positive obligation, and hence no obligation to 'respect', ie negative obligation, can be read into the provision. Implicit in this wording is that the Declaration sought to absolve States, and their agents, from any responsibility for violation of human rights, including privacy. The general emphasis on 'sovereignty' and 'international peace and security' further reinforces that point. Of course, one of the constant controversies in human rights standard setting has been that human rights, and the attendant monitoring mechanism, would undermine the domestic jurisdiction of States. This traditional argument seems to have led the East/South bloc to divert the attention of the momentum set in Tehran.[21]

---

[16] *Declaration on the Use of Scientific and Technological Progress in the Interest of Peace and for the Benefit of Mankind*, GA Res 3384 (XXX), 2400th plenary mtg, UN Doc A/RES/3384(XXX) (10 November 1975).

[17] See Christopher Weeramantry, 'Science, Technology and the Future of Human Rights' (1986) 13 India International Centre Quarterly 41, 47.

[18] Existing and Proposed Texts which could be used in the Drafting of a Further International Instrument on Human Rights and Scientific and Technological Developments, Commission on Human Rights, 33rd sess, Item 8 of provisional agenda, UN Doc E/CN.4/1233 (16 December 1976) para 2, footnote 2, quoting UN Doc E/CN.4/1199 (1975) paras 4–5.

[19] See GA Res 3384 (XXX) (n 16) para 2 cum 8–9.

[20] ibid, para 6.

[21] See Hiroko Yamane, 'Impacts of Scientific and Technological Progress on Human Rights: Normative Response of the International Community' in Christopher Weeramantry (ed), *Human Rights and Scientific and Technological Development* (United Nations University Press 1990) 91.

Ideological fault lines featured more clearly during voting on the Declaration. Unsurprisingly, States in the North/West bloc boycotted the Declaration, and they finally abstained during the voting.[22] It appears that the effort on the part of the North/West bloc to successfully push the cause of human rights was frustrated by the overwhelming majority of the South/East camp which was made up of several countries from Asia, Africa, East Europe, and the Middle East. To vent its frustration, the western bloc resorted to a politically motivated Resolution on the mistreatment of mentally ill persons in imprisonment in east European countries.[23] This was part of the trend at the time by which western countries reportedly used human rights as a 'stick to beat' socialist countries.[24] Ogata reports that due to the ideological conflict, the western camp had lacked enthusiasm to push for human rights initiatives at the time.[25] Except for Cassin who led the French delegation, western States were generally passive during the Conference for different reasons, the major being the numeric dominance of non-western States especially newly independent African and Asian States during the Conference.[26]

Perhaps, the inability to pursue a tangible (data) privacy agenda at the UN seems to be the reason for western countries to focus more on a regional approach to data privacy through the CoE and the Organization for Economic Cooperation and Development (OECD) where there exists considerable ideological convergence among member States. Noting that the idea for Convention 108 indeed began at the Tehran Conference, Hondius intimates that 'when, in 1974, it was clear that there was no hope for the moment of a worldwide instrument concerning the protection of human rights with regard to computers, the European Ministers of justice met in Vienna and recommended that steps' to be taken at the level of the CoE.[27] Indeed, in the context of human rights more broadly, Cassese writes that the Cold War confrontation had led (western) States to agree upon measures at the regional level where there frequently is greater homogeneity.[28] Soft law was the other alternate path taken to bypass the impasse of the Cold War period.[29] The adoption ultimately of the UN Data Privacy Guidelines best illustrates this point.

Reverberations of Cold War politics were also felt during the drafting of other domain-specific international data privacy instruments. One instance was during the drafting of United Nations Educational, Scientific and Cultural Organization (UNESCO) instruments relating to (data) privacy. At least in the context of the 'Universal Bio-ethics Declaration', recourse was made to a Declaration as opposed

---

[22] See Ogata (n 11) 4.
[23] ibid, 5–6.
[24] See Antonio Cassese, *International Law in a Divided World* (Clarendon Press 1986) 300.
[25] Ogata (n 11) 4.
[26] See Burke (n 14) 99–106.
[27] Frits Hondius, 'A Quarter of Century of International Data Protection' (2006) 19 Hague Yearbook of International Law 23, 24, 28.
[28] See Cassese (n 24) 198.
[29] ibid.

to a treaty due to two reasons according to Kirby, who was involved in the drafting process. One is relevant in this context. A binding treaty should be considered, it was agreed at the time, at a later stage once States have deliberated and consulted on the Declaration, like in the case of the UDHR which later was translated into two covenants.[30] The obvious resistance towards stringent human rights commitment among many States appears to have dictated a soft law approach.

Kirby reports that UN effort in the field of (data) privacy in the 1970s was limited to 'problems of developing countries.'[31] Lack of concern to the perils of privacy intrusion in developing and socialist countries, at the time, is well documented. The focus instead was on how best to reap the developmental benefits of scientific progress such as computerization.[32] The economic potential of technological advances as opposed to their human rights dangers were the prime focus at the Conference. That is nowhere more explicitly stated than in The Proclamation of Tehran, the final act of the Conference. Its preamble, for instance, notes the 'new opportunities made available by the rapid progress of science and technology'. This is indirectly reinforced in Part 13 which provides:

> Since human rights and fundamental freedoms are indivisible, the full realization of civil and political rights without the enjoyment of economic, social and cultural rights is impossible. The achievement of lasting progress in the implementation of human rights is dependent upon sound and effective national and international policies of economic and social development.

Dangers of scientific advances to human rights are envisaged only incidentally. Paragraph 18 of the Proclamation provides that 'while recent scientific discoveries and technological advances have opened vast prospects for economic, social and cultural progress, such developments may nevertheless endanger the rights and freedoms of individuals and will require continuing attention'.

In sum, the successful lobbying of the South/Eastern bloc and the lack of enthusiasm among western countries had further reduced the possibility of a major international data privacy initiative. All the UN could achieve after two decades of prolonged process was mere Guidelines.[33] A soft law instrument that provides only high-level principles of fair information practices, with no effective machinery of monitoring, is thus a result of the political compromise, one that had to be struck between ideological foes of the time.

---

[30] See Michael Kirby, 'Human Rights and Bioethics: The Universal Declaration of Human Rights and UNESCO Universal Declaration of Bioethics and Human Rights' (2009) 25 Journal of Contemporary Health Law and Policy 309, 320.

[31] Michael Kirby, 'Transborder Data Flows and the Basic Rules of Data Privacy' (1980) 16 Stanford Journal of International Law 26, 45–46.

[32] See Frits Hondius, *Emerging Data Protection in Europe* (North Holland Publishing Company 1975) 62.

[33] See UN Data Privacy Guidelines (n 3).

2.2. The Data Privacy Inattention Effect

The Cold War effect alone does not fully explain the weak structures of international data privacy law. A reluctant approach to the privacy agenda entrenched in UN processes is equally responsible for the lack of a robust data privacy regime. This problem was more visible within the former Commission on Human Rights under whose aegis the work on the UN Data Privacy Guidelines was carried out. The Commission, for instance, was not able to closely consider various studies on the subject conducted under the auspices of the Secretary-General between 1968 and 1976.[34] This had forced the UNGA to issue a Resolution expressing 'regrets' over the delay in considering the matter by the Commission in due time.[35] Although the official excuse was 'lack of time', divergence of priorities among States appears to have been the principal factor in dragging the agenda item.

Even before the actual work on the Guidelines began, States had made it clear that all that they are willing to consider was a 'general guideline' that could guide States in legislating at the national level.[36] Yet the work on these guidelines did not begin until 1980 and the first draft was submitted only four years later.[37] Several drafts of the Guidelines were circulated among member States to achieve some level of consensus before they were finally adopted in 1990.[38] Reports suggest that most States were disengaged during the drafting process and seldom did they respond to queries.[39] Even members of the Sub-Commission on the Prevention of Discrimination and Protection of Minorities, a subsidiary of the former Commission under whose auspices the UN Data Privacy Guidelines were prepared, were said to withhold their opinion on studies and reports submitted to them in the interest of 'moving along the agenda'.[40] This is indicative of the lack of enthusiasm at the time for privacy in general and the Guidelines in particular. Resistance to the Guidelines was also shown by UN specialized agencies such as the International Labour Organization (ILO) and by the International Criminal Police Organization (INTERPOL). An aspect of this resistance was that these organizations had requested exemption from the application of the Guidelines to their operations.[41] Given that these agencies are intergovernmental, where membership is

---

[34] See Yo Kubota, 'The Institutional Response' in Christopher Weeramantry (ed), *Human Rights and Scientific and Technological Development* (United Nations University Press 1990) 113–14.

[35] See *Human Rights and Scientific and Technological Developments*, GA Res 3149 (XXVIII), 2201st plenary mtg, UN Doc RES/3149(XXVIII) (14 December 1973).

[36] See Kubota (n 34) 119.

[37] ibid.

[38] ibid.

[39] ibid.

[40] See Kathrine Brennan and others, 'The Fortieth Session of the UN Sub-Commission on Prevention of Discrimination and Protection of Minorities' (1989) 11 Human Rights Quarterly 295, 312.

[41] See Wayne Madsen, *Handbook of Personal Data Protection* (Macmillan 1992) 194.

at the State level,[42] it may well be that the ideological differences witnessed within the UN were also present in these organizations.

The (data) privacy inattention effect is also latent in the way the substance of the data privacy instruments was crafted. In the case of the Data Privacy Guidelines for instance, relatively better and privacy protective initial versions of the Guidelines were later substantially watered-down. A number of rules or principles embodied in the Secretary-General's 1974 Report, which later partially were integrated with the guidelines prepared by Joinet,[43] are absent in the current version. Of principles included in the initial version of the Guidelines include the following: stringent requirements for collection of personal information including prohibition of collecting hearsay and subjective information, legal responsibility of computer manufacturers and software developers regarding security of information systems, specific rules on damages and penalties for violation of the rules, requirement for judicial control of automated decision-making, extraterritorial protection and specific obligations of national data protection authorities which included monitoring developments in the technology sector that may affect the right to privacy.[44] These norms and principles were later eliminated from the final version of the Data Privacy Guidelines. There is little reason to suggest that these rules were rolled back due to political compromises, not least because the Guidelines mere soft law. A more plausible conjecture, then, is that the overall lack of attention to privacy is partly liable. Had there been a firm commitment to introduce a robust data privacy instrument, would these rules have been eliminated? Perhaps a related explanation is the pushback from States such as Japan calling for an instrument that leaves wide latitude to States due to differing social and cultural characteristics.[45]

In the ultimate analysis, the human rights origins of the international data privacy framework, added to the ideologically divided era during which the process was set in motion, appeared to have opened the door for ideological factors to negatively influence the present shape of the international data privacy framework. Ideological differences, and the need for political compromises needed to narrow

---

[42] Note, however, that the ILO's Governing Body has a unique tripartite membership structure in which employer and employee representatives participate alongside States. See *Constitution of the International Labour Organization* (1919) art 7.

[43] Note that Louise Joinet, appointed by the Sub-Commission as a Special Rapporteur, drafted the final version of the Guidelines, after replacing Nicole Questiaux. The latter was responsible for the preparation of the initial reports and studies for the Sub-Commission that eventually led to the UN Data Privacy Guidelines. See Edward Lawson (ed), *Encyclopedia of Human Rights* (Taylor & Francis, 2nd edn 1996) 1195–96. See also Study of the Relevant Guidelines in the field of Computerized Personal File, Final Report Prepared by Mr Louis Joinet, UN Doc E/C.4/Sub.2/1983/18 (30 June 1983) para 13.

[44] See Uses of Electronics which may Affect the Rights of the Person and the Limits which Should be Placed on such Uses in a Democratic Society, Report of the UN Secretary-General, UN Doc E/CN.4/1142 (31 January 1974) paras 92, 320.

[45] Submission of the Government of Japan on the Draft UN Data Privacy Guidelines of September 1989, quoted in Guidelines for the Regulation of Computerized Personal Data Files, Report of the Secretary General, UN Doc A/44/606 (24 October 1989) para 11.

these differences, appear to be the primary factors for the current normatively and institutionally weak framework for the protection of data privacy. In considering the lack of express reference to the right to privacy in the Helsinki Final Act—a document often seen as lessening the Cold War, one wonders if the right to privacy was particularly disadvantaged. The Act, which of course is not a legally binding instrument, enshrines the agreement of States to respect human rights particularly freedom of expression, freedom of religion and other group rights but privacy rights are omitted.[46]

Indeed, while the signing of the Helsinki Final Act has had an impact in 'shoring up' the human rights agenda, its signing by the Soviets was merely of symbolic gesture, rather than a genuine commitment to human rights.[47] This observation corresponds to the instances of 'drafting inattention' that plagued the human right to privacy highlighted in chapter 2. But more generally, it reinforces the point that the UN has generally been reluctant in consistently considering the issue of whether new threats to privacy dictate an international legal response. No clear and coherent approach has been pursued when it comes to international protection of (data) privacy. While the ongoing UN privacy discourse increasingly adopts a unifying approach that touches on important aspects of privacy, including data privacy, it still exhibits a level of selectivity in its choice of themes, as shall be examined in chapter 5. The approach, thus far, has been haphazard and piecemeal that cumulatively left a patchy international data privacy regime in contrast with progressive regional approaches in Europe, and recently, in Africa.

3. Normative Sources

Before delving directly into the normative boundaries of current international data privacy law, this section offers a brief sketch of its normative sources. Following mainly the formal sources of international law envisaged in art 38(1) of the Statute of the International Court of Justice (ICJ), it discusses three sources of international data privacy law. These are treaty law, customary international law, and general principles of law. Transnational treaties such as Convention 108 are not treaties of universal scope and hence are not considered in what follows. But it further considers soft law which, as the fourth relevant normative source, forms a central part of international data privacy law.

---

[46] The Helsinki Final Act of the Conference on Security and Cooperation in Europe Final Act (1 August 1975) Sec VII.

[47] See Rosemary Foot, 'The Cold War and Human Rights' in Melvyn Leffler and Odd Westad (eds), *The Cambridge History of the Cold War* (Cambridge University Press Vol 3, 2010) 459.

3.1. Treaty Law

As alluded to in chapter 1, the lack of a truly international data privacy treaty is a longstanding topic of discussion in the privacy literature. Apart from the CoE's transnational treaty—ie, Convention 108, there currently exists no data privacy treaty of universal scope. Chapter 6 explores further the ways in which Convention 108 may be transformed into such a 'universal' treaty, but this section briefly considers to what extent other treaties of 'universal' scope envisage data privacy standards. Two types of treaties are relevant when considering data privacy in international law: general and domain-specific treaties. This functional dichotomy is based on the scope of rights that the treaties guarantee.

A typical 'general' treaty is the ICCPR, which—as examined in chapter 2—guarantees the right to privacy alongside other rights of personality. The text of Article 17 of the ICCPR does not explicitly guarantee data privacy as a subset of the right to privacy. But the jurisprudence of the Human Rights Committee (HR Committee) has gradually embraced data privacy within the penumbra of the right to privacy. In particular, General Comment (GC) 16, within its exceedingly truncated formulation, embodies a set of widely accepted principles of data privacy law.[48] The post-Snowden privacy discourse at the UN has further read more progressive data privacy principles under privacy provisions of the ICCPR as well as the UDHR. Through a process of dynamic cross-fertilization of norms, data privacy principles now feature in the series of Resolutions adopted by the UNGA and the Human Rights Council (HR Council).

Post-ICCPR human rights treaties go slightly further in embodying data privacy treaties, albeit in a rather domain-specific manner. In part, this appears to be related to the time when these treaties are adopted. In the decades after the adoption of the ICCPR, data privacy has attained significant attention globally as a matter of international concern. Formative discussions at the Nordic and Tehran Conferences in particular played a key role not least in internationalizing the subject of privacy and modern technologies. This means post-ICCPR treaties cast the scope of privacy rather broadly to capture the protection of personal data alongside traditional 'zones' of privacy protection. One such treaty is the Convention on the Rights of Persons with Disabilities (CRD), the first human rights treaty of the 21st century.

Protection of data privacy is quite important to disabled persons at many levels. Obtaining support, be it social welfare or employment, would ordinarily require them to disclose personal information, including their medical data.[49] And when

---

[48] HR Committee, *General Comment 16: Art 17—The Right to Respect of Privacy, Family, Home and Correspondence, and Protection of Honour and Reputation*, 32nd sess, UN Doc HRI/GEN/1/Rev.9 (Vol I) (8 April 1988) 10.
[49] See Molly Land and others, 'Art. 22: Respect for Privacy' in Ilias Bantekas and others (eds), *UN Convention on the Rights of Persons with Disabilities: A Commentary* (Oxford University Press 2018) 605.

third parties fail to keep such information confidential, it may also result in serious consequences to persons with disabilities, including in seeking employment.[50]
For this reason, the Convention addresses protection of personal data in different
levels. At a higher level, one of the Convention's 'General Principles'—an innovation for a human rights treaty in and of itself—is 'respect for inherent dignity,
individual autonomy including the freedom to make one's own choices, and independence of persons'.[51] In view of privacy's intrinsic link with and value in upholding dignity and autonomy, this proviso offers the normative foreground for
the protection of privacy. With respect to (data) privacy, this general principle is
unpacked in the substantive and procedural parts of the Convention. One is the
specific provision on the right to privacy. Captioned 'Respect for Privacy', the provision reads:[52]

1. No person with disabilities, regardless of place of residence or living arrangements, shall be subjected to arbitrary or unlawful interference with his or her
   privacy, family, home or correspondence or *other types of communication* or
   to unlawful attacks on his or her honour and reputation. Persons with disabilities have the right to the protection of the law against such interference
   or attacks.
2. States Parties shall protect the privacy of *personal, health and rehabilitation information* of persons with disabilities on an equal basis with others.
   [Emphasis added]

The Convention's privacy provision itself departs from the ICCPR and other subsequent human rights treaties in at least two respects. One is that 'zones' of protection include 'other types of communications' alongside 'correspondence'. That was
meant to capture 'more recent communication technologies' such as the Internet
and allied technologies.[53] In that sense, the provision is progressive. The second,
and relevant to the discussion here, is that the provision explicitly guarantees protection of personal data, among other types of data. But the meaning and scope of
data protected are far from clear. The definitional provision, Article 2, offers a definition of neither personal nor health information. Nor has the Committee on the
Rights of Persons with Disabilities issued a general comment to unpack the scope
of the provision.[54] Concluding Observations of the Committee likewise offer little

---

[50] ibid, 618.

[51] See *Convention on the Rights of Persons with Disabilities*, opened for signature 30 March 2007, 2515
UNTS 3 (entered into force 3 May 2008) art 3(a).

[52] ibid, art 22.

[53] Report of the Ad Hoc Committee on a Comprehensive and Integral International Convention on
the Protection and Promotion of the Rights and Dignity of Persons with Disabilities on its Fifth Session,
UN Doc A/RES/60/232 (31 January 2006) para 92.

[54] See details about the Committee's General Comments adopted thus far at <https://www.ohchr.
org/EN/HRBodies/CRPD/Pages/GC.aspx>.

guidance, unsurprisingly though, due to their abbreviated juridical nature. Often, the Committee uses the expression 'personal data and medical records' in sections that deal with review of a State party's performance vis-à-vis the right to privacy.[55] But the precise meaning of the terms is not clear.

In requiring States to 'protect' privacy of personal, health and rehabilitation information, the provision imposes a positive duty on State parties which would include a duty to introduce appropriate legal and institutional framework on data privacy. This should be read together with the general obligation of State parties in Article 4 'to adopt all appropriate legislative, administrative and other measures for the implementation of the rights recognized' in the Convention. No doubt, this would obviously include data privacy legislation that implements the right to privacy guaranteed in the Convention. The provision is not without other ambiguities, however. First, it suggests that rehabilitation and health data are not personal data, which may not necessarily be the case. Second, while health data is typically personal—and sometimes sensitive—data, the nature of rehabilitation data is not clear—does it, for example, include non-personal data? If that is the case, the Convention broadens the scope of data privacy protection beyond personal data.

Commentators argue that the phrase 'regardless of place of residence' in Article 22 of CRD gives it an extraterritorial scope.[56] Per this interpretation, a State party's activity within its borders but interfering with the right to privacy of a disabled person in another jurisdiction would engage its obligations under Article 22. This appears to be a sound interpretation because, unlike Article 2 of the ICCPR, the CRD does not define the scope of State obligations vis-à-vis individuals subject to its jurisdiction though outside its territory.

Data privacy is also addressed in the Convention's procedural clause dealing with statistics and data collection.[57] It reads as follows:

1. States Parties undertake to collect *appropriate information, including statistical and research data*, to enable them to formulate and implement policies to give effect to the present Convention. The process of collecting and maintaining this information shall: (a) Comply with legally established safeguards, including *legislation on data protection, to ensure confidentiality and respect for the privacy of persons with disabilities*; (b) Comply *with internationally accepted norms to protect human rights* and fundamental freedoms and ethical principles in the collection and use of statistics.

---

[55] See, eg, Committee on the Rights of Persons with Disabilities, Concluding Observations on the Initial Report of France, UN Doc CRPD/C/FRA/CO/1 (4 October 2021) para 47.
[56] See Land and others (n 49) 621.
[57] See CRD (n 51) art 31.

2. States Parties shall assume responsibility for the dissemination of these statistics and ensure their accessibility to persons with disabilities and others. [Emphasis Added]

Although not couched in human rights language, this provision offers additional protection to personal data. The term 'appropriate information' is evidently too broad to include personal data, including sensitive personal data. Indeed, the reference immediately after to data protection legislation in this provision confirms this point. As alluded to above, the privacy provision of the Convention—in contrast—clearly delineates the type of data subject to the protection of the law: personal, health and rehabilitation data. A central part of ensuring the implementation of disability rights is through timely and comprehensive collection of data by States. To that effect, the Convention imposes a duty on States to collect data which may include personal data.[58] But during the drafting of the Convention, there were concerns that statistical data, including personal data, collected in the process of realizing the rights might be misused thereby undermining data privacy rights.[59] To address this, the Convention includes a corresponding duty to ensure that collection and processing of personal data of persons with disabilities to be in line with national, regional, and international data privacy standards.[60]

The specific requirement to align state practices of data collection with data protection legislation should be read together with the Convention's 'general obligation' of State parties. States are required to 'adopt all appropriate legislative, administrative and other measures for the implementation of the rights recognized in the present Convention'.[61] Read together, these two provisions of the Convention impose a duty on State parties to the Convention to introduce data protection legislation. And in some instances, the Committee on the Rights of Persons with Disabilities has—in its Concluding Observations—called upon State parties to enact legislation for the protection of the privacy of persons with disabilities.[62] The reference 'legally established standards' is taken by some commentators to mean national and regional data privacy laws whereas 'internationally accepted norms' concern the UN Fundamental Principles of Official Statistics or the UN Principles Governing International Statistical Activities.[63] Data privacy norms are converging to a set of rights, principles, and governance norms, but any notion that the this provision of the Convention requires State parties that are not, for instance

---

[58]   ibid, art 31(1).
[59]   Mads Pedersen and Federico Ferretti, 'Art 31: Statistics and Data Collection' in Ilias Bantekas and others (eds), *UN Convention on the Rights of Persons with Disabilities: A Commentary* (Oxford University Press 2018) 936–37.
[60]   See CRD (n 51) art 31(1(1–b)).
[61]   ibid, art 4(1(a)).
[62]   Committee on the Rights of Persons with Disabilities, Concluding observations on the Initial Report of India, UN Doc CRPD/C/IND/CO/1 (29 October 2019) para 47.
[63]   Pedersen and Ferretti (n 59) 936, 944.

members of the EU to comply with the General Data Protection Regulation (GDPR), would be a stretch.

None of the Committee's jurisprudence so far engages with the data privacy aspects of this provision. Parts of its concluding observations on this provision, for instance, never alludes to obligations pertaining to data privacy. Almost always, the Committee only expresses concern on the lack of comprehensive and disaggregated data, not the attendant privacy concerns.[64] Part of the State obligation is not only to collect relevant information and statistics but also to disseminate them.[65] Persons with disabilities are among actors to which such data should be disseminated. But this does not appear to be related to the notion, or rather right, of access in data privacy legislation by which data subjects are entitled to know data held about them. This flows from the way in which the provision is framed in that access to the data can be or should be provided to 'others' as well as the relevant person with disability.

Another human rights treaty with provisions dealing with data privacy is the Enforced Disappearance Convention. The Convention touches on data privacy in two respects. First, it regulates the use and disclosure of 'personal information' as part of States' duty to 'search' the whereabouts of a disappeared person. Article 19 of the Convention provides the following:

1. *Personal information, including medical and genetic data*, which is collected and/or transmitted within the framework of the search for a disappeared person shall not be *used or made available for purposes other than the search for the disappeared person*. This is without prejudice to the use of such information in criminal proceedings relating to an offence of enforced disappearance or the exercise of the right to obtain reparation.
2. The collection, processing, use and storage of personal information, including medical and genetic data, shall not infringe or have the effect of infringing the human rights, fundamental freedoms or human dignity of an individual. [Emphasis Added]

Jurisprudence, including a general comment, is yet to be developed by the Committee on Enforced Disappearance on this provision but three observations can be made about this provision. One is that 'personal information' is not defined in the Convention but it is enunciated denotatively to include medical and genetic data. That makes it closer to the broader meaning of personal data in standard data privacy legislation. The other noteworthy point is that the provision does not

---

[64] See, eg, Concluding Observations on the Initial Report of Estonia, UN Doc CRPD/C/EST/CO/1 (5 May 2021) paras 60–61; Concluding Observations on the Combined Second and Third Periodic Reports of Australia, UN Doc CRPD/C/AUS/CO/2-3 (15 October 2019) para 57.
[65] See CRD (n 51) art 31(2).

prohibit collection of personal data as a matter of principle. All it requires is that processing of personal information should not have the effect of violating human rights. This broad framing suggests that no prohibition exists for the sheer collection of even sensitive personal data. Ultimately, it is only after collection, processing, storage and use that legality or legitimacy would be considered. This therefore leaves wide latitude to State parties. The third point is that the use and disclosure of personal information is permissible under three circumstances: where that is necessary for the purpose of facilitating the search, for prosecuting the crime of enforced disappearance or to seek reparation by victims. It is clear from this provision that while collection of personal data of a disappeared person is generally permissible, its use (which would include processing) and disclosure is subject to strict restriction.

The Convention requires State parties to maintain a database containing information of persons deprived of liberty.[66] Such information may include personal information such as information about the person's identity and state of health.[57] But the information may not be disclosed to 'persons with legitimate interest' if non-disclosure is (a) mandated by law, (b) strictly necessary and (c) likely to adversely affect the privacy of the disappeared person.[68] Even when these conditions are met, States are allowed to restrict disclosure of information only when a 'person is under the protection of the law and the deprivation of liberty is subject to judicial control'.[69] That means that (data) privacy can be a ground for non-disclosure exceptionally, that is when the 'disappeared person' is somehow under the control of the State. If the State has no knowledge or role in the disappearance of the person, privacy cannot be invoked to restrict disclosure of personal data. What this clearly suggests is that disclosure of information is the rule and non-disclosure is the exception. And this flows from the Convention's underlying objective of tracing and locating disappeared persons through all available means, including through the collection, processing, and disclosure of personal data. That means data privacy considerations are bound to take the backseat.[70]

Apart from the fact that the Convention is a modern human rights treaty, the inclusion of data privacy themes has to do with the background of its drafters. The first draft of the Convention was prepared by Joinet[71] who, as shall be noted further

---

[66] *International Convention for the Protection of All Persons from Enforced Disappearance*, opened for signature on 6 February 2007, 2716 UNTS 3 (entered into force 23 December 2010) art 17(3).

[67] ibid, art 17(3(a and f)).

[68] ibid, art 20(1). Persons with legitimate interests, per art 18(1), include relatives of the person deprived of liberty, their representatives or their counsel.

[69] ibid.

[70] See Tullio Scovazzi and Gabriella Citroni, *The Struggle Against Enforced Disappearance and the 2007 United Nations Convention* (Martinus Nijhoff 2007) 340.

[71] Emmanuel Decaux, 'The International Convention for the Protection of All Persons from Enforced Disappearance, as a Victim-Oriented Treaty' in Margaret de Guzman and Diane Amann (eds), *Arcs of Global Justice: Essays in Honour of William A. Schabas* (Oxford University Press 2018) 58–59 citing Draft International Convention for the Protection of all Persons from Enforced Disappearance, UN Doc E/CN.4/Sub.2/RES/1998/25 (26 August 1998).

in this chapter, not only did he help draft CoE and OECD privacy instruments but also the UN Data Privacy Guidelines of 1990. At the time, Joinet served as both the Chairperson and Special Rapporteur on the Sub-committee's Sessional Working Group on the Administration of Justice as part of the then UN Commission on Human Rights.[72] Not only did he present the first draft treaty for the Working Group's consideration but also presented an extensive study on the subject. But it should be pointed out that Article 19 of the current text of the Convention did not exist in his preliminary draft.[73] Nor did he mention during his presentation of the text European data privacy instruments among a list of instruments he took into account while drafting the text.[74] But there is little doubt that his vast experience in data protection policymaking in transnational organizations would have influenced his subsequent drafts, which ultimately led to a specific data protection provision in the Convention.

World Health Organization's (WHO) International Health Regulations (IHRs) is the other treaty of universal scope containing data privacy standards.[75] The treaty regulates the treatment of personal (health) data collected by State parties from each other or the WHO.[76] In that respect, the scope of the treaty's data privacy regulation is notably unique in that it does not concern personal data collected by States themselves. If the WHO had collected health data of a State's nationals or residents which the State in question has not or was not able to collect on its own, the treaty allows that State to seek such data from the WHO. But this raises the question of whether data subjects in such circumstances are nationals or residents of another State party. Equally unclear are what such circumstances in reality would look like as well as the rationale behind this conception of data processing regulation. What is clear is that the inclusion of the provision in the IHRs is with the objective of introducing human rights protections which did not exist in earlier iterations of the IHRs.[77] This provision made its way into IHRs in the 2005 revision, the process of which began a decade earlier.[78] With a protracted revision process involving various stakeholders including from Europe, one sees clear marks of European data privacy standards.

---

[72] See Draft International Convention on the Protection of All Persons from Enforced Disappearance, Resolution 1998/25 of the Sub-Commission on Prevention of Discrimination and Protection of Minorities, UN Doc E/CN.4/Sub.2/1998/L.11/Add.2 (26 August 1998).

[73] See Report of the Sessional Working Group on the Administration of Justice: Chairman-Rapporteur, Mr Louis Joinet, UN Doc E/CN.4/Sub.2/1998/19, Annex (19 August 1998).

[74] ibid, para 15.

[75] See International Health Regulations (3rd edn, 2005). At the time of writing, the treaty has 196 State parties. See details at <https://bit.ly/3qlr3cG>.

[76] ibid, art 45 cum art 2(1) [defining 'personal data' as any information relating to an identified or identifiable natural person].

[77] See David Fidler, 'From International Sanitary Conventions to Global Health Security: The New International Health Regulations' (2007) 4 Chinese Journal of International Law 325, 377.

[78] IHRs under its current nomenclature and structure was initially adopted in 1969 and has since been revised several times with the latest being in 2005. See generally Fidler, Id.

Article 45 of the IHRs regulates processing of health data in two respects, again with some normative idiosyncrasies. First, it requires for such data to be kept confidentially and processed anonymously 'as required by national law'.[79] This obligation is premised on the existence of national law laying out such requirements, typically a data privacy legislation. So, it is unclear what this would mean if the relevant State party has no data protection legislation or other law with equivalent requirements of data processing. As the law currently stands, it might be taken to exempt State parties with no such legally mandated requirements. Second, it stipulates a set of specific data privacy principles—and a conditional right governing the disclosure and processing of personal data in the context of responding to public health risks. The principles include 'fair and lawful processing', 'purpose limitation', 'data minimization', 'data quality', and 'storage limitation'.[80] The IHRs also envisage a conditional right to access personal data without undue delay or expense.[81] Conditional about this right is that the duty bearer (data controller)—ie, the WHO, not State parties—is not bound to honour the duty if providing access is not practicable.

Although not a human rights treaty, the Marrakesh Treaty also engages data privacy of persons with 'print' disabilities.[82] The aim of this treaty is to facilitate access to disable persons, referred to as beneficiary persons, to copyrighted materials in forms suitable to their conditions.[83] In a way, the treaty offers the means for realizations of rights envisaged in the CRD, namely those relating to access.[84] In turn, that means upholding the right to privacy is not the main objective of the treaty, but it still recognizes the need—albeit oddly—to protect privacy in implementing the treaty. Article 8 of the Convention provides that 'in the implementation of the limitations and exceptions provided for in this Treaty, Contracting Parties shall endeavour to protect the privacy of beneficiary persons on an equal basis with others'.

Facilitating access to works in traditional format, especially when it involves processing across borders, privacy rights of a beneficiary may be impacted. Albeit crudely, this provision requires States to uphold the privacy of beneficiaries in 'handling and record keeping'.[85] But this proviso is remarkable in at least two respects. One is that it does not explicitly refer to privacy as a fundamental human right. That an underlying objective of the Convention include upholding human rights such as non-discrimination means the aim is also to protect the right to

---

[79] See IHRs (n 75) art 45(1).

[80] ibid, art 45(2).

[81] ibid, art 45(3).

[82] *Marrakesh Treaty to Facilitate Access to Published Works for Persons Who Are Blind, Visually Impaired, or Otherwise Print Disabled*, opened for signature 28 June 2013 (entered into force 30 September 2016).

[83] ibid, preamble cum art 3

[84] See Laurence Helfer and others, *The World Blind Union Guide to the Marrakesh Treaty: Facilitating Access to Books for Print-Disabled Individuals* (Oxford University Press 2017) 9–10.

[85] See also Marrakesh treaty (n 82) art 2(c(iv)).

privacy. The other is that the duty appears to be only 'progressive' in that it requires States only to 'endeavour' to respect the right. Such obligations are associated with socio-economic and cultural rights in the realization of which States owe no immediate obligations. This would mean, then, that the Marrakesh treaty waters-down the right to privacy, a 'first generation' civil and political right, to a 'second generation right'.

3.2. Custom

Custom is the second potential source of international data privacy law. That there currently exists no data privacy treaty with a universal scope makes the question of whether data privacy has attained customary international law compelling. At its 58th session in 2006, the International Law Commission (ILC) decided to include 'protection of personal data in transborder flow of information' in its long-term program of work.[86] Inclusion in the Commission's long-term program of work means no work would begin until the Commission takes a specific decision to do so. Over a decade later, the topic remains still among a long list of the topics in the Commission's long-term program of work.[87] When the Commission's Working Group on Long-term Program of Work proposed its inclusion in 2006, it had submitted a background study that surveyed the state of the art in the field of data protection.[88] But among the key findings of the Working Group were (a) that there is a 'commonality of interests in a number of core principles' although differences in approach exist; and (b) that state practice in the field is not extensive or fully developed.[89] But the Working Group recommended the Commission to include the topic in its long-term program of work with a view a view to identity emerging trends in legal opinion and practice.[90] A point vital to note in this regard is that among the criteria for topic selection included the subject matter should be sufficiently advanced in terms of state practice and be concrete and feasible for progressive development.[91]

In light of this position of the Working Group in 2006, two pertinent questions should be raised regarding the customary law status of data privacy. One is whether one should assume that, on account of the latest decision to keep the

[86] See 'Other Decisions and Conclusions of the Commission' in Report of the Commission to the United Nations General Assembly on the Work of its Fifty-eighth Session, UN Doc A/61/10 (August 2006) para 260(o) cum paras 256–57.
[87] For a list of topics in the long-program of work as at 72nd session of the ILC (2021), see <https://legal.un.org/ilc/programme.shtml>.
[88] See Protection of Personal Data in Transborder Flow of Personal Data in Report of the Commission to the United Nations General Assembly on the Work of its Fifty-eighth Session, UN Doc A/61/10 (August 2006) Annex IV cum para 261.
[89] ibid, para 12.
[90] ibid.
[91] ibid, para 256.

topic in the Commission's long-term program of work, there is still a lack of general state practice and *opinio juris* for the formation of customary international law of data privacy. But significant developments in the fifteen or so years in the global data privacy policy arena disproves the assumption. The second—and related to the first—is whether sufficient state practice supported with *opinio juris* has emerged since its initial inclusion in 2006. With the considerable rise in the number of national data privacy legislation worldwide as well as adoption of transnational privacy treaties after 2006, it might be argued that state practice may have become sufficiently extensive or developed.[92] And the adoption of and proposals for new data privacy standards worldwide may arguably be taken to reflect *opinio juris* on the part of States.

One way to stress test such suppositions is through ILC's Draft Conclusions on the Identification of Customary International Law.[93] While still a draft, it is instructive in assessing whether data privacy has attained the status of Customary International Law (CIL). A general state practice and acceptance of that practice as law are the two constitutive elements required to establish the existence of a rule of CIL.[94] But each constituent element should be established separately. Among the ways in which state practice can be expressed is through legislative acts.[95] But such practice must be 'general' in that it must be sufficiently widespread, representative and consistent.[96] The surge in national data privacy legislation in the past decade or so can be taken to reflect a general state practice.[97] Considering the overall tendency to follow European data privacy standards in countries outside Europe, it might further be said that the practice is 'general'. Reinforcing this point further is that practices of international organizations which, in certain cases, may contribute to the formation or expression of rules of CIL.[98] From EU's robust policymaking in the field, including the GDPR, and CoE's modernization of Convention 108 to the adoption of the African Union (AU) Convention on Cybersecurity and Personal Data Protection (Malabo Convention), such extensive treaty making in the field of data privacy would arguably contribute to the formation of CIL.

What, then, remains is the requirement of *opinio juris*—are States worldwide adopting or proposing data privacy legislation as matter of right or duty? This requirement is rather hard to establish as it relates to the psychological aspect of State

---

[92] cf Monika Zalnieriute, 'An International Constitutional Moment for Data Privacy' (2015) 23 International Journal of Law and Information Technology 99, 99 [suggesting that the post-Snowden global outcry, expressed through Resolutions of international organizations such as the UN and EU, has led to the emergence of instant customary law on data privacy].

[93] Draft Conclusions on Identification of Customary International Law, Adopted by the International Law Commission at its Seventieth Session (2018).

[94] ibid, Conclusion 2.

[95] ibid, Conclusions 5, 6(2).

[96] ibid, Conclusion 8.

[97] Of a related view, see Christopher Kuner, 'The Internet and the Global Reach of EU law' in Marise Cremona and Joanne Scott (eds), *EU Law Beyond EU Borders: The Extraterritorial Reach of EU Law* (Oxford University Press 2019) 131.

[98] Draft Conclusions (n 93) Conclusion 4(2).

conduct. Among forms of evidence for acceptance as law indicated in the ILC Draft Conclusions are official State publications as well as conduct in relation to resolutions of international organizations.[99] Arguably, the official publication of an adopted or proposed data protection legislation in dozens of countries in the past decade or so might be presented to show *opinio juris*. Additionally, the adoption without a vote of the series of post-Snowden UN privacy resolutions—explored at length in chapter 5—might be taken to suggest that States are acting with a sense of duty vis-à-vis data privacy principles, rights, and governance norms. Add to this the proviso that such resolutions may serve as evidence for the existence of a rule of CIL.[100]

Overall, this brief sketch points towards an affirmative answer to the customary law status of protection of personal data.[101] Indeed, the sheer fact that the topic has not been elevated to the ILC's current program of work cannot be taken to mean lack of sufficient state practice and *opinio juris*. The inherently uncertain nature of CIL as a source of law means the question of whether data privacy has attained a status of CIL will persist for long. What should, instead, be asked is whether the rise of data privacy to that level would add any significant value to international law and its privacy problem in the digital age. The prime benefit of a rule becoming a rule of CIL is that it would be a rule of general international law. In the context of privacy, this means States not parties to one of the regional treaties would be bound by the rule. But bindingness in and of itself would add little in making international law fit for purpose in the digital age. As shall be shown in further details in chapter 7, soft legalization grounded in existing rules of international law of privacy should be one of the two pragmatic steps in attending to the 'privacy problem' in the digital age. Chapter 8 considers the second which relates to a dialogical approach to international privacy law.

3.3. General Principles

If data privacy has not conclusively become a rule of CIL, what remains is the question of whether it has attained the status of General Principles of Law (GPsL). GPsL is, as already alluded to in the preceding chapter, the least utilized source of international law including by international courts, including the ICJ.[102] Part of the

---

[99] ibid, Conclusions 9, 10(2).

[100] ibid, Conclusion 12.

[101] For a contrasting and older analysis based on a specific focus on 'transborder flow of personal data see Olga Estadella-Yuste, 'Transborder Data Flows and the Sources of Public International Law' (1991) 16 North Carolina Journal of International Law 379, 408–18.

[102] See, eg, Catherine Redgwell, 'General Principles of International Law' in Stefan Vogenauer and Stephen Weatherill (eds), *General Principles of Law: European and Comparative Perspectives* (Hart 2017) 12–13; Giorgio Gaja, 'General Principles in the Jurisprudence of the ICJ' in Mads Andenas and others (eds), *General Principles and the Coherence of International Law* (Brill 2019) 36.

reason for its nigh disuse is that treaties and custom already provide rules for the regulation of much of international affairs. Indeed, the drafters of the ICJ Statute envisaged GPsL to have mainly a 'gap filling' role in the event conventional and customary international rules offer no rules.[103] Perhaps, the absence of a comprehensive and binding international data privacy instrument may lend weight to an argument on the need to revitalizing general principles in the privacy field.

In at least three respects, normative difficulties arise in relations to general principles as sources of international law. One relates to what exactly such principles are—what makes principles of law general and hence eligible for dealing with matters of international concern? What constitutes 'recognition' in this context? What principles of law are eligible to serve as means of addressing international relations?[104] The second concerns the sources from which such principles are to be drawn—are the principles to be sourced from domestic law, international law, or both?[105] Third—and related to the second, is domestic laws of which jurisdictions or legal traditions should serve as sources of general principles. This was a bone of contention among the committee of experts during the drafting of the ICJ Statute.[106] But the general agreement was that the municipal law is the primary source of GPsL.[107]

With a view to address these persistent questions, the ILC has been considering GPsL under its current program of work since 2018.[108] A special rapporteur has been appointed to further the work who has, as highlighted in chapter 2, since tabled two reports and preliminary 'conclusions' on the identification of GPsL. In terms of scope, the special rapporteur proposes that both domestic and international law can be sources of GPsL.[109] But different requirements shall apply in the two instances. With respect to domestic law sourced principles, two requirements need to be met: the relevant principle should be (a) common to principal legal systems of the world, and (b) capable of transposition to the international legal system.[110] In ascertaining whether a particular principle is common in principal legal systems of the world, a fairly comparative survey of national law and judicial decisions is required.[111] Suitability of transposition into the international

---

[103] See Alain Pellet, 'Article 38' in Andreas Zimmermann and others (eds), *The Statute of the International Court of Justice: A Commentary* (Oxford University Press 2nd edn, 2012) 832.

[104] ibid, 835–37; see also First Report on General Principles of Law by Marcelo Vázquez-Bermúdez, Special Rapporteur, UN Doc, A/CN.4/732 (5 April 2019) paras 163–75.

[105] See, eg, Redgwell (n 102) 7–11.

[106] Imogen Saunders, *General Principles as a Source of International Law: Art 38(1)(c) of the Statute of the International Court of Justice* (Hart 2020) 38–47.

[107] ibid, 46; see also Second Report on General Principles of Law by Marcelo Vázquez-Bermúdez, Special Rapporteur, UN Doc A/CN.4/741 (9 April 2020) paras 2–3, 16.

[108] See Other Decisions and Conclusions of the Commission, 70th session held in (July 2018) chapter XIII, A <https://legal.un.org/ilc/reports/2018/english/chp13.pdf>.

[109] Consolidated Draft Conclusions in Annex to the Second Report of Vázquez-Bermúdez (n 107).

[110] ibid, Conclusion 4.

[111] ibid, Conclusion 5.

legal system is to be ascertained by considering whether the relevant principle is compatible with fundamental principles of international law and that conditions exist to operationalize the principle.[112] For a principle drawn from international law, it should be either (a) widely recognized in treaties or international instruments, (b) underlie conventional or customary international law, or (c) inherent in the basic features and fundamental requirements of the international legal system.[113]

Despite its overall disuse and the attendant uncertainties, GPsL can be a potentially viable source of international data privacy law in at least two ways. First, the proliferation of data privacy legislation worldwide in the past two decades signals recognition of data privacy principles among principal legal systems of the world. More importantly, such laws are by and large aligned with a common set of data subject rights, principles and governance norms. Put differently, normative convergence has by and large emerged in the field of data protection around the world. Studies have demonstrated in this regard the influence of European data privacy instruments. With notable exceptions such as the United States, it may be said that data privacy as a set of legal principles is widely common in major legal systems of the world. Even in the United States, the growing number of data privacy legislation at the state level resembles, to a degree, European standards.[114] There is no obvious reason to doubt that the transposition of principles drawn from domestic law sources would be contrary to fundamental principles of international law or hard to operationalize in the context of the international legal system. Second—and related to the first, is the convergence in the normative structure of data privacy treaties. As highlighted above, wider recognition of a principle in treaties and international standards can be used to determine the existence and content of general principles formed in the international legal system. From the recognition in the UDHR, European Court of Human Rights (ECtHR), the ICCPR, and other regional human rights treaties of the underlying right to privacy to the adoption of Convention 108 and the Malabo Convention, there is arguably a wider recognition of data privacy principles. Add to this the series of privacy resolutions adopted by the UN in the wake of the Snowden revelations which reinforce widely accepted principles of data privacy.

However, the fact that the nature, scope, and function of GPsL remains unsettled makes its candidacy as a source of international data privacy law uncertain. A closer look at the discussion thus far around GPsL, including in the recent

---

[112] ibid, Conclusion 6.
[113] ibid, Conclusion 7.
[114] See, eg, generally Paul Schwartz, 'Global Data Privacy: The EU Way' (2019) 98 New York University Law Review 771; Emmanuel Pernot-Leplay, 'EU Influence on Data Privacy Laws: Is the US Approach Converging with the EU Model?' (2019) 18 Colorado Technology Law Journal 101, 116–22; Stacy Cooper, GDPR Comes to the US—Nevada & California Privacy Laws (Webspec, 23 September 2019) <https://bit.ly/3KhRqb9>.

studies of the ILC's special rapporteur, reinforce this uncertainty in two respects. One is that GPsL are envisioned within a State-centered prism of international law. That does not comport well with the function of data privacy as means of regulating processing of personal data by public and private actors. Related to this is the nature of general principles in that they appear to be largely procedural as opposed to substantive. Indeed, among principles envisioned by the drafters of the ICJ Statute included 'certain principles of procedure, the principle of good faith, and the principle of *res judicata*'.[115] Further adding up to the uncertainty is the fact that data privacy is notably a recent area of law. The overall singular conception of general principles is the other cause for uncertainty. Unlike data privacy which is made up of a series of principles as well as rights and governance norms, international law doctrine, jurisprudence and discourse on GPsL speak of *a* principle. That throws any notion of data privacy as a general principle in more doubt. But more importantly, the value of data privacy being part of general principles is even minimal in addressing the 'privacy problem' in the digital age. The principal value of data privacy being elevated to GPsL is that it would be a rule of general international law binding all States. But the main argument of this book, shall be laid out in chapter 7, is that soft legalization as opposed to hard law—be it in a form of treaty law or general international law—is the appropriate step in devising an international law response to the privacy problem in the digital age.

3.4. Soft Law

Soft law forms a central part of the current international data privacy framework. The Data Privacy Guidelines of 1990, which remains to be the primary universal data privacy instrument, is a soft law. The Guidelines stipulates a set of principles of information practices as 'minimum guarantees' to be enacted by States and international organizations.[116] These guarantees are basically high-level principles of data privacy comparable to most domestic and regional data privacy principles. Key data privacy principles contained in the Guidelines include: principles of 'lawfulness and fairness', 'accuracy', 'purpose specification', 'interested-person access', 'non-discrimination', and 'security'.[117] The Guidelines further provides for rules on transborder data flows between countries with 'comparable' data privacy safeguards and on the need for an independent data protection authority.[118] The requirement of a data protection authority also applies to international intergovernmental organizations.[119]

---

[115] See Saunders (n 106) 46.
[116] UN Data Privacy Guidelines (n 3) Part A.
[117] ibid, paras 1–5, 7.
[118] ibid, paras 8–9.
[119] ibid, Part B.

A novelty of the UN Data Privacy Guidelines is that it envisages rules regarding processing of personal data by 'governmental international organizations'.[120] But the UNGA Resolution that adopted the Guidelines 'requests' respect of the Guidelines from a broader set of organizations: 'governmental, intergovernmental and non-governmental organizations'.[121] The reference to intergovernmental organizations is straightforward in that it covers intergovernmental international organizations governed by public international law. So is the reference to non-governmental organizations, which would include both national and international non-governmental organizations. Unclear however is the reference to 'governmental organizations'— does it concern organs of the State/government or public enterprises? If that is really the case, it would simply be redundant as State regulation of the data processing would obviously cover the public sector, ie, processing by public bodies, subject to some exceptions. Regulation of private sector data processing would also address practices of State commercial enterprises. In any case, the UNGA Resolution broadens the scope of application of the Guidelines in at least in covering non-governmental international organizations. The broad framing of scope is quite a remarkable point, but that Guidelines is—as shall be discussed further in the next section—a soft law reliant on voluntary compliance means it would not be of much significance normatively.

In response largely to the 'request' in the UNGA Resolution—and the requirement in the Guidelines, a number of intergovernmental organizations especially UN specialized and related agencies have issued data privacy policies in the past decade. The UN Data Privacy Guidelines also provides the 'enabling law' for the adoption of agency-level data protection policies by 'governmental international organizations' based on the Guidelines for internal and external purposes.[122] Indeed, the UNGA had—in a post-Tehran Conference Resolution—'invited' UN specialized agencies to 'pay particular attention to the protection of the broad sector of the population' from the 'harmful effects' of technological developments and the impact that they pose to human rights.[123] Over the past decade, this call has been heeded by many UN agencies as well as international organizations with, inter alia, adoption of internal data privacy policies. Thus, individuals of concern to these agencies are entitled to protection commonly afforded in national data protection legislation.

---

[120] ibid.
[121] GA Res 45/95 (n 3) para 5.
[122] ibid, Part B.
[123] See *The Use of Scientific and Technological Developments in the Interest of Peace and Social Development*, GA Res 3150 (XXVIII), 2201st plenary mtg, UN Doc RES/3150 (XXVIII) (14 December 1973) para 5.

To date, the World Food Program (WFP),[124] the UN Children's Fund (UNICEF),[125] the UN High Commission for Refugees (UNHCR),[126] the International Labour Organization (ILO),[127] International Organization for Migration (IOM),[128] the UN Development Program (UNDP),[129] and the WHO[130] have issued some form of data privacy policies. This is of course in addition to the data privacy policies and guides issued by other intergovernmental (eg, INTERPOL) and non-governmental international organizations (eg, International Committee of the Red Cross).[131] Except for ILO's Code, a defining feature of these policies is that they are intra-agency instruments regulating the processing of personal data of persons under the purview of or are of concern to the respective organization. ILO's Code, discussed further in the next section, is meant rather as a guidance to member States in legislating on the subject. As their nomenclatures suggest, the legal nature of the intra-agency data protection policies is mixed. Those dubbed 'Rules' and 'Policies' are clearly binding instruments whereas those titled 'Manual' and 'Guide' appear to be soft law. But as shall be discussed in the next section, the sole fact that they are internal instruments—regardless of their legal nature—undercuts their value in international law.

4. Falling into Disuse

Propelled mainly by historical factors outlined above, the international data privacy framework exhibits a number of normative and institutional weaknesses. This section examines the scope of data privacy protection in international data privacy law, and highlights two of its major weaknesses: (a) problems of substance and approach; (b) problems of institutionalization. A caveat is, however, in order: since existing rules are scattered across various instruments, the discussion in this section is limited to those that are universal in scope, and those containing key international data privacy norms.

---

[124] *Guide to Personal Data Protection and Privacy* (WFP, June 2016).

[125] *Policy on Personal Data Protection*, POLICY/DFAM/2020/001 (UNICEF, 15 July 2020).

[126] *Policy on the Protection of Personal Data of Persons of Concern to the UNHCR* (UNHCR, May 2015).

[127] *Code of Practice on the Protection of Workers' Personal Data* (ILO, 1997).

[128] *Data Protection Manual* (IOM, 2009).

[129] *Guidance to UNDP Country Offices on the Privacy, Data Protection and Broader Human Rights Dimensions of using Digital Technologies to Combat Covid-19* (UNDP, June 2020). Notably, this is slightly different from other policies of UN agencies, not least because it is a temporal (ie, induced by the pandemic). According to the UNDP, it has not issued a data protection policy because it rarely handles personal data. See at 2.

[130] *Data Principles* (WHO, 10 August 2020). Note, however, WHO is reportedly in the process of developing a freestanding policy on data protection, the latest draft tabled in 2020. See at 5. Another relevant WHO instrument is the Policy on the Use and Sharing of Data collected by WHO in Member States outside the Context of Public Health Emergencies (August 2017) <https://bit.ly/3raaf7v>.

[131] *Rules on the Processing of Data* (as amended), III/IRPD/GA/2011 (INTERPOL, 2019); *Rules on Personal Data Protection* (International Committee of the Red Cross, November 2015).

4.1. Problems of Substance and Approach

Normative weaknesses of the present framework relate mainly to three issues. One is the problem of normative dispersion in that existing data privacy norms are a mere patchwork of rules dispersed across various instruments. As shall be shown below, this has significantly lessened their effectiveness and accessibility. Second, existing data privacy norms are embodied in a set of exceedingly soft legal instruments which not only reduced their normative strength but also played a role in their lower practical utility. While soft legalization is an effective tool of international lawmaking, its overuse in the data privacy field has had little value or has been counterproductive. Third, existing international data privacy rules are normatively inferior to their regional counterparts, because of which the desirable level of protection has been minimal. Not only were more protective norms watered-down during the drafting process but also that lack of proper attention at the UN to data privacy over the past four decades has rendered existing standards obsolete. Particularly so in the light of significant developments in the field of data privacy law at national and regional levels since.

4.1.1. Dispersive Approach to Data Privacy

Present international data privacy norms are scattered across various sets of instruments. Not only are these norms scattered in various instruments but also that each instrument is often detached from other related instruments. One finds no unified and comprehensive universal instrument that regulates the processing of personal information and, as such, protects data privacy. Most norms appear to have come about under specific circumstances, and hence in isolation with already existing norms. This patchwork of rules is a result of piecemeal, uncoordinated and sporadic approaches to data privacy pursued by the UN and its agencies. It can also be attributed to the general apathy towards issues of privacy, as highlighted in chapter 2 and earlier in this chapter, that has been rampant in the UN standard setting processes in the past few decades. What follows considers this pervasive fragmented approach to data privacy at the UN. Based on their legal nature and scope, diffuse international data privacy instruments/norms can be grouped into four categories: 'universal/general', 'domain/subject-specific', 'agency-level', and 'human rights instrument-based' data privacy instruments and/or norms.

4.1.1.1. Universal/General Standards

The UN Data Privacy Guidelines is the primary general data privacy instrument with a universal scope of application. As alluded to above, the Guidelines envisages a series of data privacy principles and rules addressed to both States and international intergovernmental organizations. But a hallmark of the Guidelines is that the 'procedures' for the implementation of these guarantees are left to States so long as they are based on the Guidelines' 'orientations'. Added to the soft law nature of the Guidelines—and hence lack of binding force, this leaves a significant latitude to States in translating the Guidelines into domestic legislation. As shall be noted later in this chapter, this broad latitude had lent weight in the ultimate disregard of the Guidelines by almost all States in domestic lawmaking.

Other more general UN Internet governance instruments also fall in this category. Good cases in point are a set of conference outcome documents adopted following the World Summit on Information Society (WSIS) which slightly touch upon data privacy. These instruments, however, address data privacy only peripherally and indirectly. One finds mere affirmation of privacy rights, and no data privacy principles are articulated as such. The Geneva Declaration of Principles, for instance, simply affirms the need to protect 'data and privacy'.[132] Similarly, the accompanying document—the Geneva Plan of Action—merely 'encourages' research in the field of e-health to ensure respect for the right to privacy, especially in the context of international transfer of health data.[133] The Tunis Commitment—a final act of the Tunis WSIS of 2005—does not make any reference to privacy at all but its accompanying document, the Tunis Agenda, emphasizes the need for the protection of 'personal information, privacy and data'.[134] Beyond the peripheral—and at points, inaccurate references such as 'data and privacy', these international instruments do not engage with other corresponding instruments that deal with (data) privacy, including the UN Data Privacy Guidelines.

4.1.1.2. Domain/Subject-specific Standards

The second category of the international data privacy framework includes 'subject/sector-specific' data privacy norms/instruments. An example is the UN Fundamental Principles of Official Statistics, which stipulates a set of principles that must be observed in undertaking official statistics. A relevant data privacy norm is provided in Principle 6 which states that 'individual data collected by statistics agencies must be strictly confidential and used exclusively for statistical purposes'.[135] Another instrument is the UN Principles and Guidelines on Access to Legal Aid in Criminal Justice Systems whose data privacy provision provides that 'privacy and personal data protection' of children must be protected in the course of criminal proceedings and appropriate law must be enacted to that effect.[136] That these UN Principles address specific subjects, and hence nuanced in scope, means they are not typical data privacy instruments short of substance.

---

[132] The Geneva Declaration of Principles, WSIS-03/GENEVA/DOC/4-E (12 December 2003) para 35 cum 58.

[133] The Geneva Plan of Action, WSIS-03/GENEVA/DOC/5-E (12 December 2003) para 18 cum 12(f).

[134] The Tunis Agenda for the Information Society, WSIS-05/TUNIS/DOC/6(Rev. 1)-E (18 November 2005) para 39 cum 42.

[135] See Fundamental Principles of Official Statistics, GA Res 68/261, 68th sess, Agenda item 9, UN Doc A/RES/68/261 (29 January 2014).

[136] See UN Principles and Guidelines on Access to Legal Aid in Criminal Justice Systems, GA Res 67/187, 60th plenary mtg, UN Doc A/RES/67/187 (20 December 2012) para 54 cum 58(b).

4.1 1.3. Agency-level Standards

Data protection and information disclosure policies of specialized and related agencies of the UN, highlighted above, belong to the third category of the international data privacy framework. Instruments in this category are of different varieties in terms of scope and legal nature. While some are directly framed in human rights language—thereby reflective of the human rights genesis of the international data privacy framework, others have the common data privacy tone. Whereas some are sector-specific, a good case in point being the ILO Code of Practice, explained further below. The more recent intra-agency data protection policies, as shall be considered below, are notably reflective of European data privacy standards.

Several UN agencies have adopted agency-level data protection instruments in the past few years. Examples in this regard are the policies adopted by the UNHCR and the IOM. The UNHCR Policy explicitly states that it is adopted in response to the UN Data Privacy Guidelines which urges, as noted above, international-governmental organizations to apply the Guidelines in the course of their operations, albeit with some adjustments.[137] The Policy embodies widely accepted data privacy principles and data subject rights with some level of details.[138] The IOM Data Protection Manual is the other internal instrument developed by a related UN agency, which—like the UNHCR Policy—envisages progressive data privacy standards.[139] But unlike the UNHCR Policy, the UN Data Privacy Guidelines does not appear to be its inspiration. Adopted a few years after the International Conference of Data Protection and Privacy Commissioners—recently renamed the Global Privacy Assembly—made the initial call for an international data privacy instrument, the Manual seeks to contribute to the 'discussion' (re)stared by the Conference.[140]

With the increasing global attention to (data) privacy, it is likely that other UN agencies that control and process vast personal information in the course of their operations may develop similar intra-agency policies. The UN Secretary General's Data Strategy gives considerable attention to the protection of privacy in the effort to make the UN a 'data-driven' organization.[141] For instance, it foreshadows a data protection and privacy programme that would streamline data privacy in the process of 'datafying' the UN system.[142] As highlighted above, the WHO is in the process of developing a policy on personal data protection. In the wake of the Covid-19

---

[137] ibid; cf UNHCR Data Protection Policy (n 126) para 1.1.
[138] See UNHCR Data Protection Policy (n 126) Sec 2–7.
[139] See IOM Data Protection Manual (n 128).
[140] See Richard Perruchoud, 'Foreword' in IOM Data Protection Manual, Id; cf *Montreux Declaration: The Protection of Personal Data and Privacy in A Globalized World—A Universal Right Respecting Diversities* (International Conference of Privacy and Data Protection Commissioners, Montreux, Switzerland, 2005).
[141] See Data Strategy of the Secretary-General for Action by Everyone, Everywhere with Insight, Impact and Integrity: 2020–22 (2020) 4, 17, 43, 49.
[142] ibid, 59–61.

pandemic, some UN agencies have taken tailored steps relating to data privacy within their areas of competence. The UNESCO, for instance, released a Technical Guide that, inter alia, seeks to protect data privacy in the context of online education.[143] And the Guide outlines widely accepted data privacy principles.[144]

But the proliferation of agency-level standards raises a concern of fragmentation. To address this concern, the UN Data Privacy Policy Group which consists of experts drawn from different UN agencies developed a set of data privacy principles as a 'basic framework' for UN agencies in the course of processing personal data.[145] This framework was later adopted by the UN High-Level Committee on Management. Two years later, the Secretary General's Data Strategy reports that the implementation or observance of the framework by UN bodies has been 'partial'.[146] To that end, it emphasizes the need to undertake a comprehensive assessment of the framework and introduce updates with due account taken of new and emerging technologies.[147] Overall, that these policies, rules and manuals are largely aligned with widely accepted data privacy standards means normative variations, except those dictated by the institutional competence of the agencies, are unlikely. Yet the intra-agency scope of the instruments reduces their value in international law.

A related development is that some of these agencies have adopted information disclosure policies that further complement the data protection policies. While mainly aimed to facilitate access to information retained by the agencies, information disclosure policies often embody 'exceptions' to disclosure when the requested access to personal information would invade 'privacy interests' of concerned persons. The Information Disclosure Policy of the UNDP, for instance, prohibits disclosure of 'personal information' relating to 'staff and consultants' of the UNDP, including information pertaining to 'personal medical information and personal communications'.[148]

On top of their intra-agency and hence narrow scope, these policies often provide for circumstances where the impinged disclosure could be permitted for overriding 'public interest' reasons regardless of risks of privacy invasion.[149] Moreover, the 'privacy exceptions' often are couched in a manner less reflective of a genuine desire to protect privacy rights. For instance, UNDP's Policy prohibits disclosure because it would 'violate his or her rights, or invade his or her privacy', thereby

[143] See *Personal Data Security Technical Guide* (UNESCO, 2020) 2–3.
[144] ibid, 9–10.
[145] See *Personal Data Protection and Privacy Principles*, adopted by the UN High-Level Committee on Management at its 36th Meeting (11 October 2018); see also about the Group at <https://bit.ly/3Fqf9lX>.
[146] See Secretary General's Data Strategy (n 141) 11.
[147] ibid, 60.
[148] See *Information Disclosure Policy* (UNDP, 1996) (as amended in 2017) art 15(b). cf *Information/Document Access Policy* (International Telecommunication Union, 2016) art 3.1; *Directive on Information Disclosure* (WFP 2010) art 3(iv).
[149] ibid, art 16.

suggesting that privacy is worthy of protection not because it is a 'right'. This seems to have the objective of distancing the organization from any obligation, in human rights terms, which would have otherwise been the case had privacy been stated in human rights language.[150] These limit the potential of internal information disclosure policies of UN agencies in serving as a source of international data privacy law.

A variant of agency-level international data privacy instruments or norms takes the form of domain or subject-matter policies. For instance, the ILO—a specialized agency of the UN—has taken steps in adopting a 'non-legal soft law' instrument on the data privacy of workers.[151] The 'Code of Practice on the Protection of Workers' Personal Data' particularizes widely accepted data privacy principles and data subject rights to the labour sector.[152] The aim of the Code is to provide 'guidance' to States in enacting national legislation, and to other actors to take them into account while preparing work-related agreements.[153] Although adopted seven years after the UN Data Privacy Guidelines, the Code of Practice makes no reference to the Guidelines but to other regional instruments such as the EU Data Protection Directive and the CoE Data Protection Convention.[154] This is one of the instances that reflect not only the sectoral and disjointed nature of UN efforts in the field of data privacy, but also that UN has been complicit in undermining its own instruments. But as shall be highlighted later in this chapter, the ILO Code of Practice has had some significance in shaping judicial decisions at the regional level in relation to worker data privacy.

4.1 1.4. Human Rights Instrument-based Standards

In the fourth category, one finds data privacy principles embedded in some international human right treaties considered in the preceding section. A good case in point is the CRD whose data privacy provisions are discussed in section 3 above. To an extent, the Convention on Enforced Disappearance also touches on data privacy themes although it does not provide for a specific right to privacy like the CRD.[155] The value of treaty-based data privacy provisions is the potential of

---

[150] It is worth pointing out that whether international organizations, including intergovernmental organizations such as UN specialized and related agencies, are bound by international human rights has been part of the broader human rights and non-State actors debate. Recent proliferation of agency-level data privacy instruments is primarily driven by, as noted earlier, the call made in the UN Data Privacy Guidelines, but it may arguably be associated with their positive obligation in international human rights law. See more in ch 7.

[151] In discussing the diversity of soft law in international lawmaking, Chinkin refers to 'Codes of Practice' as 'non-legal soft law', as a subcategory of soft law. See Christine Chinkin, 'Normative Development in the International Legal System' in Dinah Shelton (ed), *Commitment and Compliance: The Role of Non-Binding Norms in the International Legal System* (Oxford University Press 2000) 28.

[152] See ILO Code of Practice (n 127).

[153] ibid, para 2.

[154] ibid, preamble, para 1.

[155] See detailed discussion in section 3 above.

inspiring domestic data privacy legislation, perhaps one with specific focus on persons covered in the respective instrument. But they are another manifestation of the fragmented approach to data privacy at the international level.

Data privacy themes, in human rights language, figure also in a series of instruments adopted by UNESCO. Indeed, one of the mandates of UNESCO is to 'further universal respect for human rights',[156] and this has been translated into several instruments relating to data privacy. Of UNESCO instruments, relevant to data privacy is the Universal Declaration on Human Genome and Human Rights of 1997. The Declaration, endorsed later by the UNGA in 1998, aims at safeguarding, among other human rights, privacy of genetic data in the course of genetic research.[157] It embodies a number of data privacy principles. For instance, the 'principle of lawful collection' is implied when the Declaration mandates the need to solicit the consent of data subjects in the course of collecting and processing genetic information.[158] The principle of 'data security' is patent in the Declaration where it requires that genetic data collected or being processed must be kept confidential, and any limitation thereof must be imposed only by law which is consistent with international human rights law.[159]

The Declaration has further been reinforced by another instrument, the International Declaration on Human Genetic Data of 2003. The Declaration not only embodies data privacy principles but also addresses the right to privacy more directly. On top of emphasizing the need for obtaining 'prior, free and informed consent' in the course of collecting and processing genetic data, it provides principles of 'purpose specification principle', 'use limitation principle', 'principle of data security', 'data subject participation principle', and 'principles of data quality'.[160] 'Privacy and confidentiality' are also touched on under Article 14 of the Declaration. A latest UNESCO instrument in the field of data privacy is the Universal Declaration on Bioethics and Human Rights, adopted by the General Conference. This Declaration aims to protect human rights in medical research and stipulates universal ethical principles that States must translate into domestic legislation and to provide guidance to non-State actors. Of the ethical principles, one is that confidentiality of personal medical data shall be respected, and no data shall be used or disclosed for purposes than it was initially collected or consented for, except in accordance with international human rights law.[161] The latter phrase

---

[156] *Constitution of the United Nations Educational, Scientific and Cultural Organization* (16 November 1945) (as amended) art I (1).

[157] *Declaration on the Human Genome and Human Rights*, UNESCO, 29 C/Resolutions (11 November 1997) Preamble.

[158] ibid, art 5.

[159] ibid, arts 7 and 9.

[160] *International Declaration on Human Generic Data*, UNESCO, 32 C/Resolutions (16 October 2003) arts 8–9, 13, 15–16.

[161] *Universal Declaration on Bio-ethics and Human Rights*, UNESCO, 33 C/Resolutions (19 October 2005) arts 7 and 9.

appears to invite the application of the widely agreed three-part tests of legality, necessity and legitimate aim in assessing requests for disclosure of personal data. But despite the framing of UNESCO instruments in human rights parlance, the legal softness, and of course, the apparent nuanced scope, reduce their place in international law.

4.1 1.5. Perils of a Fragmented Approach

As the above survey of the current international legal framework reveals, normative dispersion is prevalent. A fragmented approach to data privacy is problematic on many levels. A more obvious concern is that it results in redundancy of efforts when several UN bodies are involved not only in setting these norms but also in overseeing them. Normative fragmentation creates institutional dispersion, which in turn weakens the overall effectiveness of the international data privacy framework in enhancing the protection of (data) privacy. The problem of normative fragmentation is, however, different from the sectoral and domain-specific approach to data privacy regulation, or at least in the form common in the EU data privacy system.

The EU, which has the most advanced regime for the protection of data privacy, regulates the matter under various instruments. In addition to the GDPR, there are sectoral data privacy instruments. A typical example is the e-Privacy Directive which particularizes data protection rules to the communications sector.[162] Another example is the Data Protection Directive in the field of criminal proceedings and law enforcement which extends protection of data privacy to victims, suspects and witnesses of crimes.[163] Processing of data by EU institutions is also regulated under a separate instrument.[164] But, these instruments operate in a coherent and consistent manner, and that each is not completely isolated from the other. That is not the case with respect to the flurry of international data privacy norms which are deeply fragmented, and almost each instrument is disjointed from the other.

Lack of a unified and coherent framework weakens the potential of the international data protection norms in ensuring uniform protection of data privacy. This is particularly the case when normative dispersion makes applicable rules invisible to relevant adjudicative bodies and data subjects. The HR Committee, for instance, has never referred to either the UN Data Privacy Guidelines or other data

---

[162] Directive (EC) 2002/58 of the European Parliament and of the Council of 12 July 2002 on the Protection of Privacy in the Electronic Communications Sector [2002] OJ L 201/37.

[163] Directive (EU) 2016/680 of the European Parliament and of Council of 27 April 2016 on the Protection of Natural Persons with regard to the Processing of Personal Data by Competent Authorities for the Purposes of the Prevention, Investigation, Detection or Prosecution of Criminal Offenses or the Execution of Criminal Penalties and on the Free Movement of such Data [2016] OJ L 119/89.

[164] Regulation (EU) 2018/1725 of the European Parliament and of Council of 23 October 2018 on the Protection of Natural Persons with regard to the Processing of Personal Data by the Union Institutions, Bodies, Offices and Agencies and on the Free Movement of such Data [2018] OJ L 295/39.

privacy instruments in examining relevant individual communications and periodic reports of States. The lack of a clear and accessible framework of rules has the potential to bury even the patchy rules that guarantee rights of individuals from those who could oversee or invoke them in practice. The problem is that almost every fragmentary data privacy standard does not carry binding legal force, as shall be discussed further below.

4.1.2. Problem of (Over) Soft Legalization

The second normative weakness of the international data privacy framework flows from its exceedingly soft law approach. As shown in the discussion above, not only are data privacy norms diffuse but also that they are carried in soft law instruments. Except for the human right treaties noted above, almost all international data protection instruments are soft law. The obvious concern with soft legalization is that States are at liberty simply to ignore these non-binding rules. At a more general level, excessive soft legalization threatens the international legal order. As Handl and others comment, there is often a concern that excessive soft legalization pursued due to current exigencies may weaken the international legal order.[165] In part, the generally patchy structures of international data privacy law are results of the soft law approach to data privacy.

Excessive soft legalization also gives rise to practical concerns. A primary concern lies not just on the lack of legally binding force but the resultant loss of value in practice. As will be considered in chapter 7, soft law is the most pertinent candidate in reimagining the right to privacy in international law. But the excessive use of soft law tends to reduce the possibility of its rules being implemented at the local level. Precisely this is the problem of the international data privacy framework due to its overly soft approach to legalization. The concern is compounded by the lack of a robust institutional machinery to oversee the implementation of soft rules by States. Where there are monitoring bodies, they are handicapped by structural problems, including lack of adequate monitoring authority. We return to this point later in this chapter.

As alluded to above, the primary concern with excessive soft legalization is that owing to the non-binding nature of soft laws, their legislative goal may not necessarily be met in practice. This, in turn, reduces their practical utility. An illustrative example, in this regard, is the practical utility of the UN Data Privacy Guidelines in meeting their objective of serving as a 'mode law'. The overarching aim of the Guidelines is to provide a prototype for national-level legislation with a minimum set of data privacy guarantees. In adopting the Guidelines, the UNGA merely 'requested' governments on the one hand, and governmental, intergovernmental, and non-governmental organizations on the other hand, to take into account and

---

[165] Guther Handl and others, 'A Hard Look at Soft Law' (1988) 82 Proceedings of the Annual Meeting of the ASIL 371, 377.

respect the Guidelines in their domestic legislation and in the course of their activities respectively.[166] There is, however, little evidence to suggest that the Guidelines have actually been used as benchmarks in several countries that enacted data privacy legislation since the 1990s. In fact, it is only rarely that even instruments adopted within the auspices of the UN invoke the Guidelines as an enabling universal data privacy instrument.

Studies have shown that the EU Data Protection Directive, adopted five years after the Guidelines, instead served as a benchmark instrument for national data privacy laws in Asia, Africa, and Latin America.[167] The surge in data privacy legislation since the early 2000s is mostly dictated by the 'adequacy' requirement of the EU Data Protection Directive. Countries with trade relations with the EU are induced, if not compelled, to adopt a national data protection law that is proximate to European standards.[168] To be sure, accession to the CoE Data Protection Convention is one of the factors that must be taken into account in the 'adequacy' decisions of the EU under the GDPR.[169] Therefore, the recent proliferation of data privacy law worldwide is not—for the most part—a response to the rather universal UN Data Privacy Guidelines.[170]

One may well say that other soft legal instruments, particularly the OECD Privacy Guidelines, have served as a model law in a number of countries.[171] And of course, data privacy legislation in some OECD member States has been inspired by the Guidelines.[172] But, this has to be considered in context. The successes of OECD instruments have a lot to do with the small membership of the organization, and the general ideological convergence among member States.[173] This convergence, added to the principal 'economic' institutional goals of the OECD itself and its privacy guidelines,[174] appears to have paved the way for the wider acceptance of the Guidelines in member States. On the contrary, the UN is home for a diverse

---

[166] See UN Data Privacy Guidelines (n 3) paras 4–5.

[167] See Graham Greenleaf, 'Data Protection in A Globalized Network' in Ian Brown (ed), *Research Handbook on Governance of the Internet* (Edward Elgar 2012) 231.

[168] For the influence in Africa, see Alex Makulilo, 'The Context of Data Privacy in Africa' in Alex Makulilo (ed), *African Data Privacy Laws* (Springer 2016) 18–19.

[169] See *Regulation (EU) 2016/679 of the European Parliament and of the Council of 27 April 2016 on the Protection of Natural Persons with regard to the Processing of Personal Data and on the Free Movement of Such Data* [2016] OJ L 119/1, Recital 105.

[170] Perhaps one exception is that the Guidelines, along with other regional instruments, were 'overtly' taken into account by the Spanish Constitutional Court in its landmark ruling of 2000 that consolidated the 'right to data protection' as a fundamental right. See Gloria Fuster, *The Emergence of Personal Data Protection as a Fundamental Right of the EU* (Springer 2014) 179, citing *STC 292/2000*, de 30 de noviembre de 2000 del Tribunal Constitucional.

[171] See OECD *Guidelines on the Protection of Privacy and Transborder Flows of Personal Data* (23 September 1980) [as updated in 2013].

[172] See, eg, *Australian Privacy Act* 1988 (Cth) preamble. cf Explanatory Memorandum Privacy Bill 1988 (Cth) [1988].

[173] See Michael Kirby, 'The History, Achievement and Future of the 1980 OECD Guidelines on Privacy' (2011) 1 International Data Privacy Law 6, 11 (note that Kirby was a chairperson of the expert committee that drafted the OECD Privacy Guidelines).

[174] ibid, 8.

panoply of States from all corners of the world that exhibit deep ideological, socio-economic and political differences. In the face of such divergence—more so in an area like data privacy that has human rights at its core, States are free to ignore following the UN Data Privacy Guidelines. At the time of writing, close to 150 countries have adopted or are considering some form of data protection bills largely based on European standards.[175] This leaves around fifty States still without any data privacy law proper although they are required, or expected, to adopt one per the UN Data Privacy Guidelines.

Of course, the drafting of the UN Data Privacy Guidelines was influenced by European data privacy instruments, especially the CoE Data Protection Convention, which was adopted in 1981 while the Guidelines were still in gestation. What is more, the primary drafter of the Guidelines, Joinet, was—as noted above—a French data protection official and was involved with the drafting of data protection instruments of both the CoE and the OECD;[176] so European marks in the Guidelines were inevitable. But the Data Privacy Guidelines does also embody some privacy-protective rules that are not to be found in European instruments, or even OECD Guidelines. For instance, the Guidelines' 'principle of accuracy' requires data controllers to make regular accuracy checks, the 'principle of purpose specification' requires publicity of the purpose of the data collection/processing, the 'principle of interested third party access' requires the data subject to be informed of the recipients of data concerning him, and more importantly the Guidelines mandate the application of the principles to international organizations.[177] If States especially those that pursued the European approach really had the aim of introducing more human rights friendly instrument, the UN Data Privacy Guidelines would have been a good starting point, or at least an additional benchmark. Arguably, the primary legislative motive rather was largely economic, or perhaps of mere capitulation. But the soft law nature of the Guidelines, added to the economic incentives of taking the European path, seems to have played a role in limiting the practical utility of the Guidelines.[178]

Yet not only did the Data Privacy Guidelines fail in their mission to serve as a 'model law' for national legislation but also regional instruments enacted subsequently do not appear to consider them an inspiration. The EU Directive of 1995—and its recent replacement, the GDPR—do make reference to the CoE Convention but not to the Guidelines.[179] The Asia Pacific Economic Cooperation (APEC) Privacy Framework follows suit, and notes that it rather relied upon the

---

[175] See, eg, Graham Greenleaf, 'Global Data Privacy Laws 2021: Despite COVID Delays, 145 Laws Show GDPR Dominance' (2021) 169 Privacy Laws and Business International Report 3–5.

[176] See his profile at <http://bit.ly/2lwQFiL>; see also Kirby (n 173) 9.

[177] See UN Data Privacy Guidelines (n 3) paras 2–4 cum part B. For more on this, see Bygrave Lee Bygrave, *Data Privacy Law: An International Perspective* (Oxford University Press 2014) 52–53.

[178] Of a related view, see Bygrave (n 177) 53.

[179] See, eg, GDPR (n 169) Recital 105.

OECD Privacy Guidelines.[180] The absence of any reference to the UN Data Privacy Guidelines is significant given that it is universal instruments well positioned to serve as enabling law for regional and national legislation. Whether this disregard of the Guidelines was a deliberate (in)action is unclear, but it is clear that it played a role in further undermining the practical utility of the Guidelines and putting them off the global map of data privacy lawmaking. This does not, however, provide the complete explanation for the nigh isolation of the Data Privacy Guidelines. As shall be considered later in this chapter, the UN and its relevant bodies also contributed in throwing the Guidelines into disuse.

The exceedingly soft law approach to data privacy legalization further casts on the extent of attention given to the privacy agenda. Uninterrupted but again disjointed resort to soft legalization, and without ever making efforts towards progressive development of international data privacy law is problematic. More so when one considers the established pattern of gradual transition to hard law in other areas of international regulation. Soft law often serves as a precursor to and a way of short-circuiting hard law.[181] In line with this tradition, several international soft legal instruments, including Guidelines have been translated into—or have formed an important part of—subsequent hard laws in the same area. An example is the Guidelines on Environmental Impact Assessment of 1987 which were later incorporated substantially into the Convention on Environmental Impact Assessment in a Trans-border Context of 1991.[182] This has not materialized in the case of the Data Privacy Guidelines. On the contrary, what we now have—as noted have—is a partially watered-down 'lite' version of the Guidelines.

At times, the limited practical utility of the Data Privacy Guidelines—and equally other relevant data privacy instruments, is attributed to the timing of the adoption of the Guidelines. This viewpoint holds that the Guidelines were adopted (in 1990) long after the OECD Privacy Guidelines (1980) and the CoE Data Protection Convention (1981) had served as benchmark for national legislation in many countries.[183] In short, that the Guidelines were late-comers means not much domestic legislation left to inspire. But two obvious reasons cast doubt on this observation. First, owing to the limited memberships of both the OECD and CoE, there were over a hundred States (probably including some European States) without a fully fledged data privacy law by the time the Guidelines were adopted. And, the doors for accession to the CoE Data Protection Convention to non-member States opened up rather recently, in 2008.[184] That the OECD Privacy

[180] See APEC Privacy Framework (2014) Preamble, para 5.

[181] See Leo Gross, Essays on International Law and Organization (Springer Vol I/II, 2014) 176.

[182] Convention on Environmental Impact Assessment in a Transboundary Context, opened for signature 1 March 1991, 1989 UNTS 309 (entered into force 10 September 1997).

[183] See Paul De Hert and Vagelis Papakonstantinou, 'Three Scenarios for International Governance of Data Privacy: Towards an International Data Privacy Organization, Preferably a UN Agency?' (2013) 9 I/S: A Journal of Law and Policy for the Information Society 271, 282.

[184] See Committee of Ministers Decision CM/Del/Dec/2008 (2 July 2008) 1031/10.2.

Guidelines are also soft law instruments meant that its members were, or are, at liberty not to follow the Guidelines, but they did (mostly) in practice anyway.[185] Perhaps, the generally wider reception of the OECD Privacy Guidelines was also facilitated by other structural-institutional push factors, including the underlying Convention that created the organization. Kirby notes, in this regard, that the Privacy Guidelines 'on the whole, have been taken seriously by the countries that are parties to the OECD Convention'.[186]

Second, most data privacy pieces of legislation enacted since the late 1990s and early 2000s, especially in Africa and Asia as well as partly in Latin America, as noted above, are largely influenced by the EU Data Protection Directive of 1995, which is more progressive, and detailed in its regulatory patterns, than the OECD Guidelines. Therefore, the 'timing of adoption' argument cannot persuasively explain away why the UN Data Privacy Guidelines failed in spurring data privacy legislation. Instead, a host of factors, including the soft law nature of the Guidelines is to blame for their resultant limited impact.

Overall, added to the low normative quality of UN data privacy standards considered in what follows, the excessive soft law path taken by the UN has significantly limited the practical utility and efficacy of UN data privacy norms globally.

4.1.3. Problem of Juridical Quality

International data privacy law has a problem of poor normative quality in contrast with its regional counterparts. This problem of normative quality has two dimensions. One is that the data privacy norms are restricted to generic and high-level provisions. Unlike the regulatory and bureaucratic nature of data privacy legislation, present data privacy standards are contained in high-level data privacy principles. The only exception is the recent intra-agency policies of UN specialized and related agencies, which relatively reflect the substance of modern data privacy instruments. A common challenge associated with the overly brief and general nature of, for instance the UN Data Privacy Guidelines is that it opens the door for conflicting interpretations.[187] This is exacerbated by the lack of basic interpretative guidance in the Guidelines which, in turn, may lead to divergent transposition into domestic law by States. Basic weaknesses of this sort are no less significant in causing uncertainties in the application of the Guidelines. But more generally, the high-level nature of international data privacy instruments means that mechanical regulatory details of data privacy law will not be provided. The data privacy framework is less holistic would mean that its legislative goals cannot be met.

---

[185] Kirby (n 173) 11.
[186] ibid.
[187] See Perry Keller, *European and International Media Law: Liberal Democracy, Trade and the New Media* (Oxford University Press 2011) 350.

A similar observation applies with equal force to the other international data privacy instruments discussed above. In relation to genetic data for example, the CoE has a progressive regime than relevant UNESCO instruments. It regulates the matter through a binding instrument, the Convention on Human Rights and Biomedicine of 1997.[188] The Convention, which currently has twenty-nine State parties, recognizes the right to privacy in the context of health data and envisages grounds of limitation identical to ones provided in Article 8(2) of the European Convention on Human Rights and Fundamental Freedoms (ECHR).[189] The Convention further requires State parties to pass implementing domestic legislation and to provide remedial measures such as injunctions, compensation and even sanctions.[190] The Convention is elaborated in additional protocols that touch on data privacy in the context of biomedical research and genetic testing.[191]

The second aspect of poor juridical quality is that international data privacy norms have now become obsolete in the light of significant developments worldwide. Modern data privacy principles, data subject rights, and the corresponding obligations of data controllers, processors, and data protection authorities that evolved over the years are absent in many of the international instruments. This concerns also those international instruments introduced relatively recently. Little reform has occurred through UN processes to revitalize already existing norms in light of new developments in the digital age, and to make them fit for purpose. Not only is legislative reform lacking but also progressive development through the existing but dispersed institutional arrangements is unlikely.[192] This stands in stark contrast to the continued reform introduced in most regional systems, including the EU, CoE, and even the AU which has introduced an all-in-one data protection treaty.[193] The European data privacy framework has particularly been under continuous review that introduced a number of progressive data privacy standards.[194]

With no major reforms so far, and uncertain future reforms in the horizon, it is safe to state that the international data privacy framework, especially the Data Privacy Guidelines is slightly 'obsolete' as they stand.[195] In the ultimate analysis,

---

[188] *Convention on Human Rights and Biomedicine*, opened for signature 4 April 1997, 164 ETS (entered into force 1 December 1999).

[189] ibid, art 26 cum art 5.

[190] ibid, art 23.

[191] See, eg, *Additional Protocol to the Convention on Human Rights and Biomedicine Concerning Biomedical Research*, opened for signature 25 January 2005, 195 CETS (entered into force 1 September 2007) art 25 cum art 13(2)(iv); *Additional Protocol to the Convention on Human Rights and Biomedicine Concerning Genetic Testing for Health Purposes*, opened for signature 27 November 2008, 203 CETS (entered into force 1 July 2018) art 16 cum art 13(d).

[192] See below on the problem of institutional dispersion.

[193] See *AU Convention on Cybersecurity and Personal Data Protection Convention* (June 2014) ch II.

[194] See, eg, GDPR (n 169) arts 33, 25, 35; see also *Modernized Convention for the Protection of Individuals with Regard to the Processing of Personal Data*, opened for signature 10 October 2018, CETS No 223 (not yet in force).

[195] Of a related view, Cristina Casagran, *Global Data Protection in the Field of Law Enforcement: An EU Perspective* (Routledge 2016) 217.

the fact that the framework is already outmoded compared to European law means that its role in shaping the progressive development of international law will be, and has been, limited. To some degree, the ongoing discourse on right to privacy in the digital age touches on data privacy themes, but the influence of universal data privacy standards is yet to be felt. As shall be shown in chapter 5, substantive elements of Resolutions adopted as part of the discourse bear more of, as they should, marks of European data privacy law.

4.2. Problems of Institutionalization

The dispersive approach to data privacy, discussed above, is worsened by deep institutional and structural gaps. The principal shortcoming is the lack of clear institutional arrangements for overseeing the implementation of existing data privacy norms. Owing to the dispersed nature of existing norms, the monitoring responsibility falls on various bodies. The institutional arrangement for the monitoring of existing data privacy rules is as fragmented as the rules are. The other institutional weakness is that these various bodies tasked to monitor scattered information rules lack the requisite monitoring capacity that would allow them to ensure adequate respect for and protection of data privacy. This section considers these two limitations.

4.2.1. Institutional Fragmentation

Present institutional arrangements in the international data privacy framework are devolved among several entities. Data privacy principles embodied in human right treaties, for instance, are overseen by the respective treaty bodies. The Committee on the Rights of Persons with Disabilities, although yet to apply data privacy principles embodied in the Convention, is responsible for adjudging individual communications, examining periodic reports of State parties and even adopting GCs on relevant provisions of the Convention.[196] UNESCO instruments relevant to data privacy similarly are monitored by the International Bioethics Committee and the Intergovernmental Bioethics Committee.[197] In contrast, the CoE's counterpart to the UNESCO Declarations, the Convention on Human Rights and Biomedicine, is supervised by a dedicated Steering Committee which further benefits from the 'advisory' role of the ECtHR.[198] Indeed, the ECtHR has adjudged several cases that touch upon the Convention—and to that extent, it

---

[196] See CRD (n 51) art 34.
[197] See, eg, Declaration on the Human Genome and Human Rights (n 157) art 24; see more details at <http://bit.ly/2mIyFCb>.
[198] See Human Rights and Biomedicine Convention (n 188) art 29.

could be said that provisions of the Convention are also indirectly enforceable by the ECtHR.[199]

The institutional problem is slightly different when it comes to the UN Data Privacy Guidelines, which leaves matters of implementation to national governments. The 'model law' nature of the Guidelines naturally means that no central monitory body is envisaged. But the soft law nature of the Guidelines, as noted above, makes it easy for States to undermine the requirements of installing a national body to oversee legislation enacted based on the Guidelines. The former UN Commission on Human Rights had put in place a 'follow-up' procedure by which the Secretary-General would monitor the implementation of the Guidelines by States and international organizations.[200] At a practical level, the follow-up procedure was symbolic in that States and international organizations would simply be requested to provide information or updates on the progress of implementing the Guidelines to the Secretary-General, and the latter would prepare reports based on the information so received. What makes this a symbolic procedure is that States or even international organizations would simply report compliance, even without taking any measure. Or at worse, they may not even reply to the requests of the Secretary-General.

While the follow-up essentially was a tentative monitoring mechanism, it still had the potential to push the adoption of domestic law based on the Guidelines' 'orientations'. But the UN had not tapped into this potential, and the procedure was abandoned without any success. Various reports of the Secretary-General suggest that the procedure was not taken seriously. A 1998 report, for instance, states that no information has been provided by States as to whether they have translated the Guidelines into national legislation.[201] But the Commission decided a year later to terminate the follow-up procedure because 'the applicable guidelines are progressively being taken into consideration by States'.[202] Instead, it instructed the Secretary-General to focus on ensuring the implementation of the Guidelines by relevant UN organs. This comes as a rather striking decision because most data

---

[199] For a summary of cases where principles of the Convention have been considered, see Pere Vilanova, 'The Right to Privacy in the Case Law of the ECtHR' in *Proceedings of the High-Level Seminar on International Case Law in Bioethics: Insight and Foresight* (2016) 21 et seq.

[200] See Question of the Follow-up to the Guidelines for the Regulation of Computerized Personal Data Files, Commission on Human Rights Decision 1995/114, UN Doc E/CN.4/DEC/1995/114 (8 March 1995); see also Human Rights and the Follow-up to the Guidelines for the Regulation of Computerized Personal Data Files, Commission on Human Rights Decision 1997/122, UN Doc E/CN.4/1997/L.103 (16 April 1997).

[201] See Question of the Follow-up to the Guidelines for the Regulation of Computerized Personal Data Files, Report of the Secretary-General prepared Pursuant to Commission Decision 1997/122, UN Doc E/CN.4/1999/88 (18 November 1998) para 5.

[202] See Human Rights and the Follow-up to the Guidelines for the Regulation of Computerized Personal Data Files, Commission on Human Rights Decision 1999/109, UN Doc E/CN.4/1999/167 (28 April 1999).

privacy laws adopted in the 1990s, as noted above, including the EU Directive of 1995 are barely based on the UN Data Privacy Guidelines.

It is clear that the 'follow-up procedure' was meant to be a temporary procedure. Little has, however, followed it in terms of creating a proper monitoring body, be it by salvaging existing oversight bodies or installing a new one. A more pertinent monitory body, at least for overseeing the UN Data Privacy Guidelines, would have been the HR Committee, regardless of its institutional weaknesses discussed in chapter 2. This is for two reasons. One is that the Committee is responsible for overseeing the ICCPR, the major binding multilateral treaty that guarantees the right to privacy to which data privacy is one area of protection. The genealogical link between the Data Privacy Guidelines and the ICCPR, as discussed at the outset, lends weight to this point. The Committee could even justify basing its data privacy jurisprudence on the UN Data Privacy Guidelines by holding that they constitute 'authoritative interpretations' of the ICCPR's privacy provision. As will be considered in the context of post-Snowden UN Privacy Resolutions in chapter 5, the 'authoritative interpretation' argument draws from earlier doctrinal arguments that the UDHR is an 'authoritative interpretation' of the UN Charter's human rights provisions—and hence creates binding legal obligations on States.[203] Because the UN Data Privacy Guidelines is adopted through the Resolutions of the UNGA, like the UDHR, the authoritative interpretation analogy seems plausible.

Second, the Committee has taken steps to embrace data privacy principles, to some degree, through its GC 16 and concluding observations, as discussed in chapter 2. These principles are not, however, articulated fully, and as such, are incomplete. The UN Data Privacy Guidelines would have assisted by supplementing and further stimulating the Committee's data privacy jurisprudence. In examining States' periodic reports or considering individual communications, the Committee could invoke principles of the Guidelines in assessing compliance with the privacy provision of the ICCPR. This is also unlikely to raise a question of legitimacy since the Guidelines, as a soft law adopted by consensus, apply—or are at least addressed—to all member States of the UN. But the Committee has never made a reference to the Guidelines.

Ironically, the Committee often refers to and sometimes relies upon the case law of the ECtHR on data privacy issues. For instance, in the recent case of *NK v The Netherlands*, the Committee drew substantially from the decision of the Court in the case of *S and Marper v UK*, which concerned the collection and storage of cellular samples in a criminal context.[204] In contrast, the ECtHR's reference to the HR

---

[203] See Obed Asamoah, 'The Legal Effect of Resolutions of the General Assembly' (1965) 3 Columbia Journal of Transnational Law 210, 223.

[204] HR Committee, *NK v The Netherlands*, Communication No 2326/2013 (10 January 2018) paras 9.3–9.4, footnotes 13–14, 22. It is also interesting to note here that while the author's application to the ECtHR was initially declared inadmissible by the Strasbourg Court, the HR Committee found violation under art 17 of the ICCPR.

Committee's jurisprudence is rare. When it has done so, it is often in a barely decisive manner. In the data privacy front, the UN Data Privacy Guidelines has been referred to in a recent Grand Chamber judgment of the Strasbourg Court in a case relating to the workplace surveillance of employees' digital communication, but with no visible influence in the outcome.[205] It is, however, interesting to note that this case has referred to and, to some extent, relied upon the ILO Code of Practice on the Protection of Workers' Personal Data.[206]

In considering the termination of the monitoring procedure, perhaps for the wrong reasons, and reluctance of treaty bodies to heed to the Data Privacy Guidelines, it is safe to state that the UN may have played the major part in throwing the Guidelines into disuse and practical futility. And of course, even most recent UN engagements with privacy in the wake of the Snowden revelations also have completely overlooked the Guidelines. All UN Privacy Resolutions make no reference to the Guidelines despite the fact that they purport to cover data privacy.[207] Reports of the SRP do not sufficiently engage UN data privacy instruments. In his report to the HR Council for instance, the Special Rapporteur 'encourages' countries recently adopting national data privacy law to ensure that the 'minimum standards' set out in the CoE Data Protection Convention are met.[208] One would expect the UN Data Privacy Guidelines referred to, instead, not least because it sets minimum guarantees, and importantly is a UN instrument.[209] In that sense, the universal data privacy instruments, particularly the Data Privacy Guidelines, are abandoned even by the UN itself.[210]

In contrast, the institutional arrangements put in place in Europe are much advanced. The system by which each data privacy instrument is monitored is well tailored to avoid redundancy of efforts as indicated below in broad strokes. Moreover,

---

[205] ECtHR, *Barbulescu v Romania*, Application No 61496/08 (5 September 2017) para 37.

[206] ibid, paras 38–40.

[207] A 2017 Resolution of the Human Council, however, breaks the trend, and mentions the UN Data Privacy Guidelines, which might in due course put the Guidelines in sight. See *The Right to Privacy in the Digital Age*, HRC Res 34/7, 34th sess, Agenda Item 3, UN Doc A/HRC/RES/34/7 (22 March 2017) Preamble, para 5.

[208] Report of the Special Rapporteur on the Right to Privacy, Joseph Cannataci, UN Doc A/HRC/34/60 (24 February 2017) para 9. See also Report of the Special Rapporteur on the Right to Privacy, Joseph Cannataci, UN Doc A/HRC/40/63 (27 February 2019) para 47 (recommending UN member States to incorporate principles contained in Article 11 of the Modernized Convention).

[209] The October 2017 report of the Special Rapporteur to the UNGA does refer to the Guidelines but in a clearly tangential manner after the OECD Guidelines (whose principles the report details) and the CoE Data Protection Convention. See Report of the Special Rapporteur on the Right to Privacy, Joseph Cannataci, UN Doc A/72/540 (19 October 2017) paras 71–72. A recent report of the OHCHR likewise notes that the CoE Data Protection Convention 'can direct the design of adequate policy instruments'. See *The Right to Privacy in the Digital Age*, Report of the High Commissioner for Human Rights, UN Doc A/HRC/48/31 (13 September 2021) para 28.

[210] Of a related point, see Casagran (n 195) 217. In another report co-authored for UNESCO, Cannataci mentions the UN Data Privacy Guidelines as part of the international framework for the protection of privacy. See Joseph Cannataci and others, *Privacy, Free Expression and Transparency: Redefining their New Boundaries in the Digital Age* (UNESCO Series on Internet Freedom 2016) 36.

although implementation of these instruments is largely local—ie, undertaken by State parties under national legislation, the hard law nature of the data privacy instruments makes it compulsory to put in place the requisite institutional framework. At the most basic level, member States are required to install an independent national data protection authority to oversee the relevant legislation, and to entertain complaints from individuals. Additionally, European data subjects have the option of pursuing their claims in courts. Decisions of national data protection authorities are also appealable to domestic courts.[211]

In the EU framework, layers of institutions are involved in enforcing and overseeing data privacy laws. The Court of Justice of the European Union (CJEU), for instance, will be involved in individual cases when domestic courts refer cases for a preliminary ruling.[212] A member State may also be sued by the European Commission before the Court for failing to respect EU legislation, including data protection law. It may even annul legislation found to violate fundamental rights, including the right to data protection, based on action for annulment brought by the Commission, a member State or even individuals directly affected by a specific legislation.[213] A more recent annulment decision by the Court was made against the Data Retention Directive whose 'disproportionate' retention obligations were found to violate the right to data protection recognized under the EU Charter.[214]

The EU's General Court also has a jurisdiction to hear and decide on cases brought by individuals against EU agencies or against regulatory instruments.[215] Other supervisory mechanisms are also available. For instance, compliance with data protection rules by EU institutions is monitored by the Data Protection Supervisor.[216] The 'Data Protection Board' under the GDPR also has some supervisory roles in ensuring harmonized application of data protection rules throughout the Union.[217] That data protection is now a fundamental right in the EU also means that the Fundamental Rights Agency would also be involved in the web of the governance framework. Furthermore, the GDPR makes it mandatory to appoint 'Data Protection Officers' as internal supervisory authorities within each body engaged in the processing of personal data.[218] These layers of monitoring bodies enable higher protection of data privacy rights of EU citizens. In the CoE,

---

[211] See, eg, *Additional Protocol to the Convention for the Protection of Individuals with regard to Automatic Processing of Personal Data, regarding Supervisory Authorities and Transborder Data Flows*, opened for signature 8 November 2001, 181 ETS (entered into force 1 July 2004) art 1(4).

[212] See, eg, *Treaty of Lisbon, Amending the Treaty on EU and the Treaty Establishing the European Community*, opened for signature 13 December 2007 [2007] OJ C 306/1 (entered into force 1 December 2009) art 9F.

[213] ibid.

[214] See *Digital Rights Ireland and Stetlinger and others v Minister for Communication and others* (C-293/12 and C-594/12) [2014] ECLI 238.

[215] See eg, Treaty of Lisbon (n 212) art 9F.

[216] See GDPR (n 169).

[217] ibid, arts 68–76.

[218] ibid, arts 37–39.

there is no supranational body tasked to enforce or monitor the Data Protection Convention. Legitimacy questions aside, there is arguably a possibility for individuals to invoke data privacy principles of the Convention when lodging complaints before the ECtHR. Since the ECtHR has considered many cases that concern protection of data privacy based on widely accepted data privacy principles, individuals could invoke the Convention directly before the Court.[219]

In conclusion, the international data privacy framework lags far behind when it comes to an institutional arrangement for monitoring implementation. The problem is not just in the lack of clearly designated monitoring bodies but also that already existing UN bodies such as treaty bodies have not been progressive in applying existing norms in practice. The discontinuation of the 'follow-up' procedure, despite its limitations, further suggests the general reluctance, or lack of attention, at the UN towards data privacy as one area of protection. Now that universal data privacy standards are largely obsolete means that existing monitoring bodies like the HR Committee are better off to look across Europe, notwithstanding the question of competence that comes with it, until and unless the ongoing UN privacy discourse leads to a robust instrument of some sort.

4.2.2. Monitoring Challenges

The second institutional limitation relates to the weak monitoring capacity of the various bodies tasked to oversee the plethora of international data privacy standards. Like in the case of treaty bodies, the enforcement of UNESCO instruments falls in the hand of mostly part-time independent experts. The International Bioethics Committee, for instance, is a body of thirty-six independent experts elected by the Director General of the UNESCO for a four-year term, and convenes at least once in a year.[220] The Committee is basically a deliberative body that offers recommendations to the UNESCO on matters of life sciences.[221] Unlike the European regime, there is no body with the power to make enforceable determinations on complaints lodged by individuals. Structural problems that beset treaty bodies such as the part-time nature of the role and frequent reshuffles add up to the lack of adequate monitoring powers. CoE's Consultative Committee on Data Protection has largely recommendatory roles,[222] but the existence of the

---

[21]   See Graham Greenleaf, 'A World Data Privacy Treaty? "Globalisation" and "Modernisation" of Council of Europe Convention 108' in Norman Witzleb and others (eds), *Emerging Challenges in Privacy Law: Comparative Perspectives* (Cambridge University Press 2014) 100. Recent examples of cases adjudged by the ECtHR that involved data privacy principles include ECtHR, *LH v Latvia*, Application No 520 9/07 (29 April 2014) [concerning processing of health data]; ECtHR, *Uzun v Germany*, Application No 5623/05 (2 September 2010) [concerning processing of location data]. Moreover, the ECtHR routinely makes reference to and relies upon Data Protection Convention 108.

[22]   See details at <http://bit.ly/2mIyFCb>.

[22]   ibid.

[22]   See Modernized Data Protection Convention (n 194) art 18.

ECtHR provides a safety net. That is not the case in the international data privacy framework.

Data protection policies of the UNHCR and the IOM envisage relatively strong monitoring mechanisms. For instance, they mandate appointment of a 'Data Protection Officer' at the headquarters with the ultimate responsibility of oversight and 'Data Protection Focal Points' at each country office.[223] Complaints against non-compliance with the policies could also be lodged to higher offices/officers in the organizations' hierarchy, ie to the Inspector General's Office under the UNHCR and the Office of Legal Affairs under the IOM Manuals.[224] But the 'intra-agency' and essentially sectoral nature of these policies undercut the potential of these instruments to serve as a truly international institutional framework.

The SRP is a newly added layer to the UN data privacy institutional arrangement. Its roles can generally be grouped into three: providing intellectual guidance, facilitating multi-level dialogue, and monitoring developments on the right to privacy.[225] On top of being a part-time role, the mandate's effectiveness in addressing the institutional deficit is hampered by a number of structural factors, including lack of resources and non-adjudicative nature of the role. That limits the potential of the mandate in filling the institutional void. But as shall be explored in chapter 8, its roles could be reoriented towards steering the already warmed-up discourse at the UN on the right to privacy in the digital age. The mandate could, for instance, be tasked to chair the envisioned privacy forum where current and emergent privacy challenges are regularly discussed among all stakeholders.

5. Conclusion

This chapter examined boundaries of international data privacy law in protecting digital privacy. It has shown that the present framework suffers from deep normative fragmentation, lack of progressive privacy standards, and a weak institutional machinery. These weaknesses of the data privacy framework are mainly by-products of Cold War politics and the UN's generally reluctant approach to privacy in general. The chapter further uncovered that relevant UN bodies have played a role in undermining practical value of the data privacy framework. The HR Committee's privacy jurisprudence, for instance, reveals no reference to UN data privacy standards. This adds up to the thin privacy jurisprudence of the Committee developed under the ICCPR. The international data privacy framework, therefore, remains buried, and without any practical utility. With the human

---

[223] See UNHCR Data Protection Policy (n 126) Part 7.
[224] See IOM Data Protection Manual (n 128) Principle 12.
[225] See *The Right to Privacy in the Digital Age*, HRC Res 28/16, 28th sess, Agenda Item 3, UN Doc A/HRC/RES/28/16 (26 March 2015) para 4.

right to privacy system yet to properly address data privacy themes—and with a rather parasitic and yet patchy data privacy framework, the case for a modern and comprehensive data privacy treaty may seem plausible. But the feasibility and desirability of a global data privacy treaty is doubtful. As outlined in chapter 1 of this book, any hard legalization approach to digital privacy will meet stiff resistance from different corners, but it is also undesirable. The best way forward is, as shall be shown in chapter 7, is to follow the unifying approach to privacy pursued in the ongoing UN privacy discourse. A soft law that brings under one roof various privacy norms, including key data privacy norms, will fill the missing data privacy piece in international law.

PART II

GLOBAL PRIVACY INITIATIVES AND INTERNATIONAL LAW

This part explores the prospect of three global privacy initiatives in attending to international law's privacy problem laid out in part I. Chapter 4 takes up the first of these initiatives: Internet bills of rights. It argues that the progressive vision for privacy in these initiatives notwithstanding, the role of Internet bills of rights in reimagining international law is limited by a host of conceptual and practical challenges. It then submits that a more promising role for the Internet bill of rights movement is 'catalytic' by which it may shape the 'normative direction' of international privacy law reform. Chapter 5 addresses the second initiative: the ongoing discourse at the United Nations on the 'right to privacy in the digital age'. It investigates the extent to which the discourse addresses gaps in international law. The chapter argues that while Resolutions adopted as part of this discourse have little to offer in lessening gaps in the existing regime, they offer the foundation for future reform efforts. Chapter 6 examines the prospect of transnational data protection standards, especially the Council of Europe data protection framework, in evolving into an international law response to the 'privacy problem' in the digital age. The chapter argues that the slow pace of accession to the Convention by non-CoE member States thus far means enriching and shaping international data privacy jurisprudence is where its most tangible potential lies.

4

Internet Bills of Rights

1. Introduction

This chapter examines the first of global privacy initiatives that tend to envisage a progressive vision for the right to privacy: Internet Bills of Rights (IBRs). Dating roughly back to the early days of the Internet, initiatives for IBRs seek to recast human rights, principles, and governance norms in light of the new realities of the digital age. But the Snowden revelations marked a significant milestone in the evolution of the IBRs project. Not only has it garnered significant attention among policymakers and civil society groups but also appeared to maintain a momentum. In a memorable remark, inventor of the web Sir Tim Berners-Lee called for an IBRs that would be a 'global constitution' for the Internet.[1] Far from a constitutional document envisioned by Berners-Lee, the World Wide Web Foundation—which he founded—launched, instead, several years later a global plan of action called 'Contract for the Web' that offers a series of recommendations to governments, the private sector and citizens.[2] Be it in reaction to another high-profile privacy scandal or the rise of new technological advances, the IBRs tradition has continued.

Among the rights commonly addressed in IBRs initiatives is the right to privacy but in a manner that departs significantly from the normative structures of the right in international law. The chapter explores the role of IBRs in reimagining international law of privacy in the digital age. To that effect, the chapter considers the extent to which the new contours of the right to privacy envisioned in IBRs entrench, elaborate, or clarify international law, or even reinforce developing privacy norms. As shown in chapters 2 and 3, international privacy law is not largely fit for purpose in protecting digital privacy. This chapter discusses the role of IBRs in addressing weak structures of international privacy law. The argument develops in three steps.

First, this chapter demonstrates that the IBRs project is unlikely to develop into a freestanding international law response to the 'privacy problem'. This is mainly due to the diffuse and momentary nature of the overall IBRs project, which further erodes the desirability and feasibility of a global IBRs. The adoption (and tabling) of IBRs legislation only in a handful of countries so far, and mainly in reaction

---

[1] Jemima Kiss, An Online Magna Carta: Berners-Lee Calls for Bill of Rights for Web (The Guardian, 12 March 2014) <https://bit.ly/3AMIHtv>.
[2] *Contract for the Web* (World Wide Web Foundation 2019).

Privacy and the Role of International Law in the Digital Age. Kinfe Yilma, Oxford University Press. © Kinfe Yilma 2023.
DOI 10.1093/oso/9780192887290.003.0004

to the shock of the Snowden debacle, adds little in terms of progressively developing an international IBRs. Post-Snowden developments such as the Cambridge Analytica scandal, the Covid-19 pandemic, and the proliferation of Artificial Intelligence (AI) systems likewise perpetuated the momentary nature of the IBRs project. Conceptual ambiguities in many IBRs initiatives further weaken the 'freestanding' role of IBRs in international law.

Second, the chapter shows that the other possible role of IBRs is 'contributory' in that it may shape the methodological and normative directions of other ongoing or future reform initiatives. This flows from the characteristic feature of IBRs in cross-fertilizing developing privacy norms drawn from multiple sources. As this—and the next chapter on the ongoing discourse on the right to privacy in the digital age at the United Nations (UN)—shall demonstrate, marks of IBRs, shoehorned through submissions of civil society groups, are slightly visible in the series of UN Privacy Resolutions as well as the accompanying thematic reports. However, the extent to which IBRs have so far informed the ongoing UN privacy discourse is limited. This reduces the contributory role of IBRs in making international privacy law fit for purpose in the digital age.

Third, the chapter then argues that because IBRs is unlikely to result in anything tangible on its own or through cross-fertilization, the prime significance of IBRs is 'catalytic' by which its progressive vision shapes the form and content of a pragmatic approach to international privacy law. Chapters 7 and 8 explore how aspects of the IBRs project may form part of such an approach, particularly in unpacking the scope and meaning of the right to privacy in international law.[3] As this chapter will show, the significance of IBRs initiatives lies in the way in which they reimagine the right to privacy in the digital context. Most IBRs envisage the right to privacy in an elaborate manner, in contrast with vaguely charged privacy provisions of international law.

For the sake of convenience and to capture emerging terminologies in the literature, the chapter uses the terms IBRs, IBRs project, IBRs movement, and digital constitutionalism interchangeably.[4] Appendix 1 provides a full text of the Italian Declaration of Internet Rights for ease of reference.

---

[3] The term 'catalytic role' is borrowed from Brownlie by which he refers to the potential of legal instruments like Resolutions (and judicial decisions) in provoking further development of law. See, eg, Ian Brownlie, 'Legal Status of Natural Resources in International Law' (1979) 162 Recueil des Cours 1, 261 (noting the decisive 'catalytic effect' of soft law in provoking development in state practice).

[4] See, eg, Dennis Redeker and others, 'Towards Digital Constitutionalism? Mapping Attempts to Craft an Internet Bill of Rights' (2018) 80 International Communication Gazette 302 (describing multilevel IBRs initiatives as digital constitutionalism); Francesca Musiani, 'The Internet Bill of Rights: A Way to Reconcile Natural Freedoms and Regulatory Needs?' (2009) 6 Scripted 505 (describing the initiatives as a 'project'); for reference to IBRs as a 'movement', see Kinfe Yilma, 'Bill of Rights for the 21st Century: Some Lessons from the Internet Bill of Rights Movement' (2022) 26 The International Journal of Human Rights 701.

2. Making Sense of Internet Bills of Rights

As a deeply decentralized and sporadic movement, the legal nature and scope of the multi-level initiatives for IBRs are little known. Through a holistic analysis of IBRs initiatives, this section seeks to fill this void in three respects. First, it offers a brief account of how IBRs emerged in the past few decades as a constitutional project at various levels and in different forms. Second, it lays out the major areas of convergence emerging in the IBRs movement. As shall be shown, despite inevitable differences between initiatives pursued by different actors—and for various interests, the IBRs project increasingly exhibits convergence into a set of rights, principles, and governance norms. Third, this section considers the miscellany of sources from which initiatives for IBRs are drawn and manifold legal forms they take. Because IBRs are issued by various actors, including governments, civil society groups, private actors, and international organizations, they come in different legal forms, be it as a political declaration or legislation.

2.1. Origins of a Constitutional Project

The origins of the various initiatives for IBRs date back to the early days of the Internet. With a typical declaratory tone, these initiatives sought to uphold the protection of human rights to the then expanding cyberspace. The unprecedented capabilities of Information and Communication Technologies (ICTs) stirred concern that human rights would not adequately be protected in the new space. While the very nomenclature 'bill of rights' suggests the constitutional aim of these initiatives both in guaranteeing rights and setting limits to power, the initial choice of the terms was merely for symbolic purposes. Drawing on the English Bill of Rights (1689), the American Bill of Rights (1791)—and recently the 'Magna Carta' (1215), proponents of IBRs seek to symbolically assert human rights on the Internet, rather than to strictly enact them.[5] In that sense, the IBRs project may be taken as an attempt to offer a digital supplement to the global constitutionalization of human rights that took place after the Second World War. In the light of the new contexts of the digital space, it seeks to particularize the (international) human rights system to a set of rights and principles that require some unique rendition.

Unlike what its name might suggest, the 'IBRs project' is not a unified and coherent digital right movement. Rather, it is a collective label meant to capture a range of digital constitutionalism initiatives worldwide that often emerge in different contexts and fora.[6] As shall be discussed below, these initiatives emerged in

---

[5] See Stefano Rodotà, 'A Bill of Rights for the Internet Universe' (2008) 21 The Federalist Debate 15, 16–17. The term 'Magna Carta' has been used, in the context of IBRs, by inventor of the web Tim Berners-Lee in the wake of the Snowden debacle. See Kiss (n 1).

[6] See Musiani (n 4) 505–06, 510–11.

varying contexts and disparate processes but with some commonality of purpose. The growing judicial reference to these initiatives—and of course, the adoption of IBRs legislation in some jurisdictions—appear to gradually pull these initiatives towards a coherent whole, however. The disunity of goals that epitomized its initial path is gradually lessening. This is further emboldened by the half-hearted embrace of the IBRs project by various inter-governmental processes, including at the UN, the European Union (EU), and the Council of Europe (CoE).

The United States is sometimes considered a pioneer in adopting the first 'bill of rights for the computer age' when it introduced the Code of Fair Information Practices in 1973.[7] But the Code was merely a soft law that codifies data privacy principles which were then being enacted into law in some European countries, and as such, has little resemblance to typical IBRs considered in this chapter. Since the late 1980s, various actors including individual activists, media organizations, civil society groups, and academics have launched declarations of rights, principles, and manifestos that claim rights on the Internet.[8] Civil society organizations have particularly played a key role in championing IBRs since the early days of the web. The most influential IBRs initiative emerged at the Internet Governance Forum (IGF) in 2006, which has since inspired, as shall be noted below, other similar initiatives at various levels. The Snowden revelations, however, came as an important milestone in the history of the IBRs project. Not only did new typical exhortatory initiatives emerge but also that the IBRs project has slightly changed its course, especially in terms of inspiring some concrete measures at national, regional, and international levels.

In the years after the revelations, Brazil and Italy have enacted pieces of legislation that embody elements of IBRs. While these countries have long been supporters of IBRs at the IGF,[9] the enactment of national IBRs legislation has barely been a course of action they envisioned. Similar initiatives are taking foot in other countries such as Cambodia, Nigeria, the Philippines, and Guatemala. IBRs have also recently gained traction in some national and regional courts, as shall be considered later in this chapter. At the international level, IBRs are also slightly shaping the ongoing discussion at the UN on the 'right to privacy in the digital age', where elements of IBRs inform, to a certain extent, the content of the latest Privacy Resolutions. As noted above, the IBRs project postulates the right to privacy in a more nuanced and specific manner. The chapter returns to discuss the way in

---

[7] See Simson Garfinkel, *Database Nation: The Death of Privacy in the 21st Century* (O'Reilly 2000) 12; the text of the Code is available at <http://bit.ly/1CVSJmd>.

[8] Writing in 2014, Rodotà—who is one of the pioneers in the IBRs project—reported the existence of at least eighty-seven IBRs proposals worldwide. See Stefano Rodotà, Towards a Declaration of Internet Rights (European Area of Freedom, Security and Justice, 18 November 2014) <https://bit.ly/2IuWmxw>.

[9] See, eg, *Joint Declaration (of the Minister of Culture of Brazil and Undersecretary of Communication of Italy) on Internet Rights*, The Second Internet Governance Forum, Rio de Janeiro, 12–15 November 2007 (13 November 2007) <https://bit.ly/2qiWvuI>.

which the right to privacy is articulated in IBRs documents after having discussed immediately below common threads that tie the otherwise diffuse IBRs initiatives together.

2.2. Locating Convergence in IBRs Initiatives

As noted above, the IBRs movement represents a diverse array of initiatives that often emerge in varying contexts, times and levels. This section seeks to locate areas of convergence in the IBRs project with a view to provide a conceptual background against which its legal significance is examined. The discussion draws on a selection of IBRs initiatives, particularly those put forward post the Snowden revelations. This is precisely because the revelations have played a key role in the re-emergence of IBRs but also in lending some coherence to the IBRs project. Despite the fragmented and diffuse nature of the IBRs project, there are at least five common threads that tie most IBRs initiatives together, as considered below.

2.2.1. Evolutionary Project

The IBRs project has generally been an *evolutionary* endeavour when it comes to its ultimate goals and purposes. While the original idea behind the project was to promote the protection of human rights on the Internet through non-binding advocacy instruments, this appears to be shifting over the years. Most of these initiatives emerged originally as aspirational and declaratory documents aimed at influencing public policy. Unlike a typical legal instrument that gives individuals enforceable rights, IBRs were seen as tools of advocating for the respect, protection, and enforcement of rights on the Internet. In launching an IBRs more recently, Article 19—a civil society organization—for instance, notes that it is simply following the 'honourable tradition within civil society and digital communities to draft and publish declarations, statements or principles on human rights and the Internet', and based on 'visionary and inspirational' approach of the tradition.[10] Similarly, the IBRs initiative at the IGF, considered further below, originally sought to use the Charter of Internet Rights and Principles (IRP Charter) as a 'rhetorical device' that lays down an alternative vision for the Internet,[11] and to serve as an advocacy tool.[12]

This conventional aim of IBRs has, however, been gradually changing in recent years. One apparent sign for this shift is the adoption into law of IBRs in some

---

[10] See Barbora Bukovska and Niels ten Oever, #InternetofRights: Creating the Universal Declaration of Digital Rights (Article 19 Blog, 24 March 2017) <http://bit.ly/2q5wji2>.

[11] See Marianne Franklin, *Digital Dilemmas: Power, Resistance and the Internet* (Oxford University Press 2013) 143.

[12] See Rikke Jorgensen, 'An Internet Bill of Rights?' in Ian Brown (ed), *Research Handbook on Governance of the Internet* (Edward Elgar 2013) 369–70.

countries. Civil society initiatives are also showing similar signs of shift. At the 2014 IGF Istanbul meeting of the IBRs Dynamic Coalition—a group behind the launching of the IRP Charter, a member of the Coalition had, for instance, emphasized the need to translate these initiatives into 'legal standards', to take the Charter beyond aspiration.[13] A suggestion of pushing the Charter to the 'calm waters of the UN' has also been made pointing to the desire of translating the Charter into a form of a multilateral instrument.[14] The shift towards a binding IBRs is also reflected in subsequent initiatives. One example is the European Digital Rights Charter, the name of which was even intended to be likened to the EU Fundamental Rights Charter.[15] The aim has been to present it to the European Parliament,[16] and subsequently to be adopted as a binding instrument, perhaps as a digital supplement to the EU Charter—and hence enforceable by the Court of Justice of the European Union (CJEU).[17] Perhaps a delayed—and partly modified response to the Charter, the European Commission has recently released the European Declaration on Digital Rights and Principles for the Digital Decade.[18]

As the Commission's Communications states, the proposed Declaration builds on 'previous initiatives from member States and from the European Parliament and benefits from numerous contributions gathered during the public consultation'.[19] It further provides that the draft Declaration 'builds on primary EU law, in particular the Treaty on the European Union, the Treaty on the Functioning of the European Union, the EU Charter of Fundamental Rights and the case-law of the Court of Justice of the European Union'.[20] In that sense, the draft Declaration may be taken to translate binding legal norms in EU law into a soft solemn declaration of the three EU institutions: the Council, the Parliament and the Commission.[21] But as shall be noted later in this chapter, the proposed Declaration goes, in some cases, beyond current EU law especially when it comes to the right to privacy and data protection. Once it is signed by the three EU institutions, it would open for the rights and principles envisaged in the proposed Declaration to be applied by CJEU. That way, its original declaratory soft law nature may be hardened.

---

[13] See The IRP Charter of Human Rights and Principles for the Internet: Five Years On, IRP Coalition Meeting Report: IGF 2014 Istanbul (4 September 2014) <http://bit.ly/1IL6lT9>.

[14] See Marianne Franklin, *Digital Dilemmas: Power, Resistance and the Internet* (Oxford University Press 2013) 169, 180.

[15] See *Charter of Digital Fundamental Rights of the European Union* (2016).

[16] See details at <https://bit.ly/2q33dRf>.

[17] See European Digital Rights Charter (n 15) art 23.

[18] *European Declaration on Digital Rights and Principles for the Digital Decade*, COM(2022) 28 Final (26 January 2022) <https://bit.ly/3u4tZN2>.

[19] Communication from the Commission to the European Parliament, the Council, the European Economic and Social Committee and the Committee of the Regions, Establishing a European Declaration on Digital Rights and Principles for the Digital Decade, SWD(2022) 14 Final (26 January 2022) 4.

[20] ibid, 5; see also European Declaration (n 18) Preamble, para 7.

[21] ibid, 1, 5.

Italy's IBRs Declaration is also a soft law, but the long-term aim has been to use the Italian Presidency of the EU at the time as an opportunity to pursue the issue of IBRs at the EU.[22] As a high-profile IBRs initiative, it is highly likely that Italy's Declaration would be one of the initiatives on which the Commission's proposed Declaration builds. Indeed, this is partly reflected in the resemblance of rights and principles—as shall be considered later in this chapter—envisaged in both declarations. In forming part of a Union level IBRs, the Italian Declaration is essentially evolving beyond a mere soft law. These developments attest to the evolution of the IBRs project. One possible factor for this shift is the realization that threats to human rights in the digital age will not sufficiently be addressed through advocacy alone. While the net effect of this shift is yet to be seen, the increasing prominence of IBRs would gradually play a role in influencing law, policy, and practice. The chapter returns to this point later.

2.2.2. Rights Novelty

Right novelty is the second characteristic feature of IBRs initiatives in that a set of quasi-novel human rights and principles are commonly set forth. While most IBRs documents appear to affirm or adapt existing rights in the digital context, a set of novel rights that find no direct counterparts in the present human rights catalogue are also put forward. Some protagonists of the IBRs project maintain that there are contextual factors unique to cyberspace, which the human rights regime needs to take into full account.[23] IBRs initiatives, for example Article 19's Declaration, emphasis the need to 'create and articulate' new rights for the digital age.[24] The preamble of the Declaration affirms that there is a need to 'explore and expand new human rights guarantees for the future'.

In a speech that foreshadowed the recently released EU Declaration, the President of the European Commission had stated that the set of 'digital principles' to be addressed in the Declaration will 'complement' existing legal rights.[25] But she further alluded to the fact that such principles would set 'new standards'.[26] Indeed, the Commission's Communication likewise notes that while 'some' of the principles stipulated in the Declaration are already laid down in legislation, 'others may require further action at the appropriate level'.[27] Not only does this suggest that some of the principles in the proposed Declaration are novel, or quasi-novel, which do not find recognition or counterpart in existing law but also that such recognition is desirable. However, the text of the Declaration sends a mixed signal

---

[22] See Report of the Dynamic Coalition for Internet Rights and Principles (2015) 3.
[23] See David Casacuberta and Max Senges, 'Do We Need New Rights in Cyberspace? Discussing the Case of How to Define Online Privacy in an Internet Bill of Rights' (2008) 40/41 *Enrahonar* 99, 99–100.
[24] See Bukovska and Oever (n 10).
[25] President von der Leyen's speech at the High-level Opening Session of the 2021 Digital Assembly, 'Leading the Digital Decade' (1 June 2021) <https://bit.ly/3KNx8qo>.
[26] ibid.
[27] Communication from the Commission (n 19) 6.

on this point. Its preamble, for instance, provides that the proposed Declaration merely 'recall the most relevant rights' suggesting that rights already guaranteed in EU instruments are reiterated by the Declaration.[28] But this is negated by the operative parts of the Declaration where quasi-novel, if not purely novel, rights are stipulated. Overall, this reinforces, added to the set of quasi-novel rights included in the proposed Declaration—noted further below, the point that rights novelty is a common thread in IBRs initiatives.

Often, the 'right to Internet access' is seen as the only 'new' right propounded by the IBRs project.[29] The proposed EU Declaration, for instance, envisages the right of 'everyone' to access 'digital technologies, products, and services that are safe, secure, and privacy-protective by design'.[30] But rights that appear to be carved as 'subsets' of existing rights are arguably new, or at least quasi-new rights as well.[31] The exercise in novelty particularly concerns the right to privacy, which is often furthered into a subset of rights such as the 'right to (use) encryption', the 'right of anonymity', and 'freedom from surveillance'. In providing specific privacy rights, IBRs appears to redefine the scope of the classic right to privacy based on the new realities of the digital age. This approach seemingly proceeds from the assumption that respect for and the effective protection of the right to privacy require some rendition in the digital space.[32]

In the context of the right to privacy, for instance, the importance of encryption technologies—and hence the right to *use* encryption—is often emphasized, including by UN human rights officers/bodies. The more recent argument was advanced by the former UN High Commissioner for Human Rights, Hussein, who remarked that since encryption is now widely used as a tool of protecting privacy in the digital age, it deserves protection.[33] This viewpoint was later seconded by the inventor of the web Berners-Lee who reportedly claimed that encryption is now used by the 'critical mass'—and weakening it, therefore, would destroy the 'modern way of life'.[34] Reimagining the right to privacy in the digital age requires

---

[28] See European Declaration (n 18) Preamble, para 5.

[29] See, eg, Marianne Franklin, 'Mobilizing for Net Rights: The IRPC Charter of Human Rights and Principles for the Internet' in Jonathan Obar and others (eds), *Strategies for Media Reform: International Perspectives* (Fordham University Press 2016) 85.

[30] See European Declaration (n 18) ch v.

[31] As shall become clear, 'subsets' of the right to privacy considered here are slightly different from the 'typology of privacy' or 'taxonomy of privacy' discussed in the privacy literature. Bert-Jaap Koops and others, for instance, identify typology of privacies in national constitutions of nine countries such as 'bodily privacy' and 'communication privacy'. See generally Bert-Jaap Koops and others, 'A Typology of Privacy' (2017) 38 University of Pennsylvania Journal of International Law 438.

[32] See Franklin (n 29) 73–74(stating the need for more 'explicit rendering' of human right to the online context).

[33] See Apple-FBI Case Could Have Serious Global Ramifications for Human Rights: Zeid (OHCHR Press Release, 4 March 2016) <https://bit.ly/2H7vX4x>.

[34] See Matt Burgess, Tim Berners-Lee: 'We Need to Rethink the Web to Stop the Spread of Mean Ideas' (Wired, 11 April 2017) <https://bit.ly/2oyapHE>; a report of the Dutch government also emphasizes the importance of encryption for the 'functioning of society'. See Kieren McCarthy, Dutch Govt Says No to Backdoors, Slides $540k into OpenSSL Without Breaking Eye Contact (The Register, 4 January 2016) <https://bit.ly/2EYKuNs>.

some level of specificity, but it would invite questions of legitimacy. This point is discussed further later in this chapter.

The proposed EU Declaration continues this tradition of rolling out rights that specify rights, including the right to privacy. Provided in the 'privacy and individual control over data' part of the Declaration, a set of privacy rights are envisaged. It partly reads as follows:[35]

Everyone has the <u>right to the confidentiality of their communications</u> and the information on their electronic devices, and no one shall be subjected to <u>unlawful online surveillance or interception</u> measures. Everyone should be able to <u>determine their digital legacy</u>, and decide what happens with the publicly available information that concerns them, after their death. [Emphasis added].

None of these rights find proximate recognition in legislation. But the exercise in novelty in this case is particularly relevant because some of these sub-rights find no counterparts even in other IBRs documents. A good case in point is the right to determine one's digital legacy. This right raises in and of itself a challenging question on the propriety of posthumous privacy in the digital age. Generally speaking, the right to privacy does not apply after death. But if one were to have a right, or a sub-right, to determine the fate of his digital footprints after death, it may extend—in some sense—to the protection of the right to privacy after death. This is beyond the scope of this book, but reinforces the point about conceptual ambiguities, considered later in this chapter, that persist in IBRs initiatives.

Rights novelty is also common in domain-specific IBRs initiatives. The Montreal Declaration on responsible AI, for instance, envisages a series of rights that find no direct counterparts in traditional catalogue of human rights or data subject rights in data privacy law. Among rights provided under 'protection of privacy and intimacy principle' include the right not to be subjected to digital evaluation, the right to digital disconnection and the right to donate personal data for research organizations.[36] Whereas the Statement released by the European Commission's scientific advisory body introduces privacy rights or principles such as the right to be free from technologies that influence personal development, right to meaningful human contact and the right not to be profiled, measured, analyzed, coached or nudged.[37]

Overall, a defining feature of IBRs is the tendency to specify the right to privacy into a set of novel or quasi-novel rights. A caveat should, however, be made that not all IBRs initiatives introduce such an elaborate set of rights and principles. Instead,

---

[35] See European Declaration (n 18) ch v.

[36] See *Montreal Declaration for A Responsible Development of Artificial Intelligence* (2018) Principle 3.

[37] *Statement on Artificial Intelligence, Robotics and 'Autonomous' Systems of European Group on Ethics in Science and New Technologies* (March 2018) 19.

they reaffirm or restate rights and principles already recognized in legislation at various levels, be it international, regional or domestic legislation. In this regard, European data protection law offers much of the principles both in omnibus or domain-specific IBRs initiatives. An example among omnibus IBRs initiatives is the Contract for the Web which grew out of a multistakeholder process organized under the auspices of the World Web Foundation.[38] The principle dealing with privacy, for instance, offers no quasi-novel privacy rights but a restatement of common principles of data protection law.[39] Global Privacy Assembly's principles on government access to data likewise restate widely accepted principles of data protection law.[40] But the tendency to reimagine privacy and data protection in most IBRs initiatives may provide a normative source for a more robust reform of international privacy law.

2.2.3. Momentary Project

A third defining feature of IBRs concerns the way in which they emerge. Most IBRs initiatives follow major historical junctures or events, and are often momentary. Unlike conventional human rights documents that are often preceded by years of negotiation and drafting, most—if not all—IBRs are expressions of outrage at a particular incident, be it an invasive legislation or government and private sector practices. A good case in point is the Snowden revelations. The momentary nature of IBRs is also to be traced in some of the national initiatives in Brazil and the Philippines where the process was triggered by the adoption of, or proposal for, legislation thought to be human rights unfriendly.[41] These initiatives were soon abandoned, until the Snowden revelations came to light, particularly in Brazil to which the disclosures have had a particular resonance.

Public scandals regarding the practices of technology companies likewise generate IBRs initiatives. One such high-profile scandal is the Cambridge Analytica affair which unveiled illegal collection of personal data of about 87 million Facebook users for purposes of targeted political advertising.[42] In the wake of the scandal, a number of IBRs emerged but the most notable one was proposed by a US congressman, Ro Khanna.[43] Released in the aftermath of Zuckerberg's testimony

---

[38] See *Contract for the Web* (n 2).
[39] ibid, Principles 3, 5.
[40] See *Principles for Governmental Access to Personal Data held by the Private Sector for National Security and Public Safety Purposes* (Global Privacy Assembly, October 2021).
[41] See, eg, Jonathan de Santos, The Wisdom of Crowds: Crowdsourcing Net Freedom (Yahoo! News, 21 January 2013) <https://bit.ly/3g4x7A9> (detailing the rationales for the launch of the Magna Carta for the Philippine Internet); Luiz Fernando, Marrey Moncau, and Diego Werneck Arguelhes, 'The Marco Civil da Internet and Digital Constitutionalism' in Giancarlo Frosio (ed), *Oxford Handbook of Intermediary Liability* (Oxford University Press 2020) 196.
[42] Kevin Granville, Facebook and Cambridge Analytica: What You Need to Know as Fallout Widens (The New York Times, 19 March 2018) <https://nyti.ms/3G4shxA>.
[43] See Seung Lee, Rep Ro Khanna tapped by Pelosi to Draft 'Internet Bill of Rights' (The Mercury News, 21 April 2018) <https://bayareane.ws/33VZ9eD>.

before the United States Congress and in response to a request from the democratic party leadership, the proposal was endorsed by Berners-Lee who has advocated for IBRs following the Snowden debacle.[44] The proposal outlines a series of principles that are commonly provided in data protection legislation.[45] As a bill admittedly 'built' on the Consumer Privacy Bill of Rights of the Obama era,[46] Rep Khanna's proposal appears to be no more than a soft law bearing no legally enforceable rights. But its ultimate goal is not clear, and no further steps seem to have followed its initial release. This reinforces the momentary nature of the IBRs project.

Related to the above are IBRs initiatives issued by technology companies in anticipation of regulation, be it antitrust or privacy regulation. An example is the release of Facebook's Privacy principles ahead of the coming into force of the General Data Protection Regulation (GDPR).[47] Issued on Data Privacy Day, the principles simply outline how the company approaches privacy, and as such, do not introduce specific rights and principles. In anticipation of competition regulation particularly in the United States, Twitter likewise released a set of regulatory principles that should be followed to protect the open Internet.[48] No specific rights and principles are envisaged but calls for regulatory measures to be anchored on universally recognized human rights such as the right to privacy. Considering the temporal element in such initiatives, the objective appears to be either shaping regulatory discussions or as a way of posturing in the face of stringent regulatory intervention. But what this essentially attests to is the momentary nature of IBRs as a movement.

A more recent trigger factor for IBRs initiatives has been the Covid-19 pandemic. Due to the widespread use of technological tools in contact-tracing processes as well as remote learning and working, a number of IBRs that stipulate digital rights have emerged. One sees two common threads in this batch of IBRs. One relates to the particular focus on the right to privacy.[49] Unlike other preceding IBRs initiatives, pandemic-induced IBRs initiatives pay particular attention to privacy and data protection. This is indeed dictated by the unique threats that the right to privacy faces due to the routine collection of personal data in the course of combating the plague. The other is the notable lack of rights novelty. Instead of

---

[44] Rep Khanna Releases 'Internet Bill of Rights' Principles, Endorsed by Sir Tim Berners-Lee (Press Release, 4 October 2018) <https://bit.ly/3u9UfWp>.

[45] ibid.

[46] See We Can't Wait: Obama Administration Unveils Blueprint for a 'Privacy Bill of Rights' to Protect Consumers Online (Press Release, 23 February 2012) <https://bit.ly/3G9He1c>.

[47] See Katie Collins, Facebook Publishes Privacy Principles for the First Time (Cnet, 29 January 2019) <https://cnet.co/3rV072T>; Facebook's Privacy Principles (Meta Platforms, 28 January 2013) <https://www.facebook.com/about/basics/privacy-principles>.

[48] See Protecting the Open Internet: Regulatory Principles for Policymakers (Twitter, October 2021) <https://bit.ly/3LDGGEY>; see also John Eggerton, Twitter Proposes Guiding Principles for Online Regulation (Multichannel News, 15 October 2021) <https://bit.ly/3nYf6YL>.

[49] See, eg, Principles for Technology-Assisted Contact-Tracing (American Civil Liberties Union, 16 April 2020); Resolution on the Privacy and Data Protection Challenges Arising in the Context of the Covid-19 Pandemic (Global Privacy Assembly, October 2020); Recommendations on Privacy and Data protection in the Fight Against COVID-19 (Access Now, March 2020).

setting forth typical quasi-novel rights, pandemic-induced initiatives seek to elaborate how existing principles should apply in the context of the public health crisis.

A further illustration of IBRs momentary feature is the recent 'principle proliferation' for new and emerging technologies such as AI.[50] With the rapid proliferation of AI-enable technologies in the past few years, a number of actors, including States and civil society groups, have launched tailored IBRs initiatives. An example is the recent initiative of the White House Office of Science and Technology Policy to create a crowdsourced 'Bill of Rights for an AI-Powered World'.[51] The Toronto Declaration is another initiative launched by civil society organizations with a particular focus on the protection of the right to equality in the context of machine learning systems.[52] Similar initiatives have also emerged from academia and professional associations such as the Montreal Declaration and General Principles launched by the Institute of Electrical and Electronics Engineers (IEEE).[53] The hype around AI has also reached international organizations where ethical principles are proposed to guide the design and operation of AI-powered technologies.[54] By and large, such initiatives present ethical principles drawn from other fields such as bioethics and data protection law.[55] But one sees significant similarities among the principles enshrined in these initiatives.

Momentary nature of the IBRs project, highlighted above, has limited its impact in shaping policy, law, and practice. IBRs initiatives reinforce already legally guaranteed rights as much as they 'specify' them into quasi-novel digital rights. But no IBRs initiative has evolved into a meaningful legal response to the challenges of upholding human rights in the digital age. This failure flows directly from the essentially sporadic nature of the movement which rises and falls with political or technological events of the time. Perhaps, the recent recognition of IBRs by national and regional courts as well as by the ongoing UN privacy discourse may slightly address this particular concern. But as this chapter shall show, this role of IBRs has not only been limited so far but is also unlikely to have a significant role in reimagining the right to privacy in international law.

---

[50] Luciano Floridi and Josh Cowls, 'A Unified Framework of Five Principles for AI in Society' (2019) 1 Harvard Data Science Review 1, 1–2.

[51] Se Eric Lander and Alondra Nelson, Americans Need a Bill of Rights for an AI-Powered World (Wired, 8 October 2021) <https://bit.ly/35ht6pR>. While the book was in production, a 'blueprint' of the Bill has been released.

[52] See, eg, *Toronto Declaration: Protecting the Right to Equality and Discrimination in Machine Learning Systems* (Amnesty International and Access Now, May 2018).

[53] See Montreal Declaration (n 36); *Ethically Aligned Design: A Vision for Prioritizing Human Well-being with Autonomous and Intelligent Systems* (IEEE, 2019).

[54] See, eg, *Declaration on Ethics and Data Protection in Artificial Intelligence* (Global Privacy Assembly, October 2018); European Group on Ethics in Science and New Technologies (n 37); *Ethics Guidelines for Trustworthy AI* (High-Level Expert Group on Artificial Intelligence, April 2019).

[55] See Floridi and Cowls (n 50) 5.

2.2.4. Norm Cross-fertilization

A tendency to build on progressive judicial decisions, domestic laws and emerging industry practices is the other attribute of IBRs. One finds a number of rights and principles in IBRs initiatives that have already been recognized in judicial decisions and laws at various levels. The influence of European (case) law is, in this regard, particularly significant. Examples are in order. One of the commonest (Internet) rights in IBRs documents is the 'right to the confidentiality and integrity of information systems', also referred to as 'IT basic right'.[56] Before it widely featured in these documents, it was introduced by the German Constitutional Court in a 2008 decision.[57] The Court read this right within the broader 'right to personality' which is expressly recognized in the Basic Law of Germany.[58] The decision was based on the argument that the extant protection under either the right to inviolability of home or secrecy of telecommunication was not adequate to protect the right to privacy in the digital space. While this decision introduced, or carved out, a quasi-novel constitutional (digital) right, the idea behind this right already existed in European law. One finds, for instance, in European data privacy law provisions that require data controllers to put in place technical measures to ensure confidentiality of digital communications.[59] The IBRs project embraces this (European) right which, with the recent proliferation of data privacy legislation worldwide (based mostly on European standards), is being recognized in jurisdictions outside Europe.

Another example is the 'right to information self-determination', a right initially formulated by a decision of the German Constitutional Court in a 1983 decision,[60] which is now widely adopted in IBRs instruments.[61] Like the right to the confidentiality and integrity of information systems, this right was also carved out by the Court from the classic right to personality and the right to dignity of the Basic Law. A more recent example is the 'right to be forgotten', a right declared by the CJEU but based on relevant provisions of EU data privacy law.[62] The right is now commonplace in IBRs instruments.[63] With the adoption of the GDPR, the influence of

---

[56] See Wolfgang Schulz and Joris van Hoboken, *Human Rights and Encryption* (UNESCO Series on Internet Freedom 2015) 37.

[57] See Bundesverfassungsgericht (2008) *BVerfG 822*.

[58] See *Basic Law of the Federal Republic of Germany* (1949) (as amended in 2014) art 2(1).

[59] See, eg, *Directive (EC) 2002/58 of the European Parliament and of the Council of 12 July 2002 on the Protection of Privacy in the Electronic Communications Sector* [2002] OJ L 201/37, arts 1, 4–5.

[60] See Bundesverfassungsgericht (1983) *BVerfGE 65*.

[61] See, eg, *Italian Declaration of Internet Rights* (2015) art 6; European Digital Rights Charter (n 15) art 11 [note, however, the error in the heading of the article, 'data protection and data sovereignty' while the proper heading is used (wrongly) in art 12, the content of which concerns, inter alia, the right to encryption].

[62] See *Google v Agencia Española de Protección de Datos (AEPD) v Mario Costeja González* (C-131/12) [2014] ECLI 317. Note that the GDPR expressly recognizes a broader 'right to be forgotten'. See *Regulation (EU) 2016/679 of the European Parliament and of the Council of 27 April 2016 on the Protection of Natural Persons with regard to the Processing of Personal Data and on the Free Movement of Such Data* [2016] OJ L 119/1, Recital 105, art 17.

[63] See, eg, Italy's Declaration (n 61) art 11.

European data protection law has been significant in recent IBRs initiatives. Global Privacy Assembly's principles on government access to personal data held by the private sector likewise, as highlighted above, restate widely accepted data privacy principles.[64]

As the above brief sketch suggests, not all rights, principles, and norms in IBRs are novel or quasi-novel with no counterparts in legislation nor do all IBRs initiatives experiment with rights novelty. To a greater degree, the IBRs project has been a result of cross-fertilization of rights, principles, and norms drawn from different sources. Unlike the pursuit in rights novelty which—as shall be illustrated later in this chapter—tends to bring with it several difficulties, distilling norms already embodied in law in different levels is beneficial. The benefit of such a cross-fertilization approach is that it identifies best practices from different sources and projects them to a wider global audience. This opens the possibility of gradual recognition in national law and even international law. We return to this point later in this chapter.

2.2.5. Multistakeholder Experimentation

Many IBRs initiatives are products of multistakeholder processes by which inputs are drawn from various stakeholders, including governments, civil society groups, academia, and the technical community. A more recent example is the Contract for the Web initiative in the development of which more than eighty organizations representing governments, companies, and civil society groups reportedly took part.[65] Enhancing procedural legitimacy of the norms created through the process is the primary goal of a bottom-up, multi-level process. The assumption is that an instrument that heeds to the views, inputs and concerns of relevant stakeholders is likely to be treated as legitimate.[66] A multistakeholder approach must, however, be distinguished from the rather common ways of drawing input in national law-making processes such as consultation. While both seek to achieve procedural legitimacy by drawing input from relevant interest groups, the latter appears to be entirely discretionary or advisory—and hence not all inputs may make their way into the final version of the outcome. The making of some IBRs appears to have followed the conventional public consultation mechanism, as opposed to a truly bottom-up, multistakeholder process.

The multistakeholder approach is often reinforced by crowdsourcing mechanisms. While the IBRs project makes use of crowdsourcing in norm creation, it is only rarely that the drafting of IBRs ever started from scratch. Often, the crowdsourcing exercise builds on an initial draft—and in that sense, it resembles

---

[64] See Principles for Governmental Access to Personal Data (n 40).
[65] See *Contract for the Web* (n 2); see also <https://contractfortheweb.org/about/>.
[66] See, eg, Joanna Kulesza, Protecting Human Rights Online: An Obligation of Due Diligence, New York University School of Law Jean Monnet Working Paper No 24/14 (2014) 6.

the traditional 'public consultation' in domestic lawmaking. The drafting of Italy's Declaration, for instance, was undertaken by a Commission installed by the government, which then was released to gather inputs through crowdsourcing.[67] In a similar vein, Article 19 has launched a #hashtag campaign on Twitter, perhaps as a new variant of crowdsourcing mechanism, to gather input on the draft Declaration.[68] Perhaps an exception is the more recent IBRs initiative of the White House where a process to draw input from 'experts across the federal government, academia, civil society, the private sector, and communities all over the country' has been launched in late 2021.[69] To this effect, a mechanism of providing input has been put in place. But the prevalent digital divide, across geography, income level, age and gender, undercuts the promises of crowdsourcing as a reliable medium to ensure popular participation. This state of affairs, coupled with recent threats of online disinformation, further raises concerns regarding the legitimacy of a crowdsourced IBRs instrument. This point is further discussed later in this chapter.

2.3. Legal Sources and Forms in IBRs

Despite the above highlighted commonalities, initiatives for IBRs take different legal forms and draw from multiple sources. The IBRs project is, as noted above, a syndicate of initiatives launched at various levels, including by individual activists, civil society groups, the private sector and national governments. IBRs also take various forms from a legal point of view. While many are launched as non-binding civil society policy briefs or mere advocacy instruments, others are adopted (or proposed) as domestic legislation, be it in hard or soft law form. This section discusses this diversity in form and source to properly situate IBRs in the international law. The submission is that the diffusion in form hinders the prospect of IBRs developing into an international instrument in the long-run.

Initiatives for IBRs launched by civil society groups dominate the global IBRs landscape. The IRP Charter is perhaps the most influential of civil society IBRs initiatives. The genesis of the Charter was at the Tunis Summit on Information Society in 2005, a summit convened by the International Telecommunication Union. With the active support of the governments of Brazil and Italy, the Charter was developed at the Summit by the Dynamic Coalition of Internet Rights and Principles.[70] While the Coalition operates within the UN as part of the IGF, it essentially is a multistakeholder platform where the voice of non-State actors especially civil society groups is influential. Article 19, a UK based civil society group, has recently

---

[67] See details at <http://camera.civi.ci/>.
[68] See the hash tag campaign at <https://twitter.com/hashtag/InternetofRights>.
[69] Se Lander and Nelson (n 51).
[70] See Jorgensen (n 12) 353, 358–59.

launched two notable IBRs: the Universal Declaration of Digital Rights and the Global Principles on the Protection of Freedom of Expression and Privacy. The Global Principles primarily aim to offer an 'analytical framework' on the way how free speech and privacy rights reinforce each other.[71] But one finds useful articulation of digital privacy rights in the Global Principles, particularly in unpacking the respective role of States and corporations vis-à-vis the right to privacy. The African Declaration of Internet Rights and Freedoms is another civil society IBRs initiative. The Declaration seeks to promote 'human rights standards in Internet policy formulation and implementation' in Africa.[72] As shall be highlighted later in this chapter, the Declaration recently drew the attention of the African Union's (AU) human rights monitoring body, signalling the prospect of reference in its jurisprudence.

A number of countries have either adopted, or are currently considering legislation, that carries IBRs themes. The first country to adopt a law that touches on aspects of IBRs is Brazil. Launched in response to a draft cybercrime legislation perceived to be human rights unfriendly in 2009, it initially was seen as an experiment of building consensus before parliamentary deliberations.[73] The process was stalled until the Snowden disclosure came to light, which was particularly scandalous to Brazil. The country's President at the time, who was a victim of the espionage, declared a 'constitutional emergency' that revived the law. However, despite the frequent reference to this Brazilian law as a 'bill of rights', its content barely resembles typical IBRs instruments examined in this chapter. This point is further considered later in this chapter.

Italy is the first country to adopt, albeit a soft law, an IBRs legislation in the strict sense of the term. Italy's Declaration of Internet Rights was initiated by the President of the Italian Chamber of Deputies after the Snowden revelations.[74] But, the Italian IBRs experiment, as noted above, began at the IGF in collaboration with Brazil. Nigeria has also been considering a draft IBRs legislation since the Snowden debacle. The Nigerian Digital Rights and Freedom Bill, adopted by the country's legislature but later denied Presidential assent,[75] aims to 'ensure that offline rights apply online' and to ensure compliance with 'established rights and freedoms'.[76] The Bill is meant to be a broader cyber legislation, but it embodies common digital

---

[71] See *Global Principles on the Protection of Freedom of Expression and Privacy* (Article 19, 2017); another recent civil society initiative is the *International Declaration on Information and Democracy* (Reporters Without Borders 2018).

[72] *African Declaration of Internet Rights and Freedoms* (2014).

[73] See Carolina Rossini and others, The Strength and Weaknesses of the Brazilian Internet Bill of Rights (Chatham House 2015) 4.

[74] See Rodotà (n 8).

[75] See Victor Ekwealor, Nigeria's President Refused to Sign Its Digital Rights Bill, What Happens Now? (Techpoint.africa, 27 March 2019) <https://bit.ly/2UZhGRG> (reporting lack of thematic focus and coverage of proposed topics in existing law as the grounds for denial of presidential assent).

[76] See *Nigerian Digital Rights and Freedoms Bill* (2016) Part I (1).

rights, including privacy rights and principles. Substantive aspects of the Bill as well as Italy's Declaration, are considered in the section below.

The essence of IBRs has also found some expression in inter-governmental processes. As highlighted above, the EU has recently released a draft Declaration that may soon be adopted by the three EU institutions as a solemn political declaration.[77] In Africa, the regional human rights body—the African Commission on Human Rights Peoples Rights—released in 2019 a Declaration of Principles which, contrary to what its nomenclature suggests, addresses privacy rights at length.[78] It does so in three steps. First, the Declaration guarantees the right to privacy online, including communicating anonymously through the use of Privacy Enhancing Technologies (PETs).[79] It requires States to refrain from engaging in arbitrary measures that would undermine secure and private communications such as weakening encryption, mandating key escrows, and backdoors or data localization. Second, the Declaration of Principles prohibits mass surveillance and bulk collection, storage, analysis, or sharing of personal data.[80] Moreover, it stipulates that even when the surveillance is targeted, a series of safeguards must be put in place to prevent or remedy arbitrary practices. Such safeguards include prior independent oversight, due process, restriction on the time, manner, and scope of the surveillance, *post facto* notification to the surveilled subject. Third, the Declaration of Principles requires States to adopt data protection laws that stipulate principles of processing of personal data, guarantee data subject rights and institute a national data protection authority.[81]

At the UN, IBRs themes are considered, to some degree, in the reports of UN Special Rapporteurs. Some reports of the former Special Rapporteur on Freedom of Expression, La Rue, have touched on aspects of IBRs. His 2013 report, for instance, notes that restrictions on the use of PETs such as encryption amount to interference with the right to privacy.[82] He further suggested that everyone has the right to use any technological tool to ensure the security of his/her communication, and States owe a negative obligation of not interfering with such use, or to force disclosure of encryption keys.[83] The former Special Rapporteur on Human Rights and Counter-terrorism, Emerson, has endorsed this reading of Article 17 of the ICCPR in his post-Snowden disclosures report. Emerson noted that the obligation of States under Article 17 of the ICCPR is to 'respect' the privacy and security

---

[77] See also OECD's initiative: Recommendation of the Council on OECD Legal Instruments Artificial Intelligence, OECD/LEGAL/0449 (May 2019).

[78] See *Declaration of Principles on Freedom of Expression and Access to Information*, The African Commission on Human and Peoples' Rights (November 2019) Principles 40–42.

[79] ibid, Principle 40(2).

[80] ibid, Principle 41.

[81] ibid, Principle 42.

[82] See Report of the Special Rapporteur on the Promotion and Protection of the Right to Freedom of Opinion and Expression, Frank La Rue, UN Doc A/HRC/23/40 (17 April 2013) para 71.

[83] ibid, para 89.

of digital communication, further suggesting that no positive obligation exists in the context of secure communications.[84] These statements essentially read a right to *use* encryption in the classic right to privacy. To what extent these UN reports have informed, or been informed by, IBRs initiatives, is not entirely clear. Perhaps, the Special Rapporteurs' assertion might have informed civil society IBRs as part of the overall cross-pollination of digital rights norms in the IBRs project.

La Rue's successor, Kaye, has also noted that Article 17(2) of the ICCPR embraces a right to be notified when cases of compelled disclosure of user data arise.[85] Kaye further noted that the obligation involves, among other things, 'protecting' the private sector development and provision of technical measures, products, and services.[86] Unlike La Rue who read a right to *use* encryption mainly in the privacy provision, Kaye reads the right implicitly within the right to freedom of expression.[87] One also recalls the remark of the former Higher Commissioner, noted above, suggesting that encryption, as an important tool of protecting privacy, deserves protection. But he did not go far to claim the existence of a right *to* encryption or that States have a corresponding obligation therewith.[88] Overall, apart from such occasional and indirect references to IBRs, there is an apparent apathy at the UN towards IBRs in general.[89] Not only did IBRs themes surface occasionally but also that the above noted reports of Special Rapporteurs barely engage with the various IBRs documents that correspond to their mandates. This lack of consistent attention to IBRs by relevant UN bodies discounts the possible role of IBRs in the progressive development of international law.[90]

---

[84] See Report of the Special Rapporteur on the Promotion and Protection of Human Rights while Countering Terrorism, Ben Emmerson, UN Doc A/69/397 (23 September 2014) paras 28, 58.

[85] See Report of Special Rapporteur on the Promotion and Protection of the Right to Freedom of Opinion and Expression, David Kaye, UN Doc A/HRC/29/32 (22 May 2015) para 18.

[86] See Report of the Special Rapporteur on the Promotion and Protection of the Right to Freedom of Opinion and Expression, David Kaye, UN Doc A/HRC/32/38 (11 May 2016) para 86.

[87] See Report of Kaye (n 85) paras 29–35; see also David Kaye, Encryption and Anonymity Follow-up Report, Research Paper 1/2018 (June 2018) paras 5–6.

[88] In an interesting contrast, the former SRP, Cannataci, treats 'technical safeguards' like encryption as extra-legal means of privacy protection—and in so saying, appears to suggest no right to *use* encryption exists under the right to privacy. See Report of Special Rapporteur on the Right to Privacy, Joseph Cannataci, UN Doc A/HRC/31/64 (8 March 2016) para 50.

[89] Note that IBRs themes also had figured occasionally at the HR Council. See Dixie Hawtin, 'Internet Rights and Principles: Trends and Insights' in Alan Finlay (ed), *Internet Rights and Democratization: Focus on Freedom of Expression and Association Online* (Global Information Society Watch 2011) 52.

[90] Note that IBRs has also gained some traction at the CoE. A CoE digital sector official, for instance, had signalled that the best forum to realize Berner-Lee's idea of a Magna Carta is the CoE, and indeed, the Council's Internet Governance Strategy document (2016–2019) had embraced that idea, although nothing tangible has come out thus far. See Jan Kleijssen, A Magna Carta for the Internet? (LinkedIn Pulse, 17 September 2014) <http://bit.ly/2qtNTOH> cum See Internet Governance Strategy: 2016–2019 (CoE, 2016) para 8. At the EU, IBRs was considered, but not acted upon till recently with the proposal for a Declaration issued by the European Commission, at the European Parliament even before the Snowden debacle. See, eg, European Parliament Recommendation to the Council on Strengthening Security and Fundamental Freedoms on the Internet, [2008/2160(INI)] (26 March 2009) paras S and ac; see also Nate Anderson, New Internet Bill of Rights Contender Comes from ... Pirates? (Arts Technica, 12 December 2012) <http://bit.ly/2iv6SDg>.

To summarize the above discussion, the sporadic and diffuse nature of the IBRs project—added to the complex diversity of its legal sources and forms, undermine its role in the further development of privacy law at various levels. The lack of sustained consideration of IBRs in relevant intergovernmental processes, especially at the UN, further arrests its role in reimagining the international law of privacy in the digital age. The next section discusses the way in which the right to privacy is envisaged in IBRs instruments. In doing so, it seeks to explicate the substantive boundaries of IBRs in articulating the right to privacy. As shall be shown, the way in which privacy is formulated in IBRs documents offer a progressive vision for the right to privacy in international law.

2.4. Privacy in IBRs

In a 1989 piece 'Why have a Bill of Rights?', Justice Brennan of the United States Supreme Court quips that 'the utility of a bill of rights cannot easily be gauged before its contents are specified'.[91] In that spirit, this section examines the way in which the content of the right to privacy in the digital context is specified in IBRs initiatives. This provides the background against which the utility of IBRs in reimagining international privacy law can be gauged in section 3.

IBRs instruments cover a broad range of human rights, including those that find counterparts in (international) human rights law, and those that do not. Of these human rights, the right to privacy holds a prominent place in almost every initiative for IBRs. Not only is the right to privacy envisioned in these initiatives but also that it is made so in a manner that specifies the right into what we might call a 'subset of rights'. One, however, finds variations in the way in which the right to privacy is enshrined vis-à-vis those 'subset' of rights. Some IBRs documents provide a general right to privacy which then is specified into specific privacy rights,[92] while others stipulate each subset of right as a freestanding right.[93] As shall be discussed further below, the IBRs project also draws the scope of privacy rights in a manner that, to some extent, clarifies the scope of the right and the corresponding obligations of duty-bearers, particularly technology companies.

Two subset of privacy rights are commonly envisioned in IBRs initiatives: the 'right to use encryption technologies' and 'freedom from surveillance'.[94] Most IBRs documents incorporate a right to *use* encryption while a few others provide for a right *to* encryption.[95] The basic difference is that the former appears to envisage a

---

[91] William Brennan, 'Why Have a Bill of Rights?' (1989) 9 Oxford Journal of Legal Studies 425, 425.

[92] See *Charter of Human Rights and Principles for the Internet* (7th edn, 2019) art 8.

[93] See *Universal Declaration of Digital Rights* (Article 19, 2017) arts 4–6.

[94] See, eg, IRP Charter (n 92) art 8; see also African Declaration (n 72) art 8; Article 19's Declaration (n 3) arts 5–6.

[95] See, eg, European Digital Rights Charter (n 15) art 12(2).

negative freedom, allowing users to make use of those technologies. In practice, this simply would mean the right of individuals to use encryption tools such as Pretty Good Privacy. And as such, no positive obligation flows from this in a way that would require technology providers, or States, to avail those tools. But the latter, on the other hand, suggests a positive freedom that entitles a right to demand provision of encryption tools somehow.

In practical terms, the right *to* encryption would partly relate to emerging requirements in data privacy law worldwide towards privacy by design. Perhaps, what the IBRs project does is that it frames aspects of this idea in a human rights language. In EU law, the principle of 'data protection by design' concerns the embedding of (data) privacy principles in the designing of information systems used in the processing of personal data. It is described as the idea behind PETs.[96] To a certain degree, the notion of privacy by design captures recent industry practices of companies like Apple in providing encryption of data and ephemeral messaging services. As hinted above, the primary component of the right to *use* encryption technologies is the freedom to access and apply the technologies. But where the right includes an entitlement for secure products and services, it would be a right *to* encryption.

The other specific privacy right is the 'right to online anonymity'. It involves the right not to be identified while surfing the Internet. While some IBRs documents provide this right as a freestanding freedom,[97] others provide it alongside the right to *use* encryption.[98] However, both anonymity and encryption technologies reinforce the right to privacy. While most anonymization technologies hide the identity of individuals at the different ends of the communication, encryption software helps conceal the content of the communication.

'Freedom from surveillance' is another common privacy right in IBRs documents. The use of the term 'freedom' suggests a negative right, but its content appears to embrace a positive dimension as well. The freedom involves the right not to be subjected to arbitrary mass surveillance, interception, and pervasive monitoring.[99] Its positive dimension guarantees a right to *ex post-facto* notification to a person subjected to 'targeted' surveillance. Moreover, it involves the right to access laws and procedures that authorize surveillance. This right is an invention of post-Snowden IBRs initiatives meant directly as a response to revelations of mass surveillance practices of Five Eyes States.[100] But it captures an important essence of the right to privacy which the above subsets of privacy rights do not seem to cover.

---

[96] Bert-Jaap Koops and Ronald Leenes, 'Privacy Regulation cannot be Hardcoded: A Critical Comment on the "Privacy by Design" Provision in Data Protection Law' (2014) 28 International Review of Law, Computers and Technology 159, 159.

[97] See, eg, Article 19's Declaration (n 93) art 4.

[98] See, eg, IRP Charter (n 92) art 8.

[99] ibid; see also Article 19's Declaration (n 93) art 6.

[100] For purposes of this book, the term 'mass surveillance' represents practices of States, acting alone or with the assistance of technology companies, to gather intelligence including personal information of an entire or significant portion of a population in bulk. See more at <https://bit.ly/2MzKB8Y>.

Privacy principles and norms that now are common in data privacy law are also provided in many IBRs documents. This means that despite the apparent 'human rights' tone of IBRs, the IBRs project embraces, to some degree, aspects of the rather regulatory field of data privacy. Indeed, in the case of Brazil's purported IBRs law the privacy provisions were imported from the then draft data privacy legislation.[101] Italy's Declaration also embodies rights that relate to the protection of data privacy. It, for instance, embodies the 'right to the protection of personal data', the 'right to information self-determination', and the 'right not to be subjected to decisions based on automatic processing of personal data'.[102] With the increasing fusion of human rights language in data privacy legislation in the form of 'data subject rights', the unifying approach of the IBRs project is not out of place. But because of the casuistic nature of data protection legislation, IBRs do not, and probably could not, go beyond setting forth an enabling set of data privacy rights, leaving the mechanical details of regulation to secondary legislation.

The way these rights and principles are framed sometimes varies. The African Declaration, for instance, puts the right to privacy into the 'right to personal data protection', the 'right to anonymity', and the 'right to (use) appropriate technologies to ensure private, anonymous and secure communication'.[103] Whereas Article 19's Declaration stipulates the right to privacy into the 'right to anonymity', the 'right to encryption', the 'right to be free from surveillance', the 'right to control data', and the 'right to migrate and export data'.[104] The other important variation is that not all of these privacy rights are explicitly recognized in some IBRs documents. For example, while Brazil's Marco da Civil Internet addresses the right to privacy at length, one finds no rights like the right to *use* encryption in the legislation.[105] The closest it comes is when it provides for the 'inviolability and secrecy of the flow of communications over the Internet' in Article 7(II).

Italy's Declaration does not similarly recognize a specific right to encryption technologies. It embodies, however, other rights such as the right to the 'inviolability of electronic systems, devices and domiciles' which may perhaps be taken to embrace aspects of the right *to* encryption.[106] Article 10(1) of the Declaration, although situated under the caption 'protection of anonymity', reflects the spirit of a right to *use* encryption technologies: anyone may 'communicate electronically using instruments, including technical systems, which ... prevent the collection of personal data'. Considering encryption's primary role in making content data unreadable by third parties, this provision can be said to protect a right to

---

[10] See Rossini and others (n 73) 4.
[10] Italy's Declaration (n 61) arts 5–6, 8–9.
[10] African Declaration (n 72) art 8.
[10] But note that while the heading reads as 'right to encryption', the content adds the term 'use'. See art 5.
[10] *Brazilian Civil Framework for the Internet* (2014) Ch I, art 3 (II and III), Ch II, arts 7–8, Section II. Of a similar view, see Schulz and van Hoboken (n 56) 44.
[10] Italy's Declaration (n 61) art 7.

use encryption. Nigeria's Bill exhibits similar variations. While it does not embody a specific right to encryption, it includes broadly termed rights like the 'right to digital privacy'.[107]

The second issue concerns the way in which IBRs initiatives define the scope of the right to privacy. They do so by providing a limitation clause that rectifies the gap in international law. As discussed in chapter 2, no proper limitation clauses are attached to the privacy provisions of both the UDHR and the ICCPR. Limitation clauses in many IBRs invariably adapt the widely accepted three-part standards of legality, legitimate aim, and necessity.[108] There are, of course, exceptions to this. The IRP Charter, for instance, merely provides a general limitation clause that resembles Article 29 of the UDHR.[109] This lapse appears to be a result of the drafters' mechanical approach while adapting provisions of the UDHR to the digital context, article by article. The European Digital Rights Charter also refers back to Article 52 of the EU Fundamental Rights Charter which envisages requirements of legality, necessity, and proportionality.[110] Proper limitation clauses are key in ascertaining the scope of human rights, and thereby preventing overbroad restrictions by the State (and non-State) actors.

The third important aspect of the IBRs project relates to the way in which possible obligations/responsibilities of both States and non-State actors are envisioned in some IBRs documents. This mostly is framed along with each subset of privacy rights. Article 19's Global Principles, for instance, articulate the content of the right to anonymity and encryption along with obligations that purportedly rest on States and corporations. Obligations/responsibilities of States and corporations regarding encryption, for example, include recognition by law the importance of encryption technologies, promotion of end-to-end encryption, promotion of digital literacy, repeal of laws that ban or restrict use or import/export of encryption technologies, and repeal of laws requiring backdoor access or escrow systems.[111]

Principle 8 further provides the conditions under which Internet corporations may be required to disclose user data, and an obligation/responsibility to provide notification to users when such disclosure is made. Similarly, the conditions for access to, search and seizure of digital accounts of users are provided in the Global Principles, which involve judicial oversight and requirements of legality, necessity, and proportionality.[112] This attempt at articulating the possible responsibilities or obligations of Internet corporations vis-à-vis the digital rights, including privacy, might offer some guidance for future efforts of defining the role of both States and corporations vis-à-vis the right to privacy.

---

[107] Nigeria's Bill (n 76) arts 3–11.
[108] See, eg, Article 19's Declaration (n 93) art 21.
[109] IRP Charter (n 92) art 29(b).
[110] European Digital Rights Charter (n 15) art 23.
[111] Article 19's Global Principles (n 71) Principle 7.
[112] ibid, principle 10.

3. Situating IBRs in International Law

If the nature and scope of the IBRs project as a promising international privacy initiative is clearly laid out, the next step is to examine its role in reimagining current international law of privacy in the digital age. In analyzing the role of IBRs, the discussion in what follows considers three potential roles for IBRs. First, it considers whether there is any chance of IBRs developing into an international legal response to the 'privacy problem'. Second, having rejected the possibility of a global IBRs, it goes to consider its contributory role by which it may shape the pending UN privacy discourse and beyond. Third, because the contributory role has a limited normative value, it then discusses the more promising 'catalytic role' of IBRs in shaping the course of practicable reforms.

3.1. Freestanding Role

One possible path for the IBRs project to take is gradually evolving into a global instrument, probably in treaty form.[113] As highlighted at the outset, there have been occasional calls for a sort of international IBRs. De Minico, for instance, suggested for an IBRs to be adopted by a 'public supranational legislator' based on input from the private sector.[114] A different form of the proposal has been Rodotà's proposed 'charter of rights for the Internet' that a 'crowd of judges' in every jurisdiction would apply in addressing common questions of human rights on the Internet.[115] Beside ambiguities associated with these proposals considered in chapter 1, any idea of a global IBRs faces a number of hurdles. Such hurdles emanate from the nature of the IBRs project as a whole, its normative content, the process through which it often emerges. What follows discusses these concerns that reduce the chance of IBRs developing into a freestanding international law response to the privacy problem.

3.1.1. Diffuse and Momentary Project
The diffuse and momentary nature of the IBRs project is the primary obstacle in its gradual development into a global instrument. As considered in section 2 above, the IBRs project has been from the outset a multi-level endeavour pursued at various levels, by different actors and at different times. IBRs are adopted into domestic law, launched as civil society advocacy instruments and even by individual activists. IBRs national laws adopted so far, for example in Italy, are soft law and hence of no legal force. Where they are adopted in a form of hard law—for example

---

[113] For a brief discussion of whether a customary international law (of privacy) may grow out of IBRs, see section 3.2 below, but the short answer is no.

[114] See Giovanna De Minico, 'Towards an Internet Bill of Rights' (2015) 37 Loyola of Los Angeles International and Comparative Law Review 1, 19–30.

[115] See Rodotà (n 5).

in Brazil, the degree to which they reflect the conventional substance of IBRs has been limited. This diffuse nature of the project means that any hope for an international IBRs is slim.

Momentary nature of the IBRs project in that it emerges in reaction to a given incident, and dies down gradually, further reduces the possibility of an international IBRs or in even contributing towards other forms of reform. IBRs initiatives do not often linger after the hype around that particular phenomenon recedes, and as such, the underlying aim does not appear to shape the development of human rights in the digital context. Reflective of the IBRs project's momentary nature is that it is also becoming a tool of political campaign in some countries. In countries like the United Kingdom and New Zealand, political parties—including those in power—appear to find it politically advantageous to champion digital rights in their election manifestos.[116] But little seems to follow once the election season ends. The recent embrace of IBRs by some technology companies is also a manifestation of the market-driven, and hence its momentary nature.

In that sense, IBRs initiatives may have become victims of what Raz calls 'reckless activism'[117] of rights that follow some major events thought to be human rights unfriendly. But resort to rights activism without a sustained process damages the integrity of the international human rights system.[118] This relates to the problem of 'rights inflation' or 'hypertrophy of rights' which occurs due to nomination of more human rights, thereby posing the risk of cheapening the currency of the human rights.[119] As shall be discussed further below, this particular point has also a bearing on the legitimacy of IBRs. One way this may materialize is when addressees of those rights, for example duty bearers, could easily co-opt or cherry-pick among the panoply of rights with less demanding obligations. This is the effect of what Floridi calls the creation of a 'market of principles' where a flurry of principles is churned out by different actors at different levels.[120]

Overall, because of its deeply fragmentary and temporal nature, it is unlikely that an international instrument would come out of the IBRs project. As Floridi

---

[116] See, eg, Protecting Your Data Online with a Digital Rights Bill (Liberal Democrats, 11 April 2015); Change Britain's Future: Liberal Democrat Manifesto (2017) 72; Forward, Together: Our Plan for Stronger Britain and a Prosperous Future (The Conservative and Unionist Party Manifesto, 2017) 76–77, 79–80; The Digital Democratic Manifesto (The Labour Party, August 2016); Gareth Hughes MP: Government Must Do More to Close the Digital Divide (The Green Party of New Zealand, 3 February 2015).

[117] Joseph Raz, 'Human Rights in the Emerging World Order' in Rowan Cruft and others (eds), *Philosophical Foundations of Human Rights* (Oxford University Press 2015) 228.

[118] See Hurst Hannum, 'Reinvigorating Human Rights for the 21st Century' (2016) 16 Human Rights Law Review 409, 445.

[119] See Eric Posner, *The Twilight of Human Rights Law* (Oxford University Press 2014) 94; see also Michael Ignatieff, 'Human Rights as Politics and Idolatry' in Amy Gutmann (ed), *Human Rights as Politics and Idolatry* (Princeton University Press 2001) 90; James Griffin, *On Human Rights* (Oxford University Press 2009) 205–06.

[120] Luciano Floridi, 'Translating Principles into Practices of Digital Ethics: Five Risks of Being Unethical' (2019) 32 Ethics and Philosophy 185, 186–87.

anc Cowl counsel in the context of 'principle proliferation' in relation to AI, the deluge of rights and principles risks delaying formal legislative and extra-legal responses.[121] Confronted with competing rights and principles, it would take time for governments to initiate pertinent regulatory frameworks and for private actors to introduce compliant industry practices. In that sense, the momentary nature of IBRs as a movement works against its potential in contributing towards addressing the privacy problem in the digital age.

3.1 2. Conceptual Ambiguities

Perhaps a result of the diffuse and momentary nature of the IBRs project, most IBRs initiatives lack theoretical-conceptual clarity, particularly in the way they formulate rights. This is the second factor that works against the possibility of IBRs becoming a freestanding global instrument on digital rights. The problem of conceptual ambiguity has two dimensions. First, many IBRs initiatives do not clearly provide the substantive content of rights and corresponding obligations. Second, the IBRs project often overlooks the institutional framework needed for the implementation of the envisioned (Internet) rights. Third, the IBR project does not properly situate itself within the international human rights discourse. What follows is an examination of these conceptual-theoretical shortcomings of the IBRs project.

Beyond recognizing a subset of privacy rights, most IBRs documents leave undefined the specific content of each subset of right, and the corresponding obligations/responsibilities. The right to *use* encryption best illustrates this point. Despite figuring in almost every IBRs initiative discussed above, what obligation flows from this right is rarely explicitly provided. It is not also straightforward on which actor the corresponding obligations befall—ie, States, corporations or even ordinary individuals. Whether the obligation of States, for instance, is merely a negative obligation or also a positive obligation is far from clear. Would, for instance, States be required to run awareness raising campaigns on secure communications, waive import/export tariff or roll back licensing requirements? Would the obligation of businesses involve providing end-to-end encryption by default or offering free device encryption services or install Transport Layer Security such as https? Questions of this sort find little answer in most initiatives for IBRs, perhaps with the exception of Article 19's Global Principles which, as noted above, to some extent elaborates possible obligations/responsibilities that flow from some digital rights both on States and corporations.

Such conceptual ambiguities give rise to a number of questions. First, from a theoretical perspective, there can barely exist a right if no corresponding obligation could be discerned from the right stipulated. As elaborated in Hohfeld's analytical

---

12 See Floridi and Cowls (n 50) 4.

framework of rights, duty is a 'jural correlative' of a right which exists only when there is a right.[122] This means, as put by Raz, it is only when a right leaves a corresponding obligation on others that it exists, and therefore, a right exists because it gives rise to duty(ies).[123] Second, even when a corresponding obligation may be implied somehow, it would prove difficult to attribute it to a particular duty-bearer. This, in turn, makes it onerous for individuals whose rights are violated to attribute responsibility. Even more onerous in the digital realm where attribution is harder, and that violation could be committed by anyone with ill-will. What makes the above uncertainties more acute, in the IBRs context, is that no interpretive entities are envisioned in most IBRs initiatives, as will be discussed below.

Amnesty International, a human rights non-governmental organization, recently offered an expansive reading of States' positive obligations under the right to privacy in the context of encryption technologies. According to this reading, the obligation to 'protect' includes the obligation to raise awareness about Internet security issues, fixing security flaws, and to 'facilitate' the use of encryption tools and services.[124] This expansive interpretation can be problematic, however. For instance, what exactly 'facilitating' involves would be controversial. Does 'facilitating', for example, involve import tariff exemption, or State subsidized provision of PETs? What would the State obligation to 'fix security flaws' include? It is not clear whether it comes into play only when the security flaw concerns State-operated computer systems or extends to the private sector as well.

Conceptual ambiguities inhere in other rights as well: freedom from surveillance. The right to freedom from surveillance includes, for example under the IRP Charter, the right not to be tracked online. But the scope of this right is far from clear. For example, whether freedom from surveillance would require service providers not to block access to users using anti-tracking technologies or more generally to make their services interoperable is not clearly enunciated. Article 19's Declaration frames the 'right to be free from surveillance' to include a right to have access to information about policies on surveillance and to be informed when a targeted surveillance has been authorized.[125] But, the scope of the right to notification is unclear—is the notification to be given prior to or after the surveillance? No doubt, *ex ante* notification is implausible as it would defeat the very purpose of the surveillance once the target becomes aware that surveillance is underway. Perhaps, a right to notification, as repeatedly articulated by the European Court of Human Rights (ECtHR), seems more appropriate *ex post* facto, which would allow concerned users to lodge protest against the request.[126]

---

[122] Wesley Hohfeld, 'Fundamental Legal Conceptions as Applied in Judicial Reasoning' (1917) 26 The Yale Law Journal 710, 710–14.

[123] Raz (n 117) 221.

[124] See Encryption: A Matter of Human Rights (Amnesty International 2016) 3, 32–33.

[125] Article 19's Declaration (n 93) art 6.

[126] See, eg, ECtHR, *Ekimdzhiev v Bulgaria*, Application No 62540/00 (28 June 2007) para 90.

More recent IBRs are equally afflicted by conceptual ambiguities. As highlighted above, the Montreal Declaration introduces a series of rights under the rubric of the 'privacy and intimacy' principle. One such right is the right to digital disconnection.[127] This right has recently been recognized in the labour laws of several European countries by which workers are able to disengage from work-related electronic communication during non-working hours.[128] In the wake of the Covid-19 pandemic—and the shift towards teleworking, a committee of the European Parliament recommended the adoption of a directive on the right to disconnect because there is no 'specific Union law on the worker's right to disconnect'.[129] But the nature and scope of this right as envisaged in the Montreal Declaration is not clear. At the basic level, it envisages 'people'—as opposed to individuals—as right holders which is less common in human rights vocabulary and hence may generate interpretative ambiguities.

More importantly, the scope of the right is far from clear—to what would the disconnection relate? Does it concern disconnection from digital accounts, access to computer systems or devices? Also ambiguous is the corresponding duty to this right. All that is provided in the Declaration is that AI systems 'should explicitly offer the option to disconnect at regular intervals, without encouraging people to stay connected'. Read literally, this provision may be taken to mean that the duty in question falls on AI systems which the Declaration defines as 'any computing system using AI algorithms, whether it's software, a connected object or a robot'.[130] But it is sensible to suggest that the duty essentially falls on developers or designers of such systems. But it is not straightforward as to how this right would be enforced in a world where AI systems are countless, less conspicuous and developed by transnational actors.

Another right with apparent ambiguity in the Montreal Declaration is the right to donate personal data for research purposes.[131] Unlike the right to digital disconnection, this right applies to 'individuals' not people but its formulation raises concerns. One such concern stems from the nature of donation as a juridical act. Except for the absence of payment, an act of donation entails all the effects of sale such as transfer of ownership to the recipient. With protection of personal data now largely established as a fundamental human right, the idea of personal data donation negates the *extra commercium* nature of rights. Moreover, that an act of donation is irrevocable means that much of the rights that data subjects enjoy in data protection law such as the right to erasure would be moot.[132] Even if the

---

[127] See Montreal Declaration (n 36) Principle 3(3).

[128] For more on this, see, Right to Disconnect (European Observatory of Working Life, 1 December 2020) <https://bit.ly/32NaflO>; see also Bart Custers, 'New Digital Rights: Imagining Additional Fundamental Rights for the Digital Era' (2021) 44 Computer Law and Security Review 1, 6–7.

[129] European Parliament Resolution with Recommendations to the Commission on the Right to Disconnect [2019/2181(INL)] (21 January 2021) Preamble.

[130] See Montreal Declaration (n 36) Glossary.

[131] ibid, Principle 3(7).

[132] See, eg, GDPR (n 62) art 17.

Declaration envisions donation to research organizations, there is no guarantee against change of hands at a later stage. Not only, then, that the Declaration overlooks the broader implications of granting personal data ownership to individuals but also fails to condition the right to donation with a view to protect data privacy of the donor. In envisioning data donation, the underlying assumption appears to be the much-loathed idea that data subjects 'own' their data, and hence are in control to be able to make informed decisions. But the technical complexity and the stealth with which personal data is collected, stored, and processed by a web of companies in the digital ecosystem renders data ownership and control nigh impossible.[133]

A version of the ambiguity relates to institutional arrangements, or the lack thereof, for the implementation of IBRs. Most IBRs initiatives, save a few exceptions such as the Brazilian and the Nigerian legislation/Bill as well as the European Digital Rights Charter, overlook the institutional aspect of rights protection. At times, the IBRs project relegates the task of building institutions and the implementation of IBRs to a separate 'discourse'.[134] The underlying aim of most IBRs initiatives to 'translate' human rights in the digital context also appears to eliminate the conventional role of judicial bodies to 'translate' norms to particular circumstances, including in light of new conditions of the day. Notable protagonists of the IBRs project suggest that there is no need for an institutional arrangement for IBRs as its provisions would be applied by a global 'community of judges' who, in the digital age, will have to address similar legal questions.[135] IBRs would serve as a 'reference' to these, to use Rodotà's words, 'crowd of judges' in such cases.[136] But this viewpoint raises more questions than it answers. For instance, it is not clear to which IBRs instrument would serve as a model or reference to the global community of courts unless one assumes it to be the IRP Charter of the IGF or Italy's recent Declaration in the drafting of which Rodotà played a part. It is not also clear how this would work, in reality, as courts normally apply legislation of their own jurisdiction. Nor is Rodotà's vision equivalent to the rather common practice of judicial dialogue among courts of various jurisdictions.

Centrality of an institutional framework for a rights regime cannot be overemphasized. As rights without corollary duties are hardly rights, rights without an institutional framework to enforce them would be mere declaratory statements. As Raz points out, despite recognition by the black letters of the law, rights without impartial, efficient and reliable institutions that oversee their implementation

---

[133] Of a related view, Martin Tisne, It's time for a Bill of Data Rights (MIT Technology Review, 14 December 2018) <https://bit.ly/348b7SH>.

[134] See Casacuberta and Senges (n 23) 105.

[135] See Rodotà (n 5).

[136] ibid. Note also that one of the aims of the European Declaration on Digital Rights and Principles is to provide a 'reference point' or a 'global benchmark' for businesses and other relevant actors when developing and deploying new technologies. See European Declaration (n 18) Preamble, para 5; Communication from the Commission (n 19) 4.

are not (human) rights.[137] The role of an institutional monitoring is also latent in Hohfeld's analytical framework of rights. 'Power', in addition to 'right', 'privilege', and 'immunity', is the other jural component, by which it refers, among others, to the discretion of the State more broadly. According to his thesis, when 'rights' are violated, or more precisely, when 'duties' are not discharged—a putative right holder can appeal to the 'power' of the State to enforce his/her rights.[138] This reinforces the indispensable role of an institutional mechanism, be it a court, quasi-judicial body or even an administrative agency, to maintain the balance of the rights-duty correlative.

In summary, the conceptual-theoretical opacity of the IBRs project throws doubt on its practicality as an international law response to the privacy problem.

3.1.3. The Desirability Dilemma

Regardless of conceptual questions surrounding IBRs, there are also doubts as to the desirability of a global IBRs. Is there a need for an international IBRs? What justifies such an instrument? The question of desirability relates to at least two issues. One is that the IBRs project does not offer a compelling justification as to why IBRs is needed in addition to the already existing framework of rights in (international) law. It is not clear how, and where, the present framework fails to protect human rights in the digital environment, and to what extent these weaknesses will be addressed by IBRs. Whether the perceived limitations of the present rights protection regimes are that of normative weaknesses or enforcement challenges is not clearly articulated by proponents of the IBRs project.

The underlying objective of serving as an advocacy instrument of some IBRs initiatives, for example the IRP Charter, partly addresses the first point as this objective does not necessarily rely on the existence of weaknesses in the present framework. But the problem persists in those IBRs instruments whose objective appears to be more than raising awareness or influencing public policy. The concern is that rolling out human rights without sufficient certainty that they will influence practice defeats their pragmatic function.[139] In considering the various shortcomings of international privacy law in attending to the privacy problem in the digital age—addressed in chapters 2 and 3, the lack of coherent conceptual justification for a new or expansive set of human rights standards for the digital space in the IBRs project diminishes its appeal.

Second, the desirability of IBRs is also to be called into question in the light of the current reality where already guaranteed human rights are constantly violated. On account of the fact that some IBRs initiatives tend to install a parallel rights

---

[137]   Raz (n 117) 228; see also Brennan (n 91) 457 (noting that without some effective means of vindication, legal rights become mere moral claims).

[138]   See generally Hohfeld (n 122).

[139]   See Amy Gutman, 'Introduction' in Amy Gutmann (ed), *Human Rights as Politics and Idolatry* (Princeton University Press 2001) xi.

regime, it is of little value to add a new catalogue of rights which would either face the fate of being undermined or not enforced at all. The implied justification, at times, for some of the (Internet) rights lends weight for an argument against an international IBRs. The imperative of a right to encryption, for example, is often based on the supposition that encryption technologies are relied upon by 'human rights defenders, journalists and dissidents'.[140] Given that a smaller section of society uses such technologies, a question of whether it is worthy of nomination as a right arises.

This further raises doubt on the exaggerated claims, noted above, that encryption is necessary for the 'functioning of society', and that prohibition/restriction of its use would 'destroy the modern way of life'.[141] When one considers the unresolved controversies regarding socio-economic and cultural rights—both in rights theory and practice, ambitious ventures of the IBRs project particularly in introducing seemingly new rights such as the right to the Internet access or even to use encryption technologies further compounds the desirability concern.[142] The desirability concern, therefore, underpins the need for a pragmatic approach that explicitly justifies a reform without the risk of looking too ambitious, and hence stirring controversy. Chapter 7 explores the propriety of such an approach in rethinking the scope of the right to privacy in the digital age.

3.1.4. Feasibility Challenges

Uncertainties about the desirability of an international IBRs further cloud the likelihood of a globally acceptable IBRs framework. The feasibility concern takes various forms. First, the essentially 'western' origin—and hence reflection of 'western values'—of IBRs, in the face of wider digital divide, raises the question of whether IBRs could draw sufficient support worldwide to supplement, or remedy, weaknesses of international law. The sheer fact that IBRs such as Nigeria's Bill and the African Declaration, or even Brazil's Macro da Civil, are from the global south do not necessarily mean that they reflect values of those jurisdictions or are reflections of wider concern for (Internet) rights. Indeed, most IBRs initiatives outside Europe are directly influenced by the IBRs project that emerged as a European initiative, as highlighted above.

---

[140] See, eg, Amnesty International (n 124) 4, 31.

[141] cf Melissa de Zwart, 'Privacy for the Weak, Transparency for the Powerful' in Andrew Kenyon (ed), *Comparative Defamation and Privacy Law* (Cambridge University Press 2016) 244 [claiming that 'encryption may need to become the new standard, replacing common law or statutory concepts of privacy which have proven too vague and too unenforceable'].

[142] At the center of the controversy were the strong views of western States that socio-economic rights are 'new' rights, albeit to western political thought, and therefore, should not be made part of the international bill of human rights. See Ronald Burke and James Kirby, 'The Universal Declaration of Human Rights: Politics and Provisions (1945–1948)' in Gerd Oberleitner (ed), *International Human Rights Institutions, Tribunals and Courts* (Springer 2018) 32.

IBRs initiatives like the African Declaration are largely replicates of Charters with origins in the western world. The African human rights system, for instance, does not expressly recognize a right to privacy,[143] but the Declaration embodies a list of privacy rights imported from preceding IBRs documents. With the digital divide wider (and intersectional) in some parts of the world, concerns for (digital) rights are probably lower. Some States and regions would, as a result, show hesitance towards a global IBRs or an instrument with IBRs touch. Perhaps, a reluctance of the AU towards IBRs, except for a recent side note of the AU's human rights body, in contrast with the support shown by the CoE and EU, suggests the lack of strong interest, or attention, in Africa. A few countries in Latin America have recognized the right of Internet access, a typical IBRs, including in their national Constitution,[144] but it is too early to pronounce a wider appeal to IBRs in the region. In parts of the world where access to the Internet is still limited, and where other priorities are too many, there is an additional reason to resist IBRs, or at least not to take them as a matter of priority.

IBRs may still be pursued as an international measure regardless of the above feasibility concerns. And, they might be endorsed without drawing sufficient consensus, as sometimes is the case in international standards setting. But this often comes with risks. As Hannum points out, attempts by (western) activists to put in place new human rights, without efforts to draw consensus, generates a backlash in the rest of the world.[145] The backlash could take various forms but typically IBRs drawn with insufficient consensus will be taken less seriously. In the context of 'rights talk' in general—ie, proliferation of human rights, Glendon notes that impracticable demands of more human rights will gather little audience.[146] The more visionary but unrealistic demands are made, the less that such demands are taken seriously, and met in practice. In places where they obtain some audience, the lack of resources towards enforcement will dictate a hierarchy of rights.[147] This concern partly extends to the IBRs project whose demands for rights protection not only appears less realistic but also lacks a clear conceptual basis.

Recent enactment of legislation in Brazil and Italy does not necessarily reflect a strong and genuine global interest in IBRs. In fact, the success in the adoption of both pieces of legislation must be seen in context, and with a measure of care. Brazil's Marco da Civil, despite frequent references to it as the world's first IBRs, its content barely resembles typical IBRs. As noted above, a right to encryption, for

---

[143] The only exception is the rather specialized treaty, the African Child Rights Charter. See *Charter on the Rights and Welfare of the Child*, opened for signature 11 July 1990, OAU Doc CAB/LEG/24.9/49 (entered into force 29 November 1999) art 10.

[144] See, eg, *Constitution of Ecuador* (2008) (as amended) art 16; *Constitution of Mexico* (1917) (as amended) art 6.

[145] Hannum (n 118) 412–13.

[146] Mary Glendon, *Rights Talk: The Impoverishment of Political Discourse* (Free Press 1991) 14.

[147] See Dominique Clement, 'Human Rights or Social Justice? The Problem of Rights Inflation' (2013) 22 International Journal of Human Rights 155, 159.

instance, is not explicitly guaranteed under the law. Other privacy protective provisions of the legislation such as data localization rules were later rolled back due to criticism from various corners.[148] Similarly, its implementation Decree adopted in 2016 addresses privacy only peripherally as its primary focus is net neutrality.[149] Considering these nuances behind the legislation, Marco da Civil can be seen as a politically motivated legislative rebuff to the Snowden revelations. So, this raises the question of whether IBRs, in the true sense of the concept, stand a chance of being accepted fully as one device of adapting (international) human rights to the digital space.

3.1.5. Procedural and Substantive (Il)Legitimacy

If a global IBRs somehow gets adopted—despite fundamental questions raised above, it cannot circumvent the consequent question of legitimacy.[150] This is particularly so if such an instrument were to be adopted through a process often deployed in the IBRs project. The process through which most IBRs initiatives come about, and actors that take part in the process, raise issues of legitimacy and competence. In many cases, IBRs initiatives often are results of a multistakeholder process where various stakeholders, including civil society groups, governments and the private sector participate in the drafting exercise. The multistakeholder process is, as noted above, also increasingly being supplemented by crowdsourcing. That these processes of drawing up legal instruments are largely new phenomena raises the question of whether both the processes and the outcome of these processes could be accepted as legitimate. The question centers around who gets to decide what claims become human rights, and what content that such rights should have. The procedural and substantive legitimacy of a given rights regime turns, to a greater degree, on the answer to these questions.

There is no single widely accepted body to make the above sort of determinations. Perhaps, the closest is what is often referred to as a 'democratic political community' or the 'international community'.[151] This is, of course, without losing sight of the fact that these notions are largely artificial constructs, and at times, their constitution is contested.[152] Democratically installed legislative and judicial bodies at the national, regional and international levels can be taken to satisfy the criterion of 'democratic political community'.[153] At the national and regional

---

[148] See Carlos Souza and others, 'Notes on the Creation and Impacts of Brazil's Internet Bill of Rights' (2017) 5 Theory and Practice of Legislation 73, 86.

[149] ibid, 86–88.

[150] The meaning of legitimacy may vary depending on the context in which it is used. But in a more general sense used here, what is often regarded 'legitimate' is one that is 'lawful, just and rightful'. See Christopher Morris, *An Essay on the Modern State* (Cambridge University Press 1998) 102–03.

[151] See Saladin Meckled-Garcia, 'Specifying Human Rights' in Rowan Cruft and others (eds), *Philosophical Foundations of Human Rights* (Oxford University Press 2015) 300.

[152] See Alan Boyle and Christine Chinkin, *The Making of International Law* (Oxford University Press 2007) 17.

[153] See Meckled-Garcia (n 151) 302.

levels, parliaments and courts of competent jurisdiction may constitute such a body whereas bodies like the UN General Assembly (UNGA) may be the international equivalents.[154]Alston refers to the UNGA as the final 'arbiter' in deciding what claims are worthy of nomination as human rights.[155] The Assembly perhaps represents what we earlier referred to as the 'democratic political community' or the 'international community'.[156] The process through which some IBRs were launched meet these requirements, particularly those anchored at the national level.

Brazil's legislation, for instance, is said to be a 'legitimate' piece of law on account of the participatory multistakeholder legislative process.[157] And of course, it has been adopted by an elected Congress, as was the Italian Declaration. The legislative exercise in the other experiments have not been so. The participation during the making of the Italian legislation, for instance, was said not to be 'extraordinary', suggesting the limited level of participation.[158] Little is known to what extent the Nigerian or other similar initiatives in the Philippines, have been inclusive. But most civil society initiatives barely meet the requirements of legitimacy noted above, not least because they often result from casual processes with apparent little concern for diversity of views. There is a general agreement that most civil society groups are not 'even minimally transparent or accountable' and hence lack legitimacy.[159] Article 19's Twitter hashtag campaign, for instance, has gathered limited reaction, and the project seems to have been abandoned altogether. This casts doubt on the legitimacy of a global IBRs churned out of such processes of norm creation.

As highlighted in section 2 above, the IBRs project is often credited for successfully experimenting with a 'multistakeholder model', reinforced through crowdsourcing, of norm creation. But the level of stakeholder representation is constantly contested in organizations that practice 'multistakeholderism'.[160] Although the options of participation are formally open, participation is practically

[154] See John Shorupski, 'Human Rights' in Samantha Besson and John Tasioulas (eds), *Philosophy of International Law* (Oxford University Press 2010) 357.

[155] Philip Alston, 'Conjuring Up New Human Rights: A Proposal for Quality Control' (1984) 78 The American Journal of International Law 607, 607–08.

[156] In their separate opinions in the *Namibia Case*, Judges Fouad Ammoun and Padilla Nero refer to the UNGA as 'representative' of the international community and an 'organ of the international community' respectively. See *Legal Consequences for States of the Continued Presence of South Africa in Namibia Notwithstanding Security Council Resolution 276 (1970)* [Advisory Opinion] ICJ Reports 1971 (21 June 1971) 73, 112.

[157] See Rossini and others (n 73) 7.

[158] See Elisabeth Ferrari, Italy Issues a Declaration of Internet Rights—Now Let's Improve It (Center for Global Communication Studies Media Wire, 4 August 2015) <https://bit.ly/2qqyLQB>.

[159] See Samantha Besson and Jose Marti, 'Legitimate Actors of International Law-making: Towards a Theory of International Democratic Representation' (2018) 9 Jurisprudence: An International Journal of Legal and Political Thought 504, 527, 537.

[160] See, eg, Laura DeNardis and Mark Raymond, Thinking Clearly About Multistakeholder Internet Governance, Paper Submitted at the 8th Annual GigaNet symposium, Bali, Indonesia (21 October 2013) 10.

limited by several factors including funding constraints, lack of expertise, or even organizational capacity.[161] The open-door approach also exposes the process to undue influence by some interest groups, be it governments, businesses or even civil society.[162] When one considers the generally sporadic and momentary nature of the IBRs project, fault lines of its multi-stakeholder experiments compound. If multistakeholder participation is not free from flaws in well-resourced organizations like the Internet Corporation for Assigned Names and Numbers, the experiment in IBRs would probably be too flawed to be taken seriously.

Recent developments further cast doubt on the value of crowdsourcing as a mechanism of norm creation. One is the advent of online disinformation that dilutes the flow of information. The open nature of crowdsourcing platforms inherently lacks accountability mechanisms to protect legitimate contributions from being burdened by web trolls and bots.[163] This adds up to the already growing 'technological ambivalence' towards promises of the web as a platform of popular participation. The failure of the crowdsourced constitution-making process in Iceland best illustrates the ambivalence towards crowdsourcing initiatives.[164] With a failed experiment in a small country of homogeneous and highly literate population, would crowdsourcing succeed in a rather heterogeneous environment, like the international community, where legitimacy is even more needed?[165] Probably not.

Crowdsourcing also raises an issue of juridical quality. In the absence of a mechanism of quality control by which the merit of inputs is independently examined, the sheer aim of ensuring procedural legitimacy ends up producing a document that erodes substantive quality and hence legitimacy. Indeed, the juridical quality of several IBRs instruments—both those crowdsourced from scratch and those presented for collaborative redrafting—is questionable on many levels. Article 19's Declaration, for instance, incorporates a range of rights, including ones that find counterparts in neither of the preceding IBRs instruments nor international law. The problem is not with the exercise in rights novelty but the conceptual ambiguity of these rights. The Declaration contains, among others, the 'right to blog', 'right to create', 'right to share', 'right to digital protest', 'right to dissent, offend and be offended', 'right to hack', 'right to tinker', and 'right to run one's own server'.[166]

---

[161] See Jeannette Hofmann, 'Multi-stakeholderism in Internet Governance: Putting a Fiction into Practice' (2016) 1 Journal of Cyber Policy 29, 33.

[162] See Besson and Marti (n 159) 528, 538.

[163] See Helen Landemore, 'Inclusive Constitution-making: The Icelandic Experiment' (2015) 23 Journal of Political Philosophy 166, 175.

[164] See Andrea Simoncini, The Constitutional Dimensions of the Internet: Some Research Paths, EUI Working Papers, LAW 2016/16 (2016) 7–9.

[165] For a related point, see Landemore (n 163) 188–89.

[166] See Article 19's Declaration (n 93) arts 7–10, 13–5; perhaps in anticipation of surprise with some of the extraordinary rights, readers are cautioned from the outset that some of the text could be 'distressing' to lawyers and advises 'reader discretion'. See prelude.

Similarly, the European Digital Rights Charter, reportedly drafted initially by a group of German academics, civil society groups, and politicians, is poorly drafted, and is even described as a 'juridical disaster'.[167] This casts negatively on crowdsourcing as a viable means of enhancing substantive legitimacy.

Intersectional digital divides, be it geographically, across age groups, gender or disability is the other source of concern. Digital divide significantly discounts the promises of crowdsourcing as a reliable medium of ensuring popular participation. Unless crowdsourcing is supplemented by other means of gathering input, what ultimately finds expression in the IBRs would be views of a limited group of stakeholders. Indeed, some interest groups, mainly businesses, may pursue crowdsourcing, in addition to their offline lobbying strategies, to influence the outcome of the lawmaking process. And this is not far from reality, with businesses now increasingly advocating for IBRs that often are aligned with their business interests.[168] In the ultimate analysis, the legitimacy of the process, and the method through which some IBRs were launched so far—both as domestic legislation and civil society initiatives—falls short.

To summarize the above discussion, the case for a global IBRs instrument is weak for a number of reasons. The diffuse and momentary nature of IBRs means that no major initiative that gradually develops into an international instrument is likely. But notwithstanding its diffusive approach, an international IBRs would face questions of desirability. There is no compelling reason why, and how, a global IBRs would be adopted by the international community. More so if the proposed IBRs is to be developed through a process that lacks legitimacy.

3.2. Contributory Role

As shown above, the freestanding role of the IBRs project in reimagining international privacy law is limited, if not none. But will it have some contributory role through which it may shape the progressive development of privacy law and practice at various levels? This section addresses this question. The contributory role may occur in three mutually reinforcing levels: informing and steering global privacy discussions, inspiring domestic legislation and inducing judicial and industry best practices. As this section will illustrate, this role of the IBRs project is unlikely to be consequential.

---

[16]   See Franz von Weizsäcker and Norman Schräpel, Why We Should Support the 'European Charter of Digital Fundamental Rights' (Internet Policy Review Blog, 14 December 2016) <http://bit.ly/2qBgl2N>.

[16]   See the section below on such industry practices.

3.2.1. Discursive Value

One possible contributory role is that IBRs may help further the global privacy debate evoked by the Snowden revelations and subsequent revelations. More particularly, the elaborate privacy rights espoused in IBRs may shape the further development of privacy law worldwide. This may occur in inter-governmental processes, where IBRs is not an entirely new subject. As highlighted in section 2, the IBRs project now has been, to some degree, an agenda item before several inter-governmental organizations such as the Human Rights Council (HR Council), the EU, and the CoE. In practice, marks of IBRs are also slightly visible in the ongoing UN privacy discourse. The series of UN Privacy Resolutions adopted in the wake of the Snowden revelations appear to reflect, as shall be explored in chapter 5, IBRs themes. The Privacy Resolutions, for example, 'encourage' Internet corporations to 'enable secure communications' and develop 'technical solutions' to protect their users against arbitrary and unlawful privacy interference.[169] This proviso reflects elements of common rights espoused in IBRs such as the right to *use* encryption.

But the degree to which IBRs will continue to shape global privacy discussions is limited. This is because the pursuit of IBRs as an agenda in inter-governmental and multistakeholder platforms has been largely sporadic. Despite positive initial gestures to IBRs at the CoE, the EU, and the HR Council, there is little to suggest that it still is an agenda item. The role of IBRs in the pending UN privacy discourse has also been or will probably continue to be, limited. This is, however, dictated partly by the nature of the discourse. The composition of the Privacy Resolutions exhibits hybridity and selectivity of norms which means limited place for IBRs themes. Add to that the inherent unsuitability of Resolutions in being sufficiently comprehensive. Thus, regardless of the political will to embrace IBRs, there is only so much that may ultimately form part of a Resolution. Perhaps, the best chance is that other reform efforts may exploit this positive gesture in developing a more focused approach. This point is further explored below and in more details later in chapters 7 and 8.

3.2.2. Shaping Lawmaking

IBRs may also inspire the enactment of national IBRs legislation, and hence gradually (and cumulatively) enhance harmonized protection of privacy globally. One of the earliest IBRs, the IRP Charter, for instance, has inspired Brazil and Italy's IBRs instruments, albeit unsurprisingly given the historical role of the two countries at the Dynamic Coalition.[170] Of draft IBRs pieces of legislation, a draft tabled by New Zealand's Green Party is benchmarked after the IRP Charter.[171] The

---

[169] See *The Right to Privacy in the Digital Age*, GA Res 71/199, 71st sess, Agenda item 68(b), UN Doc A/RES/71/199 (25 January 2017) para 7.

[170] See Report of the Dynamic Coalition (n 22) 3.

[171] See IRP Coalition Meeting Report (n 13) 12; Cambodia's IBRs initiative is also influenced by the IRP Charter. See Mike Godwin, The Great Charter for Cambodian Internet Freedom (LinkedIn, 8 March 2015) <https://bit.ly/2GEF2UR>.

substance of IBRs initiatives in the Philippines,[172] Guatemala,[173] Cambodia,[174] as well as in Nigeria are also similarly shaped by earlier IBRs documents. But the value in the proliferation of national IBRs legislation is rather limited in terms of international privacy law. Not only is the recent adoption of and proposal for IBRs legislation restricted to a few countries but also in the usual momentary fashion. The apparent lack of persistence in the IBRs project means nothing concrete is forthcoming in terms of global privacy law.

These geographically limited legislative measures so far further eschew the possibility for the gradual development of international customary norms on privacy. As Chinkin notes, the use by States of instruments produced by civil society groups like IBRs may facilitate creation of customary norms by pressuring compliance and hence producing state practice.[175] The adoption of domestic legislation giving effect to IBRs would further reinforce the creation of a rule of customary international law. But, the limited adoption of domestic IBRs legislation so far and the lack of adequate use of civil society IBRs by States means that the possibility of IBRs-induced customary norm is unlikely.

In short, because only a few pieces of IBRs legislation have been adopted thus far, the role of IBRs in inspiring domestic legislation, and hence gradually resulting in the development of customary IBRs applicable globally, will be insignificant.

3.2.3. Stimulating Judicial and Industry Practices

Another possible role for IBRs is to shape or influence decisions of courts at the international, regional, and national levels. As highlighted in section 2, one characteristic feature of IBRs is that they are results of cross-fertilization of norms, including those drawn from decisions of regional and domestic courts. But the reverse has also been the case, albeit seldomly. Many IBRs have been considered by courts on a few occasions. In a partial realization of Rodotà's vision of IBRs serving as 'reference' to the global community of judges,[176] the Supreme Court of Argentina has reportedly made a reference to Brazil's IBRs in one of its decisions.[177] At the regional level, AU's prime quasi-judicial human rights body has 'taken note' of the African Declaration in its Resolution on Freedom of Expression on the Internet.[178] The ECtHR has also referred to IBRs themes in a number of recent cases.[179]

---

[172] See Launch of the Philippine Declaration on Internet Rights and Principles (Foundation for Media Alternatives, September 2015) <http://104.236.169.13/FMA/?p=416>.

[173] See An Inclusive Dialogue for the Internet Bill of Rights in Guatemala (Web We Want Foundation, 27 January 2017) <http://ow.ly/hvMx30c7zdC>.

[174] See Godwin (n 171).

[175] Christine Chinkin, 'Normative Development in the International Legal System' in Dinah Shelton (ed), Commitment and Compliance: The Role of Non-Binding Norms in the International Legal System (Oxford University Press 2000) 36.

[176] Rodotà (n 5).

[177] See Souza and others (n 148) 93.

[178] The Right to Freedom of Information and Expression on the Internet in Africa, ACHPR Res 362 LIX) 2016 (4 November 2016) Preamble.

[179] In the recent case of Szabo and Vissy v Hungary for instance, the ECtHR made reference to a 2013 Report of La Rue, highlighted above, where the Special Rapporteur emphasizes States' obligation of not

The legal significance of the above noted judicial references to IBRs is, however, limited. More so in the development of the right to privacy in international law. In the case of Brazil's IBRs, for instance, the reference was to a provision of the legislation dealing with network neutrality. This adds up to the fact that the Brazilian legislation, as already noted, is not a typical IBRs instrument. The references by the two regional human rights bodies are also more of symbolic, rather than substantive, value. There is nothing to suggest, in the case of ECtHR for instance, that aspects of IBRs have shaped the respective decisions. This thus means that the potential of IBRs in shaping judicial practice in a meaningful way is yet to arrive. While the willingness of regional bodies to engage IBRs is useful, its relevance in developing current international law of privacy is circumscribed.

Beyond the legal arena, IBRs may also influence the *modus operandi* of technology companies in adopting practices that protect (digital) rights of users. In the light of frequent scandals plaguing major market players, a handful of technology companies recently saw the competitive advantage of pledging IBRs. An example is the social networking site Ello which has proclaimed a 'Bill of Rights for social Network Users' for its users.[180] Ello's IBRs appears to be influenced by the 'Bill of Privacy Rights for Social Network Users' introduced by the Electronic Frontier Foundation (EFF), a digital rights advocacy organization, in 2010.[181] The other way in which Internet corporations resort to privacy protective practices is through enabling encryption by default or issuing transparency policy detailing, albeit in broad-strokes, government requests for user data.

Besides the fact that the traction to these industry practices is restricted to a section of the industry, specifically small Internet businesses and the voluntary nature of these pledges reduce their significance. But more importantly, part of the reason for the recent corporate support towards digital rights may simply be a business strategy, perhaps one meant to overcome the backlash since the Snowden debacle.[182] As Rodotà rightly cautions, (digital) rights activism championed by Internet corporations may be clouded by business priorities.[183] The future of

interfering with the use of encryption technologies. See ECtHR, *Szabo and Vissy v Hungary*, Application No 37138/14 (12 January 2016) para 24. The Concurring Opinion of Judge De Albuquerque in *Szabo and Vissy* makes extensive reference to post-Snowden developments at the UN, including the passing of Resolutions which, as noted above, touch on IBRs themes. See paras 3–7, 51.

[180] See details at <https://bill-of-rights.ello.co/>. Other social networking sites have also similar policies, an example being 'MeWe'. See <https://t.co/7DetwK2FSr>.

[181] See Kurt Opsahl, A Bill of Rights for Social Network Users (Electronic Frontier Foundation, 19 May 2010) <http://bit.ly/2s2PMFp>.

[182] See Ernesto Falcon and Jeremy Gillula, The Hypocrisy of AT&T's 'Internet Bill of Rights' (Electronic Frontier Foundation, 1 February 2018) <https://bit.ly/2qgTGY9> cf Randall Stephenson, Consumers Need an Internet Bill of Rights (AT&T Media Release, 24 January 2018) <https://soc.att.com/2DHA7ki>.

[183] Stefano Rodotà, 'Data Protection as a Fundamental Right' in Serge Gutwirth and others (eds), *Reinventing Data Protection?* (Springer 2009) 82.

international privacy law must be one that encourages such voluntary industry best practices but seeks to broaden the role of Internet corporations in the protection of human rights, including in multi-level dialogues. One form of such a dialogue was projected when the idea of an IBRs was raised by Democrats at the United States Congress in the wake of the Cambridge Analytica scandal. Regardless of the final outcome, its proponent had pledged to incorporate the input of technology companies in the drafting process.[184] But care will have to be taken to ensure that such involvements do not lead to weaker legislative responses. We return to this point in chapters 7 and 8.

3.3. Catalytic Role

As the above discussion demonstrated, the possibility of IBRs developing into a global treaty law is deeply doubtful. Nor would its role of gradually shaping further development of privacy principles go far enough to address international law's privacy problem. This section suggests that a more pertinent role for IBRs is should its progressive vision be geared towards a more focused and innovative approach to reform. If it were to be integrated with such an approach, IBRs would assist in lessening, to some degree, the weak normative contours of international privacy law. Chapters 7 and 8 explore what a pragmatic reform approach to international law of privacy would look like in greater details, but what follows points to two aspects of IBRs that would be drawn upon in those chapters.

The IBRs project envisions, as shown in section 2 above, the right to privacy in a manner that unpacks the scope of the right in international human rights law. This offers an alternate way of addressing the problems of scope, considered in chapter 2, of the human right to privacy framework. The international data privacy framework, as shown in chapter 3, is generally fragmented and outdated at many levels. The IBRs project offers useful lessons in addressing the deep normative dispersion and the normative paucity of the international data privacy framework. As IBRs instruments generally treat the 'human right to privacy' and 'data privacy' in a holistic manner, future reform efforts could rely on this approach. Normative inferiority of international data privacy law could similarly be addressed as IBRs generally embody widely accepted rights and principles of data privacy that now are grounded in domestic laws of many countries. The other major rectification offered in IBRs, as noted above, concerns the provision of pertinent limitation clauses to privacy rights. Most IBRs initiatives now clearly envisage the grounds under which the right to privacy can lawfully be restricted. This would remedy the blind spots in international law.

---

[184] See Lee (n 43) [note, though, that the Congressman reportedly said he would seek the 'help' of Tim Cook and Mark Zuckerberg in drafting the IBRs to 'demonstrate Silicon Valley's reputable force'].

Thus, the legal significance of IBRs lies in pointing towards an alternate 'normative direction' for further development of privacy in international law. In that sense, its role resembles what Alston called the 'catalyst' role of older charters of rights such as the English Bill of Rights and other subsequent national declarations of rights.[185] Like the international law of human rights that followed the Second World War was partly inspired by these monumental national documents, IBRs may also catalyze an international privacy law reform. In that way, pragmatic reform ideas, particularly the soft law supplement to international privacy law argued for in chapter 7, draws from the catalytic potential of IBRs.

4. Conclusion

The history of the IBRs project in the past two decades or so has been replete with uncertainties as to scope and goals. Most IBRs initiatives emerged in momentary, disjointed and uncoordinated fashion. Often, each initiative for IBRs including those advanced by civil society groups varied in scope, purpose and existed in isolation from one another. This approach appears to have limited, thus far, their impact in the international protection of privacy. This chapter examined the role of IBRs in reimagining the right to privacy in international law. It has shown that a more concrete role of the IBRs project is in charting a normative direction for other more focused and practical reforms. The chapter argued that IBRs will neither develop into a freestanding international instrument nor will it sufficiently shape privacy law and practice worldwide to address international law's privacy problem.

Progressive normative elements of IBRs would, instead, offer a novel way in which the scope of the right to privacy should be drawn. More particularly, the IBRs project moves past the present, to use Ignatieff's words,[186] the 'minimalist' approach of international privacy law. The relatively elaborate manner in which privacy rights are envisioned in IBRs would assist in unpacking the high-level abstract principles of international law. But, as this chapter has illustrated, the IBRs project risks slightly overstretching the human rights framework. Chapters 7 and 8 explore an approach to privacy law reform that strikes a fair balance between minimalist and maximalist visions of the right to privacy. The soft law supplement argued for in chapter 7 seeks to critically embrace quasi-new rights without eroding the integrity and credibility of the international human rights system.

---

[185] Alston (n 155) 614.
[186] See Ignatieff (n 119) 321–22.

5

Emergent Privacy Standards

1. Introduction

This chapter examines the second of international privacy initiatives: the ongoing discourse on the 'right to privacy in the digital age' at the United Nations (UN). In the wake of the Snowden revelations in mid-2013, the UN General Assembly (UNGA) broached a discourse with a resolution that brought to light concerns surrounding mass surveillance and arbitrary collection of personal data.[1] The discourse has since developed into a series of resolutions adopted both by the UNGA and the Human Rights Council (HR Council). As part of this evolving discourse, a number of thematic reports have been prepared by the UN Office of the High Commissioner for Human Rights (OHCHR).[2] The chapter interrogates the role of this discourse, particularly the series of Privacy Resolutions adopted as part of the discourse, in making international privacy law better-equipped in the digital age. In so doing, it seeks to demonstrate the extent to which normative and institutional blind spots laid out in chapters 2 and 3 are being addressed by the ongoing discourse. The chapter argues that the prime merit of the discourse lies, like Internet Bills of Right (IBRs) initiatives examined in chapter 4, in its role of catalyzing the progressive development of privacy law. The argument develops in three steps.

First, the chapter considers the 'freestanding' role of the Privacy Resolutions in reimagining the right to privacy in international law. The freestanding potential of the Resolutions primarily relates to their role in elaborating the rather vague and truncated rules of international privacy law. As shown in chapter 2, the right to privacy in international law is formulated in an exceedingly vague language, entangled with a broad set of values less related to privacy, which—to date—are yet to find adequate elaboration in treaty body jurisprudence. Nor is the international framework on data privacy sufficiently coherent and elaborate. Further considered is whether the Resolutions constitute authoritative interpretations of existing privacy provisions of international law. The chapter shows that the rather patchy,

---

[1] *The Right to Privacy in the Digital Age*, GA Res 68/167, 68th sess, Agenda item 69(b), UN Doc A/RES/68/167 (21 January 2014).

[2] See, eg, The Right to Privacy in the Digital Age, First Report of the High Commissioner for Human Rights, UN Doc A/HRC/27/37 (30 June 2014); The Right to Privacy in the Digital Age, Second Report of the High Commissioner for Human Rights, UN Doc A/HRC/39/29 (3 August 2018); The Right to Privacy in the Digital Age, Third Report of the High Commissioner for Human Rights, UN Doc A/HRC/48/31 (13 September 2021).

Privacy and the Role of International Law in the Digital Age. Kinfe Yilma, Oxford University Press. © Kinfe Yilma 2023. DOI: 10.1093/oso/9780192887290.003.0005

disjointed, and incoherent content of the Resolutions, inter alia, discounts the significance of their elaborative and interpretive potential.

Second, the chapter considers the 'contributory' role of the discourse in shaping the further development of privacy law at national, regional, and international levels. It first discusses the extent to which the Privacy Resolutions may substantively inform the making of laws and judicial decisions at different levels. Further considered is whether the Resolutions may ground the right to privacy in general international law, namely international custom and general principles. The chapter demonstrates that this contributory role of the discourse is inconsequential and probably undesirable in addressing the 'privacy problem' in the digital age. The substantive reach of the Resolutions thus far is narrow means that their possible function of grounding the right to privacy in general international law is negligible.

Third, the chapter contends that a more tangible role of the discourse is 'catalytic' by which it may shape the normative and methodological directions of future practical privacy reform efforts. Because the freestanding and contributory roles of the discourse are nominal, the best outcome would be innovative utilization of the political will exhibited in the ongoing discussions. The stimulation of a privacy agenda at the UN evoked by the discourse carries a political capital that can catalyze a more focused and practical reform effort. Chapters 7 and 8 explore such a reform alternative that critically embraces but goes beyond aspects of the privacy discourse in general and the Privacy Resolutions in particular.

2. Mapping the Discourse

As shall become clear, the UN privacy discourse is in a state of flux and its true colours are yet to fully emerge. Not only is the conversation sparked by this discourse still inchoate but also that it is entangled with other parallel UN processes dealing with human rights and new digital technologies. One such discourse relates to the protection and promotion of human rights on the Internet initiated at the HR Council.[3] Sparked in the wake of the so called the Arab Spring, this discourse preceded the privacy discourse but there is an increasing normative convergence between the two processes.[4] Likewise, the privacy discourse is slowly collapsing into a more recent initiative at the HR Council on human rights and emerging technologies.[5] Beside the drawbacks of such a disjointed approach, the role of the going UN

---

[3] See, eg, *The Promotion, Protection and Enjoyment of Human Rights on the Internet*, HRC Res 20/8, 20th sess, Agenda item 3, UN Doc A/HRC/RES/20/8HRC (16 July 2012).

[4] See, eg, *The Promotion, Protection and Enjoyment of Human Rights on the Internet*, HRC Res 47/16, 47th sess, Agenda item 3, UN Doc A/HRC/RES/47/16 (26 July 2021).

[5] See *New and Emerging Digital Technologies and Human Rights*, HRC Res 41/11, 41st sess, Agenda item 3, UN Doc A/HRC/RES/41/11 (17 July 2019); *New and Emerging Digital Technologies and Human Rights*, HRC Res 47/23, 47th sess, Agenda item 3, UN Doc A/HRC/RES/47/23 (16 July 2021).

discourse on the right to privacy in reimagining international law of privacy has not been considered.

In an attempt to lessen this void and to provide an analytical prism to subsequent sections, this section positions the discourse in context. First, it offers a background as to the origins and the overall composition of the discourse. Second, it considers the novelties introduced by the series of Privacy Resolutions adopted from 2013 to 2021 as part of the discourse. The examination offers the background against which the prospect of the discourse in making international privacy law fit for purpose in the digital age are considered in section 3. The reference in this chapter, where applicable in other chapters too, to the post-Snowden process at the UN as a 'discourse' is deliberate. The Oxford Dictionary defines 'discourse' as 'a long and serious treatment, or discussion of a subject in speech or writing'.[6] From the outset, resolutions of both the UNGA and HR Council emphasize the need to 'discuss' issues surrounding the right to privacy in the digital age as a means to 'clarify' existing standards and 'identify' best practices.[7] In a remark during the discussion on the very first Resolution, it was suggested by the Permanent Representative of Brazil to the UN that the underlying objective of the process is to 'debate' the right to privacy in the digital age.[8] It is in that spirit that the term discourse is deployed in this chapter and elsewhere where the Resolutions and the accompanying reports are considered.

2.1. Background to the Discourse

The ongoing privacy discourse represents a revival of the privacy agenda at the UN after many years of hiatus. Since the introduction of a general right to privacy in the International Covenant on Civil and Political Rights (ICCPR) in 1966, the subject has received little attention at the UN. The two major exceptions are the adoption of the Guidelines for Computerized Personal Data Files (Data Privacy Guidelines) in 1990 and General Comment (GC) 16 two years earlier. Privacy returned to the UN agenda decades later through various reports of UN Special Rapporteurs. But even in those instances, the right to privacy was treated largely as an enabler of other human rights, mainly freedom of expression.[9] An exception is the landmark

---

[6] See <https://www.oxfordlearnersdictionaries.com/definition/english/discourse_1?q=discourse>.

[7] See, eg, *The Right to Privacy in the Digital Age*, GA Res 69/166, 69th sess, Agenda item 68(b), UN Doc A/RES/69/166 (10 February 2015) para 5 cum Preamble, para 9.

[8] Remark by Antonio de Aguiar Patriota, Permanent Representative of Brazil to the United Nations, before the Third Committee of the UNGA, quoted in Summary Record of the 51st Meeting of the Third Committee, UN Doc A/C.3/68/SR.51 (26 November 2013) para 38.

[9] See Report of the Special Rapporteur on the Promotion and Protection of the Right to Freedom of Opinion and Expression, Frank La Rue, UN Doc A/HRC/17/27 (16 May 2011) paras 53–59; Report of the Special Rapporteur on the Promotion and Protection of the Right to Freedom of Opinion and Expression, Frank La Rue, UN Doc A/66/290 (10 August 2011) para 11.

report of the former UN Special Rapporteur on Freedom of Expression, La Rue. Presented a few months before the Snowden revelations, the report considered implications of States' surveillance of communications on the exercise of the human rights to privacy as well as freedom of opinion and expression.[10]

Of particular interest is that among the modalities of communications surveillance highlighted in the report, mass surveillance is one of them, but only in the specific context of the Arab Spring in the Middle East.[11] In a way, the report foreshadowed the breath-taking level of transnational mass surveillance unveiled by the Snowden papers, albeit by the so called Five Eyes States. Perhaps in recognition of this, the inaugural resolution of the UNGA on the right to privacy in the digital age specifically welcomed the report.[12] But it was not until the Snowden debacle a few months later that privacy would come to the limelight in UN processes in a manner that is sustained to date. In that sense, the Snowden revelations have played a central role in putting the right to privacy back in the UN agenda. It is this essentially 'new' privacy discourse sparked by the revelations that is the prime focus of the chapter.

In terms of scope, the discourse consists of a series of Resolutions adopted by the UNGA and the HR Council. At the time of writing, five Resolutions have been adopted by the UNGA[13] and five Resolutions by the HR Council.[14] There are two common threads in these Resolutions. One is that they are all adopted by consensus without formal casting of votes. The practice of adopting Resolutions by consensus is a relic of the Cold War era meant to offer compromise over controversial draft Resolutions.[15] It is often seen as a way of papering over differences on the text of Resolutions.[16] And this may ultimately leave its marks in vague textual formulations.[17] Fidler notes, in the context of the Privacy Resolutions, that the adoption without a vote—ie, by consensus—is a reflection of controversy among member States on the content of the Resolutions.[18] And of course, there were

---

[10] See Report of the Special Rapporteur on the Promotion and Protection of the Right to Freedom of Opinion and Expression, Frank La Rue, UN Doc A/HRC/23/40 (17 April 2013).

[11] ibid, para 38.

[12] GA Res 68/167 (n 1) Preamble, para 7.

[13] Resolutions of the UNGA chronologically are: Resolution 68/167 (18 December 2013); Resolution 69/166 (18 December 2014); Resolution 71/199 (19 December 2016); Resolution 73/179 (17 December 2018); Resolution 75/176 (16 December 2020).

[14] Resolutions (and a Decision) of the HR Council chronologically are: Decision 25/117 (27 March 2014) [Panel on the Right to Privacy in the Digital Age]; Resolution 28/16 (26 March 2015); Resolution 34/7 (23 March 2017); Resolution 37/2 (22 March 2018); Resolution 42/15 (7 October 2019); Res 48/4 (13 October 2021). For ease of reference, the appendices provides full text of the latest UNGA Privacy Resolution.

[15] See Antonio Cassese, *International Law in a Divided World* (Clarendon Press 1986) 197.

[16] See, eg, Oscar Garibaldi, 'The Legal Status of General Assembly Resolutions: Some Conceptual Observations' (1979) 73 Proceedings of the Annual Meeting of the ASIL 324, 326.

[17] See Conforti Benedetto, *The Law and Practice of the United Nations* (Martinus Nijhoff 3rd edn, 2004) 82.

[18] David Fidler, 'United Nations Resolution on the Right to Privacy in the Digital Age' in David Fidler (ed), *The Snowden Reader* (Indiana University Press 2015) 313.

reports of lobbying by the Five Eyes States at the early stages of the discussions at the UNGA's Third Committee, but the resultant change was said to be more of style and toning-down wordings.[19] With that said, the initiation, and still sustained, discussion on the privacy agenda paves the way for further engagement on privacy issues. The affirmative gesture of States, expressed when agreeing to adoption by consensus, would create an expectation of the international community that the terms of the Resolution will be taken seriously.[20] The adoption of the Resolutions *per se* is, thus, of some value when one considers the exigencies of reform in international privacy law.

A second thread is that Resolutions adopted by the HR Council are often iterations of the UNGA Resolutions and adopted as a follow-up. Generally, Resolutions of both UN bodies carry no legally binding force. But it appears that UNGA Resolutions are more authoritative, not least because the Council is a subsidiary organ of the Assembly. The UNGA is generally considered as the 'chief deliberative, policy-making and representative organ of the United Nations'.[21] That the Council operates through periodic membership (added to its exposure to politicization) further makes its Resolutions less authoritative. A drawback with the involvement of the HR Council is a tendency to combine the ongoing discourse with other parallel discussions alluded to above. The concern with this approach is that the rather promising potential of the privacy discourse may be lost in a process that is increasingly becoming disjointed.

In addition to the close to a dozen Resolutions, the privacy discourse is accompanied by a number of reports prepared by the OHCHR and UN Special Rapporteurs.[22] This means that the content of the Privacy Resolutions is shaped and informed by these various Reports. The first report of OHCHR, for instance, has been key in shaping the direction and substance of subsequent Resolutions of the UNGA. But again, that report was developed based on inputs from various sources, including submissions of civil society groups which, in turn, draw from the jurisprudence of regional courts, national legislation, and even IBRs.[23] Likewise,

---

[19] See, eg, Anupam Chander and Molly Land, 'Introductory Note to United Nations General Assembly Resolution on the Right to Privacy in the Digital Age' (2014) 53 International Legal Materials 727, 727.

[20] See Samuel Bleicher, 'The Legal Significance of Re-Citation of General Assembly Resolutions' (1969) 63 The American Journal of International Law 444, 446–47.

[21] See, eg, *United Nations Millennium Declaration*, GA Res 55/2, 55th sess, Agenda item 60(b) (8 September 2000) para 30.

[22] See, eg, First Report of the High Commissioner (n 2).

[23] ibid, paras 9–11; it is interesting to note that the third Resolution of the General Assembly 're-called' that business enterprises have a responsibility to respect 'human rights, applicable laws, international principles and standards'. The phrase 'international principles and standards' may be taken to refer to IBRs initiatives, discussed at length in chapter 4, which indeed have been submitted as part of stakeholder input during the preparation of reports of the OHCHR. But this reference was removed from subsequent Resolutions of both the UNGA and the HR Council. See, eg, *The Right to Privacy in the Digital Age*, GA Res 71/199, 71st sess, Agenda item 68(b), UN Doc A/RES/71/199 (25 January 2017). But, all Resolutions of the UNGA encourage 'further discussion' including by UN bodies with a view to, inter alia, to clarify 'existing principles and standards' and identify 'best practices' which arguably

the second and third reports are prepared based on input from different stake-holders including States, civil society groups, and international organizations.[24] In that sense, the UN privacy discourse has been a site for cross-fertilization of global privacy norms.

Forming also an important part of the discourse are reports of the UN Special Rapporteur on the Right to Privacy (SRP) which, indeed, is a product of the discourse. Created in 2015 by the HR Council, among the main functions of the mandate include submitting recommendations towards ensuring the protection of the right to privacy in the digital age.[25] To that effect, the Special Rapporteur reports annually to the UNGA and the HR Council.[26] But more importantly, the inaugural mandate holder had initiated a treaty process on government surveillance and draft soft laws dealing with health data and Artificial Intelligence (AI).[27] The current status of these initiatives is unknown, but they are indicative of the mandate's future role in triggering standard setting on the right to privacy in the digital age. The chapter makes incidental references to reports alluded to above and the accompanying discussion driven by other actors, mainly civil society groups. It should, however, be noted that the reports of the Special Rapporteur have slightly shaped the content of the Privacy Resolutions. One relates to the emphasis on the importance of the right to privacy for the free development of individual personality in his inaugural report which are later incorporated in subsequent Resolutions of the HR Council.[28]

Aspects of the privacy discourse have also gradually migrated to other longstanding initiatives of UN bodies. One such initiative is the Global

---

include privacy rights, standards, and norms often advanced in IBRs initiatives. See, eg, *The Right to Privacy in the Digital Age*, GA Res 73/179, 73rd sess, Agenda Item 74(b), UN Doc A/RES/73/179 (21 January 2019) para 10. One also sees an evolution in the influence of IBRs in the Privacy Resolutions. With the recent prominence of AI and related technologies, more recent Resolutions reflect 'ethical principles' now widely championed by various actors, including inter-governmental organization and civil society groups. See, eg, *The Right to Privacy in the Digital Age*, GA Res 75/176, 75th sess, Agenda item 72(b), UN Doc A/RES/75/176 (28 December 2020) para 6; *The Right to Privacy in the Digital Age*, HRC Res 48/4, 48th sess, Agenda Item 3, UN Doc A/HRC/RES/48/4 (13 October 2021) para 5.

[24] See Second Report of the High Commissioner (n 2) para 4; Third Report of the High Commissioner (n 2) para 5.
[25] See *The Right to Privacy in the Digital Age*, HRC Res 28/16, 28th sess, Agenda Item 3, UN Doc A/HRC/RES/28/16 (26 March 2015). The mandate has since been renewed several times with the latest in March 2021. See *Mandate of Special Rapporteur on the Right to Privacy*, HRC Res 46/16, 46th sess, Agenda item 3, UN Doc A/HRC/RES/46/9 (31 March 2021).
[26] See reports of the mandate at <https://www.ohchr.org/EN/Issues/Privacy/SR/Pages/AnnualRepo rts.aspx>.
[27] See Special Rapporteur on the Right to Privacy Presents Draft Legal Instrument on Government-led Surveillance and Privacy (28 February 2018) <https://bit.ly/3FZhDJJ>; Data Privacy Guidelines in Context of Artificial Intelligence (Draft, October 2021) <https://bit.ly/3mYp2Qr>; Recommendation on the Protection and Use of Health-related Data (5 December 2019) <https://bit.ly/3L1Qd8g>.
[28] See Report of Special Rapporteur on the Right to Privacy, Joseph Cannataci, UN Doc A/HRC/31/64 (8 March 2016) paras 7, 11, 23–27 cum *The Right to Privacy in the Digital Age*, HRC Res 34/7, 34th sess, Agenda Item 3, UN Doc A/HRC/RES/34/7 (22 March 2017) Preamble, para 14.

Counter-terrorism Strategy which was originally launched in 2006 and reviewed every two years since.[29] As part of this periodic review, the latest iterations of the Strategy are considerably influenced by the Resolutions adopted as part of this discourse. Pillar IV deals with measures to ensure respect for human rights for all and the rule of law as the fundamental basis of the fight against terrorism. This pillar 'urges' States to respect and protect the right to privacy while countering terrorism.[30] But it goes further and calls upon States to uphold the right to privacy as set out in international human rights law while countering terrorism and preventing violent extremism conducive to terrorism and to review legislation regarding the surveillance of communications, their interception and the collection of personal data, including mass surveillance, interception, and collection.[31] This largely reflects, if not replicate, the terms of the Privacy Resolutions.[32] But it should be noted that such cross-influence started to emerge once the privacy discourse gathers steam at the UN. This is manifested, for instance, in the absence of terms taken directly from the Privacy Resolutions, ie, regarding surveillance of communications, their interception, and the collection of personal data, in the Strategy adopted in June 2014.[33] This is remarkable because the third review does not even make any specific reference to privacy but simply calls upon States to uphold human rights and fundamental freedoms, as well as due process and the rule of law, while countering terrorism.[34]

The Secretary General's Call to Action for Human Rights is probably the other UN initiative influenced directly or indirectly by the ongoing privacy discourse. Launched on the occasion of the 75th anniversary of the UN, the Call pays particular attention to privacy and data protection.[35] One of the seven domains identified in the Call is 'new frontiers of human rights' where promotion of the effective protection of the right to privacy and personal data is one of the desirable actions envisaged.[36] Related to this are the Secretary General's Roadmap for Digital Cooperation and the creation of an Envoy on Technology to oversee its implementation.[37] Data privacy is one of the digital human rights themes considered in

---

[29] The *United Nations Global Counter-Terrorism Strategy: Seventh Review*, GA Res 75/291, UN Doc A/RES/75/291 (2 July 2021).

[30] ibid, para 106; see also *The United Nations Global Counter-Terrorism Strategy Review*, GA Res 72/284, UN Doc A/RES/72/284 (2 July 2018) para 19; *The United Nations Global Counter-Terrorism Strategy Review*, GA Res 70/291, UN Doc A/RES/70/291 (19 July 2016) para 19.

[31] ibid, para 107; see also GA Res 72/284 (n 30) para 20; GA Res 70/291 (n 30) para 20.

[32] Cf HRC Res 48/4 (n 23) para 6(c).

[33] See *The United Nations Global Counter-Terrorism Strategy Review*, GA Res 68/276, UN Doc A/RES/68/276 (24 June 2014) para 12.

[34] See *The United Nations Global Counter-Terrorism Strategy Review*, GA Res 66/282, UN Doc A/RES/66/282 (12 July 2012) para 9.

[35] The Highest Aspiration: A Call to Action for Human Rights, United Nations Secretary General (2020).

[36] ibid, 12.

[37] Roadmap for Digital Cooperation: Implementation of the Recommendations of the High-level Panel on Digital Cooperation, Report of the Secretary General, UN Doc A/74/821 (29 May 2020);

the Roadmap where the need for effective protection of privacy and personal data is emphasized.[38] Indeed, recent Privacy Resolutions 'takes note' of the Secretary General's Strategy.[39] Such a flurry of initiatives at the UN launched in the past few years invariably provides due emphasis to the protection of the right to privacy in the digital ecosystem. And there is little doubt that the ongoing privacy discourse has had a role in putting privacy and data protection front and center in all UN initiatives dealing with new and emerging technologies.

In summary, the ongoing privacy discourse at the UN sparked by the Snowden revelations has generally been an eclectic process. Its content is shaped by sources drawn from different sources, but also increasingly shaping the broader discussions at the UN on the topic of technology and human rights. But importantly, the series of Resolutions adopted thus far are gradually shaping the normative contours of the right to privacy in international law. What follows discusses the ways in which it does so with a focus on major novelties introduced by the discourse.

2.2. Novelties of the Discourse

A closer look at the way in which the UN privacy discussions have proceeded in the past nine years reveal at least two novelties. One relates to the overall approach of the discourse. There is an apparent unifying approach to the right to privacy by which the series of Privacy Resolutions embody hitherto disparate normative sources as well as actors involved in the protection and/or violation of the right. Not only does this import norms to a rather 'human rights' discourse from adjacent regulatory fields but also reflect modern understandings of and challenges to the right to privacy in the digital age. As shall be shown below, privacy norms, standards, and principles flagged in the Resolutions are drawn from different sources, including domestic or regional data privacy law, international human rights law, and even aspects of IBRs. Moreover, there is a tendency to bring in non-State actors, particularly Internet corporations, as important actors in the protection of the right to privacy. Secondly, the Resolutions tend to unpack the normative contours of the right to privacy in the digital context, particularly in specifying the respective obligations and responsibilities of States and technology companies respectively vis-à-vis the right to privacy. What is novel about this is its tendency to change course in the UN 'business and human rights' debate by addressing

---

see also Mr Fabrizio Hochschild Drummond of Chile: Secretary-General's Envoy on Technology (Statement, 22 January 2021) <https://bit.ly/3465tAk>.

[38] ibid, paras 43–45.
[39] See *The Right to Privacy in the Digital Age*, HRC Res 42/15, 42nd sess, Agenda item 3, UN Doc A/HRC/RES/42/15 (7 October 2019) Preamble, para 9; GA Res 75/176 (n 23) Preamble, para 6; HRC Res 48/4 (n 23) Preamble, para 6.

corporations more directly in human rights language. The discussion below elaborates these novelties of approach and substance.

2.2.1. Novelty of Approach

The privacy discourse, the outcome of which has primarily been in the form of resolutions, displays a level of novelty in approach. At a higher level of abstraction, the discourse is gradually producing Resolutions that barely resemble other UN Resolutions. The UN Charter does not explicitly mention 'Resolution' as one means of international standard setting. But traditionally it is understood to be a substitute for 'recommendation' and 'decisions' which are mentioned explicitly in the Charter.[40] In the international law literature, the term 'Resolution' is often deployed to refer to both Declarations such as the Universal Declaration of Human Rights (UDHR) which embody substantive principles and rights as well as hortatory Resolutions which contain no such substantive legal principles or rights.[41] But the Privacy Resolutions defy these niceties in practice and the literature. They do so mainly by flagging some substantive privacy principles and norms, as shall be discussed further below.

While the Privacy Resolutions clearly are not Declarations like the UDHR, they are not also mere hortatory Resolutions either. Except for the initial Resolution, the subsequent Resolutions appear to reflect some substantive principles that are not common in hortatory Resolutions. A good comparison is the ongoing discourse at the HR Council on the right to freedom of expression online which has similarly resulted in the adoption of a series of Resolutions. Under the title of 'promotion, protection and enjoyment of human rights on the Internet', the free speech Resolutions are typically hortatory, generally lacking substantive norms.[42] Indeed, this dearth in substance is slightly changing partly in the light of the recent synchronization, as hinted above, between the privacy and the free speech discourses. Elements of the Privacy Resolutions are gradually migrating to the free speech Resolutions. The most recent Resolution, for instance, reiterates a longstanding dictum in the Privacy Resolutions that encryption and anonymity are key for the

---

[40] See, eg, Marko Oberg, 'The Legal Effects of Resolutions of the UN Security Council and General Assembly in the Jurisprudence of the ICJ' (2006) 16 European Journal of International Law 879, 800.

[41] See, eg, Alan Boyle and Christine Chinkin, *The Making of International Law* (Oxford University Press 2007) ch 5.

[42] See, eg, *The Promotion, Protection and Enjoyment of Human Rights on the Internet*, HRC Res 32/13, 32nd sess, Agenda item 3, UN Doc A/HRC/RES/32/13 (1 July 2016). Intriguingly, the latest free speech Resolutions reiterate a few of the seemingly substantive themes of the Privacy Resolutions particularly those on the importance of encryption and anonymity, and even embodies a paragraph that urges States to adopt, implement and/or reform law on the protection of 'personal data and privacy'. See *The Promotion, Protection and Enjoyment of Human Rights on the Internet*, HRC Res 38/7, 38th sess, Agenda item 3, A/HRC/RES/38/7 (5 July 2018) para 17. This is, of course, part of the overall cross-feralization tendency between these two discourses. One also sees elements of the free speech discourse making their way into the Privacy Resolutions, a case in point being threats of disinformation. See, eg, GA Res 73/179 (n 23) Preamble, para 23.

enjoyment of human rights online.[43] But there is also a variation in terms of legal authority. The free speech Resolutions are adopted by the HR Council, unlike the Privacy Resolutions which are adopted by both the UNGA and the HR Council. This has a bearing on the legal value of the Resolutions. In the light of this apparent distinction, it is safe to state that the Privacy Resolutions are unique in their approach and perhaps can be called 'hybrid resolutions'.

The other novelty of approach also reflects, or reinforces, this propensity to hybridity. The discourse is informed by and cross-fertilizes different normative sources on the right to privacy. While the discourse clearly is anchored within the 'human right to privacy framework', it embraces other slightly autonomous regimes for privacy protection. One such regime is data privacy law which, as examined in chapter 3, is a disparate regulatory field, albeit to a lesser degree at the international level. Not only do the Resolutions contain data privacy themes, as shall be considered below, but also the latest Resolutions unusually 'recall' the Data Privacy Guidelines.[44] The Guidelines are the prime UN data privacy instruments, but they are rarely referred to or are considered by relevant UN bodies. Data privacy themes covered in the Resolutions are sourced mainly from European data protection law.

Elements of IBRs are also visible in the Privacy Resolutions, a good case in point being the increasing emphasis on the importance of Privacy Enhancing Technologies (PETs) for privacy protection. The migration of such norms to the UN process is a result of the consultations held by the OHCHR that preceded the adoption of Resolutions by the UNGA.[45] The consultations paved a way for submissions by civil society groups that are the main drivers of the IBRs project. In that regard, the 2014 post-consultation report of the OHCHR makes reference to a post-Snowden revelation IBRs initiative of '13 International Principles on the Application of Human Rights to Communication Surveillance'.[46] Beyond these sources, one may also trace in the Resolutions the influence of UN Special Rapporteurs particularly reports of successive UN Special Rapporteurs on Freedom of Expression, discussed in chapter 4. Thus, the discourse has a unifying approach to the right to privacy which reinforces the hybrid tendencies of the Resolutions.

A third novelty of approach concerns the way in which the Resolutions address the role of technology companies under the right to privacy. As examined in chapter 2, the role of (Internet) corporations is mostly overlooked in international law. But the UN privacy discourse gradually brings them to the fore by specifying their roles in upholding digital privacy. But this occurred rather gradually. Earlier

---

[43]   HRC Res 47/16 (n 4) Preamble, para 5.

[44]   See, eg, GA Res 73/179 (n 23) Preamble, para 2.

[45]   See Carly Nyst and Thomaso Falchatta, 'The Right to Privacy in the Digital Age' (2017) 9 Journal of Human Rights Practice *104*, 105 (noting that 'soft laws' launched by civil society groups have informed the discourse).

[46]   First Report of the High Commissioner (n 2) para 22, footnote 14.

Privacy Resolutions addressed 'business enterprises' more generically to respect the right to privacy in a manner encompassing all business enterprises regardless of the sector in which they operate.[47] Then, business enterprises were simply 'encouraged' to secure communications through technical solutions.[48] This later evolved to calling upon business enterprises to, inter alia, strengthen technical privacy safeguards and adopt transparency policies.[49] But more recent Resolutions not only further specify corporate responsibilities vis-à-vis the right to privacy but also that they are directly addressed to business enterprises that 'collect, store, use, share and process data'.[50] Doubtless, this is aimed at directly addressing technology companies.

In directly addressing technology companies—more so with a set of specific responsibilities, the privacy discourse takes the broader business and human rights discourse a step further. As alluded to in chapter 2, the extant international framework on business and human rights—mainly the Ruggie Principles—which fashions corporate human rights responsibilities through what can be called a 'generic' approach. It is generic because the Ruggie Principles applies—at least in theory— to 'all' human rights, including the right to privacy, and covers corporations of all stripes, including (Internet) corporations. In practical terms, this means that the current generic approach does not consider nuances of what corporations operating in different sectors must do or not do, to discharge their responsibilities. Yet, while the discourse usefully addresses the role of corporations vis-à-vis the right to privacy, it pays not heed to another parallel treaty process of the HR Council on business and human rights. The lack of synergy between the privacy discourse and the treaty process risks resulting in duplicity of efforts, and perhaps divergence of approach. We return to this point later in the book.

2.2.2. Novelty of Substance

The Privacy Resolutions also exhibit some novelty of substance. This novelty has two dimensions. One lies in the reflection of a few privacy principles that tend to elaborate the rather vague international rules on the right to privacy. This is occurring rather progressively. With the initial mostly hortatory Resolution that 'reaffirms' existing rules to the digital space, the subsequent Resolutions are moving towards flagging substantive principles. One sees gradually emerging marks of the jurisprudence of judicial and quasi-judicial bodies such as the Human Rights Committee (HR Committee), the European Court of Human Rights (ECtHR), and IBRs initiatives, as well as a number of thematic Reports of the UN

---

[47] See, eg, GA Res 71/199 (n 23) para 6.
[48] ibid, para 7.
[49] See, eg, GA Res 73/179 (n 23) para 7. See more below.
[50] See, eg, HRC Res 42/15 (n 39) para 8; GA Res 75/176 (n 23) para 8; HRC Res 48/4 (n 23) para 8. Note also the particular reference to 'communication service providers' (HRC Res 48/4) and 'social media enterprises and other online platforms' (GA Res 75/176).

Special Rapporteurs. As such, the novelty of the privacy principles flagged in the Resolutions is mostly to the international system of privacy protection within the UN system.[51] The other dimension of novelty is that the Resolutions specify—in a soft legal language of course—the obligations/responsibilities of States and businesses vis-à-vis the right to privacy. This section examines these novelties of the privacy discourse. As shall be shown below, the privacy discourse goes to some length in introducing modern privacy themes to international law and specifying the responsibilities of technology companies, but it does so in a selective and hence less holistic manner. What follows, first, provides an overview of (data) privacy themes, and then, the responsibilities of technology companies, as well as States flagged in the Privacy Resolutions.

2.2.2.1. (Data) Privacy Iterations
An international legal framework on data privacy is yet to fully emerge as a free-standing regime. Not only that it is addressed mainly within the human right to privacy framework but also that it is deeply fragmented. Post-Snowden discussions at the UN are, however, gradually paying some attention to data privacy themes as part of the underlying norm cross-fertilization process. What follows illustrates how data privacy themes are gradually forming part of the series of Privacy Resolutions.

(a) **Metadata and biometric information:** An important privacy theme raised in the Resolutions concerns collection of metadata. In keeping with recent revelations about bulk metadata collection, the Resolutions recognize the privacy implications of gathering and aggregating communication data, including when it is done so on a mass scale. The Resolutions provide that metadata may reveal insights into the private tests, preferences and other private aspects of a person's life when combined with other information.[52] More importantly, the subsequent iterations of the Privacy Resolutions highlight that metadata can in certain instances can be no less sensitive than the actual content of communications.[53] This proviso is imported from the Report of the OHCHR, which of course was informed by the case law of the ECtHR and the Court of Justice of the European Union (CJEU).[54] In the case of *Malone v UK*, the ECtHR held that generation of metadata records through metering solely for billing purposes does not constitute interference with the right

---

[51] It is also worth emphasizing that not all aspects of the Resolutions are novel even to international privacy law. Less novel about the Resolutions, for instance, is that they reiterate the jurisprudence of the HR Committee. One example is that they reinforce the requirement that interference by States with the right to privacy to be consistent with the principles of legality, necessity and proportionality. See, eg, GA Res 73/179 (n 23) para 4.

[52] See HRC Res 34/7 (n 28) Preamble, para 17.

[53] See, eg, GA Res 75/176 (n 23) Preamble, para 17; HRC Res 48/4 (n 23) Preamble, para 24.

[54] See First Report of the High Commissioner (n 2) paras 19–20.

to private life under Article 8 of the European Convention on Human Rights, but when such a record is shared with law enforcement, it will be and hence has to be justified.[55] The Resolutions do not go as far as to stipulate when (and whether) generation of metadata on its own constitutes interference with the right to privacy but they usefully flag an important issue to be addressed as the discourse further evolves or probably in treaty body jurisprudence.

Biometric information is the other type of personal data to receive particular attention in the Privacy Resolutions. With respect to biometric data, the Resolutions address both States and businesses but in a less clear manner. A preambular paragraph provides:[56]

> States <u>must respect their human rights obligations</u> and that business enterprises <u>should respect the right to privacy</u> and other human rights when collecting, processing, sharing and storing biometric information by, inter alia, <u>considering the adoption of data protection policies and safeguards</u>. [Emphasis Added]

One notes readily the compulsory way in which this soft law proviso is formulated. But it is ambiguous on many levels. First, it appears to limit the duty of States to 'respect'—a negative duty—and hence excludes the duty to 'protect' which is a positive duty involving regulation of businesses. Second, it similarly imposes a negative duty on business enterprises which is non-existent in international law. Not only businesses owe no duty but also that the only applicable regime, ie, the Ruggie Principles, introduces only a set of corporate responsibilities. Third, it is not clear to whom that the call to consider the adoption of 'data protection policies and safeguards' applies—is it for States or business enterprises? Reference to 'policies' may be taken to mean community guidelines of digital platforms which often contain detailed privacy clauses governing both processing of personal data by the platforms and their users. Subsequent Resolutions offer some general guidance on this point. One is that States are called upon to regularly review laws and practices governing the use of, among other technologies, biometric technologies.[57] Related to this is the need to take appropriate measures to ensure that biometric systems are designed and operated with pertinent legal and technical safeguards so as to ensure compliance with international obligations.[58]

A related substantive issue engaged by the Resolutions is the widely accepted dictum that the sole act of collecting and storing personal information constitutes interference with the right to privacy.[59] A version of this principle has been recognized by the ECtHR in the case of *Leander v Sweden* where the Court held that

---

[55] ECtHR, *Malone v UK*, Application No 8691/79 (26 April 1985) paras 63–89.
[56] See GA Res 73/179 (n 23) Preamble, para 25; see also GA Res 75/176 (n 23) Preamble, para 29.
[57] See GA Res 75/176 (n 23) para 7(c); see also HRC Res 48/4 (n 23) para 6(c).
[58] ibid, para 7(q); HRC Res 48/4 (n 23) para 6(e).
[59] See, eg, HRC Res 48/4 (n 23) Preamble, paras 12, 27.

storing of personal information alone interferes with the right to privacy.[60] This principle has later been codified in the EU data protection laws such as the General Data Protection Regulation (GDPR), and as a result, amassing personal information constitutes processing of personal information thereby engaging the right to data protection.[61] If collection in and of itself constitutes interference with the right to privacy, it would mean that the interference would have to be justified under the three-part tests of legality, legitimacy, and necessity. What makes this an important principle is the ubiquity of data collection processes that are mostly automated and less transparent.

(b) **Data protection regulation:** Legal regulation of processing of personal data is the other theme in the Privacy Resolutions. The latest Resolutions emphasize the need to regulate processing of personal data by law. Resolution 73/179, for instance, calls upon all States:[62]

> To consider <u>adopting and implementing data protection legislation</u>, regulation and policies, including on digital communication data, that complies with their international human rights obligations, which could include <u>the establishment of national independent authorities</u> with powers and resources to monitor data privacy practices, investigate violations and abuses and receive communications from individuals and organizations, and to provide appropriate remedies. [Emphasis Added]

The above clause is the most explicit call for States to enact—or implement if already enacted—data protection legislation that not only regulates processing of personal data but also installs national supervisory bodies. But this should be read with a preceding clause which calls upon States to enact and/or implement legislation that is protective of individuals from unlawful and arbitrary collection, processing, retention, or use of personal data by the public and private sectors.[63] It essentially reinforces GC 16 which reads into Article 17 of the ICCPR States' obligation to enact data protection legislation applicable to both the public and private sectors. Corollary to this are the less clear calls for businesses to adopt policies that would give effect to data privacy legislation. One relates to the transparency policies concerning the data collection, use, sharing, and retention practices.[64]

---

[60] ECtHR, *Leander v Sweden*, Application No 9248/81 (26 March 1987) para 48.

[61] See, eg, *Regulation (EU) 2016/679 of the European Parliament and of the Council of 27 April 2016 on the Protection of Natural Persons with regard to the Processing of Personal Data and on the Free Movement of Such Data* [2016] OJ L 119/1, art 4(2).

[62] See, eg, GA Res 73/179 (n 23) para 6(g); GA Res 75/176 (n 23) para 7(h).

[63] ibid, para 6(f); see also GA Res 75/176 (n 23) para 7(f).

[64] See GA Res 75/176 (n 23) para 8(b).

A set of data privacy principles and data subject rights commonly recognized in European data protection law are also set out in the latest Privacy Resolutions. And this is done so as part of the corporate responsibilities of 'business enterprises that collect, store, use, share and process data'. Among others, the Resolutions call upon technology companies to implement data subject rights to access personal data, to rectification of inaccurate data, and erasure of personal data.[65] Notions of privacy impact assessment, data protection by design and data breach notification are likewise envisaged in the latest Resolutions.[66] As part of the call on technology companies to implement administrative, technical, and physical safeguards, a series of data protection principles are recognized; namely principles of purpose limitation, data minimization, data quality, data security, and lawful processing.[67] In bringing forward such modern data privacy rules, the Privacy Resolutions are, albeit indirectly, modernizing the international data privacy framework. Except for emergent agency-level data protection policies, such progressive data privacy standards—as shown in chapter 3—are largely new to international data privacy law.

(c) **Regulation of digital surveillance:** One of the two original themes of the privacy discourse, which has now evolved to embrace a range of themes, is digital surveillance alongside collection of personal data.[68] The Resolutions address regulation of digital surveillance in two respects. First, they require States to align their domestic surveillance legislation with international legal standards. What those standards exactly are is not clearly stated, but they emphasize the need for surveillance legislation to be clear, accessible, precise, comprehensive, and non-discriminatory.[69] The emphasis here on the principle of non-discrimination, in the context of foreign surveillance, seems to be a direct response to discriminatory surveillance law and practice in Five Eyes States brought to the spotlight by the Snowden revelations. Related to this is the dicta introduced in latter Resolutions on the need to put in place independent, impartial, effective, and adequately resourced judicial, legislative, and/or administrative oversight mechanisms.[70]

Second, the Resolutions address the issue of intelligence sharing the full extent of which, at least in the context of the Five Eyes States, was laid bare by the Snowden revelations. A preambular paragraph reads that 'States must respect international human rights obligations regarding the right to privacy … when they share or otherwise provide access to data collected through, inter alia, information and intelligence-sharing agreements …'.[71]

---

[65] See, eg, GA Res 75/176 (n 23) para 8(e); HRC Res 48/4 (n 23) para 8(d). Cf GDPR (n 61) arts 13–17.
[66] See, eg, GA Res 75/176 (n 23) para 8(c) (d) (f); HRC Res 48/4 (n 23) para 8(e) (f). Cf GDPR (n 61) arts 24–25, 35.
[67] GA Res 75/176 (n 23) para 8(c).
[68] See, eg, GA Res 68/167 (n 1) para 4 cum Preamble, paras 4, 8, 9.
[69] ibid, preamble, para 22 cum para 6(h) [calling for privacy safeguards and remedies to 'all' individuals].
[70] See GA Res 75/176 (n 23) para 7(d).
[71] ibid, Preamble, para 28.

This clause is unpacked in the substantive parts of the Resolutions dealing with digital surveillance. But even then, the clause is not entirely clear when it calls for States to respect international human rights obligations. The nature, scope, and source of these obligations are far from clear. As an evolutive discourse, such matters may be elaborated in subsequent Resolutions but treaty body jurisprudence is yet to spell out the boundaries of State obligations vis-à-vis intelligence sharing between States.

(d) **New and emerging technologies:** The privacy implications of new and emerging technologies such as AI and machine learning have recently received particular attention in the latest Privacy Resolutions. It first found reference in the second Privacy Resolution of the HR Council where the need to further discuss and analyse practices of automated processing of personal data and profiling is stated.[72] But that reference was mainly in the context of non-discrimination and economic, social, and cultural rights. A 2018 UNGA Resolution makes a more direct reference. Not only does it recognize novel threats posed by the rapid growth of automated technologies like AI and machine learning but also emphasizes the need to align their 'design, evaluation and regulation' with international human rights law.[73] In part, the addition of this new theme is a result of civil society work in the area.[74]

With the prominence in public policy debates on such technologies—and hence a new discourse broached at the HR Council as alluded to above, the subject has received more attention in subsequent Resolutions. A HR Council Resolution, for instance, calls upon States to regularly review their laws as well as practices regarding automated-decision making and machine learning technologies to ensure protection of the right to privacy.[75] Part of this is the call upon States to protect individuals from harm caused by the use of automated processes.[76] This is further reinforced by a corollary call on technology companies to embed privacy safeguards in the design, operation, evaluation, and regulation of automated decision-making and machine-learning technologies, and to provide effective remedies when abuses occur.[77] Articulation of standards regarding the privacy impact of new technologies is a welcome development, but—as shall be noted later in this chapter—there is, however, a tendency in the latest Resolutions to drift from its privacy focus and focus more on the impact of such technologies on other rights such the right to equality.

---

[72] See HRC Res 34/7 (n 28) Preamble, para 16.
[73] See GA Res 73/179 (n 23) Preamble, para 19 cum para 7(d).
[74] See, eg, Privacy and Freedom of Expression in the Age of Artificial Intelligence (Privacy International, April 2018) <https://bit.ly/2Hvso7J>.
[75] See HRC Res 48/4 (n 23) paras 6(c); see also GA Res 75/176 (n 23) para 7(c).
[76] ibid, para 6(n); see also GA Res 75/176 (n 23) para 7(n).
[77] ibid, 8(e); see also GA Res 75/176 (n 23) para 8(d).

Overall, these privacy themes are merely highlighted in the Resolutions. Important details of the themes remain to be unpacked, but it is possible that they may find proper articulation in a future international instrument as the discourse evolves. Even if such a comprehensive international instrument fails to materialize in the foreseeable future, standards introduced in the Privacy Resolutions may be applied in practice by relevant bodies such as treaty bodies or other special procedures of the HR Council. We will return to such an interpretive role of the Resolutions later in this chapter.

2.2.2.2. Obligations/Responsibilities of States and Corporations

A level of clarification on the nature and scope of corporations' responsibilities as well as the obligations of States under the right to privacy is the other novelty of substance introduced by the privacy discourse. Of course, this is without losing sight of the obviously soft law nature of the Resolutions. No obligation flows from them in the strict sense of the term. But these clarifications are possible foreshadows of what 'obligations' might be specified to the human right to privacy should the discourse evolve into a more focused and concrete legal instrument. The Resolutions appear to follow the conventional types of State human rights obligations in international law: to 'respect', 'protect', and to some extent, 'fulfil'.

(a) **Obligations of States:** The articulation of obligations begun with the initial Resolution which States that the obligations of States is not just to 'respect'—ie, negative obligation—but also to 'protect'—ie, positive obligation.[78] GC 16 of the HR Committee has already affirmed this point, but the reinforcing role of the Resolutions is a welcome development particularly in dispelling the (wrong) view that Article 17 of the ICCPR guarantees merely a negative freedom. But as shown below, the Privacy Resolutions go further in specifying both the negative and positive obligations of States compared to GC 16 whose truncated nature limited its scope as well as relevance.

An important elaboration of States' negative obligation is that the Resolutions call upon States to refrain from measures that oblige businesses to take steps that interfere with the right to privacy in an unlawful and arbitrary manner.[79] This point is further reinforced by a proviso which requires States to respect their obligations under international law when they seek disclosure of personal data from third parties, including technology companies.[80] What appear to be envisioned here are circumstances where States require companies to disclose user personal data, install backdoors in their products, provide encryption key escrows, or even

---

[78] See GA Res 69/166 (n 7) para 4(a).
[79] See GA Res 73/179 (n 23) para 6(l).
[80] See GA Res 75/176 (n 23) Preamble, para 28.

disclose specific encryption keys. The latest Resolutions stipulate that any restrictions by States on the use of PETs should comply with international human rights obligations.[81] What this might mean are the requirements of legality, necessity, and legitimacy. Furthermore, the Resolutions call upon States to enact 'policies that recognize and protect the privacy of individuals digital communications'.[82] But the nature of such policies is not entirely clear, for instance whether it includes legislation that would envisage when forcing breaking of encryption is permissible. But the aim appears to be nudging States to make their overall policy on the use of secure communication methods transparent.

Positive obligations of States are provided in a relatively elaborate fashion under the latter Resolutions. In addition to the recurrent requirement to bring national law and practice in line with international law, the Resolutions provide specific obligations. One is that States should 'protect' individuals from harm, including that caused by business enterprises through data collection, processing, storage, sharing and profiling as well as the use of automated processes such as machine learning.[83] Second, the Resolutions call up on States to put in place a pertinent legal framework to give effect to the right to privacy. One concerns laws governing new and emerging technologies such as AI which mandate not only embedding privacy from the early steps of design but also remedying violations that may occur once such technologies are deployed.[84] Moreover, the Resolutions explicitly require States to enact legislation that regulates the 'collection, processing, retention or use of personal data' both in the public and private sectors.[85] This proviso requires for such a national legislation to envisage sanctions and remedies that apply when violation occurs, and the law shall cover 'individuals, governments, business enterprises and private organizations'. Moreover, it calls upon States to provide effective remedy for people whose right to privacy has been violated by digital surveillance.[86] With recent revelations about the (ab)use of surveillance technologies such as Pegasus spyware to target journalists and human rights advocates—and the growing call for regulation of the industry, the latest Resolutions call upon States to 'protect' the right to privacy through the regulation of the sale, transfer, use, and export of surveillance technologies.[87]

Four specific positive measures that are more pertinent to digital privacy are also provided in the Resolutions. First, they call upon States to promote digital literacy that would equip users with technical skills needed to protect privacy.[88] The

---

[81]   ibid, para 9.
[82]   ibid; HRC Res 48/4 (n 23) para 9.
[83]   See HRC Res 42/15 (n 39) para 8(j).
[84]   See GA Res 75/176 (n 23) para 7(g) cum para 7(n).
[85]   See GA Res 73/179 (n 23) para 6(f).
[86]   ibid, para 6(e).
[87]   See HRC Res 48/4 (n 23) para 6(k) cum Preamble, para 29 [noting with 'deep concern' the use of surveillance technologies developed by the private surveillance industry by private and State actors to engage in unlawful or arbitrary surveillance, hacking and data collection].
[88]   See GA Res 75/176 (n 23) para 7(l).

proviso, which appears to reflect an 'obligation to fulfil', mandates digital literacy training on PETs such as encryption technologies, which is often envisioned in IBFs in a human rights parlance. Related to this is the call upon States to provide training to judges, prosecutors, and other members of the justice system on 'new and emerging digital technologies and their impact on human rights'.[89] Second, they call upon States to consider measures that would enable businesses to adopt voluntary transparency measures regarding government requests for user personal data.[90] The underlying aim seems to be nudging States to abolish or modify rules that impose what are commonly called 'gag orders' which prohibit businesses from informing users about government request for personal data. Third, the Resolutions call upon States to regulate by law the manner in which user personal data may be sold, resold, or otherwise shared by businesses without the free, explicit, and informed consent of the data subject.[91] This adds up to the above noted call upon States to introduce a comprehensive data protection legislation.

In summary, the above series of calls upon States essentially specify the obligations of States both in respecting and protecting—and in certain instances, fulfilling—the right to privacy in the digital age. In a way, the Resolutions unpack the rather crude provisions of the right to privacy in international law in the light of new developments and international best practices. We return to this 'interpretive' role of the Resolutions in the next section.

(b) **Responsibilities of corporations:** To a degree, the responsibilities of technology companies under the right to privacy are specified in the Resolutions. The exercise began in the first Resolution with a hint in a preambular paragraph that 'surveillance, interception, and data collection' could well be undertaken by non-State actors such as 'companies and individuals' and later grew into elaborate principles.[92] The latter Resolutions directly address the role of businesses both as agents of protection and of violation of digital privacy. What makes this important is that the responsibility of Internet corporations in the protection of the right to privacy is, as discussed in chapter 2, often overlooked in international law and discourse.

In addressing the role of Internet corporations, the Privacy Resolutions follow a layered and, at points, incremental, approach. First, they acknowledge the risks posed to the right to privacy by the growing capability of Internet businesses in collecting, processing, and using personal data.[93] Second, they provide for general points. One is that unlike earlier Resolutions which merely 'recall' the human rights responsibility of businesses under the Ruggie Principles, the latest Resolutions definitively state that the Ruggie Principles *applies* to the human right to privacy in

---

[89] See HRC Res 48/4 (n 23) para 6(m).
[90] ibid, para 6(o).
[91] ibid, para 7(p).
[92] See GA Res 68/167 (n 1) Preamble, para 4.
[93] See GA Res 71/199 (n 23) Preamble, para 26.

the digital context. They do so by calling upon businesses to 'meet their responsibilities' under the Guiding Principles.[94] This clarifies an ambiguity in an earlier Resolution which vaguely stated that businesses *may* owe responsibilities under 'applicable laws and other international principles'.[95] It has not been clear what these laws and international principles are, but now is clear that those include the Ruggie Principles, regardless of whether they are adequate to address responsibilities of technology companies vis-à-vis the right to privacy.

Third, the Resolutions stipulate a set of specific responsibilities of corporations vis-à-vis the right to privacy, as highlighted below:

- Internet businesses are called upon to inform users about the collection, use, sharing and retention of their personal data when there are risks to the right to privacy.[96] This provision mirrors many data protection instruments worldwide, but is couched in a vague language. It is not clear, for instance, whether the requirement includes data breach notification to users or it concerns transparency with respect to government requests to personal data. The provision also leaves wide latitude to corporations in determining when to inform users. The latest Resolutions reformulate this clause in three respects. One is that technology companies are called upon to establish 'transparency policies'.[97] Such policies appear to refer to data privacy policies of digital platforms that detail the ways in which data are processed. The transparency policies should allow for the 'free, informed and meaningful' consent of users,[98] the Resolutions however appear to envision a rather narrow role for the transparency policies. But the concern is that the Resolutions merely call upon technology companies to adopt such policies, which they commonly do but in many instances are inconsistent with international law standards. In that sense, the call should also be to make such policies in line with international law standards on the right to privacy.

  Since the envisioned 'transparency policies' concern 'sharing', it probably convers access provided to governments upon request of user data as well. Part of this undertaking is to reveal the extent and nature of routine requests of personal data made by law enforcement and intelligence agencies. In that sense, it does not seem to involve disclosure at an individual level. Corollary to this proviso is the call on States to ensure that 'gag orders'—ie, statutory or judicial orders preventing disclosure—are not unduly imposed on corporations.[99] The scope of the transparency policy does not, however, appear to

---

[94] See GA Res 73/179 (n 23) para 7(a).
[95] See GA Res 71/199 (n 23) Preamble, para 28.
[96] See GA Res 73/179 (n 23) para 7(b).
[97] See, eg, GA Res 75/176 (n 23) para 8(b).
[98] See, eg, GA Res 75/176 (n 23) para 8(b); HRC Res 48/4 (n 23) para 8(b).
[99] See GA Res 75/176 (n 23) para 7(o).

specifically cover a 'right to be notified' when one has been subject to surveillance, despite the fact that this has been one of the comparative lessons drawn by the report of the OHCHR.[100] In practice, transparency reports issued by technology companies are described in a generic sense that individual users are not necessarily notified. If that is the aim of the Resolutions, it would be a significant development but practically cumbersome.

- Internet businesses are called upon to implement 'administrative, technical and physical safeguards' to ensure that the processing of personal data is undertaken in line with classic data protection principles of 'fair and lawful processing', 'use limitation', 'data quality', and 'data security'.[101] Other broader principles of data protection are also implicitly incorporated in the latest Resolutions such as impact assessment and data breach notification.[102] Part of this call, as alluded to above, is the call upon technology companies to ensure the enjoyment of data subject rights such as rights of access, correction, and erasure.[103]

- The Resolutions call upon corporations to ensure that the design, operation, and evaluation of automated decision-making technologies such as AI and machine learning respect international privacy standards.[104] Latent in this proviso is what is called in EU law the principle of 'data protection by design' by which data privacy safeguards are embedded in data processing systems. A broader responsibility envisioned in the Resolution is for technology companies to undertake human rights due diligence throughout the life cycle of AI and related technologies to mitigate the human rights impact of such technologies.[105]

- Internet corporations are encouraged to secure their communications and adopt technical solutions towards safeguarding the right to privacy of their customers.[106] Specific reference is made in this regard to encryption, pseudonymization, and anonymity as technical solutions.[107] This could include end-to-end encryption which is increasingly being implemented by some technology companies. The provision is reinforced by a proviso, highlighted above, that calls upon States to (i) offer digital literacy training on PETs and (ii) to refrain from measures that oblige businesses to take steps that interfere with the right to privacy in an unlawful and arbitrary manner through key escrow or backdoor obligations vis-à-vis encryption technologies.

---

[100] See First Report of the High Commissioner (n 2) para 40.
[101] See GA Res 73/179 (n 23) para 7(c).
[102] See GA Res 75/176 (n 23) para 8(f); HRC Res 48/4 (n 23) para 8(f).
[103] ibid, para 8(e); see also HRC Res 48/4 (n 23) para 8(d).
[104] ibid, para 8(d); HRC Res 48/4 (n 23) para 8(e).
[105] See HRC Res 48/4 (n 23) para 8(g) cum para 10.
[106] ibid, para 8.
[107] See, eg, ibid, para 9.

In sum, the above highlight of corporate responsibilities vis-à-vis the right to privacy marks a significant progress in the development of international privacy law. This is particularly so for the recent Resolutions which give some substance to the rather cruder rules of the UN Guiding Principles on Business and Human Rights and on-going reform efforts at the UN. Added to a similar attempt of specifying State obligations, highlighted above, the revival of the privacy agenda at the UN through the series of Privacy Resolutions flickers hope that normative blind spots in international law will, and can, be lessened. The discourse has brought along a set of novelties, both of substance and approach, that may assist in that effort. But what has been introduced so far does not go far enough in sufficiently attending to international law's privacy problem. As shall be demonstrated in the following section, the normative values of the discourse, particularly the Privacy Resolutions, is limited in reimagining the right to privacy in international law.

3. Situating the Discourse in International Law

To what extent can the above highlighted novelties of the privacy discourse contribute towards elaborating the right to privacy in international law in light of the new realities of the digital age? To address this question, three potential roles of the discourse are examined in this section. First, it considers two possible 'freestanding roles' of the discourse. One concerns the possibility that the Privacy Resolutions' substantive principles may offer normative guidance on the scope of the right to privacy in the digital context. The other is whether the Privacy Resolutions constitute 'authoritative interpretation' of Article 17 of the ICCPR. As will be shown, these unilateral roles of the privacy discourse are insignificant. This is mainly due to the limited normative reach of the Resolutions, and the attendant questions of competence. Second, it considers the 'contributory role' of the Resolutions in offering the possibility by which a general right to privacy may be grounded in general international law, thereby broadening its scope of application. The contributory role not only carries limited legal significance but also will prove controversial. Third, it considers the 'catalytic' role of the discourse in charting new directions towards a pragmatic privacy law reform. The submission is that this is where the most promising potential of the discourse lies.

3.1. Elaborative and Interpretive Functions

3.1.1. The Privacy Resolutions as Elaborative Soft Law
Soft law historically played a key role in illuminating otherwise crude provisions of international (hard) law. As Shelton notes, soft law often formulates and

reformulates hard law particularly in applying the latter to new circumstances.[108] Soft law enunciates broad principles in new areas of lawmaking where details of obligations remain to be elaborated.[109] Resolutions of the UNGA are good cases in point in clarifying rules of international law to a specific and unique set of circumstances.[110] To a degree, the Privacy Resolutions appear to assume a similar elaborative role. As discussed above, they tend to provide some content to existing international rules on the right to privacy. The rather vague and high-level abstract principles of Article 17 of the ICCPR and the Data Privacy Guidelines find some specificity in the Privacy Resolutions.

Peters comments that the initial Privacy Resolution does not create new law but 'merely clarifies' existing rules such as the ICCPR's privacy provision to the Internet context.[111] But what the initial Resolution does, as noted above, is perhaps a little less than clarification, which rather is done, to some extent, in the subsequent Resolutions. The more recent Resolutions embody some substantive privacy principles and specify the respective roles of States and corporations vis-à-vis the right to privacy. In that sense, they appear to be what Chinkin refers to as 'elaborative soft law', one that offers some content to and interacts with treaty law.[112] The repeated reaffirmation of and reference to privacy provisions of the UDHR and the ICCPR attest to the slightly 'elaborative soft law' nature of the Privacy Resolutions.

A primary advantage of an elaborative soft law is that it offers some normative guidance to judicial bodies in charge of monitoring implementation. In that sense, the addition of some flesh to the skeletal provisions of the international law of privacy would offer some guidance to, for example, the HR Committee. The elaborative function would be useful to the Committee in examining individual communications, periodic State reports, and even in revising GC 16. Resort by the Committee to an elaborative soft law adopted by the UNGA would be much less controversial than a comparative lesson drawn by the Committee from, say, the ECtHR.[113] States would be more heedful to principles invoked from universal

---

[108] Dinah Shelton, 'Commentary and Conclusions' in Dinah Shelton (ed), *Commitment and Compliance: The Role of Non-Binding Norms in the International Legal System* (Oxford University Press 2000) 461.

[109] ibid.

[110] See, eg, Jutaro Higashi, 'The Role of Resolutions of the United Nations General Assembly in the Formative Process of International Customary Law' (1982) 25 Japanese Annual of International Law 11, 16.

[111] Anne Peters, Surveillance Without Borders: The Unlawfulness of the NSA Panopticon—Part II (EJIL: Talk!, 4 November 2013) <http://bit.ly/2vElrhK>.

[112] Christine Chinkin, 'Normative Development in the International Legal System' in Dinah Shelton (ed) *Commitment and Compliance: The Role of Non-Binding Norms in the International Legal System* (Oxford University Press 2000) 30.

[113] Other UN institutional arrangements relevant to privacy may also draw upon the Resolutions. In one of his reports, the inaugural SRP noted that his work is being 'guided by' a Privacy Resolution adopted by the HR Council. See Report of the Special Rapporteur on the Right to Privacy, Joseph Cannataci, UN Doc A/HRC/37/62 (28 February 2018) para 5.

instruments like the Privacy Resolutions than the jurisprudence of the ECtHR when the Committee makes legal determinations.

Another advantage of an elaborative soft law is that in interacting with and referring to hard law, a soft law imports some legal authority. Resolutions like the Privacy Resolutions that are tied to a hard law instrument like the ICCPR derive authority from the latter.[114] Boyle and Chinkin suggest that the application of Resolutions by judicial and quasi-judicial bodies alters their legal nature to some degree.[115] This may be called 'judicial hardening of soft law' in that the soft nature of some instruments is, in practice, hardened by judicial and quasi-judicial interpretation of the rules.[116] According to this viewpoint, reference to or application of the Privacy Resolutions by the HR Committee in its practice would elevate their legal status.

Indeed, the Committee has a tradition of relying on relevant soft law instruments in interpreting the ICCPR. In the case of *Herbert Potter v New Zealand*, the HR Committee, for instance, relied upon—as submitted by the author of the individual communications but objected by the respondent State—a soft law on prisoners' rights in finding violation of Covenant Rights.[117] The Committee not only asserted its competence to such an extraneous soft law instrument but also noted that the Rules provided 'valuable guidelines' for the interpretation of the ICCPR.[118] What makes the idea that a soft law may be hardened when applied by the HR Committee logically fallacious is the fact that the Committee's 'views' in individual cases or concluding observations under the reporting procedure are clearly non-binding on States.

Practical influences of the Privacy Resolutions in the jurisprudence of the HR Committee are yet to fully emerge. But it is already clear that the spirit of the Resolutions has started to show in the Committee's jurisprudence, particularly through recent concluding observations. As discussed in chapter 2, concluding observations adopted in the wake of the Snowden revelations—and hence the Privacy Resolutions—appear to be informed by themes of the Resolutions. The Privacy Resolutions are also considered by judicial bodies outside the UN, but it is yet to go beyond mere reference. An example is that the initial Resolution has been listed by the ECtHR among 'applicable international laws' in recent cases on digital surveillance.[119]

---

[114]   See Chinkin (n 112) 30.

[115]   Boyle and Chinkin (n 41) 213, 220.

[116]   See Dinah Shelton, 'Introduction: Law, Non-Law and the Problem of Soft Law' in Dinah Shelton (ed), *Commitment and Compliance: The Role of Non-Binding Norms in the International Legal System* (Oxford University Press 2000) 14.

[117]   HR Committee, *Herbert Potter v New Zealand*, Communication No 632/1995 (6 April 1995) paras 4.5, 6.3.

[118]   ibid cum *UN Standard Minimum Rules for the Treatment of Prisoners (Nelson Mandela Rules)*, GA Res 70/175, 70th sess, Agenda Item 106, UN Doc A/RES/70/175 (17 December 2015).

[119]   See, eg, ECtHR, *Roman Zakharov v Russia*, Application No 47143/06 (4 December 2015) para 139.

In sum, the elaborative role of the Privacy Resolutions is yet to be fully seen in action. This state of affairs is probably because the substance of the Resolutions is not significant enough to warrant much reference. In the case of ECtHR, which has a far more advanced privacy jurisprudence, the lack of reference is unsurprising. New Zealand's objection, alluded to above, also reflects the attendant question of competence when an extraneous instrument is referred to by the Committee. But more importantly, the evolving nature of the discourse means also that the elaborative function of the Resolutions may elapse without exerting much effect.

3.1 2. Resolutions as Interpretive Tools

The other possibility by which the Privacy Resolutions may find a meaningful place in international privacy law, or obtain some legal force, is based on what may be called the 'authoritative interpretation' analogy. The analogy flows from the more general view that soft law may be a mechanism of authoritative interpretation or 'amplification' of treaty law.[120] Claims of treaty law interpretation through soft law take various forms. In the context of the UN Charter for instance, Schacter suggested that if States agree that the 'Charter means what the Resolution says it states', the Resolution may be regarded as an authoritative interpretation of the Charter.[121] The UDHR, a soft law adopted by a Resolution of the UNGA, is often presented to support such claims.

UDHR's non-binding nature and the failure of universal ratification of binding treaties like the ICCPR, inter alia, brought the claim that the Declaration acquires legally binding force because it represents an authoritative interpretation of the UN Charter's human rights provisions, which is binding.[122] The Charter's provisions on human rights are general and basically affirm the importance of respect for and promotion of human rights than specific catalogue of human rights and concomitant obligations.[123] The UDHR specifies, the argument goes, these provisions into a specific list of rights and obligations of member States, which in turn represents authoritative interpretation of the Charter's human rights provisions. The 'authoritative' nature of the interpretation derives from the fact that the UDHR was adopted by the UNGA which is considered to be a forum for the consideration and expression of the collective will of the international community.

If that claim were to be analogized to the Privacy Resolutions, it would mean that they constitute an authoritative interpretation of relevant privacy provisions in international (hard) law. The general inclination to use the term 'Resolution'

---

[120] See Boyle and Chinkin (n 41) 216.

[121] Oscar Schacther, *International Law in Theory and Practice* (Martinus Nijhoff 1991) 85.

[122] See Ronald Burke and James Kirby, 'The Universal Declaration of Human Rights: Politics and Provisions (1945–1948)' in Gerd Oberleitner (ed), *International Human Rights Institutions, Tribunals and Courts* (Springer 2018) 43–44; see also John Humphrey, 'The Universal Declaration of Human Rights' (1949) 4 International Journal 351, 357.

[123] *Charter of the United Nations* (1945) arts 1(3), 13, 55, 62, 68, 76.

in referring to Declarations such as the UDHR, added with the affirmation by the UN that no difference exists, as a matter of strict legal principle, between a Declaration and a Recommendation (ie, Resolution)[124] tends to make the analogy an appealing line of argument towards adding normative force to the Privacy Resolutions. The question, then, is if the UDHR is an 'authoritative interpretation' of the UN Charter, could the Privacy Resolutions—as hybrid as they are in their legal form and substance—be considered 'authoritative interpretations' of the ICCPR's privacy provision, other subsequent specialized human rights treaties, and even the human rights provisions of the UN Charter? The repeated references in the Privacy Resolutions to the UDHR and ICCPR as well as their privacy provisos appear to lend weight to the claim. Moreover, the reference made by each Resolution to the UN Charter in the preamble may also add to a view that the Resolutions are not just authoritative interpretations of the privacy provisions of the UDHR and the ICCPR but also the generic human rights provisions of the UN Charter.

The analogy, however, gives rise to a question of legitimacy. Can a soft legal instrument interpret provisions of a treaty and to what extent will parties to that treaty be bound by the interpretation? Can they refuse to accept interpretation that goes beyond the original intentions of State parties to the treaty? Would States that object to the adoption of the soft law or simply abstained during voting be bound by it? The Privacy Resolutions are, as highlighted above, adopted through consensus and hence without any express disclosure of agreement equivalent to affirmative votes. Should that be taken as implied agreement, and hence be bound by the Resolutions' 'interpretations'? Moreover, in engaging in an interpretive exercise, would not UNGA be doing both lawmaking and judicial interpretations?

Lauterpacht was at the forefront of the objection to the analogy. He argued that the analogy not only is illogical but also that aligning UDHR's legal force with the Charter would diminish the latter's inherent legal standing.[125] In considering the fact that a proposal to give the UNGA a legislative power was rejected, the suggestion that UNGA would somehow gain a legislative power through the adoption of a Resolution appears to be extraordinary. In short, the attempt to attach some normative value to the Privacy Resolutions via the analogy of authoritative interpretation would prove controversial. If the analogy has not entirely succeeded in altering the legal nature of an instrument as widely accepted as the UDHR, it would be more far-fetched for mere Resolutions (not even a Declaration!) like the Privacy Resolutions that embody a number of ambiguities.

---

[124] See Use of the Terms 'Declaration' and 'Recommendation', Memorandum by the Office of Legal Affairs, UN Doc E/CN.4/L.610 (2 April 1962).

[125] Hersch Lauterpacht, *International Law and Human Rights* (Stevens and Sons Limited 1950) 394 et seq.

3.2. Universalizing Privacy Standards

This section considers the second potential of the privacy discourse in contributing to the gradual development of privacy and data protection in international law. The contributory role relates to the way in which the Privacy Resolutions may shape or inform the progressive development of international law. It can be considered from two perspectives. One is the possibility of the Resolutions leading to the formation of privacy norms in general international law, either as a customary norm or general principles. The other is the extent to which the discourse in general and the Resolutions in particular may influence the making of law and judicial decisions at domestic and regional levels. As this section shall demonstrate, the legal significance of the contributory role is limited and shrouded in uncertainty.

3.2 1. Accretion of General International Law

The question of whether the Privacy Resolutions contribute towards grounding the right to privacy in general international law is worthy of consideration for the following reasons. First, grounding rights or principles in general international law would broaden the scope and impact of human rights especially when human rights treaties have not achieved universal ratification.[126] A general rule of international privacy law would apply to all States regardless of whether they are parties to treaty law. This would mean that States like China that have not ratified the ICCPR would be obliged, for instance, under a customary privacy norm. It is also important even in cases where treaties are ratified but may be derogated by legislation due to the same hierarchy that treaties and any other legislation enjoy in a State party's constitutional law.[127]

Second—and relatedly, solidifying a given human right in general international law would be a way of emphasizing the importance of the respective right.[128] Because a rule of international custom, for instance, emerges after extensive State practice over a period of time, its ultimate formation reflects the prominence of the rule and the right that it guarantees. Third, the crystallization of human rights norms into customary law would allow recourse to remedies available in general international law by those whose rights have been violated.[129] Fourth, variations in the interpretation of treaty provisions would be mitigated once a customary norm crystallizes as it would add a level of certainty to the scope of that particular rule of

---

[126] See Bruno Simma and Philip Alston, 'The Sources of Human Rights Law: Custom, Jus Cogens, and General Principles' (1989) 12 Australian Year Book of International Law 82, 82.

[127] ibid, 86.

[128] See Michael O'Boyle and Michelle Lafferty, 'General Principles and Constitutions as Sources of Human Rights Law' in Dinah Shelton (ed), *The Oxford Handbook of International Human Rights Law* (Oxford University Press 2013) 209.

[129] See Schacther (n 121) 85.

law.[130] This is in addition to the benefits of a general international law rule to serve as a 'fall back' when interpretation of treaties proves difficult.[131] A good case in point is the controversy over the extraterritorial scope of the ICCPR. Finally, a customary rule of international law moulds the content of treaty law which might not otherwise be amended to keep up to speed with new developments.[132] The latter especially is appealing to the right to privacy in the digital space where there is incessant dynamics.

The attempt at linking UNGA Resolutions with formal sources of international law emanates from their uncertain place in international law. Resolutions find no mention under Article 38(1) of the Statute of the International Court of Justice (ICJ) which is widely accepted to provide an authoritative list of international law sources. But this provision is sometimes taken to have a limited role of guiding the Court than controlling sources of international law, so that Resolutions may be drawn upon by the Court when necessary.[133] The list is also argued to be merely an illustrative one, as opposed to exhaustive, which as a result does not preclude Resolutions from being a source of international law.[134] Some commentators even situate Resolutions within the ranks of Article 38 as falling just below 'judicial decisions' but certainly above 'teachings of most highly qualified publicists', which are identified as subsidiary sources of international law under Article 38(1) (d)).[135] What follows considers how and whether the Privacy Resolutions may find a place in general international law. It does so by looking at how Resolutions may facilitate the formation of an international custom and general principles. The section builds on, but does not repeat, the analysis in chapters 2 and 3 on the ways in which Draft Conclusions of the International Law Commission (ILC) on Customary International Law and General Principles of Law (GPsL) may be applied in establishing whether privacy and data protection form part of general international law.

3.2.1.1. Customary International Law

As highlighted in chapters 2 and 3, whether the right to privacy and data protection have attained the status of customary international law (CIL) has recently become

---

[130] See Pierre-Marie Dupuy, 'Formation of Customary International Law and General Principles' in Daniel Dobansky and others (eds), *Oxford Handbook of International Environmental Law* (Oxford University Press 2007) 463.

[131] ibid, 450.

[132] See James Crawford, *Brownlie's Principles of Public International Law* (Oxford University Press 8th edn, 2012) 33–34.

[133] See, eg, Merlin Magallona, 'Some Remarks on the Legal Character of UN General Assembly Resolutions' (1976) 5 Philippine Yearbook of International Law 84, 96.

[134] See generally Christopher Joyner, 'UN General Assembly Resolutions and International Law: Rethinking Contemporary Dynamics of Norm-Creation' (1981) 11 California Western International Law Journal 445.

[135] See Leo Gross, 'The United Nations and the Role of Law' (1965) 19 International Organization 537, 557.

a recurring question in the privacy literature. Answers in the affirmative are predominant but take various forms. A more general and older version of the argument departs from the UDHR which, over the years, have had significant impact worldwide. The impact of the Declaration is said to have made all of its provisions, including Article 12 on the right to privacy, rules of customary international law.[136] This view holds that given the wider incorporation of the UDHR into national constitutions, statutory and case law, as well as the very nature of the rights embodied therein, the UDHR is part of CIL. The right to privacy guaranteed under the Declaration and later reproduced, nigh verbatim, in the ICCPR is—the argument goes—grounded in CIL. Another but a more recent version of the argument holds that wider recognition of the right to privacy in several international instruments, national laws, and the prominence of privacy in legal commentary has paved the way for creation of a 'general right to privacy' in CIL.[137]

But, the above viewpoint is problematic on many levels. At the most basic level, it overestimates the value of a customary norm based on existing international privacy norms. As demonstrated in chapter 2, the right to privacy in international law is formulated in an exceedingly vague and abstract manner. Boundaries of the international right to privacy are too vague to make its elevation to customary norm appealing. The viewpoint, moreover, tends to settle for less in international privacy law reform.[138] Added to the inherent uncertainty and fluidity of customary law a customary international law of privacy based on the UDHR may not probably be adequate to improve the existing international system of privacy protection. As Lauterpacht argued in the context of the UDHR, the focus in situating Resolutions within the existing formal sources of international law risks retracting the interest in pursuing a rather effective international legislative response.[139]

Beside the above general contemplation of privacy as a rule of CIL, the Privacy Resolutions may lend weight to the argument that, indeed, such rules have emerged. Resolutions of UNGA are often seen as incipient steps towards the

[136] See John Humphrey, 'The Universal Declaration of Human Rights: Its History, Impact and Juridical Character' in Bertrand Ramcharan (ed), *Human Rights Thirty Years After the Universal Declaration* (Brill 1979) 21, 37; see also Louis Sohn, 'The Human Rights Law of the Charter' (1977) 12 Texas International Law Journal 129, 133.

[137] See Alexandra Rengel, *Privacy in the 21st Century* (Martinus Nijhoff 2013) 108. Recent expert reports also claim that the right to privacy has become a rule of customary international law. The Tallinn Manual 2.0, for instance, concluded that despite some variance on its scope, the right to privacy is of CIL character. See Michael Schmitt (ed), *Tallinn Manual 2.0 on the International Law Applicable to Cyber Operations* (Cambridge University Press 2017) 180, 189. But see Annex D: Protection of Personal Data in Transborder Flow of Information, Report on the Work of the International Law Commission, 58th sess, May–August 2006 (2006) [holding that state practice in the area (of data protection) is not extensive or fully developed, and therefore, warrants no further work of codification]. At the time of writing, the topic remains in the ILC's long-term programme of work.

[138] See more in chapter 1 on the limitations of a 'hard legalization approach' to international privacy law reform.

[139] Hersch Lauterpacht, 'The Universal Declaration of Human Rights' (1948) 25 British Yearbook of International Law 354, 376.

creation of CIL.[140] Higgins notes that Resolutions provide a rich source of evidence when taken as indications of a general customary law.[141] The constitution of the UNGA as a global political organ with universal membership adds weight to its Resolutions. As Higashi notes, Resolutions of the UNGA are expressions of the 'collective will of the international community', reflective of 'collective practices of States'.[142] As such, they would facilitate formation of CIL. As highlighted in the preceding chapters, the Draft Conclusions of the ILC affirm that resolutions of international organizations such as the UN may provide evidence in determining the existence and content of a rule of CIL or contribute to its formation.[143] A provision in such resolutions may be taken to reflect a rule of CIL where the provision corresponds to a general practice that is accepted as law.[144]

It has recently been suggested, in this regard, that the adoption of the Privacy Resolutions and preparation of reports by UN bodies such as OHCHR are adequate to show *opinio juris* under modern theories of custom. The Resolutions, the argument goes, demonstrate consensus on the importance of data privacy and could be interpreted under modern custom theories as (1) crystalizing a customary rule of (data) privacy which is needed to keep abreast of new technological developments and (2) demonstrate emergence of consensus on the right to privacy.[145] Similar limitations of the first set of views extend to this line of argument, however. What added value, if at all, would flow from the creation of a customary (data) privacy norm based on existing international human rights instruments is not entirely clear.

Overall, the contention that the right to privacy has developed into a norm of CIL appears to be misplaced in the context of the Privacy Resolutions. The fact that existing international privacy rules, particularly Article 17 of the Covenant, are binding on the vast majority of States reduces the promises of customary international law of privacy. The argument would have held more water if the supposed customary rule would introduce more robust and progressive rules rather than sheer reinforcement of treaty law. Perhaps, the modest content introduced by the Privacy Resolutions might, if they were to facilitate the formation of customary privacy norms, come handy to support the argument. But again, this would be to overlook the evolving nature of the Resolutions. In other words, an argument for a customary international law of privacy induced by the Resolutions would have made more sense had the discourse already culminated. But it has not. Another

---

[140]   See, eg, Joyner (n 134) 459.

[141]   Rosalyn Higgins, *The Development of International Law Through the Political Organs of the United Nations* (Oxford University Press 1963) 5.

[142]   Higashi (n 110) 13–15.

[143]   Draft Conclusions on Identification of Customary International Law, Adopted by the International Law Commission at its Seventieth Session (2018) Conclusion 12(1).

[144]   ibid, Conclusion 12(2).

[145]   See Monika Zalnieriute, 'An International Constitutional Moment for Data Privacy' (2015) 23 International Journal of Law and Information Technology 99, 121 et seq.

possibility would have been if, for instance, the HR Committee relies upon the Resolutions in its jurisprudence but faces objection from States claiming that they are not bound by the provisions of the Resolutions. In the latter case, the Committee may rely on the above arguments, or one of them, to insist that the Resolutions apply to State parties to the ICCPR. This has not yet occurred and perhaps objections of those types may not arise, probably ever.

3.2.1.2. General Principles of Law

General principles are the other sources of international law next to consent-based sources of treaty and customary law.[146] But can the substantive principles flagged in the Privacy Resolutions constitute general principles of privacy law? The international law scholarship generally holds that UNGA Resolutions, particularly Declarative Resolutions, constitute important sources of general principles.[147] In particular, the UDHR is said to enunciate GPsL.[148] For Ramcharan, general principles of law can be deduced from various sources, including declarations, bodies of principles, and guidelines adopted by the UN.[149] This also finds some support in the Draft Conclusions of the ILC. As alluded to in chapters 2 and 3, the ILC's special rapporteur proposes that general principles can also be sourced from the international legal system as well as domestic legal systems. One of the instances where general principles drawn from the international legal system may be a source is where *the* relevant principle is widely recognized in 'treaties and other international instruments'.[150] In his second report, the special rapporteur states that UNGA Resolutions are examples of such 'other international instruments'.[151] As this chapter has shown, the Privacy Resolutions are gradually embracing modern data privacy principles which are also widely recognized in transnational treaties as well as domestic laws.

But the way in which general principles are conceived both in doctrine and jurisprudence makes them less suited to the field of privacy law generally. One relates to the type of principles envisioned as such: age-old principles of law and procedure. This stands in stark contrast with privacy principles which are mostly substantive. Another obstacle is that general principles come into play in the context of inter-State relations, as opposed to State-individual relations as well as relations between individuals and corporations. Privacy and data protection concerns

---

[146] See *Statute of the International Court of Justice* (18 April 1946) art 38(1(c)).
[147] O'Boyle and Lafferty (n 128) 207.
[148] See Humphrey (n 122) 357.
[149] See Bertrand Ramcharan, 'The Law-Making Process: From Declaration to Treaty and Custom' in Dinah Shelton (ed), *Oxford Handbook of International Human Rights Law* (Oxford University Press 2013) 514.
[150] See Consolidated Draft Conclusions in Annex to the Second Report on General Principles of Law by Marcelo Vázquez-Bermúdez, Special Rapporteur, UN Doc A/CN.4/741 (9 April 2021) Conclusion 7(a).
[151] See Second Report of Vázquez-Bermúdez (n 150) para 122.

a complex web of relations between the public sector and individuals, the privacy sector and individuals, as well as relations between the public and the private sectors. Add to this the focus on *a* general principle as opposed to principles which is the case in the field of privacy and data protection law. Data privacy regulation is, for instance, typically a constellation of bureaucratic principles governing different steps of personal data processing. But more fundamentally, the fact that the Privacy Resolutions are still evolving with new principles being incorporated as the discourse proceeds makes their value in the development of general principles of privacy law lower, if not unpredictable.

3.2.2. Cross-fertilizing Global Privacy Norms

Another possible contributory role for the privacy discourse is inspiring the making of law and judicial decisions at domestic and regional levels. As discussed in section 2 above, the content of the Privacy Resolutions is, to some degree, a result of cross-fertilization of norms drawn from multiple sources. From domestic privacy law and decisions of regional human rights courts to IBRs, the Privacy Resolutions synthesize modern privacy norms. This potential role of the Resolutions is important, at least theoretically, because the level of privacy protection in the world over is hardly uniform. While Europe has the most advanced privacy regime espoused through progressive legislation and regional courts, less is the case in other parts of the world. As highlighted in chapter 3, even the recent proliferation of data privacy legislation in some parts of the world is yet to be complemented by independent and well-resourced monitoring agencies.

In the light of this landscape of global privacy legislation, the role of a universal soft law like the Privacy Resolution in lessening the gap seems appealing. But importantly, the Resolutions' tendency of flagging the human rights responsibilities and/or obligations of Internet corporations as well as States brings forward some novelties worth transposing to domestic legal regimes. Partly because the discourse is still ongoing—and in the short time since it began, the extent to which the Resolutions have shaped lawmaking or judicial decisions at national and regional levels is limited. An additional reason for this lack of influence may be the limited substantive scope of the Resolutions. That the Resolutions are by-products of an inchoate and hence evolving discourse means that the reference to its narrow set of privacy principles would be lesser.

Little is known as to the actual and direct, if ever, impact of the Resolutions on domestic law. Perhaps, the signing of Presidential Policy Directive (PPD) 28 by the former United States President Obama is remotely one example of the influence. The Directive partly addresses the discriminatory nature of the American digital surveillance legal regime, albeit half-heartedly.[152] Half-heartedly because

---

[152] See David Fidler, 'Cyberspace and Human Rights' in Nicholas Tsagourias and Russell Buchan (eds), *Research Handbook on International Law and Cyberspace* (Edward Elgar 2015) 114.

the Directive simply recognizes the 'privacy interests' of non-US persons, thereby avoiding a human rights language, and its attendant implications. Its preambular paragraph partly reads:

> In addition, our signals intelligence activities must take into account that all persons should be treated with dignity and respect, regardless of their nationality or wherever they might reside, and that all persons have legitimate <u>privacy interests</u> in the handling of their personal information.[153] [Emphasis Added]

Although adopted to re-enact the Patriot Act—which was then expiring, the adoption of the Freedom Act may also be seen as a reflection, if not a result, of the privacy discourse's broader impact on domestic lawmaking. The Act introduced some privacy safeguards such as the prohibition of bulk collection of phone records or metadata of 'Americans', restriction on the collection of data, permission to Internet companies to disclose the number of orders to hand over user data under the Foreign Intelligence Surveillance Act, and creation of a public advocate before the Foreign Intelligence Surveillance Court for certain novel cases to represent public interest.[154] Some of these principles particularly those relating to gag orders have found expression in the later Privacy Resolutions, as discussed in section 2 above. But again, the Directive was more a result of the political fallout and public outrage against American intelligence practices exposed by Snowden than a product of the discourse. Moreover, apart from the general recognition of aliens' privacy interests in the Directive, the above noted privacy-protective provisions of the Freedom Act apply only to American citizens and residents.

Another remote example is the 2017 draft EU e-Privacy Regulation which codified recurring themes in the Privacy Resolutions. Amendment 116 to Article 17 of the proposed Regulation provided that States must refrain from requiring corporations to take measures weakening encryption.[155] Moreover, it required corporations to notify end users when there is risk to security of their networks and services and, where applicable, provide remedies.[156] The former proviso corresponds to a paragraph in the Privacy Resolutions which calls upon States to 'refrain from requiring business enterprises to take steps that interfere with the right to privacy in an arbitrary or unlawful way'.[157] Another paragraph in the Resolutions also resembles the latter proviso which calls up on businesses to 'inform users about the collection, use, sharing and retention of their data that may affect their

---

[153] *Presidential Policy Directive 28: Signals Intelligence Activities* (17 January 2018) <https://bit.ly/2PC8kOI>.
[154] *Freedom Act* of 2015, Pub L No 114–23, 129 Stat 268, §§ 103, 201, 401, 501, 603.
[155] Draft Report on the Proposed e-Privacy Regulation (Committee on Civil Liberties, Justice and Home Affairs, 2017/0003(COD), 9 June 2017) Amendment 116 to art 17.
[156] ibid, Amendment 117 to art 17.
[157] See, eg, GA Res 73/179 (n 23) para 6(l).

right to privacy and to establish transparency policies, as appropriate'.[158] But, a version of the draft Regulation, released in May 2018, removed those provisions for unknown reasons.

Judicial references to the Resolutions have also been limited. In a number of decisions pronounced after the Snowden debacle, the ECtHR has been incorporating the initial Resolution in a section of judgments where it lists 'relevant international law'.[159] It reproduces two paragraphs from the first Privacy Resolution that urge States to align their domestic laws with international human rights standards and introduce independent oversight mechanisms. Nothing of substance is thus contained in those referenced paragraphs. While listing the Resolution is a positive gesture particularly in recognizing its status as a pertinent international (soft) law, it was essentially inconsequential in the decision making. Inconsequential because not only did the Court not engage with the Resolution but also reference is still to the merely hortatory initial Resolution. As noted above, subsequent Resolutions have become more substantive than the original one which, though, importantly charted the discussions. The reference to a now older, and less significant, Resolution manifests the basically symbolic nature of its mention in the Court's judgments.

At the international level, the impact of the UN privacy discourse was simply stimulative. Since the discourse was set in motion, the Committee's reporting procedure has seen a spike in the number of comments on States' digital surveillance practices. As discussed in chapter 2, an independent survey by a former member of the HR Committee had revealed that concluding observations relating to digital surveillance have increased by 25 per cent since the Snowden debacle.[160] But the brief nature of concluding observations means that detailed substantive principles cannot be considered in them. The most that could come out of concluding observations is that a new GC may later be developed by the Committee. And whether such a GC will be developed, and how fast is uncertain, as already submitted.

To summarize the above discussion, partly due to the nature and the narrow normative scope of the Resolutions, their level of influence in shaping the development of law at regional or domestic level or even in informing judicial decisions, has been limited. This makes the contributory role of the privacy discourse in cross-fertilizing global privacy norms insignificant. This leaves us with the third, and probably the most meaningful role: catalytic role, considered immediately below.

---

[158] ibid, para 7(b).

[159] See, eg, ECtHR, *Big Brother Watch and Others v UK*, Application Nos 58170/13, 62322/14 and 24960/15 (13 September 2018) paras 201–02.

[160] See Yuval Shany, Online Surveillance in the Case Law of the Human Rights Committee, The Hebrew University of Jerusalem Center for Cybersecurity Research (13 July 2017) <https://bit.ly/2MECR7m>.

3.3. Charting Normative and Methodological Directions

A more tangible role for the ongoing UN privacy discourse is its potential of spurring a more pragmatic approach to international privacy law. The catalytic role of the discourse has two mutually reinforcing strands. One is that the discourse charts a process which, its shortcomings notwithstanding, may be instrumental in the progressive development of international privacy law. The political capital witnessed since the start of the discussions at the UN can be geared towards pragmatic rethinking of the right to privacy in international law. The second relates to the innovative approaches to privacy pursued, albeit with some limitations, in the Resolutions. This relates to the unifying way in which the right to privacy is envisioned and the fiat given to a multistakeholder approach to privacy. What follows discusses these two aspects of the discourse.

3.3 1. Political Capital for Meaningful Reform

The political capital shown over the past few years in the UN privacy discussions cannot simply be dismissed as reactive, temporal, and hence negligible. But what is a 'political capital', and what is its role in bringing about meaningful reform in international privacy law? The term 'political capital' is a term of art, niche to the field of political science; but its technical definition essentially captures what is intended here.[161] For purposes of the discussion here, the term is meant to represent the symbolic value of the ongoing UN privacy discourse, particularly the Privacy Resolutions, in setting the agenda of elaborating the scope and meaning of the right to privacy in international law in the light of the new realities of the digital age. In that light, a prime significance of the discourse is that it has initiated a conversation on how to best secure digital privacy.[162] With the initiation of a conversation particularly at the UN level, and remarkably in a sustained way for over eight years, the discourse presents the opportunity for gradual but meaningful international legislative response to the privacy problem in the digital age. The significant level of support that the adoption of the Resolutions has received among many States, added to the strong civil society engagement with the discourse, reflects the existence of some political capital and hence political will for reform. Long-term and practical legislative measures may gradually grow out of the discourse should the political will linger long enough, and be exploited judiciously.

In international lawmaking, there are several precedents where a discourse charted in a UNGA Resolution ultimately grew into tangible legislative outcomes. In new areas of international legalization, the work often begins with a Resolution

---

[161] Political scientist Bourdieu, for instance, defines it as 'a form of symbolic capital, credit founded on credence or belief and recognition'. See Pierre Bourdieu, 'Political Representation: Elements for a Theory of the Political Field' in Pierre Bourdieu (ed), *Language and Symbolic Power* (Polity 1991) 192.

[162] Of a related view, see Marko Milanovic, 'Human Right Treaties and Foreign Surveillance: The Right to Privacy in the Digital Age' (2014) 56 Harvard International Law Journal 81, 85.

than a treaty.[163] More particularly, resort is made to soft law when the subject matter in question is new and a proper response is yet to be determined.[164] Soft legalization, in such instances, is opted to initiate a conversation on the subject until a long-term normative response is developed.[165] The passing of a Resolution on a given subject matter, on its own right, gives rise to the need for some form of new regulation, and hence opens the door for further engagement.[166] As a stepping stone towards broader normative measures, the adoption of a soft law has also the advantage of avoiding possible 'anxieties of dealing with something new' in international legalization.[167] In that sense, a soft law prepares the stage for a long-term process of reform.

The progressive development of international space law probably offers an instructive example. UN work in the field of the Outer Space begun with a UNGA Resolution on the Outer Space adopted in 1961,[168] which later was followed by a Declaration in 1963.[169] The Declaration, then, found translation into a number of multilateral treaties.[170] Following this track, the conversation that involved the adoption of a series of Privacy Resolutions may culminate in one or more treaty law or may just conclude with a soft law. Whether the conversation started by the Privacy Resolutions will, like the Outer Space discourse, progressively develop privacy law is uncertain. The underlying argument advanced in this book is that progressive development of international privacy law is needed in light of the new realities of the digital age. But, the approach towards achieving such progress must be pragmatic in that it must go beyond the rather common hard legalization paradigm in the privacy literature.[171] Chapters 7 and 8 lay out the structures of the pragmatic approach to international privacy law, but it suffices to state here that the path taken by the international regime on the Outer Space is not the best way forward for the right to privacy in the digital age. With that said, there are still three aspects of the privacy discourse that diminish their catalytic role: lack of thematic focus, ambiguous formulation of provisions, and uncertainty of scope.

---

[163] See Higashi (n 110) 16.

[164] See Dinah Shelton, 'Introduction: Law, Non-Law and the Problem of Soft Law' in Dinah Shelton (ed), *Commitment and Compliance: The Role of Non-Binding Norms in the International Legal System* (Oxford University Press 2000) 13.

[165] See Kenneth Abbott and Duncan Snidal, 'Hard and Soft Law in International Governance' (2000) 54 International Organization 421, 423.

[166] See Joyner (n 134) 463–64.

[167] See Boyle and Chinkin (n 41) 227.

[168] See *International Co-operation in the Peaceful Uses of Outer Space*, GA Res 1721 (XVI)A-E, 1085th plenary mtg, UN Doc RES/1721(XVI) (20 December 1961).

[169] See *Declaration of Legal Principles Governing the Activities of States in the Exploration and Uses of the Outer Space*, GA Res 1962 (XVIII), 18th sess, Agenda item 28a, UN Doc A/Res/18/1962 (13 December 1963).

[170] See, eg, *Treaty on Principles Governing the Activities of States in the Exploration and Use of Outer Space, including the Moon and Other Celestial Bodies*, opened for signature 27 January 1967 (entered into force 10 October).

[171] See ch 1.

Lack of thematic focus is patent in the Resolutions' increasing tendency to address themes that go beyond the right to privacy. Such loss of direction is reflected in the way in which the Resolutions import topics from other parallel discourses at the UN. One example is the emphasis on the role of Information and Communication Technologies (ICTs) for the attainment of the Sustainable Development Goals (SDGs).[172] The issue of SDGs is a broad and cross-cutting theme at the UN in contrast with the rather specific subject of digital privacy. Cybersecurity is another theme, currently in vogue at the UN, which the privacy discourse picks up. Paragraph 5 of Resolution 73/179 of the UNGA, for instance, urges States to 'promote an open, secure, stable, accessible, and peaceful ICTs environment based on respect for international law'.[173]

Themes from the ongoing discussions at the HR Council on the right to free speech online, highlighted earlier, are also slowly creeping into the privacy discourse. For example, a preambular paragraph raises the 'fake news' phenomenon, a theme covered in the free speech Resolutions of the HR Council.[174] Likewise, themes covered in the most recently launched discourse on new and emerging technologies—as alluded to above—are migrating into the privacy discourse. In the most recent Privacy Resolution of the HR Council for instance, several provisions focusing on the broader human rights implications of data-driven technologies such as AI are introduced.[175] But particular attention is also being given to other rights such as equality/non-discrimination and freedom of assembly that face unique threats due to the proliferation of data-driven technologies.[176] Part of this tendency to embrace topical themes is the reference to the Covid-19 pandemic and the attendant human rights concerns.[177]

The concern is that the central goal of the Privacy Resolutions might be sidetracked by the above issues. When one considers the long-running controversy about some of those themes in the Internet governance discourse, the evolution of the Privacy Resolutions may be frustrated by the lack of thematic focus and ambivalence of path. The more the privacy discourse cherry-picks themes from other, albeit remotely related themes, the less core privacy themes would find proper articulation in the Privacy Resolutions and perhaps ultimately in the instrument where/if the discourse culminates. In practical terms, such a future instrument might end up failing to adequately reimagine international law of privacy in the digital age.

Ambiguous formulations are also visible when one compares the elaborative tendency of the Resolutions, on the one hand, and vague cross-referencing

---

[172] See, eg, GA Res 73/179 (n 23) para 2.
[173] ibid, para 5.
[174] ibid, preamble, para 23; see also Res GA 75/176 (n 23) Preamble, para 27.
[175] See, eg, HRC Res 48/4 (n 23) para 3 cum Preamble, paras 10, 19–23, 25.
[176] See HRC Res 48/4 (n 23) paras 6(e)(r), 8(g).
[177] ibid, Preamble, paras 32–33; HRC Res 75/176 (n 23) Preamble, para 37.

of 'obligations under international human rights law' on the other. UNGA's Resolution 73/179 in para 6(b), for instance, calls upon States '... to take measures to put an end to violations of the right to privacy ... including by ensuring that relevant national legislation complies with their obligations under international human rights law.'

Such phraseology is commonplace in the Privacy Resolutions. But the question of what these obligations are, in specific terms, remains. In considering the vaguely worded provision of the right to privacy in the ICCPR and the dearth in treaty body jurisprudence, the cross-reference to obligations in international human rights law makes little sense. But at a higher level, the Resolutions' consistent call for States to align their domestic laws, procedures, and practices with international law—the content of which is either uncertain or absent—is that they may, if implemented by States, lead to an incoherent mosaic of domestic laws and practices. The risk is not of just being ignored by States but also that they may be translated into real measures in a divergent manner. In the digital context where privacy threats are transnational in nature, the need for comparable and harmonized privacy safeguards worldwide cannot be overemphasized.

A common premise that underpins all the Privacy Resolutions is that international human rights law provides a sound basis for the protection of the right to privacy in the digital age.[178] But again, they note the need to further discuss specific principles. They, for instance, provide that there is a need to 'further discuss and analyze based on international human rights law', specific issues and principles surrounding digital privacy rights such as the 'principles of non-arbitrariness and lawfulness'.[179] This is often reinforced by a concluding paragraph that 'encourages' further discussion to identify best practices, in addition to 'clarifying existing principles and standards', on the right to privacy.[180] Such phrases reveal a sense of ambivalence in underlying the adequacy of existing international privacy norms while simultaneously acknowledging the need to examine those norms if they still are fit for purpose to the digital context as well as to look out for best practices. This suggests the ambivalence of the discourse that may reduce its catalytic role.

The thematic approach of the Resolutions—ie, 'communication surveillance, interception and collection of personal data'—is also misleading. It sends the signal that the three are essentially and necessarily distinct processes. But they might well be part of a single measure of surveillance which involves interception and collection of personal data. Of course, surveillance of digital communication on its own either without interception of the whole or part of the relevant communication or collection of personal data (which might often be part of the interception) is of little use to intelligence or law enforcement agencies. A 2013 report of La Rue,

---

[178] See also ch 2.
[179] See, eg, GA Res 73/179 (n 23) Preamble, para 11.
[180] ibid, para 10.

former UN Special Rapporteur on the Freedom of Expression, offers an instructive description of 'communication surveillance': the monitoring, interception, collection, preservation, and retention of information that has been communicated, relayed, or generated over communications networks.[181]

This description appropriately captures what is probably intended in the Privacy Resolutions. But one finds the lack of clarity in the Resolutions striking because the same report has been referred to in the opening paragraphs of the Resolutions, with approval.[182] The latest Resolutions refer, instead, to reports of La Rue's successor, which do not carry the same definition of communication surveillance.[183]

In conclusion, the ongoing UN privacy discourse carries a level of political capital that could be tapped in reforming the international law of privacy. While the Privacy Resolutions are replete with inconsistencies, uncertainties, and ambiguities, the political capital would assist in realizing a more focused and practicable reform initiative.

3.3.2. Innovative Approaches to Privacy

As considered in section 2 above, the ongoing UN privacy discourse carries not only novelty of substance but also of approach. The second catalytic role of the UN privacy discourse draws from the latter. One is the unifying approach of the Resolutions in pulling together the various normative sources of privacy. Such an approach would be instrumental in distilling and cross-fertilizing diffuse privacy norms that reflect modern understandings on the legal protection of the right to privacy in the digital age. The idea of a soft law supplement argued in chapter 7 builds on, but goes beyond, this unifying and holistic approach to privacy.

A multistakeholder approach to privacy is the other innovative notion espoused in the Resolutions. In addition to the acknowledgment of 'informal dialogues' among relevant stakeholders for having greatly facilitated the discussion on the right to privacy, the Resolutions set a process in motion to further discuss the issue of digital privacy through a multistakeholder process.[184] The Resolutions provide that challenges to the right to privacy in the digital environment must be considered in a multistakeholder process.[185] But what really 'informal dialogue', as opposed to formal dialogue, constitutes is far from clear, but it appears that the SRP is tasked to lead this dialogue.[186] As considered in the context of IBRs in chapter 4, multistakeholderism offers—its inherent limitations notwithstanding—new ways of norm-creation. References to and the support for multistakeholderism in the

---

[18]   See Report of La Rue (n 10) para 6(a).
[18]   See, eg, GA Res 68/167 (n 1) Preamble, para 7.
[18]   See, eg, GA Res 73/179 (n 23) Preamble, para 4.
[18]   ibid, para 9 cum preamble, para 13.
[18]   See, eg, GA Res 75/176 (n 23) Preamble, para 6; see also GA Res 73/179 (n 23) Preamble, para 13.
[18]   ibid, para 10.

Privacy Resolutions lack clarity, however. This is particularly the case in relation to the nature and scope of the dialogue.

Yet the support for a dialogical approach to privacy is, in its own right, a pragmatic way forward. Considering the virtues of a multi-level dialogue as a way of building consensus and then gradually improving human rights protection, the support for a multistakeholder approach is a step forward. As shall be argued in chapter 8, a dialogical approach to digital privacy is the most practical step towards lessening institutional gaps in international privacy law. Introducing a privacy forum where emerging and current privacy issues are debated would be a pragmatic and logical way of realizing the support for dialogue expressed in the Privacy Resolutions.

In summary, the Privacy Resolutions' important value lies in their role of beginning a process that may culminate in long-term international legislative measures on digital privacy. The conversation commenced by the discourse and its innovative approaches to privacy yield a catalytic role in reimagining the right to privacy in the digital age. Together with progressive aspects of the IBRs project explored in the preceding chapter, the UN privacy discourse offers the normative and methodological direction in that front.

4. Conclusion

This chapter examined the normative significance of the evolving discourse on the 'right to privacy in the digital age' initiated at the UN. With a particular focus on the series of ten Resolutions adopted between 2013 and 2021, the chapter explored the ways in which the Resolution may contribute in reimagining international law of privacy in the digital age. Three potential contributions of the discourse are considered. One is the freestanding role of the discourse by which the discourse may have elaborative and interpretive functions. As shown in this chapter, the elaborative and interpretive role of Resolutions is valuable on their own but less so in the context of international privacy law given the limited normative reach of the Privacy Resolutions. Partly dictated by the very nature of Resolutions in that they are not formally suited to capture as much regulatory details, the Privacy Resolutions address privacy themes in a selective manner. Worse, institutional aspects of international privacy law are not considered. The inchoate state of the discussions further reduces the freestanding role of the privacy discourse.

The second potential role of the discourse is largely contributory in that it may help universalize privacy standards. One way this may occur is should the Privacy Resolutions lead to the gradual accretion of general international law in the field of privacy and data protection. As this chapter has shown, inevitable uncertainties (and controversy) surrounding the possibility of a customary international law of privacy or even general principles also makes them ill-suited to reimagine the right to privacy in international law. Another contributory role is the potential for the discourse to influence lawmaking and judicial decisions at the national and regional levels. But mainly due to limited normative reach as well as the limited novelty in the Privacy Resolutions, the prospect of a contributory role will be limited. As a product of cross-fertilization of norms drawn from multiple sources including domestic and regional laws and jurisprudence, it is unlikely that the Resolutions will succeed in localizing global privacy norms.

With this comes the third rather promising role of the privacy discourse: catalyzing international privacy law reform. The chapter argued that a more promising value of the discourse is its potential of catalyzing a pragmatic privacy law reform. Resolutions have long served as incipient steps towards a hard law especially in the area of human rights, including in the form of a treaty. But that is not necessarily the pragmatic way forward for meaningful international privacy law reform. A future international legal response to the privacy problem in the digital space should not necessarily follow, for example the path of the UN Resolutions on the Outer Space, at least in the short-term. As shown at the outset, treaty law is neither desirable nor viable in effectively responding to contemporary privacy challenges in the digital environment. What is needed is a focused and practical approach that builds on but moves beyond the Privacy Resolutions. Such an approach would build on the political will exhibited in the discourse and substantive aspects of the Privacy Resolutions. Chapters 7 and 8 explore the nature, scope, and content of that pragmatic approach to international privacy law.

6

Transnational Privacy Standards

1. Introduction

This chapter turns to consider the third global privacy initiative: transnational privacy standards. It examines whether—and the extent to which—transnational privacy standards, particularly the Council of Europe (CoE) data privacy framework, contribute to the development of international law. In so doing, it seeks to show the ways in which such standards may contribute in addressing the 'privacy problem' in the digital age, particularly the shortcomings in international data privacy law. The CoE has long been considered to have contributed to the development of international law generally.[1] Such allusions have also permeated the field of privacy and data protection. Convention 108 has at times been lauded by scholars for having served as a 'backbone of international law'.[2] Taken even further, it has also been referred to as a 'universal instrument'.[3] Some United Nations (UN) bodies have also highlighted the potential global role of the Convention. The United Nations Conference on Trade and Development (UNCTAD), for instance, called the Convention the most 'promising international development in the field'.[4] But the real extent of the nexus between the Convention system and international law has not been subject to systematic analysis. This chapter seeks to fill that void. It explores the various ways in which the further globalization of the Convention 108 system may help address the 'privacy problem' in the digital age.

Three potential avenues towards the universalization of the CoE Data Protection Framework are considered. First, it discusses the extent to which further accession to the Convention and its Amending Protocol by non-CoE member States may influence international law. Since the process of accession was activated by the Committee of Ministers (CoM) in 2008, a number of non-European countries have acceded to Convention 108. But as shall be shown in this chapter, the rate of accession has been largely slow in that accession by a 'critical mass' of States in the

---

[1] Arthur Robertson, 'The Contribution of the Council of Europe to the Development of International Law' (1965) 59 Proceedings of the American Society of International Law at Its Annual Meeting 201, 201.

[2] See Sylvia Kierkegaard and others, '30 Years On—The Review of the Council of Europe Data Protection Convention 108' (2011) 27 Computer Law and Security Review 223, 223.

[3] See, eg, Cécilede Terwangne, 'Council of Europe Convention 108+: A Modernized International Treaty for the Protection of Personal Data' (2021) 40 Computer Law and Security Review 1, 2, 17.

[4] Data Protection Regulations and International Data Flows: Implications for Trade and Development (UNCTAD 2016) 26.

Privacy and the Role of International Law in the Digital Age. Kinfe Yilma, Oxford University Press. © Kinfe Yilma 2023.
DOI: 10.1093/oso/9780192887290.003.0006

near future is unlikely. This may be termed a 'freestanding' role of the Convention system in helping address the privacy problem in the digital age. Second, the chapter considers whether norms envisaged in the Convention may gradually develop into general international law, including through accession and indirect adaptation into domestic legal systems. With uncertainties and complexities on the nature and scope of custom and general principles as sources of international law the prospect of the Convention developing into general international law is limited. This is a potential 'contributory' role of the Convention.

Third, the chapter considers the 'catalytic' potential of the Convention in indirectly shaping the structure of international law of privacy through jurisprudential cross-influence. With increasing reference to the case law of the European Court of Human Rights (ECtHR) —which, in turn, often refers to Convention 108 in its privacy decisions—in the jurisprudence of the Human Rights Committee (HR Committee) and other UN bodies, the Convention may gradually shape international law. As shall be shown in the chapter, this indirect influence of the Convention has recently figured in the case law of the HR Committee, the series of UN Privacy Resolutions, and the work of UN Special Procedures. That jurisprudential influence is inherently a slow process, and tends to be hamstrung by UN bureaucracy means it is unlikely to effectively result in the progressive and coherent development of international privacy law.

The central contention of the chapter is that the three avenues of norm universalization offer little in attending to the 'privacy problem' in the digital age. A virtue often associated with these paths towards norm universalization is that they would eventually lead to a truly international data privacy standard but one that introduces binding norms. Added to the complexities of each approach, the existence of time-tested binding norms of international law on the right to privacy means that there is no need for a new set of binding norms. As shall be argued in chapter 7, soft legalization in international law is perhaps the effective tool in addressing the 'privacy problem' in the digital age. In realizing the virtues of soft law in the field, the three means of norm universalization would help in the gradual socialization and diffusion of data privacy norms. More accession to Convention 108 and reading of its standards in international instruments like the International Covenant on Civil and Political Rights (ICCPR) would gradually help build consensus on a set of widely accepted data privacy rights, principles, and governance norms.

For purposes of this chapter, the reference 'Convention 108(+) system' is meant to capture Convention 108 (1981),[5] its Additional Protocol (2001),[6] and the most

---

[5] *Convention for the Protection of Individuals with Regard to Automatic Processing of Personal Data*, opened for signature 28 January 1981, ETS No 108 (entered into force 1 October 1981).

[6] *Additional Protocol to the Convention for the Protection of Individuals with regard to Automatic Processing of Personal Data, regarding Supervisory Authorities and Transborder Data Flows*, opened for signature 8 November 2001, 181 ETS (entered into force 1 July 2004).

recent Amending Protocol (2018).[7] Otherwise, each instrument is referred to specifically where relevant. Moreover, the terms data privacy and data protection are used interchangeably. The focus in this chapter thus is primarily on the Convention 108(+) system, but the prospect of other regional standards in the development of data privacy in international law is briefly considered. In this respect, the chapter considers the African Union (AU) Convention on Cybersecurity and Personal Data Protection (Malabo Convention), the General Data Protection Regulation (GDPR), the Asia Pacific Economic Cooperation (APEC) Privacy Framework, and the Standards for Personal Data Protection for Ibero-American States. Further considered in the chapter, albeit briefly, are data protection standards of sub-regional economic communities in Africa. None of these supranational standards carry a potential to grow into universal standards. A rather limited role of such standards would be to facilitate the accretion of international custom or general principles through acculturation of data privacy standards in the laws and jurisprudence of their respective member States.

2. Background to the Convention 108(+) System

CoE data privacy initiatives date back to the early 1970s. Resolutions (73) 22 and (74) 29 of the CoM introduced the first set of data privacy principles for the private and the public sector respectively.[8] But these early legislative measures were taken as a tentative response to what was then thought an urgent development requiring swift action. Then, the goal was primarily to 'prevent further divergences between the laws of member States in this field'.[9] In Resolution (73) 22, the CoM expressly foreshadowed an 'international agreement' that would permanently address the novel regulatory challenges presented by electronic data banks.[10] This raises the question of whether Convention 108—which was later opened for signature on 28 January 1981—was the envisioned 'international agreement' or that the CoM had hoped for a universal treaty negotiated under the aegis of, for instance, the UN.

What makes the later point worth making is that, as highlighted in chapter 3, the 1968 Tehran Conference is where the idea of a global data privacy treaty first emerged. Indeed, processes leading to the adoption of Resolution (73) by the CoM were initiated by the Parliamentary Assembly of the Council of Europe

---

[7] *Modernized Convention for the Protection of Individuals with Regard to the Processing of Personal Data*, opened for signature 10 October 2018, CETS No 223 (not yet in force).

[8] Resolution (73) 22 on the Protection of the Privacy of Individuals vis-à-vis Electronic Data Banks in the Private Sector, adopted by the Committee of Ministers at the 224th meeting of the Ministers' Deputies (26 September 1973); Resolution (74) 29 on the Protection of Privacy of Individuals vis-à-vis Electronic Data Banks in the Public Sector, adopted by the Committee of Ministers at the 236th meeting of the Ministers' Deputies (20 September 1974).

[9] ibid, preamble, para 4.

[10] ibid.

(PACE)—then called the Consultative Assembly—several months before the Tehran Conference opened, in April 1968.[11] First, a Motion for Resolution on Human Rights and Modern Scientific and Technological Developments was introduced by the Austrian representatives on 26 April 1967.[12] This was followed by a Recommendation adopted on 31 January 1968 where PACE called upon the CoM to instruct the Committee of Experts on Human Rights to study the human rights implications of modern technical devices on the enjoyment of the right to privacy.[13]

Based on a survey conducted between 1968 and 1970, the Committee of Experts found that no effective protection existed in the national laws of member States as well the European Convention on Human Rights and Fundamental Freedoms (ECHR).[14] A key finding in the study was that the regional human rights mechanism, ie, ECHR, as a human rights treaty imposing duties only on States, does not apply directly to the practices of the private sector. Needless to say, it is through States' positive duty to protect that the private sector is indirectly regulated vis-à-vis its data processing practices. But the Committee's point highlighted the importance of direct regulation of the conduct of the private sector through human rights. To further study the matter, the CoM instructed a sub-committee of the European Committee on Legal Cooperation in 1971 which later, among other things, recommended the creation of a Committee on the Protection of Privacy.[15] The high-level data privacy principles appended to Resolution (73) 22—and later to (74) 29—were drafted by that Committee based on insights from data privacy legislation adopted in jurisdictions such as Germany (Hessen, 1970), Belgium (1972), Sweden (1973), and US (1970).[16]

The first set of data privacy principles in Resolutions (73) 22 and (74) 29 were aimed to provide 'minimum standards' for member States as means of legislative harmonization. But the imperatives of a global response to the problem of electronic data banks was not lost on the Committee on the Protection of Privacy. Background documents suggest that the Committee had highlighted the need to reinforce Resolutions (73) 22 and (74) 29 with a binding 'international' data privacy agreement.[17] This has become a reality, at least partly, with the adoption of Convention 108 in 1981, supplemented in 2001 with an Additional Protocol and an amendment Protocol more recently in 2018. A key aspect of Convention 108

[1] Detailed archival information about the Conference is available at <https://legal.un.org/avl/ha/fat chr/fatchr.html>.
[1] See Motion for A Resolution, Doc 2206, 19th Session (26 April 1967).
[1] Human Rights and Modern Scientific and Technological Developments, Recommendation 509, adopted by the Parliamentary Assembly at 16th Sitting (31 January 1968).
[1] DH/EXP (70) 15. See also the Right to Respect for Privacy As Affected by Modern Scientific and Technological Devices: Survey of Legislation in the Member States, H. (73) 11. (1970) cited in AC Evans, 'European Data Protection Law' (1981) 29 American Journal of Comparative Law 571, 573.
[1] Explanatory Report of Resolution (73) 22, CM (73) 110 (12 July 1973) para 5.
[1] ibid, para 8.
[1] ibid, para 12.

is its open character in that non-CoE member States may be permitted to accede, subject of course to a series of bureaucratic processes.[18]

In its four decades of existence, Convention 108 and its Additional Protocol have considerably influenced data privacy lawmaking outside Europe. But its envisioned global role through the avenue of accession is yet to be attained. Writing in 2012, Greenleaf predicated that Convention 108 is likely to be acceded by a 'critical mass' of States by the end of the decade—ie, 2020—and hence live up to its global potential.[19] At the time of writing, only eight States that are not members of the CoE have acceded to Convention 108.[20] Reception to Convention 108+ has not also been as promising. At the time of writing, Convention 108+ has attracted forty-three signatures and only fifteen ratifications. This reinforces the question of whether accession is really the most feasible way of increasing the role of the Convention 108(+) system in the development of international law. As shall be argued in this chapter, accession—through formal ratification—should not be seen as the only, if not the main, means of achieving near universal acceptance of data privacy standards embodied in Convention 108. Nor should it also be seen as the most effective means of norm globalization. In the absence of a robust oversight mechanism by which compliance with legal rules can be ensured, the sheer existence of a truly international binding instrument would do little. That is the reason, as shall be discussed further below, the most feasible, but not necessarily mutually exclusive to 'globalization via accession', tools are softer mechanisms such as jurisprudential cross-influence.

3. Norm Universalization

3.1. Meaning

Convention 108's potential in diffusing data privacy norms worldwide is often described in the literature as a form of 'globalization'. Greenleaf's scholarship in this regard is notable. But the term globalization might not probably lend itself well in any attempt to comprehensively analyse the global role of the Convention 108(+) system generally and its place in international law in particular. The main challenge in deploying the term is its meaning. Defining the term 'globalization' is obviously difficult owing mainly to its different significations in different contexts.

---

[18] See Convention 108 (n 5) art 23.

[19] Graham Greenleaf, 'The Influence of European Data Privacy Standards Outside Europe: Implications for Globalization of Convention 108' (2012) 2 International Data Privacy Law 68, 92.

[20] See details about status of accession at <https://www.coe.int/en/web/conventions/full-list?module=signatures-by-treaty&treatynum=108>. Burkina Faso is slated to be the 9th State to accede once it completes the accession process.

In the international relations literature, for instance, the term carries a particular meaning. Reus-Smit and Dunne, for instance, posit that 'globalization [occurs when] norms and practices of the sovereign order [are] spread and transposed'.[21] Globalization in the context of legislation is understood slightly differently by legal academics. Shapiro, for instance, deploys the terms 'globalization of law'—in contrast with international law—to capture the development of a set of rules applicable globally through parallel developments in different parts of the world.[22] He further relates globalization to the phenomenon of worldwide diffusion of norms and legal practices.[23] Other scholars equalize the gradual harmonization of national laws as development of international law.[24] Simpson notes that globalization of (international) law involves the modernization of the law through universalizing norms, doctrines and institutions of justice.[25]

Privacy scholars of different disciplines have also deployed the term in different manners. Bennett, a political scientist who has extensively studied norm globalization—or what he calls policy convergence—in the field of data privacy, defines it as a 'dynamic process by which countries begin at different starting points and overtime converge toward similar solutions'.[26] He characterizes the phenomenon of norm convergence as the logical progression of policy interdependence between different countries.[27] Greenleaf, a legal scholar who has long advocated for and studied possibilities of globalizing Convention 108, does not seem to offer a specific definition. But one can readily glean from his extensive scholarship on the subject that globalization of Convention 108 represents the spread of data privacy laws globally particularly through national law via accession to Convention 108.[28] This is leads us to the other reason why 'globalization' is not the pertinent concept to capture the true potential of transnational standards like Convention 108. Beyond accession, the Convention 108(+) system may contribute to the development of international law of privacy through different avenues, as this chapter shall demonstrate.

---

[21] Christian Reus-Smit and Tim Dunne, 'The Globalization of International Society' in Tim Dunne and Christian Reus-Smit (eds), *The Globalization of International Society* (Oxford University Press 2017) 18.

[22] Martin Shapiro, 'The Globalization of Law' (1993) 1 Indian Journal of Global Studies 37, 37.

[23] ibid, 39.

[24] See, eg, Hans Nilsson, 'The Council of Europe Laundering Convention: A Recent Example of A Developing International Criminal Law' (1991) 2 Criminal Law Forum 419, 419.

[25] Gerry Simpson, 'The Globalization of International Law' in Tim Dunne and Christian Reus-Smit (eds, *The Globalization of International Society* (Oxford University Press 2017) 282.

[26] See Colin Bennett, 'Convergence Revisited: Toward A Global Policy for the Protection of Personal Data?' in Philip Agre and Marc Rotenberg (eds), *Technology and Privacy: The Landscape* (MIT Press 1997) 102.

[27] Colin Bennett, 'The European General Data Protection Regulation: An Instrument for the Globalization of Privacy Standards?' (2018) 23 Information Polity 239, 244.

[28] See, eg, Graham Greenleaf, 76 Global Data Privacy Laws, Privacy Laws and Business Special Report (September 2011).

This chapter, as a result, mainly uses the term norm universalization instead in exploring the ways in which the Convention 108(+) system may be transformed from a transnational to a truly universal instrument on data privacy regulation. Unlike globalization, which may mean different things in different settings, the term 'universalization' best captures the overall goal of transforming norms of regional origin into rules of general international law. As shall become clear, the chapter considers the global role of Convention 108 from a broader international law perspective. In that sense, accession to the Convention by non-CoE member States is considered only as one tool of enhancing its international law standing. The Convention 108(+) system may contribute towards the formation of rules of Customary International Law (CIL) and General Principles of Law (GPsL). But more importantly, it may indirectly influence international data privacy law through jurisprudential cross-influence. The chapter returns to these points later in this chapter. For purposes of this chapter, universalization is not meant to represent the process of making rules conceptually and linguistically accessible to the general public. In his book 'Universalizing International Law', Weeramantry deploys the term to capture the process by which international law becomes more accessible or 'brought home to the general public' to enhance its value, effectiveness, and relevance.[29] That is not the intended meaning of the concept in this chapter and the book as a whole.

3.2. Virtues

Can one realistically imagine universalization of normative standards set by a body formed to uphold a particular set of values? This is a question that any attempt of looking at the prospect of a rather regional convention with specific regulatory objectives through the lens of international law raises. The Statute of the CoE, the constitutive document of the organization, states its founding objective as follows:

> The aim of the Council of Europe is to achieve a greater unity between its members for the purpose of safeguarding and realizing the ideals and principles which are their common heritage and facilitating their economic and social progress.[30]

Doubtless, the organization is formed to foster unity among its European member States which are said to share a common heritage on values such as human rights, rule of law and democracy.[31] The CoE is thus established to bring more cohesion

---

[29] See Christopher Weeramantry, *Universalizing International Law* (Brill 2004) xi.
[30] *Statute of the Council of Europe* (5 May 1949) art 1(a) cum Preamble, para 3.
[31] See generally Martyn Bond, *The Council of Europe: Structure, History and Issues in European Politics* (Routledge 2011).

among European countries with common sets of values. Lawmaking treaties of the organization as well its numerous soft law standards are designed in further achieving this founding objective of the organization. This is no exception to Convention 108. Paragraph 1 of the Modernized Convention's preamble reiterates the organizational aim of the CoE to 'achieve greater unity between its members, based in particular on respect for the rule of law, as well as human rights and fundamental freedoms'.[32] But it goes further in stating—as one of its *raison d'être*—the importance of promoting at the global level the fundamental values of respect for privacy and protection of personal data, thereby contributing to the free flow of information between people across borders.[33]

In a way, this might be taken to mean that even the value of promoting values like privacy to non-European countries is a worthwhile mission for self-serving interests. That is, the privacy of European citizens cannot effectively be protected in an age of transborder data processing unless such values are promoted to third countries to which they may be alien. In the same year PACE set in motion the development of a data privacy legal framework, it declared that the CoE is the 'trustee of western humanism' and that its essential function should be preparing for the Europe of tomorrow.[34] Added to the above highlighted founding objective of the CoE, such statements of a closed regional body may cast doubt on the viability of universalizing its legal instruments. Put differently, one might ask whether Convention 108 stands any real chance of transforming itself into a universal data privacy instrument.

One should approach this question in historical context, and of course, CoE's organizational evolution since. With the adoption of the Convention 108 in 1981 which explicitly contains an accession clause by third countries—and Uruguay's accession in 2013, the CoE charted the process towards a global body. This was later followed by the Human Rights and Biomedicine Convention in 1997 and the Cybercrime Convention in 2001 which, with a similar accession clause,[35] unequivocally attested to CoE's organizational transformation. The Modernized Convention further solidifies the globalization mission when it emphasizes the importance of promoting at the global level the 'fundamental values of respect for

---

[32] See also Convention 108+ (n 7) Preamble, para 1.

[33] Convention 108 (n 5) Preamble, para 5; see also Convention 108+ (n 7) Preamble, para 5.

[34] Function and Future of the Council of Europe, Recommendation 516 (1968), adopted by the Parliamentary Assembly at 19th Sitting (1 February 1968).

[35] See *Convention on Human Rights and Biomedicine*, opened for signature 4 April 1997, 164 ETS (entered into force 1 December 1999) art 34; *Convention on Cybercrime*, opened for signature 23 November 2001, opened for signature 23 November 2001, *European Treaty Series* No 185 (entered into force 1 July 2004) art 37. Note, though, that the now denounced European Convention on the International Classification of Patents for Inventions—adopted a few years after the creation of the CoE—did also allow accession by non-CoE States that are members of the International Union for the Protection of Industrial Property. See *European Convention on the International Classification of Patents for Inventions*, opened for signature 19 December 1954, European Treaty Series No 017 (entered into force 1 August 1955) art 5.

privacy and protection of personal data'.[36] In allowing non-European countries to join its treaty system, the CoE appeared to have changed course in accepting that rule of law, democracy, and human rights are values shared across the globe. Arguably, this relates to data privacy as well.

While data privacy is a more recent offshoot of privacy, the essence of the right to privacy has long been guaranteed in the domestic legal system of non-European jurisdictions. In that sense, data privacy is, or should be, as much a protected—if not practiced—value outside Europe. Indeed, the trend in the past decade or so by which European data privacy standards shaped lawmaking in many countries outside of Europe may be taken to attest to the global recognition of data privacy as an important value. The 'privacy problem' in the digital age impacts any part of the word, not least because privacy is a universally shared human value and that it faces largely similar threats in the digital age. In that sense, it might be argued that exploring ways of further globalizing—or universalizing—data privacy standards, including through accession is a tenable proposition.

Making Convention 108 a universal instrument of international law as a project appears to be prompted by the lack of and infeasibility of a UN-mediated data privacy treaty. That is to say Convention 108 was not conceived with the explicit aim of making it a universal instrument of data privacy regulation. As alluded to above, the Preamble to Convention 108—reiterated verbatim in the Modernized Convention—ties its 'global role' with the reality of transborder data flow. The envisioned global promotion of data privacy was largely a self-serving, pragmatic proviso. Even then, transborder data flow was apparently envisioned rather narrowly between CoE member States and a handful of advanced economies as opposed to the 'global mass' of States. During the drafting of the Convention, a number of Organization for Economic Cooperation and Development (OECD) member States that are not members of the CoE had actively participated in the work of the Drafting Committee.[37] The inclusion of the accession clause later in the Convention was meant specifically to enable these countries, namely the United States, Canada, and Japan, join the treaty.[38] The deliberate omission of the 'European' prefix in the treaty's nomenclature is part of this early effort to give the Convention a global character.[39] From the outset, Convention 108 was seen as a 'tool' to achieve worldwide standards on data protection.[40]

---

[36] See Convention 108+ (n 7) Preamble, para 6.

[37] See Sophie Kwasny, 'Convention 108: A Transatlantic DNA?' in Dan Jerker Svantesson and Dariusz Kloza (eds), *Transatlantic Data Privacy Relations As A Challenge for Democracy* (Intersentia 2017) 534; see also Explanatory Report to the Convention for the Protection of Individuals with regard to Automatic Processing of Personal Data (28 January 1981) 14–15; Frits Hondius, 'A Quarter of Century of International Data Protection' (2006) 19 Hague Yearbook of International Law 23, 34.

[38] ibid.

[39] See Frits Hondius, 'A Decade of International Data Protection' (1983) 30 Netherlands Review of International Law 103, 106; see also Explanatory Report to Convention 108 (n 37) para 24.

[40] Robert Uerpmann-Wittzack, 'Media and Information Society' in Stephanie Schmahl and Marten Breuer (eds), *The Council of Europe: Its Law and Policies* (Oxford University Press 2017) 712.

With the expansion of data flow routes over the past few decades, the accession clause is now being revitalized to permit other countries to join the treaty system. Apart from the eight accessions thus far, enhancing the Convention system's global role has also visibly animated the conception of the Modernized Convention.[41] But no provision of Convention 108+'s text reflects this underlying purpose of the modernization process. Perhaps prompted by the lack of such explicit wording in the text, Greenleaf suggested, during a speech before the plenary meeting of the Convention Committee in 2018, renaming—or referring to—Convention 108+ as 'Global Data Protection Convention 108+' to highlight its global nature.[42] The preambular paragraphs of the Modernized Convention are sheer iterations of Convention 108, but background documents affirm the explicit globalization mission of Convention 108(+). The Explanatory Report of Convention 108(+) highlights the 'unique potential' of the Modernized Convention in becoming a 'universal standard'.[43] This suggests that the modernization of Convention 108 had the explicit objective of universalizing its standards through accession by non-member States.

Accession as a tool of universalizing a regional data privacy treaty has, however, faced some scepticism from scholars. For some commentators, the prospect of universalizing Convention 108 is lower for two reasons.[44] First, it is argued that many non-CoE member States are at a different—or lower—level of data processing compared to their European counterparts, thereby making accession less compelling to them for at least the near future. This viewpoint is, however, at odds with the recent well documented trend around the world where countries of all stripes introducing data privacy laws. Regardless of their level of data processing—which in and of itself would need to be empirically demonstrated, data privacy lawmaking has become a global phenomenon. The question of why such level of global data privacy lawmaking by States in different levels of data processing is occurring is an important but separate line of inquiry. This is, of course, not to mention the dicta that legislation can or should be enacted not just for today but also tomorrow.

Second, some commentators argue that even if non-European countries accede to the Convention, they would not be able to meet the Convention's rigorous requirements, especially those on creation of fully independent national data protection authorities.[45] Implicit in this argument is that countries outside Europe such

---

[41] See Lee Bygrave, 'The "Strasbourg Effect" on Data Protection in Light of the "Brussels" Effect: Logic, Mechanics and Prospects' (2021) 40 Computer Law and Security Review 1, 2.

[42] Graham Greenleaf, 'Modernized Data Protection Convention 108 and the GDPR' (2018) 154 Privacy Laws and Business International Report 22, 23.

[43] See Explanatory Report to the Protocol Amending the Convention for the Protection of Individuals with regard to Automatic Processing of Personal Data (10 October 2018) para 2.

[44] Paul de Hert and Vagelis Papakonstantinou, 'The Council of Europe Data Protection Convention Reform: Analysis of the New Text and Critical Comment on its Global Ambition' (2014) 30 Computer Law and Security Review 633, 641–42.

[45] See Bygrave (n 41) 10.

as those in Africa, the Americas, and Asia fall short in their democratic commit-ments. But this argument does not address the reasons why this key component of data privacy legislation finds recognition in recent laws adopted or proposed in those parts of the world. Less explicit in this anti-globalization position is whether creation of a national data protection authority that is not fully but satisfactorily independent would make the apparent diffusion of CoE data privacy norms less of norm globalization.

Related to this point is the argument that accession would not be realistic to countries that do not share CoE's organizing principles of upholding democracy, rule of law, and human rights.[46] Additionally, the value of accession is also some-times downplayed in terms of the perceived cultural diversity among countries in-cluding in their conceptions of privacy.[47] But this argument overlooks the reality that often States dubbed authoritarian sign up to international commitments, in-cluding those imposing rigorous human rights obligations. Often such measures are taken with a view to achieve particular interests of the State or the government.[48] It might well be said that non-democratic jurisdictions would be tempted to accede to Convention 108(+), for instance, as a stepping stone to obtain adequacy decision of the European Union (EU) with economic objectives in mind. Arguably, it would be sensible for a non-democratic African, Asian, or Latin-American country to ca-pitulate to certain democratic demands that accessions would bring along so as not to lose the attendant economic benefits.

There is, however, no gainsaying that accession by third countries is a slow pro-cess. As the limited number of accessions in the past decade suggest, near uni-versal accession to the Convention 108(+) system is nigh impossible. Citing the difficulties of treaty-based harmonization, Bygrave argues that a feasible way then to globalize Convention 108(+) standards is through soft law mechanisms than accession.[49] But what form that soft law mechanism should take is not, however, entirely clear—does this include adoption of a soft law instrument as opposed to a binding treaty? What follows discusses one such 'softer' mechanism in universal-izing the Convention 108(+) system: jurisprudential cross-influence. As shall be shown, this not only is feasible but has also begun to materialize—to a degree— in practice with data privacy standards embodied in Convention 108 gradually influencing international data privacy jurisprudence. But this is not also without limitations as treaty body case law too also develops no less slowly than binding treaties.

---

[46] ibid.
[47] ibid.
[48] See, eg, Oona Hathaway, 'Why Do Countries Commit to Human Rights Treaties?' (2007) 51 The Journal of Conflict Resolution 588; Eric Posner, *The Twilight of Human Rights Law* (Oxford University Press 2014) 59–68.
[49] Bygrave (n 41) 10.

4. Avenues of Norm Universalization

Transformation of Convention 108 into a universal instrument of international data privacy regulation can take various forms. This section discusses three possible ways in which universalization may occur. First, it considers whether—and to what extent—accession by third countries may contribute towards the development of international law. This potential 'freestanding' role might help fill the missing data privacy piece in international law. Second, it explores the 'contributory' role of the Convention 108(+) system by which it may lead to the accretion of general international law. Third, it explores the 'catalytic' role by which international data privacy law jurisprudence may indirectly be catalyzed by CoE data privacy standards. The submission is that while the catalytic role is increasingly growing, neither of the three avenues of norm universalization would lead to the development of international law in a meaningful way so as to allow it to effectively and timely respond to the 'privacy problem' in the digital age.

4.1. Accession

Accession is a mechanism by which States that are not members of the CoE may join the treaty system. The Accession clause in Article 23(1) of Convention 108 provides as follows:

> After the entry into force of this Convention, the Committee of Ministers of the Council of Europe may invite any State not a member of the Council of Europe to accede to this Convention by a decision taken by the majority provided for in Article 20.d of the Statute of the Council of Europe and by the unanimous vote of the representatives of the Contracting States entitled to sit on the committee.

As this clause clearly stipulates, accession by a third country would follow a rigorous bureaucratic and political process. Not only should the majority of CoE member States approve the invitation for accession but also that all State parties to the Convention should accept the proposed invitation by the CoM. The modernization of the Convention has further strengthened the clause in at least two respects. First, the Convention is now open to accession by international organizations as well as States.[50] Second, the Convention Committee is now given an explicit advisory role by which it would offer opinion on the candidacy of a State and an international organization for accession.[51]

---

[50] See Convention 108+ (n 7) art 27(1).
[51] ibid, art 23(3).

For decades, the accession clause of Convention 108 had remained dormant. It began after the International Conference of Data Protection and Privacy Commissioners urged the CoE in its widely known Montreux Declaration to activate the Convention's accession provision.[52] This later prompted the Secretary General of the CoE to take up the task of promoting accession by non-CoE member States.[53] But the important step was taken by the Convention Committee in 2008 when it formally discussed the issue of accession by non-member States.[54] Per the Committee's Recommendation to activate the accession clause, the CoM decided in July 2008 to consider any request for accession by non-member States.[55] With the approval of Uruguay's accession in August 2013, the CoM activated the accession clause. In the decade since, only seven States that are not members of the CoE have acceded to the treaty. Often, this is attributed to the lack of focused initiatives by the Convention Committee, including regarding the Modernized Convention. Its Program of Work for the 2022–2025, for instance, offers little in in terms of further globalizing Convention 108(+), except for promoting its signature and ratification.[56] Promoting accession by UN member States would probably have resulted in a relatively steady progress in the rate of accession.

Imperatives of cooperation between the UN and CoE have long been recognized by officials of both organizations. In a speech delivered at the Constitutive Assembly of the CoE in May 1966, former UN Secretary General U Thant—known for his forward looking perspective on human rights and technology, as highlighted in chapter 3—spoke of the 'expanding regional activity' that required coordination with the UN. Importantly, he highlighted that coordination is needed not just to avoid duplication but also because it had become a dynamic process.[57] Robertson, a former official of the CoE, similarly called for 'fusion of efforts' between the UN and the CoE particularly in areas of common interest like human rights.[58] Indeed, the CoE has participated in the work and sessions of the UN General Assembly (UNGA) since 1989.[59] It takes part in the work of UNGA bodies such as the Sixth Committee through the Committee of Legal Advisors on Public International

---

[52] *Montreux Declaration: The Protection of Personal Data and Privacy in A Globalized World—A Universal Right Respecting Diversities* (International Conference of Privacy and Data Protection Commissioners, Montreux, Switzerland, 2005).

[53] See Greenleaf (n 19) 82.

[54] Consultative Committee of the Convention for the Protection of Individuals with regard to Automatic Processing of Personal Data (ETS No 108) (T-PD)—Abridged Report of the 24th Plenary Meeting (Strasbourg, 13–14 March 2008) [CM(2008)81]) (15 May 2008).

[55] Council of Europe, Committee of Ministers, CM/Del/Dec(2008)1031 (4 July 2008).

[56] Consultative Committee of the Convention for the Protection of Individuals with regard to Automatic Processing of Personal Data, Work Programme: 2022–2025 (30 June 2021).

[57] Cited in Arthur Robertson, 'Relations Between the Council of Europe and the United Nations' (1970) 18 European Yearbook 80, 111–12, 115.

[58] ibid, 111.

[59] See *Observer Status for the Council of Europe in the General Assembly*, GA Res 44/6, UN Doc A/RES/44/6 (17 October 1989).

Law (CAHDI).[60] CAHDI is a committee of experts drawn from CoE member States that advances the interests of the CoE before bodies like International Law Commission (ILC) and the Sixth Committee of the UNGA.[61]

CoE's effort in promoting accession to its global conventions through the UN system may occur at different levels. One such mechanism is through the high-level dialogue between the CoE and the UN. The UNGA and PACE ritually adopt parallel Resolutions on 'Cooperation Between the UN and the CoE' on the ongoing collaborations between the two international organizations. In a recent Resolution for instance, the UNGA acknowledges the contribution of the CoE in the development of international law.[62] In particular, it welcomes the contribution of the CoE to the work of the UNGA's Sixth Committee, which deals with legal matters, and the ILC.[63] Short of calling upon member States to accede, it further 'notes' the continued development of Convention 108 and the fact that it is open for accession by all States.[64]

Highlighting CoE' robust standard setting experience, the latest corresponding Resolution of PACE calls upon the UN to further promote CoE legal instruments open to non-member States.[65] While no mention is made of Convention 108, it is obvious that the call concerns the data protection and the cybercrime conventions. It is interesting to note that the draft Resolutions are first prepared by the CoE's Committee of Ministers which are then tabled before the UNGA for adoption.[66] It is unclear to what extent, or whether, draft Resolutions of the CoM are debated and watered down before adoption by the UNGA, but this appears to give an opportunity for the CoE to push its agenda, including universalizing its Conventions, through the UN system.

Resolutions of the UNGA routinely call upon the UN Secretary General to continue working in close co-operation with its CoE counterparts. The latest Resolution, for instance, invites the UN Secretary General and the Secretary General of the CoE to 'combine their efforts' in seeking answers to global challenges.[67] Little is known to what extent such collaboration has taken place, not least in the field of data privacy. But reports of the Secretary General prepared

---

[60] See details about the Committee at <https://www.coe.int/en/web/cahdi>. See also Stephanie Schmahl, 'The Council of Europe in the System of International Organizations' in Stephanie Schmahl and Marten Breuer (eds), *The Council of Europe: Its Law and Policies* (Oxford University Press 2017) 888.

[61] See details about the Committee at <https://www.coe.int/en/web/cahdi>.

[62] *Cooperation Between the United Nations and the Council of Europe*, GA Res 75/264, UN Doc A/RES/75/264 (6 March 2021) Preamble, para 4.

[63] ibid, para 32.

[64] ibid, para 26.

[65] Strengthening Cooperation with the United Nations in Implementing the 2030 Agenda for Sustainable Development, PACE Res 2271 [2019] (9 April 2019) para 14 cum paras 8–10.

[66] See Cooperation Between the United Nations and Council of Europe, DER/Inf (2021) 1 (CoE Directorate of External Relations, 8 March 2021) para I.

[67] See GA Res 75/264 (n 62) para 37.

as a follow up to UNGA Resolutions offer no details on the matter.[68] A memo of CoE's External Relations Directorate notes that the UN is involved in promoting accession to CoE conventions where it mentions specifically the Cybercrime Convention.[69] But it does not mention Convention 108. Per Robertson's account, even the development of a number of CoE treaties were undertaken in close co-operation with UN agencies such as the World Health Organization (WHO) and International Labour Organization (ILO).[70]

Albeit intermittently, the CoE also engages with UN bodies directly involved in the field of privacy and data protection. The newly appointed Special Rapporteur on the Right to Privacy (SRP), for instance, was invited to the Plenary Meeting of the Consultative Committee in November 2021.[71] At this meeting, both parties expressed interest to collaborate further in the field of data protection. Accession to Convention 108+ has also been recommended by the inaugural UN SRP in his 2018 report to the UNGA as 'an interim minimum response to agreeing to detailed privacy rules harmonized at the global level'.[72] Beside the fact that the mandate's suggestion related specifically to the Modernized Convention—and that the call is to 'ratify', an act not necessarily equivalent to accession, the Special Rapporteur appeared to consider accession as a temporary measure not as an alternate route to international (data) privacy treaty. What is more, the call focuses on the need to pay 'particular attention to implementing immediately those provisions requiring safeguards for personal data collected for surveillance and other national security purposes'. In a subsequent report to the Human Rights Council (HR Council), the mandate's recommendation shifted to 'incorporation by member States into their national legal systems of the standards and safeguards set out in Convention 108+, Article 11' which concerns processing of personal data for national security and defence purposes.[73] This sends mixed signals on whether UN bodies support accession as an alternative path to establishing international data privacy standards.

Beyond accession by UN member States individually, two possibilities of universalizing the Convention—including through accession—exist. One is accession by the UN—as an international organization—to Convention 108+. An innovation of Convention 108+ is, as noted above, that international organizations are permitted to accede to the treaty.[74] Per the Convention's Explanatory Report, this applies only to international organizations governed by public international law.[75]

---

[68] See, eg, Cooperation Between the United Nations and Regional and other Organizations, Report of the Secretary-General, UN Doc A/75/345 (11 September 2020) paras 50–52.

[69] See DER/Inf (2021) (n 66).

[70] Robertson (n 1) 203.

[71] An Abridged Report of Consultative Committee's 42nd Meeting (19 November 2021) 2, 7, 18, 21.

[72] Report of the Special Rapporteur on the Right to Privacy, Joseph Cannataci, UN Doc A/73/438 (17 October 2018) para 117(e).

[73] See Report of the Special Rapporteur on the Right to Privacy, Joseph Cannataci, UN Doc A/HRC/40/63 (16 October 2019) para 46.

[74] See Convention 108+ (n 7) art 27.

[75] Explanatory Report to Convention 108+ (n 43) para 173.

The threshold question of whether accession by the UN should be explored as a way of accelerating the universalization of Convention 108(+) may sound an odd proposition but there does not seem to exist any reason why this is not legally possible. The UN is an international intergovernmental organization subject to and governed by international law.[76] This gives it the right or power to enter into treaties, a point affirmed by the International Court of Justice (ICJ) in *Certain Expenses of the United Nations*.[77] International organizations are difficult to define, but Klabbers identifies four key attributes that make up an international organization: (a) a body with distinct will, (b) governed by international law, (c) created between States, and (d) on the basis of a treaty.[78] Doubtless, the UN meets these attributes. Its 'distinct will' is explicitly enshrined in the Charter, which is the treaty establishing the organization. And it obviously is governed by international law.

What would, however, prove difficult to realize accession by the UN is which organ of the organization would sign and ratify the treaty—the UNGA where all member States are represented, the Secretary General or the HR Council? The lack of any such precedent by which the UN unliterally accedes to a treaty less practicable. But the longstanding initiative to have the EU accede to the Convention system makes the idea of UN accession compelling. What is more, as alluded to in chapter 3, the UN and its several related and specialized agencies have taken steps that essentially embraced European data protection standards. Add to that the pioneering efforts in the field of data privacy at the UN in the lead up to, during and post the Tehran Conference.

Equally important to note is that the ability of the UN to enter into treaties as a subject of international law would be entirely different to the UN acceding to a regional treaty. Past ICJ decisions appear to be based on the premise that the type of treaty that the UN—or its specialized and related agencies—would be able to enter into are those relating to its own organizational operations. Stated differently, the UN would not be able to join treaties with States or other international organizations that would in any way require UN member States to assume obligations. If the UN were to accede to Convention 108(+), it would only be for its member States that are not already party to the Convention to enact a corresponding national law and install a data protection authority. But that does not seem to have a firm legal basis nor would it make logical sense. What the UN acceding to the Convention 108(+) would mean is that the organization and probably its agencies would align

---

[76] See, eg, Rosalyn Higgins and others, *Oppenheim's International Law: United Nations* (Oxford University Press 2017) 414.

[77] *Certain Expenses of the United Nations*, Advisory Opinion, ICJ Reports 1962 (20 July 1962) 168. This has also been affirmed by the ICJ in its Advisory Opinion on the Interpretation of the Agreement between the WHO and Egypt where it held that international organizations are subjects of and bound by obligations under general international law. See *Interpretation of the Agreement of 25 March 1951 between The WHO and Egypt*, ICJ Reports 1980 (20 December 1980) 73, para 37.

[78] Jan Klabbers, *An Introduction to International Institutional Law* (Cambridge University Press 2002) 7–13.

their data processing operations with standards of the Convention. In that sense, no obligation would directly fall on its member States merely because the UN acceded to the Convention.

A second avenue of making the Convention 108(+) system a universal instrument is through the ILC. To a certain extent, the issue of norm globalization relates to the notion of 'progressive development of international law'. The UN Charter empowers the UNGA to initiate studies and recommendations for the purpose of progressive development of international law and its codification.[79] This power of the UNGA is now exercised through the ILC. The Statute of the ILC defines progressive development of international law mainly as preparation of new conventions on subjects not covered by international law.[80] In that sense, it might be taken to be an alternative to the idea of norm globalization. But the ILC Statute appears to envisage a scenario where the notion of progressive development of international law may involve globalization of regional standards. Article 17(1) provides:

> The Commission shall also consider proposals and draft multilateral conventions submitted by Members of the United Nations, the principal organs of the United Nations other than the General Assembly, specialized agencies, or <u>official bodies established by intergovernmental agreement</u> to encourage the progressive development of international law and its codification, and transmitted to it for that purpose by the Secretary-General. [Emphasis Added]

This provision allows the ILC to consider proposals from intergovernmental international organizations such as the CoE. This is in addition to the possibility by which the Commission may consult with any international organization to better perform its functions.[81] Would this allow the CoE to formally table to the ILC, through the Secretary General, the agenda of accession to Convention 108(+) as part of progressive development of international data privacy law? There appears to exist no precedent by which regional intergovernmental organizations deploy this provision. But it appears to be one avenue by which the CoE could further push its globalization agenda at the UN. As highlighted in chapter 3, data privacy has been in the Commission's long-term program of work since 2006 with no progress since. With a considerable number of accessions to Convention 108 by non-CoE member States, it would be sound for the CoE to advance its globalizing mission through the ILC. This may probably be done by CAHDI. The Committee, as alluded to above, takes part in the work of the ILC as well as the UNGA's Sixth Committee.

---

[79] See *Charter of the United Nations* (1945) art 13.
[80] *Statute of the International Law Commission* (21 November 1947) art 15.
[81] ibid, art 26.

Greenleaf recommends different ways in which the UN should—as he calls it 'adopt'— Convention 108, including by promoting accession by its member States, revising its Data Privacy Guidelines and by making accession to Convention 108 conditional on ratifying the First Optional Protocol to the ICCPR which mandates an individual communications procedure.[82] Greenleaf's proposal does not consider the possibility of accession by the UN itself. His two proposals are generally feasible, and indeed, the UN has been promoting accession to Convention 108. But the third proposal would bring along several challenges. One such challenge would be how the UN— and which UN body—would be able to 'adopt' the Convention, and importantly make ratification of the Optional Protocol conditional upon accession to Convention 108. That would normally require amending the Protocol which inevitably is as onerous as initiating a new treaty process. For any amendment to succeed, a proposal must be accepted by at least a third of the State parties to the Protocol for the Secretary General to convene a Conference of State parties.[83] The proposed amendment should then be approved by a majority of the State parties present and voting at the Conference before final approval by the UNGA. Even then at least two third of the State parties to the Protocol would have to approve the amendment. This makes Greenleaf's third proposal impracticable.

A related proposition by Greenleaf (and colleagues) is the call for a mechanism by which the HR Committee may receive individual communications under the First Additional Protocol against States that are party to Convention 108.[84] In formal terms, this proposal would not be possible unless the First Optional Protocol to the ICCPR is amended, which—as alluded to above—is no easy task. The Committee's competence vis-à-vis individual communications relates only to alleged violations of rights guaranteed in the ICCPR.[85] Thus, the proposal may easily be rejected by the relevant State party. But as shall be considered further in this chapter, the HR Committee's privacy case law is increasingly being shaped by the jurisprudence of the ECtHR which—in turn—often refers to Convention 108 in (data) privacy cases. In light of this emerging normative cross-influence, reference to Convention 108 by the HR Committee when interpreting the right to privacy provision of the ICCPR might not face resistance by many State parties. Indeed, it would be odd for a State party to Convention 108 to reject interpretation of Article 17 of the ICCPR in light of Convention 108 by the Committee. If such objections were possible, it would raise questions on the value of accession as a means of norm globalization.

---

[82]   Graham Greenleaf, 'The UN Special Rapporteur: Advancing A Global Privacy Treaty?' (2015) 136 Privacy Laws and International Business Report 3–4.

[83]   See *Optional Protocol to the International Covenant on Civil and Political Rights*, GA Res 2006A (XXI), opened for signature 19 December 1966, 999 UNTS 171 (entered into force 23 March 1976) art 11.

[84]   International Data Privacy Standards: A Global Approach, Australian Privacy Foundation Policy Statement (17 September 2013) para 6.4.

[85]   See First Optional Protocol (n 83) art 1.

4.2. Accretion of General International Law

Distinction is often made in the international law literature between 'general' and 'particular' international law.[86] The former binds all States of the international community, and concerns primarily CIL and GPsL. The latter creates binding legal obligations between particular States, and typically include bilateral treaties. Oftentimes, CoE conventions are referred to as 'international agreements'. As agreements between sovereign CoE member States, such treaties are, indeed, international agreements. But the regional nature of the organization makes them less international than those treaties negotiated under the auspices of the UN and its agencies. Multilateral agreements concluded within the aegis of the UN are by and large 'universal' in scope as they emerge from the prime intergovernmental international organization with universal membership. Of course, principles of international law may have less than universal acceptance but still form part of international law.[87] For instance, the ICCPR is yet to achieve universal ratification but, on account of its universal scope, it forms part of international law.

International law itself, historically, has an undisputed European origin, which later transformed from what is sometimes referred to as 'European international law' to international law proper through centuries of evolution.[88] The inquiry in this chapter considers the potential universalization of the CoE Convention into a truly international data privacy treaty. To better capture and frame the nature of jurisprudence emanating from regional intergovernmental organizations like the CoE, the literature often uses the term 'transnational law' in contradistinction with 'international law'. Indeed, the term 'transnational law' was coined by Jessup in the 1950s as he felt international law is unsuited to refer to the area of law that governs all forms of transnational relations. For Jessup, international law signified an area of law that governs relations only between States, and hence, excludes other transnational actors such corporations and even individuals entangled in transnational situations.[89] That would mean that transnational law includes any law which regulate actions or events transcending national borders. In that sense, Jessup's notion of transnational law is not meant to capture regional treaties like Convention 108, but to find an appropriate lexicon for what is generally regarded international law,

---

[86] See, eg, Grigory Tunkin, 'Is General International Law Customary Law Only?' (1993) 4 European Journal of International Law 534.

[87] See, eg, James Crawford, *Brownlie's Principles of Public International Law* (Oxford University Press 9th edn, 2019) 25–26.

[88] See Arnulf Lorca, 'Universal International Law: Nineteenth Century Histories of Imposition and Appropriation' (2010) 51 Harvard International Law Journal 475; see also generally Alexander Orakhelashvili, 'The Idea of European International Law' (2006) 17 European Journal of International Law 315 (arguing that the idea of European international law cannot stand on its own due to the impossibility of legal exclusivity in the international legal system).

[89] Philip Jessup, *Transnational Law* (Yale University Press 1956) 1–3.

be it universal or regional.[90] Koh, on the other hand, describes 'transnational law' as a law that is neither purely domestic nor international, but a hybrid of the two.[91]

In this chapter, the question at hand is whether—and how—Convention 108, a transnational instrument, may achieve the status of a 'universal' international data privacy treaty.[92] The second possible avenue, next to accession, through which this may materialize is when/if the Convention develops into general international law. What follows discusses the ways in which the Convention 108(+) system may, first, crystalize into a rule of CIL and second, attain the status of GPsL. A caveat is, however, in order. Much of the international law discourse as well as doctrine on sources of international law is premised on the strictly statist nature of the law. As a result, it may not entirely capture the nature of data privacy regulation which involves non-State actors. What follows below builds on the discussion on sources of international privacy law in chapters 2, 3, and 5.

4.2.1. Crystallization into Customary Norms

In considering the ways in which Convention 108 may lead to the formation of international custom, the ILC's Draft Conclusions on the Identification of Customary International Law offers a useful benchmark.[93] The Draft Conclusions codify principles that guide the process of determining the existence and content of CIL. In that sense, it stipulates how and when the two constituent elements of custom, namely 'general practice' and acceptance as law (*opinio juris*) may be ascertained. But this section considers the major elements of the Draft Conclusions that are pertinent to the question at hand, ie, can a regional treaty contribute to the formation of CIL? Related to this also is the worldwide proposals for and adoption of domestic data privacy legislation that are largely aligned with Convention 108.

Treaties, including multilateral treaties, may provide the material evidence in ascertaining the existence of rules of CIL. Crawford notes that an extensive pattern of treaties may also be a material source of custom along with the practice of international organizations.[94] That is especially the case when such treaties embody or codify rules that are widely recognized.[95] The ILC's Draft Conclusions affirm that a rule set forth in a treaty may reflect a rule of CIL where it has given rise to a general practice that is accepted as law (*opinio juris*).[96] If that rule is further

---

[90] cf Humphrey's contention that what has traditionally been known as international law should now be called 'world law'. See John Humphrey, 'The Implementation of International Human Rights Law' (1978) 24 New York Law School Law Review 31, 33.

[91] Harold Koh, 'Why Transnational Law Matters' (2005) 24 Penn State International Law Review 745, 745–46; see also generally Harold Koh, 'Rosco Pound Lecture: Transnational Legal Process' (1996) 75 Nebraska Law Review 181.

[92] cf Lassa Oppenheim, *International Law: A Treatise*, Vol I: Peace (Longman Green 1905) 23.

[93] Draft Conclusions on Identification of Customary International Law, Adopted by the International Law Commission at its Seventieth Session (2018).

[94] See Crawford (n 87) 21–22.

[95] See, eg, Hugh Thirlway, *The Sources of International Law* (Oxford University Press 2nd edn, 2019) 67; Crawford (n 87) 19.

[96] Draft Conclusions (n 93) Conclusion 11 (c).

embodied in a number of treaties, it may be taken to reflect CIL. Even in the case of unratified treaties, they may in certain circumstances be regarded as evidence of widely accepted rules.[97] Convention 108 as well EU's Data Protection Directive have largely inspired data protection legislation outside Europe in the past decade or so. But these regional instruments were also essentially distillations of national data protection standards. As highlighted in earlier sections, precursors of data privacy standards in Convention 108 were embodied in Resolutions (73) 22 and (74) 29 which, in turn, drew upon several national data privacy rules. Arguably, Convention 108 codified rules that were already widely recognized in national law, at least in Europe. But more importantly, a closer look at other recently adopted data privacy conventions reveal a stark similarity of substance. A good case in point being the Malabo Convention.

Under the Draft Conclusions, the first relevant point relates to the requirement of practice. Conclusion 4 provides that in certain cases the practice of international organizations may contribute to the expression or formation of rules of CIL. But what type of practice of international organizations is envisioned here is far from clear. Doubtless, international organizations may provide the platform for the 'collective expression' of state practice.[98] Forms of practice enumerated in the Draft Conclusions appear to be framed with practice of States as opposed to international organizations in mind. Rightly so as States are the primary subjects of international law and hence whose practice matters centrally in the formation or expression of CIL.[99] Per the Commentary of the Draft Conclusions, what matters is only practice that is 'attributed to international organizations themselves, not practice of States acting within or in relation to them'.[100] Moreover, what counts is a practice that falls within the mandate of the international organizations and addressed specifically to them.[101] To that extent, the contributions of CoE practices in relation to Convention 108 towards the formation or expression of custom would be limited.

Among forms of practice indicated in the Draft Conclusions include conduct in connection with Resolutions adopted by an international organization, legislative acts and conduct in connection with treaties.[102] The practice of the CoE vis-à-vis Convention 108 would involve activities such as initiation of an accession process by a State, consideration by contracting parties and the CoM as well as the Convention Committee. Thirlway argues that 'conduct in connection with treaties' should be read broadly so as to include, for example, negotiation, adoption, ratification, and implementation of a treaty.[103] Accession to the Convention cannot be

---

[97] See Crawford (n 87) 29, 44.

[98] ibid, 181.

[99] Commentary to Conclusion 4 in Commentaries of the Draft Conclusions (2018) para 2.

[100] ibid, para 4.

[101] ibid, para 5.

[102] Draft Conclusions (n 93) Conclusion 6.

[103] Thirlway (n 95) 3.

taken to have been finalized unless signatory States ratify and implement it, inter alia, through domestic legislation. In that sense, such a series of legislative steps might be seen as contributing to the expression or formation of CIL.

The second relevant point regarding state practice is that the practice must be 'general', ie it should be 'sufficiently widespread, representative and consistent' regardless of duration of the relevant practice.[104] The ILC commentary on this point provides that the practice should have attained 'virtually uniform usage' among 'necessary number and distribution of States'.[105] Again, this phraseology is premised on state practice, and it is unclear how it would translate to the practice of international organizations. Would the fact that data privacy has been the agenda of several international organizations, including the CoE, the UN, OECD, and the AU would suffice to argue that the practice is sufficiently widespread, consistent, and representative? This further circumscribes the potential of Convention 108 as a means for the development of general international law.

Opinio juris is the second constituent element of custom. It signifies that the relevant practice must be undertaken by a State or group of States with a sense of legal right or obligation, going beyond mere usage or habit.[106] Evidence of acceptance may be found in official publications, decisions of national courts, or conduct in connection with resolutions of international organizations.[107] The ILC Commentary on Draft Conclusion 10 provides that forms of evidence of acceptance applicable to States would apply, *mutantis mutandis*, to international organizations.[108] But none of these evidences of acceptance do not lend themselves well to international organizations. This adds up to the uncertainty on the possibility of Convention 108 contributing to the formation of CIL.

In the ultimate analysis, any claim that Convention 108 has attained, or will attain, the status of CIL is riddled with uncertainties. At a substantive level, the inherent uncertainty as to the nature and scope of custom as a source of international law makes it less appealing to the overall globalization drive. Uncertainty would further mean that CIL cannot be relied upon to attend to the exigencies of the 'privacy problem' in the digital age. At a more practical level, the sheer attainment by the Convention 108(+) system of a CIL status might not bring about much value in terms of fostering global data privacy protection. A central virtue of a rule becoming CIL is that it would bind all States. In the absence of a mechanism by which the implementation of binding norms could be overseen by an independent body, bindingness would bring about little outcome. This reinforces the central argument of the book—laid out in full in chapters 7 and 8—that soft legalization

---

[104] Draft Conclusions (n 93) Conclusion 8.
[105] See Commentary to Conclusion 8 in Commentaries of the Draft Conclusions (2018) para 3.
[106] Draft Conclusions (n 93) Conclusion 9.
[107] ibid, Conclusion 10.
[108] Commentary to Conclusion 10 in Commentaries of the Draft Conclusions (2018) para 7.

reinforced by a dialogical approach is the best way forward in enhancing (data) privacy globally.

4.2.2. General Principles of Law

Next to treaty and custom, 'general principles of law recognized by civilized nations' is the third primary source of international law indicated in the Statute of the ICJ.[109] The nexus between transnational treaties and this source of international law is not straightforward. Can the prospect of Convention 108 as an instrument of international data privacy regulation be looked at from the perspective of GPsL? Much of the international law scholarship downplays the potential of general principles as a source of international law.[110] This is primarily because of the fact that treaties and CIL now cover the bulk of international relations among States. But this does not necessarily undercut the potential of this source of international law in the context of global data privacy law. This is primarily for two reasons. Firstly, not only that a data privacy treaty with universal scope does not currently exist but also that whether data privacy has, as shown in the preceding section, attained the status of CIL is far from certain. But more crucially, data privacy law as a system of rules cannot be explained in the traditional statist conception of international law. In that sense, it is worthwhile to consider general principles as sources of international law. Secondly, the history of how data privacy law evolved over the past few decades—namely its evolution from a set of national laws to a growing body of transnational instruments, lends weight to the argument that general principles can, or should, be viable sources of international privacy law.

That principles of domestic law sources were originally considered as the only sources for GPsL should not be a reason to dismiss the potential of principles drawn from non-domestic law sources. The latter particularly concerns principles that are recognized, for example, in regional or transnational law. Scholarship on sources of international law has considered the propriety of embracing principles drawn from international law.[111] Transnational treaties present an interesting case in this context. More to the point is the question of whether data privacy principles of Convention 108 may lead to the development of GPsL. Convention 108—as alluded to above— is a result of a process of cross-fertilization of national laws. It essentially 'distills' data protection principles entrenched in domestic law.[112] This holds true also to the Modernized Convention, which even draws upon modern regional instruments like the GDPR. To that extent, it may be taken to reflect domestic European legislation and beyond. That means regardless of its regional or transnational nature, Convention 108—and its recent iteration—should not, on its

---

[109] See *Statute of the International Court of Justice* (18 April 1946) art 38(1).
[110] See, eg, Thirlway (n 95) 112.
[111] See, eg, Crawford (n 87) 34.
[112] See Uerpmann-Wittzack (n 40) 711.

own, matter when it comes to their role in the development of GPsL. But this is one area where any attempt at considering Convention 108 as a system and its principles in particular would face a conceptual uncertainty.

A related uncertainty about GPsL is its temporal dimension. This concerns whether GPsL concern only those that existed when the Statute of ICJ was drafted or includes principles that emerged after or those that will emerge in the future.[113] In rejecting the propriety of relying on emergent norms as general principles, some scholars allude to the need for recognizing normative properties of general principles as permanent and stable set of principles that are selected for their virtue of 'evident and perpetual rightness'.[114] This well-meaning argument should, however, be considered in context, particularly when it comes to data privacy. While a sense of permanence is implicit in the generality of the principles, the nature and speed of transformation occurring in the twenty-first century call for a more progressive approach. The Internet and other digital technologies are evolving at a pace that considerably undermines the pertinence of time-tested principles. Much of the data privacy legal framework around the world, especially data protection principles which remain to be the backbone of the law, is sufficiently stable. However, the 'privacy problem' in the digital age, as considered in chapter 1, is borne out of the increasing sophistication of technologies as well as the rise of new centers of power in data processing. This would inevitably require innovating rules that would effectively respond to the problem. Such a valid point notwithstanding, it suggests that seeking to view Convention 108 from the angle of GPsL remains bereft of certitude.

Overall, it would be a stretch to claim that Convention 108 and its principles are now GPsL and hence binding on all States. Not only is this source of international law generally running into disuse but also that it is rife with uncertainties. But its normative value in the context of data privacy is also little. With the remarkable data privacy lawmaking worldwide, there appears to exist no added value even if Convention 108 were to become a rule of general international law. As in the case of CIL, the attainment of the status of GPsL will not have any meaningful outcome.

4.3. Jurisprudential Cross-influence

Accession and development into a rule of general international law are more direct ways in which Convention 108 may be transformed into a universal standard. This section considers the third, albeit indirect, avenue in which the Convention 108(+) system may develop into an instrument of near universal scope: jurisprudential cross-influence. This relates to the scenario where international data

---

[113] Thirlway (n 95) 110.
[114] See, eg, ibid, 111.

privacy jurisprudence can be influenced by data privacy rights, principles and governance norms of the Convention. The cross-influence may occur at two levels. First, relevant UN treaty bodies, especially the HR Committee, may rely on the data privacy case law of the ECtHR, which—in turn—often refers to Convention 108. What makes the influence indirect is that the HR Committee never referred to Convention 108 in its privacy case law. Beyond case law, effects of the Convention may be felt in the other jurisprudential outputs of treaty bodies such as general comments and concluding observations. Second, data privacy standards embodied in the Convention 108(+) system may shape broader privacy discourses at the UN. Such discourses may include the ongoing post-Snowden UN discussions on the 'right to privacy in the digital age', the work of the SRP, or the HR Council's Universal Periodic (UPR) mechanism. What follows discusses these scenarios of jurisprudential cross-influence.

4.3.1. Case Law and Beyond

Treaty body jurisprudence is an area where data privacy standards codified in CoE instruments may find application. In particular, this is more likely to occur— has already begun to occur, as shall be shown below, to an extent—in the jurisprudence of the HR Committee. The Committee is tasked to adjudge individual communications alleging violation of the right of privacy by a State party under the First Optional Protocol to the ICCPR. Through the periodic reporting mechanism, the Committee also regularly issues concluding observations which are the other useful jurisprudential outputs of UN treaty bodies. That the structure of concluding observations is dictated primarily by periodic reports of State parties means they do not lend themselves well to any influence by Convention 108. Add to this the truncated nature of concluding observations, and the fact that the review concerns many Covenant rights. A survey of recent concluding observations of the HR Committee confirms this hypothesis. This goes also to concluding observations relating to States that are parties to both the Covenant and Convention 108.[115]

The Committee also issues general comments on provisions of the Covenant, including on the Article 17 of the ICCPR which guarantees the right to privacy. The General Comment (GC) on the right to privacy, ie, GC 16, was issued in 1988, only seven years after Convention 108 was adopted. As highlighted in chapter 2, GC 16 offers little normative guidance on the right to privacy, including on the protection of personal data. Paragraph 10 of the GC, where a set of widely accepted data privacy principles are provided, partly reads as follows:

---

[115] See, eg, Concluding Observations of the HR Committee: Finland, UN Doc CCPR/C/FIN/CO/7 (3 May 2021); Concluding Observations of the HR Committee: Armenia, UN Doc CCPR/C/ARM/CO/ 3 (25 November 2021); Concluding Observations of the HR Committee: Portugal, UN Doc CCPR/C/ PRT/CO/5 (28 April 2020).

Effective measures have to be taken by States to ensure that information concerning a person's private life does not reach the hands of persons who are not authorized by law to receive, process and use it, and is never used for purposes incompatible with the Covenant. In order to have the most effective protection of his private life, every individual should have the right to ascertain in an intelligible form, whether, and if so, what personal data is stored in automatic data files, and for what purposes. Every individual should also be able to ascertain which public authorities or private individuals or bodies control or may control their files. If such files contain incorrect personal data or have been collected or processed contrary to the provisions of the law, every individual should have the right to request rectification or elimination.

Data privacy principles shoehorned in this paragraph include principles of data security, purpose limitation, and data quality. Considering the time when the GC was adopted, its content was probably influenced by Convention 108 or at least national data privacy laws of the time which, in turn, shaped the Convention. The GC was drafted by a Working Group formed among members of the Committee. Background documents suggest that the Working Group had revised the draft based on comments and proposals advanced by the members of the Committee before it was finally adopted on 23 March 1988.[116] While input from other stakeholders did not seem to be considered, the Working Group would have ordinarily reviewed national and international best practices. Indeed, the above noted principles of GC 16 are largely equivalent to those provided in Convention 108.[117] With possible revision of GC 16 in the near future, it is inevitable that the Convention 108(+) system will shape the Committee's normative discussions. But more importantly, as the Committee's case law often serves as the main source of GCs, the growing reference by the Committee to the principles of Convention 108—discussed further below—would also be reflected in a future GC on the right to privacy. The latest GC of the Committee on freedom of assembly for instance, which is significantly influenced by the case law of the ECtHR,[118] is predictive of the inevitable influence of CoE jurisprudence on a future GC on the right to privacy.

Perhaps as part of the overall 'Snowden Effect' effect on UN processes on the right to privacy in the digital age, Convention 108 has started to gradually influence the case law of the Committee in the past few years. But this occurs mostly in a subtle and indirect way. The HR Committee has never explicitly referred to Convention 108 in its jurisprudence, even when it considers individual communications

---

[116] Annual Report of the Human Rights Committee to the General Assembly, GAOR 43rd sess, UN Doc A/43/40 (26 September 1988) para 635.
[117] See Convention 108 (n 5) arts 5–9.
[118] See HR Committee, *General Comment 37: Article 21—The Right of Peaceful Assembly*, 129th sess, UN Doc CCPR/C/GC/37 (17 September 2020) paras 16–17, 24, 26, 45, 51, 54, 57–58, 72, 82, 84, 89.

against States that are party to both Convention 108 and the ICCPR. And understandably so as it is created to oversee compliance by State parties with the ICCPR. But some of its recent case law extensively refers to decisions of the ECtHR which, in turn, refer to and rely upon Convention 108. As shall be further illustrated below, two recent cases particularly rely upon the Court's decision in the case of *S and Marper v United Kingdom* which involved questions surrounding the collection, processing, and storage of fingerprints as well as DNA data in the context of criminal investigation and prosecution.[119] In this case, the Strasbourg Court not only lists Convention 108—and some of its principles—among its customary outline of 'relevant national and international materials'[120] but also applies its principles extensively when tackling legal issues in question. It does so in three main ways. First, it refers to the relevant provision of the Convention to support the point that data revealing racial origin is, indeed, sensitive personal data.[121] Second, it defines fingerprints, DNA profile and cellular samples as constituting personal data within the meaning of Convention 108.[122] Third, in highlighting the 'fundamental importance' of data protection to the enjoyment of the right to privacy, it outlines key data privacy principles provided in Convention 108 which should be guaranteed in domestic legislation.[123] This decision of the Court has substantially influenced the Committee's reasoning in two recent privacy cases revolving around processing of biometric and DNA data.

Reference to the case law of the ECtHR by the HR Committee is not new, be it by the parties or the Committee itself.[124] But it is only recently that cases involving privacy make considerable reference to the case law of the Strasbourg Court. But at times, this also caused some opposition by members of the Committee. In *NK v Netherlands* for instance, a member of the Committee objected to the extensive use of the *S and Marper v United Kingdom* decision of the ECtHR for lack of resemblance.[125] At times, the reliance on ECtHR is such that members of the Committee appear to stress the need not to question a finding of the Court. In *NK v Netherlands,* a dissenting member of the Committee argued that a holding of the ECtHR in another case should not be put to question by the Committee unless a contrary information is provided.[126] In another privacy case, a dissenting member

---

[119] ECtHR, *S and Marper v United Kingdom*, Applications Nos 30562/04 and 30566/04 (4 December 2008).

[120] ibid, para 41.

[121] ibid, paras 66, 76.

[122] ibid, para 68.

[123] ibid, para 103.

[124] See, eg, HR Committee, *Nabil Sayadi and Patricia Vinck v Belgium*, Communication No 1472/2006 (29 December 2008).

[125] See Individual Opinion (Dissenting) of Committee Member Yadh Ben Achour in Annex I of HR Committee, *NK v The Netherlands*, Communication No 2326/2013 (10 January 2018) para 2.

[126] See Individual Opinion (Partly Concurring, Partly Dissenting) of Committee Member Yuval Shany in Annex II of HR Committee, *NK v The Netherlands*, Communication No 2326/2013 (10 January 2018) para 7, citing ECtHR, *W v Netherlands*, Application No 20689/08 (20 January 2009). Note that this decision was invoked by the State party to illustrate the safeguards embedded in the Netherlands

suggested that because the ECtHR has yet decided against States that mandate ID systems involving storage of fingerprints, nor should the Committee.[127]

In *NK v Netherlands*, the Committee considered an individual communication alleging violation of the right to privacy when the State party subjected the author to DNA testing without consent.[128] In finding arbitrary interference with the right to privacy of the author, the Committee drew substantially from the decision of the ECtHR in *S and Marper v United Kingdom*.[129] Paragraph 9.3 states:

> The Committee considers that the collection of DNA material for the purpose of analyzing and storing the collected material in a database that could be used in the future for the purposes of criminal investigation is sufficiently intrusive as to constitute "interference" with the author's privacy under article 17 of the Covenant.

But the Committee goes further in the footnote to the quoted paragraph above and states that it 'concurs' with the of the ECtHR in *S and Marper v United Kingdom* where the Court held that 'in addition to the highly personal nature of cellular samples, the Court notes that they contain much sensitive information about an individual, including information about his or her health. Moreover, samples contain a unique genetic code of great relevance to both the individual and his relatives.'[130]

In referring to this particular statement of the ECtHR, the Committee appears to be drawing support for its finding. One finds similar references to the *S and Marper* decision in other parts of this case. For instance, to reinforce the point that interference which has a legal basis still needs to be in line with the aims and objectives of the Covenant, the Committee refers to *S and Marper* where the Strasbourg Court held that 'the core principles of data protection require the retention of data to be proportionate in relation to the purpose of collection and insist on limited periods of storage'.[131] In highlighting the need for special attention to the privacy of children, it likewise refers to *S and Marper*.[132]

Maharajah Madhewoo v Mauritius is the second case where one can see the influence of the jurisprudence of the ECtHR on the Committee's case law. The case concerned allegation for violation of the right to privacy of the author by the existence

---

DNA database. See HR Committee, *NK v The Netherlands*, Communication No 2326/2013 (10 January 2013) footnote 8.

[127] See Individual Opinion (Dissenting) of Committee Member Gentian Zyberi in Annex II of the HR Committee, *Maharajah Madhewoo v Mauritius*, Communication No 3163/2018 (21 July 2021) paras 4–5.

[128] *NK v Netherlands* (n 126).

[129] *S and Marper v United Kingdom* (n 119).

[130] ibid, paras 72–73.

[131] See *NK v The Netherlands* (n 126) para 9.5 cum *S and Marper v United Kingdom* (n 119) para 107.

[132] ibid, para 9.10 cum *S and Marper v United Kingdom* (n 119) para 124.

of a legally mandated national ID system which involves collection and storage of biometric data.[133] Both the author and the State party refer to *S and Marper* in their respective submissions,[134] but the Committee relies significantly on the holding of the Strasbourg Court in that case. Paragraph 7.6 of the Committee's decision, which directly quotes from *S and Marper*, partly reads:

> Given the nature and scale of the interference arising out of the mandatory processing and recording of fingerprints, the Committee finds that it is essential "to have clear, detailed rules governing the scope and application of measures, as well as minimum safeguards concerning, inter alia, duration, storage, usage, access of third parties, procedures for preserving the integrity and confidentiality of data and procedures for its destruction, thus providing sufficient guarantees against the risk of abuse and arbitrariness".[135]

In directly quoting from *S and Marper*, the Committee simply applied the set of data privacy principles outlined by the ECtHR.

Data privacy at the CoE has closely been tied with the ECHR from the outset. Resolution (74) 29 of the CoM, which introduced the first set of data privacy principles for the public sector, explicitly made reference to the Article 8 of the ECHR.[136] But the question remained, then, of whether this provision of the human rights Convention provided adequate protections against threats of privacy intrusion. One of the findings of the Committee of Experts on Human Rights in its study was that the ECHR provided no direct protection against problematic data processing practices of the privacy sector.[137] Related to this is the proposal of PACE in 1980 either to amend Article 8 of the ECHR or add a new article to the Convention on data privacy.[138] But over the years, the ECtHR has interpreted Article 8 of the ECHR in a manner that extended its scope of protection to various aspects of privacy, including the protection of personal data. Its decision in *Leander v Sweden* is the first to consider processing—or more precisely storage—of 'information relating to private life' under Article 8 of the Convention.[139] But it was in latter cases that the Court started to make explicit references to Convention 108 in its examination of

---

[133] HR Committee, *Maharajah Madhewoo v Mauritius,* Communication No 3163/2018 (21 July 2021).

[134] ibid, footnotes 2, 4, 7; note also that the author of the individual communication referred to another decision of the ECtHR, ie, *LH v Latvia*, Application No 52019/07 (29 April 2014). See footnote 5. Likewise, the State party referred to another decision of the Court, ie, ECtHR, *Leyla Sahin v Turkey*, Application No 44774/98 (10 November 2005) which was originally mentioned by the Supreme Court of Mauritius. See footnote 8.

[135] Quoted from *S and Marper v United Kingdom* (n 119) para 99.

[136] See Resolution (74) 29 (n 8) Preamble, para 6.

[137] See Explanatory Report of Resolution (73) 22, 2.

[138] See Recommendation 890 on the Protection of Personal Data, Adopted by the Parliamentary Assembly at 27th sitting (1 February 1980) para 3; see also Hondius (n 39) 127.

[139] See ECtHR, *Leander v Sweden*, Application No 9248/81 (26 March 1987).

cases involving the processing of personal data.[140] Scholars often present varying rationales for and ways of reference to Convention 108 by the Strasbourg Court in its privacy case law. At times, it is seen as an attempt by the Court to 'confirm' the wider scope of Article 8 of the Convention.[141] Per this viewpoint, the Court—by reading the right to data protection into the right to privacy—essentially 'implements' Convention 108 under the right to privacy.[142]

Revitalizing the ECHR to address issues of data protection under the rubric of the right to private life existed even before the adoption of Convention 108. In a 1980 Recommendation, PACE—as noted above—had called upon the CoM to amend Article 8 of the ECHR to include protection of personal data or to add a freestanding right to data protection in the Convention.[143] This call followed a growing constitutional recognition of a separate right to data protection in several European countries.[144] The CoM decided to keep the proposal 'at abeyance' until further experience was gained.[145] The possibility of data privacy protection via Article 8 of the Convention was never in doubt from the outset. But influential figures like Hondius had, however, cast doubt on the potential of this avenue in ensuring higher protection of data privacy.[146] But case law of the Strasbourg Court under Article 8 has effectively been applied to data processing, including with frequent references to Convention 108.

In summary, one tangible way in which the Convention 108(+) system may shape international data privacy law is indirectly through the case law of treaty bodies. The HR Committee is increasingly drawing upon the case law of the ECtHR in which the Court often refers to Convention 108. But as an inherently slow process undertaken without any framework on the part of treaty bodies, its role in filling the missing data privacy piece in international law will be insignificant.

4.3.2. Digital Privacy Discourses

Multiple parallel discussions surrounding the right to privacy is the second area where the Convention 108(+) system may exert some jurisprudential influence. In this regard, three processes can be mentioned. One is the ongoing discourse on the 'right to privacy in the digital age'. As discussed in chapter 5, this discourse—launched in the wake of the Snowden debacle—is gradually introducing progressive privacy norms into the international law of privacy. Part of this normative progress relates to the international data privacy framework. The iterative but

---

[140] See, eg, ECtHR, *Z v Finland*, Application No 22009/93 (25 February 1997) paras 95, 97.
[141] Uerpmann-Wittzack (n 40) 730.
[142] See also Greenleaf (n 19) 85.
[143] See Recommendation 890 (n 138) para 3.
[144] ibid, para 2.
[145] See Hondius (n 39) 127.
[146] ibid, 127 (noting that Article 8 'simply does not correspond with the reality of data processing').

evolving Resolutions of the UNGA and the HR Council introduce progressive data privacy principles in international law.

Brought forward through a process of norm cross-fertilization, one sees clear marks of European data privacy law, including Convention 108 in the series of Privacy Resolutions. Adopted at the 48th session of the HR Council, the latest in the series of Resolutions—for instance—embodies as set of key principles of data privacy legislation such as principles of 'lawfulness, fairness and transparency', 'purpose limitation', 'integrity and confidentiality', and 'data quality'.[147] This set of data privacy principles are directed to businesses that are involved in the collection, storage, use, sharing, and processing of personal data. Albeit a soft law, the Resolution essentially reproduces principles which, in data privacy legislation, require compliance by data processors and controllers. There is little doubt that these aspects of the Resolution are influenced directly or indirectly by Convention 108 or its later iterations like the EU Data Protection Directive of 1995, the GDPR, and/or Convention 108+ which are global standard bearers in the field.

As alluded to in chapter 5, also forming a key part of the ongoing UN digital privacy discourse are the series of reports of the UN Office of the High Commissioner for Human Rights (OHCHR) and special procedures of the HR Council. Reports of the OHCHR are prepared typically based on inputs from relevant stakeholders and make references to the jurisprudence of regional bodies. The first report, for instance, makes extensive references to the case law of the ECtHR in articulating privacy principles under international law.[148] Likewise, the second[149] and the third[150] reports of the High Commissioner draw upon the case law of the ECtHR as well as other relevant CoE instruments. More often than not, cases cited in the reports refer to Convention 108.[151] In the third report, in particular, it is provided that Convention 108+ is 'a response to the emergence of new data-processing practices'.[152] But what makes this quite remarkable is that not only are reports of the OHCHR often followed by Resolutions of the Council but also that the Resolutions import principles and norms articulated in the reports. That way, norms drawn from the Convention 108+ system would find articulation in international law, albeit in a soft law.

---

[147] *The Right to Privacy in the Digital Age*, HRC Res 48/4, 48th sess, Agenda Item 3, UN Doc A/HRC/RES/48/4 (13 October 2021) para 8.

[148] The Right to Privacy in the Digital Age, First Report of the High Commissioner for Human Rights, UN Doc A/HRC/27/37 (30 June 2014) paras 20, 22, 28 and the accompanying footnotes.

[149] The Right to Privacy in the Digital Age, Second Report of the High Commissioner for Human Rights, UN Doc A/HRC/39/29 (3 August 2018) paras 7, 17–8, 35, 37, 39–40, and the accompanying footnotes.

[150] The Right to Privacy in the Digital Age, Third Report of the High Commissioner for Human Rights, UN Doc A/HRC/48/31 (13 September 2021) para 27 and the accompanying footnotes.

[151] See, eg, First Report of the High Commissioner (n 148) para 22 citing ECtHR, *Uzun v Germany*, Application No 35623/05 (2 September 2010) para 46.

[152] Third Report of the High Commissioner (n 150) para 42, footnote 79.

Reverberations of norm cross-influence are also present in reports of UN special rapporteurs that deal with the right to privacy. As highlighted earlier, the inaugural SRP has been an avid supporter of accession to the Convention 108(+) system by UN member States. Other special rapporteurs have also indirectly referred to Convention 108. In his report on the private surveillance industry, the former special rapporteur on freedom of expression—for instance—refers to a decision of the ECtHR where Convention 108 is provided as an authoritative source.[153] In that case, the Court held that the mere existence of a secret digital surveillance system in and of itself constitutes interference with the right to privacy.[154] The former special rapporteur on human rights and counter-terrorism did make an incidental reference to Convention 108, but also recommended the adoption of a UN 'declaration' on data privacy that build on 'existing principles of data protection'.[155] A subsequent mandate holder similarly engages with reports of the High Commissioner as well as specific decisions of the ECtHR.[156]

UPR is another HR Council based mechanism by which the human rights performance of all UN member States is peer-reviewed. As already shown in chapter 2, the UPR is not by design suitable for any meaningful jurisprudential output. That essentially flows from the nature of the review process in which human rights performance of States with respect to all human rights is assessed, and as a result, the outcome is often a series of brief recommendations. It goes in such a way that a particular State's performance is evaluated by other States.[157] In many cases, a State may not be reviewed, for instance, regarding its obligation to respect and protect the right to privacy. In the current Third Cycle (2017–2022), for instance, there is no reference to privacy in the report of the Working Group that reviewed Austria.[158] In that respect, there is no room for meaningful jurisprudential cross-influence of the sort that case law would normally allow. The Convention 108(+) system is thus unlikely to exert any influence under the UPR mechanism.

In summary, a more tangible role for the Convention 108(+) system in international law is shaping data privacy jurisprudence at various levels, including via multi-level discursive processes. But not only is this a recent phenomenon but also that it is inherently a slow process. Treaty body jurisprudence is where the influence would be considerable, but structural setbacks such as the part-time role of

---

[153] Report of the Special Rapporteur on the Promotion and Protection of the Right to Freedom of Opinion and Expression, David Kaye, UN Doc A/HRC/41/35 (28 May 2019) para 40.

[154] ECtHR, *Roman Zakharov v Russia*, Application No 47143/06 (4 December 2015) para 171.

[155] Report of the Special Rapporteur on the Promotion and Protection of Human Rights and Fundamental Freedoms while Countering Terrorism, Martin Scheinin, UN Doc A/HRC/13/37 (28 December 2009) paras 47, 73.

[156] See generally Report of the Special Rapporteur on the Promotion and Protection of Human Rights while Countering Terrorism, Ben Emmerson, UN Doc A/69/397 (23 September 2014).

[157] See details about the UPR at <https://www.ohchr.org/en/hrbodies/upr/pages/uprmain.aspx>.

[158] See Report of the Working Group on the Universal Periodic Review: Austria, UN Doc A/HRC/47 12 (9 April 2021) cum Outcome of the Universal Periodic Review: Austria, HRC Decision 47/109, UN Doc A/HRC/DEC/47/109 (28 July 2021).

the HR Committee, for instance, makes the prospect of meaningful jurisprudential cross-influence less likely. This generally undercuts the value of jurisprudential
cross-influence in attending to the privacy problem in the digital age.

5. Prospect of other Regional Standards

After the adoption of Convention 108 in 1981—which was preceded by the OECD
Privacy Guidelines of 1980, several transnational data privacy regimes have been
developed. From the adoption of the EU Data Protection Directive in 1995, the
APEC Privacy Framework in 2004, the Malabo Convention in 2014 and the GDPR
in 2016 to the Ibero-American Standards in 2017, a flurry of regional and sub-
regional data privacy initiatives have emerged. But the prospect of such regional
systems of data protection evolving into a universal standard is not entirely clear.
What follows briefly considers whether and the extent to which these transnational
standards may—like the Convention 108+ system—evolve into or contribute to an
international data privacy framework.

Of regional data protection standards, the GDPR is the most comprehensive,
modern and binding legal instrument. That it inherently has a 'closed' nature applicable only in EU member States however means it cannot evolve into a universal standard. Its contribution would rather be indirect and subtle. The GDPR
is likely to continue its predecessor's role in inspiring domestic lawmaking globally. As the recent survey by the SRP illustrated, regional and national standards in Latin America are significantly being shaped by the GDPR.[159] Indeed, this
cross-fertilization role of the GDPR is already occurring with data privacy legislation around the world, including in several States in the United States. As shown
in chapter 5, the series of Privacy Resolutions adopted by the UNGA and the HR
Council are increasingly embracing rights and principles embodied in the GDPR
among other normative sources. With such iterative processes of cross-influence,
decisions of national and regional courts as well as human rights treaty bodies may
gradually be influenced. Still, there is little room for such processes to lead to the
universalization of GDPR standards.

One slim chance for GDPR universalization is via the Convention 108(+)
system. To some extent, Convention 108+ embraces some of the most progressive data privacy standards embodied in the GDPR. As Greenleaf rightly
notes, 108+ includes the most important GDPR innovations, albeit in a less pre-
scriptive form.[160] In that sense, the GDPR may find a global role through the

---

[159] See generally Privacy and Personal Data Protection in Ibero-America: A Step Towards
Globalization? Report of the Special Rapporteur on the Right to Privacy, Ana Brian Nougrères, UN Doc
A/HRC/49/55 (13 January 2022).
[160] See Greenleaf (n 42) 23.

Modernized Convention. But all the caveats with accession, and even jurispruden-tial cross-influence, would still apply. Indeed, the EU has long been a champion of Convention 108's globalization. In the wake of the activation of the accession clause, the Stockholm Program of Action, for instance, not only highlighted the need to promote accession but also that the EU should be 'the driving force' be-hind the development of international data privacy rules, including through the conclusion of multilateral treaties.[161] The latest iteration is from the European Commission which, in its communication to the European Parliament and the Council, encourages accession by third countries to Convention 108 and its add-itional Protocol.[162] If the GDPR was conceived with any global role in mind, it could only be, then, through the modernized Convention.

The picture is bleaker when it comes to the Malabo Convention. It follows an 'all in one' approach—where in addition to data privacy, the Convention addresses e-commerce and cybersecurity—means it could only provide a limited set of data privacy standards. Modern data principles such as privacy impact assessment and data breach notification are not provided in the treaty. Additionally, it does not en-visage a regional oversight body equivalent to, for instance, the CoE's Convention Committee. No less concerning is that the Convention is yet to receive the required fifteen ratifications to come into force. At the time of writing, only thirteen States have ratified the Convention.[163] And interestingly, only three of the five African States—ie, Cape Verde, Mauritius, and Senegal—that have acceded to Convention 108 have so far ratified the Malabo Convention. This supports Greenleaf's prop-osition that with Convention 108 already setting not only higher but also global standards, regional instruments such as the Malabo Convention will be ignored or be of secondary value.[164] One might even add that the Convention is unlikely be of interest to States which already are bound by sub-regional standards like the Economic Community of West African States (ECOWAS) Supplementary Act.[165]

In Latin America, the Ibero-American Data Protection framework is the only re-gional framework for data privacy protection.[166] Adopted by the Ibero-American

---

[161] European Council, Stockholm Program of Action: An Open and Secure Europe Serving and Protecting the Citizens (2 December 2009) 18.
[162] Communication from the Commission to the European Parliament and the Council, COM (2017) 7 Final (10 January 2017) 11–12.
[163] See status of ratification at <https://au.int/en/treaties/african-union-convention-cyber-security-and-personal-data-protection>.
[164] Graham Greenleaf, Global Data Privacy Laws 2021: Uncertain Paths for International Standards, 169 Privacy Laws and Business International Report (2021) 27.
[165] Of a related view, see Lukman Adebisi Abdulrauf and Charles Manga Fombad, 'The African Union's Data Protection Convention 2014: A Possible Cause for Celebration of Human Rights in Africa?' (2018) 8 Journal of Media Law 67, 94–95.
[166] Standards for Personal Data Protection for Ibero-American States (20 June 2017). Note, though, that the membership of OEI is along linguistic lines in that States outside the Latin American region such as Equatorial Guinea, Spain, Portugal, and Andorra are members of the Organization. As such, the Ibero-American data privacy framework is not a typical regional data privacy framework. See details about the Organization at <https://bit.ly/3s4zv0x>. Note, though, that the Organization of American States (OAS) has recently taken some steps to introduce a regional data protection mechanism, the

Data Protection Network, the standards are soft law meant to harmonize data protection regulation in the member States of the Organization of Ibero-American States (OEI).[167] In developing the Standards, the Ibero-American Data Protection Network used as 'reference' Convention 108 and the GDPR among other transnational standards.[168] This is also reflected in the set of data protection principles, data subject rights and institutional norms provided in the Standards.[169] But neither the legislative goals nor its legal nature would allow for further globalization of the standards. That the instrument is targeted at member States of the OEI evidently attests to the absence of any global ambition. If States not party to OEI were to follow the standards, it would be voluntary. Even then, that there already exist high-profile regional benchmarks like the GDPR means its global norm cross-fertilization potential is negligible. Perhaps the only, but yet uncertain, avenue to universalization is accretion of general international law of privacy which, with the adoption of data privacy legislation in member States, may contribute towards the formation of international custom or general principles.

Another transnational standard is the APEC Privacy Framework. Initially adopted in 2005 but updated a decade later in light of the update to the OECD Privacy Guidelines, the Framework is thus far the only framework in the Asia-Pacific region.[170] Like the OECD, the founding objective of APEC is to accelerate economic integration between members States which, in the digital age, relies heavily on seamless flow of personal data across borders.[171] The APEC Privacy Framework is a soft law that is meant to outline effective privacy protections that do not put barriers to transborder information flows.[172] Its central objective, then, is ensuring that privacy protections do not impose unreasonable barrier to the rather principal objective of APEC to enhance trade, and hence, economic growth. Substantively, the Framework provides a set of privacy principles and mechanisms for implementation.[173] An important part of the Framework is the Cross-border Privacy Rules which is a voluntary accountability mechanism involving Accountability agents who, together with relevant domestic authorities, oversee compliance with the Rules by participating businesses.[174] Added to the overall economic orientations of the Framework—and its closed nature, there are no prospects for it to become a universal standard over time. Just like the Ibero-American

---

most recent being the OAS Principles on Privacy and Personal Data Protection (2015). For more, see Carlos Souza and others, 'From Privacy to Data Protection: The Road Ahead for the Inter-American System of Human Rights' (2021) 25 The International Journal of Human Rights 147.

[167] ibid, 4, 12 cum art 1.
[168] ibid.
[169] ibid, chapters II–VII.
[170] See *APEC Privacy Framework* (2014).
[171] See details about APEC at <https://www.apec.org/about-us/about-apec>.
[172] See APEC Privacy Framework (n 170) Preamble cum foreword.
[173] ibid, parts III, IV.
[174] ibid, arts 65–68. See also more details about the mechanics of the Rules at <http://cbprs.org/>.

Standards, the APEC Framework has a limited regional goal which, again, relies on voluntary commitments.

In Africa, continental economic communities have taken several data privacy initiatives. One is the ECOWAS which introduced a binding act in 2010, even before the adoption of the Malabo Convention.[175] Influenced largely by the EU Data Protection Directive of 1995, the Act is thus far the only supranational treaty currently in force in the continent.[176] Other economic communities in southern, central and eastern Africa have likewise taken measures but mainly in the form of model law.[177] Beside the visible convergence between these instruments and European data protection standards, none of them have global ambitions. In that sense, there is no scope for such standards to contribute to the development of privacy and data protection in international law. Like the above highlighted regional standards, all such standards could contribute is in localizing transnational standards, and indirectly, facilitate the gradual accretion of general international law of privacy.

Overall, the prospect of transnational standards other than the Convention 108+ system is considerably low. As the above survey illustrated, those standards are formulated with specific regional or sub-regional remit and hence bereft of any prospect of gradually evolving into universal standards. That other transnational systems of protection such as Convention 108 and GDPR have already succeeded in providing global benchmarks for lawmaking and judicial decisions at regional and national levels further reduces the globalizing hope of other regional standards considered in this section. Perhaps a limited role for such standards is to localize GDPR and Convention 108 standards to regional and sub-regional levels. In that sense, the regional and sub-regional standards stand a chance of inspiring lawmaking in member States of regional and sub-regional organizations. And with proliferation of data privacy legislation and judicial jurisprudence may gradually lead to the formation of international custom or general principles.

6. Conclusion

In a 1965 remark at the Annual Meeting of the American Society of International Law, Robertson—who was then the head of the CoE's Directorate of Human Rights—spoke of the organization's 'European role' in the development of

---

[175] *A Supplementary Act on Personal Data Protection within ECOWAS*, A1SA.1f01f10 (16 February 2010).

[176] See Graham Greenleaf and Bertil Cottier, 'International and Regional Commitments in African Data Privacy Laws: A Comparative Analysis' (2022) 44 Computer Law and Security Review 1, 15.

[177] See, eg, *SADC Model Law on Data Protection* (2013); *EAC Framework for Cyberlaws*, Phases I (2008) and II (2011); *ECCAS Model Law/CEMAC Directives on Cybersecurity* (Data Protection, E-transactions, Cybercrime).

international law.[178] But this allusion to a European role was not certainly a reference to any contribution made to the development of international data privacy law. The reference, then, was to the dozens of CoE treaties adopted on a broad range of topics such as human rights, extradition, suppression of pirate radio stations and peaceful settlement of international disputes which, he argued, 'in the wider sense of the term, ... constituted contributions to the development of international law, because they were all international treaties containing obligations accepted by States'.[179] It would indeed take a couple of more years for the CoE to set in motion its data protection legislative initiatives. In the decades since, the CoE's data protection apparatus has considerably evolved, and doubtless, shaped policymaking worldwide. But importantly, Convention 108—alongside the Cybercrime Convention—are the type of treaties poised to make significant contributions to the development of international law. With the possibility of accession by States that are not members of the CoE, the Convention 108+ system is a treaty of universal aspirations. This chapter examined the extent to which, and whether, this potential of the system may be realized as part of addressing the privacy problem in the digital age.

At the July 2008 meeting of the Convention Committee that opened the door for accession by non-CoE States, a representative from Switzerland remarked that the accession path can be a step towards a 'universal right to data protection'.[180] A decade later, accession as an avenue of universalizing the Convention 108(−) system is yet to yield tangible results. Not only has the accession process been understandably slow but also that, thus far, it has covered a specific geographic area. As Kwansy aptly stated, the accession trend largely has been 'trans-mediterranean' as opposed to transatlantic.[181] This suggests that accession is the unlikely candidate in enhancing the global potential of the convention system. But more crucially, that accession by non-CoE States is also unlikely to result in significant dent in the global protection of data privacy. At its core, it relies mainly on domestic legal systems for implementation with no meaningful international oversight. This would presuppose a robust domestic legal system where rule of law is upheld and institutions operate under a reasonably independent and well-resourced regulatory environment. Not only is this missing in the larger part of the globe but also that there is little that the Convention Committee—the only international oversight body—could do to fill the void.

As this chapter further demonstrated, the prospect of Convention 108 and its later iterations in the development of general international law in the field of data privacy is even more uncertain. Accretion of rules of CIL is known to be a

---

[178] See Robertson (n 1) 201.
[179] ibid, 203–06.
[180] See Abridged Report of the 24th Plenary Meeting of the Consultative Committee (n 54) 9, para 53.
[181] Kwasny (n 37) 539.

complex process. Let alone in a rather recent field of law like data privacy, whether a particular rule has attained CIL often generates controversies. That is more so regarding its prospect of leading to the development of general principles. Added to their little use in practice generally, this source of international law is even more uncertain. If anything, the potential of Convention 108 in contributing to the formation of CIL would be a slow process, and hence, unsuited to the urgency that the 'privacy problem' in the digital age conjures.

Influencing the international data privacy jurisprudence at multiple levels is perhaps where the global potential of the Convention 108(+) lies. Still a gradual process, but this path enables the Convention standards to find place in the progressive development of international law. To an extent, this—as shown in this chapter—has started to occur in a meaningful way at two levels. Albeit indirectly, the case law of the HR Committee is gradually being influenced by Convention 108. The influence is also visible in the ongoing UN discourse on the 'right to privacy in the digital age' which occurs at multiple levels, and in different forms. With relevant UN bodies such as the UNGA, HR Council and treaty bodies increasingly grappling with on how best to respond to the 'privacy problem' in the digital age, the Convention 108(+)—along with other key regional standards like the GDPR—stands to offer 'international best practices' in the field of data protection.

An additional benefit of such cross-influence is that it would contribute to the development of CIL. As alluded to in chapter 3, the ILC is yet to put data protection in its current program of work. A growing embrace of data privacy standards recognized in Convention 108 in UN jurisprudence might help lift data protection out of the ILC's long-term program of work. But the rather important value of jurisprudential cross-influence is that it can build the groundwork for a sustainable international law response to the 'privacy problem'. With a growing socialization of Convention 108 standards in UN processes as well as in other regional, sub-regional, and national mechanisms, consensus on widely accepted data privacy rights, principles, and governance norms may emerge. This would then provide the normative base with which high-level principles of current international law of privacy can be expanded in international soft law. Chapter 7 further explores virtues of a soft legalization approach as a pragmatic international law response to the normative aspects of the 'privacy problem'.

PART III
TOWARDS A PRAGMATIC APPROACH

Having examined the current state of international law of privacy in part I and boundaries of emergent norms in part II, this part proposes a pragmatic approach to international privacy law. In chapter 7, it will be argued that an international soft law is needed to address normative gaps in international privacy law, to globalize emergent privacy norms, and further facilitate progressive development of privacy law in the digital age. Chapter 8 considers virtues of a dialogical approach in addressing some of the pressing structural shortcomings in international law. It explores virtues of installing a multistakeholder privacy forum as a way of building consensus and facilitating co-operation among key actors on current and emerging privacy challenges.

7

Virtues of Soft Legalization

> Successful laws normally either entrench existing norms, clarifying
> any uncertainties or ambiguities or reinforce developing norms . . .
>
> Reed, *Making Laws for Cyberspace* (OUP 2012) 12

1. Introduction

This chapter explores the first strand of the pragmatic approach towards international privacy law in the digital age: a soft law supplement. The second strand, which seeks to address institutional-structural gaps, is explored in the next chapter. This chapter considers virtues of a soft law on the right to privacy in making international privacy law better equipped in the digital age, particularly in lessening its normative gaps. It argues that a soft law is virtuous in three respects: first, it would translate the rather vague provisions of the right to privacy in international law; second, it would globalize emergent privacy norms; and third, it would enable the progressive development of (privacy) law.

Over the years, soft law has been proposed as a pertinent instrument of translating human rights, including the right to privacy, based on the new realities of the digital age. A former United Nations (UN) Special Rapporteur on Human Rights and Counter-terrorism, Scheinin, for instance, had recommended the Human Rights Council (HR Council) to initiate a process for the creation of a 'global declaration on data protection and data privacy' as a 'soft law complement to the hard law in the area.'[1] Perhaps because his proposal was part of a broader theme, the recommendation did not go far enough to outline what exactly that proposed Declaration would incorporate, and why a 'Declaration' is the appropriate instrument. In addition, whether the HR Council has a mandate to issue a Declaration, which is often adopted by the UN General Assembly (UNGA), is not entirely clear. The periodic membership of the Council, added to its vulnerability to politicization, probably makes it a less optimum body to adopt the proposed Declaration.

---

[1] Report of the Special Rapporteur on the Promotion and Protection of Human Rights and Fundamental Freedoms while Countering Terrorism, Martin Scheinin, UN Doc A/HRC/13/37 (28 December 2009) para 73. See also Martin Scheinin, Privacy and Security can be Reconciled (The Guardian, 21 January 2010) <https://bit.ly/2OmKY4C>.

Privacy and the Role of International Law in the Digital Age. Kinfe Yilma, Oxford University Press. © Kinfe Yilma 2023.
DOI: 10.1093/oso/9780192887290.003.0007

Proposals for soft law of other forms, particularly a General Comment (GC) of the Human Rights Committee (HR Committee), have also been made before and after the Snowden debacle. Most notably, the American Civil Liberties Union (ACLU) not only advocated for a GC but also tabled a draft.[2] But as shall be argued in this chapter, a GC will not be a pertinent instrument to address the 'normative gap' in the international law of privacy. Another soft law proposal has been for a broader Internet governance declaration, akin to the Universal Declaration of Human Rights (UDHR), negotiated through a multistakeholder process.[3] But this proposal not only is too broad to pay as much focus to digital privacy but also does not offer any details of its possible content.

This chapter goes beyond proposing a soft law supplement and explores the justifications, content, and legal form of an international soft law on the right to privacy. In that sense, it seeks to provide a clear conceptual basis and justification for earlier proposals, particularly the one made by Scheinin a decade ago, based on developments that have occurred since. The proposed soft law would also fulfil (cumulatively) functions of Reed's imaginary 'successful law', alluded to above in the epigraph, in entrenching existing norms—while at the same time clarifying embedded uncertainties and ambiguities—and reinforcing emerging norms.

The book in general and this chapter in particular follow Boyle and Chinkin's explication of the notion 'soft law'. They describe soft law as a catchphrase for 'a variety of non-legally binding instruments used in contemporary international relations'.[4] And as such, what essentially distinguishes it from 'hard law' like treaties is its lack of binding force. Yet, despite the lack of binding force, a soft law may enjoy in practice 'legal effect' to a varying degree. As Boyle and Chinkin further note, the use of soft law is not restricted among States, but also among States and non-State actors as well as among non-State actors alone.[5] The discussion in this chapter is, therefore, within this analytical parameter.

Soft law takes different forms in international lawmaking. From Declarations and Resolutions to GCs and policy briefs of civil society groups, they all fall under the rubric of 'soft law'. Having examined the pertinence of these forms of soft legalization in filling the normative blind spots in international privacy law, the chapter concludes that a UNGA Declaration is the most appropriate instrument for two reasons. First, compared to other types of soft law such as the UN Privacy

---

[2] See Privacy in the Digital Age: A Proposal for a New General Comment on the Right to Privacy under Article 17 of the International Covenant on Civil and Political Rights (American Civil Liberties Union, March 2014).

[3] Wolfgang Kleinwächter, Internet Governance Outlook 2014: Good News, Bad News, No News? (Circle ID, 31 December 2013) <https://bit.ly/1k8uufl>; see also Andrea Pettrachin, 'Towards a Universal Declaration of Internet Rights and Freedoms' (2018) 80 International Communication Gazette 337, 349–50.

[4] Alan Boyle and Christine Chinkin, *The Making of International Law* (Oxford University Press 2007) 212–13.

[5] ibid, 213.

Resolutions explored in chapter 5, a UNGA Declaration sits at a higher normative hierarchy and hence is normatively more authoritative, while at same time enjoying all the merits of 'softness'. Second, unlike other soft laws like Resolutions and GCs, a UNGA Declaration is structurally suited to provide relatively detailed substantive and institutional norms.

For ease of reference, core aspects of the proposed soft law are provided in the appendices.

2. Virtues of a Soft Law Supplement

What makes a soft law an apposite instrument in attending to normative limitations of the current framework flows from two underlying factors. The first relates to the place and nature of soft law in the mosaic of international lawmaking. Unlike a hard law, soft law is far more feasible and flexible in developing international legal norms. That is a widely recognized virtue of soft legalization in heeding to expediency in international lawmaking. The other, equally important, factor relates to the present state of international privacy law. As examined in chapters 2 and 3, the right to privacy already finds a high-level recognition and articulation in international (hard) law. Albeit to a lesser degree and mainly provided in dispersed soft law instruments, the international data privacy framework also embodies key data privacy norms and principles. Thus, foundational norms of international privacy law are codified in hard law, making a new hard law instrument less desirable, at least at this stage. What is acutely needed, instead, is simply a 'supplement' to those norms, in a soft law form, to revitalize the current international law of privacy in the digital age.

A soft law supplement would play a key role in unpacking the rather vague high-level abstract privacy principles based on new developments, including international privacy initiatives considered in chapters 4, 5, and 6. In translating these principles in the light of new developments in the digital age, a soft law—while avoiding the long-road to hard legalization—retains the relevance of existing international privacy law. The privacy field is also uniquely a highly fragmented area of international regulation, further aggravated by a myriad of reform initiatives pursued at various levels. A soft law would be vital in being a site of norm cross-fertilization by which it unifies and universalizes these initiatives. This section discusses these virtues of a soft law supplement on the right to privacy in more detail.

2.1. Reimagining the Right to Privacy in the Digital Age

The prime significance of a soft law would be to elaborate the scope and meaning of the right to privacy in the digital age. The argument in this chapter is that a soft law is an appropriate instrument to revitalize norms that already find a general level of recognition in hard law in the light of the new realities of the digital age. This is especially so with respect to the right to privacy in international human rights law. As explored in chapter 2, the right to privacy is guaranteed in several human rights instruments, including the International Covenant on Civil and Political Rights (ICCPR), but in an exceedingly vague manner. High-level abstract principles articulated in these instruments can be elaborated through a soft law.

Soft law historically played a key role in backing-up hard law by 'concretizing' some of its abstract notions, including in the context of human rights instruments.[6] As Saul notes in the context of the UN Declaration on Rights of Indigenous Peoples (DRIP), the Declaration particularizes general human rights for indigenous peoples.[7] It 'variously consolidates existing norms, clarifies certain rules and progressively develops others'.[8] The proposed soft law likewise would clarify and consolidate the existing international law of privacy while at the same time progressively embracing emergent norms anchored in Internet Bills of Rights (IBRs) and the series of UN Privacy Resolutions. In that sense, it might be argued that the proposed soft law on the right to privacy would function as a legislative interpretive instrument in offering an authoritative interpretation of the privacy provisions of the UDHR and the ICCPR. Similar arguments, indeed, have been made in relation to other soft laws. The DRIP, for instance, is considered an authoritative elaboration of the relevant provisions of several UN human rights instruments and sector-specific instruments with respect to the rights of indigenous peoples.[9]

The elaborative potential of a soft law is useful in at least three respects. One is that it would offer normative guidance in the implementation process. Judicial and quasi-judicial bodies could draw upon the instrument in entertaining cases or conducting periodic reviews of States. In practice, this has been the case in many areas of human rights. The jurisprudence of UN treaties bodies has, for instance, been directly informed by the relevant provisions of the DRIP.[10] In a similar way, a soft law on privacy may assist in offering normative guidance on the content of the right to privacy, for instance, to the HR Committee. In view of the ICCPR's crude privacy provisions, a soft law that specifies the scope and meaning of the right would offer some guidance to the Committee in its practice. Beyond the adjudicative fora, a soft law would also be useful in providing a roadmap for deliberations in less formal platforms, where the right to privacy is considered. Chapter 8

---

[6] See Guther Handl and others, 'A Hard Look at Soft Law' (1988) 82 Proceedings of the Annual Meeting of the ASIL 371, 380.

[7] Ben Saul, *Indigenous Peoples and Human Rights: International and Regional Jurisprudence* (Hart 2016) 8.

[8] ibid.

[9] See Mauro Barelli, *Seeking Justice in International Law: The Significance and Implications of the UN Declaration on the Rights of Indigenous Peoples* (Routledge 2016) 52–54.

[10] See Benedict Kingsbury, 'Indigenous Peoples' in *Max Planck Encyclopaedia of Public International Law* (2015) para 5.

explores how the proposed soft law would provide a blueprint by which emerging and current challenges relating to privacy in the digital age could be considered in the proposed multistakeholder privacy forum.

A second advantage is that it would constitute an important normative progression in keeping with new developments. Instead of pursuing the rather cumbersome procedure of introducing treaty amendments, the adoption of a soft law would allow embracing new normative initiatives. Good cases in point, in this regard, are IBRs and the evolving UN privacy discourse, examined in chapters 4 and 5 respectively, that—to a degree—introduce privacy norms mostly new to international law of privacy. An effective way to embrace such emergent norms within the rubric of international law is through a soft law that cross-fertilizes and then reinforces them. Not only is this effective but also innovative in the sense that these international privacy initiatives, as they currently stand, are unlikely to evolve into any reform of international privacy law on their own right. But this merit of facilitating normative progression would not be restricted to these initiatives. The soft law would additionally open the doors for future similar initiatives meant to respond to emergent privacy challenges to be incorporated.

Related to this is that the soft law would also be a key instrument in reviving the (largely) invisible international data privacy framework. Despite being an important regulatory tool for the protection of privacy, international data privacy law has received little attention. Apart from recent progressive internal data protection policies of UN agencies, as examined in chapter 3, the international data privacy framework not only is deeply fragmented but also normatively outmoded. The soft law would be a pertinent universal instrument to update and revive international data privacy rules based on significant developments in the field in the past decade or so. In that sense, in expanding existing high-level abstract privacy norms, the soft law would contribute towards lessening the normative gaps of international law of privacy identified in chapters 2 and 3.

A common weakness associated with soft law is its lack of binding force.[11] In the context of the discussion here, a question might arise: what is the point of having a soft law that does not carry enforceable obligations? This takes us to the third advantage of an elaborative soft law. A soft law that interacts with and reformulates a widely accepted hard law like the ICCPR may draw from the normative force of

---

[1]   But soft law also has its detractors at a conceptual level. See, for instance, Jan Klabbers, 'The Undesirability of Soft Law' (1998) 67 Nordic Journal of International Law 381, 381–91 [suggesting that an argument for soft law is (a) detrimental because it tends to rob the formal authority of law and circumvents formal processes to the benefit of the powerful elite and (b) undesirable because it vouches for what is often either a non-law or hard law]; see also Jean d'Aspermont, 'Softness in International Law: A Self-Serving Quest for New Legal Materials' (2008) 19 European Journal of International Law 1075, 1075–93 (claiming that international lawyer's resort to soft law as a new area of study is partly a result of professional insecurity caused by perceived saturation of the field). As this chapter will show, these criticisms of soft legalization do not necessarily apply to the proposed soft law on the right to privacy, and indeed, virtues of soft law explored here are recognized, at times, by its critics.

the latter. To the extent that the soft law is an elaboration of the ICCPR's otherwise dense privacy provision, States may arguably be bound by it. If the soft law were to be, as they should, adopted by the UNGA, it would lend weight to the authority of the instrument. An argument on the basis of the authoritative value of a soft law may be useful in countering resistance to the soft law due to its inherently non-binding nature. A soft law's authority hinges, of course, on a number of factors, including the extent to which its adoption drew consensus and support from States. The level of support and consensus will also later have a bearing on its implementation in practice, but as Shelton argues, a soft instrument that builds on already well-entrenched hard law instruments is likely to draw better reception and hence compliance.[12] This is partly because the adoption of a soft law instrument that furthers, or somehow relates to, a widely accepted instrument is an indication of 'greater commitment' on the part of States for the implementation of the law.[13]

Translation of hard law through soft law is also consistent with precedents in international lawmaking. One finds several instances where specific rights provided in a given human rights treaty are elaborated in soft law instruments. One is the 'right to freedom of religion'. Although freedom of religion, conscience, and thought has been introduced as a separate right under the UDHR and the ICCPR, a Declaration on the Elimination of All Forms of Intolerance and of Discrimination Based on Religion or Belief was adopted several years later.[14] While the Declaration appears to have a specific scope—ie, religious intolerance and discrimination—the example reveals a unique instance of normative progression from hard to soft law. Article 1 of the Declaration, for instance, replicates the three sub-articles of Article 18 of the ICCPR, and the fourth one is dealt with under Article 5. The scope and content of the right are further specified under Article 6 of the Declaration.

Similar examples of normative progression are available in other areas of human rights. The UN Declaration on the Rights of Minorities is one such example, which is meant to elaborate Article 27 of the ICCPR, which provides protection to the rights of persons belonging to minority groups.[15] The Declaration was meant to 'throw light on the various implications of Article 27 and to specify measures needed for the observance of the rights recognized in the Article'.[16] Not only is the Declaration inspired by Article 27 but also builds on, and adds to, the

---

[12] Dinah Shelton, 'Introduction: Law, Non-Law and the Problem of Soft Law' in Dinah Shelton (ed), *Commitment and Compliance: The Role of Non-Binding Norms in the International Legal System* (Oxford University Press 2000) 14.

[13] ibid.

[14] See *Declaration on the Elimination of All Forms of Intolerance and of Discrimination Based on Religion or Belief*, GA Res 36/55, 93rd plenary mtg, UN Doc A/RES/42/97 (25 November 1981).

[15] See *Declaration on the Rights of Persons Belonging to National or Ethnic, Religious and Linguistic Minorities*, GA Res 47/135, 92nd plenary mtg, UN Doc A/RES/47/135 (18 December 1992).

[16] See Patrick Thornberry, *International Law and the Rights of Minorities* (Clarendon Press 1991) 152; see also Report of Special Rapporteur of the UN Sub-Commission on Prevention of Discrimination and Protection of Minorities, Francesco Capotorti, UN Doc E/CN.4/Sub.2/384/Add.5 (28 June 1977).

rights contained in the international bill of rights.[17] Another precedent shows that the progression from Declaration to treaty could, at times, again go the other way. This has been the case for the Women Rights Convention, which began with a Declaration on the Elimination of Discrimination against Women, then a Convention. The relevant provisions of the Convention later are specified by a Declaration on Violence against Women. The Preamble of the Declaration provides that it is meant to 'strengthen and complement' the Convention—and to provide clear prohibition of violence against women.[18] In the area of child rights, there are a number of instances where treaty law has been expanded through soft law. Examples include the UN Riyadh Guidelines and the Alternative Child Care Guidelines which elaborate and expand aspects of the Convention on the Rights of the Child (CRC).[19] Thus, children's rights law is the other area of international human rights law that exhibits normative progression, and elaboration, from a treaty law to a variety of soft laws.

To summarize, the primary merit of a soft law supplement is redefining the scope and meaning of the right to privacy based on developments that have emerged since its codification in international law, particularly the new realities of the digital age. A soft law would assist in revitalizing the classic privacy principles of international law in the digital age. Beyond making the law better equipped in the digital age, the soft law would also be a suitable instrument to remedy its normative gaps. Moreover, it would offer much needed normative guidance to the HR Committee (and other non-judicial forums) where digital privacy themes are routinely debated. Not only would a soft law avoid the uncertain and time-taking process of treaty lawmaking, but also provides a normatively strong roadmap to advance the privacy agenda in the digital age.

2.2. Globalizing Emergent Privacy Standards

As the analysis in earlier chapters has shown, sources of global privacy standards are diverse. From human rights law and data privacy law to IBRs and the UN Privacy Resolutions, privacy standards find no single underlying international instrument. This, added to the already excessive normative dispersion that characterizes international data privacy law, is problematic. Progressive tendencies of international privacy initiatives like IBRs will remain buried unless they are integrated with the

---

[17] See Commentary of the Working Group on Minorities to the United Nations Declaration on the Rights of Persons Belonging to National or Ethnic, Religious and Linguistic Minorities, UN Doc E/CN.4/Sub.2/AC.5/2005/2 (4 April 2005) paras 3–4.

[18] *Declaration on the Elimination of Violence against Women*, GA Res 48/104, 85th plenary mtg, UN Doc A/RES/48/104 (20 December 1993) Preamble.

[19] *Guidelines for the Prevention of Juvenile Delinquency (Riyadh Guidelines)* GA Res 45/112, 68th plenary mtg, UN Doc A/RES/45/112 (14 December 1990); *Guidelines for the Alternative Care of Children*, GA Res 64/142, 64th sess, UN Doc A/Res/64/142 (24 February 2010).

international privacy framework. As already highlighted above—and explored further in chapters 4, 5, and 6, no viable reform of international privacy law is likely through and solely by IBRs and the ongoing UN privacy discourse. Nor will the unlikely universalization of the Convention 108(+) system come to the rescue.

In the absence of an institutional process that draws upon the merits of these initiatives, they would just remain invisible, or stall without resulting in any tangible outcome. The proposed soft law would be key in unifying, and giving some effect to, these extant and emerging global privacy standards. It would distil globally accepted privacy standards and best practices advanced under different banners. From the present framework on the human right to privacy and data privacy to IBRs, the soft law would synthesize the emerging consensus on the right to privacy. An international soft law on the right to privacy would then effectively globalize emergent privacy standards and map them onto the current international law of privacy.[20]

A novelty of the UN privacy discourse is, as highlighted in chapter 5, its 'unifying' approach to the right to privacy. Although proceeding under a 'human right to privacy framework', Privacy Resolutions adopted as part of the discourse embrace diverse sources of privacy standards: human rights law, data privacy law, and IBRs. To a certain extent, the IBRs project also pursues a unifying approach when it addresses privacy rights in tandem with the rather regulatory field of data privacy, while it essentially is a human rights project. This is not, of course, entirely out of place given that data privacy increasingly is moving towards a human rights language with recognition of enforceable 'data subject rights'. But what makes this holistic approach particularly novel and beneficial is that it attends to the problem of normative dispersion and projects privacy standards globally. Normative unification increases the accessibility and visibility of global privacy standards. More accessibility and visibility would further the goal of facilitating the protection of the right to privacy on the ground.

With more visibility and accessibility also comes the possibility that global privacy standards shape the development of national privacy jurisprudence. Often, soft law offers 'reference points' by which domestic law and judicial decision making are guided. As Dupuy notes, soft law norms normally bear impact on national legislatures as 'reference models' and are often taken into account by municipal judges.[21] In this sense, a soft law on the right to privacy can inspire local action, be it in triggering domestic legislation or guiding judicial adjudication, or even informal dialogue on the subject in question. It may also serve as a 'model law' for the enactment of an equivalent domestic legislation. Even in the absence

---

[20] Soft law sceptics also recognize the 'globalizing' role of a soft law. See, eg, d'Aspermont (n 11) 1082 (acknowledging the potential of soft law in 'internationalizing' a subject matter as well as in providing normative guidance and facilitating formation of custom).

[21] Pierre-Marie Dupuy, 'Soft Law and the International Law of Environment' (1990/91) 12 Michigan Journal of International Law 420, 434–35.

of a formal legislative incorporation of the soft law or aspects of it, domestic and regional courts could draw from it in entertaining matters relating to the right to privacy. As highlighted in earlier chapters, soft law instruments such as the UN Privacy Resolutions are, actual impact regardless, already drawing the attention of national and regional courts such as the European Court of Human Rights (ECtHR).

The globalizing mission of a soft law is in accord with the underlying assumption of international human rights law: complementarity. The notion of complementarity holds that a properly functional national human rights system is key to the realization of international human rights. The globalizing potential is significant because the recent prominence of new privacy standards is, to a greater degree, restricted to some parts of the world. IBRs legislation, for instance, has been adopted only in a handful of countries—and the majority is a product of civil society advocacy. The proposed soft law—by embracing aspects of the IBRs project, among other components—would be the first global articulation of emerging privacy standards now widely championed by various stakeholders. It would transform these standards into global standards which, in turn, may enhance the global protection of privacy over time.

'Globalizing' emergent privacy standards may also indirectly alter behaviour of technology companies. As discussed in chapter 4, there is a growing corporate appeal to IBRs by a growing number of small companies that offer competitive privacy-protecting services and pledge IBRs. By embracing Internet rights in an international instrument, the soft law would globalize and perhaps nudge technology companies towards such industry practices. Coupled with local regulatory interventions such as through competition law tools of breaking up bigger companies or forcing them to share data with smaller firms, the soft law would gradually mainstream current marginal industry practices.

In summary, the soft law would offer a potential of globalizing emergent privacy standards and promoting the applicability of privacy standards at the global level. That the proposed soft law is to be adopted by the UN, a representative body of the international community, furthers the globalizing aim.

2.3. Facilitating Progressive Development of Privacy Law

The inherent flexibility of soft legalization is another factor for its plausibility. The flexibility can be explained in at least three ways. One is that a soft law, compared to hard law, entails a lower 'contracting cost'—and hence is comparatively feasible.[22] A soft law can be negotiated and adopted—as often is the case, more easily than

---

[22]   See Kenneth Abbott and Duncan Snidal, 'Hard and Soft Law in International Governance' (2000) 54 International Organization 421, 422–23, 435.

hard law. It short-circuits what is called 'treaty fatigue' and domestic constitutional hurdles that often stand in the way of new binding international rules of cooperation.[23] Thus, unlike hard law, a soft law would not require signature and ratification by States—and could enter the statute book more quickly.

Some soft laws, of course, had taken many years before they were finally adopted. One recalls, in this regard, the DRIP and the Freedom of Religion Declaration.[24] Work on the Religious Freedom Declaration, for instance, began in 1962—while the ICCPR was being drafted and debated—but, the work on the Declaration was abandoned and it was finally adopted in 1981.[25] Similar delay had occurred in the process of negotiating and adopting the DRIP. This raises the question of whether a soft law on the right to privacy would await the same fate of delay. Despite some inevitable resistance, or even opposition, from some States and non-State actors, mainly technology companies, there are reasons to believe that the proposed soft law would be adopted relatively quickly.

To start with, the discussion set in motion at various levels by the Snowden revelations offers some hope. As considered in chapter 4, the revelations have already charted an international discourse on the right to privacy in the digital age. This discourse has so far been translated into successive Resolutions that exhibited notable consensus in addressing privacy issues at the international level. More importantly, these Resolutions appear to evolve from sheer reaffirmation of the right to privacy to embracing modern privacy standards. The various sources of global privacy protection, including data privacy and IBRs have found some form of expression in the Resolutions. Such signs of distilling and synthesizing global privacy standards would prove useful in facilitating consensus. The broader acceptance of the DRIP, despite many years of negotiation, was made possible because the drafters were careful in benchmarking the Declaration on state practices and established jurisprudence in the area.[26] A soft law on privacy that builds on well-established best practices and emerging state practices stands a good chance of being adopted sooner. It will also be a natural and logical evolution of the UN Privacy Resolutions.

A no less significant 'political capital' that can usher in more robust global privacy standards has been created by the adoption of these Resolutions. As shown in chapter 5, there was relatively wider support to these Resolutions from States on all sides of the global political axis. Except for the lobbying by Five Eyes States, particularly the US to water-down the initial Resolution, there was support from

---

[23] See Joost Pauwelyn and others, 'When Structures Become Shackles: Stagnation and Dynamics in International Law Making' (2014) 25 European Journal of International Law 733, 738–43.

[24] See *The United Nations Declaration on the Rights of Indigenous Peoples*, GA Res 61/295, 61st sess Agenda item 68, UN Doc A/61/295 (2 October 2007); GA Res 36/55 (n 14).

[25] See Bahiyyih Tahzib, *Freedom of Religion or Belief: Ensuring Effective International Legal Protection* (Martinus Nijhoff 1996) 122–65.

[26] See Saul (n 7) 7.

the overwhelming majority of States. That the discussion still continues at the UN also suggests that the momentum is far from being an ephemeral political phenomenon. Civil society advocacy which found significant place in the discussions, particularly in terms of paving the way of developing an international privacy framework based on and informed by regional and local developments, is likely to assist in sustaining the discourse. Thus, these set of circumstances surrounding the privacy discourse makes soft law more feasible than not. In light of the ongoing effort to introduce a binding treaty on business and human rights at the UN, it is plausible that technology companies would settle for the rather modest proposal of a soft law. After all, when one considers that Cold War politics was the principal factor in delaying the adoption of a soft law on freedom of religion, as reported by Cassese[27]—which now appears to be largely absent, a soft law on privacy would be feasible.

The second way to consider the flexibility of a soft law is its potential to gradually develop into hard law. While a hard law instrument on the right to privacy in the digital age might not be desirable and feasible at this stage, a soft law would still serve as a way station towards hard law, be it treaty or customary law. This would be useful in the sense that the hardening of the soft law over time enhances its normativity, particularly in creating legally binding obligations. Hard law is more likely to evolve from a soft law which promotes a trend of 'hardening' international relations.[28] Soft law is generally considered a 'precursor' to hard law, a 'probationary' candidate for eventual recognition as a fully fledged law.[29] It is possible, and perhaps desirable, that domain-specific regulatory treaty(ies) on themes relating to privacy might be negotiated and adopted. An example, in this regard, is the now stalled treaty negotiation on government surveillance initiated by the inaugural Special Rapporteur on the Right to Privacy (SRP).[30] The proposed soft law could be a springboard towards such long-term multilateral treaty processes. It is also in accord with the tradition in international law making, for a treaty to evolve from a soft law, rather than a work from scratch. One recalls here that several universal human rights treaties were preceded by Declarations, including on disability rights, child rights, and women's rights.[31]

Another pathway for the hardening of soft law is development of customary law. Soft law carries the potential to facilitate the rapid codification of emerging

---

[27] Antonio Cassese, *International Law in a Divided World* (Clarendon Press 1986) 303–04.

[28] See Tadeusz Gruchalla-Wesierski, 'A Framework for Understanding "Soft Law"' (1984) 30 McGill Law Journal 37, 37.

[29] See Leo Gross, *Essays on International Law and Organization* (Springer 2014) 176; see also Hilary Charlesworth, 'Law Making and Sources' in James Crawford and Martti Koskenniemi (eds), *The Cambridge Companion to International Law* (Cambridge University Press 2012) 198.

[30] See Special Rapporteur on the Right to Privacy Presents Draft Legal Instrument on Government-lee Surveillance and Privacy (28 February 2018) <https://bit.ly/3FZhDJJ>.

[31] See a comprehensive list of UN human rights instruments at <http://bit.ly/LAdFKU>.

State practices into customary law.[32] A long-term and uncertain process, but this could also be used to counter possible resistance from States to heed the proposed soft law owing to the lack of legally binding force. A related point is that a soft law is also a convenient mechanism of holding to account States that have not ratified the ICCPR at all. Non-ratification means that States like China would not be reviewed under the periodic reporting mechanism of the treaty bodies, not to mention the complaints procedure. That the Universal Periodic Review (UPR), another venue of periodic review of human rights performance, applies regardless of ratification of human rights treaties—and hence addresses the gap in treaty body periodic review is also questionable. This is because, as discussed in chapter 2, the UPR is conducted by high-level government officials, as opposed to experts, and hence is unlikely to be a commensurate replacement to periodic review by the HR Committee.

To summarize, the proposed soft law is flexible at many levels. On top of its inherent feasibility to be adopted relatively quickly, it is also a more pertinent instrument to develop into hard law in areas of privacy where such hardening is desirable. It could be taken as part of the natural evolution of the ongoing privacy discussions at multiple levels.

3. Normative Structures of the Soft Law

A follow-up question then would be what substantive content should the proposed soft law have? What makes this a key normative question is the apparent multiplicity of sources of privacy standards. The proposed soft law is an international human rights instrument, but how should it treat emergent privacy standards drawn from the rather regulatory field of data privacy law? To what degree should it embrace progressive elements of IBRs? More importantly, to what extent can a soft law embody such a diverse set of norms? Questions of both scale and normative reach arise in considering the normative structures of the soft law. As considered in earlier chapters, there is a considerable convergence among jurisdictions and several stakeholders on the minimum standards that a right to privacy must embody in the digital age. The IBRs project increasingly converges towards a set of digital privacy rights and principles. So are data privacy instruments, which largely are moving towards European data privacy standards. And, these two tiers of privacy protection are, to a degree, finding holistic expression in the ongoing discourse on the 'right to privacy in the digital age'. The proposed soft law would, then, be the next logical legislative step in formalizing this unifying approach.

---

[32] See Christopher Joyner, 'UN General Assembly Resolutions and International Law: Rethinking Contemporary Dynamics of Norm-Creation' (1981) 11 California Western International Law Journal 445, 459.

Based primarily on post-Snowden reform initiatives, what follows provides a modest sketch of what the content of the right to digital privacy in international law should look like. The substance of the soft law explored below seeks mainly to respond to core normative gaps of present international law of privacy explored in chapters 2 and 3. More particularly, the aim is to clarify and translate the meaning and scope of the right to privacy ambiguously formulated in current international (human rights) law. This involves specifying the respective obligations and responsibilities of States and non-State actors in the respect for and protection of the right to privacy in the digital context. A unifying approach also means that the soft law must attend to, to an extent, weaknesses of the international data privacy framework, particularly its archetypal normative fragmentation. Moreover, in reimagining the right to privacy in the digital age, the proposed soft law supplement would assist in specifying the scope of the right while at the same time holistically synthesizing modern privacy standards. In what follows, normative contours of the soft law are laid out in three steps. First, it discusses how the scope of the right to privacy must be framed in the digital context. Second, it highlights core privacy principles that must be incorporated in the proposed international soft law. Third, it outlines the respective obligations, responsibilities, and/roles of States, corporations, and other non-State actors under the right to privacy. A précis of the soft law is provided in the appendices of the book.

3.1. Clarifying Scope of the Right to Privacy

Clarifying boundaries of the right to privacy in the digital context should be the prime focus of the soft law. In view of the vague manner in which the right to privacy is stipulated in international law, as explored in chapter 2, the soft law is best-positioned to clarify, elaborate, and entrench the right based on developments that have occurred in the past few decades. More particularly, IBRs and the UN privacy discourse, among other sources, offer fertile ground to redefine the scope of the right to privacy in at least the following three respects. The first is untangling interests protected under the underlying right to privacy; second, reframing the right to privacy into a set of sub-rights consistently with emerging conceptions of the right; and third, introducing an explicit limitation clause for the right to privacy.

3.1 1. Decoupling Protected Interests
Among values and interests protected under Article 17 of the ICCPR as well as Article 12 of the UDHR are 'reputation and honour'. As highlighted in chapter 2, international human rights law bundles the right to privacy with these related but distinct interests of reputation and honour leading to confusion. Ideally, then, the soft law should disentangle the right to privacy from the distinct rights to reputation

and honour. While reputation and honour are valid interests worthy of protection, they should not be conflated with the rather broad and unique right to privacy. This is not to mention the question of whether 'honour'—an entirely subjective view of a person about oneself, and hence not generally protected even under defamation law,[33] as opposed to 'reputation'—is worthy of protection as a distinct human right. In line with the recent approach of the UN Privacy Resolutions, the content of the proposed soft law should be restricted to privacy interests. The other way forward is to envisage the circumstances where interference with reputational interests of an individual merits protection under the right to privacy. While the ECtHR, as highlighted in chapter 2, has clearly ruled that privacy and reputation are distinctive interests, certain attacks on reputation may engage the right to privacy. The most common of such instances is when attacks to one's reputation result in harm to private life. This is the other way in which the proposed soft law can reconcile these bundled interests.

Moreover, the soft law must reframe the right to privacy in a manner that clarifies the nexus between the 'zones' of privacy protection and the underlying right itself. The common zones of privacy protection—ie, 'family', 'home', and 'correspondence'—as shown in chapter 2, are framed in international law in a manner suggesting that they are not covered under the umbrella term 'privacy'. This has created confusion and hence led to erroneous interpretations, including by the HR Committee, that those zones of protection are distinct from 'privacy'. This should be rectified in a manner that clarifies the fact that the right to privacy provides protection from unlawful or arbitrary interference with 'privacy of the family, home and correspondence' as opposed to 'privacy', and 'family, home, and correspondence'. This will also be in line with the increasing tendency in the literature to adopt this understanding.[34] Additionally, it should set out how these zones of protection apply in the digital context, for instance that 'home' in cyberspace includes one's digital devices and accounts. See further on this point in the appended précis of the soft law.

3.1.2. Subset of Privacy Rights

With the launching of several IBRs initiatives, the classic right to privacy has found, as explored in chapter 4, specific formulation into a number of subset of rights. Of these rights, the right to *use* encryption technologies and freedom from surveillance are the commonest. A number of other rights that grew out of judicial interpretation of the broader right to personality, but that are essentially protective

---

[33] See, eg, Mark Armstrong and others, *Media Law in Australia* (3rd edn, Oxford University Press, 1995) 9–13; see also Manfred Nowak, *UN Covenant on Civil and Political Rights: CCPR Commentary* (NP Engel 2005) 552.

[34] See, eg, John Tobin and Sarah Field, 'Art.16—The Right to Protection of Privacy, Family, Home, Correspondence, Honour, and Reputation' in John Tobin (ed), *The Convention on the Rights of the Child: A Commentary* (Oxford University Press 2019) 559 (noting this tendency in the literature).

of privacy interests, have also emerged. An example in this regard is the right to the confidentiality and integrity of information systems. Both data privacy legislation and IBRs are increasingly embracing rights that fall under what might be referred to as 'right to personal data protection' such as the right to be forgotten. The proposed soft law instrument would be a pertinent global instrument to further develop the classic right to privacy in the digital age based on these emerging normative developments.

There are at least four benefits in incorporating these subsets of privacy rights. First, it clarifies the scope and meaning of the right to privacy based on the increasingly 'overlapping consensus' at various levels, including internationally in the ongoing UN privacy discourse. As explored in chapter 4, the normative content of these rights draws, inter alia, from IBRs, privacy legislation (national, regional, and international), and case law. This suggests the growing recognition of these subset of privacy rights globally. Second, codifying these rights as well as the corresponding obligations in an international soft law adds a sense of legitimacy, particularly when one considers that most of these rights are promoted and framed by civil society groups. Third, there is a tendency among some small technology companies to pledge IBRs as a competitive strategy. Stipulation of these rights in a (soft) law would then provide a legal basis in international law to already existing, albeit limited, industry practices supporting digital privacy rights. Fourth, enshrining some of the privacy rights would also bring harmonization in areas where there are diverging domestic rules. In the case of encryption policy, for instance, countries follow different and often conflicting approaches.[35] Enshrining in an international soft law a right to use Privacy Enhancing Technologies (PETs) may contribute towards narrowing down such divergence in approach.

But of course, this must be done with caution. In particular, the conceptual-theoretical ambiguities embedded in many of the IBRs must be weeded out. As shown in chapter 4, most IBRs documents embody a right to *use* encryption whereas a few others provide for a right *to* encryption. But no clear conceptual demarcation is drawn between these seemingly different rights. As submitted in that chapter, in terms of conceptual coherence and practicality, the right to *use* encryption is more sensible. But again, that right is not conceptually broad enough to embrace technologies that are increasingly applied to enhance privacy in the digital space. Beyond encryption, technologies such as anonymizers, ToR browser and software that filter cookies, spyware, and other tracking codes considerably enhance privacy. Because of this reality, the soft law should guarantee a broader right to *use* privacy enhancing technologies to properly capture state of the art. As elaborated in the précis of the proposed soft law, the right to *use* PETs, therefore,

---

[35] On the diverse mosaic of encryption policies in domestic law, see Wolfgang Schulz and Joris van Hooken, *Human Rights and Encryption* (UNESCO Series on Internet Freedom 2015) 29–49.

embraces not only the right to *use* encryption technologies but also the right to anonymity which feature disparately in some IBRs instruments.

3.1.3. Permissible Restrictions

Except for a generic clause in Article 29 of the UDHR and the 'arbitrary and un-lawful' clauses in the privacy provision of the ICCPR, no proper limitation clause is, as considered in chapter 2, provided in privacy provisions of international human rights law. The problem with the absence of a limitation clause is that it opens the door for a narrow interpretation of the right to privacy. To address this gap, the soft law should provide a fully fledged 'limitation clause'. Such a clause can easily be adapted from other rights in the ICCPR such as the rights to freedom of expression, peaceful assembly, and association or other regional instruments such as the European Convention on Human Rights and Fundamental Freedoms whose privacy provisions provide a limitation clause.[36] Many IBRs initiatives also offer useful samples of a limitation clause, one example being the African Declaration of Internet Rights and Freedoms.[37] An appropriate limitation clause would provide at least the following three grounds for restriction.

First, it should provide the requirement of 'legality'—ie, restrictions must be sanctioned by law that is clear, accessible, and specific. Second, it should enshrine the requirement of 'legitimate aim'—ie, the restriction must be necessary in a democratic society to achieve certain legitimate aims like public security. Third, the restriction should be 'proportional' to the legitimate aims pursued. Indeed, the HR Committee has developed—albeit in less consistent fashion—aspects of these three tests in its jurisprudence, particularly in its concluding observations. But it often faces opposition from States like the United States that constantly argue that the only grounds for restriction under the right to privacy are 'unlawful' and 'arbitrary'.[38] A soft law that is equipped with a proper limitation clause would help counter such opposition, by firmly establishing in international law permissible grounds for restriction.[39]

---

[36] The Siracusa Principles also offer a sample limitation clause comprising the requirements of 'pre-scribed by law' (legality) and 'in a democratic society' (necessity). Note, though, that it—in a complex set of principles—subsumes the requirements of proportionality and legitimate aim under necessity. See *Siracusa Principles on the Limitation and Derogation Provisions in the International Covenant on Civil and Political Rights*, American Association for the International Commission of Jurists (1988) part I.

[37] *African Declaration of Internet Rights and Freedoms* (2014) art 8.

[38] See, eg, Keith Harper, Establishment of an HRC Mandate on Privacy Rights Comes at a Critical Time: Explanation of Position by the Delegation of the United States of America (26 March 2015) <http://bit.ly/2fHl53O>.

[39] See below on the question of whether a similar limitation clause should apply when the interfer-ence is by Internet corporations.

3.2. Core Privacy Principles

In the area of digital privacy, as shown throughout the book, principles play an important role in reinforcing and furthering the underlying right to privacy. Good cases in point are principles provided in data protection instruments. Drawing on these, the soft law—in addition to embodying the subset of privacy rights considered above—should incorporate the following core minimum data privacy principles.

3.2 1. Extraterritoriality of the Right to Privacy

A defining feature of the 'privacy problem' in the digital age is the ubiquity of transnational privacy interference. The Snowden revelations have exposed far-reaching foreign surveillance practices of the Five Eyes States. But the question of whether the right to privacy applies extraterritorially has been controversial. The US, a member of the Five Eyes spy network, has consistently rejected the extraterritorial scope of the ICCPR, including the right to privacy. This has been the case despite repeated determinations of the HR Committee that Covenant rights apply extraterritorially in circumstances where States exercise jurisdiction outside their geographic territory. To address this issue, the soft law must decisively stipulate that the right to privacy applies extraterritorially.

In light of the fact that interference with personal privacy occurs remotely in the digital age, the right to privacy makes little sense unless its scope of application extends beyond geographic borders. More so when one considers, as highlighted by the Snowden revelations, that American surveillance practices affected subjects outside its territory. In the wake of the revelations, the American position has loosened to some degree. One instance has been the issuance of a 2015 Presidential Policy Directive, as highlighted in chapter 5, that appears to recognize 'privacy interests' of non-Americans located overseas. This signals the prospect of a growing global consensus on the extraterritoriality of the right to privacy. In explicitly and authoritatively codifying this important principle, the soft law would place under firm legal basis the normative position of various determinations of the HR Committee and further draw universal acceptance.

3.2.2. (Data) Privacy Principles

Baseline principles on the right to privacy in the digital age should also be incorporated in the soft law. It should, for instance, enshrine major data privacy principles and other broader procedural safeguards that have found some expression in the UN Privacy Resolutions and are widely recognized elsewhere. One such rule concerns 'metadata'. As discussed in chapter 5, the Resolutions acknowledge the now widely accepted dictum that metadata can be as revealing of private life as the content of the data, more so with the rise of sophisticated technological capabilities such as big data and Artificial Intelligence (AI). The soft law should, therefore, extend the protection of the right to privacy to 'metadata' in addition to content data. The soft law should also adopt a broader definition of what constitutes 'interference' with the right to privacy in the light of new developments worldwide. Applied in the context of data collection, this would mean that mere collection of personal data constitutes interference and hence must be justified under the three-part tests outlined above. Moreover, the soft law should impose an absolute ban on all forms of mass surveillance, including bulk collection of personal data and bulk device hacking. The absolute prohibition is justified because mass surveillance measures are inherently disproportional.

Data privacy rights and principles should also be provided in the soft law. As considered in chapter 4, most IBR initiatives—in addition to the subset of privacy rights—embody what elsewhere are to be found in data protection instruments. Examples in this regard are the 'right to be forgotten' and the 'right to information self-determination'. To some degree, the UN Privacy Resolutions have also flagged widely accepted data privacy principles, as discussed in chapter 5. The proposed soft law should go along that way to address the problem of normative fragmentation in the international data privacy framework. As shown in chapter 3, normative dispersion typifies the framework. By embracing widely recognized data privacy rights and principles, the soft law would lessen this problem.

However, the essentially regulatory, and hence casuistic nature of data privacy legislation would make it imperative to limit the scope of the soft law to a set of rights and principles. No soft law, be it a GC or a Declaration, on the right to privacy could adequately accommodate these bureaucratic aspects of data privacy legislation. This, in turn, would mean relegating the task of covering all aspects of data protection law to a separate global instrument. The soft law would also bring under one roof dispersed international data privacy standards now contained in multiple soft legal instruments, informed further by new developments elsewhere, particularly the European Union (EU). The best way forward would, therefore, be for the proposed instrument to formally recognize a fundamental right to personal data protection. Of course, international law protects data privacy under the broader right to privacy. This is, for instance, overt in the jurisprudence of the HR Committee, particularly GC 16. But the recognition of a 'right to personal data protection' would have a significant normative value. This value lies primarily in providing an enabling legal foreground to further international regulation in this area.

3.2.3. Independent Surveillance Oversight

One of the major challenges in safeguarding digital privacy has been the absence of a robust and independent oversight mechanism for government surveillance measures. Domestic surveillance legislation in many countries does not mandate independent oversight. When an oversight regime exists, the sanctioned oversight lacks independence as well as competence. To help address this gap, the soft law should provide for a mandatory requirement of judicial or at least administrative oversight for (a) conducting domestic and foreign surveillance, (b) requesting user personal data from third parties and (c) intelligence sharing among States. In line with the UN Privacy Resolutions, IBRs initiatives, and jurisprudence of the HR Committee, the soft law must stipulate a mandatory requirement of independent domestic oversight for all surveillance measures. This would allow for each instance of surveillance to pass through the scrutiny of an investigative judge to reduce risks of abuse. Prior judicial or administrative warrants must also be mandated when States seek user personal data for national security and law enforcement purposes from third parties, including Internet corporations. This would respond to the practices of warrantless access to user personal data from technology companies disclosed by the Snowden revelations.

Independent oversight is also equally desirable when States share among themselves intelligence containing user personal data. The need for oversight mechanism in the context of intelligence sharing has recently been recognized by the UN Privacy Resolutions and the post-Snowden concluding observations of the HR Committee as well as the case law of the ECtHR.[40] Unlike current prevalent practices, the oversight requirements should be applicable both before the sharing of the intelligence at the originator State, and after the sharing at the receiving State. This is justified because the intelligence is to be passed on to another State's authorities and hence potentially causing new privacy harm. Oversight upon sharing would be crucial in preventing privacy harms that might otherwise arise due to, for example repurposing of the intelligence use—eg, initially collected for terrorism and then used for organized crime investigation. This would be the best way to overcome circumvention of domestic restrictions/prohibitions—eg, for mass surveillance, in the receiving State and the risk that there might not be an independent oversight body in the receiving State.

3.3. Defining Obligations and Responsibilities

Defining the respective obligations, responsibilities and roles of State and non-State actors under the right to privacy should be the other substantive aspect of the soft law. In that regard, obligations and responsibilities of two actors should be specified in the soft law: States and Internet corporations. The existence of State obligations, both negative and positive, under the right to privacy is incontrovertible.[41]

---

[40] See, eg, *The Right to Privacy in the Digital Age*, GA Res 71/199, 71st sess, Agenda item 68(b), UN Doc A/RES/71/199 (25 January 2017) para 5(d); see also Secret Global Surveillance Networks: Intelligence Sharing Between Governments (Privacy International 2018).

[41] See, eg, generally HR Committee, *General Comment 31: Article 2—Nature of Legal Obligation Imposed on State Parties to the Covenant* 80th sess, UN Doc CCPR/C/21/Rev.1/Add.13 (26 May 2004) para 6; see also HR Committee, *General Comment 16: Article 17—The Right to Respect of Privacy, Family, Home and Correspondence, and Protection of Honour and Reputation*, 32nd sess, UN Doc HRI/GEN/1/Rev.9 (Vol I) (8 April 1988) paras 1, 9.

What the soft law would, then, do in that respect is to define those obligations based on the new realities of the digital age and emerging understandings of the right to privacy. Controversial is the horizontal obligations, or the absence thereof, of non-State actors, particularly corporations—and, to some extent, international organizations. As shall be explained below, defining or foreshadowing the possible obligations of technology companies, in a soft law is both desirable and plausible. The discussion below also briefly flags the role of international organizations focusing on the relevant UN agencies and other non-State actors that play a key role in the promotion, respect for and protection of human rights in general and privacy in particular.

In discussing the obligations of States and technology companies, the widely accepted tripartite typology of human rights obligations are employed. These are obligations to 'respect', 'protect', and 'fulfil'. The notion of obligation to 'fulfil' is often associated with economic, social, and cultural rights, as opposed to civil and political rights like the right to privacy. But, this chapter considers the obligation to 'fulfil' under the right to privacy in line with the emerging tendency in the literature as well as case law to apply them to civil and political rights.[42] Similarly, duties that are sometimes grouped under a distinct obligation to 'promote' are subsumed under the obligation to 'fulfil'. And of course, it is worth noting that there is no clear-cut distinction between the obligation to 'protect' and 'fulfil'.[43] For the sake of clarity, obligations of States and (Internet) corporations considered below follow the three subsets of privacy rights highlighted above.

3.3.1. Obligations of States
3.3.1.1. Obligation to Respect
States' primary obligation under the right to privacy is to 'respect'—ie, to refrain from measures violating the right.[44] Under the right to *use* PETs, the obligation to respect involves refraining from any measure that interferes with the *use* of such technologies by individuals and entities. This obligation should also involve restraint by States from obliging or forcing Internet businesses to install backdoors on their encrypted products, provide encryption key escrows or even to disclose encryption keys. The obligation to 'respect' under 'freedom of surveillance' primarily concerns an absolute prohibition of mass surveillance and mass data collection of personal data generally. Where the surveillance is a targeted one, it should be justified under the three-part tests of the limitation clause and be subject to independent oversight. A more recent manifestation of State mass surveillance practices is resort to 'bulk hacking' of devices such as smartphones.[45] Following the

---

[42] See, eg, Frédéric Mégret, 'Nature of Obligations' in Daniel Moeckli and others (eds), *International Human Rights Law* (2nd edn, Oxford University Press 2014) 101–03.
[43] ibid, 101.
[44] ibid, 102.
[45] See details on Privacy International's website: <https://bit.ly/2OQ98ox>.

treatment of hacking as a form of digital surveillance by the HR Committee,[46] a UNGA Resolution has classified hacking as a surveillance measure.[47] In line with this emerging consensus, the soft law should thus totally prohibit bulk hacking in all circumstances. But crucially, characterizing device hacking as a surveillance measure would fill a protection void that the right to *use* PETs leaves. Unless one is guaranteed protection against arbitrary device hacking, a mere right to use, for example encryption services, would not safeguard against access to the decrypted data already loaded on a device.

In defining State obligations under the right to the confidentiality and integrity of information systems, regard should be had to its semblance with the right to use PETs. The former appears to guarantee individuals a right to secure digital products and services. End-to-end encryption is perhaps an example of measures that ensure the security, integrity and confidentiality of digital communications. But this particular right, as noted in chapter 4, grew out of the broader right of personality in German constitutional jurisprudence. It seeks to extend the protection to information systems whose integrity and confidentiality is important for the full development of personality. So, the obligation flowing from this right is distinct from those under the 'right to PETs'. Thus, the obligation to 'respect' would require States to refrain from any measure that weakens the security, integrity, and confidentiality of digital services and products.

3.3.1.2. Obligation to Protect

A State's obligation to 'protect' under the right to privacy concerns a duty to ensure that the right to privacy is not interfered with by third parties.[48] A primary duty in that regard, then, is to put in place the requisite legal and institutional framework to uphold the right to privacy. This would involve enacting appropriate legislation to regulate the processing of personal data and government surveillance practices. Under the right to use PETs, the obligation to 'protect' concerns ensuring that the use of PETs is not obstructed by third parties, including by measures that restrict the interoperability of such technologies on digital platforms and services.

Under 'freedom of surveillance', the obligation to 'protect' primarily concerns putting in place legal and institutional arrangements that regulate online monitoring, tracking, and profiling by third parties. Regulation of, for instance, private sector data processing falls in this category. Moreover, States must put in place export control in relation to surveillance technologies sold by businesses in their respective jurisdictions. This obligation would involve a requirement of a special license to those types of businesses and rules that regulate when, how and to whom

---

[46] See, eg, Concluding Observation of the HR Committee: Italy, UN Doc CCPR/C/ITA/CO/6 (1 May 2017) paras 36–37.
[47] See *The Right to Privacy in the Digital Age*, GA Res 73/179, 73rd sess, Agenda Item 74(b), UN Doc A/RES/73/179 (21 January 2019) Preamble, para 29.
[48] See Mégret (n 42) 103.

that surveillance technologies could be exported or sold. With a view to prevent sale of these technologies to actors that might use them in a manner contrary to international human rights standards, it is also vital to include an obligation to conduct regular review of the licensing regime.

In line with the case law of the German Constitutional Court, the right to the confidentiality and integrity of information systems involves a positive obligation of 'protect'. Thus, the obligation to 'protect' requires States to take steps to protect the integrity and trustworthiness of information systems they own, operate or otherwise control to prevent interference by third parties.[49] Where applicable, the obligation would involve providing appropriate remedies when the right to privacy is undermined due to breach of security.

3.3.1.3. Obligation to Fulfil

A State's obligation to 'fulfil' concerns positive measures that facilitate the realization of the right to privacy.[50] Under the right to use PETs, the obligation to fulfil has two components. First, it includes removing unnecessary barriers to access and use of PETs such as import/export restrictions or discriminatory tariffs. Second, it includes an obligation to raise awareness on the use of technical means of safeguarding digital privacy. If formulated with such a precise scope, this positive obligation would avoid possible overlap with the right to education in the International Covenant on Economic, Social and Cultural Rights or at least read as a *sui generis* right/duty. The corresponding obligation will be more or less the same under the right to the confidentiality and integrity of information systems. It would involve a duty to promote the importance of enhancing the integrity and confidentiality of information systems, especially those operated or owned by the private sector.

Under freedom of surveillance, the obligation to 'fulfil' involves two distinct obligations. One is that States must provide a notification to the targeted individual once the surveillance has ended. This would allow the individual to ascertain the extent to which the interference with one's privacy was lawful and to further seek remedy. Secondly, States must ensure accessibility of laws that sanction surveillance to any interested party. This would require States not to sanction surveillance under secret laws and procedures, as is the case in some jurisdictions.

3.3.2. Responsibilities of Internet Corporations

3.3.2.1. Questions of Plausibility and Scale

Defining the responsibilities—or foreshadowing the obligations—of technology companies is the other important aspect of the right to privacy in the digital age. But any attempt to stipulate, or envision, obligations of Internet businesses in the proposed soft law is likely to generate controversy. This, as already discussed,

---

[49] Quoted in Schulz and van Hoboken (n 35) 38.
[50] See Mégret (n 42) 103.

is because of the absence of direct corporate human rights obligations in international law. In making corporations in general and Internet corporations in particular duty-bearers in international human rights law raises fundamental questions. A primary question, in this regard, is whether it is legally, conceptually, and practically plausible to impose direct human rights obligations on Internet corporations. Alwicker argues that the notion of extending the reach of human rights to apply horizontally is implausible because (i) it lacks any legal basis and (ii) there is no consistent and uniform state practice.[51] Specifying the responsibilities or obligations of Internet businesses in the soft law would not, however, attract as much controversy for the following reasons:[52]

First, that the corporate responsibilities would be envisaged in a soft law—ie, with no legally binding force—means the possibility of objection, particularly from Internet corporations, is remote. But beyond its lack of binding force, there are reasons to suggest that Internet corporations might not oppose it, if not support it. One is that major Internet corporations have over the years openly called for stronger privacy standards. One recalls occasional calls by tech giants for global privacy standards, more recent instances being Apple's call for General Data Protection Regulation (GDPR) type of American federal privacy law, Google's initiative for a framework for data privacy regulation and Facebook's call for a 'common global framework' on privacy.[53] Add to that emerging privacy-protective industry practices of rolling out PETs. While such corporate pro-privacy views and practices should be taken with scepticism, codifying responsibilities in the soft law that essentially reflect what they publicly preach for would give the legal basis Alwicker mentions. What the soft law seeks to do is distil these practices and articulate them in a manner that could draw widespread and consistent application by businesses. Arguably, the more legal norms resonate with already accepted practices and standards, the more they would have 'persuasive appeal' and hence of practical value.[54]

---

[51] Tilmann Alwicker, 'Transnationalizing Rights: International Human Rights Law in Cross-Border Contexts' (2018) 29 European Journal of International Law 581, 598.

[52] Note that the discussion here deliberately uses the terms 'responsibilities', 'obligations', and 'roles', interchangeably because the soft law cannot strictly impose obligations but the argument is made in a programmatic sense that international law must evolve towards unpacking corporate responsibilities or direct human obligations vis-à-vis the right to privacy on at least some corporations, particularly those operating in cyberspace.

[53] See Russell Brandsom, Tim Cook Wants a Federal Privacy Law—But so do Facebook and Google (The Verge, 24 October 2018) <https://bit.ly/2qaAYSg>; see also Framework for Responsible Data Protection Regulation (Google, September 2018) <https://bit.ly/2DoNt5m>; Mark Zuckerberg, The Internet Needs New Rules: Let's Start in Four Areas (The Washington Post, 30 March 2019) <https://wapo.st/2uEbrTT>.

[54] Of a related point, see John Tobin, 'Seeking to Persuade: A Constructive Approach to Human Rights Treaty Interpretation' (2010) 23 Harvard Human Rights Journal 1, 22 (citing Ryann Goodman, Sociological Insights into International Human Rights Law, IILJ International Legal Theory Colloquium: Interpretation in International Law, NYU School of Law (3 April 2008)).

Moreover, in view of the ongoing UN effort to draft a global treaty on the subject, Internet businesses are more likely to settle for the soft law than a treaty. In considering the debates on the international regulation of corporations, regard must be had to the fact that the opposition historically come from non-Internet corporations, typical examples being mining and oil companies. Internet corporations are new to the controversy, and the supposed opposition probably does not necessarily apply to them, more so when one considers the above noted positive gestures towards regulation. In part, the corporate push for regulation of their activities is driven by their own business interests. Operating in unregulated environments but often under scandals too damaging to their reputation is counterproductive. As Wouters and Chane note, regulation is good for transnational corporations because it provides legal certainty but importantly reduces the cost implications of reputational damages.[55] This would resonate with technology companies that are often plagued with privacy scandals.

Second, the responsibilities or obligations are drawn partly from the UN Privacy Resolutions, but with more specificity and clarification, which have not so far caused any known opposition. And of course, as discussed in chapter 5, some laws at national and regional levels, to some extent, enshrine these privacy rights or aspects of them—and their corresponding obligations. To a degree, privacy laws such as EU's GDPR apply extraterritorially, thereby covering Internet corporations that are not physically located or operate in the respective jurisdiction. There are, therefore, already some precedents by which Internet corporations are subject to enforceable obligations. The soft law would then be an international law equivalent to the increasing transnational regulation of Internet corporations. Another reason why stipulation of corporate obligations, or rather responsibilities, would be less controversial is that international human rights law already contemplates or implies an implicit negative obligation of non-State actors to 'respect'.[56]

Third, the soft law as conceived in this chapter is essentially, to use Dupuy's term, a 'programmatory law',[57] that seeks to shape the progressive development of international privacy law. The aim here, then, is to envision a future of international law that embraces Internet corporations as duty-bearers alongside States. As the law develops progressively, the obligations considered below represent the types and forms that international law should, or would, impose. Soft law, indeed, often reinforces not just what the current law on a given topic is but also reflects 'future law'

---

[55] See Jan Wouters and Anna-Luise Chance, 'Multinational Corporations in International Law' in Math Noortmann and others (eds), *Non-State Actors in International Law* (Hart 2015) 238, 250.

[56] See Manfred Nowak and Karolina Januszewski, 'Non-State Actors and Human Rights' in Math Noortmann and others (eds), *Non-State Actors in International Law* (Hart 2015) 159; see also John Knox, 'Horizontal Human Rights Law' (2008) 102 The American Journal of International Law 1, 20.

[57] René Dupuy, 'Declaratory Law and Programmatory Law: From Revolutionary Custom to "Soft Law"' in RJ Akkerman (ed), *Declaration on Principles: A Quest for Universal Peace* (Kluwer Law International 1977) 248, 254.

which becomes law proper once adequate consensus builds around it.[58] Handl et al note that a 'substantial part of soft law already describes, in an impressionistic way, par of the (hard) law of tomorrow'.[59] Codifying obligations of corporations in soft law would also facilitate the discourse and doctrine on the obligations of corporations in international law. It would provide a 'common language' in the debate on corporate human rights obligations.[60] This is what Abbott intimates as the role of a soft law in initiating an institutional process and 'normative dialogue' that might later ripen into hard legalization.[61] Thus, a programmatic vision with respect to corporate human rights obligations is methodologically useful in clarifying the nature of rights, although those rights are not enforceable.[62]

Corollary to the above question is the legal and practical implications of introducing direct human rights obligations on corporations. In particular, four core questions arise:

Does it mean corporations would directly be held to account before courts and quasi-judicial bodies like the HR Committee?

That is not what is being proposed here, for three reasons. First of all, corporations are not parties to human rights treaties like the ICCPR, and importantly its First Optional Protocol that mandates a complaints procedure, simply means corporations as respondents or defendants is inconceivable. But at a more general level, the lack of judicial recourse *per se* would not diminish the existence of a right or a correlative obligation. Even without judicial mechanisms of enforcing rights, the value of rights (and obligations) will exist when there is, as Higgins writes, an authoritative source and an accompanying expectation of the international community.[63] The second reason concerns a basic point of practicality. The principal monitoring body relevant to privacy at the international level is the HR Committee. But as considered in chapter 2, the Committee is handicapped by a host of structural setbacks. It is not only a part-time body that meets just three times in a year but also has frequent reshuffling of members. On top of its lack of authority to give authoritative decisions, it is already inundated with backlogs. For the most part, similar observations apply to other relevant treaty bodies that monitor treaties

[58] See Jutaro Higashi, 'The Role of Resolutions of the United Nations General Assembly in the Formative Process of International Customary Law' (1982) 25 Japanese Annual of International Law 11 23–24.

[59] See Handl and others (n 6) 388.

[60] See Steven Ratner, 'Corporations and Human Rights: A Theory of Legal Responsibility' (2001) 111 The Yale Law Journal 443, 545.

[61] Kenneth Abbott, 'The Many Faces of International Legalization' (1998) 92 Proceedings of the Annual Meeting of the ASIL 57, 63.

[62] Of a related point, see Eric Boot, *Human Duties and the Limits of Human Rights Discourse* (Springer 2017) 67.

[63] Rosalyn Higgins, *Problems and Process: International Law and How We Use It* (Oxford University Press 1995) 98, 102.

where the right to privacy is provided. A recent report of the Secretary General to the UNGA on the status of the treaty body system states that 'with the current staff resources, the Committees would need more than six years to clear the backlog, without considering any new individual communications received'.[64]

A related point that makes litigation or judicial/quasi-judicial recourse less realistic is the sheer number of potential duty-bearer Internet corporations. No international judicial or quasi-judicial body would withstand the deluge of suits if corporations could be sued, certainly not the HR Committee. Therefore, it would be implausible to envisage a scenario where corporations could be held to account through judicial or quasi-judicial means. The issue of practicality relates to the underlying argument made in chapter 8 that dialogue, as opposed to litigation, at the international level goes a long way in realizing human rights, including the right to privacy. But the provision of rights and obligations would be a tool to engage Internet corporations in discussions, for instance, at the proposed multistakeholder privacy forum.

Would all Internet corporations be bound by these obligations irrespective of their market share, user base or any other criteria?

In international human rights discourse, the issue of which non-State actors should be envisaged as duty-bearers is fiercely debated.[65] This is precisely because the 'more diverse the range of duty-bearers, the higher the risk that human rights get diluted'.[66] Pertinent to the case in question is the issue of 'which' Internet corporations should be duty-bearers vis-à-vis the right to privacy. The diversity of Internet corporations in terms of market share, user-base, loci of influence, and the attendant dynamism dictates some form of criteria as to who is subject to the soft law or more generally in a future treaty law. Criteria considered in the human rights literature range from one that includes 'all' non-State actors, those that possess 'institutional power', to those that are 'relevantly public'.[67] When commenting on the 'zero draft' of the business and human rights treaty, Ruggie rightly noted that the issue of 'scale' is key in determining which of the transnational corporations fall under the treaty regime.[68] The huge number of transnational corporations, and the

---

[64] Status of the Human Rights Treaty Body System, Report of the Secretary General, UN Doc A/74/643 (10 January 2020) para 18.

[65] See generally Wouters and Chance (n 55).

[66] See Wouter Vandenhole and Willem van Genugten, 'Introduction: An Emerging Multi-Duty-Bearer Human Rights Regime?' in Wouter Vandenhole (ed), *Challenging Territoriality in Human Rights Law: Building Blocks for a Plural and Diverse Duty-Bearer Regime* (Routledge 2015) 4.

[67] ibid, 4–5 and the accompanying footnotes; see also Ratner (n 60) 497–520 (discussing four criteria namely: the corporation's relations with government, nexus to the affected population, the rights at issue and the internal corporate structure).

[68] See John Ruggie, Comments on the 'Zero Draft' Treaty on Business and Human Rights (Business and Human Rights Resource Center, August 2018) <https://bit.ly/2DcDv75>; see also Knox (n 56) 41 (warning against 'overinclusion' of corporations).

complexities in the supply chain, raises a question of scale. This is because scale is crucial in the effective implementation of a treaty, particularly in attributing liability to the appropriate delinquent party. As noted above, the inclusion of 'all' non-State actors, including corporations, would render the protective regime ineffective. In the digital rights context in general and privacy in particular, at least the following three criteria must be considered in identifying which Internet corporations are bound, or rather covered, by the soft law.

One is the truly transnational nature of the relevant corporation. This concerns particularly whether the relevant corporation operates in a single or a few jurisdictions, or the world over. The proposed soft law must be restricted to those corporations that have global operations but are subject only to the laws of one or more jurisdictions. Secondly, the nature of operations of the relevant corporation should also be taken into account in that the extent to which the corporation is involved in the collection, processing, and sharing of personal data. This would exclude those whose primary operations do not pose threats to privacy rights. Thirdly, the user-base of the relevant Internet corporation should be considered. Technology companies that have users above a given threshold should fall under the remit of the soft law. In applying these criteria regard should, however, be had to the characteristically dynamic nature of the digital corporate marketplace. The not too uncommon rise and fall of Internet firms as well as fluctuation or saturation of user-base, dictated by various factors, must be taken into account in defining the 'scale'.

What happens when corporations fail to comply with obligations stipulated in the soft law?[69]

The use of the terms 'rights' and 'obligations' necessarily suggests consequent ability of individuals to seek remedies and imposition of sanctions against delinquent duty-bearers. Rights and obligations envisioned here are normatively soft which means they are theoretically nominal. But on top of the soft law's aim of foreshadowing 'future law', the underlying argument of the book for a dialogical approach reduces the role of sanctions. As shall be argued in chapter 8, an effective way of addressing institutional problems of international privacy law is by entrenching the already existing 'cooperative dialogue' framework in the UN human rights system. The transnational nature of privacy threats increasingly makes litigation a far less effective means of securing digital privacy. Envisaging

---

[69] Perhaps another question would be: *what would be equivalent to the notions of jurisdiction and/ or territorial control when it comes to corporate human rights obligations?* As Karavias rightly suggests, the decisive point is the factual situation where corporations exert functional control based on their factual relations with individuals. See Markos Karavias, *Corporate Obligations Under International Law* (Oxford University Press 2013) 173–74. As such, the proposed corporate obligations under the right to privacy would apply to all netizens/users to whom Internet corporations offer products based on, eg, contractual arrangements.

rights and obligations at the international level would, however, shape the development of privacy law at regional and domestic levels where litigation is more likely to bear fruit.

Furthermore, present institutional arrangements at the international level, for instance the part-time HR Committee, are not structurally best positioned to meaningfully enhance protection of the right to privacy through litigation. Therefore, legal effects of the digital rights and obligations stipulated in the proposed soft law would play out in three ways. First, as part of the soft law's role of providing a roadmap for the dialogical approaches to privacy explored in chapter 8, those rights and obligations would serve as a way of engaging Internet corporations in the multistakeholder privacy forum. Second, the rights and obligations would inform the making of laws and judicial decisions at domestic and regional levels, thereby localizing (but hardening) soft international norms. Third, soft law would also provide an authoritative digital privacy advocacy tool to civil society groups, including in their strategic litigations before domestic and regional courts. Over the course of time, this would embed international privacy norms at the local level and hence enhance global protection of privacy.

What balancing test, ie, limitation clause, should apply when the impinged restrictions are made by corporations?

In his theory of corporate human rights obligation, Ratner posits only a single countervailing interest: the 'rights and interests' of the relevant corporation in the restriction of the right in question.[70] No doubt, the three-step tests of 'legality', 'necessity', and 'legitimate aim' that ordinarily apply to States cannot simply be transposed to corporate rights restricting measures. But Ratner's approach gives too broad a latitude to corporations in restricting human rights. What is more appropriate, then, is a limitation clause that slightly adapts the three-part tests to the corporate world. Accordingly, the requirement of 'legality' in the corporate context would be fulfilled if the relevant corporation has a legal duty, right or some other legal basis such as contract that allows interference with privacy rights.[71] The restriction must then be 'necessary and proportionate' to achieve the legitimate aim pursued. Legitimate aims would include legitimate business interests of the corporation.

---

[70] Ratner (n 60) 512–15.
[71] cf Karavias (n 69) 189–91 [suggesting, in the context of 'balancing corporate and individual rights', that when domestic law specifies circumstances of permissible restriction by corporations, the requirement of legality would be met]. Note that the book does not envisage, unlike Karavias, corporations as rightholders.

3.3.2.2. Responsibilities

If the case for introducing direct corporate obligations under the right to privacy is persuasive, technology companies should be required to discharge the same tripartite obligations to 'respect', 'protect', and 'fulfil'. Just like State obligations outlined above, the corporate obligations should follow primarily the three subsets of privacy rights.

(a) Responsibility to respect: Corporate obligations to 'respect' under the right to use PETs and the right to the confidentiality and integrity of information systems overlap. Thus, under the obligation to 'respect', corporations owe three distinct duties under both rights. First, they should refrain from any measures—including in collusion with States—that may weaken the security of computer systems or obstruct the use of PETs. Second, they should refrain from heeding to unlawful requests from States to install backdoors to their services or provide encryption keys. Third, they should refrain from selling or otherwise making available tools that may be used by States to undermine the security of information systems or products.

Under freedom of surveillance, the obligation to 'respect' should have four elements. First, technology corporations should refrain from engaging in unlawful tracking and profiling of their users either for their own business interests or as a proxy for State law enforcement purposes. Part of this obligation must be to refrain from designing technologies in a manner that enables surveillance contrary to international privacy standards. Second, they should not arbitrarily block or deny access to users relying on anti-tracking technologies. Third, they should refrain from disclosing user personal data to States without appropriate judicial authorization. Fourth, they should refrain from selling or otherwise making available technologies to third-parties that undermine the enjoyment of privacy where there is an apparent risk of abuse.

(b) Responsibility to protect: Corporate obligations to 'protect' under the right to use PETs and the right to confidentiality and integrity of information systems are not identical. Under the right to use PETs, the obligation to 'protect' falls on those offering PETs to ensure that available security features are not exploited by third parties, including State law enforcement and intelligence agencies. This would involve a requirement to put in place a mechanism by which such exploitation is addressed within a reasonable time frame, and where applicable, to provide appropriate remedy.

The obligation to 'protect' under the right to the confidentiality and integrity of information systems is to ensure the security and confidentiality of computer systems operated or owned by Internet businesses, or other entities. One can think of here a requirement of deploying Transport Layer Security in default to ensure

the confidentiality of communication between users and service providing corporations. In addition, corporations should provide notification to users where the
security of their information systems is breached and where applicable provide appropriate remedies. More generally, the obligation to 'protect' must also include a
requirement to ensure that international privacy standards are taken into account
during the design as well as the operation of new technologies such as big data analytics, AI, and machine learning.

Under freedom from surveillance, the obligation to 'protect' has two components. First, corporations should take all reasonable steps, including through legal
action, to prevent unlawful access to the personal data of their users. Second, they
should protect their users from unlawful surveillance measures of third parties,
including State actors.

(c) **Responsibility to fulfil:** The boundary between the obligations to 'protect'
and 'fulfil' is not clear-cut. But the following obligations may fall under the corporate obligation to 'fulfil'. Under the right to *use* PETs, the obligation to 'fulfil'
requires Internet businesses to take all reasonable steps to enable the use of PETs
on their products, services, or platforms. This would include ensuring interoperability of PETs on their websites or products. Under the right to the confidentiality
and integrity of information systems, the obligation to 'fulfil' involves primarily a
duty to inform or notify users. One is that technology companies that offer e-2-e
communication services should inform users as to the nature and type of security
feature included in particular communication sessions. The latter positive obligation simply codifies recent industry practices of providing notification to users regarding whether a given communication session is encrypted and the type/level of
encryption.[72]

Unlike freedom of surveillance, the corporate obligation to 'fulfil' concerns primarily adoption of transparency policies/reports at various stages. At a more general level, corporations should be required to issue regular transparency reports
that offer the nature and extent of requests for user personal data lodged by State
organs. In individual cases, they should inform a user when his personal data has
been handed over to law enforcement agencies. Such transparency reports and notification would allow individual users to be informed when they have been subjected to surveillance or when a request for their personal data is made by State
agencies. The requirement of transparency should also extend to cases where
businesses are involved in supplying surveillance technologies to third parties, including State actors. Such reporting should indicate as to which States and other
non-State actors that such technologies have been supplied. With such disclosures,

---

[72] See, eg, How Private Are Your Messaging Apps? (Amnesty International, 3 November
2016) <https://bit.ly/2HnJ4y7>.

relevant human rights monitoring bodies can make meaningful review or scrutiny of States to whom such technologies were supplied.

3.3.3. Roles of other Non-State Actors

Ideally, the role of at least three groups of non-State actors should also be addressed in the soft law. First, the important role of civil society groups in supporting the respect for and protection of the right to privacy must be recognized. Such recognition is important because the ICCPR, unlike other human rights treaties, does not envisage a role for civil society groups. The proposed soft law must, for instance, recognize the important role of civil society organizations in upholding the right to privacy particularly in raising public awareness, assisting individuals seeking redress, and in mobilizing public opinion towards ensuring compliance by States of their human rights commitments.

In flagging emerging practices—both of States and businesses—that threaten the right to privacy, civil society organizations would play an important role in enhancing accountability and transparency. Their participation in the privacy forum proposed in the next chapter will also be important on many levels. For one, their advocacy work has the capacity to put significant social and political pressure on the 'unsteady political will of States'.[73] One way to do so would be by highlighting in the privacy forum not only emergent anti-privacy practices or measures but also civil society groups could also play a key role in offering expertise on technical and complex issues surrounding privacy.

A second category of non-State actors includes international intergovernmental organizations, particularly specialized and related agencies of the UN. As examined in chapter 3, a handful of UN specialized agencies have adopted intra-agency data protection policies. The adoption of these internal policies is mainly inspired by the Guidelines for Computerized Personal Data Files (Data Privacy Guidelines) which call upon international organizations to introduce corresponding data privacy documents based on their specific needs. Arguably, these policies—by requiring those organizations to put in place a framework through which the right to privacy, among other objectives, could be upheld—tend to come close to putting international organizations within the radar of international human rights law. Like corporations, whether international organizations, including UN agencies, are bound by international human rights law alongside States is a long-running debate.[74] But the stipulation of their obligation/role in the proposed soft law may not be as much controversial for two reasons.

---

[73] See Pierre-Marie Dupuy, 'Formation of Customary International Law and General Principles' in Daniel Dobansky and others (eds), *Oxford Handbook of International Environmental Law* (Oxford University Press 2007) 465.

[74] See, eg, Nowak and Januszewski (n 56) 156–58.

One is that there is already proscription in the Data Privacy Guidelines, albeit in soft law language, to introduce data privacy policies. Soft law would basically elevate this proscription to a higher normative status, given that a Declaration appears to sit above Guidelines in the hierarchy of soft legalization. Second, best practices of already adopting internal data privacy policies means that envisaging UN specialized agencies in the soft law would simply provide a firm legal basis to these trends. Therefore, the idea of international organizations being potential duty-bearers is plausible. Their primary duty, then, would be to introduce internal data protection policies with a view to safeguard privacy rights of their clients or persons of concern. The soft law would circumscribe the obligation only to international organizations that routinely process personal data as part of their operations. This further would mean that the privacy rights discussed above would not necessarily apply to them.

The technical community such as the Internet Engineering Task Force (IETF) and Internet Architecture Board (IAB) that set core Internet standards is the third category of non-State actors to be addressed in the soft law. Recent efforts of the IETF and IAB to set standards in manner that overcome technical attacks, including surveillance, should be backed up through the soft law. In specifying their role, it would both formalize and sustain their effort in strengthening the protection of privacy at a technical level. The role would involve ensuring that Internet and web technical standards are designed in such a way to counter unlawful surveillance. The soft law must also ideally recognize the role of these technical bodies in the proposed privacy forum. The technical community would particularly assist in providing expertise at the forum.

4. Questions of Form

If the normative boundaries of the soft law are drawn, the next question is one of form. Soft law takes various forms in the repertoire of international legislation. International instruments that are often considered under the rubric of soft law range from Declarations and Resolutions, GCs to policy briefs of civil society organizations. Chinkin points out two broad categories of soft law: legal and non-legal soft laws.[75] While declarations of the UN fall under the 'legal soft law' category, resolutions, codes of practice, GCs, and civil society policy briefs are treated as 'non-legal soft laws'. This section considers which form of soft law is more suitable in effectively carrying the normative contents of the proposed soft law discussed above. Having examined the propriety of various soft law alternatives, it

---

[75] Christine Chinkin, 'Normative Development in the International Legal System' in Dinah Shelton (ed), *Commitment and Compliance: The Role of Non-Binding Norms in the International Legal System* (Oxford University Press 2000) 25–30.

leans towards a UNGA Declaration as a pertinent instrument to enshrine the proposed elements of the soft law.

A primary candidate in terms of soft legalization is a GC. This can be achieved with the adoption of a GC on the right to privacy by relevant UN treaty bodies, more appropriately the HR Committee. As considered in chapter 2, the Committee adopted GC 16, in 1988. But given the time when it was adopted, it now has little to offer in terms of providing guidance on the broader and novel issues surrounding the right to privacy in the digital age. With the recent amplified calls upon the Committee to update the GC—including by the UNGA, the HR Council, UN Special Rapporteurs, civil society, and academia, it is likely that a new GC may be adopted in the not-too-distant future. The question, however, remains as to the extent to which such a GC would assist in filling normative blind spots in international privacy law.

The major concern relates to the normative value or status of a GC which, in turn, would determine its reception by States and other possible addressees. In contrast to, for example Resolutions or Declarations of the UNGA, GCs are less authoritative for being adopted by treaty bodies. There exists little reason to suggest that a GC would readily be accepted, and trigger implementation.[76] One must also consider the fact that GCs, unlike other soft laws, have a rather limited reach. As an instrument borne out of a dedicated human rights treaty, States not party to the relevant treaty such as the ICCPR would not be required to pay heed to it. The legitimacy and acceptance of the GC further dwindles when one considers that one possible normative source for a future GC might be—as often is the case— the case law of the HR Committee developed under the First Optional Protocol. State parties to the ICCPR, but not the Protocol, are likely to resist monitoring based on standards carved out of processes from which they purposefully opted out. One recalls, in this regard, the objection from some States when aspects of the Committee's draft GC on reservations, and more recently on the right to life, were perceived to have gone beyond the Committee's prior case law.[77] With this precedent in mind, opposition to a progressive GC on the right to privacy based on, for example ACLU's draft mentioned above, will probably stir opposition. The part-time nature of the Committee's role, added to the thin jurisprudence on the right to privacy and the work-overload, further cast doubt on the feasibility of a GC in the near future. In considering the fact that the process of adopting a GC takes a few years, the prospect of a GC on the right to privacy is remote.[78] That said, a GC has

---

[76] See Seibert-Fohr, 'The Human Rights Committee' in Gerd Oberleitner (ed), *International Human Rights Institutions, Tribunals and Courts* (Springer 2018) 129 (noting the controversy in academia over the legal nature of GCs, including the question of whether they even qualify as soft law).

[77] ibid.

[78] The work on GC 36 on the 'Right to Life' took three years (2015–2018). But it took only a little over a year to complete the latest GC on freedom of assembly (March 2019–July 2020). See details at <https://bit.ly/3HpVLGy>.

some inherent advantages, one being that it is easier to undergo amendments since it is all in the hands of the Committee to update or replace GCs.

Other alternative forms of soft law are those adopted by higher UN organs such as the UNGA such as Resolutions and Guidelines. Examples in this regard are the handful of UNGA Privacy Resolutions, examined in chapter 5, and the various UN guidelines on data privacy, examined in chapter 3. The legal nature of these instruments, however, makes them less suited to serve the role of providing normative content for the right to privacy in international law. Resolutions and Guidelines are not structurally pertinent instruments to enshrine substantive principles in sufficient details. As shown in chapter 5, the UN Privacy Resolutions exhibit a level of selectivity when it comes to substantive principles despite the overall attempt of pursuing a unifying approach. The normative force of these instruments also appears to be lower, compared to other types of soft law such as Declarations. Perhaps, similar observations apply to other less common UN standard-setting instruments such as 'Rules', 'Standard Rules', 'Standard Minimum Rules', 'Principles', 'Body of Principles', 'Guiding Principles', and 'Basic Principles'.[79] More desirable, then, is a soft law that is both structurally pertinent and normatively strong so as to draw wider acceptance.

This brings us to a UNGA Declaration. In contrast to the above highlighted soft laws, Declarations of the UNGA appear to sit in a higher normative hierarchy but with all the benefits of 'softness' in international lawmaking. While the place of Declarations in the hierarchy of international legalization is less clear, it has come to assume an important normative value in practice. Indeed, the term 'Declaration' appears nowhere in the UN Charter, except as a title to Chapter XI of the Charter. The term is often used synonymously with 'Resolution', which is also not named within the Charter. But generally, the term Resolution is taken to represent a 'Recommendation' which finds expression under the Charter. Instruments such as the UDHR are sometimes misleadingly referred to as Resolutions.[80] Resolutions, like 'Declarations' and 'Decisions', are legal instruments that are formal expressions of political will.[81] And customarily, treaties and Declarations adopted by the UNGA are prefaced by Resolutions. But there appears to exist a stark difference between Resolutions and Declarations when it comes to their normative value.

UN practice suggests that Declarations are instruments that contain important legal and political principles. An earlier memo of the UN Office of Legal Affairs issued in response to a request for clarification by the former Commission on Human

---

[79] For a list of UN instruments bearing these nomenclatures, see <http://bit.ly/LAdFKU>.

[80] See, eg, Dinah Shelton, 'Commentary and Conclusions' in Dinah Shelton (ed), *Commitment and Compliance: The Role of Non-Binding Norms in the International Legal System* (Oxford University Press 2000) 450.

[81] See Rainer Lagoni, 'Resolution, Declaration, Decision' in Rudiger Wolfrum (ed), *United Nations: Law, Policies and Practice* (Springer 1995) 1081.

Rights regarding the distinction between Declaration and Recommendation (ie, Resolution) states as follows:

> In United Nations practice, a 'declaration' is a formal and solemn instrument, suitable for <u>rare occasions when principles of great and lasting importance</u> are being enunciated, such as the Declaration of Human Rights. A recommendation is less formal. . . . However, in view of the greater solemnity of a 'declaration', it may be considered to impart, on behalf of the organ adopting it, a strong expectation that members of the international community will be abide by it. . . . a declaration may by custom become recognized as laying down rules binding upon States.[82] [Emphasis added]

The memo suggests that the underlying distinction between Declaration and Resolution is that of value in normative terms. Resolutions generally tend to be exhortations while Declarations 'codify' a subject matter.[83] A great deal of UNGA Resolutions are mere exhortations than articulation of legal norms.[84] Perhaps, an exception could be made for certain types of Resolutions what Bleicher calls 'law-giving resolutions', which move slightly beyond mere exhortatory statements on a given event, action, or inaction.[85] As highlighted in chapter 5, the latest UN Privacy Resolutions appear to be Resolutions of the latter type. But while these Resolutions appear to flag some privacy principles, and paved the way for further discussion in the area, they still fall short in adequately addressing the matter in a comprehensive manner. In part, this is for the obvious reason that Resolutions are not structurally best-placed to be instruments that articulate legal rights and principles, not to mention institutional norms. A Declaration on the right to digital privacy, therefore, would be a pertinent instrument to carry forward the aim of the Privacy Resolutions but in a more holistic manner, and higher normativity.

A Declaration would also slightly move beyond the soft language of Resolutions especially in articulating obligations and responsibilities of States and Internet corporations, respectively. This is partly because UN Declarations are often framed in such a manner that they seek observance from their addressees. One recalls, in this regard, the Declaration on the Granting of Independence to Colonial Countries and Peoples which states that it shall be observed 'faithfully and strictly'.[86] And, a subsequent UNGA Resolution authorizes the UN Decolonization Committee to

---

[8]   See Use of the Terms 'Declaration' and 'Recommendation', Memorandum by the Office of Legal Affairs, UN Doc E/CN.4/L.610 (2 April 1962).

[8]   See Jorge Castenada, 'The Underdeveloped Nations and the Development of International Law' (1961) 15 International Organizations 38, 38.

[8]   For a comprehensive list of UNGA Resolutions, see <http://bit.ly/1InBBIv>.

[8]   See Samuel Bleicher, 'The Legal Significance of Re-Citation of General Assembly Resolutions' (1969) 63 The American Journal of International Law 444, 458.

[8]   *Declaration on the Granting of Independence to Colonial Countries and Peoples*, GA Res 1514 (XV), 15th sess, UN Doc A/RES/1514(XV) (14 December 1960) para 7.

monitor the implementation of the Declaration by 'all means'.[87] Other Declarations likewise appear to seek observance unconditionally with the use of obligatory terms. The Declaration on Freedom of Religion, for instance, appears to impose obligations on States, with terms such as 'all States shall take effective measures or shall make all efforts'.[88] Moreover, a soft law instrument like a Declaration could carry more normative force when its implementation is supervised by a monitoring body.[89] As will be examined in the next chapter, the proposed institutional reform ideas would be useful in overseeing implementation of the soft law supplement proposed in this chapter.

5. Conclusion

This chapter argued that a pertinent approach towards lessening the 'normative gap' in international law of privacy is the adoption of a soft law supplement. A 'supplement' because there are already high-level privacy principles codified both in international hard laws such as the ICCPR as well as a range of soft laws on data privacy. Mapped onto these extant rules of international privacy law, the proposed soft law would make these rules better equipped in the digital age. As this chapter demonstrated, a well-framed programmatic soft law is an apposite instrument to translate international privacy initiatives, particularly the IBRs project and the ongoing UN Privacy discourse, into a meaningful reform. Because these initiatives, as shown in chapters 4 and 5, are unlikely to develop into a reform that would sufficiently reimagine the international law of privacy, this book takes the position that the best way forward is a soft law that draws upon aspects of these global privacy initiatives. In embracing substantive aspects of the IBRs and the privacy discourse as well as the latter's political capital, the soft law would reimagine the right to privacy in international law. This would effectively respond to normative blind spots in international privacy law. The next chapter explores the ways in which the structural-institutional gaps may be addressed through a dialogical approach.

---

[87] *The Situation with regard to the Implementation of the Declaration on the Granting of Independence to Colonial Countries and Peoples*, GA Res 1654 (XVI), 1066th plenary mtg, UN Doc A/RES/1654(XVI) (27 November 1961) para 6.

[88] See GA Res 36/55 (n 14) art 4.

[89] See Shelton (n 12) 14.

8
Virtues of a Dialogical Approach

1. Introduction

This chapter turns to explore the second strand of the pragmatic approach: a dialogical approach to digital privacy. As shown in chapters 2 and 3, institutional gaps are rife both in the international human right to privacy and data privacy regimes. The human right to privacy framework is overseen by the Human Rights Committee (HR Committee) not only with weak monitoring authority but also beset by structural constraints. Worse, institutional arrangements in the data privacy framework are as deeply fragmented as its norms and lack adequate monitoring capacity. The lack of an effective institutional machinery, added to the underlying normative weaknesses, makes international privacy law ill-equipped to respond to the 'privacy problem' in the digital age. Chapter 7 examined virtues of introducing a soft law supplement towards lessening the normative gaps. The present chapter explores how and why a dialogical approach is the practical way of reducing institutional, and hence implementation, challenges.

As this chapter will show, rebuilding the United Nations (UN) human rights system's 'cooperative' dialogue framework is the most effective way of remedying institutional gaps. Rejecting radical proposals such as the often-made plea for a world human rights court or hardening decisions of treaty bodies, the chapter argues that a dialogical approach wields the potential of realistically lessening the institutional lacuna, particularly in the international law of privacy. The term 'dialogical', in this context, is used in its ordinary dictionary meaning. Oxford English Dictionary defines the word 'dialogic' as 'relating to or in the form of dialogue'.[1] By 'dialogical approach' the aim here is, then, to capture a mechanism that relies on fostering and reinforcing conversations on current and emerging privacy challenges among key players in the digital privacy domain.

A key feature of the proposed dialogical approach is that it favours sustained conversation, in formal settings, among actors involved in the promotion, respect, and protection of the right to privacy. The main argument is that the nature of the 'privacy problem' requires mechanisms of enhancing compliance that relies primarily on engaging and persuading those actors that hold a unique position in the digital environment for the protection, and of course, violation of human

---

[1] See <https://en.oxforddictionaries.com/definition/dialogic>.

Privacy and the Role of International Law in the Digital Age. Kinfe Yilma, Oxford University Press. © Kinfe Yilma 2023.
DOI: 10.1093/oso/9780192887290.003.0008

rights. This notion of a dialogical approach coincides with its use in other areas of (international) law. One finds an example in international economic law where a 'dialogical approach' is meant to represent ways in which stakeholders in a given subject engage on cross-cutting issues.[2] In line with this conception, this chapter explores virtues of establishing a multistakeholder privacy forum. It argues that a privacy forum that brings together relevant stakeholders and facilitated by the Special Rapporteur on the Right to Privacy (SRP), would considerably complement and reinforce the work of existing institutional arrangements, particularly the HR Committee.

2. Virtues of a Dialogical Approach

A dialogical approach is uniquely suited to lessen implementation challenges of international privacy law for two reasons. First, it is a less radical and hence pragmatic way in which the objective of upholding the right to privacy in the digital age can be realized. Second, a dialogical approach embodies the dynamism that would allow international law to remain abreast of emerging and complex privacy issues. That makes a dialogical approach adaptive to the unique realities of upholding the right to privacy in the digital environment, where threats are complex and constantly shifting. This section unpacks these two merits of a dialogical approach.

2.1. Dialogue as a Pragmatic Future

The primary virtue of the dialogical approach is that it is pragmatic. Unlike drastic reform ideas flaunted over the years, dialogical mechanisms are modest proposals that can be realized in the present political reality. But importantly, they would not require reinventing the wheel. Installing a privacy forum, for instance, would not substantially unseat existing institutional arrangements. Installing such a forum would, of course, involve creation of a new body but, as the history of other similar forums at the UN suggests, it might not be a particularly cumbersome venture. As shall become clear, this is in stark contrast with earlier initiatives that would require fundamental restructuring of the entire human rights system.

As part of a broader reform of the UN system of human rights adjudication, various proposals have been put forward over the years. One proposal has been to abolish the HR Committee altogether and establish a world human rights court because 'views' of the Committee are not legally binding and are, as a

---

[2] See, eg, Elizabeth Trujillo, 'A Dialogical Approach to Trade and Environment' (2013) 16 Journal of International Economic Law 535, 537–44.

result, often ignored in practice.[3] To this effect, a 'Consolidated Statute for a World Court of Human Rights' has been drafted.[4] Notably unique and ambitious about this proposal is that it envisioned other 'entities', including corporations, as being subject to the court's jurisdiction, albeit on a voluntary basis.[5] Similar reasoning has also prompted suggestions for the establishment of a world human rights court in the context of the International Covenant on Economic, Social and Cultural Rights.[6]

A related proposal has been for the establishment of two permanent enforcement bodies to replace the 'ineffective' HR Committee.[7] Some scholars have also advocated for the 'reconstitution' of the entire human rights regime and creation of a system that only 'democratic States' would be invited to join.[8] Along similar lines, the former High Commissioner Arbour had proposed the creation of a Unified Standing Treaty Body that would replace all treaty monitoring bodies established under UN human rights treaties, including the International Covenant on Civil and Political Rights (ICCPR).[9] An earlier proposal, including by the HR Committee itself, has been to make views of the Committee binding by amending the First Optional Protocol to the ICCPR.[10] A more domain-specific proposal has also been made, as discussed in chapter 1, for a UN agency on data privacy to oversee the implementation of the Guidelines for Computerized Personal Data Files (Data Privacy Guidelines).[11]

As can readily be gleaned, the nature of these initiatives would require radical restructuring of the human rights system, including the making of new treaties. In light of the international political reality and common challenges of treaty processes, there is little chance for such initiatives to materialize. Nothing best illustrates the feasibility challenge as much as the hibernation of the Swiss initiative for

---

[3] See, eg, Manfred Nowak, 'It's Time for a World Court of Human Rights' in Cherif Bassiouni and William Schabas (eds), *New Challenges for the UN Human Rights Machinery: What Future for the UN Treaty Body System and the Human Rights Council Procedures?* (Intersentia 2011) 26–8.

[4] ibid, 28–32.

[5] See Martin Scheinin, Towards a World Court of Human Rights: Research Report within the Framework of the Swiss Initiative to Commemorate the 60th Anniversary of the Universal Declaration of Human Rights (22 June 2009) 19.

[6] See Manisuli Ssenyonjo, *Economic, Social and Cultural Rights in International Law* (Hart 2nd edn, 2016) 651–60.

See Makau Mutua, 'Looking Past the Human Rights Committee: An Argument for De-Marginalizing Enforcement' (1998) 4 Buffalo Human Rights Law Review 211, 258–60.

See Anne Bayefsky, 'Making Human Rights Work' (1997) 26 Studies in Transnational Legal Policy 225, 262–65; see also John Barton and Barry Carter, 'International Law and Institutions for a New Age' (1992/93) 81 Georgetown Law Journal 535, 535, 557.

See Concept Paper on the High Commissioner's Proposal for a Unified Standing Treaty Body, UN Doc HRI/MC/2006/2 (22 March 2006).

[10] See Thomas Buergenthal, 'The UN Human Rights Committee' (2001) 5 Max Planck Yearbook of United Nations Law 341, 376.

[11] See Paul De Hert and Vagelis Papakonstantinou, 'Three Scenarios for International Governance of Data Privacy: Towards an International Data Privacy Organization, Preferably a UN Agency?' (2013) 9 I/S A Journal of Law and Policy for the Information Society 271 et seq.

a world human rights court, which was launched a decade ago.[12] Except for occasional but modest reforms introduced by the UN Office of the High Commissioner for Human Rights (OHCHR) over the years and the treaty bodies themselves, none of the above reform ideas have also been taken seriously. But it is not also certain whether the creation of, for example, a human rights court, would result in significant improvement in the protection of human rights. This is precisely because several other factors, beyond lack of an authoritative global human rights body, are liable for the sustained compliance deficit in international human rights law, including lack of political will and resources constraints both in developed and developing countries.[13]

Having a world human rights court, then, or a HR Committee with a power to issue binding decisions, would not necessarily guarantee effective protection of human rights. The issue, therefore, is not just of feasibility, but also of desirability. It would be unpragmatic to invest the limited available resources on initiatives with little hope of turning around the status quo. The dialogical approach argued for in this chapter is premised on this reality in the international protection of human rights in general and the right to privacy in particular. Not only is the proposed dialogic approach feasible but also would considerably assist in mitigating the compliance deficit through engagement and building consensus among key players.

Advancing the human rights movement requires engaging not only States but also other relevant stakeholders. And engagement, and the resultant change, must involve a process one that requires, as aptly put by Alston, determined 'incrementalism and organic evolution'.[14] As this chapter will show, installing a privacy forum is essentially incremental, and constitutes an organic progression in international privacy law. What makes this dialogical approach more realistic is that it simply builds upon practices not alien to the international law discourse. The proposed privacy forum, for instance, not only has many precedents in the UN human rights system but also would not require putting in place a new institutional machinery.

Pragmatic underpinnings of the dialogical approach also draw upon the ongoing UN discussions on the right to privacy. A recognition of the virtue of a dialogical approach, or a 'sustained engagement' has been a central feature of the ongoing privacy discourse at the UN. As highlighted in chapter 5, the UN Privacy Resolutions recognize that 'effectively addressing the challenges relating to the right to privacy in the context of modern communications technology requires an ongoing, concerted multistakeholder engagement'.[15] The proposed multistakeholder

---

[12] One of the initiative's progenitors recently acknowledged that the time is not yet ripe for such a 'fundamental' reform. See Manfred Nowak, 'A World Court of Human Rights' in Gerd Oberleitner (ed), *International Human Rights Institutions, Tribunals and Courts* (Springer 2018) 288.

[13] See Philip Alston, 'Against a World Court for Human Rights' (2014) 28 Ethics and International Affairs 197, 210–11.

[14] ibid.

[15] See *The Right to Privacy in the Digital Age*, GA Res 71/199, 71st sess, Agenda item 68(b), UN Doc A/RES/71/199 (25 January 2017) Preamble, para 13 cum 8.

forum, with a proper legal basis in international law, and hence formal, would be more effective in enhancing protection of digital privacy. That way, it builds on the consensus increasingly emerging in the context of the ongoing UN privacy discourse, especially on virtues of dialogue in privacy protection.

2.2. Dialogue as a Responsive Strategy

A dialogical approach, unlike non-dialogical mechanisms such as adjudication, responds relatively effectively to the unique challenges of securing digital privacy. Dynamism is a characteristic feature of the digital environment where new technologies emerge more rapidly than what law could catch up with. New technological innovations come up with as much new threats to the right to privacy as new and obscure actors that wield significant influence over individuals. Law barely keeps pace with such incessant changes, thereby making legal protection of privacy through the traditional adjudicative means harder. Not only does international lawmaking follow a rigid process to keep up with such new developments but also that present institutional arrangements structurally are not adept to progressively apply the law through evolutive interpretation. As Weeramantry noted several decades ago, 'aggressively burgeoning' technological developments demand 'constant surveillance' to properly uphold human rights.[16] A dialogical method provides the means to surveil burgeoning technological developments which are far more sophisticated now than were when Weeramantry made that observation.

The international law of privacy, as shown in chapters 2 and 3, is ill-equipped to match this novelty of the digital space. The present institutional machinery for the international protection of privacy is basically the treaty body system primarily involving the HR Committee, the Universal Periodic Review (UPR) mechanism, and the SRP. But these bodies wield weaker institutional powers, operate on a part-time basis and suffer from compliance deficit. Worse, no dedicated institutional machinery exists at all in the international data privacy framework, as shown in chapter 3, except for the part-time expert committees under relevant instruments of the United Nations Educational, Scientific, and Cultural Organization. This institutional lacuna is best illustrated by the dearth of privacy jurisprudence at the international level that would have developed existing norms in the light of the new realities of the digital age.

As shall be explored in the next section, a privacy forum would equip current international law of privacy with a way that would considerably surveil continuous changes in the privacy landscape. Regular conversations among States, civil society groups, and Internet corporations at the forum on current and emerging privacy

---

[16] See Christopher Weeramantry, 'Science, Technology and the Future of Human Rights' (1986) 13 India International Centre Quarterly 41, 42.

issues would complement, and keep alive, the quasi-adjudicatory role of the HR Committee. In that way, a dialogical approach that is adaptive to changing circumstances would make international law flexible enough in the digital age. The argument in this chapter, then, is that a multistakeholder forum would offer a way in which international law can keep up with continuous developments in the global privacy landscape.

But the value of sustained conversation on digital privacy issues can also extend to regional and national courts. As much as regional courts like the European Court of Human Rights (ECtHR) have a progressive privacy jurisprudence, enforcement of their judgments is not all rosy. Structural problems such as case backlog further punctuate the relative successes of the Strasbourg Court.[17] When one considers the rapid pace in which technologies as well as the attendant State and corporate practices change, the inherently time-consuming and bureaucratic nature of court process is a disadvantage. At times, judicial process is outpaced by the legislative process by which laws are being litigated in court are soon replaced with even more draconian rules.[18]

The degree to which courts are accessible to ordinary individuals is also questionable as most legal actions are brought by civil society groups. Issues of judicial independence as well as resource constraints reduce the capacity of national courts in many jurisdictions. This is in addition to the fundamental question of jurisdiction over transnational privacy matters. The extent to which adjudication is effective in practically enhancing privacy protection is also circumscribed. State and corporate practices that erode privacy rights do not always discontinue despite many several legal actions in domestic and regional courts.[19] But at a more fundamental level, adjudication, in the strict sense of the term, not only is ineffective but is inexistent in international privacy law. A dialogical approach, then, would be an indispensable additional tool in the repertoire of privacy right implementation at the international level.

3. Ways of Conversation

What follows considers the scope and nature of the proposed dialogical approach to digital privacy. It considers the foundations of introducing a multistakeholder

---

[17] A recent decision of the ECtHR in the case of *Big Brother Watch and Others v UK* came almost after five years, which might even be considered quicker than other cases, perhaps, due to the fervour of the Snowden debacle. See ECtHR, *Big Brother Watch and Others v UK*, Application Nos 58170/13, 62322/14 and 24960/15 (13 September 2018).

[18] A good example here is the replacement of a UK surveillance legislation litigated in the *Big Brother Watch* case before the case was decided.

[19] See, eg, A Concerning State of Play for the Right to Privacy in Europe: National Data Retention Laws Since CJEU's Tele-2/Watson Judgment (Privacy International, September 2017) [reporting that some European States non-compliance with decision of CJEU in relation to data retention].

privacy forum. It then discusses two key functions of the forum as well as its interplay with existing institutional arrangements. Further highlighted are limits of multistakeholderism that must be considered in installing a multistakeholder forum to ensure an inclusive and participatory process. Further details about the forum, its functions, and composition are provided in the appended précis of the soft law.

3.1. Foundations of the Privacy Forum

The idea of introducing a multistakeholder privacy forum is based on three major premises. First, the notion of multistakeholderism enriches multilateral processes of the UN system. As the discussion shall show, this virtue of multi-level approach to international regulation is gradually being recognized in the international legal order. Second, a multistakeholder approach is an effective way of rebuilding the model of 'cooperative dialogue' that forms a central part of the UN treaty body system. Third, because adjudicative means of upholding the right to privacy is largely moot, dialogue is the reasonable step to encourage compliance both by State and non-State actors. These three underlying rationales of the forum help explain why a privacy forum is a realistic approach towards lessening institutional gaps in international privacy law.

3.1.1. Enriching Multilateralism with Multistakeholderism
Installing a multistakeholder body would be in line with the increasing appeal for a multistakeholder approach at the UN and its various bodies, particularly in the human rights domain. This makes the proposal of a privacy multistakeholder body a rational exercise. The UN has beckoned multistakeholderism in international relations long before the post-Snowden UN Privacy Resolutions which, as noted earlier, endorse multistakeholder dialogue on the right to privacy. One early instance has been at the World Summit on Information Society in 2005 where the role of non-State actors in Internet governance, alongside States, was recognized.[20] But one of the earliest attempts to embrace non-State actors in the treaty body system was during the reform launched by former High Commissioner Pillay. In justifying the importance of multistakeholderism, Pillay argued that inter-governmental processes of the UN can embrace multistakeholder participation in strengthening

---

[20] The Tunis Agenda for the Information Society, WSIS-05/TUNIS/DOC/6(Rev. 1)-E (18 November 2005) para 34. The role of non-State actors in the promotion and protection of human rights has also been clearly recognized in the creation of the HR Council and its mechanisms, mainly the UPR. See *Human Rights Council*, GA Res 60/251, 60th sess, Agenda items 46 and 120, UN Doc A/RES/60/251 (3 April 2006) para 5(h) cum *Institution Building of the United Nations Human Rights Council*, HRC Res 5/1 5th sess, 9th mtg, UN Doc A/HRC/RES/5/1 (18 June 2007) para 3(m).

the treaty body system.[21] Unlike previous reform efforts, her reform initiative drew a great deal from the input of various stakeholders including States, civil society organizations, and national human rights organizations through a largely transparent, bottom-up, and participatory process.[22] This pursuit of a multistakeholder approach was premised on the pragmatic assumption that the operation of treaty bodies mostly relies on the activities of these various actors, and hence that reform ideas must flow from them as well.[23]

Beyond reform efforts, multistakeholderism is increasingly becoming a new avenue of international lawmaking, perhaps an informal one. Several studies have shown that an informal international lawmaking, that embraces new actors, follows new processes, and produces new types of laws, has emerged.[24] This alternative route of international lawmaking relies on transnational networks that have expert knowledge on specific issues, adopts an inclusive consensus-based multistakeholder process and the outcome of which are flexible instruments. The merit of this process lies primarily in addressing the legitimacy deficit of traditional international law by following an inclusive and consensus-based approach—also referred to as 'thick consensus'—of lawmaking, as opposed to 'thin consensus' that is based solely on State consent.[25] That the process embraces stakeholders with expertise in particular issues further means that outcomes of these process are normatively superior and hence likely to achieve desirable goals in practice. Examples of international lawmaking where multistakeholder participation played a key role include the drafting of the Disability Rights Convention and the Ruggie Principles.[26] With such increasing appeal to multistakeholderism, the idea of installing the privacy forum is likely to materialize should it be taken seriously.

3.1.2. Rebuilding Cooperative Dialogue

The second premise is that constructive dialogue, as opposed to litigation, and persuasion, as opposed to confrontation, are practical ways of enhancing the protection of human rights. This is mainly because radical improvement in the state of human rights protection is unlikely to be achieved with the current weak structure of the institutional machinery. As much as the prospects of a world human rights court are infeasible and undesirable, frequent treaty body reform efforts are also unlikely to bring about the desirable level of effectiveness in the human rights

---

[21] Strengthening the United Nations Human Rights Treaty Body System, Report of the High Commissioner for Human Rights, UN Doc A/66/860 (26 June 2012) 11.

[22] See Suzanne Egan, 'Strengthening the United Nations Human Rights Treaty Body System' (2013) 13 Human Rights Law Review 209, 213–14.

[23] ibid, 214.

[24] See generally Joost Pauwelyn and others, 'When Structures Become Shackles: Stagnation and Dynamics in International Law Making' (2014) 25 European Journal of International Law 733; see also Joost Pauwelyn and others (eds), *Informal International Lawmaking* (Oxford University Press 2012).

[25] ibid, 740–42.

[26] See, eg, Grainne de Burca, 'Human Rights Experimentalism' (2017) 111 The American Journal of International Law 277, 283.

system. Backlog of individual communications and overdue State reports, for instance, at the HR Committee—added to the prevalent compliance problem[27]—attest to the fact that this route towards enhancing the protection of human rights is structurally inadequate. This calls for an additional mechanism that revitalizes and entrenches the co-operative dialogue practiced, to some degree, in the UN treaty body system and the UPR mechanism.

One such possible way is by investing more on fostering multistakeholder dialogue. Multistakeholder dialogue would be instrumental in raising the awareness of and persuading actors, particularly States towards the importance and strategies of strengthening human rights protection. As Alston notes, the best method in the international human rights enterprise is persuasion and building confidence in the system.[28] The benefit of a multi-level dialogue is that it would bring stakeholders from all levels and create transnational networks of dialogue and co-operation. This, as Charlesworth writes, would contribute towards improving the protection of human rights by creating a 'regulatory web of influence' that combines the efforts of various actors, including those at the grass-root level.[29] Such transnational networks wield considerable 'soft powers' which, by filling the void in hard power, may be marshalled towards incrementally solving specific cross-border challenges.[30]

A network of governance that is built among human rights groups at the local level would lead to an improvement in the level of human rights protection. Repeated interactions of States with transnational networks and other actors at the local level has the capacity to gradually 'socialize' States to accept human rights standards.[31] This iterative process would create a pattern of State behaviour that would over time find translation and internationalization in domestic law and practice.[32] The same observation applies to the private sector where interaction would facilitate understanding and consensus. In practice, such interaction between human rights communities and the technology sector will, for example, allow human rights considerations to be taken in designing new technologies.[33] In

[27] See Annual Report of the Human Rights Committee to the General Assembly, GAOR, 72nd sess, UN Doc A/72/40 (March 2017) para 39 (complaining that many States parties have failed to implement the views adopted under the Optional Protocol).

[28] Philip Alston, 'The Populist Challenge to Human Rights' (2017) 9 Journal of Human Rights Practice 1, 3.

[29] Hilary Charlesworth, 'A Regulatory Perspective on the International Human Rights System' in Peter Drhaos (ed), *Regulatory Theory: Foundations and Applications* (Australian National University Press 2017) 360.

[30] See Ian Goldin, *Divided Nations: Why Global Governance is Failing, and What We Can Do About It* (Oxford University Press 2013) 112.

[31] See Margaret Keck and Kathryn Sikkink, *Activists Beyond Borders: Advocacy Networks in International Politics* (Cornell University Press 1998) 16, 60, 214; see also Thomas Risse and Kathryn Sikkink, 'The Socialization of International Human Rights Norms in Domestic Practices: Introduction' in Thomas Risse and others (eds), *The Power of Human Rights: International Norms and Domestic Change* (Cambridge University Press 1999) 1–39.

[32] See Harold Koh, 'Rosco Pound Lecture: Transnational Legal Process' (1996) 75 Nebraska Law Review 181, 203–05.

[33] See Mathias Risse, 'Human Rights and Artificial Intelligence: An Urgently Needed Agenda' (2019) Human Rights Quarterly 1, 11.

that sense, the privacy forum would be a suitable platform to bring around the table relevant stakeholders and foster dialogue on privacy issues of mutual concern.

3.1.3. Encouragement of Human Rights

As a movement, the international human rights system is a gradual and slow process—and in that sense, it involves ongoing debates and struggle.[34] As much as there are adherents to principles of human rights protection, there has always been resistance to it. And what characterizes the movement is that it is an ongoing struggle against such resistance. This dictates an approach that is aligned to the reality of the human rights project that espouses engaging in continued dialogue among various stakeholders. Such an approach would involve ways of fostering mutual understanding and sustained dialogue. This partly captures what Higgins terms the notion of 'encouragement of human rights' which involves 'invocation, interpretation and exhortation' of human rights to cajole and nudge States and the private sector towards human rights compliance.[35] Resort, then, can be made to political pressure on States (and possibly corporations) that fail to engage or resist dialogue. Indeed, even in regional human rights systems where binding judicial decisions are made, the level of effectiveness is relative, and has a political element at the core.

Political pressure is the key tool of enforcing binding decisions of regional courts such as the ECtHR.[36] Decisions of the Strasbourg Court are overseen by the Committee of Ministers, which is a political body, and hence its enforcement involves political considerations.[37] And more often, political pressure falls short in yielding compliance. Russia, for instance, has declined to implement over 250 decisions of the ECtHR that found violations of human rights in Chechnya and the Northern Caucasus.[38] Russia has also recently questioned the authority of the Court's judgments rendered by judges in the selection of whom it did not participate at CoE's Parliamentary Assembly.[39] This adds to the increasing signs of retreat from the Court by a number of other CoE member States. But importantly, this lends weight to the argument that, instead of traditional enforcement through sanctions, dialogical mechanisms are more likely to be relatively effective. The

---

[34] See Christian Tomuschat, *Human Rights: Between Idealism and Realism* (Oxford University Press 3rd edn, 2014) 431.

[35] See Rosalyn Higgins, *Themes and Theories: Selected Essays, Speeches and Writings in International Law* (Oxford University Press Vol I, 2009) 498–99.

[36] See Eva Brems, 'Introduction: Rewriting Decisions from a Perspective of Human Rights Integration' in Eva Brems and Ellen Desmet (eds), *Integrating Human Rights in Practice: Rewriting Human Rights Decisions* (Edward Elgar 2017) 5.

[37] See Alston (n 13) 204.

[38] See Philip Leach, The Continuing Utility of International Human Rights Mechanisms? (EJIL: Talk!, 1 November 2017) <http://bit.ly/2z9lEeu>.

[39] See Andrew Drzemczewski and Kanstantsin Dzehtsiarou, Painful Relations Between the Council of Europe and Russia (EJIL: Talk!, 28 September 2018) <https://bit.ly/2RTBfoD>. In the wake of the war in Ukraine, Russia has ceased to be a State party to the European Convention on Human Rights.

proposed forum would be instrumental in facilitating such dialogue on the right to privacy.

In summary, securing human rights, including the right to privacy, must rely more on dialogue than litigation to bear fruit. Sanction as a primary tool of ensuring human rights is not always successful. More so in the international legal order where no real authority of imposing sanctions exists in the first place. Instead of pushing for drastic reform to achieve such authority, entrenching dialogical approaches is needed. Creation of the privacy forum is, therefore, the way forward on that front.

3.2. Roles of the Privacy Forum

If the underlying premises of the multistakeholder privacy forum are persuasive, the next step is considering the specific functions of the forum. The privacy forum must assume the following two set of roles. The primary role of the forum should be to facilitate consensus and co-operation among relevant actors that play key roles in the protection of the right to privacy in the digital space. Exchanging best practices among these stakeholders on the protection of digital privacy is the other possible role for the forum. These roles of the forum are consistent with the role of existing multistakeholder forums in the UN human rights system. Among existing multistakeholder UN forums, the Forum on Minority Issues assumes related roles. The forum was established in 2007 by the Human Rights Council (HR Council) to serve as a platform for dialogue among relevant stakeholders, including States, UN specialized agencies and civil society organizations.[40] Its stated aim is to be a platform for promoting dialogue and co-operation on issues pertaining to minority rights and to exchange best practices, challenges, opportunities, and initiatives for the further implementation of the Minority Rights Declaration.[41] Another example is the Forum on Business and Human Rights. This forum is created to discuss trends and challenges in the implementation of the Ruggie Principles, and to further co-operation among stakeholders.[42] As such, both forums do not have any normative role, and hence, have no decision-making mandate.

In line with these precedents, the proposed privacy forum should assume two complementary roles. The primary mission of the forum should be encouraging

---

[40] See *Forum on Minority Issues*, HRC Res 6/15, 6th sess, UN Doc A/HRC/RES/6/15 (28 September 2007). cf Mandate indefinitely renewed by *Forum on Minority Issues*, HRC Res 19/23, 19th sess, Agenda item 5, UN Doc A/HRC/RES/19/23 (10 April 2012).

[41] ibid, para 5.

[42] See *Human Rights and Transnational Corporations and Other Business Enterprises*, HRC Res 14/4, 17th sess, Agenda item 3, UN Doc A/HRC/RES/17/4 (6 July 2011) paras 12–18. As discussed in chapter 2, the Ruggie Principles (and the Working Group that oversees the framework) does not address the right to privacy—and perhaps would not in the long-run—due to the narrowly defined remit of the framework. This would not, therefore, make the proposed privacy forum a redundancy.

the emergence of broader understanding on core digital privacy issues among States, civil society groups, technology companies, and other relevant stakeholders. Guided by the key digital privacy standards enunciated in the soft law considered in chapter 7, the forum would be a useful platform to develop consensus gradually. Such dialogue will especially be useful in leading to compromises on issues where there exists competing, and sometimes, conflicting interests. Unlike litigation, dialogue is more likely to be useful in reconciling conflicting interests such as fundamental rights, national security, and commercial interests. By bringing together actors with diverging interests and ideological positions around the table, mutual understanding can be established towards balancing these competing interests. Dialogue might not result in a radical and immediate change in ideological stances or business models of those actors. But the lack of any other better alternative such as a robust adjudicative system at the international level makes it the best possible alternative.

Establishing broader consensus will have significant practical implications. Considering the transnational element in international privacy protection as well as the role of private actors, the active involvement of various stakeholders is key. As highlighted in chapter 1, a key feature of the 'privacy problem' in the digital age is the increasing prominence of technology companies. Transnational corporations hold a unique position in the digital place that affects the enjoyment of human rights, including the right to privacy. Their central role in the governance, operation, and provision of the Internet infrastructure and services thus reinforces the importance of the dialogue. Worth emphasizing here is also the complex and dynamic nature of human rights protection in the digital age, which makes the case for a multistakeholder approach even more compelling. It requires the knowledge, experience, and control of both State and non-State actors. The technical aspects of the subject make the role of the private sector as much important as that of States. States remain to be pivotal actors of international co-operation. But other actors too play an increasingly crucial role in supplementing, assisting, correcting, and continuously challenging rules of international regulation.[43] This is particularly the case for privacy given the role of technology both in its protection and invasion.

Beyond reconciling competing interests, dialogue at the forum could be a useful platform for exchanging best practices among relevant stakeholders. Results of the dialogue among participants of the forum compiled through reports could provide useful insights to human rights bodies at many levels. From the HR Committee, the UPR mechanism, regional human rights courts to domestic courts and regulators, the recommendations of the forum will be useful. What makes this particularly useful is that privacy issues in the digital age are not only complex but also

---

[43]   See Joost Paulwelyn and others, 'Informal International Lawmaking: An Assessment and Template to Keep It Both Effective and Accountable' in Joost Paulwelyn and others (eds), *Informal International Lawmaking* (Oxford University Press 2012) 504.

highly dynamic. It is obviously a challenging undertaking for part-time bodies like the HR Committee to keep fully abreast of new developments in the digital arena. Added to that is the frequent turnover of Committee members,[44] and the fact that the Committee oversees an omnibus treaty containing a diverse array of rights, as opposed to a specialized treaty on a specific human right.[45] This is in a stark contrast to regional courts such as the ECtHR, which at least does not operate on a part-time basis. And of course, the ECtHR is supported by a dedicated research division and judicial assistants as well as the Court's Registry when, for instance, a need for research of international best practices arises.[46] The establishment of the forum, by providing timely expert advice, would assist in mitigating this inherent limitation of the treaty body system. Beyond treaty bodies, the privacy forum would also provide thematic contributions to the SRP.

Perhaps an incidental role for the forum is to serve as a platform to deliberate on and highlight the formal determinations on the right to privacy of various UN bodies. This will be useful to consider whether and the extent to which they have been put into effect by relevant UN bodies, States and non-State actors. In a way, this would also complement the work of the Rapporteurs on Follow-up of Views and Concluding Observations of the HR Committee. These rapporteurs are selected among members of the Committee,[47] but the enormity of the task—due to years of backlog, added to the part-time nature of their role—makes the follow-up less effective. In complementing the work of the rapporteurs, the forum thus would be a softer mechanism of oversight. In putting the work of the Committee in the spotlight, the 'visibility' concerns of the UN treaty body system would be mitigated, which is sometimes raised as one reason for its infectiveness.[48] As the work of the HR Committee is likely to feature in the agenda of the privacy forum, visibility of the Committee would accordingly increase. Visibility, in turn, would increase the profile of the Committee, stimulate its jurisprudence and ultimately contribute towards better compliance.

---

[44] See Seibert-Fohr, 'The Human Rights Committee' in Gerd Oberleitner (ed), *International Human Rights Institutions, Tribunals and Courts* (Springer 2018) 122 (noting that half of the Committee's members are elected biannually and one third of members are replaced every two years).

[45] Treaty bodies, including the HR Committee, now face more challenges due to budgetary cuts. See UN Budget Shortfalls Seriously Undermine the Work of the Human Rights Treaty Bodies (OHCHR Press Release, 17 May 2019).

[46] See Angelika Nußberger, 'The ECtHR's Use of Decisions of International Courts and Quasi-Judicial Bodies' in Amrei Muller and Hege Kjos (eds), *Judicial Dialogue and Human Rights* (Cambridge University Press 2017) 420.

[47] See Rules of Procedure of the Human Rights Committee, UN Doc CCPR/C/3/Rev.12 (4 January 2021) Rule 106.

[48] The former UN Secretary-General Annan had, for instance, noted that the UN treaty body system remains little known. See In Larger Freedom: Towards Development, Security and Human Rights for All, UN Doc A/59/2005 (21 March 2005) para 147.

In sum, the forum would be a platform for all actors to deliberate and narrow divergences on current and emerging issues of securing digital privacy. With this, it would assist in addressing the institutional challenges in international privacy law.

3.3. Procedural Considerations

In realizing the proposed forum, two procedural matters must be addressed. The first concerns the organizational structure of the body. Membership and participation procedures of the UN forums on Minority Issues and Business and Human Rights can readily be adapted to the proposed privacy forum. There are two alternatives to creating the advisory body. One is that the proposed soft law on the right to privacy, laid out in the preceding chapter, could create this forum, ie, through a Resolution of the UN General Assembly (UNGA). The other alternative—and perhaps in line with the tradition—is that it could be established by a Resolution of the HR Council, as in the case of the Forums on Minority Issues and Business and Human Rights. In the interest of being holistic, the former is perhaps more appropriate, more so to lift the authority of the forum with the imprimatur of the UNGA.

The privacy forum should meet at least once in a year for two days. A two-day meeting annually can be considered too short. Indeed, this point has been raised in relation to the Forum on Minority Issues.[49] But given the resource strain that the creation of a new forum may have as well as the budgetary cutbacks at the UN human rights system noted above, a two-day meeting seems sensible. But one must not also lose sight of the fact that unlike the minority rights and/or the business and human rights forums, deliberations of the privacy forum would focus on a single right and hence would not be as prone to problems of time shortage.

Attendance at the privacy forum must be open to all stakeholders. But given the nature of the topic in question, all relevant UN bodies in the area of privacy should be made part of the forum. UN treaty bodies, particularly the HR Committee, should be represented in the forum by one or more of its members so as to draw relevant insights from discussions at the forum and to bring to light the jurisprudence of the Committee. Engaging the Committee would, for instance, be one way to inculcate the soft law into the jurisprudence of the Committee. Fox reports that the participation of treaty bodies in the Forum on Minority Issues has considerably increased reference to the UN Declaration on Minority Rights in their jurisprudence.[50] Similarly, the soft law on the right to privacy can shape the jurisprudence of the HR Committee through dialogue at the privacy forum.

---

[49] See Graham Fox, 'The United Nations Forum on Minority Issues and Its Role in Promoting the UN Declaration on the Rights of Persons Belonging to National or Ethnic, Religious and Linguistic Minorities' in Ugo Caruso and Rainer Hofmann (eds), *The United Nations Declaration on Minorities: An Academic Account on the Occasion of Its 20th Anniversary: 1992–2012* (Brill 2015) 90, 94.

[50] ibid, 93.

As in the case of the Forum on Minority Issues,[51] the SRP should 'guide' the privacy forum and transmit its recommendations to the HR Council and perhaps the UNGA through the formal reporting procedure. Assigning a role for the SRP at the forum is plausible on many levels. One is that, as noted above, there is a precedent by which Special Rapporteurs are assigned to steer the dialogue in several forums established by the UN. But more crucially, the SRP is already 'encouraged' by UNGA Privacy Resolutions to contribute towards multistakeholder dialogues on the right to privacy.[52] This would also be in line with the mandate's recognition of the fact that mutual co-operation and dialogue play an important role in fostering global privacy protection. With that said, it is important to ensure that thematic priorities of the Special Rapporteur do not cloud, as Fox counsels in the context of the Forum on Minority Issues, the agenda items of the privacy forum.[53] The role of the SRP must, thus, be restricted to channelling the discussion, not setting the agenda of the privacy forum. This would avoid the effect of changing thematic priorities of different mandate holders on the work of the privacy forum. And indeed, it is naturally aligned with the multistakeholder feature of the forum where agenda items are set collectively, in a spirit of consensus.

The inaugural SRP had launched a multistakeholder initiative called the International Intelligence Oversight Forum. Created in 2016, this Forum is an annual event held for the purpose of 'collective identification of challenges to privacy and freedom of expression in the gathering of intelligence as well as best practices which could provide better safeguards and remedies'.[54] But the effectiveness of the intelligence forum may be affected by its constricted remit as well as lack of inclusiveness demonstrated so far. The thematic focus is on surveillance, and as such, leaves out other aspects of privacy in the digital age such as data protection. But more importantly, the level of participation in the first two events suggests lack of inclusiveness. In the first event in 2016, for example, only twenty countries took part in the forum and only 'some members of civil society'.[55] No participation from the privacy sector, particularly the rather important stakeholders—ie, Internet corporations—has been reported. The lack of inclusive participation of relevant stakeholders reduces the capacity, and ultimately, legitimacy of the SRP's unilateral initiative.[56] The privacy forum proposed in this chapter not only attends to this

---

[51] See HRC Res 19/23 (n 40) para 10.
[52] See, eg, GA Res 71/199 (n 15) para 8.
[53] Fox (n 49) 90, 105.
[54] See Report of the Special Rapporteur on the Right to Privacy, Joseph Cannataci, UN Doc A/71/368 (30 August 2016) para 12.
[55] See Report of the Special Rapporteur on the Right to Privacy, Joseph Cannataci, UN Doc A/HRC/34/60 (24 February 2017) para 3. Participation of States rose only to thirty in the 2017 event. See Report of the Special Rapporteur on the Right to Privacy, Joseph Cannataci, UN Doc A/HRC/37/62 (28 February 2018) para 12. Representatives from governments rose to forty during the 2019 event. See Report of the Special Rapporteur on the Right to Privacy, Joseph Cannataci, UN Doc A/HRC/43/52 (24 March 2020) para 11.
[56] Moreover, the third and fourth events held in November 2018 and October 2019 respectively were said to be a closed-door event. See details at <https://bit.ly/2CEMuLG> and <https://bit.ly/3JUNmg4>.

shortcoming by envisaging a multistakeholder forum where all voices are heard but one that brings a level of legitimacy and authority to the forum through clear legal basis and mission.

A question might arise as to why there should be a multistakeholder forum for privacy but not for other rights, the protection of which faces no less significant challenges in the digital age. One such right is the right to freedom of expression. There is neither conceptual nor practical barrier for not extending the remit of the proposed forum to cover other digital rights, including freedom of expression. Indeed, there is already a parallel discourse, as alluded to in the preceding chapters, on freedom of expression on the Internet running at the HR Council since 2012. But it is vital to note that free speech jurisprudence at the UN is much more advanced in comparison with privacy. The HR Committee has, for instance, adopted an elaborate general comment and this has been further advanced by the jurisprudentially influential work of successive special rapporteurs on freedom of expression. Otherwise, broadening the scope of human rights covered in the forum would not be problematic; only a privacy forum is argued here owing to the scope of the book.

Perhaps another question is one of desirability: what is the added value of installing a new forum while there is, for example, the UN Internet Governance Forum (IGF) that could—and in fact does—consider privacy issues? Human Rights are, of course, important themes in Internet governance platforms such as the IGF. But as its name clearly indicates, the IGF is meant to deal with a number of non-human rights related themes. Complex and dynamic privacy issues could not possibly be examined in an annual four-day meeting with the required level of depth and rigour. That the notion of 'Internet governance' embraces a broad range of topics means it opens up extremely broad and unstructured discussions.[57] This is where the added value of the proposed privacy forum becomes evident as it offers the platform where more but focused discourse among stakeholders would occur.

3.4. The Forum and Limits of Multistakeholderism

To a large extent, a multistakeholder approach to governance is new to international law. As noted above, 'informal international law' is largely a new phenomenon.[58]

Due to the Covid-19 pandemic, the forum has not been held since. See Report of the Special Rapporteur on the Right to Privacy, Joseph Cannataci, UN Doc A/HRC/46/37(25 January 2021) Annex I, B.

[57] See Amanda Hubbard and Lee Bygrave, 'Internet Governance Goes Global' in Lee Bygrave and Jon Bing, *Internet Governance: Infrastructure and Institutions* (Oxford University Press 2009) 232–34.

[58] But see Christine Kaufmann, 'Multi-stakeholder Participation in Cyberspace' (2016) 26 Swiss Review of International and European Law 217, 218–21 (tracing multi-stakeholder trends in intergovernmental bodies in the nineteenth century).

But the experiment in the past decade or so in the broader field of Internet governance, even where it is regarded as an 'inchoate institution',[59] reveals that risks are present. The relevant question here, then, is whether these concerns associated with multistakeholderism would apply to the proposed privacy forum. As shall be shown below, these concerns do not necessarily extend to the privacy forum due to its organizational mission and constitution. Like the forums on minority rights and on business and human rights, the proposed privacy forum would not have a normative or decision-making role. But there are still some lessons to be drawn so as to pre-emptively lessen drawbacks of multistakeholderism in the broader Internet governance policy discourse.

Three concerns are often raised in relation to multistakeholder platforms. A primary concern is the lack of proportionate representation, particularly of actors from the global south including States and non-State Actors.[60] The Internet Corporation for Assigned Names and Numbers (ICANN), a key player in the Internet's addressing system, is one organization that practices a multistakeholder approach to governance but often comes under criticism for inequitable representation. Part of the criticism is that its stakeholder groups are significantly dominated by States, members of civil society, and the private sector from western countries, particularly the United States. This sometimes gives the impression that multistakeholderism is used as a 'cover' for American 'techno-imperialism',[61] and being used to sustain vested interests.[62] Related to the problem of inclusion are language barriers and lack of technical expertise. The latter is particularly raised in connection with Internet technical bodies like the Internet Engineering Task Force (IETF).[63] Other barriers include funding constraints and organizational capacity.[64]

Lack of representation is inevitable when it comes to the privacy forum. The all too known digital divide will come as a barrier to equitable representation from developing countries. Perhaps, these countries may be keen to invest towards bridging the divide rather than participating in the forum. But the fact that the forum is envisioned as a UN body, just like other forums currently running, means at least participation from State representatives would be broader. Resource constraint would rather be a hurdle to civil society groups from those countries. Unless some form of support towards correcting the imbalance is found, voices

---

[59] See Mary Raymond and Laura DeNardis, 'Multistakeholderism: Anatomy of An Inchoate Global Institution' (2015) 7 International Theory 572, 573.

[60] See Avri Doria, 'Use [and Abuse] of Multistakeholderism in the Internet' in Roxana Radu and others (eds), The Evolution of Global Internet Governance (Springer 2013) 123.

[61] See Richard Hill, 'Internet Governance: The Last Gasp of Colonialism, or Imperialism by other Means?' in Roxana Radu and others (eds), The Evolution of Global Internet Governance (Springer 2013) 83, 85, 90–92.

[62] See Raymond and DeNardis (n 59) 611.

[63] ibid, 597.

[64] See Jeannette Hofmann, 'Multi-stakeholderism in Internet Governance: Putting a Fiction into Practice' (2016) 1 Journal of Cyber Policy 29, 33.

of non-State actors from the global south will be limited.[65] In addressing this concern, the voluntary fund created by the OHCHR to increase participation from the developing part of the world in the Forum on Minority Issues could simply be emulated for the proposed privacy forum.[66] In that way, inclusivity of the privacy forum can be enhanced over time.

With lack of inclusive participation comes a legitimacy problem. Actors not involved in the making of decisions at multistakeholder forums may resist its legitimacy and decisions.[67] Legitimacy concerns then are more pronounced in multistakeholder fora like ICANN or IETF where consequential decisions—be it of policy or technical matters—are taken. Other multistakeholder forums like the IGF where no such decisions are made thus are mostly exempt from legitimacy deficit. Because the privacy forum is not a decision-making body, legitimacy would not, as such, be a concern. But it is possible that outcomes of the privacy forum may have a 'decisional potential', albeit indirectly. One such possibility is that outcomes of the dialogue at the privacy forum may earn 'legal effects' in practice. The HR Committee may, for instance, apply the ICCPR's privacy provision based on a view that prevailed at the forum in relation to a matter a State (and its citizens or civil society) did not take part. Such instances may ultimately generate a legitimacy concern. But the best way to prevent such a concern is to work towards gradually increasing participation at the forum, as alluded to above.

The third concern relates to transparency and accountability in decision making processes. Once decisions are taken in a multistakeholder forum, there are limited avenues to challenge decisions and even to seek remedies.[68] An aspect of this concern is that there is little room for periodic monitoring and review of decisions and policies. That the privacy forum is open to anyone, and that the outcome of its deliberations would be released in the form of regular reports, adds to its transparency. But accountability issues are unlikely to emerge because, again, the forum would not make strictly binding decisions.

In summary, most concerns associated with a multistakeholder approach to Internet governance do not fully extend to the privacy forum. However, where there are risks to inclusivity, transparency, and accountability, a sensible way to mitigate such problems is through long-term initiatives of broadening participation from relevant actors.

---

[65] See Samantha Besson and Jose Marti, 'Legitimate Actors of International Law-making: Towards a Theory of International Democratic Representation' (2018) 9 Jurisprudence: An International Journal of Legal and Political Thought 504, 538 (advocating 'affirmative action' like quotas to civil society groups representing weaker or invisible groups).
[66] See HRC Res 19/23 (n 40) para 3.
[67] See Kaufmann (n 58) 218, 224–25.
[68] See Doria (n 60) 129–30.

4. Conclusion

This chapter explored virtues of a dialogical approach as a pragmatic way of lessening the institutional void in international privacy law. It argued that installing a multistakeholder privacy forum would considerably address institutional aspects of international law's privacy problem. Drawing upon precedents in the UN human rights system and support for a multistakeholder approach in the ongoing UN privacy discourse, the chapter has outlined rationales and functions of the proposed forum. As shown in this chapter, such a forum is especially suited to the international protection of digital privacy for two reasons. One is that it is a more practical way of addressing institutional problems present in international law. Unlike hitherto radical reform ideas proposed by scholars, installing a privacy forum would not require reinventing the wheel. That makes it politically as well as economically feasible. As a dialogical mechanism, the privacy forum will also prove to be more responsive to the realities of the digital age where privacy threats are dynamic, complex, and involve multiple actors. Orthodox means of human rights adjudication such as judicial process are not suited to attend to these peculiarities of the 'privacy problem'.

A prime role for the forum would, then, be to serve as a platform where all relevant stakeholders on the right to privacy would deliberate on current and emerging issues regarding the right to privacy and share best practices. A multistakeholder privacy forum would be a supplement to the existing institutional machinery by both providing expertise on the right to privacy and facilitating creation of a consensus and facilitating co-operation among stakeholders. In steering the dialogue at the forum, the international soft law argued for in chapter 7 would provide a roadmap.

Summary and Conclusion

> [The UN system is able] to survive, grow and adapt but it achieves pro-
> gress only through historical cycles of modest adaptation and change.
>
> Weiss and Daws (eds), *The Oxford Handbook on
> the United Nations* (OUP 2018) 19

1. The 'Privacy Problem' and the Role of International Law

1.1. In Search for a Role

This book examined the question of how international law should respond to the challenges of securing the right to privacy in the digital age. In addressing that question, it focused especially on three international privacy initiatives: IBRs, the ongoing UN discourse on the 'right to privacy in the digital age', and the Convention 108(+) system. It investigated the role of such initiatives in making the international law of privacy fit for purpose in the digital age. In doing this, the book makes three contributions to the literature. First, it provides a sound foundation for practical reform by exploring the extent to which international privacy law is well-equipped in the digital age. The proliferation of reform initiatives is not matched by exploration of what is really lacking in existing law. The book has demonstrated where, how, and why international privacy law falters in securing digital privacy. Thus, it fills the void in the international law scholarship, and to an extent, the IBRs literature.

Second, the book makes an original contribution by investigating the role of international privacy initiatives in helping realize the long-sought international privacy framework. More particularly, it examined the extent to which such initiatives reimagine the current international law of privacy in the digital age. It did so by situating such rather diverse and sporadic initiatives in international law. It has demonstrated the various ways in which the IBRs project interacts with and shapes international privacy law. This lessens the gap in the international law scholarship as well as the IBRs literature. Third, the book joins the debate on how international law should respond to the 'privacy problem'. In that sense, it contributes to the

Privacy and the Role of International Law in the Digital Age. Kinfe Yilma, Oxford University Press. © Kinfe Yilma 2023.
DOI: 10.1093/oso/9780192887290.003.0009

literature in showing a plausible way of reimagining international privacy law in the digital age. But going beyond the current debate, the book builds on the foundations of the existing legal framework and progressive visions of global privacy initiatives in exploring the appropriateness of an international law response to the privacy problem. In addition, the book adopted a holistic approach to privacy by combining the disparate regimes of international law—ie, human rights law, data privacy law, and IBRs—in considering the privacy problem. This builds the discursive bridge between the fragmented discourse on the right to privacy in the digital age by combining insights from the fields of data privacy law and IBRs to the broader international law discipline which, on its own, has rarely examined the question of how international law could, or should, respond to the 'privacy problem' in the digital age.

Related to the above is the book's contribution to the privacy scholarship on the potential role of international law in upholding digital privacy. By and large, the (data) privacy literature has had a particular focus on the role, or the lack thereof, of national and regional laws. In undertaking an international law examination of themes that cross-cut privacy and data protection law, the book introduces to the literature the role of international law in securing the right to privacy in the digital environment, alongside national and regional systems of protection. In a similar vein, the examination in the book shows that privacy and data protection in the 'international' context is not restricted to the privacy provisions of the UDHR and the ICCPR. Beyond these high-level principles, the international law of privacy—as considered in this book—consists of a broad range of norms and principles as well as sources.

1.2. Looking Through the Lens of Global Emergent Law

The book is inspired by the proliferation of multi-level initiatives for a set of new or expanded human rights standards for the digital age. While such initiatives existed since the early days of the Internet, they have gained momentum in the wake of the Snowden revelations in mid-2013. Breaking away from its momentary tradition, the idea of a global privacy framework has since become more coherent and prominent in law and judicial making. Nothing better illustrates this point as the adoption of (or proposal for) IBRs legislation in several countries as well as the evolving UN privacy discourse. Nevertheless, the role of such privacy initiatives and their place in international law remain largely unexamined. With the recent prominence of such initiatives in lawmaking at various levels, there is a need for careful analysis. Even more so, given the urgent need for reform in international privacy law. This book represents an attempt in that direction, examining the role of global emergent norms in reimagining current international law of privacy. But a question might arise as to the rationale for choosing global privacy initiatives more generally and the three case studies in particular in this study.

At the most basic level, this case study approach offers a unique vantage point. As shown in this book, a common thread in global privacy initiatives is the emphasis on the need for a new international privacy framework. Although not always overtly stated, such initiatives proceed from the premise that something is missing in the current framework that makes it unfit for the digital age. But this tendency to assume gaps in existing law invites an examination of what really lacks in the present legal framework. The role of emerging privacy initiatives in addressing gaps must thus be considered against the backdrop of international privacy law. Put differently, virtues of global privacy initiatives may not clearly be grasped unless the interplay with existing law is investigated.

As explored in chapters 4 and 5, IBRs and the ongoing UN privacy discourse imagine a relatively progressive vision for the right to privacy. Unlike high-level proposals of technology companies or academic commentaries, these initiatives provide normative contours of the right to privacy in the digital age. Moving beyond the rather vague and fragmented approach in present international law, these initiatives tend to reimagine the right to privacy in the light of new developments. IBRs, for instance, unpacks the right to privacy into a set of sub-rights while the UN Privacy discourse envisions (Internet) corporations as duty bearers. Using such progressive initiatives as case studies, thus, provides the angle from which international privacy law may be reimagined in the digital age. Albeit in a different dimension, the Convention 108+ system—the third case study of the book—too wields a potential to evolve into a universal instrument of data privacy due to its 'open' character.

At a practical level, the case study approach offers a fresh perspective on how to reimagine this area of law in the digital age. When considering the extent to which gaps in existing law may be filled with emergent norms, one gets a clearer picture of what approach is likely to be practical. If the gaps in the existing law are clear— and the boundaries of emergent norms are evident, it is then possible to imagine a reform alternative that can lessen those gaps while drawing up on the progressive visions of emergent law. In that sense, the role of international law in securing the right to privacy can clearly be shown. This book, therefore, critically looked at the possibility of addressing the 'privacy problem' through the lens of three significant global privacy initiatives.

2. Findings in the Book

What follows provides a summary of the three key findings of the book.

2.1. International Law of Privacy and
Its Shortcomings in the Digital Age

The first finding in the book is that current international law of privacy is ill-equipped to address the 'privacy problem' in the digital age. As demonstrated in chapter 2, the (international) human right to privacy framework is replete with legal and structural gaps. Not only are the scope and meaning of the right to privacy vaguely defined but existing institutional arrangements are not best positioned to translate the vaguely worded right to meet the new realities of the digital age. This has, in turn, resulted in a privacy jurisprudence that is thinner than its regional counterparts. The problem is more pronounced with respect to the UN data privacy framework which, as shown in chapter 3, is characterized by deep normative and institutional dispersion as well as comparatively outmoded data privacy norms. A characteristic feature of the UN data privacy framework is that it largely is a patchwork of data privacy norms scattered across a range of soft law instruments. With no dedicated institutional machinery, fragmentary international data privacy norms are now superseded by modern data privacy rights, principles, and norms elsewhere.

Putting this finding in a historical context, the book further located causes of international privacy law's weak structures in the drafting history of key privacy instruments. As chapters 2 and 3 uncovered, Cold War politics that clouded the drafting, negotiation, and adoption of relevant privacy instruments is largely responsible for the ambiguous formulation of privacy rights, principles, and norms as well as the creations of a weaker implementation framework. More crucially, the book traced marks of 'inattention' to the right to privacy—in contrast with other human rights—during the drafting of the UDHR and the ICCPR. Lesser attention meant ambiguous formulation of the right to privacy. That Article 17 of the ICCPR simply replicated UDHR's privacy provision meant that the mis-formulations not only remain unrectified but also are repeated in privacy provisions of the ICCPR and subsequent specialized human rights treaties. The book has similarly found traces of inattention during the protracted processes of installing the international data privacy framework, particularly the UN Data Privacy Guidelines.

Regarding technology companies, the book has shown that current international law of privacy is yet to recognize and effectively constrain their unique role in the protection (and violation) of digital privacy. The current UN framework on 'business and human rights' has failed to put (Internet) corporations within its remit. While it theoretically applies to 'all' human rights, and regardless of the sector in which corporations operate, the evidence so far shows that only 'brick-and-mortar' corporations are still its sole focus. The book further demonstrated that (Internet) businesses are not within the sight of the ongoing treaty process that seeks to translate the Ruggie Principles into a binding treaty. And, the draft treaty maintains the same proviso in that it covers 'all' sectors as well as human rights, but little in the draft text seems to be geared towards corporations of 'cyberspace' and hence digital privacy.

By contrast, the role of (Internet) corporations is being addressed in the UN privacy discourse which, as considered in chapter 5, began around the same time as the treaty process. The absence of some symbiosis between the two processes may however ultimately affect prospects of a tangible global legislative response. More critically, the UN privacy discourse has heralded a new front when envisioning corporate human rights responsibilities in a novel 'right-specific' fashion. This would invite challenging questions, for example: should the future of corporate human rights obligations in the digital context be 'right-specific'—as opposed to the current 'generic' all-rights approach? What are the implications of the 'right-specific' approach to the current UN 'business and human rights' framework? What would it mean, in practice, if the Privacy Resolutions evolve into a treaty? Which corporations would be held to account, and how, under such a treaty regime? Such questions are beyond the scope of the book but merit in-depth research, both doctrinal and empirical.

2.2. Global Privacy Initiatives and Their Limits

The second main finding in the book is that emerging privacy initiatives offer a progressive vision for digital privacy, but several shortcomings limit their legal significance. The role of these initiatives in reimagining international privacy law were examined based on a three-level framework of analysis: 'freestanding', 'contributory', and 'catalytic' roles. As shown in chapter 4, the IBRs project envisions the right to privacy in an elaborate manner by which a 'subset of privacy rights' is often provided. The tendency to flesh out the content of the right to privacy clarifies the scope and meaning of the right based on its growing understanding in the digital age. To that extent, IBRs points towards a way in which normative obfuscations of the right in international law may be lessened. But, the 'freestanding' role of the IBRs project is weakened by its fragmented and unco-ordinated nature. That the IBRs project is a constellation of multi-level, but momentary initiatives, means no freestanding legislative outcome, like an 'international IBRs', is likely. This leaves it only with a limited 'contributory' role of informing the substance of other practical initiatives. To some degree, signs of this role are visible; for example, in the content of the evolving UN Privacy Resolutions. But as shown in this book, the contributory role of IBRs has been negligible. What, then, remains of IBRs is the potential for a more focused global privacy reform initiative to draw from its progressive visions: a 'catalytic' role.

Like the IBRs project, the UN Privacy discourse posits a progressive vision for the right to privacy with some modern privacy principles flagged in the

Resolutions. More importantly, the role of Internet corporations in the protection of the right to privacy are, as shown in chapter 5, increasingly being foreshadowed in the latest Resolutions adopted as part of the discourse. But several factors limit the freestanding role of the discourse in reimagining existing international law of privacy. One relates to the normative composition of the Resolutions and the way in which the discourse is progressing. Privacy Resolutions adopted as part of this discourse exhibit ambivalence and lack of thematic focus. Themes currently in vogue in international law discourse such as cybersecurity, cyber warfare, and new and emerging technologies risk side-tracking the rather progressive privacy norms flagged in the Resolutions.

Elements of the 'freedom of expression on the Internet' discourse at the HR Council are also increasingly spilling over to the Privacy Resolutions. This suggests that the degree to which the Privacy Resolutions would address key privacy principles, including those concerning the human rights responsibilities of corporations as well as States, is (and will be) limited. Such loss of direction reduces prospects of the discourse in developing into a meaningful legislative response. The discourse's limited freestanding role further undercuts its contributory role. The restricted and fuzzy normative reach of the Privacy Resolutions reduce the possibility of gradual accretion of customary norms or shaping of lawmaking and case law at national and regional levels. This leaves it with a 'catalytic' role by which it may shape the normative and methodological directions of a more focused and practical reform.

Beyond its present predicaments, the future of the ongoing UN privacy discourse does not seem entirely clear. Almost nine years since it began, there is no sign of culmination with the latest (and fourth!) UNGA Resolution urging the HR Council and the OHCHR to remain 'seized' of the matter. No effort that seeks to exploit the political capital of the discourse towards a more concrete international law measure appears to be forthcoming. One of the discourse's outcomes, the mandate of SRP, is yet to orient its work with the discourse. The mandate's surveillance treaty initiative and its several ambitious 'task forces', for instance, pay little heed to the discourse. But the catalytic role of the discourse, and the political capital exhibited in the discussions so far, would have offered some impetus to such initiatives. Thus, prospects of the privacy discourse are being frustrated not just by the usual difficulties of international lawmaking but also because of the disjoint with the mandate of the SRP.

No less bleak is the prospect of regional standards, especially the Convention 108+ system, evolving into an international law response to the privacy problem. Accession as an avenue of universalizing the Convention 108(+) system is yet to yield tangible results. Not only has the accession process been understandably slow but also that, thus far, it has covered a specific geographic area. The prospect of Convention 108 and its later iterations in the development of general international law in the field of data privacy is even more uncertain. Influencing the international data privacy jurisprudence at multiple levels is perhaps where the global potential of the Convention 108(+) system lies. Still a gradual process, but this path enables the Convention standards to find place in the progressive development of international law. To an extent, this—as shown in chapter 6—has started to occur somehow in the recent case law of the HR Committee and the ongoing privacy discourse at the UN. With a growing socialization of Convention 108 standards in UN processes as well as in other regional, sub-regional, and national mechanisms, consensus on widely accepted data privacy rights, principles, and governance norms may emerge.

2.3. Reimagining International Privacy Law in the Digital Age

The third key finding in the book is that the best way forward is to adopt a pragmatic approach to international privacy law. A central argument of the book is that a pragmatic approach that is 'incremental and historically minded', 'practical', 'multi-faceted', and 'programmatic' would make international privacy law better-equipped in the digital age. The 'incremental and historically minded' nature of the approach reflects the aim of proposed reform ideas to build on existing international legal frameworks on the right to privacy and well-established precedents in international law. 'Practicality' describes the feasibility of the reform proposals not only in the present political reality but also other attendant determining factors. What makes the overall approach 'multi-faceted' is the deliberate attempt at drawing insights from multiple sources in mapping out the right to privacy in the new realities of the digital age. The approach also has a 'programmatic' orientation by which it seeks to position international privacy law in a manner able to continually adapt to dynamism in the digital space.

Organized around these four elements, the book argued for an international soft law on the right to privacy and a dialogical approach to digital privacy. It is argued that this suite of measures would respectively lessen normative and institutional gaps in present international law of privacy. First, the book explored virtues of a soft law that would 'supplement' the right to privacy in international (hard) law. An international soft law would not only help clarify the scope of the right to privacy in the digital context, but also globalize emergent privacy standards and facilitate progressive development of privacy law. The book sets out the possible normative content of the proposed soft law, including the respective obligations and responsibilities of States and (Internet) corporations in the promotion, respect, and protection of the right to privacy in the digital context.

Second, the book considered virtues of a dialogical approach that would lessen institutional gaps. It is argued that a dialogical approach is especially suited to address challenges associated with implementation of human rights in the digital space for two reasons. One is that dialogue is a practical way forward because other radical means of addressing enforcement problems, for example through creation of a world human rights court, are unlikely to materialize in the present political reality. The other is that ongoing dialogue among key actors is a responsive and adaptive mechanism to the rather dynamic nature of the digital environment where privacy threats as well as protective mechanisms constantly change. Accordingly, the book argued for the creation of a multistakeholder privacy forum where current and emerging privacy issues are discussed on an ongoing basis. The book has emphasized the value of the forum towards building consensus, sharing best practices, and fostering co-operation among stakeholders. It has elaborated the rationales, functions, and structures of the forum. By building consensus on emerging issues, regular dialogue among relevant actors in the forum would be more effective than other avenues for ensuring implementation such as adjudication.

3. Seizing the Moment for Practical Reform

As shown throughout this book, the need for reform and that such reform should be pursued at the international level, is widely acknowledged. This is partly illustrated by the flurry of international privacy initiatives as well as calls for an international privacy framework. Nevertheless, while the proliferation of initiatives suggests the need for reform, the nature, form, and processes of such reform remain elusive. Common to most reform efforts is that they are not action-oriented and hence unlikely to result in a reform that realizes the much-desired international privacy framework. As demonstrated in this book, neither the IBRs project nor the ongoing UN privacy discourse—either in their own right or through a cross-fertilized process—would evolve into an international law response to the 'privacy problem' in the digital age. Nor will the unlikely universalization of the CoE Convention 108(+) system come to the rescue. In that sense, they do not respond to the exigencies of international privacy law reform.

There are at least two key factors that make global privacy initiatives less suited to the reform imperative. One is the occasional nature of the overall movement behind a new global privacy framework. More often than not, calls for and initiatives for such a framework emerge sporadically and then quickly disappear into obscurity. This particularly epitomizes the IBRs project which, as shown in chapter 4, has generally been a sporadic digital rights movement. The urgency of a global privacy framework cannot thus be realized via IBRs. The other factor is that global efforts of introducing some form of an international privacy framework, thus far, often proceed in a fragmented manner. With almost each reform initiative following its own path, it is unlikely that one will succeed in addressing its stated objective. As highlighted above, there is already a treaty process initiated by the SRP on government surveillance but proceeds in isolation of other reform efforts like the UN privacy discourse. Such fragmentation further frustrates possibilities of reform in the foreseeable future. But more crucially, this feature—added to the characteristically occasional nature of reform efforts—reflects a lack of clear vision for reimagining international privacy law in the digital age. The second factor is that the movement tends to overlook fundamental practical considerations. As argued in this book, while most global privacy initiatives (and the accompanying scholarship) seek to make existing law fit for a new age, they overlook an equally important feature of the digital age. That is the inherently dynamic and changing landscape of the digital space. The nature of privacy threats as well as actors involved in its protection and violation change constantly. Any international law response, thus, must be attentive to this reality. That is a major flaw of the movement behind, albeit sporadic, global privacy initiatives.

On top of being momentary and fragmented, most reform efforts are too ambitious to attend to the exigencies of reform. Any reform effort with any hard legalization approach in sight—in the present political reality of ideological contestations—is moot. What is urgently needed, as argued in this book, is a reform path that finds a way through this reality to an achievable alternative. A key component of the approach argued in this book is the 'practical' nature of the proposed reform ideas. In the face of limited political will on the part of some but influential States—added to the inevitable lobbying efforts of non-State interest groups—more ambitious reform efforts are currently implausible. But again, the concern is not limited to difficulties of having, for example, a privacy treaty adopted. Even if one or more of the privacy initiatives materialize, there is no guarantee that the state of global privacy protection would magically improve. A number of hurdles stand in the way of actually improving the enjoyment of the right to privacy (and other human rights that it enables). One is that orthodox human rights monitoring mechanisms have, time and again, proven to be inaccessible, time-taking, and hence ineffective. With such a conundrum comes the gradual decline of the momentum evoked by the Snowden revelations, which perhaps offered a historic opportunity towards rethinking the right to privacy in international law.

After a major post-ICCPR UN privacy agenda broached at the Tehran Conference on Human Rights in 1968—which eventually led to the adoption of the UN Data Privacy Guidelines in 1990—the Snowden debacle offers probably the second 'historical cycle', to use Weiss and Daws's words, of reimagining international privacy law in the digital age.[1] But this opportunity might be lost unless an achievable approach is pursued. This book was an attempt to point towards such practical reform ideas to adapt current international law of privacy to the

---

[1] Thomas Weiss and Sam Daws, 'The United Nations: Continuity and Change' in Thomas Weiss and Sam Daws (eds), *The Oxford Handbook on the United Nations* (Oxford University Press 2018) 19.

new realities of the digital age. The reform ideas are suited to the fabric of the UN system which—in line with the apt observation noted in the epigraph—is adaptive only to modest changes. Moving beyond the piecemeal, ungrounded, and haphazard nature of hitherto reform paths, this book argued for a modest but plausible reform approach that will make international privacy law better-equipped in the digital age.

Italian Declaration of Internet Rights (2015)

Preamble

The Internet has played a decisive role in redefining public and private space, structuring relationships between people and between people and institutions. It has erased borders and has created new ways of generating and utilizing knowledge. It has expanded the scope for people to participate directly in the public domain. It has changed how people work. It has fostered the development of a more open and free society. The Internet must be treated as a global resource and must satisfy the criterion of universality.

The European Union is currently the world region with the greatest constitutional protection of personal data, which is explicitly enshrined in Article 8 of the EU Charter of Fundamental Rights. This serves as a necessary point of reference for specifying the principles governing the operation of the Internet, including from a global perspective.

This Declaration of Internet Rights is founded on the full recognition of the liberty, equality, dignity and unique diversity of each individual. Preserving these rights is crucial to ensuring the democratic functioning of institutions and avoiding the predominance of public and private powers that may lead to a society of surveillance, control and social selection.

The Internet is an increasingly important space for the self-organization of individuals and groups, and it is a vital tool for promoting individual and collective participation in democratic processes as well as substantive equality.

The principles underpinning this Declaration also take account of the function of the Internet as an economic space that enables innovation, fair competition and growth in a democratic context.

A Declaration of Internet Rights is crucial to laying the constitutional foundation for supranational principles and rights.

Art. 1

(Recognition and protection of rights)

1. The fundamental rights of every individual enshrined in the Universal Declaration of Human Rights of the United Nations, the Charter of Fundamental Rights of the European Union, national constitutions and other relevant international declarations shall be protected on the Internet.
2. These rights shall be interpreted so as to ensure their enforceability on the Internet.
3. The recognition of rights on the Internet shall be based on comprehensive respect for the dignity, freedom, equality and diversity of each individual, which constitute the underlying principles for balancing these with other rights.

Art. 2

(Right to Internet access)

1. Access to the Internet is a fundamental right of all persons and a condition for their individual and social development.
2. Every person shall have the same right to access the Internet on equal terms, using appropriate and up-to-date technologies that remove all economic and social barriers.
3. The fundamental right to Internet access must be ensured with respect to its substantive prerequisites, not only as the mere possibility of connecting to the Internet.
4. Access shall include freedom of choice with regard to devices, operating systems, and applications, including distributed software.
5. Public institutions shall take the necessary measures to overcome all forms of digital divide, including those created by gender, economic condition or a situation of personal vulnerability or disability.

Art. 3

(Right to online knowledge and education)

1. Public institutions shall ensure the creation, the use and the dissemination of online knowledge, construed as a good accessible to and usable by all.
2. The rights arising from the recognition of the moral and material interests connected with the production of knowledge shall be given due consideration.
3. Every person has the right to be placed in the condition to acquire and update the skills necessary to use the Internet in an informed manner for the exercise of his or her rights and fundamental freedoms.
4. Public institutions shall promote, especially through the educational and training system, the informed use of the Internet and shall take steps to eliminate any form of cultural lag that might preclude or limit the use of the Internet by any person.
5. The informed use of the Internet is an essential guarantee of the development of equal opportunities for individual and collective growth; the democratic rebalancing of disparities in power on the Internet between economic players, institutions and citizens; the prevention of discrimination and risky behaviour as well as conduct detrimental to the freedoms of others.

Art. 4

(Net neutrality)

1. Every person has the right that the data he/she transmits and receives over the Internet be not subject to discrimination, restrictions or interference based upon the sender, recipient, type or content of the data, the device used, applications or, in general, the legitimate choices of individuals.
2. The right to neutral access to the Internet in its entirety is a necessary condition for the effectiveness of the fundamental rights of the person.

Art. 5

(Protection of personal data)

1. Everyone has the right to the protection of the data that concern them in order to ensure respect for their dignity, identity and privacy.
2. Such data consist of information that allows someone to trace the identity of a person and includes data pertaining to and generated by devices, as well as any data gathering and processing, such as that involved in the development of profiles.
3. Everyone has the right to access data that concern them, and to obtain the rectification or erasure of such data for legitimate reasons.
4. Data must be processed in accordance with the principles of necessity, purpose limitation, relevance, proportionality and, in any case, the right of every individual to informational self-determination shall prevail.
5. Data may be collected and processed only with the informed consent of the data subject or on the basis of another legitimate motivation enshrined in law. Consent shall in principle be revocable. With regard to the processing of sensitive data, the law may establish that the consent of the data subject must be accompanied by a specific authorization.
6. Consent does not constitute a legal basis for the processing of data when there is a significant imbalance of power between the data subject and the data processor.
7. Access to and processing of data for discriminatory purposes, whether directly or indirectly, is prohibited.

Art. 6

(The right to informational self-determination)

1. Every person has the right to access his or her data, irrespective of the data controller and the place where the data are stored, in order to request the supplementation, rectification or erasure of the data in the manner provided for by law. Every person has the right to know the technical procedures used in processing data that concern them.
2. Data may be collected and stored only for the length of time necessary, in any event respecting the principles of purpose limitation and proportionality and the right to self-determination of the data subject.

Art. 7

(Inviolability of electronic systems, devices and domiciles)

The IT systems and devices of every person and the freedom and confidentiality of their electronic information and communications are inviolable. Exceptions are possible only in the circumstances and in the manner established by law and with the reasoned authorization of the courts.

Art. 8

(Automated processing)

No act, judicial or administrative order or decision that could significantly impact the private sphere of individuals may be based solely on the automated processing of personal data undertaken in order to establish the profile or personality of the data subject.

Art. 9

(Right to one's identity)

1. Every person has a right to the complete and up-to-date representation of his or her identities on the Internet.
2. The definition of identity regards the free construction of personality and cannot take place without the intervention and the knowledge of the data subject.
3. The use of algorithms and probabilistic techniques shall be disclosed to the data subject who, in any case, has the right to oppose the construction and dissemination of profiles regarding him or her.
4. Every person has the right to provide only the information which is strictly necessary for complying with legal obligations, for the supply of goods and services or for accessing Internet platforms.
5. The attribution and management of digital identities by public institutions shall be governed by appropriate guarantees, especially with regard to security.

Art. 10

(Protection of anonymity)

1. Every person may access the Internet and communicate electronically using instruments, including technical systems, which protect their anonymity and prevent the collection of personal data, in particular with a view to exercising civil and political freedoms without being subject to discrimination or censorship.
2. Restrictions may be imposed only when they are based on the need to safeguard a major public interest and are necessary, proportional and grounded in law and in accordance with the basic features of a democratic society
3. In the event of violations of the dignity and fundamental rights of any person, as well as in other cases provided for by the law, the courts may require the identification the author of a communication with a reasoned order.

Art. 11

(Right to be forgotten)

1. Every person has the right to obtain the removal from search engines of references to information that, due to their content or the time elapsed from the moment of collection, no longer have public relevance.
2. The right to be forgotten cannot restrict the freedom of search and the right of the public to be informed, which are necessary conditions for the functioning of a democratic society. This right may be exercised by public figures or those who hold public functions only if the data concerning them are irrelevant with regard to their activities or the public functions they perform.
3. Where a request to be removed from search engines is granted, any person may appeal the decision before the courts to ensure that the public interest in the information is preserved.

Art. 12

(Rights and safeguards of people on platforms)

1. Digital platform operators are required to behave with integrity and fairness in dealing with users, suppliers and competitors.
2. Every person has the right to receive clear and simple information on how the platform operates, not to have contractual terms arbitrarily altered and not to be subjected to conduct that could make accessing the platform difficult or discriminatory. Every person shall be in any case notified of changes in contractual terms. In this case, they have the right to terminate the relationship, to receive a copy of the data concerning them in interoperable form and to have the data concerning them removed from the platform.
3. Platforms that operate on the Internet, if they provide services essential to the lives and activities of people, shall ensure conditions—also in accordance with the principle of competition—for the appropriate interoperability, under equal contractual terms, of their main technologies, functions and data with other platforms.

Art. 13

(Network security)

1. Network security must be guaranteed in the public interest, ensuring infrastructure integrity and protection from attacks, and in the interest of individuals.
2. Restrictions on the freedom of expression are not permitted. The protection of the dignity of persons from abuses connected with such behaviour as incitement to hate, discrimination and violence, shall be guaranteed.

Art. 14

(Internet governance)

1. Every person has the right to both national and international recognition of their rights.
2. The Internet requires rules consistent with its universal, supranational scope, aimed at fully implementing the principles and rights set out above, to safeguard its open and democratic nature, to prevent all forms of discrimination and to prevent the rules governing its use from being determined by those who hold the greatest economic power.
3. Internet rules shall take into account the various territorial levels (supranational, national, regional), the opportunities created by a variety of forms of self-regulation consistent with the above principles, the need to preserve the capacity for innovation, including through competition, as well as the manifold actors operating on the Internet, and shall encourage involvement in ways that ensure the widespread participation of all concerned. Public institutions shall adopt the appropriate instruments to ensure such participation.
4. In any case, the regulatory innovations regarding the Internet shall be subject to an assessment of their impact on the digital ecosystem.
5. The Internet shall be managed so as to ensure compliance with the principle of transparency, accountability for decisions, accessibility to public information, and the representation of those concerned.
6. Access to and the reuse of data generated and held by the public sector shall be ensured.
7. The establishment of national and international authorities is essential to effectively ensure observance of the above criteria, including through an evaluation of the compliance of the new rules with the principles of this Declaration

GA Res 75/176 on The Right to Privacy in the Digital Age (2020)

The General Assembly

Reaffirming the purposes and principles of the Charter of the United Nations, the human rights and fundamental freedoms enshrined in the Universal Declaration of Human Rights[1] and relevant international human rights treaties, including the International Covenant on Civil and Political Rights[2] and the International Covenant on Economic, Social and Cultural Rights,[3] as well as the Vienna Declaration and Programme of Action,[4]

Recalling General Assembly resolutions 68/167 of 18 December 2013, 69/166 of 18 December 2014, 71/199 of 19 December 2016 and 73/179 of 17 December 2018 on the right to privacy in the digital age, and resolution 45/95 of 14 December 1990 on guidelines for the regulation of computerized personal data files, as well as Human Rights Council resolutions 28/16 of 26 March 2015,[5] 34/7 of 23 March 2017,[6] 37/2 of 22 March 2018[7] and 42/15 of 26 September 2019[8] on the right to privacy in the digital age and resolutions 32/13 of 1 July 2016[9] and 38/7 of 5 July 2018[10] on the promotion, protection and enjoyment of human rights on the Internet, *Recalling also* the outcome document of the high-level meeting of the General Assembly on the overall review of the implementation of the outcomes of the World Summit on the Information Society,[11]

Taking note of the reports of the Special Rapporteur of the Human Rights Council on the right to privacy,[12] the reports of the Special Rapporteur of the Human Rights Council on the promotion and protection of the right to freedom of opinion and expression[13] and the relevant reports of the Special Rapporteur of the Human Rights Council on the rights to freedom of peaceful assembly and of association,[14] as well as the Special Rapporteur on contemporary forms of racism, racial discrimination, xenophobia and related intolerance,[15]

---

[1] Resolution 217 A (III).
[2] See resolution 2200 A (XXI), annex.
[3] Ibid.
[4] A/CONF.157/24 (Part I), chap. III.
[5] See *Official Records of the General Assembly, Seventieth Session, Supplement No. 53* (A/70/53), chap. III, sect. A.
[6] Ibid., *Seventy-second Session, Supplement No. 53* (A/72/53), chap. IV, sect. A.
[7] Ibid., *Seventy-third Session, Supplement No. 53* (A/73/53), chap. IV, sect. A.
[8] Ibid., *Seventy-fourth Session, Supplement No. 53A* (A/74/53/Add.1), chap. III.
[9] Ibid., *Seventy-first Session, Supplement No. 53* (A/71/53), chap. V, sect. A.
[10] Ibid., *Seventy-third Session, Supplement No. 53* (A/73/53), chap. VI, sect. A.
[11] Resolution 70/125.
[12] A/HRC/43/52 and A/75/147.
[13] A/HRC/44/49 and A/75/261.
[14] A/HRC/44/50 and A/75/184.
[15] A/HRC/44/57 and A/75/329.

Welcoming the work of the Office of the United Nations High Commissioner for Human Rights on the right to privacy in the digital age, noting with interest the report of the High Commissioner thereon,[16] and recalling the expert workshops on the right to privacy in the digital age held on 19 and 20 February 2018 and on 27 and 28 May 2020,

Taking note of the Secretary-General's strategy on new technologies and his Road Map for Digital Cooperation, and noting the discussions that take place annually in the Internet Governance Forum, which is a multi-stakeholder forum for the discussion of Internet governance issues and whose mandate was extended by the General Assembly in 2015 for another 10 years, and recognizing that effectively addressing the challenges relating to the right to privacy in the context of modern communications technology requires an ongoing, concerted multi-stakeholder engagement,

Noting that the rapid pace of technological development enables individuals all over the world to use new information and communications technologies, and at the same time enhances the capacity of Governments, business enterprises and individuals to undertake surveillance, interception and data collection, which may violate or abuse human rights, in particular the right to privacy, as set out in article 12 of the Universal Declaration of Human Rights and article 17 of the International Covenant on Civil and Political Rights, and is therefore an issue of increasing concern,

Noting also that violations and abuses of the right to privacy in the digital age may affect all individuals, with particular effects on women, as well as children, in particular girls, and those who are vulnerable and marginalized,

Recognizing that the promotion of and respect for the right to privacy are important to the prevention of violence, including gender-based violence, abuse and sexual harassment, in particular against women and children, as well as any form of discrimination, which can occur in digital and online spaces and includes cyberbullying and cyberstalking,

Noting that children can be particularly vulnerable to abuses and violations of their right to privacy,

Reaffirming the human right to privacy, according to which no one shall be subjected to arbitrary or unlawful interference with his or her privacy, family, home or correspondence, and the right to the protection of the law against such interference, and recognizing that the exercise of the right to privacy is important for the realization of the right to freedom of expression and to hold opinions without interference and the right to freedom of peaceful assembly and association, and is one of the foundations of a democratic society,

Recalling with appreciation general comment No. 16 of the Human Rights Committee on article 17 of the International Covenant on Civil and Political Rights, on the right to respect of privacy, family, home and correspondence, and protection of honour and reputation,[17] while also noting the vast technological leaps that have taken place since its adoption and the need to discuss the right to privacy in view of the challenges of the digital age,

Recognizing the need to further discuss and analyse, based on international human rights law, issues relating to the promotion and protection of the right to privacy in the digital age, procedural safeguards, effective domestic oversight and remedies, the impact of surveillance on the right to privacy and other human rights, as well as the need to examine the principles of non-arbitrariness, lawfulness, legality, necessity and proportionality in relation to surveillance practices,

---

[16] A/HRC/39/29.
[17] *Official Records of the General Assembly, Forty-third Session, Supplement No. 40* (A/43/40), annex VI.

Recognizing also that the discussion on the right to privacy should be based upon existing international and domestic legal obligations, including international human rights law, as well as relevant commitments, and should not open the path for undue interference with an individual's human rights,

Stressing the importance of full respect for the freedom to seek, receive and impart information, including the fundamental importance of access to information and democratic participation,

Recognizing that the right to privacy is important for the enjoyment of other rights and can contribute to an individual's ability to participate in political, economic, social and cultural life, and noting with concern that violations or abuses of the right to be free from unlawful or arbitrary interference with the right to privacy might affect the enjoyment of other human rights, including the right to freedom of expression and to hold opinions without interference, and the right to peaceful assembly and freedom of association,

Noting that, while metadata may provide benefits, certain types of metadata, when aggregated, can reveal personal information that can be no less sensitive than the actual content of communications and can give an insight into an individual's behaviour, social relationships, private preferences and identity,

Expressing concern that individuals, particularly children, often do not and/or cannot provide their free, explicit and informed consent to the sale or multiple resale of their personal data, and that the collecting, processing, use, storage and sharing of personal data, including sensitive data, have increased significantly in the digital age,

Noting that general comment No. 16 of the Human Rights Committee recommends that States take effective measures to prevent the unlawful retention, processing and use of personal data stored by public authorities and business enterprises,

Noting also that the use of artificial intelligence can contribute to the promotion and protection of human rights and has the potential to transform governments and societies, economic sectors and the world of work and can also have various far- reaching implications, including with regard to the right to privacy,

Noting with concern that artificial intelligence or machine-learning technologies, without proper technical, regulatory, legal and ethical safeguards, may lead to decisions that have the potential to affect the enjoyment of human rights, including economic, social and cultural rights, and affect non-discrimination, and recognizing the need to apply international human rights law and data protection frameworks in the design, evaluation and regulation of these practices,

Recognizing that, while the use of artificial intelligence can have significant positive economic and social impacts, it requires and allows for the processing of large amounts of data, often relating to personal data, including biometric data and data on an individual's behaviour, social relationships, race or ethnicity, religion or belief, which can pose serious risks to the enjoyment of the right to privacy, especially when done without proper safeguards, in particular when employed for identification, tracking, profiling, facial recognition, classification, behaviour prediction or scoring of individuals,

Noting that the use of artificial intelligence may, without proper safeguards, pose the risk of reinforcing discrimination, including structural inequalities, and recognizing that racially and otherwise discriminatory outcomes should be prevented in the design, development, implementation and use of emerging digital technologies,

Emphasizing that unlawful or arbitrary surveillance and/or interception of communications, as well as the unlawful or arbitrary collection of personal data, hacking and the unlawful use of biometric technologies, as highly intrusive acts, violate the right to privacy, can interfere with the right to freedom of expression and to hold opinions without interference, the right to freedom of peaceful assembly and association and the right to freedom of religion or belief and may contradict the tenets of a democratic society, including when undertaken extraterritorially or on a mass scale,

Recognizing that the same rights that people have offline must also be protected online, including the right to privacy,

Noting in particular that surveillance of digital communications must be consistent with international human rights obligations and must be conducted on the basis of a legal framework, which must be publicly accessible, clear, precise, comprehensive and non-discriminatory, and that any interference with the right to privacy must not be arbitrary or unlawful, bearing in mind what is reasonable with regard to the pursuance of legitimate aims, and recalling that States that are parties to the International Covenant on Civil and Political Rights must take the necessary steps to adopt laws or other measures as may be necessary to give effect to the rights recognized in the Covenant,

Expressing concern about the spread of disinformation and misinformation, particularly on social media platforms, which can be designed and implemented so as to mislead, to spread racism, xenophobia, negative stereotyping and stigmatization, to violate and abuse human rights, including the right to privacy, to impede freedom of expression, including the freedom to seek, receive and impart information, and to incite all forms of violence, hatred, intolerance, discrimination and hostility, and emphasizing the important contribution of journalists, civil society and academia in countering this trend,

Emphasizing that States must respect international human rights obligations regarding the right to privacy when they intercept digital communications of individuals and/or collect personal data, when they share or otherwise provide access to data collected through, inter alia, information- and intelligence-sharing agreements and when they require disclosure of personal data from third parties, including business enterprises,

Noting the increase in the collection of sensitive biometric information from individuals, and stressing that States must comply with their human rights obligations and that business enterprises should respect the right to privacy and other human rights when collecting, processing, sharing and storing biometric information by, inter alia, considering the adoption of data protection policies and safeguards,

Deeply concerned at the negative impact that surveillance and/or interception of communications, including extraterritorial surveillance and/or interception of communications, as well as the collection of personal data, in particular when carried out on a mass scale, may have on the exercise and enjoyment of human rights,

Emphasizing that, in the digital age, technical solutions to secure and to protect the confidentiality of digital communications, including measures for encryption, pseudonymization and anonymity, are important to ensure the enjoyment of human rights, in particular the rights to privacy, to freedom of opinion and expression and to freedom of peaceful assembly and association, and recognizing that States should refrain from employing unlawful or arbitrary surveillance techniques, which may include forms of hacking,

Noting with deep concern that, in many countries, persons and organizations engaged in promoting and defending human rights and fundamental freedoms, journalists and other media workers may frequently face threats and harassment and suffer insecurity, as well as unlawful or arbitrary interference with their right to privacy, as a result of their activities,

Noting that, while concerns about public security may justify the gathering and protection of certain sensitive information, States must ensure full compliance with their obligations under international human rights law,

Noting also, in that respect, that the prevention and suppression of terrorism is a public interest of great importance, while reaffirming that States must ensure that any measures taken to combat terrorism are in compliance with their obligations under international law, in particular international human rights, refugee and humanitarian law,

Stressing the need to address prevailing challenges to bridge the digital divides, both between and within countries, and the gender digital divide, and to harness information and communications technologies for development, and recalling the need to emphasize quality of access to bridge digital and knowledge divides, using a multidimensional approach that includes speed, stability, affordability, language, training, capacity-building, local content and accessibility for persons with disabilities, and to promote the full enjoyment of human rights, including the right to privacy,

Stressing also the need to ensure that national security and public health measures, including the use of technology to monitor and contain the spread of infectious diseases, are in full compliance with the obligations of States under international human rights law and adhere to the principles of lawfulness, legality, legitimacy with regard to the aim pursued, necessity and proportionality and the need to protect human rights, including the right to privacy, and personal data in the response to health or other emergencies,

Noting the importance of protecting and respecting the right of individuals to privacy when designing, developing or deploying technological means in response to disasters, epidemics and pandemics, especially the coronavirus disease (COVID -19) pandemic, including digital exposure notification and contact tracing,

1. *Reaffirms* the right to privacy, according to which no one shall be subjected to arbitrary or unlawful interference with his or her privacy, family, home or correspondence, and the right to the protection of the law against such interference, as set out in article 12 of the Universal Declaration of Human Rights and article 17 of the International Covenant on Civil and Political Rights;

2. *Recognizes* the global and open nature of the Internet and the rapid advancement in information and communications technologies as a driving force in accelerating progress towards development in its various forms, including in achieving the Sustainable Development Goals;[18]

3. *Affirms* that the same rights that people have offline must also be protected online, including the right to privacy, with special regard given to the protection of children;

4. *Recalls* that States should ensure that any interference with the right to privacy is consistent with the principles of legality, necessity and proportionality;

5. *Encourages* all States to promote an open, secure, stable, accessible and peaceful information and communications technology environment based on respect for international law, including the obligations enshrined in the Charter of the United Nations and human rights instruments;

6. *Acknowledges* that the conception, design, use, deployment and further development of new and emerging technologies, such as those that involve artificial intelligence, may have an impact on the enjoyment of the right to privacy and other human rights, and that the risks to these rights can and should be avoided and minimized by adapting or adopting adequate regulation or other appropriate mechanisms, in accordance with applicable obligations under international human rights law, for the conception, design, development and deployment of new and emerging technologies, including artificial intelligence, by taking measures to ensure a safe, transparent, accountable, secure and high quality data infrastructure and by developing human rights-based auditing mechanisms and redress mechanisms and establishing human oversight;

[18] See resolution 70/1.

7. *Calls upon* all States:

  (a) To respect and protect the right to privacy, including in the context of digital communications;

  (b) To take measures to put an end to violations of the right to privacy and to create the conditions to prevent such violations, including by ensuring that relevant national legislation complies with their obligations under international human rights law;

  (c) To review, on a regular basis, their procedures, practices and legislation regarding the surveillance of communications, their interception and the collection of personal data, including mass surveillance, interception and collection, as well as regarding the use of profiling, automated decision-making, machine learning and biometric technologies, with a view to upholding the right to privacy by ensuring the full and effective implementation of all their obligations under international human rights law;

  (d) To establish or maintain existing independent, effective, adequately resourced and impartial judicial, administrative and/or parliamentary domestic oversight mechanisms capable of ensuring transparency, as appropriate, and accountability for State surveillance of communications, their interception and the collection of personal data;

  (e) To provide individuals whose right to privacy has been violated by unlawful or arbitrary surveillance with access to an effective remedy, consistent with international human rights obligations;

  (f) To consider developing or maintaining and implementing adequate legislation, in consultation with all relevant stakeholders, including business enterprises, international organizations and civil society, with effective sanctions and appropriate remedies, that protects individuals against violations and abuses of the right to privacy, namely through the unlawful and arbitrary collection, processing, retention, sharing or use of personal data by individuals, Governments, business enterprises and private organizations;

  (g) To consider developing or maintaining and implementing legislation, regulations and policies to ensure that all business enterprises, including social media enterprises and other online platforms, fully respect the right to privacy and other relevant human rights in the design, development, deployment and evaluation of technologies, including artificial intelligence, and to provide individuals whose rights may have been violated or abused with access to an effective remedy, including compensation and guarantees of non-repetition;

  (h) To consider adopting or maintaining data protection legislation, regulation and policies, including on digital communication data, that comply with their international human rights obligations, which could include the establishment of national independent authorities with powers and resources to monitor data privacy practices, investigate violations and abuses and receive communications from individuals and organizations, and to provide appropriate remedies;

  (i) To further develop or maintain, in this regard, preventive measures and remedies for violations and abuses of the right to privacy in the digital age that may affect all individuals, including where there are particular effects for women, as well as children;

  (j) To consider developing, reviewing, implementing and strengthening gender-responsive policies that promote and protect the right of all individuals to privacy in the digital age;

(k) To provide effective and up-to-date guidance to business enterprises on how to respect human rights by advising on appropriate methods, including human rights due diligence, and on how to consider effectively issues of gender, vulnerability and/or marginalization;

(l) To promote quality education and lifelong educational opportunities for all to foster, inter alia, digital literacy and technical skills to effectively protect their privacy;

(m) To refrain from requiring business enterprises to take steps that interfere with the right to privacy in an arbitrary or unlawful way;

(n) To protect individuals from violations or abuses of the right to privacy, including those which are caused by arbitrary or unlawful data collection, processing, storage and sharing, profiling and the use of automated processes and machine learning;

(o) To take steps to enable business enterprises to adopt adequate voluntary transparency measures with regard to requests by State authorities for access to private user data and information;

(p) To consider developing or to maintain legislation, preventive measures and remedies addressing harm from the processing, use, sale or multiple resale or other corporate sharing of personal data without the individual's free, explicit, meaningful and informed consent;

(q) To take appropriate measures to ensure that digital or biometric identity programmes are designed, implemented and operated with appropriate legal and technical safeguards in place and in full compliance with the obligations of States under international human rights law;

≡. *Calls upon* all business enterprises that collect, store, use, share and process data:

(a) To meet their responsibility to respect human rights in accordance with the Guiding Principles on Business and Human Rights: Implementing the United Nations 'Protect, Respect and Remedy' Framework,[19] including the right to privacy in the digital age;

(b) To inform users in a clear and easily accessible way about the collection, use, sharing and retention of their data that may affect their right to privacy and to establish transparency policies that allow for the free, informed and meaningful consent of users, as appropriate;

(c) To implement administrative, technical and physical safeguards to ensure that data are processed lawfully and to ensure that such processing is limited to what is necessary in relation to the purposes of the processing and that the legitimacy of such purposes, as well as the accuracy, integrity and confidentiality of the processing, is ensured;

(d) To ensure that respect for the right to privacy and other international human rights is incorporated into the design, operation, evaluation and regulation of automated decision-making and machine-learning technologies and to provide for compensation for the human rights abuses that they may cause or to which they may contribute;

(e) To ensure that individuals have access to their personal data and to adopt appropriate measures for the possibility to amend, correct, update, delete and withdraw consent for the data, in particular if the data are incorrect or inaccurate, or if the data were obtained illegally;

[19] A/HRC/17/31, annex.

(f) To put in place adequate safeguards that seek to prevent or mitigate adverse human rights impacts that are directly linked to their operations, products or services, including where necessary through contractual clauses or notification of any relevant entities of abuses or violations when misuse of their products and services is detected;

9. *Encourages* business enterprises to work towards enabling technical solutions to secure and protect the confidentiality of digital communications, which may include measures for encryption, pseudonymization and anonymity, and calls upon States not to interfere with the use of such technical solutions, with any restrictions thereon complying with the obligations of States under international human rights law, and to enact policies that recognize and protect the privacy of individuals' digital communications;

10. *Encourages* all relevant stakeholders to participate in informal dialogues about the right to privacy, and takes note with appreciation of the contribution of the Special Rapporteur of the Human Rights Council on the right to privacy to this process;

11. *Decides* to continue its consideration of the question at its seventy-seventh session.
    46th plenary meeting 16 December 2020

A Précis of the International Soft Law on the Right to Privacy

1. Legislative Objective

The soft law aims to achieve three mutually reinforcing legislative objectives:

(a) To reformulate the scope of the right to privacy in international law in a manner that addresses its loopholes and accommodate modern understandings of the right in the digital age;

(b) To ground the right to privacy in international law in a manner able to respond to constant changes in the digital space; and

(c) To facilitate and guide dialogues on emerging and current issues affecting the enjoyment of digital privacy on an ongoing basis, and at multiple levels.

2. Subject-matter Focus

The soft law seeks to address the respect, protection and promotion of the right to privacy in the digital ecosystem. The subject matter of focus, therefore, is digital privacy broadly understood and covering two regulatory regimes:

(a) Protection of data privacy in the course of processing of personal data in the public and private sector.
Caveat: Since the rather mechanical and bureaucratic regulatory details of data protection law cannot be enshrined in a soft law, only high-level and baseline data privacy principles are envisaged. Such principles would serve as 'enabling law' for further international and national legislation.

(b) Protection of privacy in the course of government sanctioned surveillance measures.

3. Scope of the Right to Privacy in the Digital Age

With a view to accommodate nuances of the digital landscape and embrace emergent privacy norms worldwide, the scope of the right to privacy should be drawn in a fairly elaborate manner. The soft law should clearly indicate protected interests/values and 'subsets' of the right to privacy.

3 1. Protected Interests/Values

The spheres or zones of protection under the right to privacy include one's home, communications, family and personal information. The protection of these private spheres of protection extends to their digital equivalent.

(a) **Privacy of the Home**
- The right to privacy in the digital context extends to protection against interference with one's 'digital home' which includes one's online accounts and electronic equipment.

(b) **Privacy of Communications**
- The right to privacy in the digital age protects from interference against one's digital communications.

(c) **Protection of Reputation**
- The right to privacy protects from attacks against reputation online that cause or are likely to cause prejudice to the privacy of a person.

(d) **Data Privacy**
- The right to privacy protects privacy of personal data against unlawful collection, storage, analysis and disclosure.

(e) **Privacy of Family Life**

- The right to privacy provides protection from interference with the privacy of the family, including in the digital context.

3.2. Subsets of the Right to Privacy

(a) Right to Use Privacy-enhancing Technologies

The right to privacy includes a right to use and access privacy-enhancing technologies and services without unlawful interference.

(b) Freedom from Surveillance

The right to privacy includes the right to be free from unlawful surveillance, tracking and monitoring in digital spaces.

(c) Right to the Confidentiality and Integrity of information Systems

The right to privacy includes protection from unlawful interference against the security, integrity and confidentiality of information systems, devices and services.

(d) Right to Protection of Personal Data

The right to privacy includes the right to protection of personal data collected and processed both in the private and public sector. Protection of data privacy should be guaranteed through the adoption of a comprehensive legislation regulating the processing of personal data and surveillance.

3.3. Restrictions of the Right to Privacy

The right to privacy is not absolute but it should be restricted either by States or corporations when the following conditions are cumulatively met:

(a) **Legality**
- Where the impinged interference is made by the State, the requirement of legality shall be deemed satisfied when the restriction is mandated by law that is sufficiently clear, accessible and specific.
- Where the impinged interference is by Internet corporations, the requirement of legality shall be deemed satisfied when the restriction is mandated by law that is sufficiently clear, accessible and clear or mandated by contract that is entered into with clear and revocable consent.

(b) Legitimate Aim

- Where the purported interference is made by the State, the requirement of legitimate aim shall be deemed satisfied when the restriction is necessary in a democratic society to achieve aims such as maintaining public security.
- Where the interference is made by Internet corporations, the requirement of legitimate aim shall be deemed satisfied when the restriction is pursued to achieve aims such as legitimate business interests.

(c) Proportionality

Where the interference is made by both States and corporations, the requirement of proportionality shall be deemed met when the restriction taken is proportional to the legitimate aim pursued that is necessary in a democratic society.

4. Core Privacy Principles

4.1. General Principles

(a) Exterritoriality of the Right to Privacy

The right to privacy applies extraterritorially when a State exercises jurisdiction or control outside its geographic territory over all or an aspect of a person's digital communication or personal data.

(b) Dialogical Approach to Privacy

With the view to attend to the complexities of securing privacy in the digital space, the international protection of the right to privacy in the digital environment should be supported by and complemented with multi-level dialogue among relevant stakeholders, particularly States, the private sector and civil society groups. The soft law shall mandate the creation of a multi-stakeholder privacy forum where such a dialogue takes place.

4.2. Baseline Privacy Principles

The following principles that are key for the protection of digital privacy should be stipulated in the soft law.

(a) Prohibition of Mass Surveillance

Mass surveillance in the form of collecting data *en masse* or bulk hacking of communication devices should be prohibited under all circumstances.

(b) Mere Data Collection as Interference

Interference with the right to privacy shall be deemed to have occurred by the mere collection of personal data irrespective of whether no further analysis or processing follows.

(c) Protection of Metadata

The protections under the right to privacy should cover all types of personal data regardless of whether it is a metadata or content data.

(d) Independent Oversight

- All State digital surveillance measures should be undertaken with prior warrant and subject to independent judicial or quasi-judicial oversight.
- All requests for user personal data from third parties, including Internet corporations, for law enforcement purposes should be undertaken with prior warrant and independent judicial or quasi-judicial oversight.
- When intelligence containing personal data is shared among States, a two-level independent oversight should be mandated in the relevant domestic legislation. In the first instance, the sharing of intelligence should be endorsed by a court or tribunal of the source State. Once shared, the approval of a court or tribunal in the receiving State should be sought to prevent new privacy harms due to repurposing of the intelligence containing personal data.

5. Obligations under the Right to Privacy

The obligations of States and responsibilities of Internet corporations under the right to privacy should follow the tripartite categories of human rights obligations, i.e., 'to respect', 'to protect' and 'to fulfil'.

5.1. Obligations of States

(a) Obligation to Respect

- States should refrain from interfering with the use of privacy-enhancing technologies, including from compelling creation of backdoors, provision of encryption key escrows or disclosure of encryption keys.
- States should not engage in mass surveillance or bulk hacking of devices under all circumstances.
- States should refrain from measures that weaken or otherwise make ineffective the security, confidentiality and integrity of information systems.

(b) Obligation to Protect

- States should put in place appropriate legislation regulating all forms of personal data processing and government surveillance practices.
- States should ensure that the legitimate use of privacy-enhancing technologies is not obstructed by third parties, including by measures that restrict their interoperability in digital platforms.
- States should ensure that everyone is protected against unlawful surveillance, monitoring, tracking and profiling online by third parties through appropriate legislative and administrative mechanisms.
- States should regulate by law the sale and export of surveillance technologies by the private sector, including through an appropriate licensing regime that involves regular reviews and monitoring.
- States should ensure the security, integrity and confidentiality of information systems operated by their agencies or private actors by which such systems are operated on the behalf of States.

(c) Obligations to Fulfil

- States should eliminate unnecessary barriers to access and use of privacy-enhancing technologies, including import and export restrictions or discriminatory tariffs.

- States should take all reasonable steps to raise awareness on the importance and use of privacy-enhancing technologies. States should make relevant surveillance legislation readily accessible to any interested party.
- States should provide *ex post* notice to a person subjected to targeted surveillance, and where appropriate, provide appropriate remedies.
- States should take all reasonable steps to promote best practices on the protection of the security of information systems operated by the private sector.

5.2. Responsibilities of Internet Corporations

(a) **Responsibility to Respect**
- Corporations should refrain from any measure that obstructs the use of privacy-enhancing technologies on their platforms, applications or services.
- Corporations should refrain from disclosing user personal data to States without appropriate judicial authorization.
- Corporations should refrain from selling or otherwise making available technologies to third-parties that undermine the enjoyment of privacy where there is an apparent risk of abuse.
- Corporations should not engage in or assist the unlawful surveillance of users by State and non-State actors.

(b) **Responsibility to Protect**
- Corporations should ensure the security, confidentiality and integrity of their communication services and computer systems.
- Corporations should provide appropriate remedies for harms resulting from the compromise of the security and integrity of their communication services, products and systems.
- Corporations should take all reasonable steps to prevent unlawful requests for user personal data from third parties.
- Corporations should protect their users from unlawful surveillance by third parties, including States.
- Corporations should be guided by applicable international privacy standards in designing and operating technologies used in the collection and processing of personal data.

(c) **Responsibility to Fulfil**
- Corporations should take all reasonable steps to enable the use of privacy-enhancing technologies on their platforms and services.
- Corporations should provide explicit information to users as to the nature and type of security features available in their computer systems or communication services.
- Corporations should inform users where the security breach of their computer systems is likely to affect the privacy of users and provide remedies where appropriate.
- Corporations should issue regular transparency reports on government requests for user personal data and regarding provision of surveillance technologies to third parties. Where applicable, corporations should inform individual users whose data has been disclosed to law enforcement agencies.

5.3. The Role of Other Non-State Actors

(a) **Civil Society**

The international protection of the right to privacy should involve the active participation, advocacy and expertise of relevant civil society organizations. This should be recognized and enhanced through their participation in the multi-stakeholder privacy forum.

(b) International-governmental Organizations

International governmental organizations that engage in the routine collection and processing of personal data should adopt internal data protection policies in line with international standards, including the soft law.

(c) Technical communities

International organizations involved in setting Internet and web technical standards should support the global effort for the protection of digital privacy, including in designing global communication standards and protocols. The technical community should also actively be involved in dialogues to be had in the multi-stakeholder privacy forum.

6. Miscellaneous Provisions

6.1. Multi-stakeholder Privacy Forum

A multi-stakeholder privacy forum shall be created as a subsidiary body of the United Nations Human Rights Council to complement and reinforce the work of existing institutional arrangements in upholding the right to privacy in the digital age.

(a) **Purpose**
  - The privacy forum shall be a platform to deliberate, on an ongoing basis, emerging and current issues affecting the protection of the right to privacy in the digital environment.
  - Held at least once in a year, the forum shall facilitate dialogue, consensus and cooperation among actors that play a role in the respect, protection and promotion of the right to privacy in the digital space.

(b) **Composition**
  - All relevant stakeholders particularly States, Internet corporations, civil society groups, intergovernmental organizations and members of the technical community should take part in the forum.
  - The United Nations and other relevant actors shall take all reasonable steps towards ensuring fair representation, including geographic representation at the forum.

(c) **The Role of the Special Rapporteur on the Right to Privacy**
  - The forum shall be chaired and facilitated by the Mandate of the Special Rapporteur on the Right to Privacy.
  - The thematic priorities of the Mandate shall not be dictated by the Special Rapporteur.

6.2. Formal Jurisprudential Dialogue

Jurisprudential dialogue between international institutional arrangements and their national and regional counterparts shall be undertaken through formal channels and under clear guiding principles.

(a) Purpose

Formal jurisprudential dialogue shall be an important vehicle of localizing international privacy standards and enhancing harmonized global privacy protection.

(b) Role of the Office of the High Commissioner

The Office of the High Commissioner for Human Rights shall be responsible in facilitating creation of formal channels of jurisprudential dialogue.

(c) Role of Treaty Bodies

Treaty bodies particularly the Human Rights Committee shall ensure that jurisprudential dialogue is undertaken in a legitimate, consistent, transparent and coherent manner.

Select Bibliography

'The Legal Protection of Privacy: A Comparative Survey of Ten Countries by the nternational Commission of Jurists' (1972) 24 International Journal of Science 417.

A Concerning State of Play for the Right to Privacy in Europe: National Data Retention Laws Since CJEU's Tele-2/Watson Judgment (Privacy International, September 2017).

A World That Counts: Mobilizing the Data Revolution for Sustainable Development, Report Prepared at the Request of the UN Secretary General by the Independent Expert Advisory Group on a Data Revolution for Sustainable Development (November 2014).

Abbott, Kenneth and Snidal, Duncan, 'Hard and Soft Law in International Governance' (2000) 54 International Organization 421.

Abbott, Kenneth and others, 'The Concept of Legalization' (2000) 54 International Organization 401.

Abbott, Kenneth, 'The Many Faces of International Legalization' (1998) 92 Proceedings of the Annual Meeting of the ASIL 57.

Abdulrauf, Lukman Adebisi and Fombad, Charles Manga, 'The African Union's Data Protection Convention 2014: A Possible Cause for Celebration of Human Rights in Africa?' (2018) 8 Journal of Media Law 67.

African Declaration of Internet Rights and Freedoms (2014).

Alexander, Adam, Digital Surveillance 'worse than Orwell', Says New UN Privacy Chief (The Guardian, 25 August 2015) <http://bit.ly/h2bEYF>.

Alpin, Tanya and Bosland, Jason, 'The Uncertain Landscape of Article 8 of the ECHR: The Protection of Reputation as a Fundamental Right?' in A Kenyon (ed), *Comparative Defamation and Privacy Law* (Cambridge University Press 2016).

Alston, Philip, 'Against a World Court for Human Rights' (2014) 28 Ethics and International Affairs 197.

Alston, Philip, 'Beyond Them and Us: Putting Treaty Body Reform into Perspective' in P Alston and J Crawford (eds), *The Future of the UN Human Rights Treaty Monitoring* (Cambridge University Press 2000).

Alston, Philip, 'Conjuring Up New Human Rights: A Proposal for Quality Control' (1984) 78 The American Journal of International Law 607.

Alston, Philip, 'The Commission on Human Rights' in P Alston (ed), *The United Nations and Human Rights: A Critical Appraisal* (Oxford University Press 1992).

Alston, Philip, 'The Populist Challenge to Human Rights' (2017) 9 Journal of Human Rights Practice 1.

An Abridged Report of Consultative Committee's 42nd Meeting/Session (19 November 2021).

An Inclusive Dialogue for the Internet Bill of Rights in Guatemala (Web We Want Foundation, 27 January 2017) <http://ow.ly/hvMx30c7zdC>.

Anderson, Nate, New Internet Bill of Rights Contender Comes from… Pirates? (Arts Technica, 12 December 2012) <http://bit.ly/2iv6SDg>.

Annual Report of the Human Rights Committee to the General Assembly, UN Doc A/72/40 (March 2017).

Annual Report of the Human Rights Committee to the General Assembly, UN Doc A/70/ 40 (April 2015).

Annual Report of the Human Rights Committee to the General Assembly, UN Doc (A/43/ 40 (28 September 1988).

Apple-FBI Case Could Have Serious Global Ramifications for Human Rights: Zeid (OHCHR Press Release, 4 March 2016) <https://bit.ly/2H7vX4x>.

Armstrong, Mark and others, *Media Law in Australia* (Oxford University Press 3rd edn, 1995).

Asamoah, Obed, 'The Legal Effect of Resolutions of the General Assembly' (1965) 3 Columbia Journal of Transnational Law 210.

Barelli, Mauro, *Seeking Justice in International Law: The Significance and Implications of the UN Declaration on the Rights of Indigenous Peoples* (Routledge 2016).

Barendt, Eric, 'Privacy and Freedom of Speech' in A Kenyon and M Richardson (eds), *New Dimensions in Privacy Law: International and Comparative Perspectives* (Cambridge University Press 2006).

Barton, John and Carter, Barry, 'International Law and Institutions for a New Age' (1992/93) 81 Georgetown Law Journal 535.

Bassiouni, M Cherif, 'Human Rights and International Criminal Justice in the Twenty-First Century: The End of the Post-WWII Phase and the Beginning of an Uncertain New Era' in M deGuzman and D Amann, *Arcs of Global Justice: Essays in Honour of William A. Schabas* (Oxford University Press 2018).

Bayefsky, Anne, 'Making Human Rights Work' (1997) 26 Studies in Transnational Legal Policy 229.

Benedek, Wolfgang and others, The Humanization of Internet Governance: A Roadmap Towards a Comprehensive Global (Human) Rights Architecture for the Internet, Paper presented at the 3rd Annual GigaNet Symposium, Hyderabad, India (2 December 2008).

Benedetto, Conforti, *The Law and Practice of the United Nations* (Martinus Nijhoff 3rd edn, 2004).

Bennett, Colin and Raab, Charles, *The Governance of Privacy: Policy Instruments in Global Perspective* (MIT Press 2006).

Bennett, Colin, 'Convergence Revisited: Toward A Global Policy for the Protection of Personal Data?' in P Agre and M Rotenberg (eds), *Technology and Privacy: The Landscape* (MIT Press 1997).

Bennett, Colin, 'The European General Data Protection Regulation: An Instrument for the Globalization of Privacy Standards?' (2018) 23 Information Polity 239.

Besson, Samantha and d'Aspermont, Jean, 'The Sources of International Law: An Introduction' in S Besson and J d'Aspermont (eds), *The Oxford Handbook on the Sources of International Law* (Oxford University Press 2017).

Besson, Samantha and Marti, Jose, 'Legitimate Actors of International Law-making: Towards a Theory of International Democratic Representation' (2018) 9 Jurisprudence: An International Journal of Legal and Political Thought 504.

Bignami, Francesca and Resta, Giorgio, 'Human Rights Extraterritoriality: The Right to Privacy and National Security Surveillance' in E Benvenisti and G Nolte (eds), *Community Interests Across International Law* (Oxford University Press 2018).

Bleicher, Samuel, 'The Legal Significance of Re-Citation of General Assembly Resolutions' (1969) 63 The American Journal of International Law 444.

Bonafe, Beatrice and Palchetti, Paolo, 'Relying on General Principles in International Law' in C Brölmann and Y Radi (eds), *Research Handbook on the Theory and Practice of International Law Making* (Edward Elgar 2016).

Bord, Martyn, *The Council of Europe: Structure, History and Issues in European Politics* (Routledge 2011).

Bossuyt, Marc, *Guide to the 'Travaux Preparatoires' of the International Covenant on Civil and Political Rights* (Martinus Nijhoff 1987).

Bourdieu, Pierre, 'Political Representation: Elements for a Theory of the Political Field' in P Bourdieu (ed), *Language and Symbolic Power* (Polity Press 1991).

Boutros-Ghali, Boutros, 'Introduction' in *United Nations and Human Rights (1945-1995)* (United Nations Blue Book 1995).

Boyle, Alan and Chinkin, Christine, *The Making of International Law* (Oxford University Press 2007).

Brandsom, Russell, Tim Cook Wants a Federal Privacy Law—But so do Facebook and Google (The Verge, 24 October 2018) <https://bit.ly/2qaAYSg>.

Brems, Eva, 'Introduction: Rewriting Decisions from a Perspective of Human Rights Integration' in E Brems and E Desmet (eds), *Integrating Human Rights in Practice: Rewriting Human Rights Decisions* (Edward Elgar 2017).

Brennan, Kathrine and others, 'The Fortieth Session of the UN Sub-Commission on Prevention of Discrimination and Protection of Minorities' (1989) 11 Human Rights Quarterly 295.

Brennan, William, 'Why Have a Bill of Rights?' (1989) 9 Oxford Journal of Legal Studies 425.

Brown, Gordon (ed), *The Universal Declaration of Human Rights in the 21st Century: A Living Document in A Changing World* (Open Book 2016).

Brown, Ian and others, Towards Multilateral Standards for Surveillance Reforms, Oxford Internet Institute Discussion Paper (2015).

Brown, Ian, 'The Feasibility of Transatlantic Privacy-protective Standards for Surveillance' (2015) 23 International Journal of Law and Information Technology 23.

Brownlie, Ian, 'Legal Status of Natural Resources in International Law' (1979) 162 Recueil des Cours 1.

Buergenthal, Thomas, 'The UN Human Rights Committee' (2001) 5 Max Planck Yearbook of United Nations Law 341.

Bukovska, Barbora and ten Oever, Niels, *#InternetofRights: Creating the Universal Declaration of Digital Rights* (Article 19 Blog, 24 March 2017) <http://bit.ly/2q5wji2>.

Burgess, Matt, Tim Berners-Lee: 'We Need to Rethink the Web to Stop the Spread of Mean Ideas' (Wired, 11 April 2017) <https://bit.ly/2oyapHE>.

Burke, Ronald and Kirby, James, 'The Universal Declaration of Human Rights: Politics and Provisions (1945–1948)' in G Oberleitner (ed), *International Human Rights Institutions, Tribunals and Courts* (Springer 2018).

Burke, Ronald, *Decolonization and the Evolution of Human Rights* (Pennsylvania University Press 2010).

Bygrave, Lee, 'Data Protection Pursuant to the Right to Privacy in Human Rights Treaties' (1998) 6 International Journal of Law and Information Technology 247.

Bygrave, Lee, 'International Agreements to Protect Personal Data' in J Rule and G Greenleaf (eds), *Global Privacy Protection: The First Generation* (Edward Elgar 2008).

Bygrave, Lee, 'The "Strasbourg Effect" on Data Protection in Light of the "Brussels" Effect: Logic, Mechanics and Prospects' (2021) 40 Computer Law and Security Review 1.

Bygrave, Lee, *Data Privacy Law: An International Perspective* (Oxford University Press 2014).

Bygrave, Lee, *Internet Governance by Contract* (Oxford University Press 2015).

Cannataci, Joseph and others, *Privacy, Free Expression and Transparency: Redefining their New Boundaries in the Digital Age* (UNESCO Series on Internet Freedom 2016).

Casacuberta, David and Senges, Max, 'Do We Need New Rights in Cyberspace? Discussing the Case of How to Define Online Privacy in an Internet Bill of Rights' (2008) 40/41 Enrahonar 99.

Casagran, Cristina, *Global Data Protection in the Field of Law Enforcement: An EU Perspective* (Routledge 2016).

Cassel, Doug, 'The Third Session of the UN Intergovernmental Working Group on a Business and Human Rights Treaty' (2018) 3 Business and Human Rights Journal 277.

Cassese, Antonio, International *Law in a Divided World* (Clarendon Press 1986).

Castenada, Jorge, 'The Underdeveloped Nations and the Development of International Law' (1961) 15 International Organizations 38.

Cate, Fred, 'The EU Data Protection Directive, Information Privacy and the Public Interest' (1995) 80 Iowa Law Review 431.

Chander, Anupam and Land, Molly, 'Introductory Note to United Nations General Assembly Resolution on the Right to Privacy in the Digital Age' (2014) 53 International Legal Materials 727.

Charlesworth, Hilary, 'Law Making and Sources' in J Crawford and M Koskenniemi (eds), *The Cambridge Companion to International Law* (Cambridge University Press 2012).

Charlesworth, Hilary, 'A Regulatory Perspective on the International Human Rights System' in P Drhaos (ed), *Regulatory Theory: Foundations and Applications* (Australian National University Press 2017).

Charter of Digital Fundamental Rights of the European Union (2016).

Charter of Human Rights and Principles for the Internet (7th edn, 2019).

Chauville, Roland, 'The Universal Periodic Review's First Cycle: Successes and Failures' in H Charlesworth and E Larking (eds), *Human Rights and the Universal Periodic Review: Rituals and Ritualism* (Cambridge University Press 2015).

Chesterman, Simon, *One Nation Under Surveillance: A New Social Contract to Defend Freedom Without Sacrificing Liberty* (Oxford University Press 2011).

Chinkin, Christine, 'Normative Development in the International Legal System' in D Shelton (ed), *Commitment and Compliance: The Role of Non-Binding Norms in the International Legal System* (Oxford University Press 2000).

Clapham, Andrew, *Human Rights Obligations of Non-State Actors* (Oxford University Press 2006).

Clement, Dominique, 'Human Rights or Social Justice? The Problem of Rights Inflation' (2018) 22 International Journal of Human Rights 155.

Code of Practice on the Protection of Workers' Personal Data (ILO 1997).

Cole, David and Fabbrini, Federico, 'Bridging the Transatlantic Divide? The United States, the European Union, and the Protection of Privacy Across Borders' (2016) 14 International Journal of Constitutional Law 220.

Collins, Katie, Facebook Publishes Privacy Principles for the First Time (Cnet, 29 January 2019) <https://cnet.co/3rV072T>.

Commentary of the Working Group on Minorities to the United Nations Declaration on the Rights of Persons Belonging to National or Ethnic, Religious and Linguistic Minorities, UN Doc E/CN.4/Sub.2/AC.5/2005/2 (4 April 2005).

Committee of Ministers Decision, CM/Del/Dec/2008, 1031/10.2 (2 July 2008).

Committee on the Rights of the Child, *General Comment 3: HIV/AIDS and the Rights of the Child*, UN Doc CRC/GC/2003/1 (17 March 2003).

Committee on the Rights of the Child, *General Comment No. 25: Children's Rights in Relation to the Digital Environment*, UN Doc CRC/C/GC/25 2 (March 2021).

Communication from the Commission to the European Parliament, the Council, the European Economic and Social Committee and the Committee of the Regions, Establishing a European Declaration on Digital Rights and Principles for the Digital Decade, SWD(2022) 14 Final (26 January 2022).

Concept Paper on the High Commissioner's Proposal for a Unified Standing Treaty Body, UN Doc HRI/MC/2006/2 (22 March 2006).

Concluding Observations of the HR Committee: The United Kingdom of Great Britain and Northern Ireland (17 August 2015).

Concluding Observations of the HR Committee: The United States of America (23 April 2014)

Conclusions of the Nordic Conference on the Right to Privacy (23 May 1967).

Consultative Committee of the Convention for the Protection of Individuals with regard to Automatic Processing of Personal Data, Work Programme for the 2022–2025 (30 June 2021).

Consultative Committee of the Convention for the Protection of Individuals with regard to Automatic Processing of Personal Data (ETS No. 108) (T-PD), Abridged report of the 24th Plenary Meeting [CM(2008)81] (March 2008).

Contract for the Web (World Wide Web Foundation 2019).

Cooper, Daniel and Kuner, Christopher, 'Data Protection Law and International Dispute Resolution' (2017) 382 Recueil des Cours 1.

Cooper, Stacey, GDPR Comes to the US—Nevada & California Privacy Laws (Webspec, 23 September 2019) <https://bit.ly/3KhRqb9>.

Cooperation Between the United Nations and Council of Europe, DER/Inf (2021) 1, Directorate of External Relations (8 March 2021).

Cooperation Between the United Nations and Regional and Other Organizations: Report of the Secretary-General, UN Doc A/75/345 (11 September 2020).

Cooperation between the United Nations and the Council of Europe, GA Res 75/264 (6 March 2021).

Crawford, James, *Brownlie's Principles of Public International Law* (Oxford University Press 8th edn, 2012).

Crawford, James, *Brownlie's Principles of Public International Law* (Oxford University Press 9th edn, 2019).

Croce, Benedetto, 'The Rights of Man and the Present Historical Situation' in *Human Rights: Comments and Interpretations* (Columbia University Press 1949).

Custers, Bart, 'New Digital Rights: Imagining Additional Fundamental Rights for the Digital Era' (2021) 44 Computer Law and Security Review 1.

d'Aspermont, Jean, 'Softness in International Law: A Self-Serving Quest for New Legal Materials' (2008) 19 European Journal of International Law 1075.

Daly, Angela, *Mind the Gap: Private Power, Online Information Flows and EU Law* (Hart 2016).

Danileko, Gennady, *Law-Making in the International Community* (Martinus Nijhoff 1993).

Data Principles (WHO, 10 August 2020).

Data Protection Manual (IOM 2009).

Data Protection Regulations and International Data Flows: Implications for Trade and Development (UNCTAD 2016).

Data Revolution Advisory Group Named by UN Secretary General (UN Media Release, 29 August 2014) <http://bit.ly/2mycqzs>.

Data Strategy of the Secretary-General for Action by Everyone, Everywhere with Insight, Impact and Integrity: 2020–22 (2020).

de Burca, Grainne, 'Human Rights Experimentalism' (2017) 111 The American Journal of International Law 277.

De Hert, Paul and Papakonstantinou, Vagelis, 'Moving Beyond the Special Rapporteur on Privacy with the Establishment of a New, Specialized United Nations Agency: Addressing the Deficit in Global Cooperation for the Protection of Data Privacy' in Dan Svantesson and Dariusz Kloza (eds), *Transatlantic Privacy Relations as a Challenge to Democracy* (Intersentia 2017).

De Hert, Paul and Papakonstantinou, Vagelis, 'The Council of Europe Data Protection Convention Reform: Analysis of the New Text and Critical Comment on its Global Ambition' (2014) 30 Computer Law and Security Review 633.

De Hert, Paul and Papakonstantinou, Vagelis, 'Three Scenarios for International Governance of Data Privacy: Towards an International Data Privacy Organization, Preferably a UN Agency?' (2013) 9 I/S: A Journal of Law and Policy for the Information Society 271.

De Minico, Giovanna, 'Towards an Internet Bill of Rights' (2015) 37 Loyola of Los Angeles International and Comparative Law Review 1.

de Santos, Jonathan, The Wisdom of Crowds: Crowdsourcing Net Freedom (Yahoo! News, 21 January 2013) <https://bit.ly/3g4x7A9>.

Decaux, Emmanuel, 'The International Convention for the Protection of All Persons from Enforced Disappearance, as a Victim-Oriented Treaty' in M deGuzman and D Amann (eds), *Arcs of Global Justice: Essays in Honour of William A Schabas* (Oxford University Press 2018).

Decision of the Committee of Ministers of the Council of Europe, CM/Del/Dec(2008)1031 (4 July 2008).

Declaration of Legal Principles Governing the Activities of States in the Exploration and Uses of the Outer Space, GA Res 1962 (XVIII), 18th sess, Agenda item 28a, UN Doc A/Res/18/ 1962 (13 December 1963).

Declaration of Principles on Freedom of Expression and Access to Information, The African Commission on Human and Peoples' Rights (November 2019).

Declaration on Ethics and Data Protection in Artificial Intelligence (Global Privacy Assembly, October 2018).

Declaration on the Elimination of All Forms of Intolerance and of Discrimination Based on Religion or Belief, GA Res 36/55, 93rd plenary mtg, UN Doc A/RES/42/97 (25 November 1981).

Declaration on the Elimination of Violence against Women, GA Res 48/104, 85th plenary mtg, UN Doc A/RES/48/104 (20 December 1993).

Declaration on the Granting of Independence to Colonial Countries and Peoples, GA Res 1514 (XV), 15thsess, UN Doc A/RES/1514(XV) (14 December 1960).

Declaration on the Human Genome and Human Rights (UNESCO, 11 November 1997).

Declaration on the Rights of Persons Belonging to National or Ethnic, Religious and Linguistic Minorities, GA Res 47/135, 92nd plenary mtg, UN Doc A/RES/47/135 (18 December 1992).

Declaration on the Use of Scientific and Technological Progress in the Interest of Peace and for the Benefit of Mankind, GA Res 3384 (XXX), 2400th plenary mtg, UN Doc A/RES/ 3384(XXX) (10 November 1975).

Deeks, Ashley, 'An International Legal Framework for Surveillance' (2015) 55 Virginia Journal of International Law 291.

Deeks, Ashly, 'Regulating Foreign Surveillance Through International Law' in F Cate and J Dempsey (eds), *Bulk Collection: Systematic Government Access to Private-Sector Data* (Oxford University Press 2017).

DeNardis, Laura and Raymond, Mark, Thinking Clearly About Multi-stakeholder Internet Governance, 8th Annual GigaNet Symposium, Brpali, Indonesia (21 October 2013).

DeNardis, Laura, *The Global War for Internet Governance* (Yale University Press 2014).

Diggelmann, Oliver and Cleis, Maria, 'How the Right to Privacy Become a Human Right' (2014) 14 Human Rights Law Review 441.

Directive on Information Disclosure (WFP 2010).

Donnelly, Jack, 'International Human Rights: A Regime Analysis' (1986) 40 International Organization 599.

Doria, Avri, 'Use [and Abuse] of Multistakeholderism in the Internet' in R Radu and others eds), *The Evolution of Global Internet Governance* (Springer 2013).

Draft Conclusions on Identification of Customary International Law, Adopted by the International Law Commission at Its Seventieth Session (2018).

Draft Data Privacy Guidelines for the Development and Operation of Artificial Intelligence Solutions (SRP 2020).

Draft International Convention for the Protection of all Persons from Enforced Disappearance, UN Doc E/CN.4/Sub.2/RES/1998/25 (26 August 1998).

Draft International Convention on the Protection of all Persons from Enforced Disappearance, Resolution 1998/25 of the Sub-Commission on Prevention of Discrimination and Protection of Minorities, UN Doc /CN.4/Sub.2/RES/1998/25 (26 August 1998).

Draft Recommendation on the Protection and Use of Health-Related Data (SRP, June 2019).

Draft Report on the Proposed e-Privacy Regulation, Committee on Civil Liberties, Justice and Home Affairs, 2017/0003(COD) (9 June 2017).

Drzemczewski, Andrew and Dzehtsiarou, Kanstantsin, Painful Relations Between the Council of Europe and Russia (EJIL: Talk!, 28 September 2018) <https://bit.ly/2RTBfoD>.

Dupuy, Pierre-Marie, 'Formation of Customary International Law and General Principles' in D Dobansky and others (eds), *Oxford Handbook of International Environmental Law* (Oxford University Press 2007).

Dupuy, Pierre-Marie, 'Soft Law and the International Law of Environment' (1990/91) 12 Michigan Journal of International Law 420.

Dupuy, René, 'Declaratory Law and Programmatory Law: From Revolutionary Custom to "Soft Law"' in RJ Akkerman (ed), *Declaration on Principles: A Quest for Universal Peace* (Kluwer Law International 1977).

Eoot, Eric, *Human Duties and the Limits of Human Rights Discourse* (Springer 2017).

Edmundson, William, *An Introduction to Rights* (Cambridge University Press 2004).

Edwards, Lilian, 'Reconstructing Consumer Privacy Protection Online: A Modest Proposal' (2004) 18 International Review of Law, Computers and Technology 313.

Egan, Suzanne, 'Strengthening the United Nations Human Rights Treaty Body System' (2013) 13 Human Rights Law Review 209.

Eggerton, John, Twitter Proposes Guiding Principles for Online Regulation (Multichannel News, 15 October 2021) <https://bit.ly/3nYf6YL>.

Eichensehr, Kristen, 'Digital Switzerlands' (2019) 167 University of Pennsylvania Law Review 665.

Ekwealor, Victor, Nigeria's President Refused to Sign Its Digital Rights Bill, What Happens Now? (Techpoint.africa, 27 March 2019) <https://bit.ly/2UZhGRG>.

Elaboration of an International Legally Binding Instrument on Transnational Corporations and other Business Enterprises with Respect to Human rights, HRC Res 26/9, 26thsess, Agenda item 3, UN Doc A/HRC/RES/26/9 (14 July 2014).

Elements of the Draft Legally Binding Instrument on Transnational Corporations and Other Business Enterprises with respect to Human Rights (September 2017).

Ferrari, Elisabeth, Italy Issues a Declaration of Internet Rights—Now Let's Improve It (Center for Global Communication Studies Media Wire, 4 August 2015) <https://bit.ly/2qqyLQB>.

Watt, Eliza, 'The Right to Privacy and the Future of Mass Surveillance' (2017) 21 The International Journal of Human Rights 773.

Encryption: A Matter of Human Rights (Amnesty International 2016).

Estadella-Yuste, Olga, 'Transborder Data Flows and the Sources of Public International Law' (1991) 16 North Carolina Journal of International Law 379.

Ethically Aligned Design: A Vision for Prioritizing Human Well-being with Autonomous and Intelligent Systems (IEEE 2019).

Ethics Guidelines for Trustworthy AI, High-Level Expert Group on Artificial Intelligence (April 2019).

European Declaration on Digital Rights and Principles for the Digital Decade, COM (2022) 28 Final (26 January 2022).

European Parliament Resolution with Recommendations to the Commission on the Right to Disconnect [2019/2181(INL)] (21 January 2021).

Evans, A.C., 'European Data Protection Law' (1981) 29 American Journal of Comparative Law 571.

Existing and Proposed Texts which could be used in the Drafting of a Further International Instrument on Human Rights and Scientific and Technological Developments, Commission on Human Rights, 33rd sess, Item 8 of provisional agenda, UN Doc E/CN.4/1233 (16 December 1976).

Explanatory Memorandum of the Australian Privacy (Private Sector) Amendment Bill 2000 (Cth) [2000].

Explanatory Memorandum of the Australian Privacy Bill 1988 (Cth) [1988].

Explanatory Report of Resolution (73) 22, CM (73) 110 (12 July 1973).

Explanatory Report to the Convention for the Protection of Individuals with Regard to Automatic Processing of Personal Data (28 January 1981).

Explanatory Report to the Protocol Amending the Convention for the Protection of Individuals with regard to Automatic Processing of Personal Data (10 October 2018).

Facebook's Privacy Principles (28 January 2018) <https://www.facebook.com/about/basics/privacy-principles>.

Falcon, Ernesto and Gillula, Jeremy, The Hypocrisy of AT&T's "Internet Bill of Rights" (Electronic Frontier Foundation, 1 February 2018) <https://bit.ly/2qgTGY9>.

Farer, Tom and Gaer, Felice, 'The UN and Human Rights: At the End of the Beginning' in A Roberts and B Kingsbury (eds), *United Nations, Divided World: The UN's Roles in International Relations* (Clarendon Press 2nd edn, 1993).

Fidler, David (ed), *The Snowden Reader* (Indiana University Press 2015).

Fidler, David, 'Cyberspace and Human Rights' in N Tsagourias and R Buchan (eds), *Research Handbook on International Law and Cyberspace* (Edward Elgar 2015).

Fidler, David, 'From International Sanitary Conventions to Global Health Security: The New International Health Regulations' (2007) 4 Chinese Journal of International Law 325.

Final Act of the International Conference on Human Rights, Tehran, The Islamic Republic of Iran (May 1968).

First Report on General Principles of Law by Marcelo Vázquez-Bermúdez, Special Rapporteur of the International Law Commission, UN Doc, A/CN.4/732 (5 April 2019).

Fischer-Lescano, Andreas, 'Struggles for a Global Internet Constitution: Protecting Global Communication Structures Against Surveillance Measures' (2016) 5 Global Constitutionalism 145.

Floridi, Luciano and Cowls, Josh, 'A Unified Framework of Five Principles for AI in Society' (2019) 1 Harvard Data Science Review 1.

Floridi, Luciano, 'Translating Principles into Practices of Digital Ethics: Five Risks of Being Unethical' (2019) 32 Ethics and Philosophy 185.

Flynn, Eilionoir, From Rhetoric to Action: Implementing the UN Convention on the Rights of Persons with Disabilities (Cambridge University Press 2011).

Foot, Rosemary, 'The Cold War and Human Rights' in M Leffler and O Westad (eds), The Cambridge History of the Cold War (Cambridge University Press Vol 3, 2010).

Forsythe, David, 'The United Nations and Human Rights: 1945-1985' (1985) 100 Political Science Quarterly 249.

Fox, Graham, 'The United Nations Forum on Minority Issues and Its Role in Promoting the UN Declaration on the Rights of Persons Belonging to National or Ethnic, Religious and Linguistic Minorities' in U Caruso and R Hofmann (eds), The United Nations Declaration on Minorities: An Academic Account on the Occasion of Its 20th Anniversary (1992–2012) (Brill 2015).

Framework for Responsible Data Protection Regulation (Google, September 2018) <https://bit.ly/2DoNt5m>.

Musiani, Francesca, 'The Internet Bill of Rights: A Way to Reconcile Natural Freedoms and Regulatory Needs?' (2009) 6 Scripted 505.

Franklin, Marianne, 'Mobilizing for Net Rights: The IRPC Charter of Human Rights and Principles for the Internet' in J Obar and others (eds), Strategies for Media Reform: International Perspectives (Fordham University Press 2016).

Franklin, Marianne, Digital Dilemmas: Power, Resistance and the Internet (Oxford University Press 2013).

Function and Future of the Council of Europe, Recommendation 516 (1968) of the Parliamentary Assembly (1 February 1968).

Fuster, Gloria, The Emergence of Personal Data Protection as a Fundamental Right of the EU (Springer 2014).

Gaja, Giorgio, 'General Principles in the Jurisprudence of the ICJ' in M Andenas and others (eds), General Principles and the Coherence of International Law (Brill 2019).

Garfinkel, Simson, Database Nation: The Death of Privacy in the 21st Century (O'Reilly 2000).

Garibaldi, Oscar, 'The Legal Status of General Assembly Resolutions: Some Conceptual Observations' (1979) 73 Proceedings of the Annual Meeting of the ASIL 324.

Georgieva, Ilina, 'The Right to Privacy Under Fire—Foreign Surveillance under the NSA and the GCHQ and Its Compatibility with Art. 17 ICCPR and Art. 8 ECHR' (2015) 31 Utrecht Journal of International and European Law 104.

Glendon, Mary, A World Made New: Eleanor Roosevelt and the Universal Declaration of Human Rights (Random House 2001).

Glendon, Mary, Rights Talk: The Impoverishment of Political Discourse (Free Press 1991).

Global Principles on the Protection of Freedom of Expression and Privacy (Article 19, 2017).

Godwin, Mike, The Great Charter for Cambodian Internet Freedom (LinkedIn, 8 March 2015) <https://bit.ly/2GEF2UR>.

Goldin, Ian, Divided Nations: Why Global Governance is Failing, and What We Can Do About It (Oxford University Press 2013).

Goldsmith, Jack and Wu, Tim, Who Controls the Internet? Illusions of a Borderless World (Oxford University Press 2006).

Granville, Kevin, Facebook and Cambridge Analytica: What You Need to Know as Fallout Widens (The New York Times, 19 March 2018) <https://nyti.ms/3G4shxA>.

Greenleaf, Graham and Cottier, Bertil, 'International and Regional Commitments in African Data Privacy Laws: A Comparative Analysis' (2022) 44 Computer Law and Security Review 1.

Greenleaf, Graham, 'A World Data Privacy Treaty? "Globalization" and "Modernization" of Council of Europe Convention 108' in N Witzleb and others (eds), *Emerging Challenges in Privacy Law: Comparative Perspectives* (Cambridge University Press 2014).

Greenleaf, Graham, 'Data Protection in A Globalized Network' in I Brown (ed), *Research Handbook on Governance of the Internet* (Edward Elgar 2012).

Greenleaf, Graham, 'The Influence of European Data Privacy Standards Outside Europe: Implications for Globalization of Convention 108' (2012) 2 International Data Privacy Law 68.

Greenleaf, Graham, 76 Global Data Privacy Laws, Privacy Laws and Business Special Report (September 2011).

Greenleaf, Graham, Global Analysis of Data Privacy Laws and Bills, 145 Privacy Laws and Business International Report (2017).

Greenleaf, Graham, Global Data Privacy Laws 2021: Despite COVID Delays, 145 Laws Show GDPR Dominance, 169 Privacy Laws and Business International Report (2021).

Greenleaf, Graham, Global Data Privacy Laws 2021: Uncertain Paths for International Standards, 169 Privacy Laws and Business International Report (2021).

Greenleaf, Graham, Modernized Data Protection Convention 108 and the GDPR, 154 Privacy Laws and Business International Report (2018).

Greenleaf, Graham, The UN Should Adopt Data Protection Convention 108 as Global Treaty, University of New South Wales Law Research Series No 24 (2018).

Greenleaf, Graham, The UN Special Rapporteur: Advancing A Global Privacy Treaty?, 136 Privacy Laws and International Business Report (2015).

Griffin, James, *On Human Rights* (Oxford University Press 2009).

Gross, Leo, 'The United Nations and the Role of Law' (1965) 19 International Organization 537.

Gross, Leo, *Essays on International Law and Organization* (Springer 2014).

Gruchalla-Wesierski, Tadeusz, 'A Framework for Understanding "Soft Law"' (1984) 30 McGill Law Journal 37.

Guidance to UNDP Country Offices on the Privacy, Data Protection and Broader Human Rights Dimensions of Using Digital Technologies to Combat Covid-19 (UNDP, June 2020).

Guide on Article 8 of the European Convention on Human Rights: Right to Respect for Private and Family (CoE, 31 August 2021).

Guide to Personal Data Protection and Privacy (WFP, June 2016).

Guidelines for the Alternative Care of Children, GA Res 64/142, 6rth sess, UN Doc A/Res/64/142 (24 February 2010).

Guidelines for the Prevention of Juvenile Delinquency (Riyadh Guidelines), GA Res 45/112, 68th plenary mtg, UN Doc A/RES/45/112 (14 December 1990).

Guidelines for the Regulation of Computerized Personal Data Files, Report of the Secretary General, UN Doc A/44/606 (24 October 1989).

Hale, Thomas and others, *Gridlock: Why Global Cooperation Is Failing When We Need It Most* (Polity Press 2013).

Hamilton, Michael and Antoine, Buyse, 'Human Rights Courts as Norm-Brokers' (2018) 18 Human Rights Law Review 205.

Hardl, Guther and others, 'A Hard Look at Soft Law' (1988) 82 Proceedings of the Annual Meeting of the ASIL 371.

Hannum, Hurst, 'Reinvigorating Human Rights for the 21st Century' (2016) 16 Human Rights Law Review 409.

Harper, Keith, Establishment of an HRC Mandate on Privacy Rights Comes at a Critical Time, Explanation of Position by the Delegation of the United States of America' (26 March 2015) <http://bit.ly/2fHl53O>.

Hathaway, Oona, 'Why Do Countries Commit to Human Rights Treaties?' (2007) 51 The Journal of Conflict Resolution 588.

Hawtin, Dixie, 'Internet Rights and Principles: Trends and Insights' in A Finlay (ed) *Internet Rights and Democratization: Focus on Freedom of Expression and Association Online* (Global Information Society Watch2011).

Helfer, Laurence and others, *The World Blind Union Guide to the Marrakesh Treaty: Facilitating Access to Books for Print-Disabled Individuals* (Oxford University Press 2017).

Higashi, Jutaro, 'The Role of Resolutions of the United Nations General Assembly in the Formative Process of International Customary Law' (1982) 25 *Japanese Annual of International Law* 11.

Higgins, Rosalyn and others, *Oppenheim's International Law: United Nations* (Oxford University Press 2017).

Higgins, Rosalyn, *Problems and Process: International Law and How We Use It* (Oxford University Press 1995).

Higgins, Rosalyn, *The Development of International Law Through the Political Organs of the United Nations* (Oxford University Press 1963).

Higgins, Rosalyn, *Themes and Theories: Selected Essays, Speeches and Writings in International Law* (Oxford University Press Vol I, 2009).

Hill, Richard, 'Internet Governance: The Last Gasp of Colonialism, or Imperialism by other Means?' in R Radu and others (eds), *The Evolution of Global Internet Governance* (Springer 2013).

Hohfeld, Wesley, 'Fundamental Legal Conceptions as Applied in Judicial Reasoning' (1917) 26 The Yale Law Journal 710.

Hondius, Frits, 'A Decade of International Data Protection' (1983) 30 Netherlands Review of International Law 103.

Hondius, Frits, 'A Quarter of Century of International Data Protection' (2006) 19 Hague Yearbook of International Law 23.

Hondius, Frits, *Emerging Data Protection in Europe* (North Holland Publishing Company 1975).

How Private Are Your Messaging Apps? (Amnesty International, 3 November 2016) <https://bit.ly/2HnJ4y7>.

HR Committee, *General Comment 16: Article 17—The Right to Respect of Privacy, Family, Home and Correspondence, and Protection of Honour and Reputation*, 32ndsess, UN Doc HRI/GEN/1/Rev.9 (Vol I) (8 April 1988).

HR Committee, *General Comment 31: Article 2—Nature of Legal Obligation Imposed on State Parties to the Covenant)*, 80thsess, UN Doc CCPR/C/21/Rev.1/Add.13 (26 May 2004).

HR Committee, *General Comment 34: Article 19—Freedom of Opinion and Expression*, 102ndsess, UN Doc CCPR/C/GC/34 12 (September 2011).

HR Committee, *General Comment 35: Article 9—Liberty and Security of Person*, 112thsess, UN Doc CCPR/C/GC/35 (16 December 2014).

HR Committee, *General Comment 37: Article 21—The Right of Peaceful Assembly)*, 129th sess, UN Doc CCPR/C/GC/37 (17 September 2020).

Hubbard, Amanda and Bygrave, Lee, 'Internet Governance Goes Global' in L Bygrave and J Bing (eds), *Internet Governance: Infrastructure and Institutions* (Oxford University Press 2009).

Human Rights and Modern Scientific and Technological Developments, Recommendation 509, adopted by the Parliamentary Assembly (31 January 1968).

Human Rights and Scientific and Technological Developments, GA Res 2450 (XXIII) (19 December 1968).

Human Rights and Scientific and Technological Developments, GA Res 3149 (XXVIII) (14 December 1973).

Human Rights and Scientific and Technological Developments, Resolution XI, adopted at the Tehran Conference (12 May 1968).

Human Rights and the Follow-up to the Guidelines for the Regulation of Computerized Personal Data Files, Commission on Human Rights Decision 1997/122 (16 April 1997).

Human Rights and the Follow-up to the Guidelines for the Regulation of Computerized Personal Data Files, Commission on Human Rights Decision 1999/109 (28 April 1999).

Human Rights and Transnational Corporations and other Business Enterprises, HRC Res 17/ 4 (16 June 2011).

Human Rights and Transnational Corporations and Other Business Enterprises, HRC Res 14/ 4 (6 July 2011).

Humphrey, John, 'The Implementation of International Human Rights Law' (1978) 24 New York Law School Law Review 33.

Humphrey, John, 'The International Bill of Rights: Scope and Implementation' (1976) 17 William and Mary Law Review 527.

Humphrey, John, 'The Universal Declaration of Human Rights: Its History, Impact and Juridical Character' in B Ramcharan (ed), *Human Rights Thirty Years After the Universal Declaration* (Brill 1979).

Humphrey, John, 'The Universal Declaration of Human Rights' (1949) 4 International Journal 351.

Huneeus, Alexandra, 'Human Rights and the Future of Being Human' (2018) 112 AJIL Unbound Symposium on UDHR at 70 and the Future of Being Human 324.

Hussain, Murtaza, 'Snowden Treaty' Calls for End to Mass Surveillance, Protections for Whistle-blowers (The Intercept, 25 September 2015) <http://bit.ly/1OZZn3I>.

Ignatieff, Michael, 'Human Rights as Politics and Idolatry' in A Gutmann (ed), *Human Rights as Politics and Idolatry* (Princeton University Press 2001).

In Larger Freedom: Towards Development, Security and Human Rights for All, UN Doc A/ 59/2005 (21 March 2005).

Information Disclosure Policy (UNDP 1996) [as updated in 2017].

Information/Document Access Policy (ITU 2016).

International Co-operation in the Peaceful Uses of Outer Space, GA Res 1721 (XVI)A-E (20 December 1961).

International Declaration on Information and Democracy (Reporters Without Borders 2018).

Internet Governance Strategy: 2016–2019 (CoE 2016).

Italian Declaration of Internet Rights (2015).

Jessup, Philip, *Transnational Law* (Yale University Press 1956).

Joint Declaration (of the Minister of Culture of Brazil and Undersecretary of Communication of Italy) on Internet Rights, The Second Internet Governance Forum, Rio de Janeiro (November 2007) <https://bit.ly/2qiWvuI>.

Joint Proposal for a Draft of International Standards on the Protection of Privacy and Personal Data: The Madrid Resolution (November 2009) <https://bit.ly/2QOXtqQ>.

Jorgensen, Rikke, 'An Internet Bill of Rights?' in I Brown (ed), *Research Handbook on Governance of the Internet* (Edward Elgar 2013).

Jorgensen, Rikke, 'Can Human Rights Law Bend Mass Surveillance?' (2018) 3 Internet Policy Review 1.

Joseph, Sarah and Castan, Melissa, *The International Covenant on Civil and Political Rights: Cases, Materials and Commentary* (Oxford University Press 3rd edn, 2013).

Joseph, Sarah, 'Social Media, Political Change and Human Rights' (2012) 35 Boston College International and Comparative Review 145.

Joyner, Christopher, 'UN General Assembly Resolutions and International Law: Rethinking Contemporary Dynamics of Norm-Creation' (1981) 11 California Western International Law Journal 445.

Kalin, Walter and Kunzli, Jorg, *The Law of International Human Rights Protection* (Oxford University Press 2009).

Karavias, Markos, *Corporate Obligations Under International Law* (Oxford University Press 2013).

Kaufmann, Christine, 'Multi-stakeholder Participation in Cyberspace' (2016) 26 Swiss Review of International and European Law 217.

Keck, Margaret and Sikkink, Kathryn, *Activists Beyond Borders: Advocacy Networks in International Politics* (Cornell University Press 1998).

Keller, Perry, *European and International Media Law: Liberal Democracy, Trade and the New Media* (Oxford University Press 2011).

Kerwin, Gregory, 'The Role of United Nations General Assembly Resolutions in Determining Principles of International Law in US Courts' (1983) 32 Duke Law Journal 876.

Kierkegaard, Sylvia and others, '30 Years On—The Review of the Council of Europe Data Protection Convention 108' (2011) 27 Computer Law and Security Review 223.

Kingsbury, Benedict, 'Indigenous Peoples' in *Max Planck Encyclopedia of Public International Law* (2015).

Kirby, Michael, 'The History, Achievement and Future of the 1980 OECD Guidelines on Privacy' (2011) 1 International Data Privacy Law 6.

Kirby, Michael, 'Transborder Data Flows and the Basic Rules of Data Privacy' (1980) 16 Stanford Journal of International Law 26.

Kiss, Jemima, An Online Magna Carta: Berners-Lee Calls for Bill of Rights for Web (The Guardian, 12 March 2014) <https://bit.ly/3AMIHtv>.

Klabbers, Jan, 'The Undesirability of Soft Law' (1998) 67 Nordic Journal of International Law 381.

Klabbers, Jan, *An Introduction to International Institutional Law* (Cambridge University Press 2002).

Kleijssen, Jan, A Magna Carta for the Internet? (LinkedIn Pulse, 17 September 2014) <http://bit.ly/2qtNTOH>.

Kleinwächter, Wolfgang, Internet Governance Outlook 2014: Good News, Bad News, No News? (Circle ID, 31 December 2013) <https://bit.ly/1k8uufI>.

Knox, John, 'Horizontal Human Rights Law' (2008) 102 The American Journal of International Law 1.

Koh, Harold, 'Rosco Pound Lecture: Transnational Legal Process' (1996) 75 Nebraska Law Review 181.

Koh, Harold, 'Why Transnational Law Matters' (2005) 24 Penn State International Law Review 745.

Koops, Bert-Jaap and Leenes, Ronald, 'Privacy Regulation cannot be Hardcoded: A Critical Comment on the "Privacy by Design" Provision in Data Protection Law' (2014) 28 International Review of Law, Computers and Technology 159.

Koops, Bert-Jaap and others, 'A Typology of Privacy' (2017) 38 University of Pennsylvania Journal of International Law 438.

Koskenneimi, Martti, *From Apology to Utopia: The Structure of International Legal Argument* (Cambridge University Press 2006).

Krotoszynski Jr., Ronald, *Privacy Revisited: A Global Perspective on the Right to Be Left Alone* (Oxford University Press 2016).

Kubota, Yo, 'The Institutional Response' in C Weeramantry (ed), *Human Rights and Scientific and Technological Development* (United Nations University Press 1990).

Kulesza, Joanna, Protecting Human Rights Online: An Obligation of Due Diligence, New York University School of Law Jean Monnet Working Paper No. 24/14 (2014).

Kuner, Christopher, 'An International Legal Framework for Data Protection: Issues and Prospects' (2009) 25 Computer Law and Security Review 307.

Kuner, Christopher, 'The European Union and the Search for an International Data Protection Framework' (2014) 2 Groningen Journal of International Law 54.

Kuner, Christopher, 'The Internet and the Global Reach of EU Law' in M Cremona and J Scott (eds.), *EU Law Beyond EU Borders: The Extraterritorial Reach of EU Law* (Oxford University Press 2019).

Kwasny, Sophie, 'Convention 108: A Transatlantic DNA?' in D Jerker Svantesson and D Kloza (eds), *Transatlantic Data Privacy Relations As A Challenge for Democracy* (Intersentia 2017).

Lachmayer, Konard, 'Rethinking Privacy Beyond Borders: Developing Transnational Rights on Data Privacy' (2015) 20 Tilburg Law Review 78.

Lagoni, Rainer, 'Resolution, Declaration, Decision' in R Wolfrum (ed), *United Nations: Law, Policies and Practice* (Springer 1995).

Lan, Raymond and others, 'Implementing the United Nations Convention on the Rights of Persons with Disabilities: Principles, Implications, Practice and Limitations' (2011) 5 ALTER: European Journal of Disability Research 206.

Land, Molly and others, 'Art. 22—Respect for Privacy' in I Bantekas and others (eds), *UN Convention on the Rights of Persons with Disabilities: A Commentary* (Oxford University Press 2018).

Land, Molly, 'Toward International Internet Law' (2013) 54 Harvard International Law Journal 394.

Landemore, Helen, 'Inclusive Constitution-making: The Icelandic Experiment' (2015) 23 Journal of Political Philosophy 166.

Lander, Eric and Nelson, Alondra, Americans Need a Bill of Rights for an AI-Powered World (Wired, 8 October 2021) <https://bit.ly/35ht6pR>.

Launch of the Philippine Declaration on Internet Rights and Principles (Foundation for Media Alternatives, September 2015) <http://104.236.169.13/FMA/?p=416>.

Lauren, Paul, *The Evolution of International Human Rights: Visions Seen* (University of Pennsylvania Press 3rd edn, 2011).

Lauterpacht, Hersch, 'The Universal Declaration of Human Rights' (1948) 25 British Yearbook of International Law 354.

Lauterpacht, Hersch, *International Law and Human Rights* (Stevens and Sons Limited 1950).

Lawson, Edward (ed), *Encyclopedia of Human Rights* (Taylor & Francis 2nd edn, 1996).

Leach, Philip, The Continuing Utility of International Human Rights Mechanisms? (EJIL: Talk!, 1 November 2017) <http://bit.ly/2z9lEeu>.

Lee Seung, Rep. Ro Khanna tapped by Pelosi to Draft 'Internet Bill of Rights' (The Mercury News, 21 April 2018) <https://bayareane.ws/33VZ9eD>.

Legally Binding Instrument to Regulate, in International Human Rights Law, the Activities of the Transnational Corporations and Other Business Enterprises, Third Revised Draft (17 August 2021) <https://bit.ly/3i2yTD1>.

Legally Binding Instrument to Regulate, in International Human Rights Law, the Activities of he Transnational Corporations and Other Business Enterprises, Zero Draft (16 July 2018).

Legislative History of the Convention on the Rights of the Child (OHCHR Vol I, 2007).

Lorca, Arnulf, 'Universal International Law: Nineteenth Century Histories of Imposition and Appropriation' (2010) 51 Harvard International Law Journal 475.

Lynskey, Orla, 'Deconstructing Data Protection: The "Added-Value" of A Right to Data Protection in the EU Legal Order' (2014) 63 International and Comparative Law Quarterly 569.

Lynskey, Orla, 'Grappling with "Data Power": Normative Nudges from Data Protection and Privacy' (2019) 20 Theoretical Inquiries in Law 189.

Lynskey, Orla, *The Foundations of EU Data Protection Law* (Oxford University Press 2015).

Madrid Privacy Declaration (3 November 2009).

Madsen, Wayne, *Handbook of Personal Data Protection* (Macmillan 1992).

Magallona, Merlin, 'Some Remarks on the Legal Character of UN General Assembly Resolutions' (1976) 5 Philippine Yearbook of International Law 84.

Makulilo, Alex, 'The Context of Data Privacy in Africa' in A Makulilo (ed), *African Data Privacy Laws* (Springer 2016).

Makulilo, Alex, 'The Future of Data Protection in Africa' in A Makulilo (ed), *African Data Privacy Laws* (Springer 2016).

Malik, Charles, 'Human Rights in the United Nations' (1951) 6 International Journal 275.

Malik, Charles, 'Human Rights in the United Nations with Text of Draft Covenants' (1952) 1 United Nations at Work 1.

McCarthy, Kieren, Dutch Govt Says No to Backdoors, Slides $540k into OpenSSL Without Breaking Eye Contact (The Register, 4 January 2016) <https://bit.ly/2EYKuNs>.

McDougal, Myres and others, 'Aggregate Interest in Shared Respect and Human Rights: The Harmonization of Public Order and Civic Order' (1977) 23 New York Law School Law Review 183.

Measures to Improve the Situation and Ensure the Human Rights and Dignity of All Migrant Workers, Report of the Open-ended Working Group, UN Doc A/C.3/36/10 (23 November 1981).

Meckled-Garcia, Saladin, 'Specifying Human Rights' in R Cruft and others (eds), *Philosophical Foundations of Human Rights* (Oxford University Press 2015).

Meeting Report of the Consultative Committee of the Convention for the Protection of Individuals with Regard to Automatic Processing of Personal Data [ETS 108 (T-PD)] (15 May 2008).

Mégret, Frédéric, 'Nature of Obligations' in D Moeckli and others (eds), *International Human Rights Law* (Oxford University Press 2nd edn, 2014).

Mégret, Frédéric, 'The Disabilities Convention: Towards a Holistic Concept of Rights' (2008) 12 The International Journal of Human Rights 61.

Meron, Theodor, *Human Rights Instruments and Customary Law* (Clarendon Press 1989).

Michael, James, *Privacy and Human Rights: An International and Comparative Study with Special Reference to Developments in Information Technology* (Dartmouth1994).

Milanovic, Marko, 'Human Right Treaties and Foreign Surveillance: The Right to Privacy in the Digital Age' (2014) 56 Harvard International Law Journal 81.

Millard, Christopher, 'Data Privacy in the Clouds' in M Graham and W Dutton (eds), *Society and the Internet: How Networks of Information and Communication are Changing Our Lives* (Oxford University Press 2014).

Mitsilegas, Valsamis, 'Surveillance and Digital Privacy in the Transatlantic "War on Terror": The Case for A Global Privacy Regime' (2016) 47 Columbia Human Rights Law Review 1.

Moncau, Luiz Marrey and Arguelhes, Diego, 'The Marco Civil da Internet and Digital Constitutionalism' in G Frosio (ed) *Oxford Handbook of Intermediary Liability* (Oxford University Press 2020).

Montreal Declaration for a Responsible Development of Artificial Intelligence (2018).

Montreux Declaration: The Protection of Personal Data and Privacy in a Globalized World—A Universal Right Respecting Diversities, International Conference of Privacy and Data Protection Commissioners (2005).

Morris, Christopher, *An Essay on the Modern State* (Cambridge University Press 1998).

Morsink, Johannes, *The Universal Declaration of Human Rights: Origins, Drafting and Intent* (University of Pennsylvania Press 1999).

Moskowitz, Moses, *International Concern for Human Rights* (Oceana Publications 1974).

Motion for A Resolution, Doc 2206, 19th Session (26 April 1967).

Moyn, Samuel, *The Last Utopia: Human Rights in History* (The Belknap Press 2010).

Mutua, Makau, 'Looking Past the Human Rights Committee: An Argument for De-Marginalizing Enforcement' (1998) 4 Buffalo Human Rights Law Review 211.

New and Emerging Digital Technologies and Human Rights, HRC Res 41/11 (17 July 2019).

New and Emerging Digital Technologies and Human Rights, HRC Res 47/23 (16 July 2021).

Niblett, G B F, Digital Information and the Privacy Problem, OECD Information Studies No 2 (1971).

Nigeria: Draft Resolution in Annex to the Final Act of the Tehran Conference on Human Rights, UN Doc A/CONF.32/C.2/L.28 (May 1968).

Nigerian Digital Rights and Freedoms Bill (2016).

Nilsson, Hans, 'The Council of Europe Laundering Convention: A Recent Example of A Developing International Criminal Law' (1991) 2 Criminal Law Forum 419.

Nowak, Manfred, 'It's Time for a World Court of Human Rights' in C Bassiouni and W Schabas (eds), *New Challenges for the UN Human Rights Machinery: What Future for the UN Treaty Body System and the Human Rights Council Procedures?* (Intersentia 2011).

Nowak, Manfred, *UN Covenant on Civil and Political Rights: CCPR Commentary* (NP Engel 2005).

Nowak, Manfred, and Januszewski, Karolina, 'Non-State Actors and Human Rights' in M Noortmann and others (eds), *Non-State Actors in International Law* (Hart 2015).

Nußberger, Angelika, 'The ECtHR's Use of Decisions of International Courts and Quasi-Judicial Bodies' in A Muller and H Kjos (eds), *Judicial Dialogue and Human Rights* (Cambridge University Press 2017).

Nyst, Carly and Falchatta, Thomaso, 'The Right to Privacy in the Digital Age' (2017) 9 Journal of Human Rights Practice 104.

O'Boyle, Michael and Lafferty, Michelle, 'General Principles and Constitutions as Sources of Human Rights Law' in D Shelton (ed), *The Oxford Handbook of International Human Rights Law* (Oxford University Press 2013).

Oberg, Marko, 'The Legal Effects of Resolutions of the UN Security Council and General Assembly in the Jurisprudence of the ICJ' (2006) 16 European Journal of International Law 879.

Observation of the United States on General Comment 31 of the Human Rights Committee (December 2007).

Observer Status for the Council of Europe in the General Assembly, GA Resolution 44/6 (17 October 1989).

Ogata, Sadako, 'Introduction: United Nations Approaches to Human Rights and Scientific Developments' in C Weeramantry (ed), *Human Rights and Scientific and Technological Development* (United Nations University Press 1990).

Oppenheim, Lassa, *International Law: A Treatise*, Vol I: Peace (Longman Green 1905).

Opsahl, Kurt, A Bill of Rights for Social Network Users (Electronic Frontier Foundation, 19 May 2010) <http://bit.ly/2s2PMFp>.

Orakhelashvili, Alexander, 'The Idea of European International Law' (2006) 17 European Journal of International Law 315.

Outline for an International Convention on the Protection of the Rights of All Migrant Workers and Their Families, Working Paper Presented by the Chairman of the Working Group, UN Doc A/C.3/35/WH.1/CRP.5 (12 November 1980).

Paust, Jordan, 'Can You Hear Me Now? Private Communication, National Security, and the Human Rights Disconnect' (2015) 15 Chicago Journal of International Law 612.

Pauwelyn, Joost and others, 'When Structures Become Shackles: Stagnation and Dynamics in International Law Making' (2014) 25 European Journal of International Law 733.

Pedersen, Mads and Ferretti, Federico, 'Art 31—Statistics and Data Collection' in I Bantekas and others (eds), *UN Convention on the Rights of Persons with Disabilities: A Commentary* (Oxford University Press 2018).

Pellet, Alain, 'Article 38' in A Zimmermann and others (eds), *The Statute of the International Court of Justice: A Commentary* (Oxford University Press 2nd edn, 2012).

Pernot-Leplay, Emmanuel, 'EU Influence on Data Privacy Laws: Is the US Approach Converging with the EU Model?' (2019) 18 Colorado Technology Law Journal 101.

Personal Data Protection and Privacy Principles (UN High-Level Committee on Management, 11 October 2018).

Personal Data Security Technical Guide (UNESCO 2020).

Peters, Anne, Surveillance Without Borders: The Unlawfulness of the NSA Panopticon—Part II (EJIL: Talk!, 4 November 2013) <http://bit.ly/2vElrhK>.

Pettrachin, Andrea, 'Towards a Universal Declaration of Internet Rights and Freedoms' (2018) 80 International Communication Gazette 337.

Policy on Personal Data Protection (UNICEF, 15 July 2020).

Policy on the Protection of Personal Data of Persons of Concern to the UNHCR (UNHCR, May 2015).

Policy on the Use and Sharing of Data Collected by WHO in Member States outside the Context of Public Health Emergencies (WHO, August 2017).

Posner, Eric, *The Twilight of Human Rights Law* (Oxford University Press 2014).

Preparatory Work on Article 8 of the European Convention on Human Rights, DH [56] 12 (1956).

President von der Leyen's speech at the High-level Opening Session of the 2021 Digital Assembly, 'Leading the Digital Decade' (EU, 1 June 2021) <https://bit.ly/3KNx8qo>.

Principles for Governmental Access to Personal Data held by the Private Sector for National Security and Public Safety Purposes (Global Privacy Assembly, October 2021).

Principles for Technology-Assisted Contact-Tracing (American Civil Liberties Union, 16 April 2020).

Principles on Freedom of Expression and Privacy (Global Network Initiative 2008).

Privacy and Computers, Report of a Task Force Established Jointly by the Department of Communications and the Department of Justice of the Federal Canadian Government, Ottawa, Information Canada (1972).

Privacy and Freedom of Expression in the Age of Artificial Intelligence (Privacy International, April 2018) <https://bit.ly/2Hvso7J>.

Privacy Developments in Europe and Their Implications for United States Policy, A Staff Report of the Committee on Government Operations, United States Senate (March 1975).

Privacy in the Digital Age: A Proposal for a New General Comment on the Right to Privacy under Article 17 of the International Covenant on Civil and Political Rights (American Civil Liberties Union, March 2014).

Proclamation of Tehran, U.N. Doc. A/CONF. 32/41 (May 1968).

Protecting the Open Internet: Regulatory Principles for Policymakers (Twitter, October 2021) <https://bit.ly/3LDGGEY>.

Protection of Personal Data in Transborder Flow of Personal Data in the Report of the Commission to the United Nations General Assembly on the Work of its Fifty-eighth Session, UN Doc A/61/10 (August 2006).

Question of the Follow-up to the Guidelines for the Regulation of Computerized Personal Data Files, Commission on Human Rights Decision 1995/114 (8 March 1995).

Question of the Follow-up to the Guidelines for the Regulation of Computerized Personal Data Files, Report of the Secretary-General prepared Pursuant to Commission Decision 1997/122 (18 November 1998).

Ramcharan, Bertrand, 'The Law-Making Process: From Declaration to Treaty and Custom' in D Shelton (ed), *Oxford Handbook of International Human Rights Law* (Oxford University Press 2000).

Rampell, Catherine, Google Calls for International Standards on Internet Privacy (The Washington Post, 15 September 2007) <http://wapo.st/2kXZAZz>.

Randall, Maya, 'The History of the Covenants: Looking Back Half a Century and Beyond' in D Moeckli and others (eds), *Human Rights Covenants At 50: The Past, Present and Future* (Oxford University Press 2018).

Ratner, Steven, 'Corporations and Human Rights: A Theory of Legal Responsibility' (2001) 111 The Yale Law Journal 443.

Raustiala, Kal, 'Governing the Internet' (2016) 110 The American Journal of International Law 491.

Raymond, Mary and DeNardis, Laura, 'Multistakeholderism: Anatomy of An Inchoate Global Institution' (2015) 7 International Theory 572.

Raz, Joseph, 'Human Rights in the Emerging World Order' in R Cruft and others (eds), *Philosophical Foundations of Human Rights* (Oxford University Press 2015).

Rechota, Vratislav, 'The Development of the Covenant on Civil and Political Rights' in L Henkin (ed), *The International Bill of Rights: The Covenant on Civil and Political Rights* (Columbia University Press 1981).

Recommendation 890 on the Protection of Personal Data, Parliamentary Assembly of the Council of Europe (1980).

Recommendation of the Council on OECD Legal Instruments Artificial Intelligence, OECD/LEGAL/0449 (May 2019).

Recommendations on Privacy and Data protection in the Fight Against COVID-19 (Access Now, March 2020).

Redeker, Dennis and others, 'Towards Digital Constitutionalism? Mapping Attempts to Craft an Internet Bill of Rights' (2018) 80 International Communication Gazette 302.

Redgwell, Catherine, 'General Principles of International Law' in S Vogenauer and S Weatherill (eds), *General Principles of Law: European and Comparative Perspectives* (Hart 2017).

Reed, Chris, *Making Laws for Cyberspace* (Oxford University Press 2012).

Rehof, Lars, 'Article 12' in A Eide and others (eds), *The Universal Declaration of Human Rights: A Commentary* (Scandinavian University Press 1992).

Rengel, Alexandra, *Privacy in the 21st Century* (Martinus Nijhoff 2013).

Rep. Khanna Releases 'Internet Bill of Rights' Principles, Endorsed by Sir Tim Berners-Lee Press Release, 4 October 2018) <https://bit.ly/3u9UfWp>.

Report of Special Rapporteur of the UN Sub-Commission on Prevention of Discrimination and Protection of Minorities, Francesco Capotorti, UN Doc E/CN.4/Sub.2/384/Add.5 (28 June 1977).

Report of Special Rapporteur on the Promotion and Protection of the Right to Freedom of Opinion and Freedom of Expression, David Kaye, UN Doc A/HRC/29/32 (22 May 2015).

Report of Special Rapporteur on the Promotion and Protection of the Right to Freedom of Opinion and Freedom of Expression, David Kaye, UN Doc A/HRC/32/38 (11 May 2016).

Report of Special Rapporteur on the Right to Privacy, Joe Cannataci, UN Doc A/HRC/31/64 (8 March 2016).

Report of the Ad Hoc Committee on a Comprehensive and Integral International Convention on the Protection and Promotion of the Rights and Dignity of Persons with Disabilities on its Fifth Session, UN Doc A/AC.265/2005/2 (23 February 2005).

Report of the Dynamic Coalition for Internet Rights and Principles (2015).

Report of the Open-ended Working Group on the Drafting of an International Convention on the Protection of the Rights of All Migrant Workers and Members of Their Families, UN Doc A/C.3/41/3 (10 October 1986).

Report of the Sessional Working Group on the Administration of Justice: Chairman-Rapporteur: Mr. Louis Joinet, UN Doc E/CN.4/Sub.2/1998/19 (19 August 1998).

Report of the Special Rapporteur on the Promotion and Protection of Human Rights and Fundamental Freedoms while Countering Terrorism, Martin Scheinin, UN Doc A/HRC/13/37 (28 December 2009).

Report of the Special Rapporteur on the Promotion and Protection of the Right to Freedom of Opinion and Expression, Frank La Rue, UN Doc A/HRC/23/40 (17 April 2013).

Report of the Special Rapporteur on the Promotion and Protection of the Right to Freedom of Opinion and Expression, Frank La Rue, UN Doc A/HRC/17/27 (16 May 2011).

Report of the Special Rapporteur on the Promotion and Protection of the Right to Freedom of Opinion and Expression, Frank La Rue, UN Doc A/66/290 (10 August 2011).

Report of the Special Rapporteur on the Promotion and Protection of the Right to Freedom of Opinion and Expression, Frank La Rue, UN Doc A/HRC/23/40 (17 April 2013).

Report of the Special Rapporteur on the Promotion and Protection of the Right to Freedom of Opinion and Expression, David Kaye, UN Doc A/HRC/41/35 (28 May 2019).

Report of the Special Rapporteur on the Promotion and Protection of Human Rights and Fundamental Freedoms while Countering Terrorism, Ben Emmerson, UN Doc A/69/397 (23 September 2014).

Report of the Special Rapporteur on the Right to Privacy, Joseph Cannataci, UN Doc A/71/368 (30 August 2016).

Report of the Special Rapporteur on the Right to Privacy, Joseph Cannataci, UN Doc A/HRC/34/60 (24 February 2017).

Report of the Special Rapporteur on the Right to Privacy, Joseph Cannataci, UN Doc A/72/43103 (19 October 2017).

Report of the Special Rapporteur on the Right to Privacy, Joseph Cannataci, UN Doc A/HRC/40/63 (27 February 2019).

Report of the Special Rapporteur on the Right to Privacy, Joseph Cannataci, UN Doc A/HRC/37/62 (28 February 2018).

Report of the Special Rapporteur on the Right to Privacy, Joseph Cannataci, UN Doc A/HRC/46/37(25 January 2021).

Report of the Special Rapporteur on the Right to Privacy, Joseph Cannataci, UN Doc A/73/438 (17 October 2018).

Report of the Special Rapporteur on the Right to Privacy, Joseph Cannataci, UN Doc A/HRC/40/63 (16 October 2019).

Report of the Special Rapporteur on the Right to Privacy, Joseph Cannataci, UN Doc A/HRC/31/64 (24 November 2016).

Report of the Working Group on the Issue of Human Rights and Transnational Corporations and other Business Enterprises, UN Doc A/71/291 (4 August 2016).

Report of the Working Group on the Issue of Human Rights and Transnational Corporations and other Business Enterprises, UN Doc A/HRC/26/25 (5 May 2014).

Report on the Second Session of the Open-ended Intergovernmental Working Group on Transnational Corporations and other Business Enterprises with respect to Human Rights, UN Doc A/HRC/34/47 (4 January 2017).

Report on the Third Session of the Open-ended Intergovernmental Working Group on Transnational Corporations and other Business Enterprises with Respect to Human Rights, UN Doc A/HRC/37/67 (24 January 2018).

Resolution (73) 22 on the Protection of the Privacy of Individuals vis-à-vis Electronic Data Banks in the Private Sector, adopted by the Committee of Ministers at the 224th meeting of the Ministers' Deputies (26 September 1973).

Resolution (74) 29 on the Protection of Privacy of Individuals vis-à-vis Electronic Data Banks in the Public Sector, adopted by the Committee of Ministers at the 236th meeting of the Ministers' Deputies (20 September 1974).

Respect for the Privacy of Individuals and Integrity and Sovereignty of Nations in the Light of Advances in Recording and Other Techniques, Report of the Secretary-General, UN Doc E/CN.4/1116 (23 January 1973).

Reus-Smit, Christian and Dunne, Tim, 'The Globalization of International Society' in T Dunne and C Reus-Smit (eds), *The Globalization of International Society* (Oxford University Press 2017).

Richards, Neil, 'The Dangers of Surveillance' (2013) 126 Harvard Law Review 1934.

Richardson, Megan, *The Right to Privacy: Origins and Influence of a Nineteenth Century Idea* (Cambridge University Press 2017).

Risse, Mathias, 'Human Rights and Artificial Intelligence: An Urgently Needed Agenda' (2019) Human Rights Quarterly 1.

Risse, Thomas and Sikkink, Kathryn, 'The Socialization of International Human Rights Norms in Domestic Practices: Introduction' in T Risse and others (eds), *The Power of Human Rights: International Norms and Domestic Change* (Cambridge University Press 1999).

Roadmap for Digital Cooperation: Implementation of the Recommendations of the High-level Panel on Digital Cooperation, Report of the Secretary General, UN Doc A/74/821 (29 May 2020).

Roberts, Christopher *The Contentious History of the International Bill of Human Rights* (Cambridge University Press 2014).

Robertson, Arthur, 'Relations Between the Council of Europe and the United Nations' (1970) 28 European Yearbook 80.

Robertson, Arthur, 'The Contribution of the Council of Europe to the Development of International Law' (1965) 59 Proceedings of the American Society of International Law at Its Annual Meeting 201.

Rocotà, Stefano, 'A Bill of Rights for the Internet Universe' (2008) 21 The Federalist Debate 1.

Rocotà, Stefano, 'Data Protection as a Fundamental Right' in S Gutwirth and others (eds), *Reinventing Data Protection?* (Springer 2009).

Rodotà, Stefano, 'Protecting Informational Privacy: Trends and Problems' in W Ates and others (eds), *Information Law Towards The 21st Century* (Kluwer Law and Taxation Publishers 1992).

Rodotà, Stefano, Towards a Declaration of Internet Rights (European Area of Freedom, Security and Justice, 18 November 2014) <https://bit.ly/2IuWmxw>.

Roessler, Beate, 'Privacy as a Human Rights' (2017) 117 Proceedings of the Aristotelian Society 187.

Rossini, Carolina and others, The Strength and Weaknesses of the Brazilian Internet Bill of Rights (Chatham House 2015).

Rozenshtein, Alan, 'Surveillance Intermediaries' (2018) 70 Stanford Law Review 99.

Ruggie, John, Comments on the 'Zero Draft' Treaty on Business and Human Rights (Business and Human Rights Resource Center, August 2018) <https://bit.ly/2DcDv75>.

Ruiz, Carlos, *La Configuración Constitucional del Derecho a la Intimidad* (1992).

Rules of Procedure of the Human Rights Committee (4 January 2021).

Rules on Personal Data Protection (ICRC, November 2015).

Rules on the Processing of Data (INTERPOL 2019).

Saadat, Lauren and Ballard, Shannon, A Way Ahead for Global Privacy Standards?—Thoughts on a UN Convention on Data Protection, International Standards and International Agreements: Which is the Best Option? 89 Privacy Laws and Business (2007).

Sartor, Giovanni, 'Human Rights and Information Technologies' in R Brownsword and others (eds), *The Oxford Handbook of Law, Regulation and Technology* (Oxford University Press 2017).

Saul, Ben, *Indigenous Peoples and Human Rights: International and Regional Jurisprudence* (Hart 2016).

Saunders, Imogen, *General Principles as a Source of International Law: Art 38(1)(c) of the Statute of the International Court of Justice* (Hart 2020).

Schabas, William (ed), *The Universal Declaration of Human Rights: The Travaux Préparatoires* (Cambridge University Press Vol I, 2013).

Schabas, William, *The European Convention on Human Rights: A Commentary* (Oxford University Press 2015).

Schabas, William, *The Customary International Law of Human Rights* (Oxford University Press 2021).

Schachter, Oscar, 'International Law Implications of U.S. Human Rights Policies' (1978) 24 New York Law School Law *Review* 63.

Schacther, Oscar, *International Law in Theory and Practice* (Martinus Nijhoff 1991).

Scheinin, Martin, Privacy and Security can be Reconciled (The Guardian, 21 January 2010) <https://bit.ly/2OmKY4C>.

Scheinin, Martin, Towards a World Court of Human Rights, Research Report within the Framework of the Swiss Initiative to Commemorate the 60th Anniversary of the Universal Declaration of Human Rights (22 June 2009).

Schieder, Siegfried, 'Pragmatism and International Law' in H Bauer and E Brighi (eds), *Pragmatism in International Relations* (Routledge 2009).

Schieder, Siegfried, 'Pragmatism as a Path Towards A Discursive and Open Theory of International Law' (2000) 11 European Journal of International Law 663 [Translated by Iain Fraser].

Schmahl, Stephanie, 'The Council of Europe in the System of International Organizations' in S Schmahl and M Breuer, *The Council of Europe: Its Law and Polices* (Oxford University Press 2017).

Schmitt, Michael (ed), *Tallinn Manual 2.0 on the International Law Applicable to Cyber Operations* (Cambridge University Press 2017).

Schmitt, Michael, 'Introduction' in N Tsagourias and R Buchan (eds), *Research Handbook on International Law and Cyberspace* (Edward Elgar 2015).

Schulhofer, Stephen, 'An International Right to Privacy? Be Careful What You Wish For' (2016) 14 International Journal of Constitutional Law 238.

Schulz, Wolfgang and Hoboken, Joris van, *Human Rights and Encryption* (UNESCO Series on Internet Freedom 2015).

Schwartz, Paul, 'Global Data Privacy: The EU Way' (2019) 98 New York University Law Review 771.

Scovazzi, Tullio and Citroni, Gabriella, *The Struggle against Enforced Disappearance and the 2007 United Nations Convention* (Martinus Nijhoff 2007).

Second Report on General Principles of Law by Marcelo Vázquez-Bermúdez, Special Rapporteur, UN Doc A/CN.4/741 (9 April 2020).

Seibert-Fohr, Anja 'The Human Rights Committee' in G Oberleitner (ed), *International Human Rights Institutions, Tribunals and Courts* (Springer 2018).

Seibert-Fohr, Anja, 'Digital Surveillance, Meta Data and Foreign Intelligence Cooperation: Unpacking the International Right to Privacy' in J David and others (eds), *Strengthening Human Rights Protections in Geneva, Israel, the West Bank and Beyond* (Cambridge University Press 2021).

Shany, Yuval, Online Surveillance in the Case Law of the Human Rights Committee, The Hebrew University of Jerusalem Center for Cybersecurity Research (13 July 2017) <https://bit.ly/2MECR7m>.

Shapiro, Martin, 'The Globalization of Law' (1993) 1 Indian Journal of Global Studies 37.

Sheinine, Martin, 'The International Covenant on Civil and Political Rights' in G Ulfstein and others (eds), *Making Treaties Work: Human Rights, Environment and Arms Control* (Cambridge University Press 2007).

Shelton, Dinah and Carozza, Paolo, *Regional Protection of Human Rights* (Oxford University Press Vol I, 2nd edn, 2013).

Shelton, Dinah, 'Commentary and Conclusions' in D Shelton (ed), *Commitment and Compliance: The Role of Non-Binding Norms in the International Legal System* (Oxford University Press 2000).

Shelton, Dinah, 'Introduction: Law, Non-Law and the Problem of Soft Law' in D Shelton (ed), *Commitment and Compliance: The Role of Non-Binding Norms in the International Legal System* (Oxford University Press 2000).

Shorupski, John, 'Human Rights' in S Besson and J Tasioulas (eds), *Philosophy of International Law* (Oxford University Press 2010).

Simma, Bruno and Alston, Philip, 'The Sources of Human Rights Law: Custom, Jus Cogens and General Principles' (1992) 12 Australian Yearbook of International Law 82.

Simoncini, Andrea, The Constitutional Dimensions of the Internet: Some Research Paths, EUI Working Papers No LAW 2016/16 (2016).

Simpson, Gerry, 'The Globalization of International Law' in T Dunne and C Reus-Smit (eds), *The Globalization of International Society* (Oxford University Press 2017).

Sinnreich, Aram, An International Approach to Data Privacy, American University Center for Media and Social Impact Policy Briefing Note (August 2018).

Siracusa Principles on the Limitation and Derogation Provisions in the International Covenant on Civil and Political Rights, American Association for the International Commission of Jurists (1988).

Sohn, Louis, 'The Human Rights Law of the Charter' (1977) 12 Texas International Law Journal 129.

Soriano, Leanor, 'A modest Notion of Coherence in Legal Reasoning: A Model for the European Court of Justice' (2003) 16 Ratio Juris 296.

Sourgens, Frédéric, 'The Privacy Principle' (2017) 42 The Yale Journal of International Law 345.

Souza, Carlos and others, 'Notes on the Creation and Impacts of Brazil's Internet Bill of Rights' (2017) 5 Theory and Practice of Legislation 73.

Special Rapporteur on the Right to Privacy Presents Draft Legal Instrument on Government-led Surveillance and Privacy (February 2018) <https://bit.ly/2ZcNe4Y>.

Ssenyonjo, Manisuli, *Economic, Social and Cultural Rights in International Law* (Hart 2nd edn, 2016).

Statement on Artificial Intelligence, Robotics and 'Autonomous' Systems of the European Group on Ethics in Science and New Technologies (March 2018).

Status of the Human Rights Treaty Body System, Report of the Secretary General, UN Doc A/74/643 (10 January 2020).

Steiner, Henry, 'Individual Claims in A World of Massive Violations: What Role for the Human Rights Committee?' in P Alston and J Crawford (eds), *The Future of the UN Human Rights Treaty Monitoring* (Cambridge University Press 2000).

Stephenson, Randall, Consumers Need an Internet Bill of Rights (AT&T Media Release, 24 January 2018) <https://soc.att.com/2DHA7ki>.

Strengthening Cooperation with the United Nations in Implementing the 2030 Agenda for Sustainable Development, PACE Res 2271 (2019).

Strengthening the United Nations Human Rights Treaty Body System, A Report by the United Nations High Commissioner for Human Rights, Navi Pillay, UN Doc A/66/860 (26 June 2012).

Strümholm, Stig, Right to Privacy and Rights of Personality: A Comparative Survey, Working Paper Prepared for the Nordic Conference on Privacy Organized by the International Commission of Jurists, Stockholm May 22–23 1967 (Instituti Upsaliensis Iurisprudentiae Gomparativae 1967).

Study of the Relevant Guidelines in the field of Computerized Personal File, Final Report Prepared by Mr. Louis Joinet, UN Doc E/C.4/Sub.2/1983/18 (30 June 1983).

Sub-Commission on the Promotion and Protection of Human Rights, Norms and Responsibilities of Transnational Corporations and other Business Enterprises with re-gard to Human Rights, UN Doc E/CN.4/Sub.2/2003/12/Rev.2 (13 August 2003).

Summary Record of the 51st Meeting of the Third Committee, UN Doc A/C.3/68/SR.51 (26 November 2013).

Sumption, Lord, The Limits of Law, 27th Sultan Azlan Shah Lecture, Kuala Lumpur (20 November 2013).

Tahzib, Bahiyyih, *Freedom of Religion Or Belief: Ensuring Effective International Legal Protection* (Martinus Nijhoff 1996).

Tene, Omer, 'Privacy: The New Generations' (2011) 1 International Data Privacy Law 15.

Terwangne, Cécilede, 'Council of Europe Convention 108+: A Modernized International Treaty for the Protection of Personal Data' (2021) 40 Computer Law and Security Review 1.

The Geneva Declaration of Principles (WSIS, 12 December 2003).

The Geneva Plan of Action (WSIS, 12 December 2003).

The Global Surveillance Industry (Privacy International) <https://bit.ly/2Isuqde>.

The Helsinki Final Act: Conference on Security and Cooperation in Europe Final Act (1 August 1975).

The Highest Aspiration: A Call to Action for Human Rights by the United Nations Secretary General (2020).

The IRP Charter of Human Rights and Principles for the Internet: Five Years On, IRP Coalition Meeting Report (4 September 2014).

The Promotion, Protection and Enjoyment of Human Rights on the Internet, HRC Res 20/8 (16 July 2012).

The Promotion, Protection and Enjoyment of Human Rights on the Internet, HRC Res 47/16 (26 July 2021).

The Promotion, Protection and Enjoyment of Human Rights on the Internet, HRC Res 47/16 (26 July 2021).

The Right to Freedom of Information and Expression on the Internet in Africa, ACHPR Res. 362(LIX)2016 (4 November 2016).

The Right to Privacy in the Digital Age, Report of High Commissioner for Human Rights, UN Doc A/HRC/39/29 (3 August 2018).

The Right to Privacy in the Digital Age, Report of the High Commissioner for Human Rights, UN Doc A/HRC/39/29 (30 June 2014).

The Right to Privacy in the Digital Age: Report of the High Commissioner for Human Rights, UN Doc A/HRC/48/31 (13 September 2021).

The Right to Respect for Privacy As Affected by Modern Scientific and Technological Devices: Survey of Legislation in the Member States, H. (73) 11 (1970).

The Road to Dignity by 2030: Ending Poverty, Transforming All Lives and Protecting the Planet, Synthesis Report of the Secretary-General on the Post-2015 Agenda, UN Doc A/69/700 (December 2014).

The Situation with regard to the Implementation of the Declaration on the Granting of Independence to Colonial Countries and Peoples, GA Res 1654 (XVI) (27 November 1961).

The Snowden Treaty: A New International Treaty on the Right to Privacy, Protection Against Improper Surveillance and Protection of Whistle-blowers (September 2015) <http://www.snowdentreaty.org/>.

The Tunis Agenda for the Information Society (WSIS, 18 November 2005).

The United Nations Declaration on the Rights of Indigenous Peoples, GA Res 61/295 (2 October 2007).

The United Nations Global Counter-Terrorism Strategy Review, GA Res 66/282 (12 July 2012).

The United Nations Global Counter-Terrorism Strategy Review, GA Res 72/284 (2 July 2018).

The United Nations Global Counter-Terrorism Strategy Review, GA Res 70/291 (19 July 2016).

The United Nations Global Counter-Terrorism Strategy Review, GA Res 68/276 (24 June 2014).

The United Nations Global Counter-Terrorism Strategy Review, GA Res 75/291 (2 July 2021).

The Use of Scientific and Technological Developments in the Interest of Peace and Social Development, GA Res 3150 (XXVIII), 2201st plenary mtg, UN Doc RES/3150 (XXVIII) (14 December 1973).

The WTO and Internet Privacy, Fact and Fiction: Misunderstanding and Scare Stories (WTO) <https://bit.ly/2P9arPD>.

Thirlway, Hugh, *The Sources of International Law* (Oxford University Press 2nd edn, 2019).

Thornberry, Patrick, *International Law and the Rights of Minorities* (Clarendon Press 1991).

Tilmann Alwicker, 'Transnationalizing Rights: International Human Rights Law in Cross-Border Contexts' (2018) 29 European Journal of International Law 581.

Tisne, Martin, It's Time for a Bill of Data Rights (MIT Technology Review, 14 December 2018) <https://bit.ly/348b7SH>.

Tobin, John and Field, Sarah, 'Art.16—The Right to Protection of Privacy, Family, Home, Correspondence, Honour, and Reputation' in J Tobin (ed) *The Convention on the Rights of the Child: A Commentary* (Oxford University Press 2019).

Tobin, John, 'Seeking to Persuade: A Constructive Approach to Human Rights Treaty Interpretation' (2010) 23 Harvard Human Rights Journal 201.

Tomuschat, Christian, *Human Rights: Between Idealism and Realism* (Oxford University Press 3rd edn, 2014).

Toronto Declaration: Protecting the Right to Equality and Discrimination in Machine Learning Systems (Amnesty International and Access Now, May 2018).

Toward a Social Compact for Digital Privacy and Security: Statement by the Global Commission on Internet Governance (Chatham House 2015).

Trujillo, Elizabeth, 'A Dialogical Approach to Trade and Environment' (2013) 16 Journal of International Economic Law 535.

Tunkin, Grigory, 'Is General International Law Customary Law Only?' (1993) 4 European Journal of International Law 534.

Tyagi, Yogesh, *The Human Rights Committee: Practice and Procedure* (Cambridge University Press 2011).

Tzanou, Maria, *The Fundamental Right to Data Protection: Normative Value in the Context of Counter-Terrorism Surveillance* (Hart 2017).

Uerpmann-Wittzack, Robert, 'Media and Information Society' in S Schmahl and M Breuer, *The Council of Europe: Its Law and Policies* (Oxford University Press 2017).

UN Budget Shortfalls Seriously Undermine the Work of the Human Rights Treaty Bodies (OHCHR Press Release, 17 May 2019).

UN Standard Minimum Rules for the Treatment of Prisoners (Nelson Mandela Rules), GA Res 70/175, UN Doc A/RES/70/175 (17 December 2015).

United Nations Conference on Human Rights: Report by Miss Muireann McHugh, Barrister-at-Law, Approved by Mr Sean McBride, Secretary-General of the International Commission of Jurists, S.2021.

United Nations Millennium Declaration, GA Res 55/2 (8 September 2000).

Universal Declaration of Digital Rights (Article 19, 2017).

Universal Declaration on Bio-ethics and Human Rights (UNESCO, 19 October 2005).

Universal Periodic Review (2013) 1 Human Rights Monitor Quarterly 1.

Use of the Terms 'Declaration' and 'Recommendation', Memorandum by the Office of Legal Affairs, UN Doc E/CN.4/L.610 (2 April 1962).

Uses of Electronics which may Affect the Rights of the Person and the Limits which Should be Placed on such Uses in a Democratic Society, Report of the UN Secretary-General, UN Doc E/CN.4/1142 (31 January 1974).

Vandenhole, Wouter and Genugten, Willem van, 'Introduction: An Emerging Multi-Duty-Bearer Human Rights Regime?' in W Vandenhole (ed), *Challenging Territoriality in Human Rights Law: Building Blocks for a Plural and Diverse Duty-Bearer Regime* (Routledge 2015).

Velu, Jacques, 'The European Convention on Human Rights and the Right to Respect for Private Life, The Home and Communications' in A Robertson (ed), *Privacy and Human Rights* (Manchester University Press 1973).

Vilanova, Pere, 'The Right to Privacy in the Case Law of the ECtHR' in *Proceedings of the High-Level Seminar on International Case Law in Bioethics: Insight and Foresight* (2016).

Volio, Fernando, 'Legal Personality, Privacy and the Family' in L Henkin (ed), *The International Bill of Rights: The Covenant on Civil and Political Rights* (Columbia University Press 1981).

Wacks, Raymond, *Privacy: A Very Short Introduction* (Oxford University Press 2015).

Wade, Ariel, A New Age of Privacy Protection: A Proposal for An International Personal Data Privacy Treaty (2010) 42 George Washington International Law Review 659.

We Can't Wait: Obama Administration Unveils Blueprint for a 'Privacy Bill of Rights' to Protect Consumers Online (Press Release, 23 February 2012) <https://bit.ly/3G9He1c>.

Weeramantry, Christopher, 'Science, Technology and the Future of Human Rights' (1986) 13 India International Centre Quarterly 41.

Weeramantry, Christopher, *Universalizing International Law* (Brill 2004).

Weeramantry, Lucian, *The International Commission of Jurists: The Pioneering Years* (Kluwer Law International 2000).

Weiss, Thomas and Daws, Sam, 'The United Nations: Continuity and Change' in T Weiss and S Daws (eds), *The Oxford Handbook on the United Nations* (Oxford University Press 2018).

Weizsäcker, Franz von and Schräpel, Norman, Why We Should Support the 'European Charter of Digital Fundamental Rights' (Internet Policy Review Blog, 14 December 2016) <http://bit.ly/2qBgl2N>.

Witzleb, Normann and others, 'An Overview of Emerging Challenges in Privacy Law' in N Witzleb and others (eds), *Emerging Challenges in Privacy Law: Comparative Perspectives* (Cambridge University Press 2014).

Wouters, Jan and Chance, Anna-Luise, 'Multinational Corporations in International Law' in M Noortmann and others (eds), *Non-State Actors in International Law* (Hart 2015).

Yamane, Hiroko, 'Impacts of Scientific and Technological Progress on Human Rights: Normative Response of the International Community' C Weeramantry (ed), *Human Rights and Scientific and Technological Development* (United Nations University Press 1990).

Yilma, Kinfe, 'Bill of Rights for the 21st Century: Some Lessons from the Internet Bill of Rights Movement' (2022) 26 The International Journal of Human Rights 701.

Yilma, Kinfe, The United Nations' Evolving Privacy Discourse and Corporate Human Rights Obligations (ASIL Insights 2019) <https://bit.ly/3tGg3bV>.

Zalnieriute, Monika, 'An International Constitutional Moment for Data Privacy' (2015) 23 International Journal of Law and Information Technology 99.

Zittrain, Jonathan, A Bill of Rights for the Facebook Nation (The Chronicle of Higher Education, 20 April 2009) <https://bit.ly/2Jj8gpq>.

Zuckerberg, Mark, A Privacy-Focused Vision for Social Networking' (Facebook, 6 March 2019) <https://bit.ly/2TmiQWv>.

Zuckerberg, Mark, The Internet Needs New Rules: Let's Start in Four Areas (The Washington Post, 30 March 2019) <https://wapo.st/2uEbrTT>.

Index

For the benefit of digital users, indexed terms that span two pages (e.g., 52–53) may, on occasion, appear on only one of those pages.

accession 9–10, 42, 113, 210–11, 214, 221–27, 242–43
authoritative interpretation 72, 120, 169–70, 190, 193–94, 254

backdoors 145, 185–86, 270–71, 279
bill of rights 18–19, 131, 132, 140, 144, 147, 166, 168, *see also* Internet bills of rights
bulk collection 145, 201, 267–68
bulk hacking 270–71, *see also* hacking

catalytic role 20, 130, 151, 190, 202–3, 204, 206, 207, 208, 221, 310
civil society groups 42, 131–32, 140–44, 160–61, 173–74, 281, 303–4
Cold War 6–7, 29–34, 79–82, 84, 260–61, 309
communication surveillance 206–7
contributory role 20, 163–64, 195, 200, 208–9, 210–11, 221, 310
cooperative dialogue 277–78, 287, 293, 294–96, *see also* informal dialogues
cross-fertilization of norms 9, 22, 89, 165, 208–9
crowdsourcing 142–43, 160, 161–63
customary international law 11, 42, 43–46, 97–99, 165, 170, 195–99, 228, 229, 246–47
customary international law of privacy 44, 198–99, 208–9

data breach notification 183
data localization 145, 159–60
data protection policies 24, 103–4, 107–8, 124, 181, 183, 255, 281–82
dialogical approach 69, 99, 208, 231–32, 277–78, 287–88, 290–92
digital constitutionalism 130
digital human rights 175–76, *see also* digital rights
digital literacy 150, 186–87, 189
digital privacy 24–25, 186–87, 203, 205, 207–8, 252
digital rights 9, 139–40, 144–45, 153, 276–77, 278, 302, 313–14

dispersive approach to data privacy 105–12

emergent law 307–8
emergent privacy standards 17, 258, 259
encryption 18, 136–37, 145–46, 147–48, 150, 154, 158, 166, 177–78, 185–86, 264–66, 270–71, 280, *see also* right to encryption

Five Eyes States 3–4, 148, 172–73, 183, 260–61, 267
freedom from surveillance 136, 147–48, 154, 264–65, 280
freestanding role 151–63, 169–70, 190, 208, 210–11, 221, 310
future law 274–75, 277–78

gag orders 186–87, 188–89, 201
general comment 7, 38–39, 40, 72–73, 89, 93–94, 171–72, 233–34, 252, 302
general international law 11, 24, 43, 50, 101–2, 170, 228–33
general principles of law 11, 47–50, 99–102, 195, 196, 199–200, 216
general principles of privacy law 199–200
global privacy initiatives 7–10, 30, 129, 286, 306–7, 308, 310–12
global privacy norms 173–74, 202, 208–9

hacking 186, 270–71
hard legalization 11–16, 46, 52, 124–25, 204, 253, 274–75, 314
health data 91, 95–96, 106, 117, 174, *see also* personal data
human right to privacy, the 76–78, 81–82, 88, 167, 178, 180, 187–88, 258
Human Rights Committee (HR Committee) 7, 17–18, 32, 51, 54–55, 57–58, 67–69, 70–71, 120–21, 185, 192, 227, 234–39, 252, 257, *see also* treaty bodies
Human Rights Council (HR Council) 24, 69–70, 74–76, 89, 121, 164, 239–40, 297, 300
hybrid resolutions 177–78, *see also* privacy resolutions

informal dialogues 207–8, 258–59
information disclosure 107, 108–9
innovative approaches to privacy 203, 207–8
institutional gaps 23, 208, 286, 287, 293, 312–13
intelligence sharing 11–12, 183–84, 268–69
interactive dialogue 71, 74
interception and collection of personal
    data 206–7
international data privacy law 24, 37–38, 80–
    82, 167, 216, 221, 255, 257–58
international human rights law 6–7, 22–23, 24,
    29, 52, 110, 147, 174–75, 253–54, 289–90
international law of privacy 4–5, 24, 32, 52, 99,
    129, 170–71, 211, 252
international law's privacy problem 5, 23, 52,
    167, 168, 190, 305
international lawmaking 105, 203–4, 252–53,
    256, 284, 291, 294, 311
international privacy law 6, 24, 81, 129, 169–70
Internet bills of rights 4–5, 129, 254
Internet businesses 64, 65, 67, 166–67, 187–88,
    270–71, 272–73, 309–10, see also Internet
    corporations
Internet corporations 17–18, 64–67, 150, 176–
    77, 187–88, 269–70, 291–92, 301–2, see also
    technology companies

Joinet, Louis 87, 94–95
juridical quality 116–18, 162–63
jurisprudential gaps 69–76

legitimacy 13, 93–94, 136–37, 142–43, 152,
    160–63, 265, 283–84, 294, 301–2, see also
    procedural legitimacy
localizing transnational standards 245

mass surveillance 145, 148, 169, 172, 174–75,
    267–68, 269, 270–71
metadata 180–81, 201, 267–68
momentary project 138–40, 151–53
multi-level dialogue 124, 166–67, 208, 295
multistakeholder approach, a 142–43, 203,
    207–8, 293–94, 298, 302–4

new and emerging technologies 108, 140, 175–
    76, 184, 186, 205, 310–11
norm cross-fertilization 141–42, 180,
    240, 243–44
norm cross-influence 241
norm globalization 214, 215, 219–20, 226, 227
norm universalization 211, 214–20, 221–42
normative and methodological directions 170,
    203–8, 311
normative dialogue 274–75
normative direction 9–10, 168

normative dispersion 105, 111–12, 167, 257–
    58, 268
normative gaps 53–67, 251, 255, 257, 263, 287
normative inferiority 167
normative progression 77, 255, 256–57

oversight 41, 71, 120, 124, 145, 150, 183, 202,
    214, 243, 246, 268–69, 270–71, 299, 301–2,
    see also surveillance oversight

personal data 1–2, 80–81, 89, 137, 182–
    224, 267–68
political capital 170, 203–7, 260–61, 286, 311
pragmatic approach, a 22–24, 130, 158, 203,
    251, 287, 312, see also pragmatism
pragmatic approach to international privacy
    law, a 22, 130, 204, 209, 312
pragmatic privacy law reform 190, 209, see also
    pragmatic reform
pragmatic reform 167, 168
pragmatism 22, 23
privacy and data protection 24, 134, 137–38,
    175–76, 210, 224, 245, 307
privacy discourse 15, 30, 81, 130, 164, 170–
    76, 239–42, 255, 290–91, 307–8, see also
    United Nations (UN) discourse
privacy enhancing technologies 145–46, 178,
    185–86, 189, 265–66
privacy forum 124, 208, 276, 281, 290, 293,
    301–2, 312–13
privacy impact assessment 243
privacy inattention effect, the 34–37, 39–
    40, 86–88
privacy problem, the 1, 2–5, 14, 50, 99, 267,
    287, 306–8
privacy reform 170, 310
privacy resolutions 11, 164, 169–70, 177–79,
    190–96, 197–200, 258, 290–91
privatization of privacy threats 2–3
procedural legitimacy 142, 162–63, see also
    substantive legitimacy
progressive development of privacy law 163,
    169, 312

reimagining international privacy law 11, 20–
    21, 147, 306–7, 310, 314–15
reputation and honour 54–56, 70–71, 263–64
rights of personality 38, 89
right to anonymity 149, 150, 265–66
right to encryption 146, 147–48, 149–50, 157–
    58, 159–60, 265–66, see also right to use
    encryption technologies
right to privacy in the digital age, the 3–4,
    39, 117–18, 130, 171, 235–36,
    253–54, 308

right to use encryption technologies 147–48, 149–50, 264–66
rights inflation 152
rights novelty 135–36, 137, 139–40, 142, 162–63
rights theory 158, *see also* theories of rights
Ruggie Principles 6, 52, 179, 187–88, 294, 309–10, *see also* United Nations (UN) Guiding Principles

Snowden revelations 1–2, 63, 101, 129, 169, 260, 307–8, 314
soft law 6, 18–19, 51–52, 102–4, 135, 143, 190–93, 251–57, 292–93, 309, *see also* soft legalization
soft law supplement 168, 207, 251, 252, 253, 257, 263, 285–86, 287
soft legalization 18–19, 51, 99, 112–13, 203–4, 252–53, 283
sophistication of privacy threats 3
substantive legitimacy 160, 162–63
surveillance technologies 3, 6, 186, 271–72, 280–81

technology companies 2–3, 51, 138–39, 176–77, 178–79, 259, 279, 298, 308, 309–10

Tehran Conference 36–37, 79–81, 82, 84, 89, 103, 212–13, 225, 314–15
Thant, U 79–80, 222–23
theories of rights 21–22
transnational privacy standards 210
transnationalization of privacy threats 1–2
transparency policies 178–79, 182, 188–89, 201–2, 280–81
treaty bodies 7, 32, 118–19, 185, 233–34, 261–62, 287, 300
treaty body jurisprudence 51, 169–70, 180–81, 184, 234, 241–42

unifying approach to privacy 124–25
United Nations Guiding Principles (UN Guiding Principles) 52, 67, 190
United Nations discourse (UN discourse) 4–5, 170–71, 233–34, 247, 306
United Nations (UN) General Assembly (UN General Assembly) 9, 31–32, 79–80, 160–61, 169, 222–23, 251, 300
universalizing privacy standards 195–202

zones of privacy protection 57–58, 59, 89, 264